Microsoft®
Excel VBA
Professional Projects

Microsoft® Excel VBA
Professional Projects

Duane Birnbaum

Premier
Press

ISBN: 1-59200-065-7

Library of Congress Catalog Card Number: 2003105362

Printed in the United States of America

03 04 05 06 07 BH 10 9 8 7 6 5 4 3 2 1

Premier Press, a division of Course Technology

25 Thomson Place

Boston, MA 02210

SVP, Retail Strategic Market Group:
Andy Shafran

Publisher:
Stacy L. Hiquet

Senior Marketing Manager:
Sarah O'Donnell

Marketing Manager:
Heather Hurley

Manager of Editorial Services:
Heather Talbot

Acquisitions Editor:
Todd Jensen

Associate Marketing Manager:
Kristin Eisenzopf

Project Editor:
Melba Hopper

Technical Reviewer:
Greg Perry

Retail Market Coordinator:
Sarah Dubois

Interior Layout:
Chris Iacono
Laura Eddings

Cover Designer:
Mike Tanamachi

Indexer:
Angie Miccinello

Proofreaders:
Jennifer Roehrig
Marissa Mathieson

About the Author

Duane Birnbaum teaches courses in data analysis and introductory database design at Indiana University-Purdue University Indianapolis (IUPUI) and also works as a VB/VBA specialist for System Design Group, Inc. He received a B.A. degree from Augsburg College (Minnesota) in 1986 with a major in chemistry and a Ph.D from the University of California, Riverside in 1991 in physical chemistry. He then spent one and one-half years at the University of Michigan as a postdoctoral scientist. After a short time as an adjunct professor of chemistry at Mary Washington College (Virginia), he moved to his current location in Indiana and worked in the biotechnology industry for several years. Duane has authored approximately two dozen scientific articles in the areas of chemical physics, biochemistry, and chemical engineering and a beginner's programming book in Excel VBA. He lives in Indianapolis with his wife, Jill, and their two boys, Aaron and Joshua.

Contents at a Glance

Contents

Appendix C Basic SQL Tutorial 683

Introduction

Goal of the Book

The goal of this book is to provide a solid introduction to the VBA programming language and show how it can be applied to create practical applications for Excel. The book is targeted to intermediate and advanced programmers; however, since VBA is arguably the easiest language out there to learn, beginning programmers with a strong Excel background should also be reasonably comfortable with this book.

The book is divided into six parts, with Part I providing an introduction to the VBA language and the Excel object model. Parts II through V each consist of three to four chapters that introduce new concepts, objects, and programming methods in considerable detail. The last chapter in each part illustrates the use of the newly introduced objects and methods in designing a practical application for Excel. Part VI contains three appendixes that provide basic tutorials on Excel, HTML/XHTML, and SQL.

The first project is an Excel-to-HTML converter that creates a static Web page from an Excel worksheet. The second project creates a data retrieval and analysis program for a mythical company that sells used cars. The program inputs sales data from an Access database for viewing and analysis in Excel worksheets and pivot tables. The third project creates a stock ticker that retrieves quotes from a Web site and displays them in a highly customized form. The stock ticker also charts the quotes in a specified time increment and copies the chart to the same form that contains the ticker. The last project is a custom data analysis program designed for a real company and involves routine data automation procedures as well as more advanced curve-fitting techniques.

The advantage of reading this book is that you get numerous examples illustrating the use of programming objects and methods that you can study as they are applied to real projects (as opposed to one or two code snippets). This advantage serves the ultimate goal of this book, which is to make you a proficient and successful VBA-Excel programmer.

Required Software

As I write this introduction, Microsoft is preparing to release its latest version of Office (tentatively called Office 2003). Like most new versions of Office, it is only a minor upgrade from the previous version (XP). VBA has not changed significantly since Office 97 was released and once again has received only minor upgrades in Office 2003. At some point, VBA will migrate to the .NET platform. In fact, with the new version of Visual Studio, developers will be able to write applications for Word and Excel using C# and VB.NET. However, major changes to VBA have not yet arrived and won't for at least a couple more years. As VBA programmers, it is important that we keep up-to-date with the latest technology. However, with the high price of a site license, many companies (of all sizes) upgrade their versions of Office only every four to five years. As a result, I still write a considerable amount of code for Office 97. Consequently, I agreed to write this book because the code it contains will still be applicable to the new version of Office and VBA.

All code included in this book was written in Excel XP with the idea that readers would be working in Excel 2000 or later. Although most of the code in this book is applicable to the version of VBA in Excel 97, few of the programs in this book will execute in Excel 97 without error. With each new version of Office, there are minor upgrades to existing objects and new objects and functions are added. Consequently, if you try to execute the code from this book in Excel 97, you will encounter errors. Most of these errors involve modal Userforms, new VBA functions, and new file I/O objects not included with Excel 97. Once you are a proficient VBA programmer, you will see that it is not difficult to transform the code in this book to execute in Excel 97 without error.

Part III of this book involves numerous code examples that input and output data from Excel to an Access database. So, it is a good idea to have Access installed on your computer when working through this section of the book. Access is part of the Office suite of programs (Windows version), so if you have installed Office, Access has also been installed on your computer. However, having Access installed on your computer is not required if the Microsoft Jet database engine and ADO or DAO object libraries are installed on your computer. With some knowledge of SQL, you can use VBA to create and define a relational database for your Excel applications.

Finally, for those of you who want to develop Excel applications for the Macintosh, I can tell you that the Macintosh version of VBA does not differ significantly from the Windows version. Of course, it doesn't take much of a difference to render a program written for the Windows version useless for the Macintosh. One of the major differences in VBA between Windows and Macintosh operating systems is in the specification of file I/O paths (Windows uses the backward slash, and Macintosh uses colons). Besides file I/O paths, the Macintosh version of VBA does not include as many objects, and there are occasional differences between the members of various object classes in the two versions. As a user of both Windows and Macintosh, I have written Excel-VBA programs for both operating systems. In fact, the data automation analysis program in Part V of this book was originally written for the Macintosh version of Excel. I have found it relatively easy to convert my Excel-VBA programs from Windows to Macintosh and vice versa, although the relative ease in converting programs from one operating system to another is certain to be a function of your comfort level with each operating system and relative proficiency with Excel-VBA.

How to Use This Book

This book is specifically organized to facilitate a good grasp of everything it covers. The conventions used in the book include the following:

TIP

Tips provide special advice or point out unusual shortcuts available using a particular product.

NOTE

Notes give additional information that may be of interest to the reader but is not essential to performing the task at hand.

CAUTION

Cautions are used to warn users of possible disastrous results if they perform a task incorrectly.

In addition, you will find all source code from the book's examples and projects at http://www.premierpressbooks.com/downloads.asp.

As a final note, you need to know that a significant amount of code in this book contains long programming statements. In some cases, long statements are simply unavoidable, especially when long object paths or Windows API functions are involved. Because long lines of code may potentially be hyphenated during production of the book (therefore, introducing an error in the code), I have used the underscore (_) to signify that the statement continues on the next line. In fact, VBA uses the underscore as its *line continuation character* so that no errors are introduced into the code. Just remember that when you see the underscore, the statement continues on the next line.

PART I

Introduction to VBA

Visual Basic for Applications (VBA) has been an integral part of the last few versions of Office and has provided developers with the ability to create custom solutions for Office applications. VBA was originally available only in Office applications but can now be licensed by third-party vendors for integration in their applications.

VBA is a practical rapid-application-development language because it is easy to learn and can be integrated into any desktop application. Therefore, instead of learning a new language for each application, all you need to learn is its object model.

In Part I, you learn the elements of the VBA programming language and the Excel object model required to begin building Excel-VBA applications. The first six chapters in Part I of this book introduce you to the VBA language elements available to any desktop application that has integrated VBA. The last two chapters in Part I introduce you to the top-level objects in the Excel object model and the objects available in VBA, Excel, and Office for file input and output. The topics you learn about include the following:

- ◆ The VBA integrated development environment (IDE)
- ◆ Declaring and using variables and constants
- ◆ VBA's built-in functions
- ◆ Creating VBA procedures
- ◆ Programming with event procedures
- ◆ Adding Userforms to a program
- ◆ Writing decision structures
- ◆ Writing loops
- ◆ Declaring and using arrays
- ◆ Top-level Excel objects
- ◆ File I/O with VBA and Excel

Chapter 1

A few years ago, Microsoft added a programming language to its Office suite of products (Access, Word, Excel, PowerPoint, and so on). The language, called Visual Basic for Applications (VBA), was built from Microsoft's popular Visual Basic (VB) language, minus a few objects and with other small differences. The integration of VBA into Microsoft Office applications not only allowed non-programming users of Office to continue recording macros for automating repetitive tasks, but also enabled programmers to significantly extend the capabilities of Office applications.

In this chapter, you examine the development environment used to create applications for Excel using the VBA language. You will begin to understand what VBA is and how to use it with your Excel applications.

VBA versus VB

Both VB and VBA are based on the old BASIC programming language that was popular a couple of decades ago because it was so easy to learn. VB and VBA are popular for the same reason. What distinguishes VB and VBA from the old BASIC programming language are their Object-based nature and the event-driven paradigm used in these languages.

 NOTE

In order to make it a true object-oriented language, Microsoft dramatically changed the latest version of VB (VB.NET). As a result, it is not really a beginner programming language, but is on a level with Java, C++, and other object-oriented programming languages.

With VBA's correlation to VB, it seems inevitable that it too will migrate to object-oriented status in the near future. However, with the latest versions of Office (XP, and 2003), VBA remains as a simpler object-based language more closely related to VB version 6.0.

VBA is a complete programming language, but you can't use it outside the application in which it is integrated, as you can VB. This does not mean VBA can be integrated only with Microsoft Office programs. Any software vendor that decides to implement VBA can include it with their application.

VBA is easy to learn, but to use it in a new application, you must first become familiar with the *object model* of the application. For example, the Document and Dictionary objects are specific to the Word object model, whereas the `Workbook`, `Worksheet`, and `Range` objects are specific to the Excel object model. As you proceed through this book, you will see that the Excel object model is fairly extensive; however, if you are familiar with Excel, you will find that using these objects is generally straightforward.

NOTE

If you have programming experience with Visual Basic version 6.0 and earlier, you will be immediately familiar with VBA. Knowing VB gives you the advantage of using your knowledge of ActiveX controls and the Windows API to add functionality to your Office applications.

Object-Based versus Object-Oriented Programming

Object-based languages such as VBA, Javascript, and Perl follow a model based on the semantics of spoken languages, with programming *objects* represented as nouns, *properties* that describe an object represented as adjectives, and *methods* that control the behavior of an object represented as verbs. The advantages of an object-based language include the following:

- ◆ **Intuitive objects.** Objects refer to the building blocks of the operating system and application. Objects are assigned intuitive names that make it easy for the programmer to understand their design and function.

- ◆ **Practical.** Once an object is created, it can be reused as often as needed. Objects are very flexible, and many of them can be easily adapted to new applications simply by altering their properties and methods. This is a dramatic timesaver as it significantly cuts down on the amount of code that must be written.

- ◆ **User-driven.** Many objects also have event procedures that are usually triggered by user actions (for example, a mouse click), so the user dictates the flow of the program. This creates a much more satisfying experience for the user than the old programs in which programmers dictated the flow.

Consider the example of a car. A car is an object that can be described by its make (for example, Ford, Chevy), model (Mustang, Taurus), type (SUV, compact, mid-size), color, and so on. A car also performs actions such as accelerating, stopping, turning, and the like. The car is the object; its make, model, type, and color are properties; and its capability to accelerate, stop, and turn are methods. You can have more than one instance of the car object (for example, a red Ford SUV and a blue Chevy compact), but they are all car objects with numerous similarities. They are distinguished by their appearance and behavior, but they are basically the same object. A car manufacturer does not start from scratch when designing a new model, but builds on the existing knowledge of engines, frames, and dozens of other systems to create a new instance of a car. As a VBA programmer, you will take advantage of many existing objects in order to build new applications.

Although object-based languages represent a vast improvement over previous programming languages, they do have limitations when compared to a true object-oriented programming language (OOP) such as C++, Java, and VB.NET. The most notable limitation is VBA's inability to perform inheritance (derive new classes from a base class or object definition). However, the details of OOP languages will not be discussed here because this book focuses on Excel-VBA.

Examining the Excel-VBA IDE

All Office applications come with their own development environment for writing VBA programs. In Excel, you can access the IDE (Integrated Development Environment) via the Visual Basic toolbar (from the main Menu Bar, select View, Toolbars; the toolbar will appear in its previously viewed location). You can also access the IDE through the Tools menu as shown in Figure 1.1 (select Tools, Macros, Visual Basic Editor).

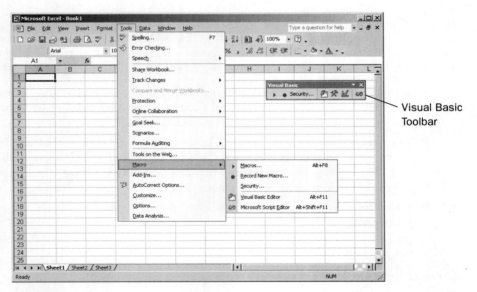

FIGURE 1.1 *Accessing the IDE from the Excel application.*

After you select the IDE, it is loaded, and a window similar to the one shown in Figure 1.2 appears.

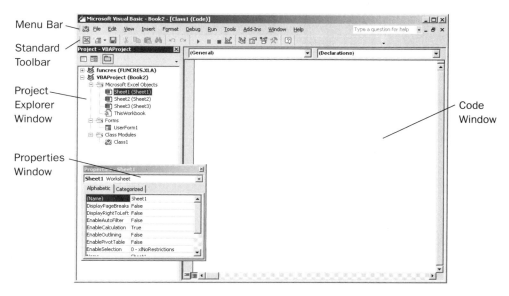

FIGURE 1.2 *The Excel-VBA IDE window in a typical configuration.*

Using the Major Components of the IDE

The major components of the IDE are the menus, toolbars, and windows most frequently used while writing a program. VBA allows you to select which components the IDE displays. Although you may choose to hide them, the major components include the following:

◆ Menu bar

◆ Standard toolbar

◆ Project Explorer window

◆ Properties window

◆ Code windows

The Menu Bar

The IDE main Menu Bar contains some of the features you expect to find in any application and is shown in Figure 1.3. The File menu enables you to save and import project files. The View menu allows you to open or select various windows in the IDE, and the Insert menu enables you to add new components (Userforms, modules, and procedures) to your project. As you probably have guessed, the Debug and Run menus allow you to debug and test code. Finally, the Help menu enables you to access the online help for the VBA programming language in Excel. I explain all these features (and several more) in detail as they arise in the programming examples and projects in this book.

FIGURE 1.3 *The main Menu Bar in the Excel-VBA IDE.*

Toolbars

If you prefer clicking icons rather than selecting menu items, you can use toolbars for debugging, editing your code, altering the appearance of Userforms, and selecting various components within the IDE. The Standard toolbar is normally displayed by default (refer to Figure 1.2) and contains buttons for running and debugging your code and for displaying some of the common components in the IDE. Select View, Toolbars to access the other toolbars (Debug, Edit, and UserForm).

Project Explorer Window

The Project Explorer window displays a list of all projects that are currently open, including all workbooks and add-ins opened from the Excel application. Every open Excel file is listed as a distinct project in the Project Explorer window. To display the Project Explorer window, select View, Project Explorer or press Ctrl+R.

A Project Explorer window listing several VBA objects is shown in Figure 1.4.

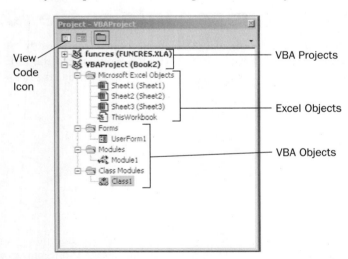

FIGURE 1.4 *The Project Explorer window in Excel.*

The Project Explorer also lists the components of opened projects. Within the projects, you will find a listing for all Excel objects that include the workbook and all worksheets contained in the workbook. For example, Figure 1.4 shows two projects currently open, FUNCRES.XLA and Book2. The project named FUNCRES.XLA is an add-in that contains several data analysis tools, and it is loaded by selecting Tools, Add-Ins, Analysis ToolPak.

Microsoft secured the FUNCRES.XLA file, so its components and code cannot be viewed in the IDE. The project Book2 is the default name created by Excel for a newly opened workbook. The Book2 project initially contained four objects: Sheet1, Sheet2, Sheet3, and ThisWorkbook representing a workbook containing three worksheets in Excel. From the Insert menu in the IDE, I added a Userform (named UserForm1), a standard module (Module1), and a class module (Class1). These are examples of VBA objects and are explained in detail throughout this book.

Properties Window

The Properties window displays all the design-time properties for the currently selected object. The selected object may be one listed in the Project Explorer window or an ActiveX control on a Userform. To display the Properties window for the current object, select View, Properties Window or press F4. The Properties window associated with the worksheet named Sheet1 is shown in Figure 1.5.

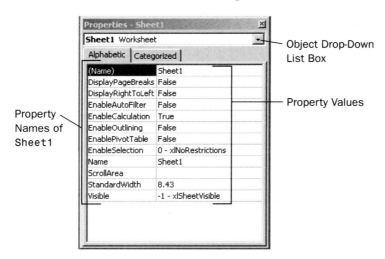

FIGURE 1.5 *The Properties window.*

The Properties window has only a couple of components and is relatively easy to use. The property names are listed on the left side of the grid, and their corresponding values are listed on the right side of the grid. You can change the values of these properties from their defaults at design time (prior to code execution) or at run time (while the program is executing). For example, changing the Name property of Sheet1 to MySheet changes the name of the worksheet as shown in Figure 1.6. Changing the Name property of a worksheet is a relatively simple example and probably would not be done at design time because the name of a worksheet is easily changed from the Excel application window. However, changing the name of an object from the Properties window does illustrate how to change properties of objects using the IDE at design time — something you will have to do often when working with ActiveX controls and (see Chapter 4, "Understanding VBA Procedures").

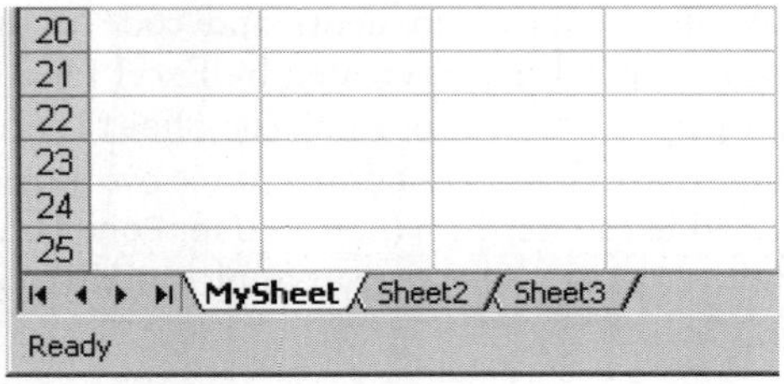

20			
21			
22			
23			
24			
25			

I◀ ◀ ▶ ▶I \ **MySheet** ╱ Sheet2 ╱ Sheet3 ╱

Ready

FIGURE 1.6 *Here is the result of changing the* Name *property of a* Worksheet *object in the VBA IDE.*

 NOTE

In the Properties window (refer to Figure 1.5), notice the two Name properties used for a Worksheet object. The Name property without the parentheses represents the name of the worksheet as it appears in Excel. The Name property with the parentheses represents the object name you can use in VBA code to reference the worksheet.

At the top of the Properties window, a drop-down list box displays the currently selected object from the Project Explorer. If the selected object is a container object, you can use this list box to select other objects within the container object (if any exist). For example, the Workbook object serves as a container for Worksheet objects. So, if you select the Workbook object named ThisWorkbook in Figure 1.4 from the Excel Objects folder in the Project Explorer window, you can use the drop-down list box in the Properties window (refer to Figure 1.5) to select any Worksheet object contained in the object named ThisWorkbook.

 NOTE

Some objects, such as the Workbook, Worksheet, and Userform objects, can serve as containers for other objects. This simply means that the GUI interface associated with these objects can hold other objects as dictated by the interface you design.

Modules and Code Windows

A *module* is essentially a related set of declarations and procedures. You can store a module as a separate file, or you can, more typically, store all modules within a project in the same Excel file. The declarations and procedures within a module are related in the sense that they are part of a single object. These objects are listed in Table 1.1, and, when added to a project, each object listed will have an associated code window.

Table 1.1 VBA Module Types

Object Module	Container	File Type
Worksheet	Yes	.cls
Workbook	Yes	.cls
Userform	Yes	.frm
Standard	No	.bas
Class	No	.cls

I will refer to code windows for `Workbook`, `Worksheet`, and `Userform` objects as form modules because they all have a GUI interface, serve as containers for other objects, and have the same rules governing variable and procedural scope (see Chapter 2, "Working with Variables and Constants in VBA," and Chapter 4, "Understanding VBA Procedures," for more on variable and procedural scope).

 NOTE

Technically speaking, form modules are class modules with predefined objects. The other major difference is the lack of a GUI interface with a class module.

All modules can contain programmer-defined procedures, but only form modules will contain predefined event procedures (for example, the `Change()` event procedure of a `Worksheet` object or `Activate()` event procedure of a `Userform` object). Event procedures are executed when triggered by a specific user action. Class modules may also contain event procedures, but the programmer must define them.

To open the Code window for an object, select View, Code, or press F7. You can also select the View Code icon at the top of the Project Explorer window (refer to Figure 1.4) or double-click the Object's name listed in the Project Explorer. Figures 1.7 and 1.8 show examples of the same Code window for an Excel `Worksheet` object.

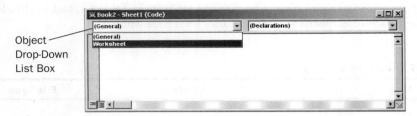

FIGURE 1.7 *Selecting the* Worksheet *object from a code window for an Excel* Worksheet *object.*

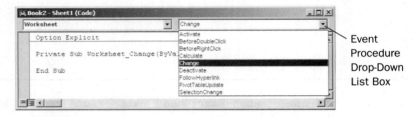

FIGURE 1.8 *Selecting the* Change() *event procedure from a code window for an Excel* Worksheet *object.*

You must enter all the code for your application in the appropriate Code window(s). Your program algorithm will be used to decide which code window is the best place for the code.

Two drop-down list boxes are located at the top of Code windows (refer to Figures 1.7 and 1.8). The list box on the left is for all objects contained within the selected object, and the list box on the right is for the associated event procedures. To view your choices of event procedures for a particular object, first select the object from the list box on the left and then view its event procedures in the list box on the right.

After selecting an event procedure, you will see two lines of code entered into the Code window. These two lines of code constitute a procedure definition. The first line will start with something like `Private Sub ProcedureName_EventName`, and the last line will start with something like `End Sub`. You must enter the code for this event procedure between these two lines of code. If you do not need an event procedure, you will have to create your own procedure using the `Sub` and `End Sub` keywords. You must enter program declarations into the general declarations section (refer to the Object list box in Figure 1.7) in the Code window. The general declarations section of a Code window is any area outside of a procedure definition (see Figure 1.9). The code module in Figure 1.9 shows the opening and closing statements for two event procedures and one Sub procedure. Because it belongs to a `Worksheet` object, this is an example of a form module.

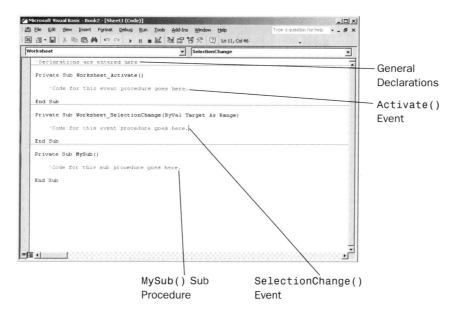

FIGURE 1.9 *A Worksheet module showing two event procedures and one Sub procedure.*

Accessing Online Help

As any good programmer knows, you must have reference material handy in order to successfully complete a project. Of course, the quality of the reference makes a difference, but you don't have much control in that area. You can, of course, buy books and many of them will be very helpful. However, when you just need to look up the syntax for a keyword or code structure, it's hard to beat online help. It's fast, easy to use, and it ships with the application. A sample Help window is shown in Figure 1.10.

 NOTE

If you have access to Microsoft Visual Studio or Microsoft Visual Basic 6.0, you will find its online help useful for some of your VBA projects. This is especially true when programming with the Windows API and some of its associated interfaces.

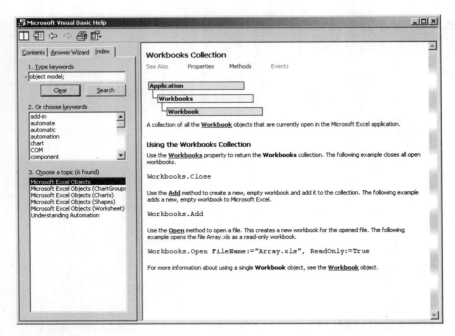

FIGURE 1.10 *The VBA help window.*

You have three choices for searching online help: a table of contents, an answer wizard, or an index. The index is typically the fastest choice because you simply enter a keyword to access a list of potential documents.

Unfortunately, if you used the normal or recommended installation procedure for Excel or Office, the help for VBA is not installed on your computer. To install online help for VBA in Office XP/Windows XP, follow this procedure:

1. Click Start and select Control Panel.

2. Select Add or Remove Programs.

3. Select Microsoft Office XP, Microsoft Excel, or similar item, and then click Change.

4. Select Add or Remove Features and click Next.

5. From the displayed list of components, open Office Shared Features and then open Visual Basic for Applications.

6. Select Visual Basic Help and click Update.

After the help files are installed, you can access them from the VBA IDE using the Menu Bar, Standard toolbar, or by pressing F1.

> **TIP**
>
> If you want help on a specific VBA keyword in your code, place the cursor on the desired keyword and press F1. The help window for that keyword will be displayed.

Utilizing VBA Components in Excel

You do not have to develop your Excel-VBA applications entirely from the IDE. There are a few components available from the Excel application window that can help you build an interface and even write your code. These components are the Macro recorder and the objects found on the Visual Basic, the Control Toolbox, and Forms toolbars.

The Visual Basic Toolbar

The Visual Basic toolbar (see Figure 1.11) is provided as a convenience to allow for fast access to several VBA components. You use the buttons on the Visual Basic toolbar to access the VBA IDE, the macro recorder, the Control Toolbox, and the Microsoft Script Editor.

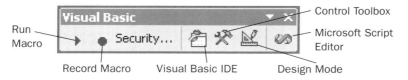

FIGURE 1.11 *The Visual Basic toolbar.*

You use the Script Editor to edit the HTML script generated by Excel when you save a worksheet as a Web page. (I don't discuss editing HTML scripts because it is beyond the scope of this book. For information on the Microsoft Script Editor, you might check out the Microsoft developer network at http://msdn.microsoft.com.) The Design mode toggle button allows you to edit the properties of ActiveX controls placed on a worksheet. ActiveX controls are found on the Control Toolbox toolbar (see Figure 1.12).

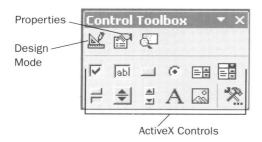

FIGURE 1.12 *The Control Toolbox toolbar.*

The Control Toolbox

The Control Toolbox contains ActiveX controls that can be added to a worksheet and controlled via a VBA program. The Control Toolbox contains several ActiveX controls that are summarized in Table 1.2. To place an ActiveX control on a worksheet, simply select the desired control and draw it on the worksheet.

Table 1.2 Standard ActiveX Controls That Come with Excel

ActiveX Control	Description
Check Box	Provides a user with one or more choices among many choices.
Text Box	Provides a user with the ability to input text.
Command Button	Triggers an action with a mouse click.
Option Button	Provides the user with only one choice among many.
List Box	Displays a list of values to the user.
Combo Box	Displays a list of values and can also accept new items.
Toggle Button	Displays whether an item is selected.
Spin Button	Changes a value. The value may be applied to another control.
Scroll Bar	Changes a value or moves an object.
Label	Provides a label for other controls or displays a message to the user.
Image	Used to display images.

ActiveX controls are objects with specific functionalities that you can use to build an interface in your VBA programs. For example, you can use a List Box to display a list of values from which the user can select one or more items in the list. Consider the sample worksheet shown in Figure 1.13.

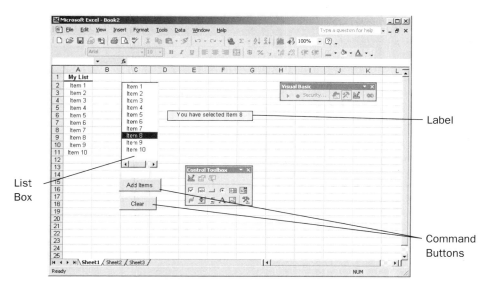

FIGURE 1.13 *An Excel worksheet containing several ActiveX controls.*

Using the Control Toolbox, I placed a List Box, `Label`, and two Command Button controls on the worksheet. I changed the `Name` and `Caption` properties of the controls from their default values by using the Properties window as it displayed the properties of a specific ActiveX control. The Properties window is opened by clicking the Properties icon on the Control Toolbox. Before altering any properties, I had to toggle into Design mode using the Design Mode icon on the Control Toolbox. Table 1.3 shows the ActiveX controls that I used and the properties whose default values I edited for the sample program. I left all other properties to retain their default values.

Table 1.3 Altered Properties of the ActiveX Controls Used in a Sample VBA Program

ActiveX control	Property	Value
List Box	Name	lstItems
Command Button	Name	cmdAddItems
List Box	Caption	Add Items
Command Button	Name	cmdClear
Command Button	Caption	Clear
Label	Name	lblOutput
Label	Caption	No Selection

The purpose of this worksheet is to add the items listed in column A to the List Box by clicking a Command Button. The user can then clear the contents of the List Box or select an item from the list that results in the selection being displayed in the Label control. The program code for this worksheet application is entered into the code module representing Sheet1 in the VBA IDE and is listed next. You must toggle out of Design mode before code will be triggered.

```
Private Sub cmdAddItems_Click()
    Dim I As Integer
    For I = 2 To 11
        lstItems.AddItem Cells(I, "A").Value
    Next I
End Sub


Private Sub cmdClear_Click()
    lstItems.Clear
    lblOutput.Caption = "No Selection"
End Sub


Private Sub lstItems_Click()
    lblOutput.Caption = "You have selected " & lstItems.Value
End Sub
```

I used the code module for Sheet1 because this worksheet serves as a container for the ActiveX controls. So, these objects and their events are listed in the code module for Sheet1.

I used the Click() event procedures of the List Box and Command Buttons to hold all program code. Don't worry about syntax, event procedures, or the specifics of the code just yet. You will learn about the VBA language specifications in the next few chapters. For now, this program serves as a simple illustration of how to use ActiveX controls on an Excel worksheet.

The Forms Toolbar

The Forms toolbar, shown in Figure 1.14, is similar to the Control Toolbox in that it holds many of the same ActiveX controls. To select the Forms toolbar, click View, Toolbars, Forms.

FIGURE 1.14 *The Forms toolbar.*

The controls on the Forms toolbar are for the typical Excel user rather than programmers. You use these controls to initiate macros and display data on a worksheet. The properties and events associated with these controls are severely limited as compared to controls in the Control toolbox. Nevertheless, the Forms toolbar controls offer a simple set of tools for simply initiating a procedure in a VBA application.

Macros

Macros as applied to VBA refer to recorded programs. Utilizing the Record New Macro feature (shown in Figure 1.15), any user can create a VBA program. While the recorder is on, just perform the tasks in Excel that you want to record (for example, create a chart, create a formula, format a few cells, and so on). When you stop the recorder, you can then run the macro to repeat the tasks that were just recorded. This is a very useful feature for typical Excel users because it allows them to do repetitive tasks quickly and easily. Developers also find recorded macros helpful when they need to learn how to program a specific Excel function.

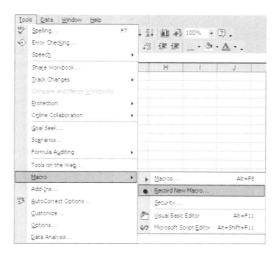

FIGURE 1.15 *Selecting the Record New Macro feature in Excel.*

Recording a Macro

If you want to learn how to program a specific component or function in Excel, your quickest and easiest way is to record a macro and examine the resulting code. Recording a macro in Excel is easy. Just follow these steps:

1. To start Excel's macro recorder, select Tools, Macro, Record New Macro. You may also select Record Macro from the Visual Basic toolbar (refer to Figure 1.11).

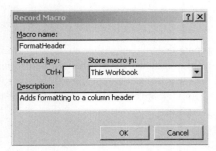

FIGURE 1.16 *Naming and storing a macro.*

2. Name the macro in the Macro name text box as shown in Figure 1.16.

   When you first select Record New Macro from the Tools menu or the Visual Basic toolbar, you are prompted to name your macro, select a workbook in which to store the recorded macro, and enter a description of the macro. None of this is very important if you are recording the macro only to generate code for examination or pasting into a project. Just remember the name and location so that you can easily find the macro after recording.

3. Select a workbook for storing the macro and click OK.

   The macro can be stored in the currently selected workbook, a new workbook, or a personal macro workbook. These workbooks are listed in the Project Explorer window and can be accessed within the IDE.

   After you enter the requested information, a small toolbar appears with two buttons (see Figure 1.17). The first button allows you to stop recording, and the second tells Excel to use relative instead of absolute cell references in the generated code. Until you click the Stop button, all actions performed in Excel are recorded.

4. Perform the sequence of tasks in Excel that you want to record just as you normally would. For example, you can select from menus, enter worksheet data, and click with your mouse, and the macro will record each of these actions.

5. Stop the recorder.

Stop Recording  Relative Reference

FIGURE 1.17 *The stop recording toolbar.*

6. Open the VBA IDE and find the recorded code. The recorded macro code is located in a standard module listed in the Project Explorer under the workbook project selected in Step 3.

7. Edit the recorded code and add it to your program.

Viewing and Editing a Recorded Macro

After recording your macro, you will want to examine the recorded code in the IDE. I recommend that you edit the code to remove unnecessary lines and add comments before copying it to your project.

The entire process of recording and editing a macro is illustrated in the following example in which several formatting options are applied to a worksheet cell with the macro recorder on (the worksheet cell is selected before the recorder is turned on). Use the Formatting toolbar in Excel to apply these formats to a worksheet cell.

1. Change the font style to bold.

2. Change font size to 14.

3. Change the font color to dark blue.

4. Autofit the column width (select Format, Column, AutoFit Selection).

The resulting macro code is stored automatically in a standard module (named `Module1`), which you can access via the Project Explorer window in the IDE (double-click the name of the module listed in the Project Explorer) as shown in Figure 1.18.

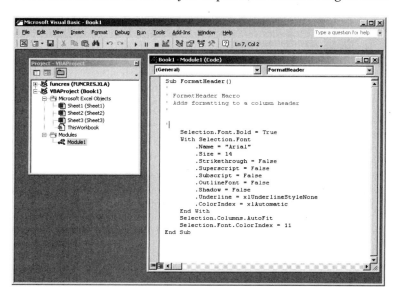

FIGURE 1.18 *Accessing a recorded macro.*

As might be expected, the recorder generates more code than needed to carry out the formatting tasks listed previously. Excel generates the extra code when it records the default values for the properties you alter while recording. It is always a good idea to record only a few steps in your macro to prevent the code from becoming too long and more difficult to read and edit. You can shorten the code in Figure 1.18 to the following without changing the result when it is executed:

```
Sub FormatHeader()
'Edited macro for formatting a header
    With Selection.Font
        .Bold = True
        .Size = 14
        .ColorIndex = 11   'Dark blue color. xlAutomatic will be black
    End With
    Selection.Columns.AutoFit
End Sub
```

 NOTE

The `With`/`End With` code structure is discussed in Chapter 7, "VBA Objects Specific to Excel Programming."

Although I have not yet discussed VBA syntax and code structures, you should be able to see what is happening in the preceding procedure. The name of the macro is assigned to a procedure name (`FormatHeader`) that begins with the keyword `Sub` and ends with `End Sub`. The first line of the procedure is a comment (comments begin with an apostrophe), which is followed by five lines of code that modify the font used for the currently selected worksheet cell. Finally, Excel automatically sets the column width to the width of the text entered in the cell (assuming you enter text in the cell before running the macro).

Running a Macro

After editing your macro, it is a good idea to test it to be certain it performs as expected. It may take a couple of attempts to record the macro to a desired result. After recording, you can execute a the macro following these steps:

1. Open the workbook in which the macro is stored.
2. Select Tools, Macro, Macros, or press Run Macro from the Visual Basic toolbar.
   A dialog box appears listing the available macros (see Figure 1.19).
3. Select the desired macro and click Run to execute the code.

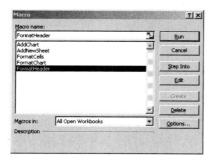

FIGURE 1.19 *Selecting a macro from Excel.*

A nice alternative to running a macro from the Tools menu or the Visual Basic toolbar is to assign the macro to a button that will make the function of the macro more obvious to the user. For example, you can assign the macro to the `Click()` event procedure of a Command Button control as described earlier, or you can just as easily assign the macro to a Button control from the Forms toolbar. Remember, the controls on the Forms toolbar are similar in appearance and function to those on the Control Toolbox. They differ in their versatility as a programming tool because they have far fewer properties and only one event procedure to work with.

You can run the `FormatHeader` macro simply by clicking a button placed on the worksheet. Just draw a button from the Forms toolbar on the worksheet and assign the macro to its `Click()` event procedure. In fact, when you draw a button on a worksheet, Excel prompts you to assign a macro (see Figure 1.20).

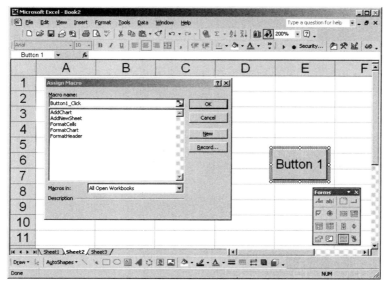

FIGURE 1.20 *Assigning a macro to a button from the Forms toolbar.*

TIP

Not all Form toolbar controls will automatically prompt you to assign a macro. However, you can right-click the control and select a macro procedure in order to assign it to the default event procedure of the control.

After you draw the button on the worksheet, a dialog box appears asking you to assign a macro. Select a macro from the list and click OK.

After you assign the FormatHeader macro to Button1, any click on the button executes the macro code. Figure 1.21 shows the worksheet before (top image) and after (bottom image) the FormatHeader macro is executed by clicking the button.

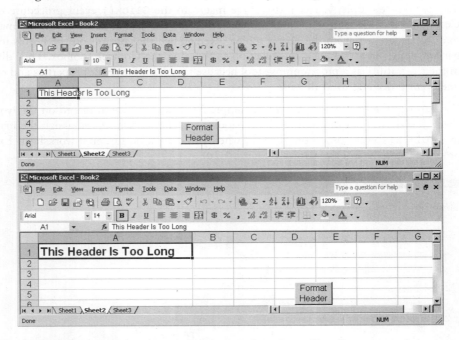

FIGURE 1.21 *Executing the* FormatHeader *macro from a Form Button control.*

NOTE

In order to assign a macro to a control on the Control Toolbox, you have to copy and paste the recorded macro from its module procedure to the event procedure associated with the worksheet module on which the control was placed.

Creating Custom Toolbars

As an alternative to using ActiveX controls placed on a worksheet to initiate program execution, you can use a custom toolbar. The advantage to using a toolbar rather than ActiveX controls is that the toolbar is independent of the Excel worksheet or workbook. That is, you can create a custom toolbar that contains buttons for initiating your VBA applications without having first to open a specific Excel workbook.

To create a custom toolbar, select Customize from the toolbars listed under the Tools menu in Excel. The Customize dialog box appears, as shown in Figure 1.22.

FIGURE 1.22 *Creating a custom toolbar.*

After pressing New and naming your custom toolbar, an empty toolbar appears on your screen. In the Customize dialog box, choose the Commands tab to add buttons and menus to your newly created toolbar. For a new custom button, select Macros from the list displayed in Figure 1.23 and drag the Custom Button selection onto the new toolbar.

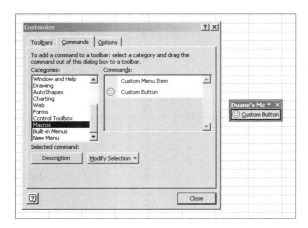

FIGURE 1.23 *Adding a button to a custom toolbar.*

You can edit the button's appearance (icon and text) and style and assign a macro by clicking Modify Selection and making the appropriate selection from the list (see Figure 1.24).

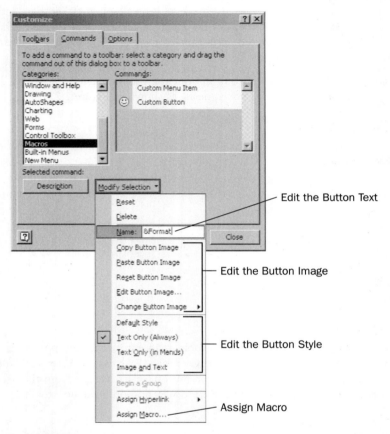

FIGURE 1.24 *Configuring a toolbar button for appearance and assigned macro.*

After assigning the macro, you can close the Customize dialog box, and the toolbar button will be functional. The custom toolbar remains available to Excel, even if you close the workbook containing the macro. If you press the button with the assigned macro, Excel automatically loads the workbook containing the macro, if it isn't already available. In Chapter 9, "Custom Menus and Toolbars," I show you how to make your custom toolbars open and close as required by your applications.

Summary

This chapter should have helped you become familiar with the VBA programming environment. I introduced you to the IDE and several of its common components. You also found out how to place ActiveX controls on an Excel worksheet and began to see how they are used in VBA applications. Finally, I demonstrated how to record a macro and attach it to ActiveX controls and toolbars. In subsequent chapters, you will discover how to use these components to create your VBA applications.

Chapter 2

The basic elements of the VBA programming language are variables and constants. Variables are the basic element of any computer language, and because this book focuses on Excel, you can think of a variable as a *worksheet cell* whose content is readily changed. Conversely, constants are values that never change.

This chapter describes how to declare variables and assign values to them. I also discuss the data types that are available in VBA for your variables. Lastly, I cover VBA and programmer-defined constants.

Creating Variables and Understanding Their Scope

Before discussing variables, I would like you to consider worksheet cells. Worksheet cells can hold different types of data, such as numbers, text, and images. Furthermore, you can format the data in many ways. For example, in Excel, a numerical value entered into a worksheet cell can be an integer, a currency, a percentage, and a fractional value, among others. Figure 2.1 shows the Excel Format Cells dialog box, which lists the categories of data formats that you can enter into a spreadsheet.

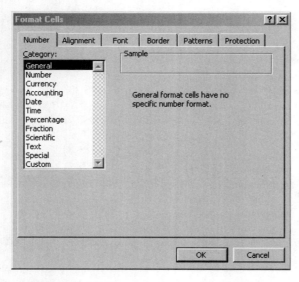

FIGURE 2.1 *The Number tab of the Format Cells dialog box listing the data formatting options available in Excel.*

You can also change or delete the content of a worksheet cell at any time. So, you can think of a worksheet cell as a temporary storage location for numbers and text.

A program variable is essentially the same thing as a worksheet cell regardless of the programming language (with the exception that it can hold more types of data — for example, images and objects — and is generally invisible to the user). Variables are used to hold some type of value for as long as the program needs it. You can manipulate or delete a variable at any time during program execution.

When to create, manipulate, and delete a variable depends on the requirements of your program, and, while doing so, you must obey a few rules specific to the programming language you are using. I will now examine those rules.

Before you work with a variable in VBA, I suggest that you first declare it, although this is not required. *Declaring a variable* tells the computer to reserve memory for some type of data. To declare a variable in VBA use the `Dim` (short for Dimension) statement.

```
Dim myVar As Integer
```

In the preceding statement, the name of the variable is `myVar`. The name must begin with an alphanumeric character and cannot exceed 255 characters. Avoid using punctuation marks or other unusual characters in the variable name because most of them are not allowed. However, you can use the underscore character, which many programmers like to use to separate distinct words (for example, `Last_Name`). You cannot use VBA keywords as variable names or duplicate a variable name within the same scope (for more on variable scope, see the next section "Understanding Variable Scope").

 TIP

Use the statement `Option Explicit` in the general declarations section of a code module to force explicit variable declaration. Without `Option Explicit`, variables can be dimensioned implicitly (without a `Dim` statement) as they are used in code. This is poor programming practice because it makes your code more difficult to read and consequently debug. To ensure that `Option Explicit` is automatically entered into each code module for your project, select Tools, Options in the VBA IDE. The Options dialog box opens. In that dialog box, check Require Variable Declaration and click OK.

Several conventions are commonly used to name variables. Of course, these are optional, but I encourage you to adopt some kind of convention because doing so will make it easier for you to read and debug your programs. Some of the conventions I've used and seen in VBA code are listed here:

◆ Use a descriptive name. For example, if a variable is going to hold someone's first name, declare it as `firstName`, `fName`, or something similar.

◆ Begin the name with a lowercase letter and then capitalize the first letter of subsequent words appearing in the name.

◆ Begin the name with a lowercase letter that reminds you of the variable's data type (for example, sFName for a string variable).

◆ Keep the number of characters in the variable name to a minimum without losing its descriptive nature. Hey, there's no point in typing all those characters if they're not needed!

Finally, the variable declaration should also specify the data type (String, Integer, Single, and so on). Specifying the data type tells VBA how much memory to reserve for the variable. Without specifying the data type, the variable will be a variant, and VBA will reserve the maximum amount of memory required for the largest data type. This not only wastes memory but also can decrease the speed of your application and make your program harder to debug.

You can declare more than one variable in one line of code. However, be sure to include the data type for each variable; otherwise, it will be dimensioned as a Variant. The following line of code declares two Integer variables and one String variable:

```
Dim myVar1 As Integer, myVar2 As Integer, fName As String
```

 NOTE

You can also specify a variable's data type using one of VBA's type-declaration characters. For example, Dim val1& specifies a variable of type Long because the ampersand (&) is the type-declaration character for the Long data type. Other type-declaration characters include ! (Single), % (Integer), @ (Currency), # (Double), and $ (String).

I discuss VBA data types in the section "VBA's Data Types," later in this chapter.

Understanding Variable Scope

The scope of a variable refers to its availability to your program. When a variable is within its scope, your program can access or manipulate it. When a variable is out of scope, it is unavailable. Any attempt to access it will generate a run-time error and code execution will stop. Three levels of variable scope are within a VBA application.

Procedure-Level Scope

A variable declared within the code block of a procedure (event, Sub, or Function procedure) is a procedural level variable. Consider the following sample Sub procedure:

```
Private Sub MyProcedure()
    Dim myVar As Integer
    myVar = myVar + 1
End Sub
```

The variable `myVar` is declared as an integer inside the `Sub` procedure `MyProcedure()`.
The variable `myVar` does not exist until this procedure is executed, and the variable is
dimensioned with the `Dim` statement. After the variable `myVar` is dimensioned, it can be
manipulated by additional code within the procedure. When program execution proceeds
to the line `End Sub`, the procedure is exited, and the memory reserved for the variable
`myVar` is released. So, the variable `myVar` is no longer available to the program. Each time
this procedure is called, the variable `myVar` is created and destroyed. In this example, the
variable `myVar` will never exceed a value of 1 (numerical variables are initialized to zero
when first declared).

If you need a procedural level variable to retain its value between calls to the procedure,
declare the variable using the `Static` keyword, as shown here:

```
Private Sub MyProcedure()
    Static myVar As Integer
    myVar = myVar + 1
End Sub
```

In the `Sub` procedure named `MyProcedure()`, the variable `myVar` is declared with
`Static`. So, the integer value stored in `myVar` will increment by one every time this procedure is executed until the program is reset.

Module-Level Scope

A variable is module-level scope if declared outside a procedure in the general declarations
section of a code module (see Chapter 1, "VBA Overview and the IDE") using the keyword `Dim` or `Private`.

 NOTE

Declaring module-level variables with `Dim` is equivalent to declaring the variable with
`Private`. Using `Private` is preferable because it leaves no ambiguity about the
scope of the variable.

If the following code is entered into a standard or form module, the variable myVar will be available to all procedures that are within the module in which it is declared but unavailable to all other procedures:

```
Private myVar As Integer
Private Sub SetVar()
    myVar=10
End Sub
Private Sub AddTwo()
    myVar = myVar + 2
End Sub
Private Sub SubtractOne()
    myVar = myVar - 1
End Sub
```

If the order of code execution follows the Sub procedures SetVar(), AddTwo(), and finally SubtractOne(),the final value of myVar will be 11 because myVar is a module-level variable and so available to all Sub procedures in the module. Any attempt to access the variable myVar from a procedure outside the module in which it was declared will result in an error.

Public Scope

The highest level of scope a variable can be assigned is Public. A Public variable (you may also know it as a global variable) is available to all procedures in all modules in your project. Public variables must be declared in the general declarations section of a standard module using the keyword Public. Avoid using Public variables if possible because they tend to make reading and debugging your code more difficult. Always ask yourself whether the variable needs to be available to procedures in more than one module. If not, don't declare the variable as Public.

 NOTE

You can use the keywords Private and Public only in the general declaration section of a code module to declare a variable. In a procedure, you must use Dim when declaring a variable.

 TIP

Avoid using the keyword Public to declare a variable in a form module because these variables will still have private module-level scope.

VBA's Data Types

Data types refer to the kind (numerical, text, and so on) of data that can be stored within the memory allocated for a variable. You can use several data types in the VBA programming language (see Table 2.1).

Table 2.1 VBA Data Types

Data Type	Storage Size (bytes)	Range
Byte	1	0 to 255
Boolean	2	True or False
Integer	2	−32,768 to 32,767
Long	4	−2,147,483,648 to 2,147,483,647
Single	4	−3.402823E38 to −1.401298E−45 for negative values; 1.401298E−45 to 3.402823E38 for positive values
Double	8	−1.79769313486231E308 to −4.94065645841247E−324 for negative values; 4.94065645841247E−324 to 1.79769313486232E308 for positive values
Currency	8	−922,337,203,685,477.5808 to 922,337,203,685,477.5807
Decimal	14	+/−79,228,162,514,264,337,593,543,950,335 with no decimal point; +/−7.9228162514264337593543950335 with 28 places to the right of the decimal; smallest non−zero number is +/−0.0000000000000000000000000001
Date	8	January 1, 100 to December 31, 9999
Object	4	Any Object reference
String (variable−length)	10 + string length	0 to approximately 2 billion
String (fixed−length)	Length of string	1 to approximately 65,400
Variant (numerical)	16	Any numeric value up to the range of a Double
Variant (string)	22 + string length	Same range as for variable−length String
User-defined	Sum of what is required by elements	Range of each element the same as the range of its data type

Numerical Data Types

Numerical data types include `Byte`, `Integer`, `Long`, `Single`, `Double`, `Currency`, and `Decimal`. You use the `Byte`, `Integer`, `Long`, `Currency`, and `Decimal` data types to store whole or non-fractional numbers of different magnitudes and `Single` and `Double` data types to store fractional, or *floating point*, numbers of different magnitudes.

 NOTE

The `Currency` and `Decimal` data types may appear as floating point numbers, but they are really stored as integers scaled by factors of 10. Also, you can't use the `Decimal` data type in variable declarations; use them only within a variant.

Care must be taken to ensure that a variable used to store a numerical value has sufficient memory and is of the right type. For instance, the following example attempts to store the numbers 512 and 5.12 in a variable declared as type `Byte`.

```
Dim myVar As Byte
myVar = 512
myVar = 5.12
```

The first assignment (`myVar = 512`) will generate an overflow error and halt program execution because the value 512 is outside the range allowed by the `Byte` data type (refer to Table 2.1 for the range of the `Byte` data type). The second assignment (`myVar = 5.12`) will not generate an error but will truncate the decimal portion of the number so that the variable holds the number 5.

You should also be careful about mixing numerical data types in mathematical operations, as shown in the following example:

```
Dim myAnswer As Byte
Dim num1 As Single
Dim num2 As Byte
num1 = 4.1
num2 = 5
myAnswer = num1 * num2
```

After the previous code executes, the final value stored in `myAnswer` is 20 because it was declared as type `Byte`. If a floating-point value is desired for `myAnswer`, it must be declared as type `Single`. This will change the final value of `myAnswer` to 20.5. The asterisk (*) is the multiplication operator in VBA. For a list of available mathematical operators in VBA see Table 2.2.

Table 2.2 VBA Mathematical Operators

Operator	Function	Example	Result
+	Addition	result = 10 + 3	13
–	Subtraction	result = 10 - 3	7
*	Multiplication	result = 10 * 3	30
/	Division with a floating point result	result = 10 / 3	3.333333
\	Division with an integer result	result = 10 \ 3	3
^	Exponent	result = 10 ^ 3	1000
Mod	Modulus	result = 10 Mod 3	1

 NOTE

The equal sign (=) in Table 2.2 serves as an assignment operator. That is, the expression result = 10 + 3 can be read as the variable result gets the value of 10 + 3.

String Data Types

String data types are used to hold a sequence of characters in a variable. The characters can be numbers, letters, and symbols or just about anything you can type on your keyboard. There are two types of string variables, fixed and variable length.

```
Dim myString As String*10
Dim myString2 As String
myString = "Fred Flintstone"
myString2 = "Fred Flintstone"
```

When declaring a fixed length string, you must specify the number of characters the string is allowed to hold. Values assigned to a string variable must be enclosed in quotes. In the preceding code, the variable myString can hold up to 10 characters. Anything longer will be truncated at 10 characters in length. Therefore, the string assigned to the variable myString is actually Fred Flint. Fixed length strings are less common because, in most situations, you will not know the length of the string that needs to be stored.

Variable length strings are declared without specifying a length. They can hold up to two billion characters (refer to Table 2.1), which is more space than you will ever need for any one-string variable.

NOTE

Variable length strings are initialized to a zero-length string (" ") when dimensioned. Fixed length strings are initialized to the length specified in the declaration.

You will usually need to manipulate or extract information from the contents of a string variable in a VBA program. Thankfully, a plethora of functions are built into VBA just for this purpose. I discuss these functions in Chapter 3, "Using VBA's Built-In Functions."

Variant Data Types

Variants are analogous to the general category in Excel (see Figure 2.1), which you use to format data in cells. The general category is the default category, and it essentially means that Excel will guess the data type for the value entered into a cell. Likewise, a variant means that VBA will choose the data type for you. Variants can contain any type of data except a fixed-length string. The variant data types are not explicitly declared in VBA (no type-declaration character). If you simply declare a variable with a `Dim` statement and leave off the type-declaration keyword or character, the variable is a variant, as shown here:

```
Dim myVar
```

Variant data types provide some flexibility when you are not sure what type of data needs to be stored in a variable. For example, if you need a variable to hold numerical data but you don't know the limits the data might reach, using a variant is one option. Variants holding numerical data will maintain the data type assigned to them. If you assign the integer value 32 (`Byte`) to a variant, the variable will be maintained as the `Byte` data type. However, if at some later time in the program, the same variable is assigned a larger integer (say 1000) or a floating-point number (5.6), the variant will be automatically promoted to an `Integer` or `Single`, respectively. So, using variants may reduce the risk of a run-time overflow error.

Despite the flexibility variants provide, avoid using them in your VBA programs. Variants use more memory than needed, may slow program execution speed, and make your code more difficult to read and debug. However, there are those rare occasions when variants are required — for example, when using VBA's `Array()` function (see Chapter 8, "Understanding File I/O, Debugging, and Error Handling in VBA").

More Data Types

Although not as common as the numerical and string data types, you will often use a few other data types in your VBA programs. Most notable of the remaining data types is the `Boolean` type. I will also discuss `Date`, user-defined, and the `Object` data types.

Boolean Data Types

The `Boolean` data type accepts one of two values, `True` or `False`. You may also assign the value 1 (`True`) or 0 (`False`) to a `Boolean` variable.

```
Dim myVal as Boolean
myVal = True
```

Boolean variables are initialized to `False` when dimensioned. They are commonly used in conditional expressions with decision structures (see Chapter 6, "Creating VBA Loops and Arrays").

Date Data Types

Values stored as type `Date` are actually floating point numbers. The number to the left of the decimal point represents a date between December 31, 1899, and December 31, 9999. The number to the right of the decimal represents a time between 0:00:00 and 23:59:59. So, the floating-point value `366.5` represents `12:00 PM on December 31, 1900` (366 days after December 31, 1899, and half way through the day). You will appreciate the convenience of the `Date` data type if you have to write many programs that handle dates and times. The convenience is a result of several VBA functions designed to work with the `Date` data type. I discuss these functions in Chapter 3.

User-Defined Data Types

A user-defined data type is one that is constructed from instances of several other parts. Each individual part of a user-defined type is defined with its own data type. Consider the example of a checkbook ledger with check number, description, debit, credit, and balance columns. If desired, you could use a variable of user-defined type to hold all the data from a single row in the ledger.

```
Type Ledger
      Number As Integer
      Description As String
      Debit As Currency
      Credit As Currency
      Balance As Currency
End Type
```

A user-defined type is defined with the `Type` and `End Type` keywords. The name of the data type is listed immediately after the `Type` keyword, `Ledger`, in the preceding example.

CAUTION

You use the `Type` statement only in the general declarations section of a code module to define a data type.

You can then declare a variable of the defined type anywhere within the scope of the definition using `Dim`, `Private`, or `Public` as though it were any other variable declaration.

```
Dim ledgerRow As Ledger
ledgerRow.Number = 1001
ledgerRow.Description = "Rent"
ledgerRow.Debit = 750
ledgerRow.Balance = ledgerRow.Balance - ledgerRow.Debit
```

You access the components of a variable declared as a user-defined type by using the variable name with the dot operator (`.`) followed by the component name. User-defined types are typically used as data records with random access files and occasionally with API calls.

Object Data Types

The last data type I will discuss is the `Object` data type. Variables of the `Object` data type store a reference to an object. Object variables are initially declared in the same manner as other variable types.

```
Dim myObject As Object
```

However, assigning a value to an `Object` data type differs from assignments to variables of other data types in that the reference to the object variable must be assigned with a `Set` statement.

```
Set myObject = Range("A1:B10")
```

The preceding statement assigns the object variable `myObject` to a `Range` object (see Chapter 7, "VBA Objects Specific to Excel Programming") consisting of 20 worksheet cells (A1 through B10). You can them manipulate the object using its properties and methods. For example, to change the background color of the range A1:B10, you could use the following:

```
myObject.Interior.Color = 16711680
```

This statement selects the `Interior` object of the `Range` object represented by the variable `myObject`. The `Color` property of the `Interior` object is then assigned a long integer value of `16711680` (Blue).

Declaring object variables using the generic `Object` data type is generally not a good idea. The problem is that the object will not be bound to the variable until run time (when program execution begins). If VBA has trouble resolving references to various properties and methods of the object at run time, performance can be decreased significantly. To avoid this problem, declare an object variable using the specific data type. The previous example can then be written as follows:

```
Dim myObject As Range
Set myObject = Range("A1:B10")
myObject.Interior.Color = 16711680
```

This time the object variable will be referenced at compile time, and VBA will easily work out references to properties and methods of the object because it has been specifically declared as a `Range` object. If desired, you can even give VBA a little more help by specifying the library in which it can find the object, as shown here:

```
Dim myObject As Excel.Range
```

Referencing the object library will avoid any ambiguity, but in most cases doing so is not necessary. You need to specify the object library if multiple objects with the same name exist in more than one library.

The Object Browser

To view a list of object libraries and the objects they contain, open the VBA IDE and press F2 to access the Object Browser (see Figure 2.2).

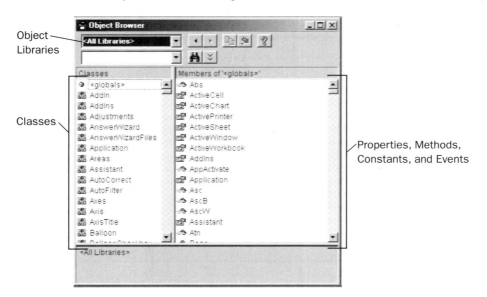

FIGURE 2.2 *The Object Browser.*

The Object Browser lists the currently loaded object libraries in a drop-down list box at the top of the window. On the left pane of the window is a list of available classes (objects). After you select a class from the list, a list of members (properties, methods, events, and constants) for that object appear in the right pane of the window.

TIP

For help on a specific object or one of its components, select the object or member name in the Object Browser and press F1.

For a detailed description on how to find and use objects in your VBA programs, see Chapter 7. Of course, the projects discussed throughout this book make extensive use of these objects.

VBA-Defined Constants

Two types of constants are available to you as a VBA programmer. First are those constants already defined by VBA. VBA-defined constants represent those constants defined in the VBA (names start with vb) object library and are available anywhere in your VBA code. For example, defined constants are available for some of the more common colors as shown in Table 2.3.

Table 2.3 Global VBA Color Constants

Constant Name	Value
vbBlack	0
vbBlue	16711680
vbCyan	16776960
vbGreen	65280
vbMagenta	16711935
vbRed	255
vbWhite	16777215
vbYellow	65535

Constants are a convenience because they don't require you to remember some obscure and often very large number for assigning a property value. For example, previously I showed you how to set the background color of a range of cells by setting the `Color` property of the `Interior` object to the value `16711680`, a number I had to look up. It's much easier to use the VBA color constant `vbBlue`, because I can remember the name of the constant.

```
myObject.Interior.Color = vbBlue
```

You can find available constants in the Object Browser. You can list global constants (constants that are available anywhere in your VBA code) by selecting globals at the top of the Classes list in the Object Browser. VBA constants are declared with global scope, so they are always available to your program.

The second type of constant is the constant you define in your VBA program. You may declare constants with procedural, module-level, or public scope just as you would a variable. Unlike variables, the value of a constant cannot be changed dynamically (while your program is running). Use constants to assign a meaningful name to a numerical or string value that may occur frequently in your program (which is analogous to using a named range in a spreadsheet formula). A named range in a spreadsheet makes your formulas more readable, and because named ranges are absolute references to specific cells, they are essentially constant values.

You declare constants using the `Const` keyword. Entering the following code into the general declarations section of a standard code module makes the global constant `HEADER` available throughout my program.

```
Public Const HEADER = "Duane Birnbaum" _
& vbCrLf & "317-111-2222" & vbCrLf _
& "email: myusername@myisp.com"
```

TIP

Use the string concatenation operator (&) to append strings. You can also use (+), but I don't recommend doing so because the plus sign may be ambiguous with addition.

I can then output the information stored in `HEADER` as often as needed without having to retype all the information it contains.

```
Cells(1, 1).Value = HEADER
```

Notice that I used the VBA constant `vbCrLf` twice in the definition of the `HEADER` constant to insert a carriage return and line feed.

TIP

Use the line continuation character (_) to continue a single code statement on the next line. As a result, VBA will treat the declaration of the constant HEADER as a single statement rather than three.

The value of a constant can never be changed in code. So use constants when you may frequently need the value the constant stores and you don't want to run the risk of that value being corrupted by a logic error in your code. You can capitalize the name of the constant, but that convention is not a requirement of the VBA language.

Summary

In this chapter, I discussed how to declare and assign values to variables and constants in a VBA program. I also provided considerable detail about VBA's data types. Chapter 3 explains how to use many of VBA's built-in functions that are designed for use with variables of a specific type, as well as functions designed for more general purposes.

Chapter 3

*Using VBA's
Built-In Functions*

Functions in VBA are similar in structure to functions in other programming languages. Most VBA functions require specific input (data type, quantity of data, and so on), and they all return at least one value. VBA contains numerous functions to assist you with your programming tasks. In this chapter, I discuss a few general-purpose functions as well as those functions designed to work with literals and variables of a specific data type. This chapter by no means includes all VBA's built-in functions, but it does introduce some of the most frequently used functions and shows you how to find functions designed for use with specific objects.

Handling Basic I/O with VBA

You will often need to prompt users with a message that helps them make a choice or directs them on how to proceed. Occasionally, you will also need user input. One of the simplest ways to send output to a user in VBA is to use the MsgBox() function. The MsgBox() function is used to display a window prompt with an informative message to the user. The user must respond to this prompt by clicking a button before continuing. You can easily obtain user input using the InputBox() function. The InputBox() function displays a window prompt to the user that includes a text box that is meant to collect user input through the keyboard.

 NOTE

The function name followed by empty parentheses signifies that functions require some type of input (often one or more variables). You will come upon a few examples in this book where input isn't required; these functions are written without parentheses and are noted as such.

The MsgBox() Function

You use the MsgBox() function to provide critical information to users and to force them to make decisions — for example, to click OK, Yes, No, or Cancel. The MsgBox() function outputs a message in a small window, like the one shown in Figure 3.1. Based on a user's response, the program continues as required.

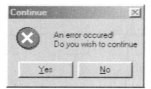

FIGURE 3.1 *A message box.*

The syntax for the `MsgBox()` function follows:

```
MsgBox(prompt[, buttons] [, title] [, helpfile, context])
```

The parameters (also called *arguments*) of the function include *prompt*, *buttons*, *title*, *helpfile*, and *context*. You must include a string value for the *prompt* argument that will serve as the message to a user when the message box is displayed. All other arguments are optional; however, it is usually a good idea to include values for the *buttons* and *title* arguments. You can also provide help information with the *helpfile* and *context* arguments. Input for the *buttons* argument tells VBA the type, icon, and number of buttons to display. The *buttons* argument can be one or more of the VBA constants listed in Table 3.1.

Table 3.1 Constants for the *buttons* Argument in the MsgBox() Function

Constant	Value	Description
VbOKOnly	0	Display OK button only.
VbOKCancel	1	Display OK and Cancel buttons.
VbAbortRetryIgnore	2	Display Abort, Retry, and Ignore buttons.
VbYesNoCancel	3	Display Yes, No, and Cancel buttons.
VbYesNo	4	Display Yes and No buttons.
VbRetryCancel	5	Display Retry and Cancel buttons.
VbCritical	16	Display Critical Message icon.
VbQuestion	32	Display Warning Query icon.
VbExclamation	48	Display Warning Message icon.
VbInformation	64	Display Information Message icon.
vbDefaultButton1	0	First button is default.
vbDefaultButton2	256	Second button is default.

continues

Table 3.1 Constants for the *buttons* Argument in the MsgBox() Function *(continued)*

Constant	Value	Description
vbDefaultButton3	512	Third button is default.
vbDefaultButton4	768	Fourth button is default.
VbApplicationModal	0	Application modal; a user must respond to the message box before continuing to work in the current application.
VbSystemModal	4096	System modal; all applications are suspended until a user responds to the message box.
VbMsgBoxHelpButton	16384	Adds Help button to the message box.
VbMsgBoxSetForeground	65536	Specifies the message box window as the foreground window.
VbMsgBoxRight	524288	Text is right-aligned.
VbMsgBoxRtlReading	1048576	Specifies that text should appear as right-to-left reading on Hebrew and Arabic systems.

In the following example, the program conveys to the user that an error occurred in the program and that input is required on how to proceed:

```
Dim msgString As String
Dim retValue As Integer
msgString = "An error occurred!" & vbCrLf & "Do you wish to continue"
retValue = MsgBox(msgString, vbCritical + vbYesNo, "Continue")
```

The message box will display the critical message icon along with buttons for Yes and No. A return value is required so that the program will know how to proceed based on the user's input (Yes or No). The MsgBox() function returns a different integer value depending on the button the user selects. The values returned by the MsgBox() function are also stored as VBA constants (listed in Table 3.2), which is useful only if the message box contains more than one button.

Table 3.2 MsgBox() Return Values

Constant	Value	Description
VbOK	1	OK
VbCancel	2	Cancel

Constant	Value	Description
VbAbort	3	Abort
VbRetry	4	Retry
VbIgnore	5	Ignore
VbYes	6	Yes
VbNo	7	No

If a user clicks Yes in the message box, a value of 6 will be assigned to the variable retValue. The program can then use the return value from the MsgBox() function to set a course of code execution (see Chapter 5, "Program Branching with VBA Decision Structures," for more on this topic).

CAUTION

Avoid using too many message boxes in your program — users often find them annoying. Reserve them for critical situations. Never use them for input or output that your program doesn't require in order to continue.

The InputBox() Function

Use the InputBox() function in your program when you need to force user input before program execution can proceed. The InputBox() function creates a window similar to the one shown in Figure 3.2.

FIGURE 3.2 *An input box.*

As with the MsgBox() function, the *prompt* is the only required argument.

```
InputBox(prompt[, title] [, default] [, xpos] [, ypos] [, helpfile, context])
```

However, it is a good idea to include the *title* and *default* arguments to provide the user with a little help in knowing what to enter. You might also specify the position of the dialog box using *xpos* and *ypos* along with references to a help file (*helpfile* and *context*).

```
Dim retValue As String
retValue = InputBox("Enter your name.", "Name", "First, Last")
```

In the preceding code, I assigned strings to the *prompt, title,* and *default* arguments of the InputBox() function, which resulted in the input box shown in Figure 3.2. I could have used string variables for the *prompt, title,* and *default* arguments. However, using the *default* argument provides users with help on how I want their names entered in the text box.

 CAUTION

Even if you provide help, I strongly encourage using input validation with the InputBox() function.

The InputBox() function returns as a string whatever the user enters into the text box. If the text box is empty or the user clicks the Cancel button, the InputBox() function returns a zero-length string (" ").

Changing Variable Types with Type-Conversion Functions

If you want to force a variable of one type to become a variable of another type, you can use one of several type-conversion functions (see Table 3.3 for a list of these functions).

You typically use these functions to help document code. For example, when you want to ensure that a mathematical operation returns an integer data type, use the CInt() function. The following code makes it clear that the result of the multiplication will be an integer:

```
val1 = 3.14
val2 = 6.63
val3 = CInt(val1 * val2)
```

The CInt() function is not needed in this example to return an integer result. Simply declaring the variable val3 as an integer will ensure the integer result. However, using the CInt() function does help self-document the code.

Table 3.3 Type-Conversion Functions

Function	Return Type	Example
CBool()	Boolean	CBool(1) returns True.
CByte()	Byte	CByte(5.6) returns 6.
CCur()	Currency	CCur(10.3245567) returns 10.3246.
CDate()	Date	CDate(366.5) returns 12/31/1900 12:00:00 PM.
CDbl()	Double	CDbl(99.2 ^ 28) returns 7.98595429489212E+55.
CDec()	Decimal	CDec(2 ^ 32) returns 4294967296.
CInt()	Integer	CInt(25 * 5.623) returns 141.
CLng()	Long	CLng(2 ^ 30) returns 1073741824.
CSng()	Single	CSng(25 * 5.5) returns 137.5.
CStr()	String	CStr(10019) returns "10019".
CVar()	Variant	

CAUTION

If the value of the expression passed to a type-declaration function is outside its range (for example, CInt(33000)), an overflow error will result.

VBA's Basic Math and Trigonometric Functions

With an application such as Excel, you may find yourself writing programs that require a fair amount of math. If needed, VBA provides several trigonometric and other math-related functions for use in your programs (Table 3.4 lists these functions). Their use is generally straightforward. You just provide an argument to the function, and it returns the result. In the following example, the Atn() function (arctangent) calculates the value of pi. This result is fairly useful because VBA does not directly supply pi with its own function (you can use an Excel worksheet function to return the value of pi).

```
Dim pi As Double
pi = 4 * Atn(1)
```

Table 3.4 VBA Math Functions

Function	Description	Example
Abs()	Returns the absolute value of a number.	Abs(-10) returns 10.
Atn()	Returns the arctangent of a number (radians).	4 * Atn(1) returns 3.14159265358979.
Cos()	Returns the cosine of a number (radians).	Cos(0) returns 1.
Exp()	Returns the base *e* exponential of a number.	Exp(1) returns 2.71828182845905.
Fix()	Returns the integer portion of a number.	Fix(-9.1) returns -9.
Int()	Returns the integer portion of a number.	Int(-9.1) returns -10.
Log()	Returns the natural logarithm of a number.	Log(2.718281828) returns 1.
Rnd()	Returns a random number between 0 and 1.	
Sgn()	Returns the sign of a number.	Sgn(-9) returns -1.
Sin()	Returns the sine of a number (radians).	Sin(3.14159265/2) returns 1.
Sqr()	Returns the square root of a number.	Sqr(9) returns 3.
Tan()	Returns the tangent of a number (radians).	Tan(3.14159265/4) returns 1.

The random number function Rnd() is a commonly used function. The Rnd() function returns a pseudo random number (**Single**) between 0 and 1. You can pass an optional argument to the Rnd() function as a seed value; however, each call to the Rnd() function will then trigger the same sequence of random numbers. The sequence is repetitive because the Rnd() function always uses the previous random number as a seed value. To prevent repetitive sequences, use the **Randomize** statement to initialize the random number generator with a seed value based on the system clock.

```
Dim val1
Randomize
val1 = Int(100 * Rnd + 1)
```

You can use the preceding code statements to generate integer random numbers between 1 and 100.

Manipulating Strings with VBA's String Functions

Manipulating strings is one of an application's most common tasks. Whether searching for specific substrings, altering the content of a string, or just returning the number of characters in a string, VBA includes a number of functions that you can use to handle these tasks. Most of the string functions are easy to use and require one or more arguments that include the string that is to be tested or manipulated. This section covers many of the large number of string functions that you can use to manipulate strings (see Table 3.5 for many of these string functions).

Table 3.5 VBA String Functions

Function	Description	Example
Str()	Converts a number to a string.	Str(12) returns the string 12.
Val()	Converts a string to a number.	Val("5XJT") returns 5.
LTrim(), RTrim(), Trim()	Removes leading and trailing spaces from a string.	Trim(" My String ") returns "My String".
Left()	Returns a substring from the left side of a string.	Left("Test",2) returns "Te".
Right()	Returns a substring from the right side of a string.	Right("Test",2) returns "st".
Mid()	Returns a substring from inside a string.	Mid("Test", 2,2) returns "es".
InStr()	Returns the location of the first character of a substring within another string.	InStr("Test", "e") returns 2.
Len()	Returns the number of characters in a string.	Len("Test") returns 4.
LCase()	Converts the string to lowercase.	LCase("ABCD") returns "abcd".
UCase()	Converts the string to uppercase.	UCase("abcd") returns "ABCD".

continues

Table 3.5 VBA String Functions (continued)

Function	Description	Example
StrConv()	Converts a string as specified by several possible choices.	Debug.Print StrConv("fred", vbProperCase) returns "Fred".
StrComp()	Returns the result of comparing two strings.	Debug.Print StrComp(str1, str2, vbTextCompare) returns 0 if two strings are equal, –1 if str1 is greater than str2, or 1 if str1 is less than str2.
StrReverse()	Reverses the order of the characters in a string.	StrReverse("Test") returns "tseT".
Format()	Formats strings, dates, and numbers as specified.	Format("ABCD", "<") returns "abcd".
Space()	Returns a string built from a specified number of spaces.	
Asc()	Returns the character code representing the first character in a string.	Asc("A") returns 65.
Chr()	Returns the character represented by the character code.	Chr(65) returns "A".
Dir()	Returns a string representing the name of a file or directory with specified pattern.	Dir("C:\Windows*.ini") returns first file found with specified extension.
CurDir()	Returns a string representing the current drive path.	CurDir() returns current directory.

String Formatting Functions

There are actually so many string functions that you often have more than one choice for carrying out a task. This is especially true with the formatting functions (LCase(), UCase(), StrConv(), and Format()). For example, each line of the following code formats a given string with all lowercase characters:

```
Cells(1, "A").Value = LCase("ALL LOWERCASE")
```

```
Cells(2, "A").Value = Format("ALL LOWERCASE ", "<")
Cells(3, "A").Value = StrConv("ALL LOWERCASE ", vbLowerCase)
```

The output of the preceding code is shown in Figure 3.3. The functions `LCase()`, `Format()`, and `StrConv()` can all be used to convert a string to all lowercase characters. The difference between these three functions is that `Format()` and `StrConv()` have more formatting options. In particular, you can use the `Format()` function to format numbers and dates, and it is, in fact, more useful for those purposes.

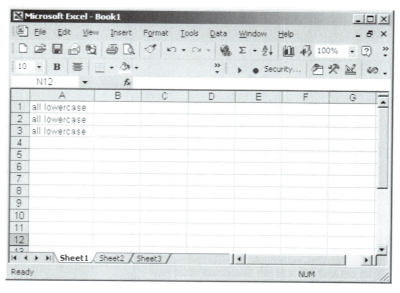

FIGURE 3.3 *Converting strings to lowercase.*

 NOTE

Rather than take up space providing *all* the required and optional syntax for the string functions discussed in this chapter, I'll just refer you to the online help. My intention, instead, is to cover the options for solving common problems.

String Concatenation: Str() and Val()

You can concatenate strings in VBA using either the addition (+) or the ampersand (&) character. To avoid confusion with addition, always use the ampersand (&) to concatenate strings. In the following code, using the ampersand for string concatenation makes it clear that the resulting string stored in the variable `newStr` will be `"55"`.

```
string1 = "5"
```

```
string2 = "5"
newStr = string1 & string2
```

You use the functions `Str()` and `Val()` to convert between numerical and string data. In most cases, you won't need them because VBA will cast the data to its proper type for the operation. In the following example, the `Val()` function is not required to convert the variable `str1` to a numerical value before it is added to `num1` because VBA will assume that an addition operation is desired. However, using `Val()` in this case does help document the code, leaving no ambiguity as to the desired operation.

```
num1 = 5
str1 = "5"
num2 = num1 + Val(str1)
```

Similarly, use the `Str()` function to help document your code when concatenating strings.

```
zip = 55555
zipx = 4444
newzip = Str(zip) + Str(zipx)
```

Without the `Str()` functions in the last line of code, the operation performed is addition. Using `Str()` ensures that the operation is concatenation. Of course, it's a mute point if the ampersand is used for concatenation.

Chr() and Asc()

You use the `Chr()` and `Asc()` functions to convert between the numerical and string representations of VBA's character code set (see Table 3.6 for certain selected characters). The character code set is essentially the ASCII standard set with 256 characters; however, many of the characters are not supported by VBA. The `Chr()` function is particularly useful in Excel VBA because it can be used to represent column indices in a spreadsheet. In an Excel VBA program, there is often a need to loop through a range of rows and columns in a worksheet. So, you can use the `Chr()` function to return characters representing a worksheet column, as shown in the following line of code:

```
Range(Chr(65 + I) & "1").Value
```

If `I = 0` in this example, then the reference is to cell A1 because the value 65 represents uppercase A. As long as the variable `I` is between 0 and 25, the previous code will return a proper reference (A–Z).

Similarly, you can use the `Asc()` function to convert a character to its numerical representation. The variable `num1` will hold the integer value 65 in the following example:

```
num1 = Asc("A")
```

NOTE

You can find more on looping in VBA in Chapter 6, "Creating VBA Loops and Arrays."

Table 3.6 Selected Characters from VBA's Character Code Set

Character Code	Character	Character Code	Character	Character Code	Character
8	backspace	61	=	94	^
9	tab	62	>	95	_
10	linefeed	63	?	96	`
13	carriage return	64	@	97	a
32	[space]	65	A	98	b
33	!	66	B	99	c
34	"	67	C	100	d
35	#	68	D	101	e
36	$	69	E	102	f
37	%	70	F	103	g
38	&	71	G	104	h
39	'	72	H	105	i
40	(	73	I	106	j
41	)	74	J	107	k
42	*	75	K	108	l
43	+	76	L	109	m
44	,	77	M	110	n
45	–	78	N	111	o
46	.	79	O	112	p
47	/	80	P	113	q

continues

Table 3.6 Selected Characters from VBA's Character Code Set *(continued)*

Character Code	Character	Character Code	Character	Character Code	Character
48	0	81	Q	114	r
49	1	82	R	115	s
50	2	83	S	116	t
51	3	84	T	117	u
52	4	85	U	118	v
53	5	86	V	119	w
54	6	87	W	120	x
55	7	88	X	121	y
56	8	89	Y	122	z
57	9	90	Z	123	{
58	:	91	[	124	|
59	;	92	\	125	}
60	<	93	]	126	~

Nesting Functions

You can nest functions in VBA virtually to any degree. However, the readability of your code will suffer. Examine the following code and see if you can understand what it is supposed to do:

```
cell2 = Mid(rangeStr, InStr(1, rangeStr, ":") + 1, _
    Len(rangeStr) - InStr(1, rangeStr, ":"))
```

If you figured out that the previous line of code returns a string representing the second part of a reference to a cell range, you are correct. For example, if the worksheet range represented by the variable `rangeStr` is "A1:C10", the variable `cell2` will hold C10 after this code executes. In this example, the function `Len()` is nested once and the function `Instr()` is nested twice within the function `Mid()`. The first occurrence of the `Instr()` function is used to set the starting value for the `Mid()` function. The combination of the `Len()` and `Instr()` functions are then used to determine the length of the string returned by `Mid()`. Clearly, this is a difficult line of code to read, and you should avoid nesting this many functions if possible.

Using VBA's Date and Time-Related Functions

VBA includes several functions that you can use to return and manipulate dates and times. Some of these functions do not accept arguments and are denoted by omitting the parentheses after the function name. Other functions require arguments in numerical or string formats that represent a date or time. Table 3.7 lists the VBA functions that are designed for use with dates.

Table 3.7 VBA Date and Time Functions

Function	Description
Time	Returns current system time.
Now	Returns current system date and time.
Date	Returns current system date.
DateDiff()	Returns the difference between two dates.
DateAdd()	Returns a date to which a timer interval has been added.
Year()	Returns an integer representing the year.
Month()	Returns an integer (1–12) representing the month of the year.
Weekday()	Returns an integer (1–7) representing the day of the week.
Day()	Returns an integer (1–31) representing the day of the month.
Hour()	Returns an integer (0–23) representing the hour of the day.
Minute()	Returns an integer (0–59) representing the minute of the hour.
Second()	Returns an integer (0–59) representing the second of the minute.
TimeSerial()	Returns a date for the specified hour, minute, and second.
DateSerial()	Returns a date for the specified year, month, and day.
TimeValue()	Returns a date containing the time specified.
DateValue()	Returns a date containing the date specified.

You use the Time, Now, and Date functions to return the current system time, time and date, and date, respectively. (Note: These three functions don't accept arguments, so I didn't use parentheses with them.) Many of the date functions are designed to return part of a date or time from a value input as a date or string. The Year(), Month(), Weekday(), Day(),

`Hour()`, `Minute()`, and `Second()` functions all return integers representing their namesake from a date or time input. The argument for these functions must be either a date or a string formatted as a date. The following example uses the `Month()` function to return an integer representing the current month. The `Now` function returns the current system date and time and is passed to `Month()`.

```
curMonth = Month(Now)        'returns current month as an integer
prevMonth = Month("Feb 4, 1900")      'returns 2
```

Other functions listed in Table 3.7 are used to return a date from a string or numerical input. The `TimeSerial()`, `DateSerial()`, `TimeValue()`, and `DateValue()` functions all return dates representing either a time or a date.

```
myTime = TimeValue("9:00")     'returns 9:00:00 AM

myDate = DateValue("Nov, 23 04")      'returns 11/23/2004

myTime = TimeSerial(9, 0, 0)       'returns 9:00:00 AM

myDate = DateSerial(4, 11, 23)       'returns 11/23/2004
```

Another date function that can be quite useful is the `DateDiff()` function. As you may have guessed from the name, the `DateDiff()` function returns the difference between two dates. The unit for the difference is specified as a string (for example, `"s"` for second, `"m"` for month, `"yyyy"` for year, and so on).

```
myInterval = DateDiff("s", Now, "10/10/03")

myInterval = DateDiff("m", Now, "10/10/03")

myInterval = DateDiff("yyyy", Now, "10/10/03")
```

The preceding examples will return the number of seconds, months, and years between October 10, 2003, and the current time and date, respectively. Be careful to use a data type with sufficient range for the return value in order to avoid an overflow error.

Using Excel Worksheet Functions in Your VBA Code

If you are a regular Excel user, you are aware of the functions that can be used in spreadsheet formulas. The Excel application includes more than 300 worksheet functions that will carry out date, time, textual, and numerous mathematical operations on a data set. These functions are conceptually the same as a VBA function in that you pass a worksheet function one or more arguments (in most cases), and it returns a single value (see Appendix A, "Basic Excel Tutorial").

You can find a list of available worksheet functions in the Insert Function dialog box shown in Figure 3.4.

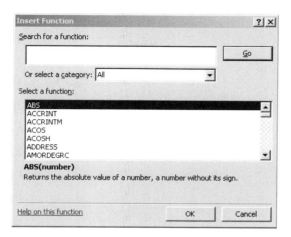

FIGURE 3.4 *Excel's Insert Function dialog box.*

Many of the worksheet functions complement VBA's collection of functions such as the `PI()` function, which returns the value of pi. Other worksheet functions, such as the `SQRT()` function, repeat what is already available in VBA. Obviously, it is the complementary functions that are of interest, and you can easily access these functions, just by doing the following:

```
myAvg = Application.WorksheetFunction.Average(5, 6, 7)      'returns 6
mySum = Application.WorksheetFunction.Sum(5, 6, 7)      'returns 18
```

You must access the functions through the `Application` and `WorksheetFunction` objects in Excel VBA. You then add the function name to the object path and supply the appropriate arguments. The `Application` object is discussed in Chapter 7, "VBA Objects Specific to Excel Programming," and there are several examples of the `WorksheetFunction` object throughout the book.

Summary

This chapter looked closely at the `MsgBox()` and `InputBox()` functions used for simple input and output in VBA. Then I discussed several VBA functions you can use for math, string, and date functions. I also briefly discussed type-conversion as the method for changing a variable's data type in your code. The functions discussed in this chapter, although quite common, comprise only a small percentage of the functions available in VBA. The thing to remember is that functions are available in VBA for nearly every aspect of programming you will encounter. In later chapters, many other VBA functions are put to use.

Chapter 4

Chapter 1, "VBA Overview and the IDE," briefly introduces VBA modules, and the three previous chapters occasionally reference the use of a Sub or event procedure. This chapter provides a more detailed description of VBA procedures (events, Subs, and Functions) and the code modules in which you will find or write them. In this chapter, you learn about common event procedures associated with the `Workbook`, `Worksheet`, and `Userform` objects, as well as ActiveX controls. Procedure scope, passing arguments between procedures, calling procedures, and executing procedures from the Excel application are also discussed.

Writing VBA Event Procedures

Before explaining event procedures, allow me to set a context by explaining what a procedure is and how you use it. A *procedure* is a small program that handles a specific task. You define a procedure with opening and closing statements and by adding code within those opening and closing statements, as shown here:

```
ProcedureType ProcedureName(optional argument list)
    'Block(s) of code here
End ProcedureType
```

You use procedures to encapsulate your program by dividing it into manageable tasks. Designing a program that makes proficient use of procedures can significantly reduce your workload and consequently ease frustrations brought on by debugging code.

With that background, you are ready to begin writing event procedures. *Event procedures* are blocks of code that are associated with programming objects and triggered by a specific action. Many of the existing objects in Excel and VBA have predefined event procedures to which you, as a programmer, add code.

Unlike Sub or Function procedures that are entirely defined by the programmer, VBA defines event procedures with opening and closing statements, a procedure name, and an argument list (if any). VBA also handles the trigger or action that initiates an event procedure. It is the programmer's job to select the event procedure that will be used to handle a specific task and then to write the code within the selected event procedure. The user directly initiates most event triggers by means of a specific action (button click, mouse move, and so on). In Chapter 1, I introduced one example of an event procedure in the `Click()` event of the Command Button control. In the following sections, you learn about a few of the more common and useful event procedures available with VBA Userforms, ActiveX controls, and Excel `Workbook` and `Worksheet` objects.

Workbook Events

Workbooks, which are stored as separate files in Excel, encompass a large set of VBA objects. Workbooks can contain numerous worksheets, chart sheets, embedded charts, ActiveX controls, and anything else an Excel file is capable of storing. Consequently, the `Workbook` object is a top-level object in Excel's object model (see Chapter 7, "VBA Objects Specific to Excel Programming"). Because it's a top-level object, you expect the `Workbook` object to have its own code module and an extensive set of predefined events, and this is the case. Table 4.1 provides a partial list of the many events associated with the `Workbook` object. For a complete list of workbook event procedures, open the code module for the `Workbook` object (default name of `ThisWorkbook`) listed in the Project Explorer, select the `Workbook` object from the object drop-down list, and select the event drop-down list (see Figure 4.1). The names for these event procedures are defined by VBA and cannot be changed if you want Excel to trigger the procedure. In most cases, the name is indicative of the action that triggers the procedure.

Table 4.1 Select Event Procedures of the Workbook Object

Procedure Name	Trigger
Activate()	Activating or selecting the workbook when it was not already the top-level workbook.
BeforeClose()	Closing the workbook. The code executes before the workbook closes.
BeforeSave()	Saving the workbook. The code executes before the workbook is saved.
Deactivate()	Deactivating the workbook by selecting another workbook.
NewSheet()	Adding a new worksheet to the workbook.
Open()	Opening the Excel workbook file (.xls).
SheetActivate()	Selecting a new sheet within the workbook.
SheetCalculate()	Recalculating the formulas in a worksheet.
SheetChange()	Changing the contents of a cell in any worksheet.
SheetDeactivate()	Deactivating the sheet by selecting another sheet within the same workbook.
SheetSelectionChange()	Selecting a new cell in a worksheet.

continues

Table 4.1 Select Event Procedures of the Workbook Object (continued)

Procedure Name	Trigger
WindowActivate()	Activating or selecting a workbook window. Identical to the Activate() event when only one workbook window exists.
WindowResize()	Resizing a workbook window.

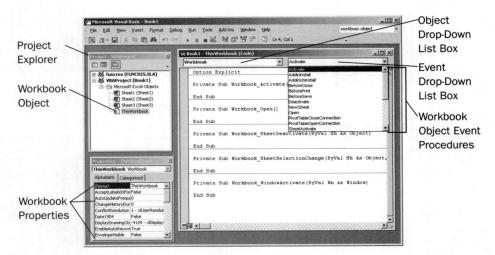

FIGURE 4.1 *A code module for the Workbook object.*

Workbook event procedures are convenient for holding initialization and validation code. For example, if you need to display a custom toolbar with a particular workbook, use the Open() event procedure. First, select this procedure from the event drop-down list in the code module for the Workbook object and then enter the code. The user triggers the Open() event procedure by opening the Excel file that contains the event procedure.

```
Private Sub Workbook_Open()
    Application.CommandBars("My Custom Toolbar").Enabled = True
End Sub
```

To hide the toolbar, use the BeforeClose() event of the Workbook object. The user triggers this procedure by selecting an item that will close the workbook. In this example, the name of the custom toolbar is "My Custom Toolbar," which was assigned when it was created (see Chapter 1 to learn how to create and name a custom toolbar). You can also use an index number if it is known. The CommandBars object is associated with menus and toolbars, and you use its `Enabled` property (type `Boolean`) to show and hide the object, as illustrated here:

```
Private Sub Workbook_BeforeClose(Cancel As Boolean)
    Application.CommandBars("My Custom Toolbar").Enabled = False
End Sub
```

 NOTE

Procedures that set program variables and objects to required values on startup are generally referred to as *initialization routines*. Procedures that validate user input are referred to as *validation routines*.

If your program needs to validate user input, one possible location for the code is the `SheetChange()` event procedure of the `Workbook` object. The user triggers this procedure by changing the contents of a cell in a worksheet. The altered worksheet must be contained within the workbook whose `SheetChange()` event procedure has been modified to include the validation code. The specific cell altered by the user is passed to the `SheetChange()` event procedure by VBA via its `Target` argument (see "Passing Arguments with ByVal and ByRef" later in this chapter).

```
Private Sub Workbook_SheetChange(ByVal Sh As Object, ByVal Target As Range)
    'Validation code is entered here.
End Sub
```

 TIP

Objects, properties, and methods are called with the dot (`.`) operator in VBA. The sequence is *object.property* or *object.method*. You may also list more than one method when returning subordinate objects (for example, `Workbooks(1).Worksheets(1).Range("A1").Value = 5`). For a complete discussion of the Excel object model, see Chapter 7.

You can use the code in the `SheetChange()` event procedure of the `Workbook` object to validate the values entered or altered by the user. A decision structure (see Chapter 5, "Program Branching with VBA Decision Structures") can be used to direct program execution based on the results of the validation.

In the previous code example, notice that the `SheetChange()` event procedure contains an argument list. The list declares two variables: `Sh` (type `Object`) and `Target` (type `Range`). VBA defines the argument list, and you should not edit it in any way. These variables are designed for use in the event procedure. When the procedure is triggered, VBA passes object references to these variables. The variable `Sh` holds a reference to the `Worksheet` object in which the user is working, and the variable `Target` holds a reference to the `Range` object (cell or range of cells) whose contents were altered. These parameters are very helpful because you can use them to test which cell or range of cells was altered by the user. The program can then decide on a course of action based on the values held by `Sh` and `Target`. If you enter the following line of code in the `SheetChange()` event procedure, the cell references and sheet name altered by the user will be output in a message box. Test this code in Excel by altering the contents of different cells in multiple worksheets. The example displayed in Figure 4.2 shows the output from the message box after the contents of five cells are deleted.

```
MsgBox (Sh.Name & " " & Target.Address)
```

You use the `Name` property of the `Worksheet` object to output the name of the worksheet, and the `Address` property of the `Range` object contains the cell references of the range altered by the user.

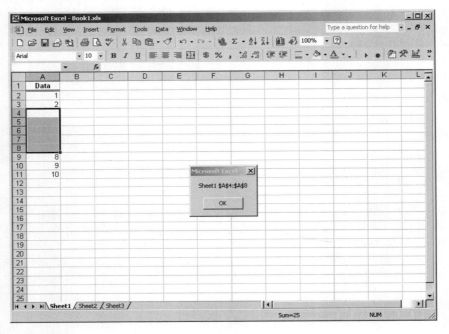

FIGURE 4.2 *Output from the* `SheetChange()` *event.*

NOTE

I discuss the ByVal keyword in the section "Passing Arguments with ByVal and ByRef" later in this chapter.

You will see other examples of Workbook object event procedures in the programming projects discussed later in this book.

Worksheet Events

Every worksheet in a workbook is represented as a single Worksheet object in Excel-VBA, and each worksheet has its own code module, which you can select from the Project Explorer. Worksheet event procedures are triggered by an action specific to a single worksheet. You can select a worksheet event procedure from the event drop-down list in the object's code module (see Figure 4.3). Table 4.2 provides a list of the available worksheet event procedures.

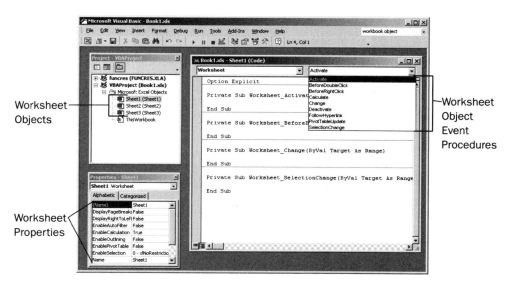

FIGURE 4.3 *A code module for the* Worksheet *object.*

Table 4.2 Event Procedures of the Worksheet Object

Event	Trigger
Activate()	Activating or selecting the worksheet when it was not previously selected
BeforeDoubleClick()	Double-clicking the worksheet
BeforeRightClick()	Right-clicking the worksheet
Calculate()	Recalculating formulas in a worksheet
Change()	Changing the contents of a cell in the worksheet
Deactivate()	Selecting another worksheet
FollowHyperlink()	Selecting a hyperlink in a worksheet
PivotTableUpdate()	Updating a pivot table in a worksheet
SelectionChange()	Selecting a new cell or range of cells in a worksheet

Many of the worksheet event procedures listed in Table 4.2 are essentially the same as those associated with the Workbook object, only with a narrower scope. For example, every worksheet has its own SelectionChange() event, so the SelectionChange() event of the Worksheet object is triggered when the user selects a new range in a specific worksheet, whereas the SheetSelectionChange() event of the Workbook object is triggered when the user selects a new range in a worksheet contained within a specific workbook. It then follows that worksheet event procedures are used in a similar fashion as workbook event procedures (that is, for validation and initialization).

Enter the following code into the code module for a worksheet and then select the worksheet in Excel. With each range selection you make in the worksheet, the background color of the selection will turn blue.

```
Private Sub Worksheet_SelectionChange(ByVal Target As Range)
    Target.Interior.Color = vbBlue
End Sub
```

The procedure uses the reference to the Range object passed into the variable Target to change the color of the user-selected range to blue. An example of a worksheet resulting from the use of this procedure is shown in Figure 4.4.

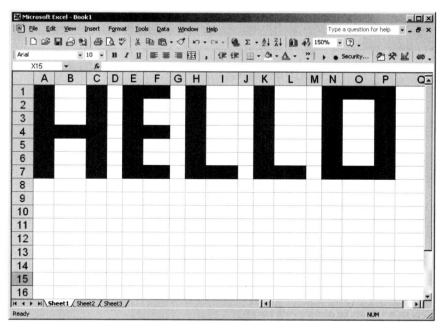

FIGURE 4.4 *Using the* SelectionChange() *event procedure.*

ActiveX Controls

ActiveX controls are reusable objects with their own set of properties, methods, and events. As I mention in Chapter 1, you can use worksheets as containers for ActiveX controls. Because ActiveX controls are placed within another object, their event procedures can be found in the code module of the object in which they are placed. So, you will find the event procedures of an ActiveX control placed on a worksheet within the code module of the Worksheet object. The code module for the Worksheet object from Chapter 1 containing the List Box, Label, and two Command Button controls is shown in Figure 4.5. The event procedures of any of these four ActiveX controls are selected from the event drop-down list box after selecting the name of the control from the object drop-down list box. The three event procedures that the program uses (all Click() event procedures) are listed within the code window for the Worksheet object that contains the controls.

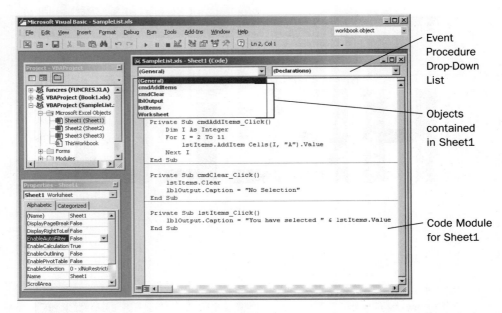

FIGURE 4.5 *Object drop-down list and code module for a worksheet containing several ActiveX controls.*

You can quickly access the default event procedure of an ActiveX control by double-clicking the control on the worksheet while in design mode. Each ActiveX control has a default event procedure. This will launch the VBA IDE (if it is not already open) and open the code module for the `Worksheet` object containing the ActiveX control. The default event procedure of an ActiveX control is the procedure for which you typically will have to write code because it is the procedure that is most often triggered by the user. For example, the `Click()` event is the default procedure for a Command Button control. Table 4.3 lists the default event procedures for the ActiveX controls included with Excel.

Table 4.3 Default Event Procedures for ActiveX Controls

ActiveX Control	Default Event
Check Box	`Click()`
Text Box	`Change()`
Command Button	`Click()`
Option Button	`Click()`
List Box	`Click()`

ActiveX Control	Default Event
Combo Box	Change()
Toggle Button	Click()
Spin Button	Change()
Scroll Bar	Change()
Label	Click()
Image	Click()

Now consider another simple programming example using the default event procedures of the Option Button and Scroll Bar controls. The program uses Option Button controls to set the chart type and a Scroll Bar control to change the color of the data series on an embedded chart in a worksheet. Option buttons provide the user with a single choice from several possibilities. You can provide the user with a large range of values to choose from with Scroll Bar control. Table 4.4 lists the properties of the Option Button and Scroll Bar controls that typically are altered at design time.

Table 4.4 Common Properties of the Option Button and Scroll Bar Controls

Control	Property	Description
Option Button	Name	Name used to access the control in code. Convention is to start the name with opt.
Option Button	Caption	Text displayed to the user.
Option Button	Font	Font style and type for the Caption property.
Option Button	Value	True or False depending on whether the control is selected.
Scroll Bar	Name	Name used to access the control in code. Convention is to start the name with scr.
Scroll Bar	Min	Minimum number that can be stored in the Value property.
Scroll Bar	Max	Maximum number that can be stored in the Value property.
Scroll Bar	Value	Current value of the scroll bar. Will always be an integer between the Min and Max properties.

continues

Table 4.4 Common Properties of the Option Button and Scroll Bar Controls (continued)

Control	Property	Description
Scroll Bar	SmallChange	Increments/decrements the Value property of the scroll bar when the user selects either arrow at the ends of the scroll bar.
Scroll Bar	LargeChange	Increments/decrements the Value property of the scroll bar when the user selects the area within the scroll bar.

The worksheet is shown in Figure 4.6, and the content of the code module for the worksheet is listed here:

```
Option Explicit
Private myChart As Chart
```

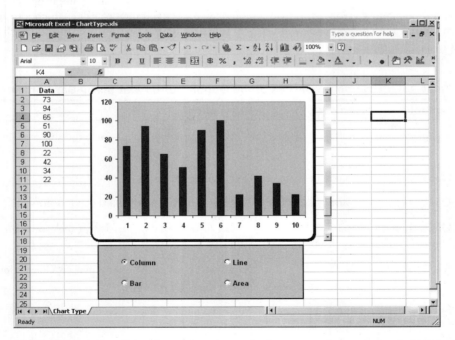

FIGURE 4.6 *Using ActiveX controls to change the chart type and color of an embedded chart.*

Because the chart must be accessed in each event procedure in the code module, the module-level object variable myChart (type Chart) is declared. The Name properties of the Option Button controls were changed to more descriptive values at design time (optArea, optBar, optColumn, and optLine). Their Click() event procedures are triggered when the user selects the option button. The program then edits the chart by changing its type appropriately.

Specifically, each Click() event procedure of the Option Button controls sets a reference to the embedded chart on the worksheet via the ChartObjects collection object and the Chart object. The ChartType property is then set with a VBA-defined constant (xlArea, xlBarClustered, xlColumnClustered, and xlLine). The Click() event procedures of the Option Button controls are listed next.

```
Private Sub optArea_Click()
    Set myChart = ActiveSheet.ChartObjects(1).Chart
    myChart.ChartType = xlArea
End Sub
Private Sub optBar_Click()
    Set myChart = ActiveSheet.ChartObjects(1).Chart
    myChart.ChartType = xlBarClustered
End Sub
Private Sub optColumn_Click()
    Set myChart = ActiveSheet.ChartObjects(1).Chart
    myChart.ChartType = xlColumnClustered
End Sub
Private Sub optLine_Click()
    Set myChart = ActiveSheet.ChartObjects(1).Chart
    myChart.ChartType = xlLine
End Sub
```

The Change() event of the Scroll Bar control provides the user with the ability to change the color of the charted data series. In the following Change() event procedure, the ColorIndex property of the Interior object is accessed via a host of Excel objects (Worksheet, ChartObject, Chart, SeriesCollection, and finally Series) to assign its value to that of the Value property of the Scroll Bar control (60 possible values set via the Min and Max properties).

```
Private Sub scrColor_Change()
    Set myChart = ActiveSheet.ChartObjects(1).Chart
    myChart.SeriesCollection(1).Interior.ColorIndex = scrColor.Value
End Sub
```

The Interior object represents the interior area of an object for those objects that have borders (for example, ChartArea, Range, Series, and so on). Note that this procedure will generate a run-time error if the value of the scroll bar is changed when the chart is a line type, because you cannot return an Interior object for this specific Series object. This nuance is just one many when working with Excel's Chart object.

NOTE

The remaining ActiveX controls are discussed as they occur in examples and programming projects later in this book. I discuss the Chart object in Chapter 7.

Userforms

You use *Userforms* in VBA to design custom dialog boxes in your Office application. You add them using the Insert menu in the VBA IDE. If you are familiar with Visual Basic, Userforms will remind you of the forms in that language, albeit with fewer properties and methods. As is the case with their Visual Basic counterparts, Userforms are container objects and, as such, are listed separately in the Project Explorer. So Userforms have their own code module. A blank Userform and its associated code module are shown in Figure 4.7.

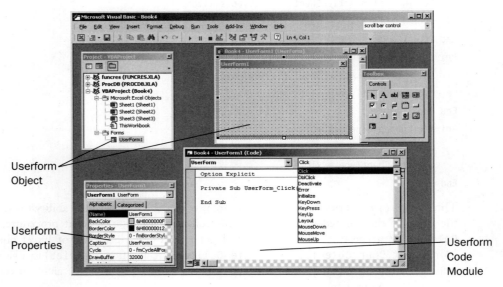

FIGURE 4.7 *The Userform object and its code module from the VBA IDE.*

 TIP

Userforms have numerous properties that are normally set at design time. Many of these properties adjust the appearance of the Userform. Some of the properties of the Userform that you may want to set at design time include Name, BackColor, BorderColor, BorderStyle, Caption, StartUpPosition, SpecialEffect, Width, and Height.

Userform Events

The Userform object has 22 predefined event procedures, but you will seldom use most of them. The default event procedure of the Userform object is the Click() event, but it is not particularly useful. More helpful are the Activate() and Initialize() events that can be used to initialize variables and objects when these events are triggered. Both the Activate() and Initialize() event procedures are triggered by loading the Userform, but they execute before the Userform is shown. Similarly, the user triggers the QueryClose() event procedure by closing the Userform, but the QueryClose() event executes just before the Userform closes so it can be used to reset or remove objects from memory. I cover some of the less common events as they occur in the projects later in this book, but you will use the previously mentioned event procedures with nearly every Userform that you add to a project.

Userforms and ActiveX Controls

You build custom dialog boxes with Userforms and ActiveX controls. When you select a Userform in the VBA IDE, the Control Toolbox appears (this toolbox is located at the upper-right corner of Figure 4.7). Alternatively, you can select the Control Toolbox from the View menu in the IDE. Notice that some additional controls are available to use with Userforms relative to what is available from the Control Toolbox in the Excel application. Table 4.5 lists the additional controls.

Table 4.5 Additional AcitveX Controls Available for Use with Userforms

ActiveX Control	Description
Frame	Used to group controls on a Userform. Makes Option Button controls mutually exclusive.
TabStrip	Used to group data on a Userform. This control does not serve as a container for ActiveX controls. So data must be updated programmatically as the user selects each tab.
MultiPage	Similar to TabStrip control, but each page serves as a container object for more ActiveX controls.
RefEdit	Used to return the range of cells selected by the user on a worksheet.

You can draw ActiveX controls on a Userform just as you draw them on Excel worksheets. When the control is selected, properties of the ActiveX controls are displayed in the Properties window, and event procedures are available from the code module of the Userform that contains them.

With the exception of the cmdGetUserForm_Click() Sub procedure, the remaining code in this section is from the form module associated with the Userform shown in Figure 4-8. This Userform contains a RefEdit control (named refStats) and four Label controls (named lblMin, lblMax, lblSum, and lblAverage). The Name property and a few appearance properties of the Userform were set at design time. The Userform is loaded from the Excel worksheet via a Command Button control named `cmdGetUserForm` (it appears with the caption "Stats" in Figure 4.8) whose `Click()` event procedure contains the following code. Note that this `Click()` event procedure is contained within the code module of the `Worksheet` object that holds the Command Button control.

```
Private Sub cmdGetUserForm_Click()
    frmStats.Show vbModal
End Sub
```

If the Userform is not already loaded, the `Show` method loads and shows the Userform (named `frmStats`). The `Show` method accepts one argument specifying the Userform as modal or modeless. A modeless Userform is one that can be deselected without having to be closed first. I passed the constant `vbModal` to the `Show` method because it is a requirement of the RefEdit control to be used on a modal Userform. To show a modeless Userform, use the VBA constant `vbModeLess`.

TIP

Use the `Hide` method of the `Userform` object to hide it from the user without removing it from memory.

The worksheet from which the Userform is loaded is also shown in Figure 4.8. For demonstration purposes, the worksheet contains randomly generated numbers. The function of the Userform is to allow the user to select a range on the worksheet and automatically see some basic statistics calculated from the data in the selected range.

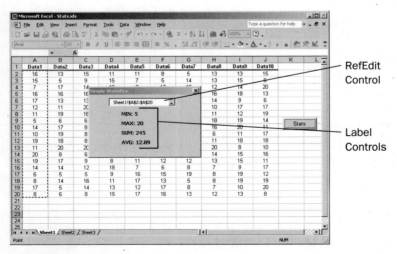

FIGURE 4.8 *Sample worksheet demonstrating Userforms and the RefEdit control.*

The `Initialize()` event procedure of the Userform initializes the `Value` property of the RefEdit control to the range `$A$2:$A$20` on the worksheet. This reference to a worksheet range is displayed in the RefEdit control as soon as the Userform is shown. With the RefEdit control selected, the user can select any range on the worksheet, and the reference will be displayed immediately.

```
Option Explicit
Private Sub UserForm_Initialize()
    refStats.Value = "Sheet1!$A$2:$A$20"
End Sub
```

The `Change()` event of the RefEdit control is triggered whenever its value changes, so it is convenient to use this procedure for updating the label controls that display the statistics. You calculate these statistics using Excel worksheet functions. The worksheet functions are passed a reference to the range object representing the selected range on the worksheet. Create the reference to the `Range` object by passing the string value contained in the `Value` property of the RefEdit control to the `Range` property of the `Worksheet` object. Note that line continuation characters are used in the `Change()` event procedure of the RefEdit control.

```
Private Sub refStats_Change()
    lblMin.Caption = "MIN: " & Application.WorksheetFunction. _
                        Min(Range(refStats.Value))
    lblMax.Caption = "MAX: " & Application.WorksheetFunction. _
                        Max(Range(refStats.Value))
    lblSum.Caption = "SUM: " & Application.WorksheetFunction. _
                        Sum(Range(refStats.Value))
    lblAverage.Caption = "AVG: " & Format(Application.WorksheetFunction. _
                        Average(Range(refStats.Value)), "#0.00")
End Sub
```

The user triggers the `QueryClose()` event procedure of the Userform by closing the Userform. If you want to remove the Userform from the computer's memory, you must use the `Unload` statement; otherwise, the Userform is only hidden.

```
Private Sub UserForm_QueryClose(Cancel As Integer, CloseMode As Integer)
    Unload Me      'Removes Userform named frmStats from memory.
End Sub
```

 TIP

Use the keyword Me to reference the current active object in the program. The equivalent code without the reference to Me is Unload frmStats.

Userforms and ActiveX controls are tremendously useful VBA programming tools. They are in nearly every programming project in this book.

Private, Public, and Procedure Scope

The `Private` and `Public` keywords used previously (see Chapter 2, "Working with Variables and Constants in VBA") with variable declarations also apply to procedure definitions. Earlier, I defined all the event procedures with `Private` scope. At a minimum, any procedure is available to all other procedures within the module in which it is defined, and if that is the limit of its scope, such a procedure is defined with the `Private` keyword. A procedure defined with the `Public` keyword is available to all other procedures in all modules in the project (called *global scope*). However, depending on the type of module in which the procedure is defined, you may need additional object qualifiers to access a `Public` procedure.

Calling a Procedure

You can direct program execution to another procedure simply by calling it with a single line of code. The following examples all call the procedure named `MyProcedure()`:

```
Call MyProcedure(argument list)
MyProcedure argument list
Object.MyProcedure argument list
```

In some cases, parts of the syntax used to call a procedure are optional. For example, to call a procedure with module-level scope (defined with the `Private` keyword), you can use either of the following statements from within another procedure in the same module:

```
MyProcedure
Call MyProcedure
```

If the procedure contains arguments, you can use the following:

```
MyProcedure argument list
Call MyProcedure(argument list)
```

The `Call` keyword is optional if no arguments must be passed. If arguments are passed, you must use `Call` if you also include the parentheses. These rules also apply to calling a procedure defined with `Public` scope in a standard module. However, when calling a procedure in a form module (Userform) defined with `Public` scope from another module in your project, you must also specify the object qualifier (name of the Userform). Use the following line of code to call the procedure `MyProcedure` declared with `Public` scope in a Userform module (named `frmUserform`) from another module in the same project:

```
frmMyUserform.MyProcedure
```

When calling a procedure defined with an argument list, you must pass a value of the appropriate type for each argument in that list. For example, if `MyProcedure()` is defined with a list of two arguments that includes a string and a number, a call to that procedure should pass a string and numerical value as shown here:

```
MyProcedure "My String", 25
```

You can also pass variables as long as their data types match the types defined in the procedure definition. Each argument is separated by a comma in the calling statement, and the sequence of values must match the procedure's declarations.

 TIP

When calling a procedure that has been defined with an argument list, you can pass values to the procedure using *named arguments*. A named argument consists of the name of the argument followed by a colon and an equal sign (`:=`), and the value assigned to the argument. For example, if the `MyProcedure()` Sub procedure is defined with arguments called `myString` and `myNum`, then a call to this procedure can appear as follows:

```
MyProcedure myString:="My String", myNum:=25
```

You can list named arguments in any order, and they also help to self-document your code.

Writing VBA Sub Procedures

I refer to custom VBA procedures or Sub procedures as those procedures defined entirely by the programmer in a standard or form module but that are not function procedures (see the section "Writing VBA Function Procedures" later in this chapter). You define Sub procedures with the `Sub` and `End Sub` keywords along with a name for the procedure. You should also declare the procedure scope with `Private` or `Public`. If you do not declare the scope, the procedure is `Public` by default.

```
Private/Public Sub MySub(argument list)
     'Code is entered here
End Sub
```

You can type the procedure directly into a code module, or you can do the following:

1. In the VBA IDE, click the Insert menu.
2. From the menu click Procedure. The Add Procedure dialog box appears (see Figure 4.9).
3. Type the name of the procedure in the text box, choose the desired options, and click OK.

FIGURE 4.9 *The Add Procedure dialog box.*

Sub procedures help encapsulate your program by solving relatively small problems. Sub procedures can be called repeatedly and do not return a value to the calling procedure. Sub procedures may be passed a list of arguments (usually as variables), but that is not required. When passing variables to another procedure, you have the choice of passing them by value or by reference.

The argument list is optional, but when included, it should contain a list of variable declarations complete with data types as shown for the MyProcedure() Sub procedure listed here:

```
Private Sub MyProcedure(myString As String, myNum As Integer,_
     Optional myVal As Single)
     'Code Block
End Sub
```

Calls to MyProcedure() must include a list of at least two arguments, the first argument being a string and the second argument a number. A third argument specifying a number of type Single can be included, but it is not required because the argument is defined with the Optional keyword.

 TIP

Keep your procedures as short as possible. As procedures get longer and more involved, they become harder to read and debug. As a general rule, I keep my procedures short enough so that all the code fits on my screen. I will break this rule on occasion when writing code with redundant logic that is very easy to follow.

Passing Arguments with ByVal and ByRef

Earlier in this chapter, you learned about the SheetChange() event procedure with two arguments listed with the ByVal keyword. The opening statement of the SheetChange() event procedure is repeated here:

```
Private Sub Workbook_SheetChange(ByVal Sh As Object, _
    ByVal Target As Range)
```

You use the ByVal keyword to pass variables by value, which means VBA will make a copy of the passed variable for use in the called procedure. When passed by value, the called procedure can change only its copy of the variable, and the calling procedure's variable remains unchanged.

Alternatively, you can pass variables by reference using the ByRef keyword. You can also omit ByVal or ByRef to pass a variable by reference. When you pass a variable by reference, you are essentially passing the original variable. Thus, if a procedure changes a variable passed by reference, the change takes place in the calling *and* the called procedures.

To test the behavior exhibited by passing variables by value and by reference in VBA, enter the following code into a standard module. You can quickly test the program by inserting the cursor in the Sub procedure Main() and clicking Run Sub/UserForm on the Standard toolbar or by pressing F5.

```
Private Sub Main()
    Dim num1 As Integer
    Dim num2 As Integer
    num1 = 10
    num2 = 20
    Call PassByValue(num1)
    Call PassByReference(num2)
    MsgBox num1 & "   " & num2
End Sub
```

The Sub procedure Main() initializes two integer variables and passes one each to the Sub procedures PassByValue() and PassByReference(). The variable num1 is passed by value to another variable declared with the same name. (Note: The name of the variable in the called procedure does not have to have the same name.) The value of the copied variable is then squared so that the value stored in the variable num1 is 100 in the scope of the PassByValue() Sub procedure.

```
Private Sub PassByValue(ByVal num1 As Integer)
    num1 = num1 ^ 2
End Sub
```

The variable num2 is passed by reference to the `PassByReference()` Sub procedure where it is assigned the new name num3. The variable num3 is then squared so that it now holds the value 400.

```
Private Sub PassByReference(num3 As Integer)
    num3 = num3 ^ 2
End Sub
```

When program execution returns to the Sub procedure `Main()`, the message box outputs the values 10 and 400 for the variables num1 and num2, respectively. The variable num1 has not changed because it was passed by value. However, the variable num2 was changed because it was passed by reference, even though a new variable name was used to represent it in the called procedure.

NOTE

As with any variable declaration, you should declare the variable type in the argument list of a called procedure. Without a type declaration, the variable will be treated as a variant in the called procedure. When passing a variable by reference, the data types must match in order to prevent a run-time error.

Writing VBA Function Procedures

When you need a procedure to return a result of some operation or set of operations, create a Function procedure. Function procedures work very much like VBA's or Excel's built-in functions in that they are usually passed one or more arguments and they always return at least one value. The difference is that they are programmer-defined. Function procedures in VBA are defined with the `Function` and `End Function` keywords.

```
Private/Public Function FunctionName(argument list) As type
    'Code is entered here
    FunctionName = Return Value
End Function
```

You should define Function procedures with a data type to prevent their return value from being typed as a variant. You assign a value to a Function procedure by using the procedure's name and an assignment statement (typically at the end of the procedure). When calling a Function procedure, you need to assign its return value to a variable. The variable that accepts the return value from the Function procedure should match its data type.

```
myVal = MyFunction(argument list)
```

In the following example, the Sub procedure `Main()` calls the Function procedure `SqRoot()` and assigns its return value to the variable `myRoot`. The variable is formatted before its value is output in a message box. I passed the variable num1 by value in order to output its original value in the message box. All variables are declared as type `Double` to match the data type requested by VBA's `Sqr()` function, although this is not required as long as VBA can cast the value to the new data type.

```
Private Sub Main()
    Dim num1 As Double
    Dim myRoot As Double
    num1 = 10
    myRoot = SqRoot(num1)
    myRoot = Format(myRoot, "#0.00")
    MsgBox "The square root of " & num1 & " is " & myRoot
End Sub
```

The Function procedure `SqRoot()` accepts a single value (passed by value) and returns its square root.

```
Public Function SqRoot(ByVal num1 As Double) As Double
'Calculates and returns the square root of a number
    num1 = Sqr(num1)
    SqRoot = num1
End Function
```

The `SqRoot()` Function procedure can also be written with a single line of code rather than two lines by directly assigning the square root of the variable num1 to the Function procedure's name.

```
SqRoot = Sqr(num1)
```

TIP

Use `Exit Sub` or `Exit Function` to immediately return program execution to the calling procedure.

Executing Public Procedures from Excel

If you define procedures with `Public` scope, they are accessible from the Excel application. Sub procedures defined in standard, worksheet, and workbook modules with `Public` scope are available as macros from the Excel application. You can select these procedures from the Macro dialog box, as shown in Figure 4.10. Alternatively, you can go to the Forms toolbar and assign the macros to the default event procedures of ActiveX controls.

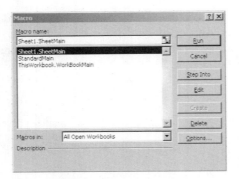

FIGURE 4.10 *Selecting Public Sub procedures from Excel.*

Sub procedures defined in modules associated with `Workbook` and `Worksheet` objects are listed with their object reference. Sub procedures defined in standard modules are listed with only the name of the procedure. Sub procedures defined in modules associated with a Userform object are not available from the Excel application.

Function procedures declared with `Public` scope in a standard module are also available in Excel for use in formulas. You will find your custom Function procedures listed with the other Excel worksheet functions in the Insert Function dialog box. The `SqRoot()` Function procedure discussed earlier in this chapter is listed in Figure 4.11. You can use custom-built Function procedures in Excel worksheet formulas just as you do with other worksheet functions.

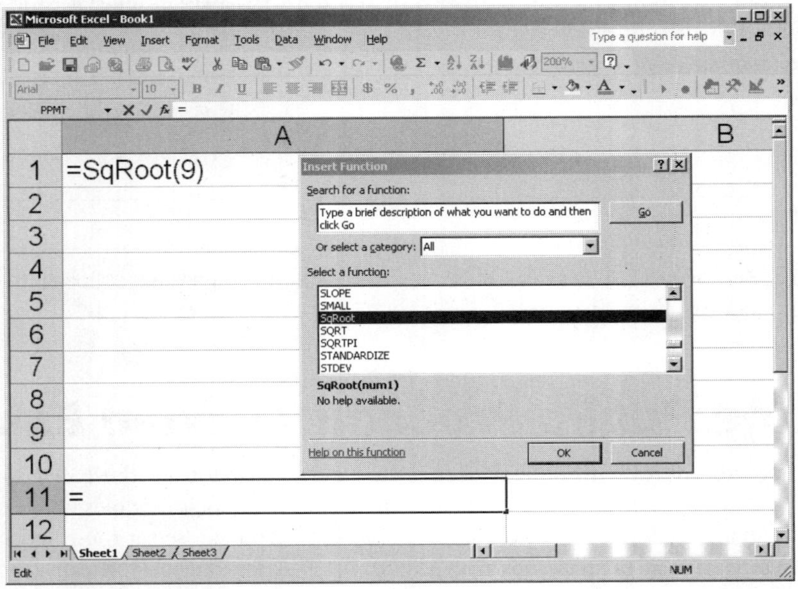

FIGURE 4.11 *Selecting Public Function procedures from Excel.*

Summary

After reading this chapter, you should have a basic understanding of VBA procedures. Specifically, I covered the predefined event procedures for the `Workbook` and `Worksheet` objects as well as Userforms and ActiveX controls. Although it isn't practical (or even necessary) to cover every event procedure available in VBA for Excel, you should now know how to find a list of all available event procedures for a specific object and understand the fundamentals for selecting the appropriate event procedure for your program algorithm.

I also showed you how to create and call custom Sub and Function procedures. After reading this chapter, I hope you realize that creating these procedures is not difficult. The more difficult task is deciding when you need a custom procedure, what scope it should be defined with, and what type of code module it should be placed in.

Finally, my discussion of VBA procedures is not yet complete. I have not covered Function and Sub procedures used to define the properties and methods of a custom object defined in a class module. These topics are covered in Chapter 11, "VBA Class Modules: Creating Custom Objects," which provides more advanced programming examples.

Chapter 5

Decision structures are fundamental to any computer programming language. They are used to execute one block of code over another based on the evaluation of a conditional statement. The use of decision structures in a program is commonly referred to as *program branching*.

Conditional statements are the focus of any decision structure. They are built from one ore more logical expressions that are used to compare two values and return a `Boolean` result. This chapter introduces two common decision structures: `If/Then/Else` and `Select/Case` and the components of the conditional statements from which they are constructed — namely, the comparison operators used in the evaluation of two values in a logical expression and the logical operators used to combine multiple expressions in a single statement.

Evaluating Conditional Statements

Conditional statements are programming language statements built from one or more logical expressions. A logical expression is a comparison of two values using a comparison operator (see Table 5.1) and evaluates as `True` or `False` (for example, "Ten is greater than or equal to five" is a true statement and can be written in VBA as `10>= 5`). Logical operators are used in conditional statements so VBA will evaluate a series of logical expressions in order to return a single `Boolean` result. A decision structure then uses the evaluation of a conditional statement to branch program execution.

Logical Expressions

The basic logical expression is a comparison carried out between two values. A logical expression can be evaluated as `True`, `False`, or, in some cases, `Null`, but most of the time, you will be seeking a result of `True` or `False`. The operators used to compare two values in VBA are listed in Table 5.1.

Table 5.1 VBA Comparison Operators

Operator	Example	True if . . .
=	*Value1* = *Value2*	*Value1* is equal to *Value2*.
<	*Value1* < *Value2*	*Value1* is less than *Value2*.
>	*Value1* > *Value2*	*Value1* is greater than *Value2*.

Operator	Example	True if . . .
<=	*Value1* <= *Value2*	*Value1* is less than or equal to *Value2*.
>=	*Value1* >= *Value2*	*Value1* is greater than or equal to *Value2*.
<>	*Value1* <> *Value2*	*Value1* is not equal to *Value2*.
Is	*Object1* Is *Object2*	*Object1* and *Object2* refer to the same object.
Like	*String* Like *Pattern*	*String* matches the *Pattern*.

 NOTE

The equal symbol (=) functions as both an assignment and a comparison operator in VBA.

With the exception of Is and Like, the values being compared can be of any numerical or string data type. When using Is, the comparison must be between two object variables, and when using Like, the comparison must be between a string and a pattern that relates to a string. Consider the following examples that compare variables and literals of numerical, string, and object data types using the operators listed in Table 5.1. The first part of the program declares and initializes numerical, string, and object variables for later comparison, and is listed here:

```
Dim num1 As Integer
Dim num2 As Single
Dim str1 As String
Dim str2 As String
Dim obj1 As Object
Dim obj2 As Object
Dim result As Boolean
num1 = 10
num2 = 10
str1 = "10"
str2 = "Excel"
Set obj1 = Range("A1")
Set obj2 = Range("A1")
```

Numerical comparisons are straightforward. The two values are either equal or not equal regardless of the numerical data type (`Integer`, `Single`, `Double`, and so on).

```
result = (num1 = num2)      'result holds True
result = (num1 < num2)      'result holds False
result = (num1 > num2)      'result holds False
result = (num1 >= num2)     'result holds True
result = (num1 <= num2)     'result holds True
result = (num1 <> num2)     'result holds False
```

Be aware that when comparing a numerical data type to a string data type, VBA can evaluate the expression only when the string contains all numerical characters; otherwise, a type mismatch error will occur. You can use the `Val()` function to convert the string to a number, but the result of the conversion will always be zero if the first character in the string is not numerical.

```
result = (num1 = str1)      'result holds True
result = (num1 = str2)      'Type mismatch error
```

When comparing strings, by default, VBA performs a binary comparison. A binary string comparison is based on the computer's binary representation of the characters. For example, uppercase "A" is stored as the binary representation of the number 65 (1000001) and lowercase "a" as the binary representation of the number 97 (1100001). Therefore, lowercase "a" is greater than uppercase "A." (Most of the characters you will ever want to compare are listed in the 0–127 character set found in Table 3.6 in Chapter 3, "Using VBA's Built-In Functions.") The following code uses several comparison operators to compare the strings stored in the variables `str1` and `str`:

```
result = (str1 = str2)      'result holds False
result = (str1 > str2)      'result holds False
result = (str1 < str2)      'result holds True
result = ("a" < "A")        'result holds False
result = (str1 >= str2)     'result holds False
result = (str1 <= str2)     'result holds True
result = (str1 <> str2)     'result holds True
```

 TIP

Use `Option Compare Text` in the general declarations section of a module to force textual comparisons of strings. Textual comparisons are case insensitive.

The Is operator compares object variables. The result of an object comparison will be True only if the object references are set equal to each other, either indirectly through another object reference, or directly, as shown in the following:

```
result = (obj1 Is obj2)        'result holds False
result = Set obj1 = obj2
result = (obj1 Is obj2)        'result holds True
```

The Like operator compares a string to a pattern built from characters and optional wild cards. You can use the wild cards (see Table 5.2) to build patterns of single and multiple characters, character lists, and character ranges.

```
result = (str1 Like "E*")      'result holds False
result = (str2 Like "E*")      'result holds True
result = (str2 Like "?x?*")    'result holds True
result = (str1 Like "##")      'result holds True
result = (str2 Like "[E,e]*")  'result holds True
```

Table 5.2 Wild Cards Used to Build Patterns with Like

Character	Matches
*	Zero or more characters
?	Any single character
#	Any single digit (0–9)
[list]	Any single character in the specified list
[!list]	Any single character not in the specified list

Logical Operators

Depending on the needs of the decision structure in your program, you may want to evaluate multiple expressions before executing one block of code rather than another. Logical operators allow you to evaluate multiple expressions as True, False, or Null. Table 5.3 lists the logical operators available in VBA.

Table 5.3 VBA Logical Operators

Operator	Example	True if . . .
And	*Expression1* And *Expression2*	Both expressions are True.
Or	*Expression1* Or *Expression2*	Either expression is True.

continues

Table 5.3 VBA Logical Operators (continued)

Operator	Example	True if . . .
Xor	*Expression1* Xor *Expression2*	One expression is True.
Not	Not *Expression1*	*Expression1* is False.
Eqv	*Expression1* Xor *Expression2*	Both expressions are True or both expressions are False.
Imp	*Expression1* Imp *Expression2*	Both expressions are True, both expressions are False, *Expression2* is True, *Expression1* is False, and *Expression2* is Null.

This discussion focuses only on the three logical operators And, Or, and Not because they do the bulk of the work in most VBA programs. Use logical And when both expressions must evaluate as True before the entire statement is True. In the following example, the value stored in the Boolean variable result will be True only if num1 is less than or equal to 10 *and* num2 is not equal to 50.

```
num1 = Cells(1, 1).Value
num2 = Cells(1, 2).Value
result = (num1 <= 10) And (num2 <> 50)
```

If logical Or is used, then only one expression must evaluate as True before the entire statement is True. This time, the value of the variable result will be True if num1 is less than or equal to 10 *or* num2 is not equal to 50. It does not matter which expression is True; the value of result will be True if either or both expressions are True.

```
result = (num1 <= 10) Or (num2 <> 50)
```

Use the Not operator when you want the opposite value of a logical expression. Typically, you will use the Not operator to make your code self-documenting. For example, the EOF() function in VBA returns a Boolean value and is used when accessing a computer's file. The EOF() function returns False until the end of a file has been reached, at which point it returns True. Therefore, the following programming statement reads as follows: If I am not at the end of the file, then keep reading it; otherwise, close the file.

```
If Not EOF(1) Then
      'continue reading in data
Else
      Close(1)
End If
```

If the EOF() function returns False, the program has not yet reached the end of the data file, so the logic Not False evaluates as True. You can also write the preceding example as If EOF(1) = False Then, but now the goal of the statement is not as obvious, so the previous example is preferred.

Note that in the previous example, I used VBA's If/Then/Else programming structure. In the following section, I discuss this decision structure, followed by Select/Case, the second decision structure in VBA.

Programming with Decision Structures

Now that you have a grasp on how to write conditional statements in VBA, take a look at the available decision structures. (Decision structures are sometimes referred to as *branching structures* because the path of program execution will change with the evaluation of a conditional statement.) Decision structures are common to all languages, are used extensively in all programs, and are very easy to learn.

If/Then/Else

If you want your program to execute one block of code rather than another based on certain criteria, you can use the If/Then/Else programming structure. Here is the basic form of this structure:

```
If (expression) Then
      'Block of programming statements
End If
```

The block of code between the If and End If statements will execute only if the expression evaluates as True; otherwise, the entire block is skipped. If you prefer, you can write this expression with a single line of code by entering the programming statement immediately after Then and omitting End If, as shown here:

```
If (expression) Then statement1
```

You can also write multiple lines of code on a single line in the editor window by using a colon to separate each statement:

```
If (expression) Then statement1 : statement2
```

This practice is acceptable if your statements are very short, but be aware that it tends to make your program harder to read and debug.

For situations when your program must decide between executing only one of two blocks of code, add the Else statement to the If/Then structure. In this case, the first block of programming statements will execute if the expression evaluates as True. If the `expression` evaluates as `False`, the block of statements between `Else` and `End If` will execute. Using `Else` ensures that at least one block of code executes regardless of the logical result of the expression.

```
If (expression) Then
        'Block of programming statements
Else
        'Block of programming statements
End If
```

The following example is a simple Sub procedure that plays a number guessing game with the user:

```
Public Sub NumberGuess()
    Dim ranNumber As Integer
    Dim userGuess As Integer
    Randomize
    ranNumber = Int(Rnd * 10) + 1
    userGuess = InputBox("Guess a number between 1 and 10", _
        "Number Guess")
    If ranNumber = userGuess Then
        MsgBox ("You got it!")
    Else
        MsgBox ("No, the correct answers was " & ranNumber)
    End If
End Sub
```

Using an `InputBox()` function, the procedure prompts the user to input a number between 1 and 10. A random integer between 1 and 10 is generated and compared to the user's guess in an `If/Then/Else` decision structure. Based on the evaluation of the logical expression (`ranNumber = userGuess`), the program proceeds to one of two statements that utilize a `MsgBox()` function. If the user guesses the correct answer, the appropriate message box is displayed. If the user guesses wrong, a brief message is displayed with the correct answer.

It is also possible to nest `If/Then/Else` structures to as many levels as desired, but be sure to keep the number of nested structures to a minimum so that your code remains readable. In the following example, the `NumberGuess()` Sub procedure is once again listed, only this time nested `If/Then/Else` structures are used to give the user a second guess at the number.

```
Public Sub NumberGuess()
    Dim ranNumber As Integer
```

```
Dim userGuess As Integer
Randomize
ranNumber = Int(Rnd * 10) + 1
userGuess = InputBox("Guess a number between 1 and 10", _
     "Number Guess")
If ranNumber = userGuess Then
    MsgBox ("You got it!")
Else
    If ranNumber < userGuess Then
        userGuess = InputBox("Too high, guess again ", "Number Guess")
        If ranNumber = userGuess Then
            MsgBox ("You got it!")
        Else
            MsgBox ("No, the correct answer was " & ranNumber)
        End If
    Else
        userGuess = InputBox("Too low, guess again ", "Number Guess")
        If ranNumber = userGuess Then
            MsgBox ("You got it!")
        Else
            MsgBox ("No, the correct answer was " & ranNumber)
        End If
    End If
End If
End Sub
```

Even though the If/Then/Else structure is nested only two levels deep in the NumberGuess() Sub procedure, the code is difficult to read. Fortunately, the If/Then/Else structure can be expanded to accommodate multiple code blocks without having to nest structures.

ElseIf

Including ElseIf with If/Then enables you to test multiple expressions without having to repeatedly nest If/Then structures. The logical expressions used with ElseIF can be different, giving you more flexibility to build a more intelligent structure.

Before examining a Function procedure that uses an If/Then/ElseIf structure, consider the worksheet shown in Figure 5.1 that calculates the monthly payment and cumulative interest for fixed rate loans that differ in amount and number of payments. The interest rate is fixed at 6 percent annually, but this can be changed to any value, in which case, the rest of the worksheet will be automatically updated. The spreadsheet contains 93 combinations of loan amounts and loan lengths (not all rows are shown in the figure).

	A	B	C	D	E	F
1	Loan Amount	Months	Rate (Yearly)	Monthly Payment	Total Interest	Accept
2	$5,000.00	36	6	-$127.11	-$475.95	TRUE
3	$6,000.00	36		-$152.53	-$571.14	TRUE
4	$7,000.00	36		-$177.95	-$666.33	TRUE
5	$8,000.00	36		-$203.38	-$761.52	TRUE
6	$9,000.00	36		-$228.80	-$856.71	TRUE
7	$10,000.00	36		-$254.22	-$951.90	TRUE
8	$11,000.00	36		-$279.64	-$1,047.09	TRUE
9	$12,000.00	36		-$305.06	-$1,142.28	TRUE
10	$13,000.00	36		-$330.49	-$1,237.47	TRUE
11	$14,000.00	36		-$355.91	-$1,332.66	TRUE
12	$15,000.00	36		-$381.33	-$1,427.85	TRUE
13	$16,000.00	36		-$406.75	-$1,523.04	FALSE
14	$17,000.00	36		-$432.17	-$1,618.23	FALSE
15	$18,000.00	36		-$457.59	-$1,713.42	FALSE
16	$19,000.00	36		-$483.02	-$1,808.61	FALSE
17	$20,000.00	36		-$508.44	-$1,903.80	FALSE
18	$21,000.00	36		-$533.86	-$1,998.98	FALSE
19	$22,000.00	36		-$559.28	-$2,094.17	FALSE
20	$23,000.00	36		-$584.70	-$2,189.36	FALSE
21	$24,000.00	36		-$610.13	-$2,284.55	FALSE
22	$25,000.00	36		-$635.55	-$2,379.74	FALSE
23	$26,000.00	36		-$660.97	-$2,474.93	FALSE
24	$27,000.00	36		-$686.39	-$2,570.12	FALSE
25	$28,000.00	36		-$711.81	-$2,665.31	FALSE

F2 =LoanCriteria(A2,B2,D2,E2)

Microsoft Excel - LoanDemo.xls

FIGURE 5.1 *A sample spreadsheet that calculates financial information for fixed rate loans.*

NOTE

The spreadsheet in Figure 5.1 uses the PPMT( ) worksheet function to calculate the monthly payment and a custom VBA Function procedure to calculate the cumulative interest. The custom Function procedure is discussed in Chapter 6, "Creating VBA Loops and Arrays."

Although this spreadsheet can be greatly simplified, it would help people determine how much they could borrow, for example, to purchase a car based on strict criteria governing the monthly payment, the total interest paid, and the length of the loan. Consider an example in which the user wants to know how much to borrow based on the following criteria:

◆ The monthly payment must be less than $400.

◆ The number of monthly payments must be 48 or less.

◆ The total interest paid over the length of the loan must not exceed a value of 10 percent of the initial loan amount.

It would take some effort to scan 90–100 rows looking for combinations of loan amount and number of payments that satisfy the criteria listed. It is easier to write a VBA Function procedure that will test the values for you. The LoanCriteria() Function procedure accepts four arguments as input that include the loan amount, number of payments, monthly payment, and cumulative interest for the length of the loan. The LoanCriteria() Function is declared as a Boolean and evaluates as True only if all criteria are met. Declaring the LoanCriteria() Function with Public scope allows it to be used as a worksheet function in Excel (note the formula bar in Figure 5.1). The worksheet in Figure 5.1 shows that only 11 combinations satisfy all criteria. Furthermore, the worksheet shows that a person could borrow up to $15,000 at 6 percent for three years and still keep the monthly payment under $400 and the cumulative interest for the loan below 10 percent of the initial loan amount.

```
Public Function LoanCriteria(loanAmt As Single, numPayments As Integer, _
        moPayment As Integer, totInterest As Single) As Boolean
    'Payment less than $400
    'Total interest less than 10% of the initial loan
    'Number of payments 48 or less
```

An If/Then/ElseIf decision structure that tests several expressions and assigns a Boolean value to this Function procedure when one of these expressions evaluates as True does all the work in this procedure. Note that the first 11 rows in the worksheet satisfy all criteria, so the LoanCriteria() Function returns True to the worksheet.

The If/Then/ElseIf structure proceeds until it finds an expression that evaluates as True. The corresponding block of code is then executed, and the rest of the structure is ignored. If none of the expressions evaluates as True, the last block can simply use the Else clause to ensure that at least one block of code in the structure is executed. You must take care to establish logic in the If/Then/ElseIf structure in such a way that program execution does not exit the structure before executing the correct block of code. You must develop logic that ensures only one expression evaluates as True or write the structure with the proper order of ElseIf blocks so that the correct expression is the first expression to evaluate as True. The following If/Then/ElseIf structure is designed to ensure that at least one block of code executes when the opening expression (Abs(moPayment)>400) is True:

```
    If Abs(moPayment) > 400 Then
        LoanCriteria = False
    ElseIf Abs(totInterest) > (0.1 * loanAmt) Then
        LoanCriteria = False
    ElseIf numPayments > 48 Then
        LoanCriteria = False
    Else
        LoanCriteria = True
    End If
End Function
```

Clearly, If/Then/ElseIf is easier to follow than a set of nested If/Then/Else structures. The If/Then/ElseIf structure is most useful when there are several different criteria that must be tested before deciding which block of code to execute. You can also use the If/Then/Else structure to repeatedly test the same expression, but, in this case, the Select/Case decision structure is the better choice.

Select Case

The Select/Case decision structure allows for the execution of one block of code statements based on the value of a single expression. The Select/Case decision structure is similar to that of If/Then/ElseIf in that it allows a program to choose between multiple code blocks based on conditional statements. It differs from If/Then/ElseIf in that the Select/Case structure can test only a single expression against several different values. The basic syntax for the Select/Case structure follows:

```
Select Case (test expression)
        Case (arguments tested against expression)
                'Block of programming statements
        Case Else
                'Block of programming statements
End Select
```

The opening statement Select Case is followed by a *test expression*. The *test expression* is a numeric or string expression whose value will be tested within the remaining parts of the structure. Each distinct code block is separated by a different Case expression. The number of Case statements you can list within a structure is unlimited. Following each Case statement is an expression that is evaluated against the main *test expression* for True or False. The expression following the Case statement can take one of three forms:

- ◆ *expression* (evaluate for equality to the *test expression*)
- ◆ *expression* To *expression* (evaluate for *test expression* within a range)
- ◆ Is comparison operator *expression* (evaluate *test expression* with comparison operators except for Is and Like)

NOTE

Using Is in a Select/Case structure is not the same as using the Is comparison operator.

The following VBA Function procedure uses a Select/Case structure to assign a letter grade to a percentage representing a student's numerical score. The Function procedure is meant to be used as an Excel worksheet function. The test expression for the `Select/Case` structure is the variable `studScore` that is passed to the Function procedure from a worksheet (see Figure 5.2). If the value passed to the Function procedure is within the range specified after a `Case` statement, the expression evaluates as `True` and the block of code is executed. In this case, the Function procedure is assigned a string value corresponding to a letter grade.

```
Public Function AssignGrade(studScore As Single) As String
    Select Case studScore
        Case 90 To 100
            AssignGrade = "A"
        Case 80 To 89
            AssignGrade = "B"
        Case 70 To 79
            AssignGrade = "C"
        Case Else
            AssignGrade = "F"
    End Select
End Function
```

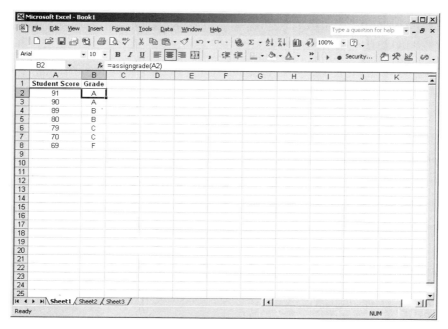

FIGURE 5.2 *Using the* `AssignGrade()` *Function in an Excel worksheet.*

In the previous `AssignGrade()` Function procedure, the order of the `Case` statements within `Select Case` is not important. The `To` keyword is used in the `Case` expression to specify a range of values for testing the variable `studScore`. Therefore, only one `Case` expression can evaluate as `True`, and it will always be the correct expression regardless of the order of `Case` expressions within the `Select/Case` structure. If the `AssignGrade()` Function procedure is rewritten using `Is` instead of `To` in the `Case` expressions, the order of expressions within the structure is critical, as shown in the following:

```
Public Function AssignGrade(studScore As Single)
    Select Case studScore
        Case Is >= 90
            AssignGrade = "A"
        Case Is >= 80
            AssignGrade = "B"
        Case Is >= 70
            AssignGrade = "C"
        Case Else
            AssignGrade = "F"
    End Select
End Function
```

Now, several `Case` expressions can evaluate as `True` for any given value of the variable `studScore`. For example, if `studScore` is less than 70, all `Case` expressions are `True`. As written, the Function will always return the correct letter grade because of the order of the `Case` expressions within the `Select/Case` structure. Remember that the first block of code whose expression evaluates as `True` is the only block that is executed. Therefore, if `studScore` is 85.6, a letter grade of "B" is returned because the previous expression (`Case Is >= 90`) is `False`. Even though the next expression (`Case Is >= 70`) is also `True`, its code block is never executed because a `True` expression has already been encountered.

If you were to change the order of `Case` expressions in the previous example, the Function would fail to always return the correct letter grade, as shown in the following:

```
Public Function AssignGrade(studScore As Single)
    Select Case studScore
        Case Is >= 70
            AssignGrade = "C"
        Case Is >= 80
            AssignGrade = "B"
        Case Is >= 90
            AssignGrade = "A"
```

```
        Case Else
            AssignGrade = "F"
    End Select
End Function
```

In this case, if the variable studScore holds the value 97.5, a letter grade of "C" is returned by the Function because that is the first Case expression that evaluates as True. So, you have to be careful about how you write the order of Case expressions when using the Is keyword.

Summary

Even if you are completely unfamiliar with VBA or VB, you should have found the information in this chapter fairly straightforward. The logical operators and If/Then/Else and Select/Case decision structures are common to all languages. This chapter provided an introduction to the syntax and nuances of these structures as applied to VBA. As with all programming languages, logical operators and decision structures are workhorse elements in VBA, and you see them throughout the book.

Chapter 6

**Creating VBA
Loops and Arrays**

Loops and arrays are fundamental programming structures common to most languages. They expand the capabilities of a language by allowing a program to repeatedly execute the same series of statements and by providing easier access to related sets of data. Loops and arrays make a programmer's task much easier because they significantly decrease the amount of code that would otherwise have to be written. In fact, in many cases, loops and arrays allow programmers to complete tasks that otherwise could not be done.

This chapter specifically covers VBA Do/Loops and For/Next loops, as well as single, multidimensional, and dynamic arrays.

Writing VBA Loops

Program *looping* refers to the repeated execution of the same block of code. The number of times a loop executes (also known as *iterations*) can be a fixed value or based on a programming condition. Loops are common to most languages because they are great for solving problems that involve the repeated execution of the same code. With regard to an Excel spreadsheet application, imagine a situation in which you need to test the value stored in the first 100 cells of column A in a worksheet. Testing a cell value is easy. For example, you can obtain the value of cell A1 using the following statement:

```
Range("A1").Value
```

What a pain it would be to have to write 99 more statements similar to this one for testing the required values in column A. Now consider a situation in which you don't know exactly how many cells you have to test because the number of cells that must be tested depends on the value of a conditional statement:

```
If Range("B1").Value > Range("C1").Value Then
      numRows = 50
Else
      numRows=25
End If
```

Because you don't know the number of cells until after the If/Then/Else block executes, it is nearly impossible to write a program without a looping structure that will test only the required cells.

For/Next Loops

You use VBA `For/Next` loops when you know the number of iterations required from the loop when writing the program. `For/Next` loops are easy to write and follow the basic syntax:

```
For counter = start To end [Step value
      'Block of statements
Next [counter]
```

The keywords `For`, `To`, and `Next` are required as is the counting variable `counter`. The variable `counter` is an `Integer` that must be assigned a range of values from `start` to `end`. After the counter is initialized to `start`, the block of statements inside the loop is executed. When the program encounters the keyword `Next`, the counter is incremented or decremented by the value specified after the keyword `Step`. `Step` is optional and, if omitted, `counter` is incremented by one. The block of statements inside the loop is repeatedly executed until `counter` reaches its maximum value specified by `end`. Several examples illustrating the use of the `For/Next` loop are listed next. The first loop iterates 11 times outputting 11 message boxes with the numbers 0–10.

```
For I = 0 To 10
      MsgBox(I)
Next I
```

The following loop iterates six times outputting the numbers 0, 2, 4, 6, 8, and 10 in a message box:

```
For I = 0 To 10 Step 2    6 iterations: 0, 2, 4, 6, 8, and 10
      MsgBox(I)
Next I
```

The next loop iterates four times outputting the numbers 0, 3, 6, and 9 in a message box:

```
For I = 0 To 10 Step 3    4 iterations: 0, 3, 6, and 9
      MsgBox(I)
Next I
```

Finally, in the next example, the loop iterates just three times outputting the numbers 10, 5, and 0 in a message box:

```
For I = 0 To 10 Step -5    3 iterations: 10, 5, and 0
      MsgBox(I)
Next I
```

In Chapter 5, "Program Branching with VBA Decision Structures," I use the cumulative interest from a loan based on constant monthly payments at a fixed interest rate as a determinate for a decision structure in an `If/Then/ElseIf` code block. The Function procedure

`TotalInterest()`, designed to be used as a worksheet function, calculates the cumulative interest for this type of loan. The `TotalInterest()` Function procedure accepts as arguments the loan amount (`loanAmt`), number of payments (`numPayments`), and interest rate (`rate`). The cumulative interest is calculated using a `For/Next` loop that continually adds a month's interest to the variable `totInterest`, as shown in the following:

```
Public Function TotalInterest(loanAmt As Currency, numPayments As Integer, _
                            rate As Single)
    Dim totInterest As Currency
    Dim I As Integer
    'Use IPmt function to calculate monthly interest. Loop through months
    'to calculate total interest.
    For I = 1 To numPayments
        totInterest = totInterest + Application.WorksheetFunction.IPmt( _
                            rate / 100 / 12, I, numPayments, loanAmt, 0)
    Next I
    TotalInterest = totInterest
End Function
```

 NOTE

The Excel worksheet function `CUMIPMT()` contained in the Analysis ToolPak add-in (select Tools, Add-Ins) is equivalent to the `TotalInterest()` Function procedure.

Do Loops

The VBA `Do/Loop` executes a block of code based on the evaluation of a conditional statement. The `Do/Loop` may execute its code block whether the conditional statement is `True` or `False`, depending on the design. It is also possible to design a `Do/Loop` that will either execute its code block at least once, regardless of the conditional statement, or not at all. The basic syntax for the `Do/Loop` must use the keywords `Do` and `Loop`. In addition, you will almost always use an optional keyword `While` or `Until` with a conditional statement.

```
Do
    'Block of statements
Loop While or Until condition
```

Placing the condition at the end of the loop ensures that the `Do/Loop` will execute at least once because the condition is not evaluated until after the block of code inside the loop executes. If the condition is at the beginning of the `Do/Loop`, the program will evaluate the condition first before proceeding.

```
Do While or Until condition
      'Block of statements
Loop
```

 TIP

Because of the use of a conditional statement with the Do/Loop, the danger of writing an infinite loop is much greater than with a For/Next loop. If you find your program stuck in an infinite loop while debugging and testing, use Ctrl+Alt+Break to interrupt program execution.

While

A Do/Loop that uses the keyword While essentially means "execute the code block while the condition is True." The loop stops when the conditional statement evaluates as False. The following example uses a Do/Loop to copy the values in column A of a worksheet to column B. The loop executes until an empty cell is found in column A. Placing the While keyword and condition at the beginning of the loop ensures that the block of code inside the loop will not execute if the first cell of column A is empty. A counting variable I is initialized just prior to the loop and incremented inside the loop to ensure that the value tested by the loop's condition is read from the next cell in column A of the worksheet.

```
Dim I As Integer
I = 1
Do While Cells(I, "A").Value <> ""
      Cells(I, "B").Value = Cells(I, "A").Value
      I = I + 1
Loop
```

To ensure that the code block executes at least once, you may place the While keyword and conditional statement at the end of the Do/Loop. This loop will perform essentially the same task as the previous example: copy the values in column A to column B. The one difference is that this loop executes its code block at least once; therefore, cell A1 can be empty and the loop will continue if cell A2 contains a value.

```
Dim I As Integer
I = 1
Do
      Cells(I, "B").Value = Cells(I, "A").Value
      I = I + 1
Loop While Cells(I, "A").Value <> ""
```

NOTE

For/Next and Do/Loops are inefficient structures for looping through worksheet cells. When possible, use the For/Each loop to iterate through a range of cells (especially if it is a large number of cells) on a worksheet. The For/Each loop is discussed in Chapter 7, "VBA Objects Specific to Excel Programming."

Until

You can also write a Do/Loop using the keyword Until. The statement now follows the logic "execute the code block until the conditional statement is True." Therefore, the loop executes as long as the conditional statement evaluates as False. You can always write the same loop using Until instead of While; doing so is usually just a matter of changing the comparison operator. The previous Do/Loop can be rewritten with Until and by changing the comparison operator from not equal to (<>) to equal to (=).

```
Dim I As Integer
I = 1
Do
        Cells(I, "B").Value = Cells(I, "A").Value
        I = I + 1
Loop Until Cells(I, "A").Value = ""
```

TIP

Use Exit For or Exit Do to force code execution to immediately leave the looping structure and proceed with the first line of code after the loop. Normally, Exit For or Exit Do will be within a decision structure inside of the loop.

Worksheet Formulas

A chapter on program looping in Excel would not be complete without a discussion about creating worksheet formulas. If you are just beginning to program in Excel, you will inevitably have to use VBA to write formulas to a worksheet. Creating formulas with VBA is easy enough; it is essentially the same as creating a String and assigning that String to a specific cell. However, before you create the formula String, you have to know how to build it. That is why you need a thorough understanding of Excel formulas and the use of absolute and relative references. Appendix A, "Basic Excel Tutorial," contains information on how to use some of the essential features in Excel, including formulas.

The first step in creating formulas with VBA is deciding what style notation to use: A1 or R1C1.

A1 Style References

The A1 style notation is the more intuitive style to use because it uses the row and column headers as they appear in Excel to reference specific cells in a worksheet (for example, A1, F22, and so on). The A1 style notation uses dollar signs ($) to denote absolute references (see Appendix A) for a row or column index (for example, $A1, A$1, or $A$1, and so on). Since formulas are strings, you can write a formula to a cell using either the `Value` or `Formula` properties of the `Range` object.

```
Range("D5").Value = "=SUM(D1:D4)"
Range("D5").Formula = "=SUM(D1:D4)"
```

These examples write a formula to cell D5 in the active worksheet. Excel evaluates a formula after it is written to the cell.

TIP

Although you can use both the `Value` and `Formula` properties to write formula strings to a worksheet cell, the `Formula` property is the better choice because it helps self-document your code. Furthermore, you must use the `Formula` property to read an existing formula from a worksheet because the `Value` property will return the result of the formula.

When essentially the same formula must be written to several cells in the same column or row of the worksheet, use a loop and the `Cells` property of the `Range` object. For example, to write a formula in the first 10 columns of row 21 in a worksheet that calculates the standard deviation of the values in rows 2 through 20, use the following:

```
For I = 1 To 10
        Cells(21, I).Formula = "=STDEV(" & Chr(I + 64) & "2:" & Chr( _
            I + 64) & "20)"
Next I
```

Don't confuse this example with the use of an Excel worksheet function in VBA code. The `String "=STDEV("` is only the first part of a concatenation that builds the entire formula `String` to be entered into a cell. Excel does not recognize this as anything but a `String` until after it is written into a cell.

I've already mentioned that `For/Next` and `Do/Loops` are inefficient methods for looping through a range of cells. This is especially true when writing any kind of value to a cell, including formula strings. However, it is not always possible to avoid loops, depending on the cell references in the formula and the spatial relationships between these references and the cell in which the formula is entered. In general, if you can't obtain the correct formulas with a copy and paste of the cell in Excel, you must use a looping structure to write the formulas.

As another example, consider a situation in which, in effect, the same formula must be entered in successive cells in a worksheet column, but one of the references in the formula must be incremented by more than one row. The spreadsheet shown in Figure 6.1 is such an example. The spreadsheet contains 12 blocks of data in columns A–D. Each block is separated by four rows. The average of each column in the data block is to be calculated and entered in the first 12 rows of columns F through I. Thus, the formula strings for rows 2 and 3 in column F must be " =AVERAGE(A2:A6) " and " =AVERAGE(A11:A15) ", respectively. The reference to the row index in these formulas increases by 9, but the difference in the cells that hold the formulas is only 1. Therefore, the correct formula for cell F3 cannot be obtained with a copy and paste of cell F2.

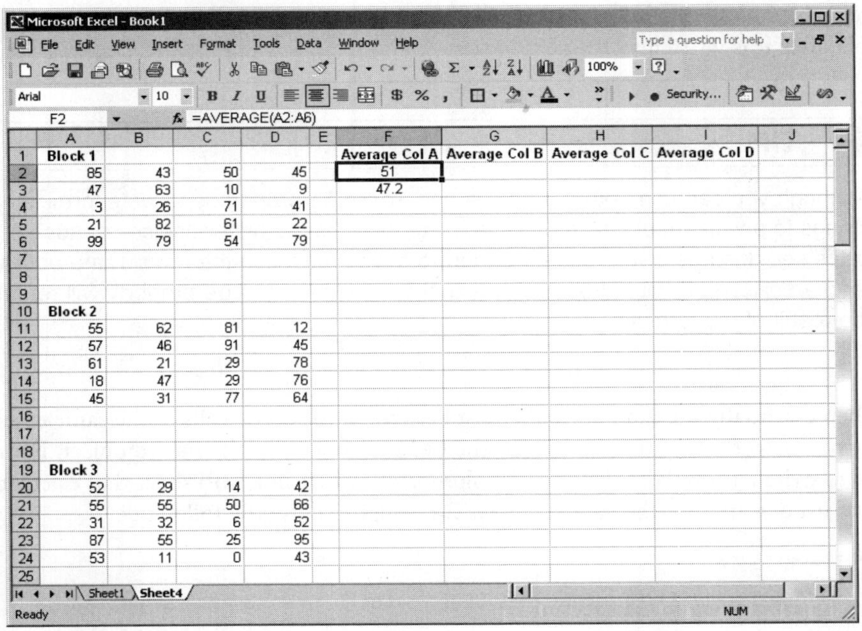

FIGURE 6.1 *A sample spreadsheet that requires a looping structure to write the correct formulas in VBA.*

Because the difference between the row indices in successive formulas is a constant, a looping structure will work very well for creating the correct formulas in column F, as shown in the following:

```
For I = 0 To 11
        Cells(I + 2, "F").Formula = "=Average( _
        A" & (I + 2) + (I * 8) & ":A" & (I + 6) + (I * 8) & ")"
Next I
```

When I=0, the resulting formula entered into cell F2 is =AVERAGE($A$2:$A$6).

The remaining formulas for columns G through I do not have to be entered with a loop. In this case, the VBA equivalent of a copy and paste runs much faster:

```
Range("F2:F13").Copy Range Destination:=Range("F2:I13")
```

You use the Copy method of the Range object to copy and paste the specified range ("F2:F13") to the destination range ("F2:I13"). Alternatively, you can use the AutoFill method, which also accepts a destination range as a parameter. The destination range is the only required parameter, but you can also specify the type (see Table 6.1 for the Excel-VBA constants for the fill type).

```
Range("F2:F13").AutoFill Destination:=Range("F2:I13")
```

Table 6.1 Available Constants for the Type Argument of the AutoFill Method

Constant	Value
xlFillDays	5
xlFillFormats	3
xlFillSeries	2
xlFillWeekdays	6
xlGrowthTrend	10
xlFillCopy	1
xlFillDefault (default)	0
xlFillMonths	7
xlFillValues	4
xlFillYears	8
xlLinearTrend	9

 TIP

Use the HasFormula property of the Range object to read a Boolean value that tells you if the cell or cells in the specified range contain formulas.

R1C1 Style References

The R1C1 style notation uses the letters R and C to denote the row and column reference of a worksheet cell. The numbers that follow R and C specify the exact cell. Brackets around the numbers denote a relative reference; no brackets denote an absolute reference. For example, R[-1]C[2] refers to the cell one row lower and two columns higher than the cell holding this reference. In addition, the absolute reference R5C2 is the equivalent of $B$5 in the A1 style notation.

Use the `FormulaR1C1` property of the `Range` object when reading or writing formulas to a worksheet with the R1C1 style notation. (You can also use the `Value` and `Formula` properties to write the formula `String`.) The equivalent statements for the previous `For/Next` loop written using the R1C1 style notation instead of the A1 style notation follows:

```
For I = 0 To 11
        Cells(I + 2, "F").FormulaR1C1 = "=Average(R" & (I + 2) + (I * 8) _
            & "C1" & ":R" & (I + 6) + (I * 8) & "C1" & ")"
Next I
```

When I=0, the resulting formula entered into cell F2 is =AVERAGE(R2C1:R6C1).

Whether you use A1 style or R1C1 style notation makes no difference to the user. The user will see whichever style they have set in Excel. There is no reason to use one style rather than another; it is simply a matter of personal preference. I will use the A1 style throughout the rest of this book because, in my opinion, it is more intuitive and easier to use than the R1C1 style. I only include a discussion of the R1C1 style because it appears in VBA code generated by Excel's macro recorder.

 NOTE

To set Excel to display formulas with the R1C1 style notation, select Tools, Options, General and click the checkbox labeled "R1C1 Reference style."

Creating Arrays in VBA Programs

It is always easy to introduce arrays in the context of a spreadsheet application because arrays are directly analogous to spreadsheets in that both are used to store associated sets of data. Arrays are essentially variables that can hold multiple values rather than only one. VBA supports one-dimensional and multidimensional arrays that can hold data of any type. A single column in an Excel worksheet is analogous to a one-dimensional array variable, and multiple columns in a worksheet are analogous to a two-dimensional array. Likewise, it follows that a workbook with multiple worksheets is analogous to a three-dimensional array.

NOTE

Unlike Visual Basic, control arrays are not supported in VBA.

One-Dimensional Arrays

A *one-dimensional array* is a single column of related data (or row, if you prefer). The array is assigned a name and has an index value used to reference specific elements in the array, much like a row number is used to reference a specific element in a worksheet column. Arrays are declared in VBA just as variables are except that the size of the array (number of elements) is also specified. The following statement declares an `Integer` array with 10 or 11 elements:

```
Dim myArray(10) As Integer
```

You can declare an array with `Private` or `Public` scope as you would any variable. You should also specify a data type to prevent the array from being declared as a `Variant`. All elements of the array will be of the data type specified in the declaration. The number of elements depends on the setting of the `Option Base` in the general declarations section of the code module. You can use `Option Base 0` (default) or `Option Base 1` to set the lower bound of an array. Thus, without setting the `Option Base`, the previous statement declares and `Integer` array with 11 elements (0 to 10). If preferred, you can override the `Option Base` setting by specifically setting the lower bound in the array declaration, as shown in the following:

```
Dim myArray(1 to 10) As Integer
```

Now the lower bound is specifically set to 1, so there are 10 elements in the array named `myArray`. VBA initializes arrays on declaration as is done with variables. `Integer` arrays are assigned the value 0 to each element and empty strings (`""`) are assigned to `String` arrays.

Of course, you will use some type of loop to populate the elements in an array you create with VBA. The following loop copies the values of cells A1 through A10 into a `String` array named `myArray`. Note that `Option Base 0` is implied in this example.

```
Dim I As Integer
Dim myArray(9) As String
For I = 0 To 9
    myArray(I) = Cells(I + 1, "A").Value
Next I
```

```
'------------------
      Do                              'Outer Do/Loop iterates until array _
                                          is sorted
          anotherIteration = False
          For I = 0 To 8                    'Inner For-loop exchanges array elements
              If sortArray(I) > sortArray(I + 1) Then
                  tempVar = sortArray(I)
                  sortArray(I) = sortArray(I + 1)
                  sortArray(I + 1) = tempVar
                  anotherIteration = True
              End If
          Next I
          iterationNum = iterationNum + 1
          '
          '-------------------------
          'Copy array to next column
          '-------------------------
          Cells(1, iterationNum + 2).Value = iterationNum
          For I = 0 To 9
              Cells(I + 2, iterationNum + 2).Value = sortArray(I)
          Next I
      Loop While anotherIteration = True
End Sub
```

The data to be sorted is copied into a one-dimensional array named sortArray. You don't have to use this array because the data is already in a worksheet column, but referencing the array variable is less tedious than repeatedly using the Cells property of the Range object. Next, the BubbleSort() procedure uses a For/Next loop to successively compare and exchange (if necessary) two elements in the array holding the data. The For/Next loop is nested inside a Do/Loop that is used to repeat the process if the array is not yet sorted. Finally, the array that results from each iteration is output to the adjacent column in the worksheet. The result of the BubbleSort() procedure operating on a set of ten randomly generated numbers is shown in Figure 6.2. Notice that this particular data set took only six of a maximum ten iterations of the Do/Loop to be sorted.

Data	Iteration-->	1	2	3	4	5	6
4		4	2	2	2	2	2
78		2	4	4	4	4	4
2		70	52	7	7	5	5
70		52	7	52	5	7	7
52		7	59	5	52	52	52
7		59	5	59	59	59	59
59		5	70	67	67	67	67
5		72	67	70	70	70	70
72		67	72	72	72	72	72
67		78	78	78	78	78	78

FIGURE 6.2 *Using the* `BubbleSort()` *procedure to sort worksheet data.*

This version of the `BubbleSort()` procedure is not particularly useful because it sorts only ten elements entered into specific cells on a worksheet. In the section "Finding Contiguous Blocks of Data," later in this chapter, I modify the `BubbleSort()` procedure to sort a small dynamic array used to help find contiguous blocks of data in a worksheet.

Multidimensional Arrays

With VBA, you can declare arrays with up to 60 dimensions. I'm not sure why you would need or want 60, as it is conceptually difficult for most people to visualize past three or four dimensions. With Excel, you will probably find considerable use for two-dimensional arrays because they can represent all the data in a single worksheet. Adding a third dimension allows the duplication of data in all worksheets within a workbook. Rarely (if at all) will you need to use arrays declared with more than two or three dimensions, so I show only examples of arrays with these sizes.

The following statement declares a two-dimensional `Integer` array with ten rows and three columns (assuming the lower bound is zero):

```
Dim myArray(9,2) As Integer
```

Data is copied to a two-dimensional array using nested loops. In the next example, data in the first 100 rows and 100 columns of the active worksheet are copied to the array name myArray. The inner loop uses the `Integer` variable `I` to select the row associated with the column represented by the `Integer` variable `J` in the outer loop.

```
Dim I As Integer
Dim J As Integer
Dim myArray(99, 99) As Integer
For J = 0 To 99       'Column index
    For I = 0 To 99      'Row index
        myArray(I, J) = Cells(I + 1, J + 1).Value
    Next I
Next J
```

Similarly, by nesting one more loop, you can use a three-dimensional array to hold the data from the rows and columns in multiple worksheets. In the following example, the first 100 rows and 100 columns of the first three worksheets in the active workbook are copied to the array named `myArray`:

```
Dim I As Integer
Dim J As Integer
Dim K As Integer
Dim myArray(99, 99, 2) As Integer
For K = 0 To 2       'Worksheet index
    For J = 0 To 99      'Column index
        For I = 0 To 99      'Row index
            myArray(I, J, K) = Worksheets(K + 1).Cells(I + 1, J + 1).Value
        Next I
    Next J
Next K
```

You add the expression `Worksheets(K + 1)` to the assignment statement in order to access the cells in different worksheets. Chapter 7, provides a full discussion of Excel objects, including the `Workbook`, `Worksheet`, and `Range` objects.

Array Functions

As might be expected, a handful of functions are included with VBA that you can use to manipulate and extract information from arrays. Some of these functions work only with one-dimensional arrays and may require that the array be of type `String`. You can use other functions to return the bounds on an array or build an array from a specified list of values. Curiously, there are no functions for sorting the values in an array, so you will have to build these functions. Table 6.2 lists the VBA functions designed to work on or with arrays.

Table 6.2 VBA Array Functions

Function	Description
UBound()	Returns the upper bound of an array for the specified dimension.
LBound()	Returns the lower bound of an array for the specified dimension.
Array()	Returns an array built from a comma-delimited list of values.
IsArray()	Returns a Boolean value indicating whether a variable is an array.
Split()	Returns a one-dimensional array built from a delimited String.
Filter()	Returns an array based on filtering criteria that represents a subset of an existing String array.
Join()	Returns a String concatenated from the elements of an existing array and a delimiter.

The UBound() function is particularly useful with For/Next loops when working with dynamic arrays (discussed in the next section, "Dynamic Arrays"). You can use the UBound() function with an array of any dimension to return the upper bound of the specified dimension. Used in conjunction with the three-dimensional array variable myArray from the previous example, UBound(myArray,1) returns 99 for the upper limit of the looping variable I in the following For/Next loop. The second argument of the UBound() function in the following code specifies the first dimension of the array variable myArray:

```
For I = 0 To UBound(myArray, 1)
    'Block of statements
Next I
```

The Array() function creates an array of type Variant from a comma-delimited list of values. The variable used to represent the array must be declared as a Variant. The following code is an example of one of the few instances in which you have no choice for using a Variant:

```
Dim varArray As Variant
varArray = Array("Element1", 2, "Another string")
```

Because the array is a Variant, the data added to the array can be of any data type except fixed-length strings and user-defined types. The specification in the Option Base statement determines the lower bound on the array.

The previous statements create a Variant variable named varArray that later is used to hold an array of values. This is different than creating an array whose elements are of type Variant (Dim varArray(2) As Variant); however, the elements in both arrays are accessed the same way, so you will not notice the difference.

TIP

You can pass a `Variant` variable holding an array to another procedure just as you pass any other variable.

Dynamic Arrays

So far I have shown examples only of fixed length arrays (size is predefined in the declaration). The size of fixed length arrays cannot be changed during run time, so you are stuck with using the declared size. There is nothing wrong with using fixed-length arrays as long as you are certain of the required length and that the array size will not have to change. When you do not know the size requirements of an array (either before or during run time), you should declare a dynamic array rather than a fixed array. In the examples I've shown so far, arrays are initialized from a specific number of cells at a specific location (address) on the active worksheet. To make array initialization more robust, you can use dynamic arrays that are resized during run time to accommodate the required input.

TIP

To return a selected range from the active Excel worksheet, use `ActiveWindow.Selection`. This returns a `Range` object representing the user's selection. I discuss the `Window` and `Range` objects in Chapter 7.

To declare a dynamic array, remove the value or values used to indicate lower and upper bounds in a fixed array declaration.

```
Dim myArray() as Integer
```

Later in the program, after the required size of the array is determined, re-dimension the array with the `ReDim` keyword, as shown here:

```
ReDim myArray(mySize)
```

CAUTION

Avoid using `ReDim` as a declarative statement with arrays because of potential conflicts with variables that have the same name as the array, even if the variables are of different scope.

Using `ReDim` will reinitialize all elements in the array. If you must preserve the existing values, use the `Preserve` keyword, as shown here:

```
ReDim Preserve myArray(mySize)
```

When using `Preserve`, you can change only the size of the last dimension; you cannot change the number of dimensions, and values at the end of the array are lost if you re-dimension the array smaller than the original size.

Now that you are familiar with VBA loops and arrays, take a look at some interesting and useful procedures that rely heavily on them.

Transposing Data in a Worksheet

Transposing is taking a rectangular block of data and rotating it so that columns become rows and vice versa. To transpose a block of data in a worksheet, you must first select and copy the range and then select Edit, Paste Special. In the Paste Special dialog box, select the Transpose checkbox before clicking OK (see Figure 6.3).

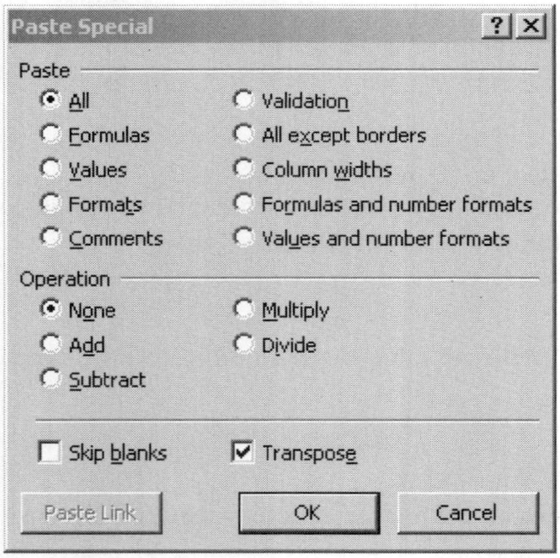

FIGURE 6.3 *Using the Paste Special dialog box to transpose data in a worksheet.*

You can also use Excel's worksheet function `TRANSPOSE()`, but either way, the process of transposing data in Excel is a little annoying, and I wanted to show you something easier, so I've written a custom Sub procedure called `Transpose()`.

The `Transpose()` Sub procedure transposes a selected block of data (values only, no formulas) in a worksheet keeping the upper-left cell as the first cell in the transposed block. The results of transposing a 3x7 block of data are shown in Figures 6.4 and 6.5.

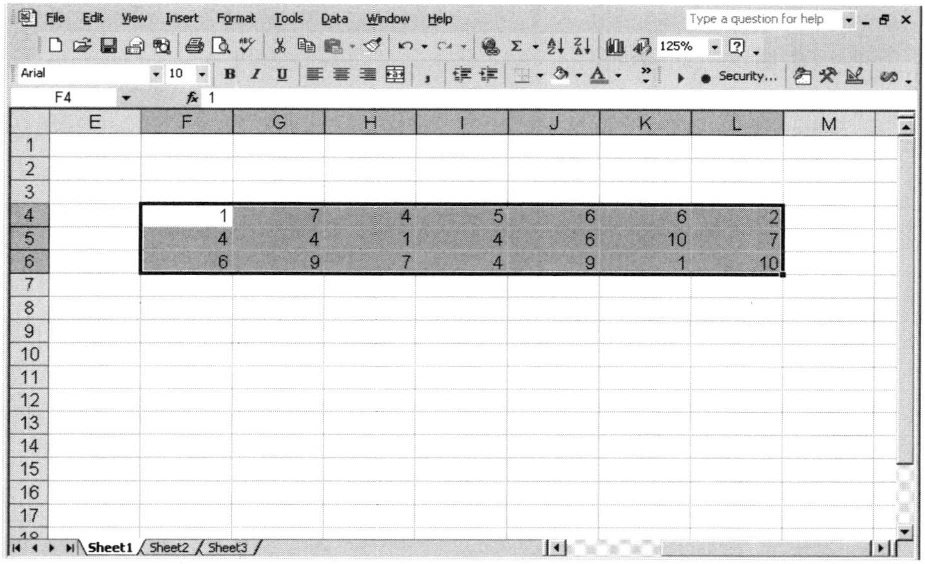

FIGURE 6.4 *A block of data selected to be transposed.*

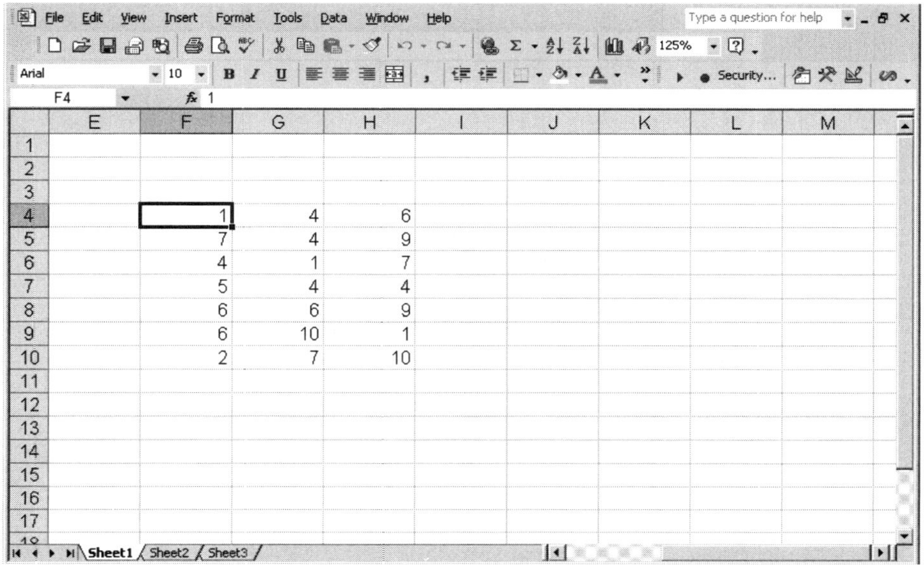

FIGURE 6.5 *The block of data shown in Figure 6.4 after being transposed.*

The `Transpose()` Sub procedure is fairly short, and its design follows these steps:

1. **Declare variables.** This includes a dynamic array named `transArray` declared as a `Variant` data type. I declared the array as a `Variant` because I wanted to be able to transpose numerical and `String` data.

2. **Determine the size and location of the selected range.** The worksheet range representing the data selected by the user is read using the `Selection` property of the `Window` object. When the object selected in Excel represents a group of cells on a worksheet, the `Selection` property returns a `Range` object. The `Row` and `Column` properties of this `Range` object return the first row and column of the selected range. The size of the selected range is read using the `Rows`, and `Columns` properties of the `Range` object. These properties return `Collection` objects representing the collection of rows and columns selected by the user. The `Count` property returns the number of selected rows and columns.

3. **Copy the selected values into an array.** The `transArray` array is re-dimensioned as a two-dimensional array using the bounds determined in Step 2. After re-dimensioning, the array is loaded with the selected worksheet data using nested `For/Next` loops.

4. **Output the transposed data back to the worksheet.** The range is cleared using the `ClearContents` property of the `Range` object before copying the data back to the worksheet in transposed form with nested `For/Next` loops. The data block is transposed by switching the looping variables used to represent rows and columns in the worksheet and the array.

The `Transpose()` Sub procedure is listed next as a `Public` procedure that should be executed after a block of worksheet cells has been selected:

```
Public Sub Transpose ()
    Dim I As Integer
    Dim J As Integer
    Dim transArray() As Variant
    Dim numRows As Integer
    Dim numColumns As Integer
    Dim colIndex As Integer
    Dim rowIndex As Integer
    Dim inputRange As Range
    '
    Set inputRange = ActiveWindow.Selection
    colIndex = inputRange.Column
    rowIndex = inputRange.Row
    '--------------------------------
```

```
'Get the size of the data block
'...............................
numRows = inputRange.Rows.Count
numColumns = inputRange.Columns.Count
ReDim transArray(numRows - 1, numColumns - 1)
'...........................
'Copy values into the array.
'...........................
For I = colIndex To numColumns + colIndex - 1
    For J = rowIndex To numRows + rowIndex - 1
        transArray(J - rowIndex, I - colIndex) = Cells(J, I).Value
    Next J
Next I
'...................................................
'Copy the array to the worksheet in transposed form
'...................................................
inputRange.ClearContents
For I = colIndex To numRows + colIndex - 1
    For J = rowIndex To numColumns + rowIndex - 1
        Cells(J, I).Value = transArray(I - colIndex, J - rowIndex)
    Next J
Next I
Cells(rowIndex, colIndex).Select
End Sub
```

A nice feature of the `Transpose()` Sub procedure is that it can transpose any size block of data almost (see note) anywhere on a worksheet.

 NOTE

Here, the `Transpose()` Sub procedure does not work everywhere on a worksheet because I did not include error handling to deal with potential problems at the boundaries of the worksheet. The maximum number of rows and columns in a worksheet is 65,536 and 256, respectively. Attempts to copy the transposed data block to rows or columns with higher index values will crash the program. I discuss error handling in VBA in Chapter 8, "Understanding File I/O, and Debugging and Error Handling in VBA."

Finding Contiguous Blocks of Data

Whether you program with VBA as a hobby or professionally, you will eventually need to use something similar to the FindBlocks() Sub procedure for locating contiguous blocks of data on a worksheet. This procedure locates all rectangular blocks of data on a worksheet and was developed using the following algorithm:

1. Determined the range of used cells on the active worksheet. The used range will set the variables for looping through each cell in the worksheet that may contain data. Because I will be using For/Next loops and Do/Loops, I want to minimize the number of cells searched to make the application execute as fast as possible. The UsedRange property of the Range object makes this task easy.

2. Looped through the used range to find cells that contain data. I used nested Do/Loops to iterate through each cell in the used range. When a cell that contains data is found, it is assumed to be the upper-left corner of a new block of data. It is then a relatively simple task to call another procedure that increments the row and column indices of the cell until an empty cell is found within the same row and column as the original cell (see Figure 6.6).

3. Stored the range that holds the data block. Once the final row and column indices of the data block are known, a String representing the range of cells containing the data block is stored to an array. Program execution proceeds back to the original procedure to continue looping through the used range of cells on the worksheet. Whenever a cell containing data is found, it is first checked against the ranges of cell blocks already stored to make sure it hasn't already been counted. To make this search easier, I used a two-dimensional array to hold the range strings and the row and column indices of the data block.

4. Sorted the array holding the strings representing data blocks. I used a bubble sort procedure to sort the array according to the first column reference in the String.

5. Presented the data blocks. I used a message box to output a list of strings representing the ranges occupied by each block of data on the worksheet.

6. Assumed there is no data in the last column (256) or row (65536) of the worksheet.

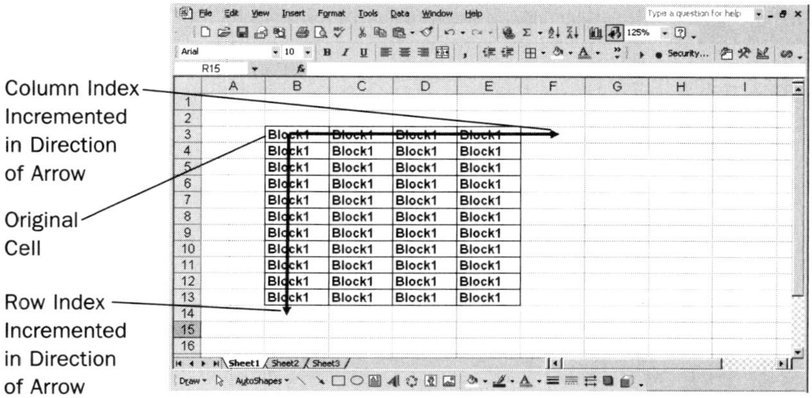

Column Index Incremented in Direction of Arrow

Original Cell

Row Index Incremented in Direction of Arrow

FIGURE 6.6 *Method used to determine the size of a contiguous block in a worksheet.*

The FindBlocks() Sub procedure loops through the used range on the active worksheet searching for cells that contain data. When a cell containing data is found, program execution is passed to the GetBlock() Sub procedure in order to locate the entire block associated with the cell. After all cells in the used range have been tested, the array holding the strings representing the discovered blocks of data is sorted before output.

```
Public Sub FindBlocks()
    Dim numRows As Long
    Dim numCols As Integer
    Dim colIndex As Integer
    Dim rowIndex As Long
    Dim J As Integer
    Dim theUsedRange As Range
    Dim cellBlocks() As String
    Dim msg As String
    '
    '------------------------------------
    'Find the used range on the worksheet
    '------------------------------------
    Set theUsedRange = ActiveSheet.UsedRange
    numRows = theUsedRange.Rows.Count
    numCols = theUsedRange.Columns.Count
    '
    '-----------------------------------------------
```

```
'Loop through the used range to find data cells
'- - - - - - - - - - - - - - - - - - - - - - - - - - - - - - - - - - - - -
colIndex = 1
rowIndex = 1
Do
    Do
        If Cells(rowIndex, colIndex).Value <> "" Then
            Call GetBlock(rowIndex, colIndex, cellBlocks())
        End If
        colIndex = colIndex + 1
    Loop While colIndex <= numCols
    colIndex = 1            'Reset indices
    rowIndex = rowIndex + 1
Loop While rowIndex <= numRows
    '
    '- - - - - - - - - - - - - - - - - - - - - - - - - - - - - - - - - - - - -
'Sort the array and output used ranges in a message box
'- - - - - - - - - - - - - - - - - - - - - - - - - - - - - - - - - - - - -
BubSort cellBlocks, 3, False
For J = 0 To UBound(cellBlocks, 2)
    msg = msg & vbCrLf & cellBlocks(0, J)
Next J
MsgBox msg
End        'Required to clear static variables from memory.
End Sub
```

The `GetBlock()` Sub procedure is called from `FindBlocks()` and accepts the row and column indices of a single cell on the worksheet. The array used to hold the strings representing blocks of cells already found is also passed to this procedure. If the discovered cell passes a test to see whether it has already been included in a discovered block of data, this cell must represent the upper-left corner of a new block of data. The range of the new block is then determined by incrementing row and column indices until empty cells are found as illustrated in Figure 6.6. The new block of cells is then written to the `cellBlocks` array, which is the ultimate goal of the `GetBlock()` Sub procedure.

```
Private Sub GetBlock(rowIndex As Long, colIndex As Integer, _
                                cellBlocks() As String)
    Dim I As Long
    Dim J As Integer
    Dim K As Integer
```

```
Static numBlocks As Integer
Dim r1 As Long
Dim r2 As Long
Dim c1 As Integer
Dim c2 As Integer


'------------------------------------------------------------
'Test the cell to see if it already exists in a stored range
'------------------------------------------------------------
ReDim Preserve cellBlocks(4, numBlocks)
For K = 0 To UBound(cellBlocks, 2) - 1
    r1 = cellBlocks(1, K)
    r2 = cellBlocks(2, K)
    c1 = cellBlocks(3, K)
    c2 = cellBlocks(4, K)
    If rowIndex >= r1 And rowIndex <= r2 And colIndex >= c1 _
        And colIndex <= c2 Then Exit Sub
Next K


'------------------------------------------------------------
'Loop thru rows and columns to find first empty cell in each
'------------------------------------------------------------
I = rowIndex
Do While Cells(I, colIndex) <> "" And I < 65536
    I = I + 1
Loop


J = colIndex
Do While Cells(rowIndex, J) <> "" And J < 256
    J = J + 1
Loop


'---------------------------
'Build the range as a string
'---------------------------
cellBlocks(0, numBlocks) = GetColumnRef(colIndex) & rowIndex & _
        ":" & GetColumnRef(J - 1) & I - 1
cellBlocks(1, numBlocks) = rowIndex
```

```
        cellBlocks(2, numBlocks) = I - 1
        cellBlocks(3, numBlocks) = colIndex
        cellBlocks(4, numBlocks) = J - 1
        numBlocks = numBlocks + 1
End Sub
```

The `GetColumnRef()` Function procedure is called from `GetBlock()` and accepts an `Integer` representing a column index. This Function converts the `Integer` to a `String` representation of the same column. The `GetColumnRef()` Function is necessary in case a column index is greater than 26 (column Z). For example, you cannot use the `Chr()` function to convert the column index 27 to the `String` "AA".

```
Private Function GetColumnRef(columnIndex As Integer) As String
'Converts a column index number to a textual reference
    Dim numAlpha As Integer
    Dim firstLetter As String
    Dim secondLetter As String
    Dim remainder As Integer

    'Calculate the number of characters needed
    numAlpha = columnIndex \ 26
    Select Case columnIndex / 26
        Case Is <= 1      'Column ref is between A and Z
            firstLetter = Chr(columnIndex + 64)
            GetColumnRef = firstLetter
        Case Else      'Column ref has two letters
            remainder = columnIndex - 26 * (columnIndex \ 26)
            If remainder = 0 Then
                firstLetter = Chr(64 + (columnIndex \ 26) - 1)
                secondLetter = "Z"
                GetColumnRef = firstLetter & secondLetter
            Else
                firstLetter = Chr(64 + (columnIndex \ 26))
                secondLetter = Chr(64 + remainder)
                GetColumnRef = firstLetter & secondLetter
            End If
    End Select
End Function
```

The `BubSort()` Sub procedure is much the same as the `BubbleSort()` procedure discussed earlier in this chapter, except that it sorts a two-dimensional array on a specific column. The `BubSort()` procedure is more robust than `BubbleSort()` in that it can sort any size array of two dimensions and sort the array using any column. The `BubSort()` Sub procedure will also sort `String` or numerical values, and is listed in the following:

```
Private Sub BubSort(myArray() As String, sortCol As Integer, _
                                    strType As Boolean)
'Sorts a two-dimensional array using either column
'Array to be sorted is the variable myArray. This variable
'also holds the sorted array.
    Dim tempVar() As String
    Dim anotherIteration As Boolean
    Dim I As Integer
    Dim J As Integer
    Dim arraySize As Integer
    Dim tempVarSize As Integer
    '
    arraySize = UBound(myArray, 2)
    tempVarSize = UBound(myArray, 1)
    ReDim tempVar(tempVarSize)
    Do      'Outer Do/loop iterates until the array is sorted
        anotherIteration = False
        For I = 0 To arraySize - 1    'Inner loop exchanges array elements
            If strType Then       "if data is a string
                If myArray(sortCol, I) > myArray(sortCol, I + 1) Then
                    For J = 0 To UBound(myArray, 1): tempVar( _
                        J) = myArray(J, I): Next J
                    For J = 0 To UBound(myArray, 1): myArray( _
                        J, I) = myArray(J, I + 1): Next J
                    For J = 0 To UBound(myArray, 1): myArray( _
                        J, I + 1) = tempVar(J): Next J
                    anotherIteration = True
                End If
            Else    'If data is numerical
                If Val(myArray(sortCol, I)) > Val( _
                    myArray(sortCol, I + 1)) Then
```

```
            For J = 0 To UBound(myArray, 1): tempVar( _
                    J) = myArray(J, I): Next J
            For J = 0 To UBound(myArray, 1): myArray( _
                    J, I) = myArray(J, I + 1): Next J
            For J = 0 To UBound(myArray, 1): myArray( _
                    J, I + 1) = tempVar(J): Next J
            anotherIteration = True
         End If
      End If
   Next I
   Loop While anotherIteration = True
End Sub
```

An Excel worksheet constructed with meaningless information was used to test the procedures for finding contiguous blocks of data. The result is shown in Figure 6.7.

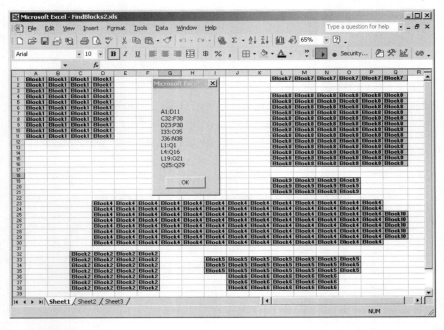

FIGURE 6.7 *Output from the program used to find contiguous blocks of data on a worksheet.*

Quick Sort

The bubble sort procedures already discussed work fine for sorting relatively small lists of strings or numbers. However, as the number of elements in a data set increases, the bubble sort becomes increasingly inefficient. The inefficiency is due to the nonlinear dependence of the number of required exchanges on the number of elements in the data set (approximately N^2 dependence, where N is the number of elements). So, the bubble sort is very slow when the data set is large.

Sorting procedures that are much more efficient than the bubble sort can be written in VBA. The quick sort is one of these fast sorting procedures and is relatively simple to write. The QSort() Sub procedure is a recursive procedure (calls itself) and operates on an exchange mechanism just as the BubbleSort() procedure does. However, the dependence of the number of exchanges on the number of elements in the data set is significantly less (approximately $N \log N$).

The QSort() procedure partitions the array into two sections and compares the elements in each section to a partition value. Ideally, the partition value is the median of the data set passed into the array, but I am using the median index value of the array here for simplicity. Values on the left of the partition index (those values with a lower array index than that of the partition value) that are greater than the partition value are exchanged with values on the right that are less than the partition value. Each partition is then passed recursively to the QSort() procedure until the array is sorted. For an example, check the table in Figure 6.8, which illustrates the process for sorting a list of 10 integers.

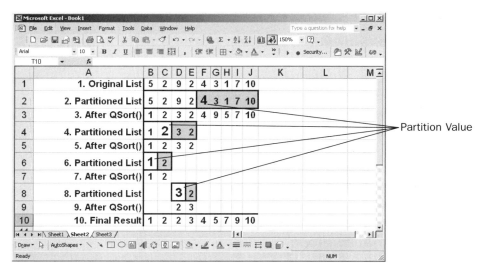

FIGURE 6.8 *Sorting a list using the* QSort() *Sub procedure.*

The original list of numbers to be sorted is shown in the top row of Figure 6.8. The second row shows how QSort() partitions the list into two sections. The partition value is shown in a larger font size, and the result of one pass through the QSort() procedure is shown in the third row. Next, a recursive call to QSort() passes in the index values representing the four values in the left partition. The process of exchanging values is then repeated, and the result is shown in the fourth and fifth rows. More recursive calls to the QSort() procedure pass in even smaller partitions (two values) until the first four values in the original list are sorted (rows 6 through 9 of Figure 6.8). Finally, the same process sorts the right partition from the original list.

Although the QSort() procedure is short, here are a few items worth noting:

◆ **The procedure accepts three parameters.** The three parameters include the array to be sorted and two integers representing the first and last index values of the array.

◆ **The array must be passed by reference.** This ensures that values in the original array variable are exchanged with each call to QSort().

◆ **The variables representing the left and right index values passed to the QSort() procedure must be passed by value.** This prevents these variables from being altered when code execution returns to the instance of the QSort() procedure that made the call.

Remember that only the original call to the QSort() procedure passes the entire array. Subsequent recursive calls are passing smaller and smaller partitions for sorting. The QSort() Sub procedure is listed in the following:

```
Private Sub QSort(sortArray() As Double, ByVal leftIndex As Integer, _
                            ByVal rightIndex As Integer)

    Dim compValue As Double
    Dim I As Integer
    Dim J As Integer
    Dim tempNum As Double


    I = leftIndex
    J = rightIndex
    compValue = sortArray(Int((I + J) / 2))


    Do
        Do While (sortArray(I) < compValue And I < rightIndex)
            I = I + 1
```

```
        Loop
        Do While (compValue < sortArray(J) And J > leftIndex)
            J = J - 1
        Loop
        If I <= J Then
            tempNum = sortArray(I)
            sortArray(I) = sortArray(J)
            sortArray(J) = tempNum
            I = I + 1
            J = J - 1
        End If
    Loop While I <= J


    If leftIndex < J Then QSort sortArray(), leftIndex, J
    If I < rightIndex Then QSort sortArray(), I, rightIndex
End Sub
```

With an application such as Excel, you may find the `QSort()` Sub procedure handy for sorting large arrays of numbers. Yes, there is a `Sort` method of the `Range` object that you can use to sort data; but the data will have to be in a worksheet, and that just isn't always practical.

Summary

This chapter discussed the `For/Next` and `Do/Loop` programming structures and array data structures included in VBA. These structures demonstrated some useful programs that included sorting and transposing data as well as finding contiguous blocks of data in an Excel worksheet.

Chapter 7

The first six chapters of this book focus on VBA's basic programming structures. Although, in those chapters, I use several examples that incorporate objects from Excel, the structures are common to all applications that integrate VBA. This chapter provides a detailed discussion of some of the objects referred to in the earlier chapters and introduces new objects that are specific to Excel.

Because Excel's object model is fairly extensive, I cannot discuss all of its component objects in this chapter. Instead, I will focus on those objects most commonly used — the `Application`, `Workbook`, `Worksheet`, and `Range` objects. You learn about other VBA- and Excel-specific objects as you encounter them in the programming projects later in this book.

Understanding the Excel Object Model

Approximately 200 objects are included in Excel's object model that VBA programmers can use to create applications. You use these objects to build the data and manipulate the appearance of an Excel spreadsheet and its related components. To make programming easier, Excel objects come with properties that you can use to manipulate Excel's behavior and appearance. In addition, many of the objects have methods for carrying out some type of action, and a handful of objects have event procedures that the user, code, or system can trigger. For a graphical representation of the Excel object model, go to the online help and enter **object model** in the keyword field. Figure 7.1 shows the chart of Excel's object model as it appears in the online help.

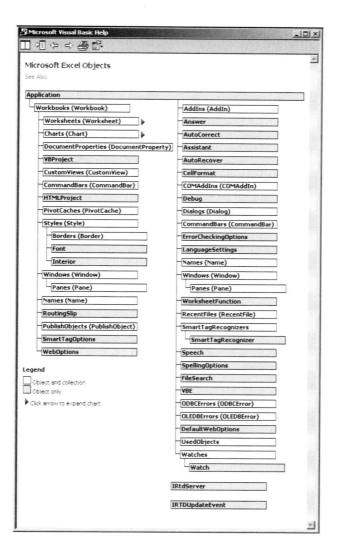

FIGURE 7.1 *Graphical representation of the Excel object model.*

The Object Browser Revisited

In Chapter 2, "Working with Variables and Constants in VBA," I briefly introduce you to the Object Browser (available from the IDE by pressing F2), which you use to view all available programming objects and their members (properties, methods, and events). You can use the Object Browser (see Figure 7.2) when you need help on the objects available for use in your program.

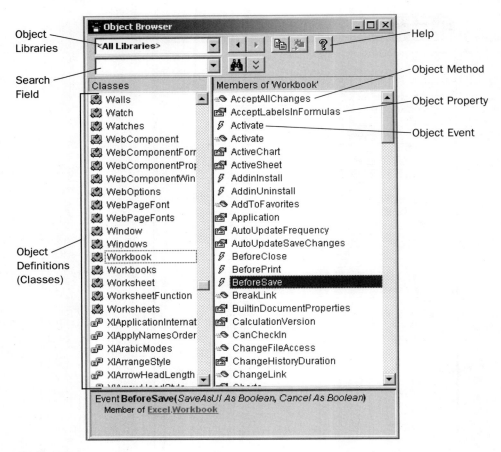

FIGURE 7.2 *The Object Browser listing the members of the* Workbook *object.*

Objects are categorized as *type libraries,* which are computer files that hold the program code required for building the objects. An object library is grouped by a type that usually refers to the application that uses it (for example, the Excel object library stores the code that is used to build objects specific to the Excel application). In the Object Browser, the library drop-down list includes all object libraries with current references. At a minimum, the Excel and VBA libraries must be referenced in order to write a functional program. In fact, the references to these libraries are set automatically, and you cannot remove them. References that may be set automatically on your computer include the Microsoft Office (if installed), the Microsoft Forms, and the OLE Automation object libraries. The Office and OLE Automation libraries are relatively small and include objects common to all Office applications and some interfaces available through *automation.*

NOTE

The version number of the Microsoft Office Object Library may be different on your computer. Version 9.0 is Office 2000, version 10.0 is Office XP, and version 11.0 is Office 2003.

The Forms library will be referenced whenever a Userform is added to a project. To reference other libraries, go to the IDE menu bar and select Tools, References. The dialog box that appears (see Figure 7.3) lists all libraries registered with the operating system.

 NOTE

Automation is a feature of the Component Object Model (COM), a standard technology that applications use to expose their objects to other development tools such as VBA. For example, the Excel object model is exposed through automation making it possible to access Excel objects, properties, methods, and events from another application.

When an application supports Automation, the objects exposed by an application can be accessed by VBA. Object libraries exposed through automation are referenced in a VBA project by selecting a specific library from the References dialog box (see Figure 7.3).

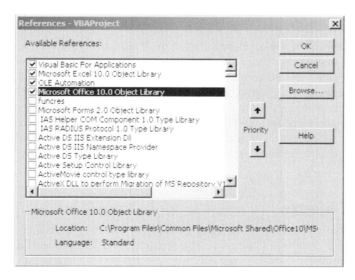

FIGURE 7.3 *Adding a reference to an object library in the References dialog box.*

You can set a reference to an object library by selecting the checkbox next to its name. The objects available in the selected library are then listed in the Object Browser and are available for you to use in your program. If you are not using objects from the selected library, you should clear its reference so that VBA will not search this library when resolving references in your project at compile time.

CAUTION

A run-time error will result if your program uses an object from a library without a set reference.

If the object library is not listed in the References dialog box, click the Browse button to search the directories on your computer for the desired file and add the reference. Relevant file types are libraries (*.olb, *.tlb, and *.dll), executables (*.exe and *.dll), and ActiveX controls (*.ocx).

NOTE

Be aware that setting a reference to an object library does not necessarily mean that you will be able to use the objects it contains. The objects may be restricted by licensing requirements. Furthermore, if you intend to install your program on another computer, any additional objects your program requires will also have to be installed on the target computer.

After you select a library in the Object Browser, a list of all available objects (classes) and their members (properties, methods, and events) will appear. The listed classes are filtered according to the selected library. To view all available classes, select All Libraries (refer to Figure 7.2). After you select a class from the list, its members are displayed on the right side of the Object Browser. Icons specify the member type (pointing hand for properties, moving green cube for methods, and lightening bolt for events). For immediate help on a selected component, click the question mark or press F1. The Object Browser's utility lies is in its capability to provide a handy list of available objects and its quick access to the online help.

Top-Level Excel Objects

The Excel object model is hierarchical in nature. To apply an object's methods or change the value of its properties, you must identify the object path in your VBA code. If the path to the desired object immediately follows the currently selected object in the hierarchy, the full path can be omitted. However, if there is any ambiguity in the object path, you must qualify it with as many references as required to remove the uncertainty.

The references specified in the object path must follow the established hierarchy. You access objects in Excel through the hierarchy using the dot (.) operator. For example, the following statement changes the value of the Name property of the first worksheet in the first workbook of the Excel application:

```
Application.Workbooks(1).Worksheets(1).Name = "My Sheet"
```

The statement follows Excel's object hierarchy, starting with the Application object and proceeding through the Workbook and Worksheet objects before changing the value of the Name property of the specific Worksheet object. This statement avoids potential ambiguity by explicitly referencing each object in the path starting from the top of Excel's object model (the Application object). If the first worksheet in the first workbook that was opened also happens to be the currently selected or active worksheet, the next statement accomplishes the same task.

```
ActiveSheet.Name = "My Sheet"
```

This statement is more risky because it increases the potential of accessing the wrong worksheet. So, when using a more ambiguous object path, take care to ensure that the active object is the desired one.

Now it's time to get started with Excel's object model at the top of the hierarchy and then to work through the most commonly used objects.

The Application Object

The Application object is the top-level object in Excel's object model and represents the entirety of the Excel application (refer to Figure 7.1). The Application object's properties and methods manipulate the appearance and behavior of the Excel application. You can set some of these properties in the Options dialog box, which you access by selecting Tools, Options (see Figure 7.4).

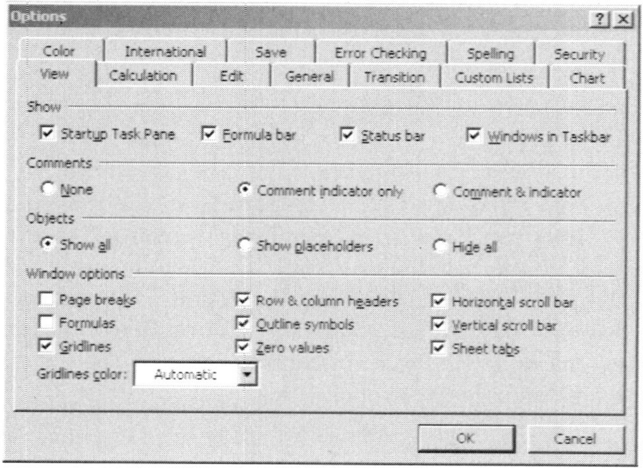

FIGURE 7.4 *The Options dialog box from Excel.*

Because the `Application` object is at the top of the object hierarchy, you don't need to reference it in code except when dealing with it exclusively. For example, to change the values of the `WindowState`, `Width`, and `Height` properties of the Excel application window, you must explicitly reference the `Application` object, as shown in the following:

```
Application.WindowState = xlNormal
Application.Width = 600
Application.Height = 450
```

However, when changing the `Width` and `Height` properties of a workbook window, the reference to the `Application` object is implied, so an explicit reference to it is not required (though you can include it if you want). The `Workbooks` property is a member of the `Application` object and returns a reference to the `Workbook` object specified by the index value given in the parentheses.

```
Workbooks(1).Windows(1).WindowState = xlNormal
Workbooks(1).Windows(1).Width = 500
Workbooks(1).Windows(1).Height = 300
```

If you need access to the currently selected object (for example, `Workbook`, `Worksheet`, `Chart` or `Cell`), you can use the active properties (`ActiveCell`, `ActiveChart`, `ActiveSheet`, `ActiveWorkbook`) of the `Application` object. Each of these properties returns a reference to the currently selected object in Excel. These properties are convenient and prevent you from having to type a long object path when all you need is access to the currently selected object. Of course, the selected object must match the property (for example, if you use `ActiveChart`, you must first select a `Chart` object). The following two lines of code use the `ActiveCell` and `ActiveSheet` properties of the `Application` object to return a `Range` and `Worksheet` object, respectively. The `Value` property of the `Range` object (representing the currently selected cell in the active worksheet) is changed to `"HELLO"`, and the `Name` property of the `Worksheet` object is changed to `"My Sheet"`.

```
ActiveCell.Value = "HELLO"
ActiveSheet.Name = "My Sheet"
```

In total, the `Application` object has about 250 properties, methods, and events. Although you will probably never use most of its members, the `Application` object should not be overlooked. Properties and methods dealing with system memory, the application's display, and the computer's file structure can be found as members of the `Application` object. You may also find that the `Worksheets`, `WorksheetFunction`, and `ScreenUpdating` properties (among others) to be of considerable use. You see examples of these properties and methods throughout the book.

NOTE

> Several event procedures are also members of the `Application` object. Most of these procedures encapsulate the event procedures of the `Workbook` object in a larger scope.
>
> The event procedures of the `Application` object are not activated by default. The activation of the event procedures requires some additional code and the creation of a class module. Because this is also the case for the `Chart` object, a discussion on activating the events of the `Application` and `Chart` objects is in Chapter 10, "Creating and Manipulating Excel Charts."

Collection Objects

The use of collection objects in VBA is relatively straightforward. They are exactly what the name implies — a group or collection of objects of the same type. Not all Excel objects can be part of a collection, but many can, and some of these objects include the `Workbook` (`Workbooks`), `Worksheet` (`Worksheets`), `Sheet` (`Sheets`), `Chart` (`Charts`), and `Shape` (`Shapes`) objects. You can usually recognize a collection object as the plural form of the object word. One notable exception to this rule is the `Range` object, which can represent a single cell or a collection of cells on a worksheet.

Collection objects typically have only a few members. Common members include `Add`, `Delete`, `Select`, and `Copy` methods along with `Count` and `Item` properties. Note that not all collection objects will contain these members (consult the Object Browser).

The following code creates a new workbook and adds it to the collection, reads the number of workbooks into a variable, and selects all worksheets in the active workbook:

```
Workbooks.Add
numWorkbooks = Workbooks.Count
Worksheets.Select
```

As you will see in the section, "For Each Loops," later in this chapter, collection objects are particularly useful with looping structures when returning individual objects from the collection.

The Workbook and Window Objects

The `Workbook` object is one of the workhorse objects in Excel's object model. You will use the `Workbook` object often when writing VBA code for Excel applications. On the other hand, you seldom use the `Window` object, but I include it here to point out the confusion that may exist between these two objects.

NOTE

The `Workbook` and `Window` objects are subordinate to the `Application` object. However, because of the uniqueness of the `Application` object, its reference is implied and does not have to be included when referencing subordinate objects.

A `Workbook` object represents a single open workbook in Excel. All `Workbook` objects are included in the `Workbooks` collection object. Therefore, a new `Workbook` object is created whenever you use the `Add` method of the `Workbooks` collection object (or the user selects File, New in Excel). You can select a `Workbook` object from the `Workbooks` collection object with the `Activate` method and an index value to specify the desired workbook.

```
Workbooks(1).Activate
```

The index values run from 1 to the number of `Workbook` objects in the collection and are ordered in the sequence in which the workbooks were added to the collection. To select the last `Workbook` object in the collection, use the following:

```
Workbooks(Workbooks.Count).Activate
```

Alternatively, if the name of the `Workbook` object is known, you can use a `String` rather than an index value, as shown here:

```
Workbooks("MyWorkbook.xls").Activate
```

All `Window` objects are included in the `Windows` collection object, so a `Window` object also represents a single open workbook in Excel. In fact, all `Workbook` objects are also `Window` objects. The distinction between the `Workbook` and `Window` objects lies in an additional method that can be used to create a `Window` object. You can create new `Window` objects using the `NewWindow` method of the `Window` object. This is the equivalent of the user selecting Window, New Window in Excel.

```
Windows(1).NewWindow
```

 TIP

Unlike the `Workbooks` collection object, the `Windows` collection object always reserves the index value 1 for the currently selected or active window.

The `NewWindow` method creates a copy of the selected `Window` object and renames each window by concatenating a colon and number to the end of the name. For example, a `Workbook` object (which is also a `Window` object) with the name `MyWorkbook.xls` will be renamed

MyWorkbook.xls:1, and its copy will be named MyWorkbook.xls:2. After the new window is created, the Windows collection object contains two windows (MyWorkbook.xls:1 and MyWorkbook.xls:2), and the Workbooks collection object contains only one workbook (MyWorkbook.xls). It follows that the next two lines of code are equivalent:

```
Workbooks("MyWorkbook.xls").Activate
Windows("MyWorkbook.xls:1").Activate
```

The Workbook and Window objects have a large number of members that can be viewed in the Object Browser or online help. The following Sub procedure uses a few of these members to open a workbook and then size it to fit just within the application window:

```
Public Sub OpenBook()
    Workbooks.Open ActiveWorkbook.Path & "\MyWorkbook.xls"
    FitWindow
End Sub
Private Sub FitWindow()
    Dim winWidth As Integer
    Dim winHeight As Integer
    winWidth = Application.UsableWidth 'Get the usable width of app window
    winHeight = Application.UsableHeight
    '
    Windows(1).Width = winWidth
    Windows(1).Height = winHeight
    Windows(1).Left = 0
    Windows(1).Top = 0
End Sub
```

The OpenBook() Sub procedure opens the workbook named MyWorkbook.xls using the Open method of the Workbooks collection object. The file MyWorkbook.xls must be saved in the same directory as the active workbook because the Path property of the Workbook object is used to return the file path for the Open method. The FitWindow() Sub procedure then uses several properties of the Window object (Width, Height, Left, and Top) to fit the workbook window to the application window.

The Worksheet Object

The Worksheet object is just under the Workbook object in Excel's object hierarchy. This makes sense because any single workbook can contain multiple worksheets. The Worksheets collection object contains all the Worksheet objects in the selected or specified Workbook object. To activate a worksheet, you can use either the Activate or Select methods of the Worksheet object.

```
Workbooks("MyWorkbook").Worksheets("Sheet2").Select
```

The previous code selects the worksheet named Sheet2 in the workbook named MyWorkbook in Excel. If the workbook qualifier is omitted, the worksheet will be selected from the active workbook.

> **NOTE**
>
> Don't confuse the Sheets collection object with the Worksheets collection object. The Worksheets collection object contains all worksheets in a workbook. The Sheets collection object contains all worksheets and chart sheets in a workbook.

Looping through worksheets in order to set or return specific properties of the Worksheet object (or subordinate Range objects) is one of the more common tasks when programming in Excel-VBA. The following example uses nested For/Next loops to count the total number of cells used in all open worksheets:

```
Public Sub numCells()
    Dim I As Integer
    Dim K As Integer
    Dim numCells As Long

    For K = 1 To Workbooks.Count    'Loop through workbooks
        Workbooks(K).Activate
        For I = 1 To Worksheets.Count  'Loop through worksheets
            numCells = numCells + Worksheets(I).UsedRange.Count
        Next I
    Next K
    MsgBox (numCells)
End Sub
```

The outer loop iterates through each Workbook object in the collection, activating each workbook before the inner loop iterates through each Worksheet object contained in the active workbook. The UsedRange property of the Worksheet object returns a Range object representing the range of cells (as a rectangular block) that contain values or formulas in the worksheet. A Range object is also a collection object, so the Count property is used to return the number of cells in the range.

Typically, you will set only a few properties of the Workbook and Worksheet objects. These objects are more commonly used to return a specific worksheet contained in a specific workbook to provide access to a specific range of cells. This makes sense because most of the work done by an Excel user involves adding data, formulas, and formatting to a range of cells in a worksheet.

NOTE

I discuss event procedures for the `Workbook` and `Worksheet` objects in Chapter 4, "Understanding VBA Procedures."

The Range Object

The `Range` object represents a collection of one or more contiguous cells in a worksheet. The `Range` object is just below the `Worksheet` object in Excel's object hierarchy and will be the most extensively used object in your programs. It is through the `Range` object that you will manipulate and read values, formulas, and formatting in a worksheet. This constitutes a majority of the work that has to be done by a typical VBA program. Consequently, familiarity with the `Range` object is an absolute requirement for any VBA programmer.

You can use the `Range` and `Cells` properties of the `Worksheet` object to return a `Range` object. The `Range` property is better for returning a specific collection of cells, and the `Cells` property can be used to return all cells in a worksheet or just one cell. For example, the following statement uses the `Range` property of the `Worksheet` object to set the font color of every cell in columns A and B of the worksheet:

```
Range("A:B").Font.Color = vbRed
```

TIP

The fastest way to learn how to format cells in a worksheet is to record a macro and examine the resulting code.

The same task cannot be accomplished with the `Cells` property because it returns a `Range` object that represents either all (no indices) or just one (specific row and column) of the cells in the parent object. In the first of the next two statements, the font color of all cells in the active worksheet is set to red, while the second statement sets just the color of cell C1 to red.

```
Cells.Font.Color = vbRed
Cells(1, "C").Font.Color = vbRed
```

You should use the `Cells` property with the `Application` or `Worksheet` objects only because it is redundant, so you don't have to use it with the `Range` object. Both of the following statements return the same `Range` object consisting of 20 cells (the first ten cells in columns A and B):

```
Range("A1:B10").Cells
Range("A1:B10")
```

The `Cells` property is best suited for use with loops because it accepts numerical parameters representing the row and column indices in a worksheet (the column index can be a `String` or number). Nested `For/Next` loops work well for looping through multiple rows and columns in a worksheet.

```
Dim I As Integer
Dim K As Integer
For K = 1 To 5
    For I = 1 To 10
        Cells(I, K).Value = I * K
    Next I
Next K
```

The nested `For/Next` loops generate 50 values that are entered into the first ten rows of the first five columns in the active worksheet (see Figure 7.5).

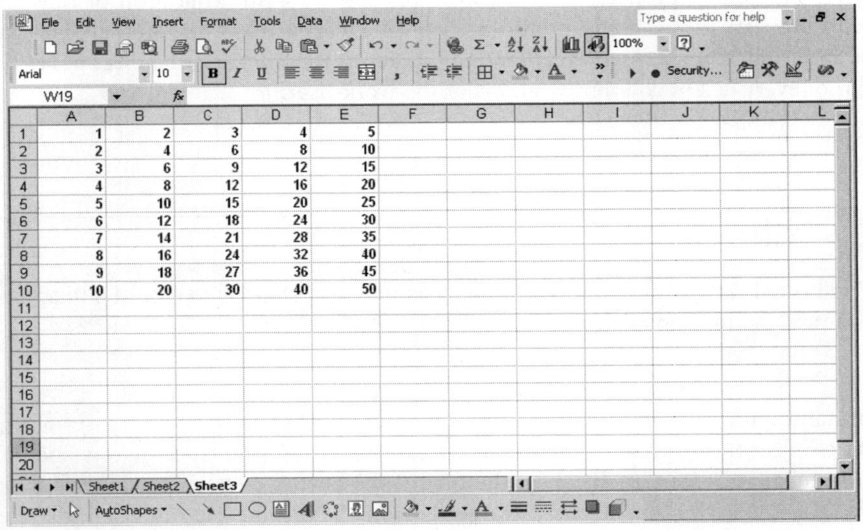

FIGURE 7.5 *Resulting values from multiplying the row and column indices in nested* `For/Next` *loops.*

You have already seen several examples using the `Range` object, and you will see many more throughout this book. After a brief discussion of two more structures that help simplify coding objects, I will discuss a sample program that makes significant use of the `Range` object.

Working with Objects

Previous chapters provide numerous examples that invoke the methods and set the properties of Excel objects. However, now I want to introduce two programming structures explicitly designed to be used with objects. The With/End With structure enables you to write a series of statements that reference a specific object without having to repeatedly reference the object in the path. The With/End With structure makes your procedures run faster, decreases the amount of typing you have to do, and makes your code easier to read. In addition, the For/Each loop is a looping structure that lets you access individual objects from a collection. The For/Each loop is more efficient than the For/Next and Do/Loop and should be used to loop through a collection of objects whenever possible.

The With/End With Structure

When you need to set the values of several properties of the same object, use the With/End With programming structure to reduce the amount of typing required and to speed up your code. Consider the following statements that set the values of several properties of the Font object for a range of worksheet cells:

```
Range("A1:A10").Font.Bold = True
Range("A1:A10").Font.Color = vbBlue
Range("A1:A10").Font.FontStyle = "Italic"
Range("A1:A10").Font.Size = 14
Range("A1:A10").Font.Name = "Comic Sans Serif"
```

You can rewrite the preceding code with just one reference to the Font object by using With/End With. Once the object has been specified, you can set the values of any property or invoke any of its methods without having to qualify the object in each line of code. You can also access subordinate objects and their members if any exist. Each statement inside the With/End With structure must begin with the dot operator (if qualifying a member or subordinate object).

```
With Range("A1:A10").Font
    .Bold = True
    .Color = vbBlue
    .FontStyle = "Italic"
    .Size = 14
    .Name = "Comic Sans Serif"
End With
```

The resulting code is easier to read and will run faster because VBA does not have to repeatedly resolve references to the same object. Use the With/End With structure whenever you need to set several properties or invoke several methods of a single object.

For Each Loops

Up to now, I have used the For/Next and Do/Loop to iterate through collections of Workbook, Worksheet, and Range objects. Although these loops work fine for looping through collections, there is an easier and better way. The For/Each loop is designed specifically for looping through collections. The syntax of the For/Each loop is similar to, but simpler than, the For/Next loop.

```
For Each object In collection
    'Statements
Next [object]
```

Following the required For Each keywords is a reference to a single object that is typically a variable of type object. The object must be of a type that can be part of a collection object. The collection is specified after the keyword In. The code block inside the loop may set and read properties, or invoke methods of each object in the collection. The loop ends with the Next keyword followed by an optional object reference. The For/Each structure is preferred for looping through a collection of objects because VBA automatically loops through every object in the collection without a counting variable. So, you don't have to worry about index values and making sure you are specifying the correct object in the collection. The For/Each structure is also more efficient than the other looping structures.

The straightforward nature of the For/Each structure is illustrated in the following example. Earlier in this chapter, I used nested For/Next loops to set the Value property of 50 cells (as Range objects) in a worksheet (refer to Figure 7.5). The same result is obtained with a single For/Each loop.

```
Dim c As Range
For Each c In Range("A1:E10")
    c.Value = c.Row * c.Column
Next
```

I show the declaration of the object variable c (type Range) to remind you that this variable must be declared prior to the loop. The object collection is also a Range object, and it contains 50 cells. The loop will start with cell A1 and set its Value property to the product of its Row (=1) and Column (=1) properties before proceeding through the remaining columns and rows of the collection. Even with this simple example, the superior readability and simplicity of the For/Each loop over the For/Next loop is clear.

Comparing Workbooks

One assignment commonly asked of Excel-VBA programmers is to automate lengthy data analysis procedures. The idea is to relieve a user from considerable repetitive work by automating the analysis with a VBA program. Automating the analysis can save a great deal of time (and money) because it allows the user to proceed directly to interpretation rather than spending a lot of time on calculation. Of course, the reliability of the program must be verified, which you accomplish by comparing a workbook generated by the program to an original workbook created by hand.

You can use the following program to compare the values and formulas in two Excel workbooks. This program is based on the premise that one workbook was created entirely within the Excel application (no VBA or recorded macros) and the other workbook by a VBA program written for an exact reproduction of the analysis. So, if the same raw data is used in both workbooks, the workbooks should be identical. I define *identical workbooks* as symmetrical in terms of the number of worksheets, used cell ranges, and cell content.

Designing the Interface

When creating a VBA application in Excel, your options for creating an interface include any combination of a worksheet, Userform, and toolbars. The program interface for the workbook comparison application is built almost entirely from a Userform (a Button control on a worksheet is used to show the Userform). The Userform is designed so that it allows the user to select two open workbooks for comparison. Equivalent worksheet cells between the two workbooks (same worksheet number and cell address) that hold different values or formulas will be listed in a text box when the program runs. After the comparison of all cells is completed, the user can copy the addresses of cells that differ by value or formula to a worksheet. The design of the Userform is shown in Figure 7.6, and the properties of the ActiveX controls that were altered from their default values are listed in Table 7.1 (with the exception of `Label` controls that have no programmatic functionality).

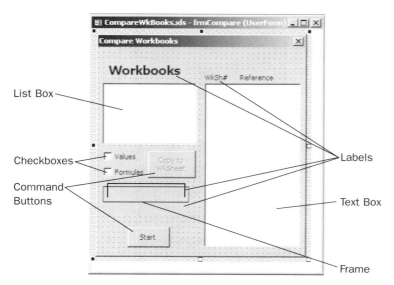

FIGURE 7.6 *Userform designed for VBA program that tests the equivalence of two Excel workbooks.*

Table 7.1 ActiveX Controls on the Userform and Their Relevant Design-Time Properties

ActiveX Control	Property	Value
Userform	Name	frmCompare
Userform	Caption	Compare Workbooks
Userform	StartupPosition	CenterOwner
List Box	Name	lstWorkbooks
List Box	MultiSelect	fmMultiSelectMulti
List Box	SpecialEffect	fmSpecialEffectSunken
Check Box	Name	ckValue
Check Box	Caption	Values
Check Box	Value	False
Check Box	Name	ckFormulas
Check Box	Caption	Formulas
Check Box	Value	False
Command Button	Name	cmdCopy
Command Button	Enabled	False
Command Button	Caption	Copy to WkSheet
Frame	Caption	None
Frame	BorderStyle	fmBorderStyleSingle
Label	Name	lblP1 through lblP8
Label	BorderStyle	fmBorderStyleNone
Label	BackStyle	fmBackStyleOpaque
Label	SpecialEffect	fmSpecialEffectFlat
Label	Name	lblNumCells
Label	ForeColor	&H00FF0000&
Label	Caption	None
Text Box	Name	txtReferences

ActiveX Control	Property	Value
Text Box	Text	None
Text Box	MultiLine	True
Text Box	SpecialEffect	fmSpecialEffectSunken

Form Module Code

The Workbook Comparison program uses the `Initialize()` and `QueryClose()` event procedures of the Userform and the `Click()` event procedures of the two Command Button controls (`cmdCopy` and `cmdStart`) contain on the Userform. All four event procedures are contained in the code module for the Userform name `frmCompare`.

The `Initialize()` event procedure of the Userform is triggered when the Userform is first loaded and before it is shown. This is the ideal location for initializing program variables and ActiveX controls on the Userform. In the Workbook Comparison program, the names of all open workbooks are added to the List Box control with its `AddItem` method and a `For/Each` loop.

```
Option Explicit
Private Sub UserForm_Initialize()
'Add names of all open workbooks to the list box
    Dim wkBook As Workbook
    For Each wkBook In Workbooks
        lstWorkbooks.AddItem wkBook.Name
    Next
End Sub
```

The `QueryClose()` event procedure is triggered just before a Userform is closed. It is used in the Workbook Comparison program to unload the Userform object from system memory and end the program.

 TIP

The `Hide` method of the Userform does not remove the object from system memory, but simply from the display.

```
Private Sub UserForm_QueryClose(Cancel As Integer, CloseMode As Integer)
'Free memory and end the program
    Unload Me
    End
End Sub
```

The `Click()` event of the Command Button control named `cmdCopy` clears the contents of the worksheet with the `Clear` method of the `Range` object. The `SelStart` and `SelLength` properties of the Text Box control (run-time properties only) are used to select the entire contents of the Text box control before it is copied to the worksheet via the clipboard (`Copy` method of the Text Box control and `Paste` method of the `Worksheet` object).

```
Private Sub cmdCopy_Click()
'Copy workbook differences to the worksheet
    Workbooks("Compare WorkBooks.xls").Worksheets("Sheet1").Activate
    Cells.Clear
    Range("A1").Select
    txtReferences.SelStart = 0
    txtReferences.SelLength = Len(txtReferences.Text)
    txtReferences.Copy
    ActiveSheet.Paste
End Sub
```

The `Click()` event of the Command Button control named `cmdStart` determines the names of the workbooks selected by the user in the List Box control named `lstWorkbooks`. Multiple selections can be made in the List Box because its `MultiSelect` property was set to `fmMultiSelectMulti`. The procedure loops through all items listed in the List Box and checks the `Boolean` state of the `Selected` property (run-time only). If the `Selected` property is `True` and the user has selected two workbooks, the names of the selected workbooks are stored in the `Public` array named `wkBooks`. Next, the `CompareWkBooks()` Sub procedure contained in a standard module is called to compare the values and/or formulas in the workbooks.

```
Private Sub cmdStart_Click()
'Store workbook names in public array. Error check user selections
    Dim I As Integer
    Dim J As Integer

    cmdCopy.Enabled = False
    '-----------------------------
```

```
'Get all the selected workbooks
'- - - - - - - - - - - - - - - - - - - - - - - - - - -
For I = 0 To lstWorkbooks.ListCount - 1
    If lstWorkbooks.Selected(I) Then
        If J >= 2 Then
            MsgBox ("Two files only!")
            Exit Sub
        End If
        wkBooks(J) = lstWorkbooks.List(I)
        J = J + 1
    End If
Next I
If J <= 1 Then
    MsgBox ("Select two workbooks!")
    Exit Sub
End If


txtReferences.Text = ""
CompareWkBooks
If txtReferences.Text = "" Then txtReferences.Text = "No References"
End Sub
```

Standard Module Code

The remaining code for the Workbook Comparison program is contained in a single standard module. The module contains two `Public` (`SelectWkBooks()` and `CompareWkBooks()`) and three `Private` procedures (`GetColumnRef()`, `ProgBar()`, and `Delay()`). In addition, the `Public` array variable `wkBooks` (used to hold the names of the two workbooks being compared) is declared in the general declarations section of this module.

```
Option Explicit
Public wkBooks(1) As String
```

The Sub procedure `SelectWkBooks()` is simply used to load and show the Userform named `frmCompare` that was previously described. The Button control drawn on the worksheet (see Figure 7.7) triggers this procedure when clicked.

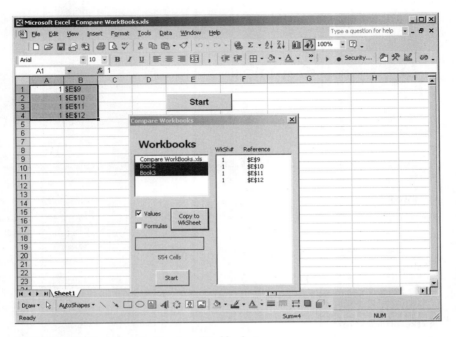

FIGURE 7.7 *Running the Compare Workbooks program.*

```
Public Sub SelectWkBooks()
    frmCompare.Show vbModeless
End Sub
```

NOTE

Versions of Excel prior to and including Excel 97 do not support modeless Userforms.

The `CompareWkBooks()` Sub procedure does the majority of the work in this program. It must be of `Public` scope so that it can be accessed from the form module code. The procedure is a bit longer than I prefer, but the logic is straightforward and follows these steps:

1. Determine the number of worksheets in each workbook and hold in a variable. I used the `Count` property of the `Worksheet` object to accomplish this task.

2. Determine the number of cells that will be compared between the two workbooks and output the value to the Userform. Again, the `Count` property returns the number of cells in the `Range` object returned from the `UsedRange` property of the `Worksheet` object.

3. Inform the user if workbooks are not symmetrical in terms of the number of worksheets, but take no action.

4. Loop through the minimum number of worksheets (determined by the workbook with the fewest number of worksheets) to access the used cells in each worksheet. Because the loop may take a considerable amount of time to execute, the `DoEvents` function is included in the loop so that the operating system will temporarily suspend program execution in order to process other events (for example, if the user closes the Userform or selects another application).

5. Determine the maximum range used in each worksheet, then loop through each cell and compare values and formulas according to the user's selection on the Userform (Check Box controls). If the used ranges are not symmetrical, the test range is set to the minimum/maximum row and column indices of the used ranges in the two worksheets being compared. For example, if the used ranges in the two worksheets are A1:X50 and B2:Y40, the test range will be A1:Y50. If a cell does not contain a formula, the `Formula` property of the `Range` object still returns the value of the cell. So, the conditional expression that tests for identical formulas must also use the `HasFormula` property of the `Range` object to verify the presence of a formula in the cell being tested.

6. Calculate the progress of the program as a fraction of the total number of cells tested and update the progress bar. Comparing the values and formulas in thousands of cells (or more) can take a great deal of time. I added a progress bar to the Userform to inform the user of the relative fraction of cells tested as the program is running. I created the progress bar from a Frame control and eight Label controls. The `BackColor` and `SpecialEffect` properties of the Label controls are altered when the progress of the program is updated.

7. Clear the progress bar and enable the Command Button control named `cmdCopy`.

 NOTE

You can probably find ActiveX controls that serve as progress bars on the Internet or even on your computer. However, the ActiveX control may come with licensing restrictions.

The `CompareWkBooks()` Sub procedure listed next loops through all used cells in a workbook and compares their value and/or formula to that of the value and/or formula in the corresponding cell of a second workbook. If the values or formulas compared between two cells are not equivalent, the cell reference is output to a Text Box control.

```
Public Sub CompareWkBooks()
'Compares two workbooks for equality
    Dim I As Integer, J As Integer
```

```vba
Dim cells1 As Range, cells2 As Range
Dim c1 As Range, c2 As Range
Dim numSheets1 As Integer, numSheets2 As Integer
Dim numCells As Long, fracCells As Single, totCells As Long
Dim minRow As Long, maxRow As Long
Dim minCol As String, maxCol As String


'------------------------------------------------
'Find the number of worksheets in both workbooks
'and the number of cells for the comparison
'------------------------------------------------
numSheets1 = Workbooks(wkBooks(0)).Worksheets.Count
numSheets2 = Workbooks(wkBooks(1)).Worksheets.Count
For I = 1 To numSheets1
    totCells = totCells + _
        Workbooks(wkBooks(0)).Worksheets(I).UsedRange.Count
Next I
frmCompare.lblNumCells.Caption = totCells & " Cells"


'------------------------------------------------
'Inform user if workbooks are not symmetrical
'------------------------------------------------
If numSheets1 <> numSheets2 Then
    MsgBox ("Selected workbooks do not have " & _
        "the same number of worksheets")
End If


'------------------------------------------------
'Loop through worksheets to make cell comparisons
'------------------------------------------------
For I = 1 To Application.WorksheetFunction.Min( _
                numSheets1, numSheets2)
    DoEvents
    Set cells1 = Workbooks(wkBooks(0)).Worksheets(I).UsedRange
    Set cells2 = Workbooks(wkBooks(1)).Worksheets(I).UsedRange
    '
    '------------------------------------------------------------
```

```vba
'If used ranges are unequal then reset the search range to
'the maximum possible size.
'-----------------------------------------------------------
If cells1.Address <> cells2.Address Then
    minRow = Application.WorksheetFunction.Min( _
                    cells1.Row, cells2.Row)
    minCol = Application.WorksheetFunction.Min( _
                    cells1.Column, cells2.Column)
    maxRow = Application.WorksheetFunction.Max(minRow + _
                cells1.Rows.Count, minRow + cells2.Rows.Count)
    maxCol = GetColumnRef(Application.WorksheetFunction.Max( _
                minCol + cells1.Columns.Count, minCol + _
                cells2.Columns.Count))
    minCol =GetColumnRef(Val(minCol))
    totCells = totCells - cells1.Count
    Set cells1 = Workbooks(wkBooks(0)).Worksheets(I).Range( _
                    minCol & minRow & ":" & maxCol & maxRow)
    totCells = totCells + cells1.Count
    frmCompare.lblNumCells.Caption = totCells & " Cells"
End If


    '-----------------------------------------------------------
    'Loop through cells in worksheet and compare values/formulas
    '-----------------------------------------------------------
For Each c1 In cells1
    DoEvents
        'Set ref to cell in 2nd sheet
    Set c2 = cells2.Range(GetColumnRef(c1.Column) & c1.Row)
    If frmCompare.ckFormulas.Value = True And _
            frmCompare.ckValue = True Then
        If c1.Value <> c2.Value Then
            frmCompare.txtReferences.Text = _
                frmCompare.txtReferences.Text & I & vbTab & _
                c1.Address & vbTab & "V" & vbCrLf
        End If
        If c1.Formula <> c2.Formula And _
            (c1.HasFormula = True Or c2.HasFormula = True) Then
```

```
                    frmCompare.txtReferences.Text = _
                        frmCompare.txtReferences.Text & I & vbTab & _
                        c1.Address & vbTab & "F" & vbCrLf
                End If
            ElseIf frmCompare.ckFormulas.Value = True Then
                If c1.Formula <> c2.Formula And (c1.HasFormula = _
                    True Or c2.HasFormula = True) Then
                    frmCompare.txtReferences.Text = _
                        frmCompare.txtReferences.Text & I & _
                        vbTab & c1.Address & vbCrLf
                End If
            Else
                frmCompare.ckValue = True
                If c1.Value <> c2.Value Then
                    frmCompare.txtReferences.Text = _
                        frmCompare.txtReferences.Text & I & vbTab _
                        & c1.Address & vbCrLf
                End If
            End If


            '-------------------------------------
            'Calculate progress and update the bar
            '-------------------------------------
            numCells = numCells + 1
            fracCells = numCells / totCells
            If fracCells >= 1 / 8.1 Then
                ProgBar
                numCells = 0
            End If
        Next
    Next I

    Delay 0.25
    ProgBar (-1)      'Clear the bar
    frmCompare.cmdCopy.Enabled = True
End Sub
```

The `GetColumnRef()` Function procedure returns the character representation of a column index passed in as an `Integer`. For example, the index value 27 represents column "AA" on a worksheet. This is a handy little procedure that I use when I need a character reference for a column. In this case, I need the character reference because I am using the `Range` property of the `Worksheet` object to return a `Range` object in the `CompareWkBooks()` Sub procedure.

```vba
Private Function GetColumnRef(columnIndex As Integer) As String
'Converts column index number to a textual reference
    Dim numAlpha As Integer
    Dim firstLetter As String
    Dim secondLetter As String
    Dim remainder As Integer

    numAlpha = columnIndex \ 26   'Calculate number of letters needed
    Select Case columnIndex / 26
        Case Is <= 1      'One-letter reference to column
            firstLetter = Chr(columnIndex + 64)
            GetColumnRef = firstLetter
        Case Else      'Two-letter reference to column
            remainder = columnIndex - 26 * (columnIndex \ 26)
            If remainder = 0 Then
                firstLetter = Chr(64 + (columnIndex \ 26) - 1)
                secondLetter = "Z"
                GetColumnRef = firstLetter & secondLetter
            Else
                firstLetter = Chr(64 + (columnIndex \ 26))
                secondLetter = Chr(64 + remainder)
                GetColumnRef = firstLetter & secondLetter
            End If
    End Select
End Function
```

The progress bar on the Userform is built from a Frame control and eight Label controls. The bar is somewhat crude, but it's easy to use in a program where calculating the progress is simple. In the Workbook Comparison program, the progress is calculated as the fraction of the total cells tested. When the fraction exceeds another ⅛ of the total cells, the appearance of another label control is altered via its `BackColor` and `SpecialEffect` properties.

NOTE

A control array of Label controls would greatly simplify the `ProgBar()` Sub procedure. Unfortunately, control arrays are not supported in VBA.

```vba
Private Sub ProgBar(Optional clearBar As Integer)
'Updates the make-shift progress bar
    Static I As Integer

    If clearBar = -1 Then I = clearBar
    I = I + 1
    Select Case I
        Case 1
            frmCompare.lblP1.BackColor = RGB(50, 50, 100)
            frmCompare.lblP1.SpecialEffect = fmSpecialEffectSunken
        Case 2
            frmCompare.lblP2.BackColor = RGB(50, 50, 100)
            frmCompare.lblP2.SpecialEffect = fmSpecialEffectSunken
        Case 3
            frmCompare.lblP3.BackColor = RGB(50, 50, 100)
            frmCompare.lblP3.SpecialEffect = fmSpecialEffectSunken
        Case 4
            frmCompare.lblP4.BackColor = RGB(50, 50, 100)
            frmCompare.lblP4.SpecialEffect = fmSpecialEffectSunken
        Case 5
            frmCompare.lblP5.BackColor = RGB(50, 50, 100)
            frmCompare.lblP5.SpecialEffect = fmSpecialEffectSunken
        Case 6
            frmCompare.lblP6.BackColor = RGB(50, 50, 100)
            frmCompare.lblP6.SpecialEffect = fmSpecialEffectSunken
        Case 7
            frmCompare.lblP7.BackColor = RGB(50, 50, 100)
            frmCompare.lblP7.SpecialEffect = fmSpecialEffectSunken
        Case 8
            frmCompare.lblP8.BackColor = RGB(50, 50, 100)
            frmCompare.lblP8.SpecialEffect = fmSpecialEffectSunken
```

```
        Case Else     'Clear the bar
            I = 0
            frmCompare.lblP1.BackColor = -2147483633
            frmCompare.lblP1.SpecialEffect = fmSpecialEffectFlat
            frmCompare.lblP2.BackColor = -2147483633
            frmCompare.lblP2.SpecialEffect = fmSpecialEffectFlat
            frmCompare.lblP3.BackColor = -2147483633
            frmCompare.lblP3.SpecialEffect = fmSpecialEffectFlat
            frmCompare.lblP4.BackColor = -2147483633
            frmCompare.lblP4.SpecialEffect = fmSpecialEffectFlat
            frmCompare.lblP5.BackColor = -2147483633
            frmCompare.lblP5.SpecialEffect = fmSpecialEffectFlat
            frmCompare.lblP6.BackColor = -2147483633
            frmCompare.lblP6.SpecialEffect = fmSpecialEffectFlat
            frmCompare.lblP7.BackColor = -2147483633
            frmCompare.lblP7.SpecialEffect = fmSpecialEffectFlat
            frmCompare.lblP8.BackColor = -2147483633
            frmCompare.lblP8.SpecialEffect = fmSpecialEffectFlat
    End Select
End Sub
```

The last Sub procedure is used to delay program execution by a specified input time. I use this procedure to create short delays (less than one second) to give the user a chance to view an effect that is otherwise unobservable because of program execution speed. In this case, I use the Delay() Sub procedure to ensure that the user sees the progress bar finish before it is cleared. The procedure uses VBA's Timer function to return the number of seconds since midnight. A Do/Loop actually creates the delay in the program. Alternatively, you could use the Sleep function in the Windows API, but I prefer not to use the API exclusively for adding delays to a program. I discuss the Windows API in Chapter 17, "Accessing the Windows API with VBA."

 NOTE

In Windows, the Timer function's resolution is about 30–50 milliseconds and represents the only VBA function that allows for fractional values of a second.

```
Public Sub Delay(pauseTime As Single)
'This simply delays program execution by the specified time
    Dim begin As Single
    begin = Timer
    Do While Timer < (begin + pauseTime)
        DoEvents
    Loop
End Sub
```

That concludes the Workbook Comparison program. It has been a fairly useful program for me and serves as a good introduction to the top-level objects in Excel's object hierarchy, the Range object in particular.

Summary

The top-level objects discussed in this chapter represent the most functional objects in the Excel object model. Although you will use these objects extensively in your VBA programs, you will seldom use most of their properties and methods (some of them not at all). However, you should still be aware that these objects contain numerous properties and methods and that you only need to consult the Object Browser to locate them. It is not such a bad idea to peruse these objects in the Object Browser and gain some familiarity with their members.

In this chapter, I discussed some of the top-level objects in Excel's object model, including the Application, Workbook, Window, Worksheet, and Range objects. I also discussed how to find objects and their members in the Object Browser, as well as how to set new object references in a VBA project. The concept of collection objects was also discussed as it applies to the Excel object model and the objects contained within. I also introduced two new code structures (With/End With and For/Each loops) designed to be used specifically with object variables. These structures are used extensively throughout the rest of this book. Finally, I used a sample program that does a cell-by-cell comparison of all worksheets between two workbooks to illustrate the use of many of these objects.

Chapter 8

**Understanding File
I/O, Debugging,
and Error Handling
in VBA**

This chapter covers two common programming tasks that are not necessarily dependent on each other but that certainly go hand in hand. First, I discuss the objects and methods used for file input and output (I/O) in Excel-VBA before proceeding to debugging and error handling. File I/O is fundamental to any programming language, and VBA is no exception. This chapter looks at the different tools available in Excel-VBA that allow the programmer to read and write data to a disk. Data can consist of Excel workbooks, components of a workbook, and simple text files. Also, because File I/O errors are among the most common errors raised in any application, this chapter discusses additional tools used for error handling and debugging VBA programs.

Inputting and Outputting Data to a File

File input and output (I/O) has never been one of VBA's strong points. Originally, you could do little more than repeat the tasks from the Office application or use Visual Basic's archaic Open method for sequential and random file access. With successive editions of Office, programming objects have been added and updated to make file I/O easier for the developer.

VBA now includes several objects that can be used for file I/O. You have probably surmised that one of these objects is the Workbook object and its methods for saving and opening files. However, other file I/O tools are available in VBA, ranging from the outdated Open method from Visual Basic to the FileSearch object that was recently updated in Office XP.

You will typically use file I/O operations in your VBA applications to open and close workbooks and to read and write small text files containing information required for your application. You may also use file I/O to search for specific files and/or directories. When a VBA application requires file I/O, it often involves a relatively small amount of data stored in program variables and not in a worksheet or document. With Excel, the programmer has the choice of copying the data to a worksheet so that the user can save the data in the usual way (by selecting File, Save) or of saving the content of the variables directly to a file. Simply writing the data directly to a file on the hard drive so that the user does not have to be concerned with the task is often more convenient. In fact, giving users access to the data may be undesirable, as they might alter it before saving. In this case, reading and writing simple text files within the program code offers an attractive solution. This chapter looks at ways of accessing text files and Excel files using VBA program code and ways to search the computer's file structure for specific files and folders.

The Excel Workbook

The Workbook object contains methods for opening, closing, and saving workbooks in the same manner a user might perform these operations from the Excel application window. You can open and save workbook files using a variety of formats with VBA code.

Opening, Closing, and Saving Workbooks

You use the Open method of the Workbooks collection object to open Excel-compatible files. The Open method accepts numerous arguments, but the only required argument is the FileName. The syntax for the Open method of the Workbooks collection object, including all arguments, follows:

```
Workbooks.Open(FileName, UpdateLinks, ReadOnly, Format, Password, WriteResPassword,
IgnoreReadOnlyRecommended, Origin, Delimiter, Editable, Notify, Converter, AddToMru,
Local, CorruptLoad, OpenConflictDocument)
```

TIP

Use the OpenText, OpenXML, and OpenDatabase methods of the Workbooks collection object to open text files, XML files, and database tables, respectively.

The following example opens a workbook named MyWorkbook.xls located in the same directory as the active workbook. An error is generated if the file cannot be found.

```
Dim filePath As String
filePath = ActiveWorkbook.Path
Workbooks.Open (filePath & "\" & "MyWorkbook.xls")
```

To close all open workbooks, use the Close method of the Workbooks collection object. The Close method does not accept arguments, so the user will be prompted to save changes to any workbook that was edited but not resaved.

```
Workbooks.Close
```

To close a single workbook, use the Close method of the Workbook object. The Close method accepts three optional arguments (SaveChanges, FileName, and RouteWorkbook).

```
Workbooks("MyWorkbook.xls").Close SaveChanges:=False
```

Setting the SaveChanges argument prevents the user from having to answer the prompt. However, if SaveChanges is False, all changes will be lost! Use the FileName argument to save the workbook with a new filename, and the RouteWorkbook argument specifies whether the workbook is routed to the next recipient (if a routing slip exists).

To save a workbook from a VBA program, use either the `Save` or `SaveAs` methods of the `Workbook` object. The `Save` method does not accept arguments and will save a new workbook to the default directory.

```
Workbooks("MyWorkbook.xls").Save
```

The `SaveAs` method accepts many of the same arguments as the `Open` method, including `FileName`, `Password`, `WriteResPassword`, `ReadOnlyRecommended`, `AddToMru`, and `Local`. In addition, the `SaveAs` method accepts `FileFormat` and `CreateBackup` arguments. The `FileFormat` argument can be one of several named constants referring to the format that will be used to save the workbook (for example, `xlCSV` for comma-separated-value, `xlTemplate` for an Excel template, and `xlWorkbookNormal` for the standard Excel format using the current version). See the online help for remaining formats. When you save a workbook using a textual format, only the active worksheet will be saved. The following line of code saves the active worksheet in the workbook named `MyWorkbook.xls` as a comma-delimited text file named `test.csv`:

```
Workbooks("MyWorkbook.xls").SaveAs Filename:=ActiveWorkbook.Path & _
        "\test.csv", FileFormat:=xlCSV
```

The `Chart` (as chart sheet) and `Worksheet` objects also contain a `SaveAs` method that is used in essentially the same way as the `SaveAs` method of the `Workbook` object. However, only the specified chart sheet or worksheet is saved.

Excel Dialogs

Approximately 800 `Dialog` objects that can be accessed via the `Dialogs` collection object are built into Excel XP. These dialog boxes are the ones that appear when selecting an option from a menu and toolbar or when double-clicking various objects. There are dialog boxes for formatting the worksheet, formatting various components of a chart, creating custom menus, and so on — for example, the Format Number and Chart Options dialog boxes found under the Format and Chart menus in Excel. Of course, there are also Open and Save As dialog boxes used for opening and saving files in Excel. To load a specific `Dialog` object from a VBA program, use the `Show` method of the `Dialog` object selected from the `Dialogs` collection object. The `Show` method accepts various arguments depending on the dialog box used and returns an optional `Boolean` value that you can use to determine which button on the dialog box was selected by the user (OK or Cancel). The next example displays the Open dialog box and places the string `"MyWorkbook"` in the text box used to hold a file's name (see Figure 8.1).

```
Application.Dialogs(xlDialogOpen).Show ("MyWorkbook.xls")
```

The VBA object library includes named constants for most of the built-in dialog boxes (see "Built-In Dialog Box Argument Lists" in the online help). You use the named constant `xlDialogOpen` to show the Open dialog box and `xlDialogSaveAs` or `xlDialogSaveWorkbook` to show the Save As dialog box (shown in Figure 8.1). You can use these dialog boxes to prompt the user to open or save an Excel compatible file.

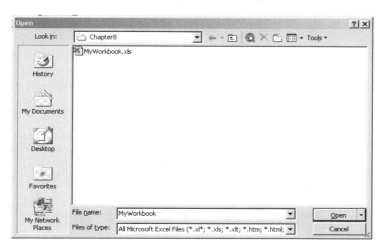

FIGURE 8.1 *The Open dialog box displayed via the* Show *method of the* Dialog *object.*

The FileDialog Object

Included in the Office library of objects is the `FileDialog` object. The `FileDialog` object is essentially the standard dialog used in Office applications for opening and saving files. The `FileDialog` object provides more functionality than the Open and Save dialog boxes associated with Excel's `Dialogs` collection object discussed in the last section. The dialog boxes from the `FileDialog` object allow users to specify the files and folders that a program should use and will return the paths of the selected files or folders. You can also use the `FileDialog` object to execute the associated action of the specified dialog box.

 NOTE

A reference must be set to the Microsoft Office object library before you can use the `FileDialog` object. Select Tools, References, Microsoft Office 10.0 Object Library from the VBA IDE.

The `FileDialog` object is not included with Office 97.

The `FileDialog` object contains two methods called `Show` and `Execute`. You use the `Show` method to show one of four possible dialog boxes (see Table 8.1) depending on the constant passed to the `FileDialog` property of the `Application` object.

```
Application.FileDialog(FileDialogType)
```

Table 8.1 Dialog Types Used with the FileDialog Object

Dialog Type	VBA Constant (FileDialogType)
Open	msoFileDialogOpen
Save	msoFileDialogSaveAs
File Picker	msoFileDialogFilePicker
Folder Picker	msoFileDialogFolderPicker

The Execute method allows the user to carry out the specified action of the dialog box for files that are compatible with the Excel application (for example, files of type .xls, .xtl, .csv, and so on). For example, the Open dialog box allows the user to select one or more files to open when the Execute method of the FileDialog object is invoked.

TIP

Be careful to set the properties of the FileDialog object appropriately for the desired action. For example, you cannot set the FilterIndex property of the FileDialog object when showing the Folder Picker dialog box because this dialog box shows only folders and does not allow file extension filters.

The FileDialogFilters and FileDialogSelectedItems Collection Objects

The FileDialog object has two subordinate collection objects — the FileDialogFilters and the FileDialogSelectedItems collection objects. The FileDialogFilters collection object contains a collection of FileDialogFilter objects that represent the file extensions used to filter what files are displayed in the dialog box (used with the Open and Save As dialog boxes). Use the Filters property of the FileDialog object to return the FileDialogFilters collection and the Item property of the FileDialogFilters collection object to return a FileDialogFilter object. The Description and Extensions properties of the FileDialogFilter object return the description (for example, All Files) and the file extension used to filter the displayed files (for example, *.*).

```
Dim fc As FileDialogFilters
Dim ff As FileDialogFilter
Set fc = Application.FileDialog(msoFileDialogOpen).Filters
Set ff = fc.Item(1)
MsgBox ff.Description & ff.Extensions     'Displays "AllFiles" and *.*
```

The `FileDialogSelectedItems` collection object contains the paths to the files or folders selected by the user. Use the `SelectedItems` property of the `FileDialog` object to return the `FileDialogSelectedItems` collection.

```
Dim si As FileDialogSelectedItems
Set si = Application.FileDialog(msoFileDialogOpen).selectedItems
```

You can use the `Add` method of the `FileDialogFilters` collection object to create your own list of filters. The following code example shows the File Picker dialog box after clearing the `FileDialogFilters` collection and adding two new filters (*.*, and *.jpg). The `Show` method of the `FileDialog` object returns −1 if the user presses the action button (Open in this example) and 0 if the action is cancelled.

```
Dim fd As FileDialog
Dim imagePath As String
Set fd = Application.FileDialog(msoFileDialogFilePicker)
With fd
    .AllowMultiSelect = False
    .Filters.Clear
    .Filters.Add "All files", "*.*"
    .Filters.Add "Image", "*.jpg", 1
    .FilterIndex = 1
    .InitialFileName = ""
    .Title = "Select JPEG file"
    If .Show = -1 Then        'User pressed action button
        imagePath = .selectedItems(1)
    End If
End With
```

The path to the file selected by the user is returned from the `FileDialogSelectedItems` collection and stored in the `String` variable `imagePath`. If the `Execute` method of the `FileDialog` object is omitted in the program, your program will need this path. Do not use the `Execute` method of the `FileDialog` object when selecting files that are not compatible with Excel — doing so will either result in a run-time error or open a workbook containing incomprehensible data.

If the `AllowMultiSelect` property of the `FileDialog` object is set to `True`, the `FileDialogSelectedItems` collection will hold more than one file path. The `ShowFileDialog()` Sub procedure loads the Open dialog box and allows the user to select multiple files. The paths to the selected files are stored in the array variable `selectedPaths` before the `Execute` method attempts to open them.

```
Public Sub ShowFileDialog()
    Dim fd As FileDialog
```

```
        Dim selectedPaths() As String
        Dim I As Integer

        Set fd = Application.FileDialog(msoFileDialogOpen)
        With fd        'Configure dialog box
            .AllowMultiSelect = True
            .FilterIndex = 2
            .Title = "Select Excel File(s)"
            .InitialFileName = ""
            'Show the dialog and collect file paths selected by the user
            If .Show = -1 Then    'User clicked Open
                ReDim selectedPaths(.selectedItems.Count - 1)
                'Store file paths for later use.
                For I = 0 To .selectedItems.Count - 1
                    selectedPaths(I) = .selectedItems(I + 1)
                Next I
            End If
            .Execute        'Open selected files
        End With
        Set fd = Nothing
    End Sub
```

The dialog box resulting from the ShowFileDialog() Sub procedure is shown in Figure 8.2.

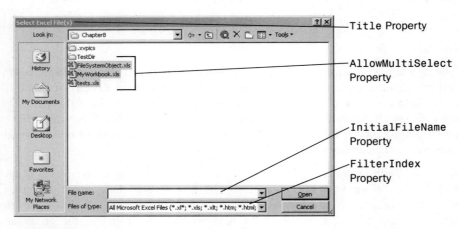

FIGURE 8.2 *The Open dialog box that results from using the* Show *method of the* FileDialog *object.*

The FileSystem Object

The FileSystem object is a collection of methods that you can use to set and obtain information about files, directories, and drives. You can find the members of the FileSystem object listed in the Object Browser and in Table 8.2. You can use them as though they were just another group of VBA built-in functions. That is, you do not need to qualify the object when using these methods in your program.

Table 8.2 Members of the FileSystem Object

Member	Description	Example	Return Value
ChDir	Changes the current directory.	ChDir "C:\Documents and Settings" or ChDir ".."	N/A.
ChDrive	Changes the current drive.	ChDrive "D:"	N/A.
CurDir	Returns the current directory path.	MsgBox CurDir	Outputs the current directory path in a message box.
Dir	Returns the name of a file, directory, or folder that matches a pattern, file attribute, or the volume label of a drive.	fileName = Dir("C:\test.txt", vbNormal)	The file name if it exists; otherwise, an empty string.
EOF	End of file.	EOF(fileNum)	A Boolean value indicating whether the end of an opened file (specified with a file number) has been reached.
FileAttr	The mode used to open a file with the Open statement.	Mode = FileAttr (fileNum, 1)	Returns a Long integer indicating the mode used to open a file (Input, Output, Random, and so on).

continues

Table 8.2 Members of the FileSystem Object *(continued)*

Member	Description	Example	Return Value
FileCopy	Copies a file from a source path to a destination path.	FileCopy "C:\TestFile.txt", "D:\TestFile.txt"	N/A.
FileDateTime	Returns the date and time that a file was created or last modified.	fileDate = FileDateTime ("C:\test.txt")	For example, 1/23/2004 10:25:14 AM.
FileLen	Returns the length of a file in bytes.	fileSize = FileLen ("C:\test.txt")	For example, 4.
FreeFile	Returns an Integer representing the next file number available for use by the Open statement.	FileNumber = FreeFile	For example, 2.
GetAttr	Returns an Integer representing the attributes of a file or directory.	myAttr = GetAttr(CurDir)	0=Normal, 1=Read-Only, 2=Hidden, 4=System, 16=Directory, 32=Archive.
Kill	Deletes a file or files.	Kill "C:\test.txt"	N/A.
Loc	Specifies the current read/write position within an open file.	MyLocation = Loc(1)	A Long integer.
LOF	Returns a Long integer specifying the length of an open file in bytes.	FileLength = LOF(1)	For example, 4.
MkDir	Creates a new directory.	MkDir "TestDir"	N/A.
Reset	Closes all disk files opened using the Open statement.	Reset	N/A.
RmDir	Deletes an empty directory.	RmDir "TestDir"	N/A.

Member	Description	Example	Return Value
Seek	Returns a Long integer specifying the current read/write position within an open file.	Seek(1)	If the file is opened in Random mode, it returns the number of the next record; otherwise, it returns the current byte position in the file.
SetAttr	Sets attribute information for a file.	SetAttr "C:\test.txt", vbReadOnly	N/A.

These methods are primarily designed to be used with the Open statement, but you may also find them useful with the other objects and methods discussed in this chapter.

The Open Statement

The Open statement has been around since the early days of BASIC (even prior to Visual Basic) and is probably outdated. Yet, the Open statement is still supported and is easy to use; therefore, it presents another option to the programmer for use in simple file I/O operations.

You use the Open statement to read or write data to a file. Table 8.3 summarizes the type of access modes and functions available for reading and writing data to a file with the Open statement.

Table 8.3 File Access Modes with VBA

Access Mode	Writing Data	Reading Data
Sequential/Append	Print#, Write#	Input#, Input
Random	Put	Get
Binary	Put, Write#	Get, Input#, Input

The Open statement takes several arguments that include the file path, access mode, and file number. Optional arguments include an access argument (Read\Write), lock (used to restrict operations on the file from other programs), and reclength (specifies the length of the buffer or record).

```
Open "C:\Test.txt" For Input As #1
```

The preceding line will open a file named `Test.txt` found at the designated path for input and assign the file to the file number 1. If the file is not found, one will be created. Files opened in this manner should always be closed with the `Close` statement.

```
Close #1
```

Sequential Access Files

Sequential access files can be written with `Print#` or `Write#` statements and read with the `Input` or `Input#` statements. Data is written to a sequential access file in the order it is output with the `Print#` or `Write#` statements. The following example outputs the contents of the first row in columns A through E of the active worksheet to a text file called `MyHeaders.txt`. The procedure uses the `Write#` statement, which inserts quotes around strings and a new line character at the end of each statement. The resulting file will contain five lines of data with one item per line.

```
Public Sub CreateSeqFile()
    Dim filePath As String
    Dim I As Integer
    filePath = ActiveWorkbook.Path & "\MyHeaders.txt"
    Open filePath For Output As #1
        For I = 1 To 5
            Write #1, Cells(1, I).Value
        Next I
    Close #1
End Sub
```

More than one value can be output with `Write#` by separating the list with commas, and it is the order of the data output with `Write#` that sets the structure of the file. Because the structure of the file is known, it is a simple task to alter the preceding procedure to create a new procedure that reads the data into the active worksheet.

```
Public Sub ReadSeqFile()
    Dim filePath As String
    Dim I As Integer
    Dim myHeader As String
    I = 1
    filePath = ActiveWorkbook.Path & "\MyHeaders.txt"
    Open filePath For Input As #1
```

```
    Do While Not EOF(1)
        Input #1, myHeader
        Cells(1, I).Value = myHeader
        I = I + 1
    Loop
    Close #1
End Sub
```

In the `ReadSeqFile()` Sub procedure, the file `MyHeaders.txt` is opened for input, and the data is read into a variable with `Input#` before being copied to the worksheet. The `Boolean` value returned from the `EOF()` function is used as the conditional test to see whether the end of the file has been reached.

Random Access Files

Random access files enable you to access specific records within a file without having to load the entire file into memory. This is accomplished by ensuring that the individual data elements are of the same length before writing to the file. You can use random access files as database tables with each output value representing a single record in the table. So, you should use user-defined variable types with random access files. Consider a simplified example of an employee table containing fields for employee ID, name, age, status, and salary class. You declare the user-defined type in the general declarations section of a code module as follows. You use fixed length strings to ensure that each record will require the same amount of memory.

```
Private Type Employee
     empID As String*8
     empName As String*20
     empAge As Integer
     empStatus As String*10
     empSalaryClass As String*1
End Type
Private recNum As Integer
```

The fields in the user-defined type are used to match the worksheet displayed in Figure 8.3. Note that three form buttons have been added to the worksheet and are used to add new records to and display existing records from the file named Employees.txt.

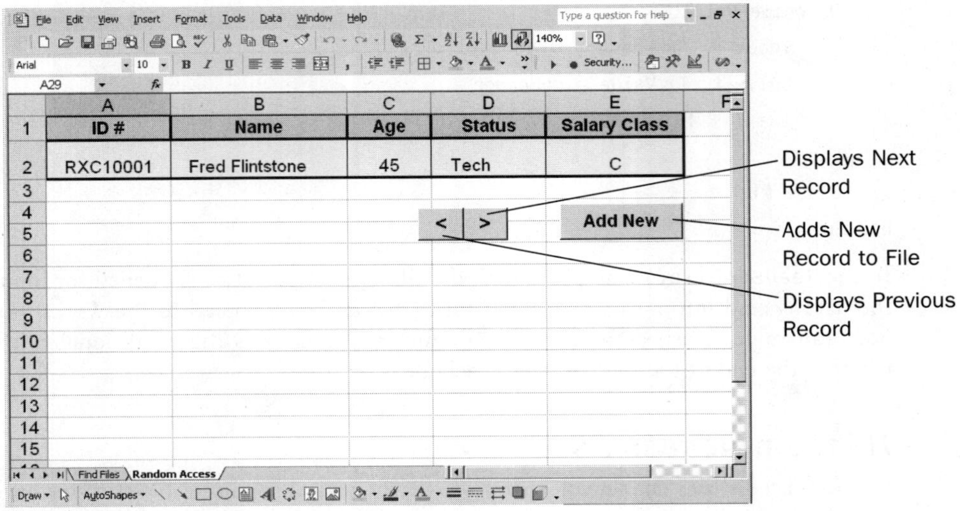

FIGURE 8.3 *An Excel worksheet used to display employee records.*

The Sub procedure `WriteEmployeeInfo()` is attached to the Button control with the caption `Add New` and is used to write a new employee record to the end of the data file. The file is opened for random access before the user-defined type (declared as the variable `empdata`) is loaded with data and written to the file with the `Put#` statement. Random access files require a record number, so the module-level variable `recNum` is used to track the current record number.

```
Public Sub WriteEmployeeInfo()
'Writes a new record to the Employees.txt file using data in the worksheet
    Dim empData As Employee
    Dim filePath As String
    recNum = GetMaxRecNum      'Get the next available record number
    filePath = ActiveWorkbook.Path & "\Employees.txt"
    Open filePath For Random As #1 Len = Len(empData)    'Open file
        empData.empID = Cells(2, "A").Value
        empData.empName = Cells(2, "B").Value
        empData.empAge = Cells(2, "C").Value
        empData.empStatus = Cells(2, "D").Value
        empData.empSalaryClass = Cells(2, "E").Value
        Put #1, recNum, empData     'Write the data
    Close #1
End Sub
```

The Function procedure `GetMaxRecNum()` returns the next available record number for the data file. Because the user-defined data type is of a known size, the `FileLen()` and `Len()` functions are used to calculate the number of records contained in the file.

```
Private Function GetMaxRecNum() As Integer
    Dim empData As Employee
    Dim empDataLen As Long
    Dim filePath As String
    filePath = ActiveWorkbook.Path & "\Employees.txt"
    empDataLen = FileLen(filePath)
    GetMaxRecNum = empDataLen / Len(empData) + 1
    If GetMaxRecNum < 0 Then GetMaxRecNum = 0
End Function
```

The Sub procedures `IncRecNum()` and `DecRecNum()` are attached to the Button controls used to display the next (caption of > — refer to Figure 8.3) and previous (caption of <) record in the file, respectively. After setting the `recNum` variable, both procedures call the Sub procedure `GetEmployeeInfo()`, which displays the next or previous record in the worksheet.

```
Public Sub IncRecNum()
    Dim maxRecNum As Integer
    recNum = recNum + 1
    maxRecNum = GetMaxRecNum
    If recNum > maxRecNum Then
        recNum = maxRecNum
    End If
    GetEmployeeInfo
End Sub
Public Sub DecRecNum()
    recNum = recNum - 1
    If recNum <= 0 Then recNum = 1
    GetEmployeeInfo
End Sub
```

The `GetEmployeeInfo()` Sub procedure opens the data file for random access, retrieves the desired record, and loads the data into the variable `empData` before writing each field to the worksheet.

```
Private Sub GetEmployeeInfo()
'Gets the desired record from the file and writes the fields to the worksheet.
    Dim empData As Employee
```

```
    Dim filePath As String
    filePath = ActiveWorkbook.Path & "\Employees.txt"
    Open filePath For Random As #1 Len = Len(empData)
        Get #1, recNum, empData
        Cells(2, "A").Value = empData.empID
        Cells(2, "B").Value = empData.empName
        Cells(2, "C").Value = empData.empAge
        Cells(2, "D").Value = empData.empStatus
        Cells(2, "E").Value = empData.empSalaryClass
    Close #1
End Sub
```

The preceding is a simple example of random file access using Excel and VBA. In most situations involving database applications and importing data into Excel, you will want to use a dedicated database application (such as Microsoft Access) and a database object for retrieving the data (see Chapter 13, "Data I/O Between Excel and Access"). However, if such a database application is unavailable and your data files are relatively small, VBA's Open statement is a viable alternative.

The FileSystemObject Object

The FileSystemObject object and related objects were added to VBA 6.0 (Office 2000) to provide VBA programmers with a complete set of objects for accessing and modifying a computer's file structure. The FileSystemObject object model is contained in a type library called Scripting, located in the file scrrun.dll. You can add the FileSystemObject object and its subordinate objects to a project in the IDE. Just click Tools, References in the VBA IDE. The References dialog box appears. In the Available References list, select Microsoft Scripting Runtime (see Figure 8.4).

The objects included in the FileSystemObject object model and their descriptions are listed in Table 8.4.

 NOTE

You will not be able to use the FileSystemObject object model with Excel 97 unless the scripting runtime library is installed on your computer by another application (for example, Visual Basic 6.0).

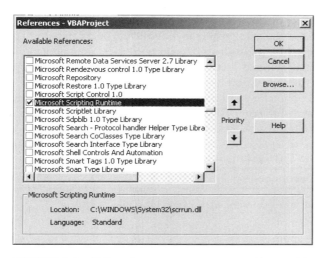

FIGURE 8.4 *Adding the* FileSystemObject *object model to a VBA project.*

Table 8.4 The FileSystemObject Object Model

Object	Description
FileSystemObject	The top-level object of the model. It provides access to a computer's file system and contains methods that allow you to manipulate drives, folders, and files.
Drives	Collection object consisting of all available drives (read-only).
Drive	Provides access to the properties of any disk drive connected to the system (hard-drives, floppies, CD-ROMs, network, and so on).
Folders	Collection object consisting of all Folder objects contained within a specified Folder object.
Folder	Provides access to the properties of a folder. It contains methods for creating, deleting, copying, and moving folders.
Files	Collection object consisting of all File objects within a folder.
File	Provides access to all the properties of a file. It contains methods for deleting, copying, and opening files.
TextStream	Provides sequential access to a file allowing you to read and write text files.

The `FileSystemObject` object contains several methods and one property that you can use to retrieve information from and manipulate the file structure on a computer. The lone property (the `Drives` property) returns a `Drives` collection object containing all `Drive` objects on the local computer. Selected methods of the `FileSystemObject` object are listed in Table 8.5, to point out the capabilities of the `FileSystemObject` object model. These methods are used in conjunction with the other objects in the model and many of them are repeated as members of the other objects.

Table 8.5 Methods of the FileSystemObject Object

Method	Description
CopyFile	Copies a file from one location to another.
CreateFolder	Creates a folder in the specified location.
CreateTextFile	Creates a text file and returns a `TextStream` object that can be used to write data to the file.
DeleteFile	Deletes a file.
DeleteFolder	Deletes a folder and all its contents.
DriveExists	Returns a `Boolean` value indicating whether the specified drive exists.
FileExists	Returns a `Boolean` value indicating whether the specified file exists.
FolderExists	Returns a `Boolean` value indicating whether the specified folder exists.
GetBaseName	Returns a `String` representing the last component in a specified path.
GetDrive	Returns a `Drive` object representing the drive in a specified path.
GetDriveName	Returns a `String` containing the name of the drive in a specified path.
GetExtensionName	Returns a `String` containing the extension for the last component in a specified path.
GetFile	Returns a `File` object representing the file in a specified path.
GetFileName	Returns a `String` representing the last component in a specified path that is not part of the drive specification.
GetFolder	Returns a `Folder` object representing the folder in a specified path.
GetParentFolderName	Returns a `String` representing the path to the parent folder of the last component in a specified path.
OpenTextFile	Opens a text file and returns a `TextStream` object that can be used to read from or append to the file.

The TextStream Object

The `TextStream` object is included in the `FileSystemObject` object model and provides another method in VBA for creating and reading sequential access text files. The `CreateTextFile` and `OpenTextFile` methods of the `FileSystemObject` object are used to return a `TextStream` object for reading or writing data to or from a file. The `TextStream` object contains several properties and methods that provide considerable flexibility to the programmer relative to the `Open` statement and associated statements discussed earlier in this chapter.

The Sub procedure `CreateTxtFile()` uses the `FileSystemObject` object and the `TextStream` object to create a text file holding tab-delimited data read from the selected range of the active worksheet. The `CreateTextFile` method of the `FileSystemObject` object creates and opens the text file while returning a `TextStream` object to the variable `aFile`. A `For/Each` loop accesses the data in the selected range (obtained from the `Selection` property of the `Window` object) and uses the `WriteLine` method of the `TextStream` object to write the data to the file. Tab characters are written to the file after each value to create a tab-delimited text file.

```vba
Public Sub CreateTxtFile()
    Dim fso As FileSystemObject
    Dim aFile As TextStream
    Dim c As Range
    Dim curRow As Integer

    '-------------------------------------------------
    'Set object references and loop through selected range
    'to write each value to the file.
    '-------------------------------------------------
    Set fso = New FileSystemObject
    Set aFile = fso.CreateTextFile("C:\myFile.txt", True)
    curRow = ActiveWindow.Selection.Row
    For Each c In ActiveWindow.Selection
        If c.Row <> curRow Then       'Test for the next row
            aFile.WriteLine
            curRow = c.Row
        End If
        aFile.Write (c.Value & vbTab)    'Write tab-delimited text
    Next
    aFile.Close          'Close file and clear memory
    Set fso = Nothing
    Set aFile = Nothing
End Sub
```

> **TIP**
>
> If you do not want to set a reference to the Microsoft Scripting Runtime library, you can still access the objects in the `FileSystemObject` model by using the `CreateObject()` function.
>
> ```
> Dim fso As Object
>
> Set fso = CreateObject("Scripting.FileSystemObject")
> ```
>
> The `CreateObject()` function returns a reference to an object when passed the application name (`Scripting`, in this example) and the class of object to create (`FileSystemObject`).
>
> One drawback to this method is that you have to use generic object types for your variable definitions, which causes late binding of the variables and can slow down the execution speed of your program. Another drawback is that you will not get the pop-up menu of properties and methods displayed when typing variable names associated with the objects in the `FileSystemObject` model.

The Sub procedure `ReadTxtFile()` reads the data from the tab-delimited text file and writes it to the selected range on the active worksheet. The `OpenTextFile` method of the `FileSystemObject` object opens the file and returns a `TextStream` object to the variable `aFile`. A `Do/Loop` iterates through each line of the file testing for the end of the file with the `AtEndOfStream` property of the `TextStream` object. The `ReadLine` method of the `TextStream` object returns each line of data in the file to the `String` variable `fileContent`, which is then written to a single cell in the worksheet. Each line of data in the file is written to a new row in the worksheet; however, the entire line of data remains in a single cell. After the file is closed, the worksheet range containing the data is selected, and the data is redistributed across the proper number of columns using the `TextToColumns` method of the `Range` object.

```
Public Sub ReadTxtFile()
    Dim fso As FileSystemObject
    Dim aFile As TextStream
    Dim fileContent As String
    Dim rowIndex As Integer
    Dim colIndex As Integer
    Dim colStr As String
    Dim I As Integer


    '-----------------------------------------------
```

```
'Find the selected cell in which to copy data
'and open the file
'-----------------------------------------------
I = ActiveCell.Row
rowIndex = I
colIndex = ActiveCell.Column
colStr = Chr(colIndex + 64)
Set fso = New FileSystemObject
Set aFile = fso.OpenTextFile("C:\myFile.txt", 1)


    '-------------------------------------------
    'Read each line of file until the end
    'and write data to selected range.
    '-------------------------------------------
Do While Not aFile.AtEndOfStream
    fileContent = aFile.ReadLine
    Cells(I, colIndex).Value = fileContent
    I = I + 1
Loop
aFile.Close      'Close file and convert lines of data to columns
Range(colStr & rowIndex & ":" & colStr & I - 1).Select
Selection.TextToColumns Destination:=Range( _
        colStr & rowIndex), DataType:=xlDelimited, Tab:=True
Set fso = Nothing
Set aFile = Nothing
End Sub
```

The TextStream object is a superior object for creating and reading sequential access files from VBA relative to the Open statement because of the additional flexibility provided by its properties and methods. So, you should use the TextStream object whenever possible for creating such text files.

Building a Custom File Dialog

You can use the FileSystemObject object and subordinate objects to access the entire directory structure of a computer. With these objects and a few ActiveX controls, I have built a custom file dialog box to illustrate the basic use of the FileSystemObject object model. The Userform design contains List Box controls for the drives, folders, and files on the computer and Command Button controls are used to add various functionalities. Figure 8.5 shows the design of the Userform. Except for the Name, Caption, Width, Height, Left, and

Top properties, which typically must be changed to accommodate the program, I altered only a few other design-time properties of the ActiveX controls from their default values.

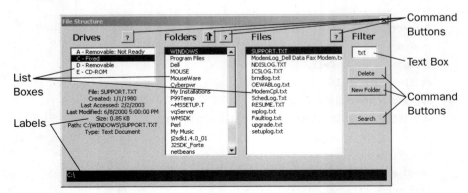

FIGURE 8.5 *A custom file dialog box built from a Userform and several ActiveX controls.*

The program must start by showing the Userform, which then triggers its `Initialize()` event. The `Initialize()` event of the Userform calls the Sub procedure `AddDrives()`, which lists the available drives on the local computer. I discuss the `AddDrives()` Sub procedure in the next section.

```
Private Sub UserForm_Initialize()

    AddDrives

End Sub
```

The Drive and Drives Collection Objects

The `Drives` collection object is subordinate to the `FileSystemObject` object and consists of a collection of all available disk drives. The `Drives` collection object has no methods and only two properties — `Item` and `Count`, which you can use to access a specific drive or return the number of drives in the collection, respectively. The `Drive` object also has no methods, but does have several properties that you can use to set and return information about a drive.

The Sub procedure `AddDrives()` uses the `FileSystemObject` object, `Drives` collection object, and `Drive` object to locate and list all available disk drives on a computer in a List Box control (named `lstDrives`) on a Userform. The variable `dColl` holds the collection of drives on the local computer returned from the `Drives` property of the `FileSystemObject` object. The `DriveLetter`, `DriveType`, and `IsReady` properties of the `Drive` object are used to learn the letter, type, and status of each local drive, respectively. The values of these three properties are then added to the List Box control using its `AddItem` property.

NOTE

The `Drives` property of the `FileSystemObject` object does not return shared network drives to the collection. You must hard-code shared network drives into your program when using this object.

```vba
Private Sub AddDrives()
'Add all drives to the drives list box
    Dim fso As FileSystemObject, aDrive As Drive, dColl As Drives
    Dim dType As String, dLetter As String, status As String


    '-------------------------------------------------------
    'Loop through each drive on the local computer and add it
    'to the List Box along with its type and status
    '-------------------------------------------------------
    Set fso = New FileSystemObject
    Set dColl = fso.Drives
    For Each aDrive In dColl
        dLetter = aDrive.DriveLetter & " - "
        Select Case aDrive.DriveType
            Case Is = 1
                dType = "Removable"
            Case Is = 2
                dType = "Fixed"
            Case Is = 3
                dType = "Network"    'Not returned by Drives property
            Case Is = 4
                dType = "CD-ROM"
            Case Is = 5
                dType = "RAM Drive"
            Case Else
                dType = "Unknown Drive"
        End Select
        If Not aDrive.IsReady Then
            status = ": Not Ready"
```

```
        Else
            status = ""
        End If
        lstDrives.AddItem dLetter & dType & status
    Next
    Set fso = Nothing
    Set dColl = Nothing
End Sub
```

Information about a drive selected in the List Box is easily output to a Label control via the `Click()` event of a Command Button control. The `VolumeName`, `FreeSpace`, `TotalSize`, and `IsReady` properties of the selected drive are output to a Label control named `lblInfo`.

```
Private Sub cmdDriveInfo_Click()
'Display selected drive information in label
    Dim fso As FileSystemObject, aDrive As Drive
    Dim infoStr As String
    'If nothing selected in the list box then exit the sub
    If IsNull(lstDrives.Value) Or Len(lstDrives.Value) = 0 Then
        MsgBox ("Select a drive.")
        Exit Sub
    End If
    If Right(lstDrives.Value, 9) = "Not Ready" Then Exit Sub
    '.................................................................
    'Set the objects and build the string with the selected drives properties
    '.................................................................
    Set fso = New FileSystemObject
    Set aDrive = fso.GetDrive(Left(lstDrives.Value, 1) & ":\")
    With aDrive      'Create a string to hold properties of the drive
        infoStr = lstDrives.Value & vbCrLf
        infoStr = infoStr & "Volume Name: " & .VolumeName & vbCrLf
        infoStr = infoStr & "Free Space: " & Format( _
            .FreeSpace / 1000000000#, "#0.00") & " GB" & vbCrLf
        infoStr = infoStr & "Total Size: " & Format( _
            .TotalSize / 1000000000#, "#0.00") & " GB" & vbCrLf
        infoStr = infoStr & "Ready: " & .IsReady
    End With
```

```
    'Output the drive info to a label control
    lblInfo.Caption = infoStr
    Set fso = Nothing
    Set aDrive = Nothing
End Sub
```

After finding all the drives and determining their properties, the next step is to locate all folder objects in a particular drive.

The Folder and Folders Collection Objects

The Folders collection object represents all subfolders contained with a specific Folder object. The Folders collection object contains two properties (Item and Count) and one method (Add), which are used in the usual way with collections. The Folders collection object holds a collection of Folder objects that represent the subfolders in another folder. You can then use the properties and methods of the Folder object to gather information or manipulate specific folders in the collection.

The AddFolders() Sub procedure accepts a String variable representing the path to a folder or drive and then lists its subfolders in another List Box control (lstFolders). The GetFolder method of the FileSystemObject object returns a Folder object representing the folder or drive passed into the procedure. The SubFolders method of the Folder object is then used to return its subfolders to the variable fcoll declared as a Folders collection object. A For/Each loop then adds the folders to the list.

```
Private Sub AddFolders(ByVal aPath As String)
'Add folders from input path to a list box
    Dim fso As FileSystemObject, curFolder As Folder, folder As Folder
    Dim fcoll As Folders

    Set fso = New FileSystemObject
    Set curFolder = fso.GetFolder(aPath)
    Set fcoll = curFolder.SubFolders
    For Each folder In fcoll
        lstFolders.AddItem folder.Name
    Next
    Set fso = Nothing
    Set curFolder = Nothing
    Set fcoll = Nothing
End Sub
```

Again, the Click() event of a Command Button control is used to display the information read from the properties of a Folder object in a Label control.

```
Private Sub cmdFolderInfo_Click()
'Display selected folder info in label
    Dim fso As FileSystemObject, curFolder As folder
    Dim infoStr As String
    If IsNull(lstFolders.Value) Or Len(lstFolders.Value) = 0 Then
        MsgBox ("Select a folder.")
        Exit Sub
    End If
    '------------------------------------------------------
    'Build string containing info. on selected folder
    '------------------------------------------------------
    Set fso = New FileSystemObject
    Set curFolder = fso.GetFolder(lblPath.Caption & lstFolders.Value)
    With curFolder
        infoStr = "Folder: " & lstFolders.Value & vbCrLf
        infoStr = infoStr & "Created: " & .DateCreated & vbCrLf
        infoStr = infoStr & "Last Accessed: " & .DateLastAccessed & vbCrLf
        infoStr = infoStr & "Last Modified: " & .DateLastModified & vbCrLf
        infoStr = infoStr & "Size: " & Format(.Size / 1000#, "#0.00") & " KB"
    End With
    '
    lblInfo.Caption = infoStr
    Set fso = Nothing
    Set curFolder = Nothing
End Sub
```

There are a number of ways to create new folders in the file structure of the computer, including using the Add method of the Folders collection object. Another method for creating a new folder is listed in the Click() event procedure of the Command Button named cmdCreateFolder. This procedure uses the CreateFolder method of the FileSystemObject object to create a new folder within the folder currently selected in the folder List Box control. The folder list box is then updated to display the folder collection containing the newly created folder.

```
Private Sub cmdCreateFolder_Click()
'Creates a new folder in current path
    Dim folderName As String
    Dim fso As FileSystemObject
```

```
        If IsNull(lstFolders.Value) Or lstFolders.Value = "" Then
            MsgBox ("Make a selection!")
            Exit Sub
        End If
        Do
            folderName = InputBox("Name of new folder?", "New Folder")
        Loop While Len(folderName) = 0

        Set fso = New FileSystemObject
        fso.CreateFolder (lblPath.Caption & lstFolders.Value & "\" & folderName)
        NewLevel
    End Sub
```

You use the Sub procedure NewLevel() to update the list boxes whenever a new level in the computer's file structure has been selected. The currently selected directory path is always output to a Label control named lblPath.

```
Private Sub NewLevel()
    lstFiles.Clear
    folderPath = lblPath.Caption & lstFolders.Value
    lstFolders.Clear
    AddFolders folderPath
    AddFiles folderPath
    folderPath = folderPath & lstFolders.Value & "\"
    lblPath.Caption = folderPath
End Sub
```

The File and Files Collection Objects

The Files collection object represents a collection of File objects contained within a specific Folder object. The Files collection object contains two properties (Item and Count) that are used to access specific File objects within a folder.

The AddFile() Sub procedure accepts a String variable representing the path to the currently selected folder and updates the List Box control used to display files (lstFiles). In this case, the Files property of the Folder object is used to return a collection of File objects to the Files collection variable fileColl. Files are listed against a filter entered in a Text Box control named txtFileFilter.

```
Private Sub AddFiles(aPath)
'Add files from selected folder to list box
    Dim fso As FileSystemObject, curFolder As Folder, aFile As File
    Dim fileColl As Files
```

```vba
    Set fso = New FileSystemObject
    Set curFolder = fso.GetFolder(aPath)
    Set fileColl = curFolder.Files
    'Loop through the files in the current folder.
    For Each aFile In fileColl
        If txtFileFilter.Text <> "" Then
            'If file extension matches filter then add file to list box
            If LCase(Right(aFile.Name, 3)) = LCase( _
                    txtFileFilter.Text) Then
                lstFiles.AddItem aFile.Name
            End If
        Else    'Add all files to list box
            lstFiles.AddItem aFile.Name
        End If
    Next
    Set fso = Nothing
    Set curFolder = Nothing
    Set fileColl = Nothing
End Sub
```

Properties of a selected File object are displayed in a Label control when the Command Button cmdFileInfo is selected.

```vba
Private Sub cmdFileInfo_Click()
'Display selected file info in label
    Dim fso As FileSystemObject, aFile As File
    Dim infoStr As String

    'Test if file has been selected or if any are listed
    If IsNull(lstFiles.Value) Or Len(lstFiles.Value) = 0 Then
        MsgBox ("Select a file.")
        Exit Sub
    End If

    Set fso = New FileSystemObject
    Set aFile = fso.GetFile(lblPath.Caption & lstFolders.Value & _
                "\" & lstFiles.Value)
```

```
    'Build information string containing file Info.
    ' for output to label control.
    With aFile
        infoStr = "File: " & lstFiles.Value & vbCrLf
        infoStr = infoStr & "Created: " & .DateCreated & vbCrLf
        infoStr = infoStr & "Last Accessed: " & .DateLastAccessed & vbCrLf
        infoStr = infoStr & "Last Modified: " & .DateLastModified & vbCrLf
        infoStr = infoStr & "Size: " & Format(.Size / 1000#, "#0.00") & " KB" &
vbCrLf
        infoStr = infoStr & "Path: " & .Path & vbCrLf
        infoStr = infoStr & "Type: " & .Type
    End With

    lblInfo.Caption = infoStr
    Set fso = Nothing
    Set aFile = Nothing
End Sub
```

Selected folders or files are deleted in the `Click()` event procedure of the Command Button `cmdDelete` using the `DeleteFolder` or `DeleteFile` method of the `FileSystemObject` object. You can also use the `Delete` methods of the `File` or `Folder` objects to accomplish the same task.

 CAUTION

Be aware that deleting a folder with these methods will also delete the contents of the folder without warning!

```
Private Sub cmdDelete_Click()
    Dim ms As Integer
    Dim fso As FileSystemObject

    'Test if folder has been selected.
    If IsNull(lstFolders.Value) Or lstFolders.Value = "" Then
        MsgBox ("Make a selection!")
        Exit Sub
    End If
```

```
'Prompt user to ensure they want to delete folder or file.
ms = MsgBox("Delete the folder or file?", vbYesNo, "Delete")
If ms = 7 Then
    Exit Sub
End If


Set fso = New FileSystemObject
'Delete the folder and update folder list box
If IsNull(lstFiles.Value) Or lstFiles.Value = "" Then
    fso.DeleteFolder (lblPath.Caption & lstFolders.Value)
    lstFolders.Clear
    AddFolders (lblPath.Caption)
Else    'Delete the file and update file list box
    fso.DeleteFile (lblPath.Caption & lstFolders.Value & _
        "\" & lstFiles.Value)
    lstFiles.Clear
    AddFiles (lblPath.Caption & lstFolders.Value)
End If
Set fso = Nothing
End Sub
```

Remaining procedures include `Click()` and `DblClick()` events of the List Box controls and one Command Button control to add the ability to navigate through the file structure of the computer. The `Click()` event procedure of the Command Button control named **cmdBack** moves the current directory path up one level and updates the folder and file lists.

```
Private Sub cmdBack_Click()
    Dim curPath As String
    curPath = lblPath.Caption
    If Len(curPath) <= 3 Then Exit Sub       'if at root drive then exit
    curPath = Left(curPath, InStrRev(curPath, "\") - 1)
    'remove one level from path
    curPath = Left(curPath, InStrRev(curPath, "\"))
    lblPath.Caption = curPath
    lstFolders.Clear
    lstFiles.Clear
    AddFolders (curPath)
    AddFiles (curPath)
End Sub
```

The `Click()` event of a List Box control is triggered when the user selects an item in the list. When the user selects a specific drive, the following procedure is triggered and the folder and file lists are updated.

```
Private Sub lstDrives_Click()
    lstFolders.Clear
    lstFiles.Clear
    If Right(lstDrives.Value, 9) = "Not Ready" Then Exit Sub
    AddFolders Left(lstDrives.Value, 1) & ":\"
    AddFiles Left(lstDrives.Value, 1) & ":\"
    folderPath = Left(lstDrives.Value, 1) & ":\" & lstFolders.Value
    lblPath.Caption = folderPath
End Sub
```

Selecting a single folder from the list, triggers the `Click()` event of `lstFolders`, and the list of files within the selected folder is updated. Double-clicking on a single folder from the list triggers the `DblClick()` event of `lstFolders` that calls the `NewLevel()` Sub procedure listed earlier and updates the folder and file lists.

```
Private Sub lstFolders_Click()
    lstFiles.Clear
    AddFiles lblPath.Caption & "\" & lstFolders.Value
End Sub
Private Sub lstFolders_DblClick(ByVal Cancel As MSForms.ReturnBoolean)
    NewLevel
End Sub
```

The last Sub procedure included in the form module for the file dialog box activates another Userform that is used to search for a specific file on the local computer's C drive.

```
Private Sub cmdSearch_Click()
    frmSearch.Show vbModal
    lblPath.Caption = filePath
End Sub
```

Recursive Search Using the FileSystemObject Model

The file dialog box shown earlier in Figure 8.5 contains a Command Button control with the caption `Search` that displays a simple Userform (`frmSearch`) when clicked. The Userform contains a Text Box control named `txtSearchStr` and a Command Button control named `cmdStartSearch`. When the user selects the Command Button, the file entered in the Text Box control is searched for using the Sub procedure `FindFile()`.

```
Private Sub cmdStartSearch_Click()
    Call FindFile(txtSearchStr.Text, "C:\", False)
    Unload frmSearch
End Sub
```

The `FindFile()` Sub procedure recursively calls itself until the desired input `String` (`target`) is found. The procedure begins at the root directory (C:\) and recursively searches all folders and subfolders until a file whose name matches the `String` variable `target` is found. The procedure then writes that path to the Label control named `lblPath` found on the original Userform (`frmFileSystem`).

```
Private Sub FindFile(target As String, ByVal aPath As String, _
                                    foundTarget As Boolean)
    Dim fso As FileSystemObject, curFolder As Folder, folder As Folder
    Dim folColl As Folders, file As File, fileColl As Files

    Set fso = New FileSystemObject
    Set curFolder = fso.GetFolder(aPath)
    Set folColl = curFolder.SubFolders
    Set fileColl = curFolder.Files


    'Search for target file by looping through files in current folder
    'Exit sub when target is found.
    For Each file In fileColl
        If file.Name = target Then
            foundTarget = True
            frmFileSystem.lblPath.Caption = file.Path
            Exit Sub
        End If
    Next


    If Not foundTarget Then
        'Make recursive call until file is found
        For Each folder In folColl
            DoEvents        'Yield execution so other events may be processed
            If Not foundTarget Then
                FindFile target, folder.Path, foundTarget
            End If
        Next
    End If
```

```
        Set fso = Nothing
        Set curFolder = Nothing
        Set folColl = Nothing
        Set fileColl = Nothing
    End Sub
```

The file dialog box and file search procedures presented here are obviously a bit rough and could use a few enhancements. Namely, the searching algorithm could be improved to include finding all files with desired specifications (name and type) in any directory, but I'll leave it up to you to add these enhancements.

The FileSearch Object

Although the `FileSearch` object has been around since Office 97, it has received significant upgrades over time. The `FileSearch` object and related objects are probably a little easier to use than the `FileSystemObject` object model, but their applications are limited to searching a computer's file structure. In applications that require file and folder searches, the two object models are competitive; otherwise, they are complementary.

The `FileSearch` object is a member of the Office library of objects, so you must set a reference to the Office library before using the `FileSearch` object. Use the `FileSearch` property of the `Application` object to return a `FileSearch` object.

```
Dim fs As FileSearch
Dim numFiles As Long
Set fs = Application.FileSearch
With fs
    .NewSearch
    numFiles = .Execute
End With
```

The `NewSearch` method of the `FileSearch` object resets the search criteria to their default values, and the `Execute` method starts the search. The `Execute` method returns a value (type `Long`) representing the number of files found in the search. Although file searches can be carried out using only the properties of the `FileSearch` object, you have more flexibility if you use the subordinate objects in the model. I discuss these objects in the following sections.

The SearchScopes Collection and SearchScope Objects

The `SearchScopes` collection object is a simple collection of `SearchScope` objects. You cannot add or remove objects from this collection because it is predefined. The `Count` and

`Item` properties of the `SearchScopes` collection object return the total number of `SearchScope` objects and individual `SearchScope` objects, respectively.

```
Dim sss As SearchScopes
Dim numSSS As Integer
Set sss = Application.FileSearch.SearchScopes
numSSS = sss.Count
```

The `SearchScope` object is contained in the `SearchScopes` collection object and represents the type of folder that can be searched using the `FileSearch` object. There are four basic types of `SearchScope` objects as determined by the `Type` property of the `SearchScope` object (see Table 8.6).

Table 8.6 Search Scope Types

Type (as VBA constant)	Description
`msoSearchInCustom`	Custom search scope
`msoSearchInMyComputer`	All local drives (for example, A:\, C:\, D:\, and so on)
`msoSearchInMyNetworkPlaces`	All network drives
`msoSearchInOutlook`	Microsoft Outlook folders

To return a `SearchScope` object to a variable, use the `Item` property of the `SearchScopes` collection object.

```
Dim ss As SearchScope
Set ss = sss.Item(1)
```

You can use one or more of the predefined search scopes to set the "scope" for a file search. Inevitably, you will need to narrow your search to a specific folder and possibly any sub-folders it contains. In such a case, you must create `ScopeFolder` objects and add them to the `SearchFolders` collection object.

The SearchFolders Collection and ScopeFolder Objects

The `SearchFolders` collection object contains the `ScopeFolder` objects that define which folders are searched when the `Execute` method of the `FileSearch` object is invoked. In designing a custom file search, you should clear the `SearchFolders` collection before adding the specific `ScopeFolder` objects required for the search.

The `SetRootFolders()` Sub procedure first clears the `SearchFolders` collection using its `Remove` method. Next, a single `ScopeFolder` object is added back to `SearchFolders` collection. The specific `ScopeFolder` object is determined by the variable `rootFolder` that is passed to the SetRootFolders() Sub procedure as a String. The rootFolder variable is meant to be one of the local drives included in the My Computer search scope (for example, A:\, C:\, D:\, and so on). To add the right ScopeFolder object to the SearchFolders collection, set the variable sf to hold the ScopeFolder object representing the first item in the SearchScopes collection (that is, My Computer). The ScopeFolders collection object subordinate to the ScopeFolder object representing My Computer is searched until the desired path is found and then added to the SearchFolders collection via the AddToSearchFolders method of the ScopeFolder object. In a nutshell, the SetRootFolders() Sub procedure adds one ScopeFolder to the SearchFolders collection representing one of the local drives on the computer.

```
Private Sub SetRootFolder(rootFolder As String)
    Dim sfs As SearchFolders
    Dim sf As ScopeFolder
    Dim subsf As ScopeFolder
    Dim I As Integer

    Set sfs = Application.FileSearch.SearchFolders
    Set sf = Application.FileSearch.SearchScopes.Item(1).ScopeFolder
    With sfs              'Clear search folders collection
        For I = .Count To 1 Step -1   'Always remove the last item from a
            .Remove (I)               'collection first.
        Next I
    End With
    With sf
        'loop through subfolders in My Computer
        For Each subsf In .ScopeFolders
            If subsf.Path = rootFolder Then
                subsf.AddToSearchFolders
            End If
        Next subsf
    End With
End Sub
```

In addition to setting the root drive, you may want to set the file types and some specific file properties before conducting a search.

The FileTypes and PropertyTests Collection Objects

The FileTypes collection object contains a collection of VBA constants (msoFileType) that represent the file types returned in a search invoked by the Execute method of the

FileSearch object. You can specify about two dozen file types in a search, including all files (msoFileTypeAllFiles), databases (msoFileTypeDatabases), Excel workbooks (msoFileTypeExcelWorkbooks), Power Point presentations (msoFileType _ PowerPointPresentations), and Word documents (msoFileTypeWordDocuments), among others (see the Item property of the FileTypes object in the online help).

 NOTE

You can also clear the FileTypes collection by invoking the FileType property of the FileSearch object. The first item of the FileTypes collection object is then set to the file type defined by the FileType property.

```
Application.FileSearch.FileType = msoFileTypeExcelWorkbooks
```

The SetFileTypes() Sub procedure listed next removes all items from the FileTypes collection before adding three items representing Power Point presentations (*.ppt), Excel workbooks (*.xls), and Word documents (*.doc).

```
Private Sub SetFileTypes ()
    Dim ft As FileTypes
    Dim I As Integer
    Set ft = Application.FileSearch.FileTypes
    With ft
        'Always remove the last item from a collection first
        For I = .Count To 1 Step -1
            .Remove (I)
        Next I
        .Add msoFileTypePowerPointPresentations
        .Add msoFileTypeExcelWorkbooks
        .Add msoFileTypeWordDocuments
    End With
End Sub
```

The PropertyTests collection object represents a collection of PropertyTest objects that describe the search criteria for a file search. The properties of the PropertyTest object represent the values set by users in the Advanced Search dialog box (see Figure 8.6), which they access by going to the standard toolbar and clicking Search.

FIGURE 8.6 *Excel's Advanced Search dialog box.*

The properties of the `PropertyTest` object enable you to add additional search criteria in a file search. The Sub procedure `SetPropertyTests()` adds additional search criteria that will result in a file search finding only those files that were created or modified within seven days of the current date. As written, the `SetPropertyTests()` Sub procedure is meant to be executed after the `SetFileTypes()` Sub procedure.

```
Private Sub SetPropTests()
    Dim pt As PropertyTests
    Dim I As Integer

    Set pt = Application.FileSearch.PropertyTests
    With pt
        For I = .Count To 1 Step -1
            .Add Name:="Last Modified", _
                Condition:=msoConditionOnOrAfter, _
```

```
                    Value:=DateAdd("d", -7, Date)
          Next I
      End With
End Sub
```

In addition to the `Name`, `Condition`, and `Value` arguments, the `Add` method of the `PropertyTests` object accepts `SecondValue` and `Connector` arguments used to add an upper bound to the search criteria when the `Condition` is `msoConditionAnyTimeBetween` or `msoConditionAnyNumberBetween`. See the online help for a complete list of constants to use with the `Condition` argument. You can also select a property in the Advanced Search dialog box. Just click the down arrow beside the Property drop-down list to see which conditions are available for a specific property.

The FoundFiles Collection Object

The `FoundFiles` collection object holds the paths (as strings) to the files found in a file search. Use the `FoundFiles` property of the `FileSearch` object or the `Item` property of the `FoundFiles` collection object to return the path to the file or files found in a search.

```
Dim ff As FoundFiles
Dim fs As FileSearch
Dim I As Integer
Set fs = Application.FileSearch
Set ff = fs.FoundFiles
With ff
    For I = 1 To ff.Count
        MsgBox ff.Item(I)
    Next I
End With
```

 NOTE

The `PropertyTests` and `FoundFiles` objects are the only two objects included in the `FileSearch` object model with Office 97 and Office 2000.

Recursive Search Using the FileSearch Object

As was the case with the `FileSystemObject` object, to carry out a proper file search using the `FileSearch` object, you will have to write a recursive procedure similar to the `SetSubFolders()` Sub procedure listed here. But, first, use the `FindTheFiles()` Sub procedure to initialize the parameters for the search. The `FindTheFiles()` Sub procedure calls the `SetRootFolder()`, `SetFileTypes()`, and `SetPropTests()` Sub procedures listed earlier to initialize a new search for the FileSearch object. Specifically, files of type .xls, .ppt, and .doc located anywhere in the root directory D:\ created or modified within seven days of the current date will be returned to the FoundFiles object. After the search criteria are set, a call to the Sub procedure SetSubFolders() adds all subfolders of the root folder to the SearchFolders collection object. Paths to all files found in the search are output in a message box.

```
Public Sub FindTheFiles()
    Dim sf As ScopeFolder
    Dim I As Long
    Dim fs As FileSearch
    Dim msg As String

    Set fs = Application.FileSearch
    'Set properties of the filesearch object
    With fs
        .NewSearch
        SetRootFolder ("D:\")   'Set root folder for search
        SetFileTypes    'Set file types for search
        SetPropTests    'Set additional file properties for search
        Set sf = fs.SearchFolders.Item(1)
        Call SetSubFolders(sf.ScopeFolders, "")   'Find the subfolders
        If .SearchFolders.Count > 0 Then
            If .Execute <> 0 Then   'Files were found if >0
                msg = "Files found: " & .FoundFiles.Count & vbCrLf
                For I = 1 To .FoundFiles.Count
                    msg = msg & .FoundFiles.Item(I) & vbCrLf
                Next I
            End If
        End If
    End With
    MsgBox msg
End Sub
```

The SetSubFolders() Sub procedure loops through all the ScopeFolder objects in the ScopeFolders collection passed to the procedure. Any folder that has the same name as the value of strFolder is added to the SearchFolders collection. If strFolder is an empty string, all subfolders are added to the SearchFolders collection. The recursive call then passes each ScopeFolders collection associated with the newly added ScopeFolder objects back to the procedure to repeat the process until no more ScopeFolder objects are found (or exist).

```
Private Sub SetSubFolders(ByVal sfs As ScopeFolders, _
                      ByRef strFolder As String)
    Dim sf As ScopeFolder
    'Loop through scope folders to find desired sub folders
    For Each sf In sfs
        If strFolder <> "" Then  'Search for specific sub-folders
            If LCase(sf.Name) = LCase(strFolder) Then
                sf.AddToSearchFolders
            End If
        Else      'Add all sub-folders to the search
            sf.AddToSearchFolders
        End If
        DoEvents     'Yield execution so other events may be processed
        'Make recursive call to find more sub-folders
        If sf.ScopeFolders.Count > 0 Then
            Call SetSubFolders(sf.ScopeFolders, strFolder)
        End If
    Next sf
End Sub
```

Error Handling

Inevitably, your programs will contain errors (bugs). When caused by violation of the rules of the language, the errors are called _syntax errors_ (for example, misspelled keywords, missing components of a code structure, improper declaration of a variable, and so on). Syntax errors are easy to find in VBA because they will prevent a program from compiling properly and the editor will send you right to the source of the problem. Other errors occur as a result of poor program logic (for example, infinite loops, wrong variable initialization, and so on). These types of errors are referred to as _logic errors_. Logic errors do not prevent the program from compiling and executing; therefore, they can be difficult to find. However, with proper debugging, you can significantly reduce the number of errors in a program.

In addition to syntax and logic errors, programs may contain errors that can only be anticipated. Examples might include a "divide by zero" error or a "file not found" error. Left unchecked, these errors will cause a program to crash. Furthermore, you may not be able to fix errors of this type by altering the logic of the program. In situations such as these, the program requires additional error handling code and procedures. Error handling code should be included whenever the program interacts with the user or other components of the computer. This section focuses on special statements and objects available in VBA for handling anticipated errors.

On Error/Goto and the Err Object

To enable error handling in a VBA program, use the On Error statement. The On Error statement must be followed with another statement instructing the program on where to proceed when a run-time error is encountered. You have a couple of options when deciding on the direction of program execution after encountering an error.

 TIP

The On Error statement must precede the code that is anticipated to generate the run-time error. The On Error statement is normally placed near the beginning of a procedure.

The Resume Next clause sends program execution to the next line of code following the line that generated the error. Although using this clause is the simplest solution for handling run-time errors, in many cases, doing so is not a good idea. The Resume Next clause does nothing to resolve the error that may continue to cause trouble in your program.

 TIP

To learn the nature of a run-time error, you can access the Err object and read its properties. The Err object is a member of the VBA object library and can be accessed anywhere in a program without special declarations. The Err object is filled with information about a run-time error whenever one is generated. Two of the most useful properties of the Err object are the Number and Description properties.

Err.Number

Err.Description

In some cases, you may be able to fix the error or, at the very least, output some information to the user on the nature of the error using an error handling routine. To send program execution to an error handling routine, use the Goto statement after On Error.

```
On Error GoTo ErrorHandler
```

The term ErrorHandler refers to a line label used to direct program execution to the block of code specifically created for handling the run-time error. Line labels must start at the leftmost position in the editor window and end with a colon. The error handling code follows the line label. The order of program execution within a procedure with error handling code is similar to that listed next and illustrated in Figure 8.7.

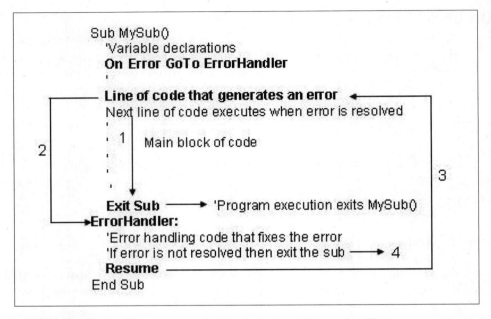

FIGURE 8.7 *Order of program execution in a procedure with error handling.*

The order of program execution in a procedure containing error handling code is as follows:

1. If no error is generated, code execution proceeds as normal and exits before reaching the error handler.

2. If an error is raised, code execution proceeds immediately to the error handler.

3. If the error handler resolves the error, code execution proceeds back to the line of code that raised the error.

4. If the error handler cannot resolve the error, code execution exits the Sub procedure without executing the main block of code in the procedure. Some type of output should be included to inform the user of the nature of the error.

 NOTE

Because of the danger of creating "spaghetti" code with the `Goto` statement, limit its use to error handling routines only. *Spaghetti code* refers to a program that branches in so many directions that it becomes twisted like a plate of spaghetti, making it very difficult to maintain.

Now, reconsider the `ReadTxtFile()` Sub procedure listed earlier in the section "The TextStream Object," only now with an error handling code block. An error will be raised by this procedure if the file or path to the desired file cannot be found. The statement `On Error`

GoTo ErrorHandler is placed immediately after variable declarations so that program execution will be sent to the error handling code block at the end of the procedure as soon as an error is raised. The rest of the procedure is essentially the same as before, except that the file path is now stored in a variable and the error handling block of code is placed at the end.

```
Private Sub ReadTxtFile()
    Dim fso As FileSystemObject, aFile As TextStream
    Dim fileContent As String, colStr As String
    Dim rowIndex As Integer, colIndex As Integer
    Dim I As Integer, ms As Integer
    Dim fPath As String

    On Error GoTo ErrorHandler
    '-----------------------------------------------
    'Find the selected cell in which to copy data
    'and open the file
    '-----------------------------------------------
    I = ActiveCell.Row
    rowIndex = I
    colIndex = ActiveCell.Column
    colStr = Chr(colIndex + 64)
    Set fso = New FileSystemObject
    fPath = "D:\myFile.txt"
    Set aFile = fso.OpenTextFile(fPath, 1)
    '-----------------------------------------
    'Read each line of file until the end
    'and write data to selected range.
    '-----------------------------------------
    Do While Not aFile.AtEndOfStream
        fileContent = aFile.ReadLine
        Cells(I, colIndex).Value = fileContent
        I = I + 1
    Loop
    aFile.Close      'Close file and convert lines of data to columns
    Range(colStr & rowIndex & ":" & colStr & I - 1).Select
    Selection.TextToColumns Destination:=Range( _
        colStr & rowIndex), DataType:=xlDelimited, Tab:=True
    Set fso = Nothing
    Set aFile = Nothing
```

If no errors are raised in the procedure, `Exit Sub` must be used to ensure that the error handling code is not executed.

```
    Exit Sub
ErrorHandler:
    If Err.Number = 53 Or Err.Number = 76 Then
        ms = MsgBox(Err.Description & vbCrLf & _
                "Do you want to look for the file?", vbYesNo)
        If ms = 6 Then
            fPath = ShowFileDialog(fPath)
            If fPath <> "Cancelled" Then Resume
        Else
            MsgBox "Resolve file error before continuing."
        End If
    Else
        MsgBox Err.Number & ": " & Err.Description
    End If
End Sub
```

The error handling code follows the line label `ErrorHandler:` and presents one of several possible messages to the user. If the error raised is due to an incorrect file path (error 53) or drive not found (error 76), the user has the option of looking for the file or canceling the operation altogether.

TIP

To get a list of VBA error codes and descriptions, see "Trappable Errors" in the online help.

Regardless of the error, the user is at least informed of its nature via the `Description` property of the `Err` object. If the user decides to look for the file, program execution proceeds to the `ShowFileDialog()` Function procedure that allows the user to navigate the computer's file structure and locate the file. If the user selects a file, its path is returned to the error handler, which resets the variable `fPath` and sends program execution back to the line of code that originated the error. If the user does not select a file, the procedure is exited without taking action.

```
Private Function ShowFileDialog(fName As String) As String
    Dim fd As FileDialog
    Dim I As Integer
```

```
        Set fd = Application.FileDialog(msoFileDialogOpen)
        With fd
            .AllowMultiSelect = False
            .FilterIndex = 2
            .Title = "Find File"
            .InitialFileName = fName
            If .Show = -1 Then
                ShowFileDialog = .SelectedItems(1)
            Else
                ShowFileDialog = "Cancelled"
            End If
        End With
        Set fd = Nothing
End Function
```

Debugging

By now, you have certainly encountered errors in your programs and perhaps wondered what was available for correcting them. Fortunately, VBA has several easy-to-use tools to help you debug a program. You will probably rely heavily on only one or two of the following tools to debug your program.

Break Mode

When a run-time error is generated while testing a program, a message box similar to the one shown in Figure 8.8 is displayed.

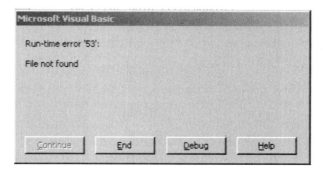

FIGURE 8.8 *The run-time error message box.*

Selecting the Debug option from the message box will call up the VBA IDE and display the program in break mode with the line of code that generated the error highlighted. Break mode pauses program execution at a specific line of code so that you can closely examine factors such as order of code execution and the current values stored within variables. To intentionally enter break mode, insert a breakpoint at the desired location in the program using the Debug menu item or Debug toolbar (select View, Toolbars, Debug) in the VBA IDE (see Figure 8.9). You can also toggle a breakpoint by clicking the left margin of the code window next to the line of code where you want program execution to pause, or you can press F9.

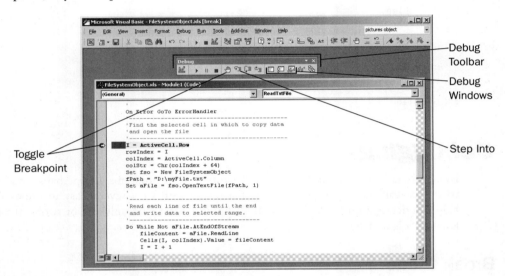

FIGURE 8.9 *The VBA IDE in break mode.*

You can insert break points at locations in your code where bugs are suspected or known to exist. After inserting all break points, you can execute the program or procedure containing the break points. Break mode is entered when program execution proceeds to a line of code containing a breakpoint. In break mode, you have the option of resetting the program, stepping through the program one line at a time, or continuing normal operation of the program. While in break mode, the value currently stored in a variable can be checked by holding the cursor over the name of that variable. Checking the contents of a variable can help find logic errors in a program that may have been caused by code that assigns the wrong value to a variable.

While in break mode, you can also step through code one line at a time. Use the Step Into option on the Debug toolbar or press F8 to execute one line of code at a time starting from the location of the break. The order of program execution can be verified and values stored within variables checked as code execution proceeds through each line.

The Immediate Window

Stepping through code one line at a time can be tedious if the error is not found immediately. The Immediate window allows you to view current values or test new values of program variables under normal program execution. You can access the Immediate window from the Debug toolbar by selecting View, Immediate window, or by pressing Ctrl+G in the IDE.

The Debug Object

You can add debugging statements at suspected trouble spots in your code that, when executed, write the value of a variable or variables to the Immediate window. Debugging statements use the `Assert` and `Print` methods of the `Debug` object. You can use the `Assert` method to break program execution based on a `Boolean` expression. Use the `Print` method to write values to the Immediate window.

 NOTE

The compiler ignores debugging statements, so there is no harm in leaving them in your code.

The `IncRecNum()` Sub procedure listed in the section "Random Access Files," earlier in this chapter, is repeated with additional statements using the `Debug` object. Use the `Boolean` expression `recNum < maxRecNum` with the `Assert` method of the `Debug` object to break program execution when it evaluates as `False`. Use the `Print` method of the `Debug` object to write the value of the variables `recNum` and `maxRecNum` to the Immediate window whenever this procedure is called. If desired, you can pass a `String` to the `Print` method to identify the variable output to the Immediate window. After or during program execution, you can view the Immediate window and its contents from the VBA IDE, as shown in Figure 8.10.

```
Public Sub IncRecNum()

    Dim maxRecNum As Integer


    recNum = recNum + 1

    maxRecNum = GetMaxRecNum

    Debug.Assert recNum < maxRecNum

    Debug.Print "recNum = " & recNum; "   maxRecNum = " & maxRecNum

    If recNum > maxRecNum Then

        recNum = maxRecNum

    End If

    GetEmployeeInfo

End Sub
```

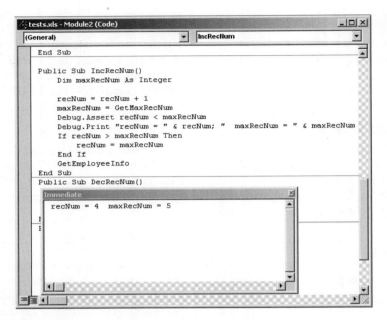

FIGURE 8.10 *The Immediate window with values written to it using Debug.Print.*

Program execution in the `IncRecNum()` Sub procedure will enter break mode whenever the procedure is called and the expression `recNum < maxRecNum` evaluates as `False`. Having the program in break mode allows you to step through the remaining lines of code to ensure that the procedure performs as expected. In this example, the idea is to ensure that the variable `recNum` never exceeds the actual number of records in the file.

You can also use the Immediate window to enter code statements while the program is in break mode. You can enter statements directly into the Immediate window that change the value of a variable or the property of an ActiveX control or that call a procedure. The statements take effect after you press Enter. For example, the value of the variable `recNum` can be changed while in break mode by entering `recNum = maxRecNum + 1` in the Immediate window. Doing so can be useful for redirecting program execution and testing the results of changing a variables value without having to alter code.

The Watch Window

Another useful tool for debugging VBA programs is the Watch window. The Watch window makes it possible to track the value of a variable or expression (property, function call, and so on) from anywhere in a program. Add a watch to an expression from the Debug menu or right-click the expression and choose Add Watch from the shortcut menu that appears. The resulting dialog box is shown in Figure 8.11.

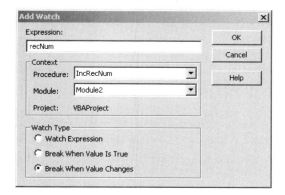

FIGURE 8.11 *The Add Watch dialog box.*

In the Procedure drop-down list, choose the procedure in which you want to watch the expression or choose All Procedures. Next, in the Module drop-down list, choose the module in which you want to watch the expression or select All Modules. Finally, select the watch type (Watch Expression , Break When Value Is True, or Break When Value Changes). The watch expressions selected will be displayed in the Watch window only when the program enters break mode. So, if Watch Expression is selected, you must insert a break point in the procedures containing the expression before running the program. The other two watch types automatically pause the program at the specified location. The Watch window in Figure 8.12 shows the value of an expression while the program is in break mode.

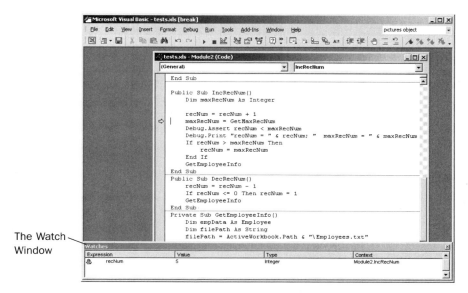

FIGURE 8.12 *The Watch window set to watch the value of a variable.*

The Locals Window

You use the Locals window (see Figure 8.13) to display the value of the declared variables local to the procedure in which program execution pauses with a break point. Module-level variables are listed under the object Me in the Locals window (not shown in Figure 8.13). To display the Locals window, select View, Locals Window or select the Locals Window icon from the Debug toolbar.

When a procedure is suspected of containing an error, insert a breakpoint in the procedure, run the program, and display the Locals window before stepping through the procedure's code. This is a handy tool for debugging a procedure because it allows you to view the values of all local variables while stepping through the code.

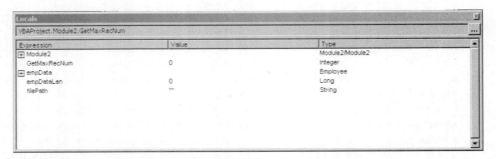

FIGURE 8.13 *The Locals window showing the values of all local variables in a procedure.*

Summary

This chapter covered a lot of information especially in regard to file input and output. Specifically, you learned how to open and save Excel workbooks using methods of the Workbook object as well as the dialog boxes available from the Dialogs collection object and the FileDialog object. You also learned how to create sequential and random access text files using the Open statement and some of the functions included with the FileSystem object. An extensive discussion of the FileSystemObject and FileSearch models showed you how to navigate and manipulate a computer's file structure as well as recursively search for specific files. Finally, you learned how to handle run-time errors and debug your VBA programs.

PART

II

Professional Project 1 — Excel-to-HTML Converter

The last few versions of Excel have included tools that allow users to save workbooks (or parts thereof) as Web pages and publish the resulting documents to a local or networked drive. The resulting HTML files create nice reproductions of the original spreadsheets when saved as either static or dynamic Web pages. However, the HTML files generated by Excel can be very long and difficult to decipher for even the most experienced Web developer. The most recent versions of Excel have made significant strides in removing a lot of the clutter that was included in the generated HTML files in earlier versions; yet these files are still longer than necessary and difficult for someone with little to moderate HTML experience to follow. Furthermore, the number of required options the user must set before publishing a workbook can be a bit intimidating and, if misunderstood, might result in the generation of extra files or code.

The goal of this project is to create a convenient VBA application that generates an easy-to-read HTML file from an existing Excel worksheet. The resulting Web page should be static and accurately reproduce the original worksheet. The HTML file should be simple enough that even a beginner can effectively edit the data content in the file. With this application, users will be able to easily publish Web pages to a local or networked drive and even edit the content of the resulting HTML file (if so desired).

The intended user of this program is anyone who needs to post the analyses from Excel worksheets to the Internet or an intranet for dissemination throughout their business or school or worldwide.

The next four chapters introduce you to some new objects and code modules that will be used in the construction of the Excel-to-HTML converter program. The topics you learn about include the following:

- Creating custom menus and toolbars
- Programming with the `Chart` object
- Creating reusable objects with class modules

The last chapter in Part II uses these newly introduced and previously discussed VBA programming tools to construct the Excel-to-HTML converter program.

Chapter 9

The Excel-to-HTML converter project constructed in this part of the book includes a number of VBA programming components that I have not yet discussed. The next three chapters introduce the programming components required to build the Excel-to-HTML converter program. In this chapter, I show you how to create custom toolbars and menus that appear and disappear as your VBA programs are loaded and unloaded. In addition, I show you how to store your VBA programs as add-ins that the user can load as needed. After an add-in is loaded, your custom toolbar or menu items will appear. The Excel-to-HTML converter program will include a custom toolbar and will be saved as an Excel add-in.

Creating Menus and Toolbars with VBA

Chapter 1, "VBA Overview and the IDE," explains how to create a custom toolbar from the Excel application window. You can add custom menus to the menu bar in the same way. Creating menus and toolbars as explained in Chapter 1, however, has a potential drawback: The customized menu or toolbar might remain in the Excel application window, even if the user closes the application with which the customized menu or toolbar is designed to work. Often, it is more desirable to design your program so that a toolbar is added when the user opens the program and is removed when the user exits the program, and you can do this easily with VBA.

The CommandBar, CommandBarControl, and Related Objects

The CommandBars collection object represents a collection of CommandBar objects and a CommandBar object represents any menu or toolbar in the application (for example, the Worksheet Menu Bar or the Standard and Formatting toolbars). Likewise, the CommandBarControls collection object is a collection of CommandBarControl objects that represents items within a particular menu (for example, the Save command in the File menu) or toolbar (for example, the Bold button on the Formatting toolbar).

As with all collections, you can use the Add method to create a new object within the CommandBars and CommandBarControls collection objects. The idea is to first create the menu bar or toolbar and then add menu items (usually as buttons) to it.

Custom Menus

Creating a new menu that replaces the existing menu bar in the Excel application window is an easy task with VBA. The NewMenu() Sub procedure listed next is used to create a new menu bar via the Add method of the CommandBars collection object. The object variable myMenu (type CommandBar) represents the new menu bar to which items are added. You can place your new menu bar at the top of the Excel application window using the Position argument of the Add method (msoBarTop). Other choices for the Position argument of the Add method include msoBarLeft, msoBarRight, msoBarBottom, msoBarFloating, and msoBarPopup. To replace the active menu bar, set the MenuBar argument of the Add method to True). The new menu bar will be automatically deleted when Excel is closed if you set the Temporary argument to True.

```
Private myMenu As CommandBar
Private subControl1 As CommandBarButton
Public Sub NewMenu()
'Create a new menu bar that replaces the existing menu bar
    Dim myControl1 As CommandBarControl
    Dim subControl1 As CommandBarControl

    'First create an empty menu bar
    Set myMenu = Application.CommandBars.Add ( _
        Name:="My Menu Bar", _
        Position:=msoBarTop, _
        MenuBar:=True, _
        Temporary:=True)
    myMenu.Visible = True
```

After the Visible property of the CommandBar object is set to True, but before any items have been added to the new menu, a blank menu bar appears in Excel, as shown in Figure 9.1.

Empty Custom Menu

FIGURE 9.1 *A custom menu bar before items are added to it.*

Once the menu bar is created, you can add CommandBarControl objects to it with the Add method of the CommandBarControls collection object (returned with the Controls property). The object path must include a reference to the CommandBar object to which the CommandBarControl object is being added, in this case, myMenu. The Add method of the CommandBarControls collection object accepts up to five optional arguments (Type, ID, Parameter, Before, and Temporary). The Type argument represents the kind of object that will be added to the menu bar. Choices for the `Type` argument include `msoControlButton`, `msoControlEdit`, `msoControlDropdown`, `msoControlComboBox`, or `msoControlPopup`, and they represent `CommandBarButton`, `CommandBarComboBox`, or `CommandBarPopup` objects. You typically use a pop-up control for the major menu items because all pop-up controls contain a `CommandBar` object. This allows you to add more `CommandBarControl` objects to the major menu item as sub-items.

TIP

Use a `CommandBarComboBox` object (of type `msoControlComboBox`) when you need to display a list of choices for one particular object. For example, the font type and size in the standard toolbar of Microsoft Office are examples of `CommandBarComboBox` objects.

After the `NewMenu()` Sub procedure adds the new menu bar, the object variable `myControl1` is set to represent a new menu item on the new menu bar.

```
Set myControl1 = myMenu.Controls.Add( _
    Type:=msoControlPopup, _
    ID:=1, _
    Before:=1, _
    Temporary:=True)
myControl1.Caption = "Menu Header &1"
```

After the `CommandBarControl` object `myControl1` is added, the custom menu bar appears as shown in Figure 9.2.

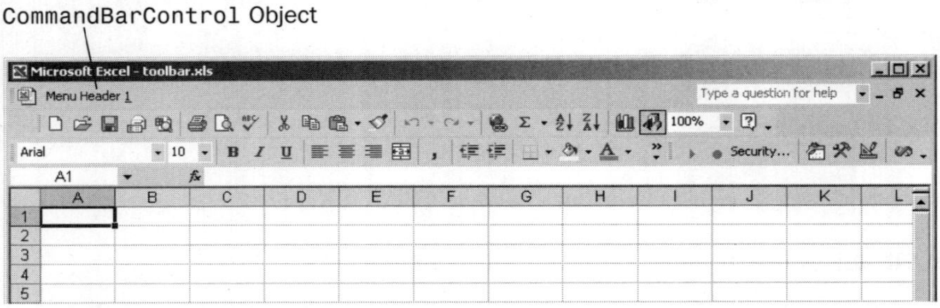

CommandBarControl Object

FIGURE 9.2 *A custom menu bar containing one item as a* `CommandBarControl` *object.*

The ID argument of the Add method represents a built-in control (existing CommandBarControl object such as File, Edit, or View) and should be omitted or set to 1 when adding a custom control. The Before argument specifies the position of the control on the menu bar, and you can use the Parameter argument to store information (as a string) about the control. After the control is added to the menu bar, you can set its properties in the usual way. A caption is always a good idea for a menu item. The ampersand (&) used in the Caption property of the CommandBarControl object representing a menu item will not show up in the menu item's caption; instead, it denotes the shortcut key for accessing the menu item from the keyboard. Thus, you can use *alt+1* to select the menu item with the caption Menu Header 1 (the 1 will appear underlined in the caption; refer to Figure 9.2).

TIP

You can add existing Excel menus (also know as *built-in menus*) to your menu bar or toolbar by specifying the associated value with the ID argument of the Add method for the CommandBarControls collection object. Unfortunately, the ID numbers are not well documented in the online help. To learn the ID value for a particular built-in menu, you need to record a macro while creating a custom menu or toolbar from Excel.

After adding a major item to the menu bar, you can add sub-items to each pop-up control. The added control represents a sub-item and will be displayed to the user only when the major item (myControl1) is selected. In this example, the added control is a button (object type CommandBarButton) that executes a specified Sub procedure (DeleteMenu) when the user selects it:

```
    Set subControl1 = myControl1.Controls.Add( _
        ID:=1, _
        Parameter:=" You have chosen to delete the custom menu!", _
        Before:=1, _
        Temporary:=True)
    subControl1.Caption = "Delete Menu"
    subControl1.Visible = True
    subControl1.OnAction = "DeleteMenu"
End Sub
```

Figure 9.3 shows the menu bar that appears when the NewMenu() Sub procedure is executed.

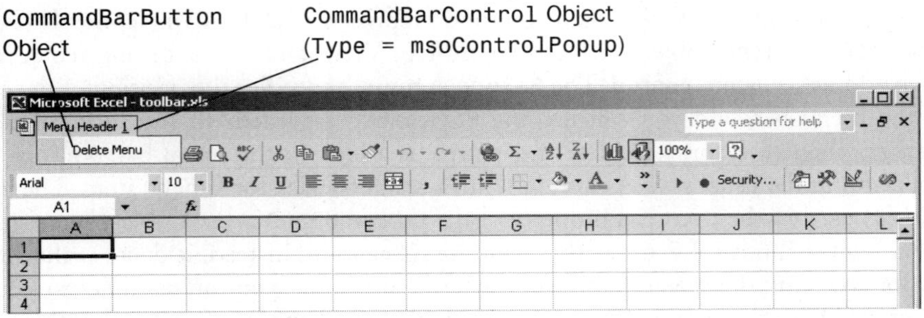

CommandBarButton
Object

CommandBarControl Object
(Type = msoControlPopup)

FIGURE 9.3 *Creating a custom menu bar with a VBA program.*

The `DeleteMenu()` Sub procedure is called when the user selects the sub-item (`subControl1`) from the major item (`myControl1`) on the menu bar and serves to delete the custom menu bar. The `OnAction` property of the `CommandBarControl` object `subControl1` sets this procedure call.

```
Private Sub DeleteMenu()
    MsgBox subControl1.Parameter
    myMenu.Delete
End Sub
```

As you can see, creating custom menu bars is easy. You can also use these methods to add major items and sub-items to Excel's worksheet menu bar. Instead of adding a new menu bar, select the existing menu from the `CommandBars` collection object and add a new `CommandBarControl` object.

```
CommandBars("Worksheet Menu Bar").Controls.Add
```

You can also select existing menu items and add sub-items. For example, to add a menu item to the Excel File menu, use the following.

```
CommandBars("File").Controls.Add
```

Follow the methods used in the `NewMenu()` Sub procedure to set the properties of the `CommandBarControl` objects added to an existing menu or menu item.

 TIP

To add a picture to a custom menu item, use the `Picture` property of the `CommandBarButton` object. The `LoadPicture` method is a member of stdole library found in the Stdole2.tlb file (to access this file, select OLE Automation in the References dialog box).

```
subControl1.Picture = LoadPicture("C:\MyPath\myImage.bmp")
```

Custom Toolbars

Custom toolbars are really no different than custom menus; they are all `CommandBar` objects and part of the same `CommandBars` collection. The difference normally attributed to menus and toolbars is only perceived — because of the different appearances that programmers create. You typically create menu captions by using text or, in some cases, icons, whereas, typically you create toolbar options with just icons (although they may also contain text).

You can add the following procedures to the code module of a `Workbook` object in order to create a custom toolbar containing a single button. When you open the workbook file that contains these procedures, the `Open()` event procedure of the `Workbook` object is triggered. The `Open()` event procedure calls the `AddToolbar()` Sub procedure, which creates a new `CommandBar` object with one button in much the same way the custom menu bar was created earlier. The difference is that the new `CommandBar` object is not docked (`Position:=msoBarFloating`), and its button (`CommandBarButton` object named `tlbMyButton`) is assigned both a caption and an image. The Sub procedure `RemoveToolbar()` ensures that the custom toolbar is deleted when the user closes the workbook. Without the `RemoveToolbar()` Sub procedure, the toolbar remains visible to the user even after the workbook is closed and will be included in the list of toolbars from the Excel application window (View menu). This may or may not be your objective. If not, using procedures similar to these is a good way to provide a custom toolbar or menu as an interface to the user for exclusive use with a particular VBA project or projects included in a workbook. Figure 9.4 shows the toolbar resulting from the execution of the `AddToolbar()` Sub procedure.

```
Private tlbMyToolbar As CommandBar
Private Sub Workbook_BeforeClose(Cancel As Boolean)
'Remove the toolbar before closing the workbook.
    RemoveToolbar ("Example Toolbar")
End Sub
Private Sub Workbook_Open()
'Remove toolbar (if it exists) before creating
'a new toolbar of the same name.
    RemoveToolbar ("Example Toolbar")
    AddToolbar
    Application.DisplayAlerts = False
End Sub
Private Sub AddToolbar()
    Dim tlbMyButton As CommandBarButton
```

```
'Set module-level toolbar variable to create a new empty toolbar
    Set tlbMyToolbar = Application.CommandBars.Add( _
        Name:="Example Toolbar", _
        Position:=msoBarFloating, _
        Temporary:=True)
    tlbMyToolbar.Visible = True

'Add a button to the new toolbar. Include image and text
    Set tlbMyButton = tlbMyToolbar.Controls.Add( _
        Type:=msoControlButton, _
        Temporary:=True)
    tlbMyButton.Style = msoButtonIconAndCaption
    tlbMyButton.Picture = LoadPicture( _
                        ActiveWorkbook.Path & "\myImage.bmp")
    tlbMyButton.Caption = "Test"
End Sub


Private Sub RemoveToolbar(tlbarName As String)
'Removes a toolbar specified by the name passed in
    Dim cBar As CommandBar
    For Each cBar In Application.CommandBars
        If cBar.Name = tlbarName Then
            cBar.Delete
            Exit For
        End If
    Next
End Sub
```

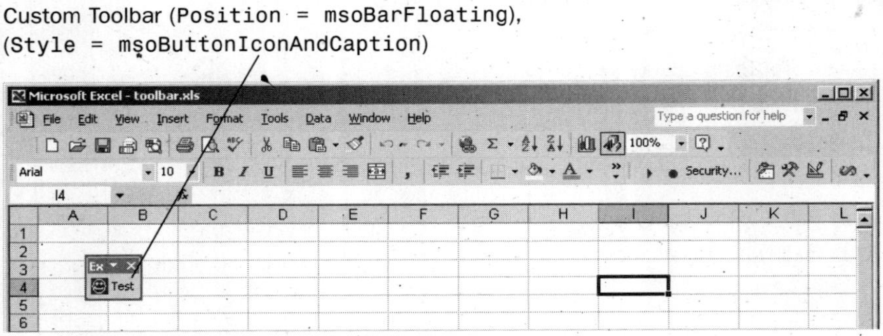

Custom Toolbar (Position = msoBarFloating),
(Style = msoButtonIconAndCaption)

FIGURE 9.4 *Creating a custom toolbar with a VBA program.*

Using and Creating Excel Add-Ins

Add-ins are files containing functions and programs that can be loaded into Excel to provide additional features for the user. Excel comes with several add-in programs, including a data analysis pack that provides numerous statistical functions and applications, a solver function for performing nonlinear optimization of a user-defined model on a data set, and more. Figure 9.5 shows the Add-Ins dialog box, which you access by selecting Tools, Add-Ins.

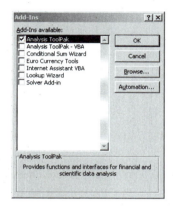

FIGURE 9.5 *Loading Excel add-ins.*

You can write programs in VBA that use the objects and functions from add-ins, but prior to doing so, the add-in must be loaded by either the user or the program. To load an add-in from a VBA program, use the `AddIns` property of the `Application` object to return the `AddIns` collection object and set the `Installed` property to `True`. The following example loads the Analysis ToolPak add-in that comes with Excel:

```
Application.AddIns("Analysis ToolPak").Installed = True
```

After the add-in is installed, its functions and objects are available for use in your VBA program. The next line of code generates 100 random numbers in a normal distribution and places them in the range A2:A101 in the active worksheet.

```
Application.Run "Random", ActiveSheet.Range("$A$2"), 1, 100, 2, 55, 72, 7
```

The Analysis ToolPak contains several functions; therefore, you use the `Run` method of the `Application` object to access the `Random()` function contained in the add-in file. The arguments passed to the `Random()` function in the preceding example represent the location in the worksheet in which to place the random numbers (`$A$2`), the number of variables (`1`), the number of random numbers to generate (`100`), the type of distribution (`2=Normal`), the random seed (`55`), the average value (`72`), and the standard deviation (`7`).

NOTE

Excel add-ins are stored with the .xla extension and are usually found in the Library folder of the Office directory on your hard drive. The number of installed add-ins may vary from one computer to the next depending on the installation procedure followed. So you may need to include an error handler in your code that catches errors that result from trying to access an add-in that is not installed. To learn how to write an error handler, see Chapter 8, "Understanding File I/O, Debugging, and Error Handling in VBA."

Space does not allow me to discuss the multitude of add-ins in detail, and programming techniques can vary significantly from one add-in to another. Furthermore, depending on the add-in, the online documentation may be sparse or nonexistent. If you want to use one of the features available from an add-in in your program, record a macro and examine the resulting code. For functions available from the Analysis ToolPak, you just need to know how many arguments must be passed to the function.

Although functions and programs from existing Excel add-ins are available for use in your VBA programs, of more interest to VBA programmers is creating your own add-ins to represent a library of useful VBA programs and functions. Saving your VBA programs as add-ins is another way to deliver your functions and programs to the user. Creating an add-in from a VBA project is easy — just create your VBA program as usual and then save it using the .xla extension (see Figure 9.6).

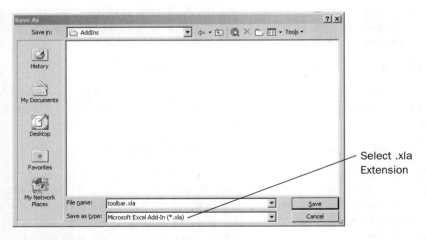

FIGURE 9.6 *Creating an Excel add-in file from the Save As dialog box.*

To see your add-in listed in the Add-Ins dialog box, you must install the add-in in the proper directory, which is normally the Library subfolder included in the Office folder created upon installation (for example, C:\Program Files\Microsoft Office\Office10\Library). To find the correct directory, search for an existing add-in file (EUROTOOL.XLA, HTML.XLA, LOOKUP.XLA, or SUMIF.XLA) and place your custom add-in within the same directory.

Summary

In this chapter, you learned how to create custom menus and toolbars to expand the user interface for your VBA programs. Although custom menus and toolbars can be created in Excel and displayed with any workbook, it is less intrusive to users if you use a VBA program so that they are created and deleted on demand. This way, users never have to see the toolbar unless a program requiring it is loaded. You also learned how to begin programming with existing Excel add-ins such as the Analysis ToolPak. Finally, I showed you how to save your VBA programs as add-ins that the user can load as desired.

Chapter 10

harts are valuable tools for data analysis and presentation in Excel and other spreadsheet applications. Excel's Chart object is substantial, and you will find that its learning curve is a bit longer and steeper than other components in the Excel object model.

Although this chapter takes you through the basics on creating and manipulating charts with VBA, before attempting to program using Excel's Chart object, you need to understand the common chart types and their components. So, before proceeding, I suggest that you turn to Appendix A, where you will find a brief tutorial describing the more common types of Excel charts.

Programming with Excel's Chart Object

If you have created charts in high-end spreadsheet applications other than Excel, you know that the charting tools in Excel are not as good as in other applications. Furthermore, working with Excel charts is not always an intuitive process. It is difficult to format some components of an Excel chart simply because it is difficult to access the correct dialog box.

Programming with Excel's Chart object can (at times) be an equally frustrating process because the names of the objects in the Chart object model don't always make sense. In addition, the Chart object model is quite extensive and can be a bit intimidating. Figure 10.1 shows a graphical representation of Excel's Chart object model as found in the online help.

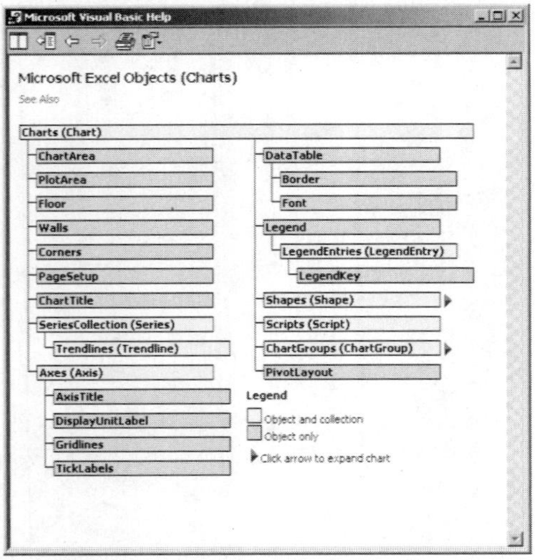

FIGURE 10.1 *The Chart object model.*

However, you should not be intimidated by the breadth of Excel's `Chart` object model since its use follows the same programming rules as other VBA and Excel objects. Understanding Excel's `Chart` object model is simply a matter of becoming familiar with the objects and gaining experience with them via your programming.

Excel has several types of charts, including, among others, column, bar, line, and scatter charts. Each type of chart has several subtypes. For example, the column chart type contains clustered, stacked, and 100% stacked subtypes. In addition, most chart types have three-dimensional versions of their subtypes, which adds to the total number of chart types to choose from when creating a chart.

When programming with the `Chart` object, depending on the chart type and its subtype, different objects will be available for use in your program. For example, unlike the area, column, and bar charts, a line chart does not have an `Interior` object subordinate to its `Series` object. As a result, you cannot set the `ColorIndex` property of the `Interior` object of the `Series` object for a line chart.

Another decision regarding charts is whether to create an embedded chart or a chart sheet. An *embedded chart* is one that is placed on the drawing layer of a worksheet. A given worksheet can contain any number of embedded charts. A *chart sheet* is a separate sheet in the workbook and can contain only one chart. As you are about to see, there are differences between programming with embedded charts and chart sheets; however, you access both via the `Chart` object.

Accessing Existing Charts

Using VBA to programmatically control chart sheets and embedded charts involves using different objects that, at first, can be a little confusing. Ultimately, you access chart sheets and embedded charts using the `Chart` object, but the path to an embedded chart differs significantly from the path to a chart sheet.

Accessing Chart Sheets and Embedded Charts

Chart sheets are members of the `Sheets` collection object and, as such, must be accessed using the `Sheets` collection. The `Sheets` collection also contains all `Worksheet` objects in a workbook, so you must use the `Charts` property of the `Workbook` object to access just the chart sheets. For example, consider a workbook that contains multiple worksheets and chart sheets. To access a particular chart sheet, use the `Charts` property of the `Workbook` object and an index value or chart sheet name, as shown in the following:

```
ActiveWorkbook.Charts(1).Select
```

The `Charts` property returns the `Charts` collection containing all chart sheets in the specified workbook. Specifying an index with the `Charts` property returns a specific chart sheet from the collection.

The `GetChartSheets()` Sub procedure accesses only those sheets from the `Sheets` collection that are chart sheets. The object variable `myCharts` is declared as a collection object (type `Sheets`) and is set to contain all chart sheets in the active workbook using the `Charts` property of the `Workbook` object. A `For/Each` loop iterates through each chart sheet in the collection and outputs the value of the `Name` property of each `Chart` object to the Immediate window (see Figure 10.2). The `Name` property corresponds to the text entered into the tab at the bottom of a chart sheet, and the `GetChartSheets()` Sub procedure will output as many chart names as there are chart sheets in the active workbook.

```
Public Sub GetChartSheets()
    Dim myCharts As Sheets
    Dim chSheet As Chart
    Set myCharts = ActiveWorkbook.Charts
    For Each chSheet In myCharts
        Debug.Print chSheet.Name
    Next
End Sub
```

FIGURE 10.2 *VBA's Immediate window showing output from the* `GetChartSheets()` *Sub procedure.*

To access embedded charts, use the `ChartObjects` collection object and the `ChartObject` object.

```
ActiveSheet.ChartObjects(1).Select
```

The `ChartObjects` collection object represents all `ChartObjects` in a single worksheet. The `ChartObject` object is a container object for a single `Chart` object, so the code to access the actual chart is slightly different than the preceding code. Confusion between the `ChartObject` object and the `Chart` object will be a common source of error in your VBA code when programming using the Chart object. Consider the GetEmbeddedCharts() Sub procedure listed next:

```
Public Sub GetEmbeddedCharts()
    Dim myChart As ChartObject
    Dim myCharts As ChartObjects
    Set myCharts = ActiveSheet.ChartObjects
    For Each myChart In myCharts
        Debug.Print myChart.Chart.Name
    Next
End Sub
```

You declare the variable myChart as a ChartObject object and use it to access each embedded chart in the active worksheet. The variable myCharts represents a ChartObjects collection referenced to the ChartObjects contained in the active worksheet. Again, a For/Each loop iterates through each ChartObject object. However, to access the actual chart object and not just the container object, you must use the Chart property (myChart.Chart.Name) of the ChartObject object. Without the reference to the Chart object, the preceding procedure would output the value of the Name property of a ChartObject object, which is not the same as the Name property of the Chart object.

Table 10.1 summarizes the objects in VBA used to access Excel charts.

Table 10.1 VBA Objects Used to Access Excel Charts

Object	Function
Sheets collection	Represents a collection of all sheets in the specified workbook including chart sheets and worksheets.
Charts collection	Represents a collection of all chart sheets in the specified workbook.
Chart	Represents a single chart (embedded or as a chart sheet).
ChartObjects collection	Represents a collection of all ChartObject objects in the specified worksheet.
ChartObject	Represents the container object for an embedded chart.

Manipulating Charts

The Chart object contains numerous properties and subordinate objects that you can use to alter the appearance of an Excel chart. Examples of the ChartType and SeriesCollection properties are included in Chapter 4, "Understanding VBA Procedures." The properties and objects that are common to most chart types and the components of a chart they represent are shown in Figure 10.3.

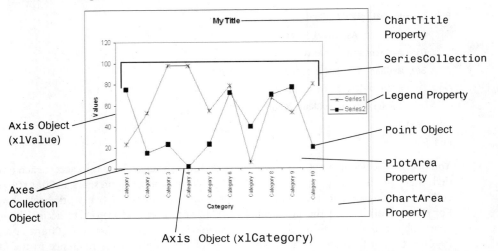

FIGURE 10.3 *A line chart illustrating the components represented by objects in Excel's* Chart *object model.*

The Sub procedures ChartInterior(), SetXAxis(), TestSeries(), and TestPoint() are written to alter a few properties of the line chart shown in Figure 10.3. The chart is embedded on a worksheet, so you must access it using the ChartObjects collection.

The ChartInterior() Sub procedure uses the RGB() function to set the interior of several chart components to a randomly selected color. The ChartArea, PlotArea, Legend, and ChartTitle properties of the Chart object return their corresponding objects before setting their interior to the same randomly selected colors. Running this procedure will homogeneously fill the chart with color. Note that you must test the chart for the existence of a ChartTitle object before altering any of the properties of the ChartTitle object.

```
Public Sub ChartInterior()
    Dim myChart As Chart
    Dim ranNum1 As Integer, ranNum2 As Integer, ranNum3 As Integer
    Randomize      'Use system clock
    ranNum1 = Rnd * 256: ranNum2 = Rnd * 256: ranNum3 = Rnd * 256
    'Reference embedded chart
    Set myChart = ActiveSheet.ChartObjects(1).Chart
    With myChart    'Alter interior colors of chart components
        .ChartArea.Interior.Color = RGB(ranNum1, ranNum2, ranNum3)
        .PlotArea.Interior.Color = RGB(ranNum1, ranNum2, ranNum3)
```

```
        .Legend.Interior.Color = RGB(ranNum1, ranNum2, ranNum3)
        If .HasTitle Then
            .ChartTitle.Interior.Color = RGB(ranNum1, ranNum2, ranNum3)
        End If
    End With
End Sub
```

The SetXAxis() Sub procedure sets several properties of an Axis object selected from the Axes collection object. An Axis object represents a single axis in a chart. By using the constant xlCategory, you select the x-axis (horizontal axis) in a univariate chart (use xlValue to select the y-axis).

 NOTE

A *univariate* chart is one that charts a single set of values in any one data series instead of charting two sets of data as a single series. Examples of univariate charts include the column, bar, pie, and area charts. A multivariate chart, such as Excel's scatter chart, plots a single data series as x,y points representing two sets of values.

A Range object is passed to the CategoryNames property for setting the categories displayed on the chart. The CategoryNames property only applies to charts that include categories, and then only when the Axis object is of type xlCategory. This is another example that serves to emphasize that you have to understand the structure of the chart you are manipulating in order to effectively set its properties.

```
Public Sub SetXAxis()
'Adds major gridlines, title, and x-axis labels to an embedded chart
    Dim myAxis As Axis
    Dim ranNum1 As Integer, ranNum2 As Integer, ranNum3 As Integer
    Randomize
    ranNum1 = Rnd * 256: ranNum2 = Rnd * 256: ranNum3 = Rnd * 256
    'Set object reference to category axis on existing embedded chart
    Set myAxis = ActiveSheet.ChartObjects(1).Chart.Axes( _
                        xlCategory, xlPrimary)
    With myAxis      'Set properties of x-axis
        .HasMajorGridlines = True
        .HasTitle = True
        .AxisTitle.Text = "My Axis"
        .AxisTitle.Font.Color = RGB(ranNum1, ranNum2, ranNum3)
        .CategoryNames = Range("C2:C11")
```

```
        .TickLabels.Font.Color = RGB(ranNum1, ranNum2, ranNum3)
    End With
End Sub
```

The result of executing the SetAxis() Sub procedure on the embedded chart shown in Figure 10.3 is shown in Figure 10.4.

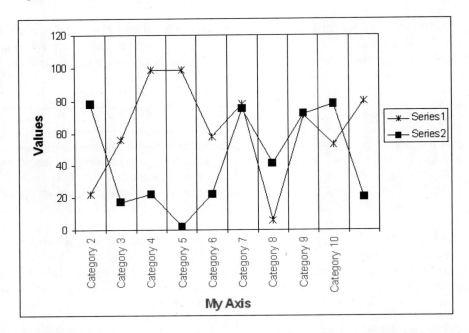

FIGURE 10.4 *Result of executing the* SetAxis() *Sub procedure on the embedded chart shown in Figure 10.3.*

Manipulating the aesthetic properties of charts is necessary for presentation, but ultimately charts are graphical representations of data. VBA therefore must provide objects that can be used to manipulate not only the appearance of the charted data, but their values as well. These objects include the SeriesCollection and Points collection objects that include Series and Point objects as their members, respectively.

A Series object is a member of the SeriesCollection collection object and represents a "series" of charted data. For example, you can tell that the chart in Figure 10.3 contains two Series objects because there are two data series charted and both are included in the chart legend. The Series object includes properties used to manipulate the markers, bars, columns (or other markers used to chart the data, depending on the chart type), and values in a data series.

The TestSeries() Sub procedure uses the SeriesCollection object to access each Series object in a chart and changes the color of the points and connecting lines in each data series. The color of the marker and connecting lines will remain uniform for each series, but each series is randomly assigned a different color. This code will execute properly only on chart types that include markers and lines (line and scatter).

```
Public Sub TestSeries()
    Dim mySeries As Series
    Dim seriesCol As SeriesCollection
    Dim ranNum1 As Integer, ranNum2 As Integer, ranNum3 As Integer
    Dim I As Integer
    Randomize
    I = 1
    'Set reference to the series collection
    Set seriesCol = ActiveSheet.ChartObjects(1).Chart.SeriesCollection
    'Loop through each series in chart and alter marker colors
    For Each mySeries In seriesCol
        ranNum1 = Rnd * 256: ranNum2 = Rnd * 256: ranNum3 = Rnd * 256
        Set mySeries = ActiveSheet.ChartObjects(1).Chart.SeriesCollection(I)
        With mySeries
            .MarkerBackgroundColor = RGB(ranNum1, ranNum2, ranNum3)
            .MarkerForegroundColor = RGB(ranNum1, ranNum2, ranNum3)
            .Border.Color = RGB(ranNum1, ranNum2, ranNum3)
        End With
        I = I + 1
    Next
End Sub
```

The `Series` object provides access to the values and markers associated with the entire data set. To access a single datum in a series, you need the `Points` collection object and `Point` object. A `Points` collection object represents the collection of data points in a series, and a `Point` object represents an individual point.

The `TestPoint()` Sub procedure accesses the third point in a `Points` collection and adds the data label for the point to the chart before changing the color of the marker. Note that the path to the individual point follows from the `Chart` object to the `Series` object before referencing the specific `Point` object.

```
Public Sub TestPoint()
    Dim myPoint As Point
    Dim ranNum1 As Integer, ranNum2 As Integer, ranNum3 As Integer
    Randomize
    ranNum1 = Rnd * 256: ranNum2 = Rnd * 256: ranNum3 = Rnd * 256
```

```
    Set myPoint = ActiveSheet.ChartObjects(1).Chart. _
                            SeriesCollection(1).Points(3)
    With myPoint
        .ApplyDataLabels xlDataLabelsShowValue
        .MarkerBackgroundColor = RGB(ranNum1, ranNum2, ranNum3)
        .MarkerForegroundColor = RGB(ranNum1, ranNum2, ranNum3)
    End With
End Sub
```

The result of executing the `TestPoint()` Sub procedure on the embedded chart shown in Figure 10.3 is shown in Figure 10.5.

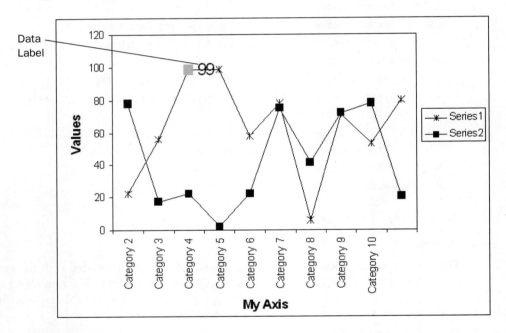

FIGURE 10.5 *Result of executing the* `TestPoint()` *Sub procedure on the embedded chart shown in Figure 10.3.*

The Pie Clock

The following short VBA program simulates an analog clock by using a pie chart. I first created the pie chart non-programmatically (from the Excel application window) as an embedded chart on a worksheet named "Pie Clock." I formatted the pie chart with colors for its chart area and plot area and added shapes (numbers for the clock) using the text box tool on the drawing toolbar. The resulting worksheet is shown in Figure 10.6.

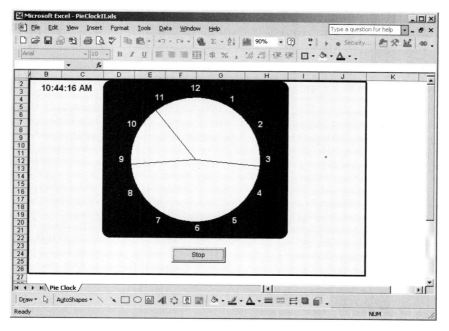

FIGURE 10.6 *A pie chart simulation of an analog clock.*

The idea is to create three pie slices for the chart orientated at the proper angle to represent the blocks of time between the second, minute, and hour hands. Placing a Command Button control (named cmdStart) on the worksheet activates and deactivates the clock via its Click() event procedure by calling the Sub procedure StartTime().

```
Private Sub cmdStart_Click()
    If cmdStart.Caption = "Start" Then
        cmdStart.Caption = "Stop"
        StartTime
    Else
        cmdStart.Caption = "Start"
    End If
End Sub
```

The Sub procedure StartTime() does most of the work by calculating the size of the slices for the pie and their proper orientation. The OnTime method of the Application object calls the StartTime() Sub procedure every second. The OnTime method accepts up to four arguments (EarliestTime, Procedure, LatestTime, and Schedule) that set the time the designated procedure is to be executed. Setting the EarliestTime argument to one second later than the current system time, the Procedure to the StartTime() Sub procedure, and the Schedule argument to True ensures that the StartTime() Sub procedure is executed every second. Note that the minimum resolution for the `OnTime` method of the `Application` object is one second.

 TIP

Always use an error handler with the `OnTime` method of the `Application` object that will disable the procedure call if an error occurs. Otherwise, if an error occurs, you will repeatedly see an error message displayed as the `OnTime` method calls the procedure.

```
Public Sub StartTime()
     Dim minutesPassed As Single, hoursPassed As Single, secondsPassed As Integer
     Dim perMinPass As Single, perHourPass As Single, perSecPass As Single
     Dim pieSlice(2) As Single
     Dim sliceAngle As Integer
     Dim PieClock As Chart

     On Error GoTo ErrorHandler
     'Call this procedure every second.
     Application.OnTime EarliestTime:=Now + TimeValue("00:00:01"), _
                        Procedure:="PieClock.StartTime", Schedule:=True


     '-------------------------------------------------
     'Find hours, minutes and seconds for analog clock.
     '-------------------------------------------------
     Range("B2").Value = Time
     If Hour(Time) > 11 Then
          hoursPassed = Hour(Time) - 12
     Else
          hoursPassed = Hour(Time)
     End If
     minutesPassed = Minute(Time)
     secondsPassed = Second(Time)
     '
     '-----------------------------------------------------
     'Calculate %'s of 60 minutes for hours minutes and second
     'relative to 12:00:00.  Use a 12 hour clock.
     '-----------------------------------------------------
```

```vb
    perHourPass = 100 * (hoursPassed + minutesPassed / 60 + _
                            secondsPassed / 3600) / 12
    perMinPass = 100 * (minutesPassed + secondsPassed / 60) / 60
    perSecPass = 100 * secondsPassed / 60


    '---------------------------------------------
    'Calculate %'s of time passed for 3 pie slices
    '---------------------------------------------

    pieSlice(0) = Application.WorksheetFunction.Min( _
                perHourPass, perMinPass, perSecPass) _
                + (100 - Application.WorksheetFunction.Max( _
                perHourPass, perMinPass, perSecPass))
    pieSlice(1) = 100 - pieSlice(0) - (Application.WorksheetFunction _
                .Max(perHourPass, perMinPass, perSecPass) _
                - Application.WorksheetFunction.Large( _
                Array(perHourPass, perMinPass, perSecPass), 2))
    pieSlice(2) = 100 - pieSlice(1) - pieSlice(0)


    '-------------------------------------------
    'Calculate angle for first pie slice.
    'Base it on max % value of hour, min, or sec.
    '-------------------------------------------

    sliceAngle = 360 * Application.WorksheetFunction.Max( _
                perHourPass, perMinPass, perSecPass) / 100


    Set PieClock = Worksheets("Pie Clock").ChartObjects("Chart 2").Chart
    With PieClock
        .ChartGroups(1).FirstSliceAngle = sliceAngle
        .SeriesCollection(1).Values = Array(pieSlice(0), pieSlice(1), _
                pieSlice(2))
    End With


    If cmdStart.Caption = "Start" Then
        Application.OnTime EarliestTime:=Now + TimeValue("00:00:01"), _
                Procedure:="PieClock.StartTime", Schedule:=False
    End If


    Exit Sub
```

```
ErrorHandler:
    MsgBox (Err.Description & vbCrLf & "The clock will be stopped.")
    Application.OnTime EarliestTime:=Now + TimeValue("00:00:01"), _
              Procedure:="PieClock.StartTime", Schedule:=False
End Sub
```

After establishing the frequency of the procedure calls with the OnTime method, the StartTime() Sub procedure calculates the percentage of a clock passed by for the hour, minute, and second hands. For example, at 30 seconds past the minute, 50% of the clock is passed by the second hand; and at 30 minutes and 30 seconds past the hour, 50.83% of the clock is passed by the minute hand, and so on.

From these percentages, the size of the three slices for the pie chart are calculated and stored in the array pieSlice. The first line on the pie chart will always be at 12:00:00 if the angle of the first slice is set to its default value of zero degrees. Thus, the angle of the first pie slice must be adjusted such that the line originally at 12:00:00 will always represent the hand of the clock at the maximum percentage. For example, when the time is 3:21:54, the second hand has traversed the largest percentage of the clock (90%), so the second hand must be used to calculate the angle of the first slice, which, in this example, is 324 degrees.

You update the Chart object with the correct time by setting the FirstSliceAngle property and then setting the Values property of the Series object to the previously calculated percentages. You use a parameter array to set the Values property of the Series object, but you could use a Range object if you first write the values to the worksheet. Finally, if the user clicks the Command Button control when its Caption property reads Stop, the OnTime method (with its Schedule argument set to False) disables all future calls to the StartTime() Sub procedure.

Creating Charts

To write a VBA procedure that creates a chart, you must decide whether to create a chart sheet or embed the chart in an existing worksheet. The difference between creating a chart sheet and an embedded chart is subtle, as you will see in the following code listings.

Creating a Chart Sheet

The Sub procedure AddChartSheet() creates a new chart sheet with a column chart (ChartType = xlColumnClustered) of data selected from a worksheet by the user. The Add method of the Charts collection object creates a new chart sheet. Remember that the Charts collection object represents a collection of chart sheets in a workbook (refer to Table 10.1 for VBA objects that are used to access Excel charts). After the chart sheet is added, the chart it contains automatically becomes active because it is the only component of the sheet. Next, a With/End With structure modifies the properties of the Chart object. Many of these subordinate objects and properties have common sense names, so their function is intuitive. There are a large number of chart types available to choose from. Table 10.2 lists some of the more common types.

Table 10.2 Common Excel Chart Types

Chart	VBA Constant (ChartType **property of** Chart **object**)
Column	xlColumnClustered, xlColumnStacked, xlColumnStacked100
Bar	xlBarClustered, xlBarStacked, xlBarStacked100
Line	xlLine, xlLineMarkersStacked, xlLineStacked
Pie	xlPie, xlPieOfPie
Scatter	xlXYScatter, xlXYScatterLines

The Axes method of the Chart object returns a specific Axis object by passing defined constants for the type (xlCategory, xlSeries, or xlValue) and group (xlPrimary or xlSecondary). The axis type xlCategory represents the x-axis on the chart, and xlValue represents the y-axis. The axis type xlSeries applies only to 3-D charts and represents the z-axis. The axis group is either xlPrimary (default) or xlSecondary (may be applied to charts containing multiple Series objects).

The rest of the objects and properties set via the Axis object are fairly straightforward and include setting tick marks and chart labels. You set the upper limit of the y-axis scale using Excel worksheet functions that return the maximum value from the dataRange range variable (defined at the beginning of the procedure) rounded up to single digit precision. Finally, you add the data to the chart by setting the Values property of the Series object (returned from the SeriesCollection collection object) to the range variable dataRange.

```
Public Sub AddChartSheet()
    Dim dataRange As Range
    'Chart the selected worksheet data
    Set dataRange = ActiveWindow.Selection
    Charts.Add    'Create a chart sheet
    With ActiveChart    'Set chart properties
        .ChartType = xlColumnClustered
        .HasLegend = True
        .Legend.Position = xlRight

        .Axes(xlCategory).MinorTickMark = xlOutside
        .Axes(xlValue).MinorTickMark = xlOutside
        .Axes(xlValue).MaximumScale = _
```

```
                    Application.WorksheetFunction.RoundUp( _
                    Application.WorksheetFunction.Max(dataRange), -1)
        .Axes(xlCategory).HasTitle = True
        .Axes(xlCategory).AxisTitle.Characters.Text = "X-axis Labels"
        .Axes(xlValue).HasTitle = True
        .Axes(xlValue).AxisTitle.Characters.Text = "Y-axis"

        .SeriesCollection(1).Name = "Sample Data"
        .SeriesCollection(1).Values = dataRange
    End With

End Sub
```

When you select worksheet data and run the `AddChartSheet()` Sub procedure, a chart sheet similar to the chart sheet shown in Figure 10.7 is created. Of course, the number of columns will change with the number of values selected.

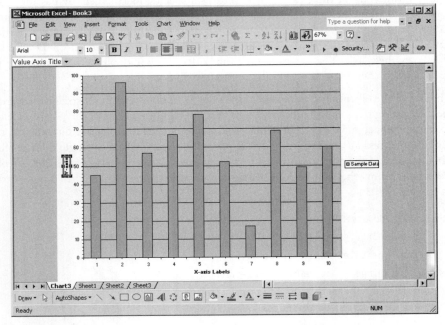

FIGURE 10.7 *A chart sheet created by the* `AddChartSheet()` *Sub procedure.*

Creating an Embedded Chart

To add an embedded chart to a worksheet, use the `Add` method of the `ChartObects` collection object. When you add an embedded chart, the `Add` method accepts four arguments that define the position of the upper-left corner of the chart on the worksheet as well as the chart width and height. The position properties of the Add method (Left and Top) are relative to the upper-left corner of cell A1 and are in units of points. Using the Activate method of the ChartObject object is equivalent to selecting the chart because only one Chart object is contained in a ChartObject object.

Before setting properties of the Chart object, the chart must contain at least one Series object. Therefore, you use the NewSeries method of the SeriesCollection object to add an empty Series object to the chart. This is another difference between creating embedded charts and creating chart sheets — upon creation of a chart sheet, a Series object is automatically added. The properties of the Chart object representing an embedded chart are set in the same manner as is done with a chart sheet.

```
Public Sub AddEmbeddedChart()
    Dim dataRange As Range
    Set dataRange = ActiveWindow.Selection    'Chart selected data
    ActiveSheet.ChartObjects.Add Left:=200, Top:=50, Width:=500, _
                                    Height:=350
    ActiveSheet.ChartObjects(1).Activate
    With ActiveChart       'Set chart properties
        .ChartType = xlColumnClustered
        .SeriesCollection.NewSeries
        .HasLegend = True
        .Legend.Position = xlRight
        .Axes(xlCategory).MinorTickMark = xlOutside
        .Axes(xlValue).MinorTickMark = xlOutside
        .Axes(xlValue).MaximumScale = Application _
                .WorksheetFunction.RoundUp( _
                Application.WorksheetFunction.Max(dataRange), -1)
        .Axes(xlCategory, xlPrimary).HasTitle = True
        .Axes(xlCategory, xlPrimary).AxisTitle.Characters.Text = _
            "X-axis Labels"
        .Axes(xlValue, xlPrimary).HasTitle = True
        .Axes(xlValue, xlPrimary).AxisTitle.Characters.Text = "Y-axis"
        .SeriesCollection(1).Name = "Sample Data"
        .SeriesCollection(1).Values = dataRange
    End With
End Sub
```

When you select worksheet data and run the AddEmbeddedChart() Sub procedure, an embedded chart similar to that shown in Figure 10.8 is created.

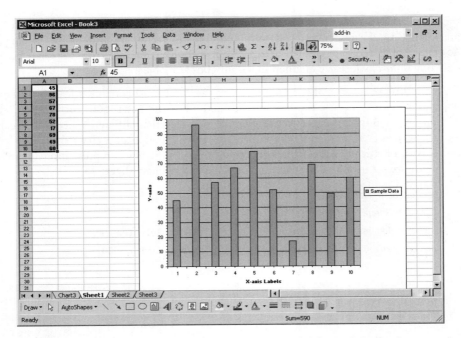

FIGURE 10.8 *A chart sheet created by the* `AddEmbeddedChart()` *Sub procedure.*

The examples for adding a chart sheet and embedded chart demonstrate only a small fraction of the objects, properties, and methods available in a `Chart` object. However, once you learn how to access a chart, setting the properties of any of its component objects is basically the same. The hard part is learning what objects are available to the specific chart being manipulated. The number of component objects in a `Chart` object varies with the chart type (column, bar, scatter, and so on) and with the sub-category of chart type (clustered, stacked, 3-D, and so on). For example, a 3-D column chart has `Wall`, `Floor`, and `Corners` objects, but a clustered column chart does not have these objects.

To learn the differences between chart types, or to just learn what is available for specific chart types, use recorded macros. First, create the chart from the Excel application and then alter its appearance with the macro recorder turned on. Be careful to record only a small number of actions (2–3) at one time because the macro recorder adds a lot of unnecessary code (setting default values). Keep in mind that as you select a component of the chart with the mouse, you are really selecting a component object of the `Chart` object. The dialog box that appears when the component object is double-clicked (or selected from the chart menu) sets the properties of that object. For example, the Format Axis dialog box shown in Figure 10.9 appears when the user double-clicks a chart axis.

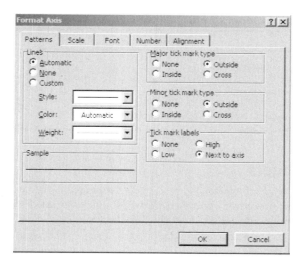

FIGURE 10.9 *The Format Axis dialog box.*

Figure 10.9 shows some of the properties of the Axis object. The area labeled Lines sets the Border property of the Axis object, and the remaining areas of the figure set the MajorTickMark, MinorTickMark, and TickLabelPosition properties. If the macro recorder is on while these properties are altered, the VBA code used to set these properties will be recorded when you click OK. After recording a small macro, proceed to the VBA IDE to examine the recorded code. If you need help understanding any of the recorded code, select the VBA keyword of interest within your recorded macro code and press F1 to retrieve its documentation from the online help. Accessing the online help directly from a VBA keyword is a big help when learning how to program specific Excel components, so be sure to exploit the advantage it provides.

Chart Events

The Chart object has several events that are triggered by various user actions. Some of the events are familiar (Activate, MouseDown, MouseUp, and so on), but a few are unique to the Chart object. Table 10.3 summarizes the unique events associated with the Chart object.

Table 10.3 Chart Object Events

Event	Trigger
Calculate()	When new or changed data is charted
DragOver()	When a range of cells is dragged over a chart
DragPlot()	When a range of cells is dragged and dropped on a chart

continues

Table 10.3 Chart Object Events _(continued)_

Event	Trigger
Resize()	When the chart is resized
Select()	When a chart element is selected
SeriesChange()	When the value of a charted data point changes

Events with Chart Sheets

Chart sheets automatically enable chart events. To catch events triggered by the user in a chart sheet, add code to an event procedure contained in the module associated with the chart sheet. You open a code window for a chart sheet the same way you open a code window for a worksheet. Figure 10.10 shows the code window of a chart sheet selected from the Project Explorer. The active project displayed in Figure 10.10 is an Excel workbook containing a single chart sheet.

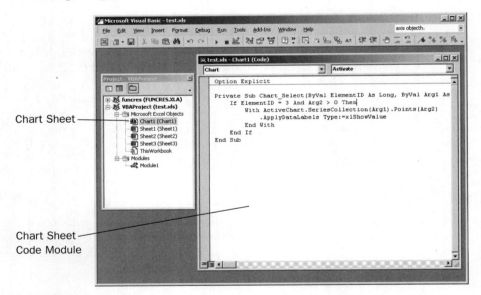

FIGURE 10.10 _Adding code to an event procedure of a chart sheet._

Unfortunately, most of the events unique to the Chart object cannot be used with a chart sheet because a user has no means of triggering them. For example, a user cannot drag and drop a range of cells over the chart when the data is in another worksheet. However, the other chart events work as expected. Here is an example using the Select() event procedure of the Chart object:

```
Private Sub Chart_Select(ByVal ElementID As Long, ByVal Arg1 As Long, _
                    ByVal Arg2 As Long)
    If ElementID = 3 And Arg2 > 0 Then
        With ActiveChart.SeriesCollection(Arg1).Points(Arg2)
            .ApplyDataLabels Type:=xlShowValue
        End With
    End If
End Sub
```

The Select() event procedure of the Chart object accepts three arguments: ElementID is a Long integer that refers to the component or element selected by the user (ChartArea, PlotArea, Series, and so on), and Arg1 and Arg2 are Long integers that refer to specific components of the selected object. In the preceding example, when the user selects a single data point on the chart, Arg1 holds the index value of the selected Series object, and Arg2 holds the index value of the selected Point object (both values must be greater than zero). The purpose of the procedure is to add a label to any point in a data series selected by the user. To accomplish this purpose, the argument ElementID is tested for equivalence to three (VBA-defined constant xlSeries; see online help for additional constants). If the user has selected a single point in a data series, the selected point is labeled with its value by using the ApplyDataLabels method and setting the Type argument to the constant xlShowValue. In this example, Arg2 holds the value −1 if the entire series is selected and will not hold a meaningful value until the user selects an individual point from the data series. When the user does select an individual data point, the value of Arg2 is passed to the Points method, which returns a Point object from the Points collection object. In this case, the Points method returns the specific data point selected by the user.

 TIP

To learn how to use the Select() event procedure of the Chart object, I added the statement Debug.Print ElementID; Arg1; Arg2 to the procedure and watched the Immediate window while I selected various components of the Chart object.

Events with Embedded Charts

To use all the event procedures of the Chart object, the chart must be embedded on a worksheet. Unfortunately, chart events are not automatically enabled for embedded charts. To enable the events of an embedded chart, you must insert a class module (in the VBA IDE, select Insert, Class Module) into the project and declare an object of type Chart.

You must declare the `Chart` object using the keyword `With Events` in the general declarations section of the class module.

```
Public WithEvents myChartClass As Chart
```

After you enter the preceding statement, the `myChartClass` object appears in the object drop-down list of the class module code window, and its event procedures are listed in the event drop-down list (see Figure 10.11).

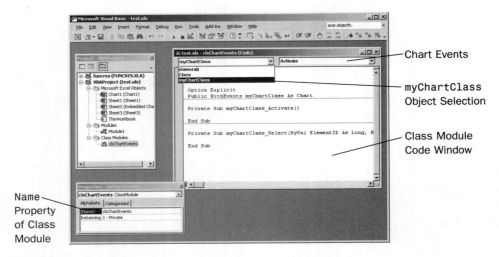

FIGURE 10.11 *Enabling event procedures of an embedded chart.*

You use class modules to define a new class. In Chapter 7, "VBA Objects Specific to Excel Programming," I note that a class represents an object definition. The task of defining new objects is discussed in the next chapter. In this case, there is no need to create a new object because the `Chart` object is already defined in VBA. All you need to do is to enable the events for the embedded chart. After declaring the `Chart` object with events in the class module, connect it to the embedded chart with the following declaration and initialization Sub procedure. The `InitializeChart()` Sub procedure can be added to any code module except a class module; however, it is best placed in a standard module.

```
Private myClassModule As New clsChartEvents
Public Sub InitializeChart()
    Set myClassModule.myChartClass = Worksheets( _
            "Embedded Chart").ChartObjects(1).Chart
End Sub
```

In this example, the class module was named `clsChartEvents` (changed from `Class1`) using the Properties window. So, the preceding declaration creates an instance of an object variable of type `clsChartEvents`, much like any other variable declaration. Before the event procedures created in the class module will work, the specific embedded chart must be connected to the myClassModule object. This is accomplished with the InitializeChart() Sub procedure that contains a single line of code used to set the object reference. In this case, the object reference is set to the first chart embedded on the worksheet named Embedded Chart. The InitializeChart() Sub procedure must run before the event procedures of the Chart object defined in the class module will work.

After the InitializeChart() Sub procedure is executed, the event procedures of the referenced chart object contained in the clsChartEvents class module are enabled. Some of the event procedures are listed in the following code. Each procedure contains a single line of code that outputs a message to the worksheet telling users when they have triggered a specific chart event.

```
Option Explicit
Public WithEvents myChartClass As Chart
Private Sub myChartClass_DragOver()
    Range("L34").Value = "You have activated the DragOver() " _
            & "sub procedure."
End Sub
Private Sub myChartClass_DragPlot()
    Range("L34").Value = "You have activated the DragPlot() " _
            & "sub procedure."
End Sub
Private Sub myChartClass_MouseDown(ByVal Button As Long, _
        ByVal Shift As Long, ByVal x As Long, ByVal y As Long)
    Range("L34").Value = "You have activated the MouseDown() " _
            & "sub procedure."
End Sub
Private Sub myChartClass_MouseMove(ByVal Button As Long, _
        ByVal Shift As Long, ByVal x As Long, ByVal y As Long)
    Range("L34").Value = "You have activated the MouseMove() " _
            & "sub procedure."
End Sub
Private Sub myChartClass_MouseUp(ByVal Button As Long, _
        ByVal Shift As Long, ByVal x As Long, ByVal y As Long)
    Range("L34").Value = "You have activated the MouseUp() " _
            & "sub procedure."
End Sub
Private Sub myChartClass_Select(ByVal ElementID As Long, _
        ByVal Arg1 As Long, ByVal Arg2 As Long)
    If ElementID = 3 And Arg2 > 0 Then
```

```
        ActiveChart.SeriesCollection(Arg1).Points(Arg2) _
            .ApplyDataLabels Type:=xlShowValue
    End If
End Sub
Private Sub myChartClass_Resize()
    Range("L34").Value = "You have activated the Resize() " _
            & "sub procedure."
End Sub
Private Sub myChartClass_SeriesChange(ByVal SeriesIndex As Long, _
        ByVal PointIndex As Long)
        Range("L34").Value = "You have activated the SeriesChange() " _
            & "sub procedure."
End Sub
```

Users trigger the `DragOver()` and `DragPlot()` event procedures when they drag and release selected data over the chart, respectively. Users trigger the `SeriesChange()` event procedure when they select and move a single point on the chart, changing its value. Finally, users trigger the `Resize()` event procedure when they resize the chart. Before using the preceding sample code, you may want to comment out the `MouseMove()` event procedure as it interferes with the messages output by the `SeriesChange()` and `Resize()` event procedures.

Summary

In this chapter, you learned how to access, manipulate, and create Excel charts using the `Chart` object and its subordinate objects. You also learned the differences between chart sheets and embedded charts and how these differences affect your VBA code. Finally, you learned how to use event procedures for chart sheets and how to activate the event procedures of an embedded chart.

Chapter 11

Class modules in VBA provide programmers with the ability to define custom classes when creating new objects. A class is an object definition, so essentially class modules serve as object templates. By inserting a class module and properly including properties, methods, and events, you can create custom objects from your class for any VBA project.

Using class modules, you can simplify VBA programs by encapsulating processes that are too complex to handle with conventional programming techniques. Once defined, referencing and using a class module in your VBA programs is as easy as using any other object. Class modules are also convenient because they can be included with any VBA programming project that can make use of their objects.

This chapter shows you how to create, define, and use class modules in your VBA programs using an object model that mimics some of the formatting objects available with worksheet cells.

Benefiting by Using Class Modules

There are several benefits to defining your own VBA classes. One benefit is that a custom class enables you to put code and data in the same module, which results in objects that protect and validate their own data. You will find it easier to manage complex data handling processes with a class module because the data and procedures that access the data are contained within a single programming structure. As a result, it is easier to ensure that your data is protected and cannot be inadvertently altered by an external procedure. This greatly reduces the risk of errors in data management applications.

In addition, creating custom objects through the use of class modules actually simplifies programming because you can develop and test your custom object for appropriate behavior independent of the project. Once a custom object behaves as desired, you can include it in any project simply by importing the class module. In short, class modules allow you to create reusable objects that are more manageable, self-documenting, and easier to maintain.

NOTE

As I mention in Chapter 1, "VBA Overview and the IDE," VBA is not a true object-orientated language because it doesn't support things such as polymorphism and inheritance (don't worry if you don't know what these terms mean). However, VBA is considered to be much easier to learn than are true object-orientated languages. Furthermore, VBA's focus on objects and their relationships within a high-end application such as Excel allows for faster development of practical tools and applications for users.

The only disadvantage of using class modules is that you must learn how to create them. But, as you are about to see, creating a workable class is not that difficult. More challenging is creating a class that is easy to program and that is robust enough to be useful in numerous projects with little or no maintenance.

Creating an Object Class

As with any programming task, you want a well-defined plan in place before beginning to write a program. When creating a custom class, consider the following questions:

♦ How will the data be handled? That is, what are the requirements for the storage, retrieval, and processing of data?

♦ What properties and methods are required of an object defined by the class being created? Try to think of all intuitive properties and methods and not just those required for a current project.

♦ Is the new class part of an object hierarchy, and if so, how is the hierarchy defined?

♦ Should the objects created from the new class be part of a collection?

To begin programming a new class, follow this step: Insert a class module into your VBA project by selecting Insert, Class Module. The new class module appears as a new item in the Project Explorer under the Class Modules folder (see Figure 11.1).

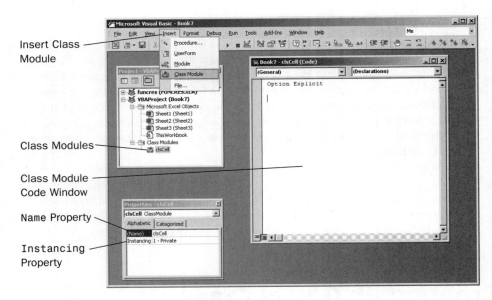

FIGURE 11.1 *Inserting a class module into a VBA project.*

After inserting a class module, you immediately change its name in the Properties window. As always, use a descriptive name and follow your favorite convention (I like to begin a class name with "cls"). After adding a new class module, you can open the code editor window in the same manner as you do any code module (for example, double-click on its icon in the Project Explorer window).

You will also notice an `Instancing` property for the class module that can take one of two possible values (`Private` or `PublicNotCreatable`). The `Instancing` property sets a value that specifies whether you can create instances of a `Public` class outside a project. If you select `Private`, other applications aren't allowed access to type library information about the class and cannot create instances of it. `Private` objects are only for use within your component. If you select `PublicNotCreatable`, other applications can use objects of this class only if your component creates the object first. Other applications cannot use the `CreateObject` function or the `New` operator to create objects from the class. So, the `Instancing` property is of limited utility to VBA programmers, and you will probably never need to change it from its default value of `Private`.

TIP

To use a custom class in multiple projects, first save the class module with the .cls extension by selecting File, Export File from the VBA IDE. To import the file into a new project, select File, Import File from the File menu.

The Cell Class Object Model

In this part of the book, you create the Excel-to-HTML converter project. You will build custom classes that manage the data (values, charts, and formats) in an Excel worksheet that has been selected for conversion to an HTML page. (See Chapter 12, "Constructing the Excel-to-HTML Converter," for the entire Excel-to-HTML converter object model.) For now, consider components of that object model, the `clsCells` collection class, `clsCell` class, and subordinate classes used to manage the formatting and content contained in a worksheet. Figure 11.2 shows a diagram of the object model.

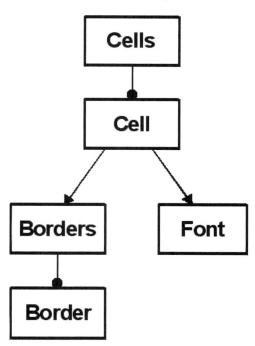

FIGURE 11.2 *The* `Cell` *object model used in building the Excel-to-HTML converter.*

Objects created from the `clsBorders` and `clsCells` classes are collection objects designed to contain objects created from the `clsBorder` and `clsCell` classes, respectively.

Table 11.1 lists the members required for the `clsCell` class. Review this table to see how these members are declared as the `clsClass` is constructed in the next section.

Table 11.1 Members of the clsCell Class

Property/Method	Description
Borders	Returns a `Border` object used to set attributes of a cell's border.
Font	Returns a `Font` object used to set attributes of a cell's font.
Alignment	Reads/writes the horizontal alignment of the text contained in the cell (`String`).
BackColor	Reads/writes the background color of the cell (`String`).
CellHeight	Reads/writes the height of the cell (`Integer`).
CellID	Reads/writes a unique identifier for the cell (`String`).
CellRange	Reads/writes the cell reference (`Range`).
CellValue	Reads/writes the contents of the cell (`String`).
CellWidth	Reads/writes the width of the cell (`Integer`).
HasBorder	Reads/writes whether the cell object has a border (`Boolean`).
HasChart	Reads/writes whether the cell object will contain a tag used to display the image of a chart in the Web page (`Boolean`).
ReadBorders	Method used to set the property values of the `Border` object for the cell.
ReadFont	Method used to set the property values of the `Font` object for the cell.
WriteCell	Reads/writes whether the cell is to be written to the HTML file. Should be set to `False` if the cell is covered by an image of a chart (`Boolean`).

Creating Properties

Virtually all objects have at least one property. *Properties* are members of a class that describe an attribute of the object (color, size, and so on). Although most properties have read/write capabilities, you are not required to design them that way (it depends on the requirements of your object). The easiest means of creating a property is by declaring a `Public` variable in the general declarations section of a class module. Properties declared in this manner are read/write.

```
Public CellValue As String
```

Although creating properties by declaring `Public` variables is easy, this approach has one major drawback: The class will have no control over processes that change the value of the variable. There is no way to validate or respond to changes made to a property's value. To solve this problem, you must write at least one property procedure.

Property procedures are VBA procedures that set or retrieve the value of a property when executed. You gain control over the processes that change the value of a variable by adding the appropriate code to the procedure. Here are the three types of property procedures:

- ◆ `Property Get`
- ◆ `Property Let`
- ◆ `Property Set`

The three types of property procedures are important because you use them to connect external code to objects instantiated from a custom class.

Property Get

You use the `Property Get` procedures to retrieve property values, thus allowing for read access to a property. You write a `Property Get` procedure similar to the way you write a VBA Function procedure. The procedure begins with a declaration using `Public` scope, the `Property Get` keywords, the procedure name, and a return type. The body of the procedure follows, after which the `End Property` keywords define the end of the procedure.

```
Public Property Get BackColor() As String
    BackColor = backColorP
End Property
```

The name and return type of the procedure define the name and data type of the property, respectively. You assign the procedure's return value to the name of the property in the same manner as you assign the return value of Function procedures. The preceding example defines a property called `BackColor` that is assigned the value of the variable `backColorP` when called. The property is called from a VBA program in the usual way, using the `object.property` notation.

```
myObj.BackColor = "FF00FF"
```

The variable `backColorP` represents a `Private` instance variable that was declared in the general declarations section of the class module.

```
Private backColorP As String
```

NOTE

I distinguish `Private` instance variables from property names by their scope (`Private` versus `Public`) and by appending an uppercase P to the end of their names. You can, of course, use another convention if you like.

To allow for write access to a property, set the value of the instance variable using a `Property Let` procedure.

Property Let

You use `Property Let` procedures to assign the values of class properties, giving write access to a property. The `Property Let` procedure is paired with `Property Get` (not required, but it's rare to allow just write-only access to a property), and their data types must match. Passing at least one argument to the procedure is required for assigning to the `Private` instance variable of the property. Any code required to validate or control the property's value should be added to the `Property Let` procedure. The following example from the `clsCell` class assigns a `String` to the instance variable (`backColorP`) of a property called `BackColor` after some manipulation of the input value (`cellColor`).

```
Public Property Let BackColor(ByVal cellColor As String)
    cellColor = Hex(cellColor)
    Select Case Len(cellColor)
        Case Is = 1
            backColorP = cellColor & "00000"
        Case Is = 2
            backColorP = cellColor & "0000"
        Case Is = 4
            backColorP = Right(cellColor, 2) & Left(cellColor, 2) & "00"
        Case Is = 6
            backColorP = Right(cellColor, 2) & Mid( _
                    cellColor, 3, 2) & Left(cellColor, 2)
        Case Else
            backColorP = cellColor
    End Select
End Property
```

The `BackColor` property in the `clsCell` class is passed a `Long` integer that is converted to a `String` of numerical characters that is further converted to a hexadecimal `String`. The `cellColor` variable passed to the `BackColor` property is meant to originate from the `Color` property of a VBA object or the `RGB()` function. The `Long` integer returned from these two functions is converted to the hexadecimal `String` required to reproduce the color in an HTML document.

Realistically, you need to add more code to validate the value of the argument passed to the property procedure. For example, if the value returned by the `ColorIndex` property of a VBA object is passed to the `BackColor` property, the resulting hexadecimal `String` will not represent the same color.

Property Set

Use `Property Set` procedures instead of `Property Let` to set the values of class properties that represent objects. `Property Set` should also be paired with `Property Get` and used when the argument or return type of the property is an object type.

```
Private rangeP As Range
Public Property Get CellRange() As Range
    Set CellRange = rangeP
End Property
Public Property Set CellRange(ByVal cRange As Range)
    Set rangeP = cRange
End Property
```

The `CellRange` property of the `clsCell` class sets and reads a reference to a `Private` instance variable (`rangeP`) that stores the `Range` object representing the location of the cell in a worksheet. Note the use of the `Set` keyword in all assignment statements involving object references.

TIP

Use `Property Get` and omit `Property Let` or `Property Set` procedures to make a property read-only.

Creating Methods

When an object performs an action, it is executing a method. For example, the `ClearContents` method of the `Range` object clears formulas and values from a specified range. To create a method for a custom class, write a Sub or Function procedure within the class module. The only difference is that a Function procedure returns a value to the calling program statement.

The `ReadFont` method of the `clsCell` class is a Sub procedure written in the usual way and serves to copy properties of a `Font` object from a range variable (`origCell`) to a variable of type `clsCell` (`aCell`). There is nothing special about this method; it simply performs tasks that could just as easily be done from the calling procedure. However, it encapsulates a process that would otherwise require more statements in the calling procedure and ensures that all the necessary properties of the `Font` object are copied to the `aCell` object variable.

```
Public Sub ReadFont(aCell As clsCell, origCell As Range)
    aCell.Font.Bold = origCell.Font.Bold
    aCell.Font.Color = origCell.Font.Color
    aCell.Font.Name = origCell.Font.Name
    aCell.Font.Size = origCell.Font.Size
    aCell.Font.Style = origCell.Font.FontStyle
End Sub
```

Creating an Instance of a Class

After creating a custom class via a class module, you can create objects of the class in a VBA program using the standard declaration for an object variable.

```
Dim myCell As clsCell
Set myCell = New clsCell
```

Or, if you prefer, you can declare and set the object variable using one statement.

```
Dim myCell As New clsCell
```

When the statement that sets the object reference is executed, an *instance* of the `clsCell` class is created. Its properties and methods are then programmatically available using the dot notation.

```
myCell.CellValue = 55
myCell.ReadFont myCell, Range("A1")
```

If the first method for creating an object variable is used, the declarative statement `Dim myCell As clsCell` does not create an instance of the `clsClass`. An instance of the class is not created until the statement that sets the object (`Set myCell = New clsCell`) is executed. This is the preferred method for creating an instance of a class because it provides more control of when the new instance of the object is created.

 TIP

Always use the New keyword to create a new instance of a VBA class. Without New, the error "Object variable or With block variable not set" is raised. If you receive this error on a statement involving your custom class, check to be sure you created the object using New.

Initialize and Terminate Class Events

VBA includes two event procedures in all custom class modules. You will find the `Initialize()` and `Terminate()` event procedures in the event drop-down list box of a class module. The `Initialize()` event is triggered when a new instance of the class is created in a program. So, the `Initialize()` event procedure is an excellent location in which to initialize class variables or create references to other objects.

Use the `Initialize()` event procedure of the `clsCell` class to initialize the `CellID` and `WriteCell` properties of a new instance of this class.

```
Private Sub Class_Initialize()
    CellID = "Cell" & CLng(Rnd * (2 ^ 31))
```

```
     WriteCell = True
End Sub
```

The Terminate() event of a custom class is triggered when an instance of the class is released or destroyed. The following statement releases the object myCell and triggers the Terminate()event of the clsCell class.

```
Set myCell = Nothing
```

The Terminate() event procedure frees system resources. If an instance of a class is not explicitly released in the program, it should be done in the Terminate() event. Use the Me keyword to reference the current instance of the class.

```
Private Sub Class_Terminate()
     Set Me = Nothing
End Sub
```

Learning when the Terminate() event of a custom class is triggered is important because VBA does not necessarily free system resources after program execution. For example, if an object variable is declared with module-level scope, instances of this object will not be destroyed unless the object is explicitly released by the program (for example, setting the variable to Nothing). If the object is not released, the Terminate() event is never triggered and system memory is not freed.

Establishing Object Hierarchies

You will often find relationships among objects when creating custom classes in an object-based programming language. Furthermore, these relationships will typically fall into an intuitive hierarchy. Throughout this book, I refer object hierarchies as object models (for example, Excel object model, Chart object model, and so on). Figure 11.2 shows the clsCell object model.

To create an object hierarchy, first create each class module and then declare properties to subordinate objects in the general declarations section of the parent class module. The following statement added to the general declarations section of the clsCell class module creates a Font property that creates a new instance of the clsFont class, making the clsFont object subordinate to the clsCell object in the hierarchy.

```
Public Font As New clsFont
```

To access a new instance of the clsFont class through the clsCell class, use the dot notation.

```
Dim myCell As New clsCell
myCell.Font.Size = 12
```

This works fine for providing read-write access to the properties of a new instance of the `clsFont` class. However, what if a program needs to access an existing instance of a custom class from a collection? In such cases, you must write a `Property Get` procedure that returns the desired instance from a collection object. I discuss collection classes in the next section.

Creating a Collection Class

There are numerous examples of collection objects in the Excel object model, including among others the `Workbooks`, `Worksheets`, and `Range` objects. A *collection class* is a class used to reference many instances of another class. For example, one instance of the `Worksheets` collection class references as many instances of the `Worksheet` class as exist in an Excel workbook. As with the `Worksheets` collection and `Worksheet` objects in the Excel object model, a pair of classes normally represents custom collections: One class defines the object to be contained in the collection, and the other class represents the collection.

You create a custom collection class in VBA much like you create any other class — by first inserting a class module into the project and then adding properties and methods. A collection class is differentiated by its methods and the data type of its instance variable. VBA includes a `Collection` object type, and every custom collection class should have at least one `Private` instance variable declared with this type. The `Private` instance variable represents a collection of instances of another class. The `clsCells` collection class is meant to hold instances of the `clsCell` class. Declare the `Private` instance variable of the `clsCells` collection class as follows:

```
Private cellsP As Collection
```

A VBA `Collection` object contains four members as described in Table 11.2. Most custom collection objects should also include these members. You can do so easily by wrapping the existing members of VBA's `Collection` object as new members of the custom collection class. By creating a custom collection class, you protect the collection object from external processes that might add invalid object instances.

Table 11.2 Members of the VBA Collection Object

Member	Description
Add	Method used to add an object to the collection. Arguments include a reference to the object, a unique identifier or key, and the location in which to add the object within the collection.
Remove	Method used to remove an object from the collection.
Item	Method used to return a single object from the collection.
Count	Read-only property that returns the number of objects in the collection.

TIP

Always declare instance variables of a collection object as `Private`. The problem is that any object type can be added to a VBA collection. Creating a custom collection class with `Private` instance variables and custom methods ensures that objects of the wrong type cannot be added to the collection.

The clsCells Collection Class

The `clsCells` collection class holds a collection of objects instantiated from the `clsCell` class. The Excel-to-HTML converter program uses the `clsCells` collection class to hold the object references to each worksheet cell that must be reproduced on a Web page. First, the data is copied from the worksheet into an object variable of type `clsCell` and then added to a collection object variable of type `clsCells`. Later, the data stored in the objects contained in the collection is used to create the text files that represent the Web page.

NOTE

VBA collections are based on the value one, and there is no option for changing this. The first object added to the collection is object 1, the second is 2, and so on. If objects are removed from the middle of the collection, higher numbers are adjusted downward to maintain a continuous sequence.

The `clsCells` collection class contains a `Private` instance variable (type `Collection`) named `cellsP`. This variable will serve as the object variable that holds each instance of the `clsCell` class added to the collection. The read-only `Count` property simply puts a wrapper around the existing `Count` property of the `Collection` object and returns the number of objects in the collection. The `Item` method returns a `clsCell` object from the `Private` collection object specified by the index value (`cIndex`) passed to this Function procedure. The `Add` and `Remove` methods also serve as wrappers of the existing methods of the VBA `Collection` object. Note that the `Add` method is passed both the instance of an object to be added to the collection and a `String` value returned from the object's `CellID` property. Recall that the `CellID` property is set in the `Initialize()` event procedure of the `clsCell` class, and it is an absolute requirement that the value of `CellID` be unique when passed to the `Add` method of a `Collection` object. A run-time error results when you attempt to add two objects with the same key to a collection. The properties and methods of the `clsCells` collection class are listed in the following:

```
Option Explicit
Private cellsP As Collection
Public Property Get Count() As Integer
```

```
        Count = cellsP.Count    'Return Count property of instance var
End Property
Public Function Item(ByVal cIndex As Long) As clsCell
        Set Item = cellsP(cIndex)    'Return obj via index value
End Function
Public Sub Add(aCell As clsCell)
        On Error GoTo AddError
        'Add obj to collection. Provide unique key
        cellsP.Add aCell, aCell.CellID
        Exit Sub
AddError:
        Err.Raise Number:=vbObjectError + 514, Source:="clsCells.Add", _
            Description:="Unable to Add clsCell object to the collection"
End Sub
Public Sub Remove(ByVal cIndex As String)
'Input argument may be a Long or a string
        On Error GoTo RemoveError
        'Remove obj from collection via provided index
        cellsP.Remove cIndex
        Exit Sub
RemoveError:
        Err.Raise Number:=vbObjectError + 515, Source:="clsCells.Remove", _
            Description:="Unable to Remove clsCell object from the collection"
End Sub
Private Sub Class_Initialize()
        'Initialize collection var with each new instance of the object
        Set cellsP = New Collection
End Sub            .
Private Sub Class_Terminate()
        Dim c As clsCell
        For Each c In cellsP      'Free system memory when obj is released
            Set c = Nothing
        Next
        Set cellsP = Nothing
End Sub
```

The `Initialize()` event of the `clsCells` collection class initializes the `Private` instance variable `cellsP`, and the `Terminate()` event frees system memory of all objects contained in the collection before releasing the collection object.

Raising Errors

In the `clsCells` collection class, error handling routines were included in the `Add` and `Remove` methods. These error handlers set a custom error type and number for run-time errors that occur in the procedure. This is accomplished with the `Raise` method of the `Err` object.

The `Raise` method of the error object raises a run-time error. It accepts up to five arguments that include a `Number` (required), `Source`, `Description`, and help file information.

```
AddError:
    Err.Raise Number:=vbObjectError + 514, Source:="clsCells.Add", _
        Description:="Unable to Add clsCell object to the collection"
```

The `AddError` error handler is called whenever a run-time error is encountered in the procedure. An error in this procedure will most likely result from improper logic in a process that calls the method (probably a type mismatch). The error handler then fills the `Err` object with custom information. The `Number` argument is set to 514 but can lie anywhere in the range 513–65535 (0 to 512 are reserved for system errors). The VBA constant `vbObjectError` is added to the number automatically by VBA for any error in a class module; therefore, it is included here so that it can be subtracted in the error handler of the calling process. The `Source` and `Description` arguments are strings that specify the location and nature of the error. If an error handler is included in the calling procedure, the `Raise` method of the `Err` object will set the error parameters but will not halt program execution. Instead, program execution is directed to the error handler in the calling procedure.

```
ErrorHandler:
    MsgBox Err.Number - vbObjectError & "  " & _
        Err.Description, , Err.Source
```

In the preceding example, the custom error number, source, and description are output in a message box.

The `Raise` method of the `Err` object provides you with the ability to generate custom error information in a class module that can then be used by a calling process to handle a run-time error.

The clsCell Class

An instance of the `clsCell` class represents a single cell in a worksheet whose contents and formatting may need to be applied to a table cell in an HTML document. Each cell within the used or selected range on a worksheet is scanned for its value and format (color, font, and border). After the properties of a `clsCell` object are set, the object is added to a `Collection` object of `clsCells`.

The class definition includes basic properties for the cell: interior color, range, value, width, and height. The `CellID` property provides a unique key for the `Add` method of the `Collection` object as discussed earlier in this chapter. The `Font` and `Borders` properties return `clsFont` and `clsBorder` objects for a cell. Note that the `Borders` property returns the `clsBorder` object from a collection and, therefore, requires a `Property Get` procedure. Finally, the `Boolean` properties indicate whether the HTML tag representing this object should be included in the document (`WriteCell`) and, if so, whether it should include a formatted border (`HasBorder`) or an image tag for a chart image (`HasChart`).

```
Option Explicit
Private alignP As String
Private backColorP As String
Private bordersP As clsBorders
Private rangeP As Range
'------------------------------
'Simple read/write properties
'------------------------------
Public CellID As String
Public CellValue As String
Public CellWidth As Integer
Public CellHeight As Integer
Public HasBorder As Boolean
Public WriteCell As Boolean
Public HasChart As Boolean
Public Font As New clsFont        'Return a Font object


Public Sub ReadBorders(aCell As clsCell, c As Range)
'Method used to set values of each Border object in the Borders
'collection object for a cell.
    aCell.Borders(1).BorderColor = c.Borders(xlEdgeTop).Color
    aCell.Borders(1).BorderStyle = c.Borders(xlEdgeTop).LineStyle
    aCell.Borders(1).BorderWeight = c.Borders(xlEdgeTop).Weight
    aCell.Borders(2).BorderColor = c.Borders(xlEdgeRight).Color
    aCell.Borders(2).BorderStyle = c.Borders(xlEdgeRight).LineStyle
    aCell.Borders(2).BorderWeight = c.Borders(xlEdgeRight).Weight
    aCell.Borders(3).BorderColor = c.Borders(xlEdgeBottom).Color
    aCell.Borders(3).BorderStyle = c.Borders(xlEdgeBottom).LineStyle
    aCell.Borders(3).BorderWeight = c.Borders(xlEdgeBottom).Weight
    aCell.Borders(4).BorderColor = c.Borders(xlEdgeLeft).Color
```

```vba
        aCell.Borders(4).BorderStyle = c.Borders(xlEdgeLeft).LineStyle
        aCell.Borders(4).BorderWeight = c.Borders(xlEdgeLeft).Weight
End Sub
Public Sub ReadFont(aCell As clsCell, origCell As Range)
'Method used to set values of the Font object for a cell.
        aCell.Font.Bold = origCell.Font.Bold
        aCell.Font.Color = origCell.Font.Color
        aCell.Font.Name = origCell.Font.Name
        aCell.Font.Size = origCell.Font.Size
        aCell.Font.Style = origCell.Font.Italic
End Sub
Public Property Get Borders(ByVal borderID As String) As clsBorder
'Property used to return a Border object via the Borders collection
        If bordersP Is Nothing Then
            Set bordersP = New clsBorders
        End If
        Set Borders = bordersP.Item(borderID)
End Property


Public Property Get Alignment() As String
        Alignment = alignP
End Property
Public Property Let Alignment(ByVal cAlign As String)
'Alignment property sets horizontal alignment only.
        If cAlign = "-4131" Then
            alignP = "left"
        ElseIf cAlign = "-4108" Then
            alignP = "center"
        ElseIf cAlign = "-4152" Then
            alignP = "right"
        Else
            alignP = "center"
        End If
End Property
Public Property Get BackColor() As String
        BackColor = backColorP
End Property
```

```
Public Property Let BackColor(ByVal cellColor As String)
'BackColor property sets the interior color of the cell.
'Hex function reverses red and blue components of long integer
'returned from RGB function and Color property.
    cellColor = Hex(cellColor)
    Select Case Len(cellColor)
        Case Is = 1
            backColorP = cellColor & "00000"
        Case Is = 2
            backColorP = cellColor & "0000"
        Case Is = 4
            backColorP = Right(cellColor, 2) & Left(cellColor, 2) & "00"
        Case Is = 6
            backColorP = Right(cellColor, 2) & Mid( _
                    cellColor, 3, 2) & Left(cellColor, 2)
        Case Else
            backColorP = cellColor
    End Select
End Property
Public Property Get CellRange() As Range
    Set CellRange = rangeP
End Property
Public Property Set CellRange(ByVal cRange As Range)
    Set rangeP = cRange
End Property
Private Sub Class_Initialize()
    CellID = "Cell" & CLng(Rnd * (2 ^ 31))
    WriteCell = True
End Sub
```

The Borders Collection and Border Classes

The clsBorders collection class and clsBorder class are paired classes used to represent the border formats of a worksheet cell. The border formatting copied from the worksheet includes the style (solid, dashed, dotted, and so on), weight, and color. The clsBorder class does not provide as many options as Excel for formatting a cell border, but these three properties will provide a reasonable reproduction of a typical cell border.

Note that the clsBorders collection class does not contain Add or Remove methods. This is because the collection is defined by the class to include four clsBorder objects that represent the borders at the top, bottom, right, and left sides of a cell. The collection is never allowed to contain more than or less than four clsBorder objects. The Initialize() event adds the four clsBorder objects to the collection without setting any of their properties. Without Add and Remove methods, a program will only have read-write access to the properties of existing objects in the collection. This protects the collection from improper external processes that could add or remove its objects and eventually result in run-time errors. Specifically, the ReadBorders method of the clsCell object requires that the clsBorders object contain four objects. Although a program can specify any index value between one and four to access a clsBorder object that represents any side of the cell, the ReadBorders method requires that index 1 refer to the top, index 2 to the right, and so on.

```vba
Option Explicit
Private bordersP As Collection
Public Property Get Item(ByVal borderID As Long) As clsBorder
    Set Item = bordersP(borderID)
End Property
Private Sub Class_Initialize()
'Add four Border objects to the collection
    Dim I As Integer
    Dim id As String
    Dim aBorder As clsBorder

    Set bordersP = New Collection
    For I = 1 To 4
        Set aBorder = New clsBorder
        If I = 1 Then
            id = "Top"
        ElseIf I = 2 Then
            id = "Right"
        ElseIf I = 3 Then
            id = "Bottom"
        Else
            id = "Left"
        End If
        bordersP.Add aBorder, id
        Set aBorder = Nothing
    Next I
End Sub
Private Sub Class_Terminate()
    Dim bor As Object
```

```
    For Each bor In bordersP      'Clear memory
        Set bor = Nothing
    Next
    Set bordersP = Nothing
End Sub
```

The clsBorder class provides properties for the border style, weight, and color. These properties are represented by numerical constants in VBA and must be converted to strings for the HTML document.

```
Option Explicit
Private borderStyleP As String
Private borderWeightP As String
Private borderColorP As String
Public Property Get BorderStyle() As String
    BorderStyle = borderStyleP
End Property
Public Property Let BorderStyle(ByVal bStyle As String)
'Convert VBA constants to HTML attribute string
    Select Case bStyle
        Case Is = "1"
            borderStyleP = "solid"
        Case Is = "4"
            borderStyleP = "dashed"
        Case Is = "5"
            borderStyleP = "dotted"
        Case Is = "-4115"
            borderStyleP = "dashed"
        Case Is = "-4118"
            borderStyleP = "dotted"
        Case Is = "-4119"
            borderStyleP = "double"
        Case Else
            borderStyleP = "none"
    End Select
End Property
Public Property Get BorderWeight() As String
    BorderWeight = borderWeightP
End Property
```

```vba
Public Property Let BorderWeight(ByVal bWeight As String)
'Convert VBA constants to HTML line weights
    borderWeightP = bWeight
    Select Case bWeight
        Case Is = 1
            borderWeightP = "1px"
        Case Is = 2
            borderWeightP = "thin"
        Case Is = 4
            borderWeightP = "thick"
        Case Is = -4138
            borderWeightP = "medium"
        Case Else
            borderWeightP = "2px"
    End Select
End Property
Public Property Get BorderColor() As String
    BorderColor = borderColorP
End Property
Public Property Let BorderColor(ByVal bColor As String)
'Convert long integers to hexadecimal strings
    bColor = Hex(bColor)
    Select Case Len(bColor)
        Case Is = 1
            borderColorP = bColor & "00000"
        Case Is = 2
            borderColorP = bColor & "0000"
        Case Is = 4
            borderColorP = Right(bColor, 2) & Left(bColor, 2) & "00"
        Case Is = 6
            borderColorP = Right(bColor, 2) & Mid( _
                    bColor, 3, 2) & Left(bColor, 2)
        Case Else
            borderColorP = bColor
    End Select
End Property
```

The Font Class

The clsFont class includes properties that describe the font used in a worksheet cell. The Name property specifies the font face (for example, Times, Arial, and so on), and the Size property specifies the size of the font in points. You must convert the Color, Style, and Bold properties from the VBA types (Long or Boolean) to String values for the HTML document.

```
Option Explicit
Public Name As String
Public Size As Integer
Private colorP As String
Private styleP As String
Private boldP As String
Public Property Get Bold() As String
    Bold = boldP
End Property
Public Property Let Bold(ByVal fBold As String)
'Convert Boolean value to proper HTML string
    If fBold = "True" Then
        boldP = "bold"
    Else
        boldP = "normal"
    End If
End Property
Public Property Get Style() As String
    Style = styleP
End Property
Public Property Let Style(ByVal styleType As String)
'Convert Boolean value to proper HTML string
    If styleType = "True" Then
        styleP = "italic"
    Else
        styleP = "normal"
    End If
End Property
Public Property Get Color() As String
    Color = colorP
End Property
Public Property Let Color(ByVal fontColor As String)
```

```
'Convert long integer to hexadecimal string
    fontColor = Hex(fontColor)
    Select Case Len(fontColor)
        Case Is = 1
            colorP = fontColor & "00000"
        Case Is = 2
            colorP = fontColor & "0000"
        Case Is = 4
            colorP = Right(fontColor, 2) & Left(fontColor, 2) & "00"
        Case Is = 6
            colorP = Right(fontColor, 2) & Mid(fontColor, 3, 2) & _
                Left(fontColor, 2)
        Case Else
            colorP = fontColor
    End Select
End Property
```

Testing the Cell Class Object Model

As mentioned earlier, one of the advantages to custom classes is that they can be tested independently before their inclusion into a program. Generally, this means creating a short Sub procedure that creates an instance of a class and tests its properties and methods for proper behavior.

To test the `clsCell` class object model, add a short Sub procedure that creates instances of the `clCell` class and `clsCells` collection class to a standard module. The Sub procedure `TestCellClass()` reads the properties of the active cell in an Excel worksheet and then uses several `Debug.Print` statements to test whether the correct values for each property in the `clsCell` and subordinate objects were recorded. Rather than executing the Sub procedure all at once (by pressing F5), you step through the procedure one line at a time (by pressing F8) to verify the reading and writing of properties and the execution of the methods. The values stored in the properties of the `clsCell` objects are output to the Immediate window (see Figure 11.3).

```
Sub TestCellClass()
'A simple procedure designed to test the clsCell and clsCells classes
    Dim myCell As clsCell
    Dim myCells As clsCells
    Dim I As Integer

    On Error GoTo ErrorHandler
```

```
    Set myCell = New clsCell
    Set myCells = New clsCells

    myCell.Alignment = ActiveCell.HorizontalAlignment
    myCell.BackColor = ActiveCell.Interior.Color
    myCell.ReadBorders myCell, ActiveCell
    myCell.ReadFont myCell, ActiveCell
    myCell.CellHeight = ActiveCell.Height
    myCell.CellValue = ActiveCell.Value
    myCell.CellWidth = ActiveCell.Width

    Debug.Print "Alignment: "; myCell.Alignment
    Debug.Print "BackColor: "; myCell.BackColor
    For I = 1 To 4
        Debug.Print "BorderColor: "; myCell.Borders(I).BorderColor
        Debug.Print "BorderStyle: "; myCell.Borders(I).BorderStyle
        Debug.Print "BorderWeight: "; myCell.Borders(I).BorderWeight
    Next I
    Debug.Print "CellHeight: "; myCell.CellHeight
    Debug.Print "CellValue: "; myCell.CellValue
    Debug.Print "CellWidth: "; myCell.CellWidth
    Debug.Print "Bold: "; myCell.Font.Bold
    Debug.Print "Color: "; myCell.Font.Color
    Debug.Print "Name: "; myCell.Font.Name
    Debug.Print "mSize: "; myCell.Font.Size
    Debug.Print "Style: "; myCell.Font.Style

    myCells.Add myCell
    Debug.Print "Count: "; myCells.Count
    myCells.Remove myCell.CellID
    Debug.Print "Count: "; myCells.Count

    Set myCell = Nothing
    Exit Sub
ErrorHandler:
    MsgBox Err.Number - vbObjectError & "   " & Err.Description, , Err.Source
End Sub
```

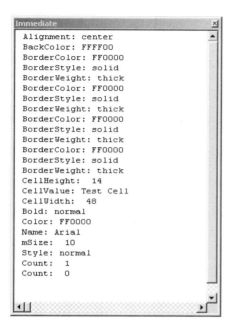

```
Immediate                                    ×
Alignment: center
BackColor: FFFF00
BorderColor: FF0000
BorderStyle: solid
BorderWeight: thick
BorderColor: FF0000
BorderStyle: solid
BorderWeight: thick
BorderColor: FF0000
BorderStyle: solid
BorderWeight: thick
BorderColor: FF0000
BorderStyle: solid
BorderWeight: thick
CellHeight:   14
CellValue: Test Cell
CellWidth:   48
Bold: normal
Color: FF0000
Name: Arial
mSize:   10
Style: normal
Count:   1
Count:   0
```

FIGURE 11.3 *Testing the* `clsCell` *and* `clsCells` *custom classes.*

Alternatively, you can test individual classes for proper behavior, but ultimately you must also test for proper connections between classes in an object model.

Summary

In this chapter, you learned how to create custom classes for inclusion in your VBA projects. Custom classes serve as templates for reusable objects with properties, methods, and events. The addition of property procedures and method procedures to a custom class module defines an object. You learned how to build a custom class, a collection class, and a hierarchical object model. You also learned how to create these objects by instantiating a class.

Chapter 12

Constructing the Excel-to-HTML Converter

The last several versions of Excel have included a feature that allows a user to save a workbook or worksheet as a Web page. With each new version of Excel, this tool has been improved with additional features (for example, interactivity) and is gradually moving toward full XML support.

Although the ability to save spreadsheets as a Web page is useful, Excel has always received one major criticism: The HTML files generated by Excel are poorly formed and are filled with unnecessary formatting and style tags that make the documents difficult to read, even for an experienced Web developer. This is not really an issue for users who create and edit HTML documents exclusively with Excel. However, people who maintain Web sites often use text editors such as Notepad, Pico, and Emacs to quickly edit an HTML document. However, the task of editing HTML documents created from Excel using a text editor is frustrating because of the poorly formed structure of the document, which leads to the motivation for creating an Excel-to-HTML converter.

An Excel-to-HTML converter application enables you to produce simple, well-formed HTML documents that yield a fair reproduction of an Excel worksheet. (See Appendix B for a tutorial covering the basic HTML/XHTML markup tags, tag attributes, and syntax, along with a brief introduction to cascading style sheets.) A well-formed HTML document is one with adequate indention and proper spacing as opposed to a badly formed HTML document that is too bunched together and difficult to read and maintain.

Chapters 9–11 describe components within VBA and the Excel object model that you use to construct the Excel-to-HTML converter program. You use custom class objects (see Chapter 11, "VBA Class Modules: Creating Custom Objects") to manage the data (values and formatting) contained in an Excel worksheet and its subsequent transformation into a Web page. You use methods of the `Chart` object (see Chapter 10, "Creating and Manipulating Excel Charts") to export embedded charts as image files for display in a Web page, and the `CommandBar` object (see Chapter 9, "Custom Menus and Toolbars") enables you to create a custom toolbar that will serve as an interface for initiating the program. In this chapter, you put all this together to build the custom toolbar and custom class modules that the Excel-to-HTML converter program uses to save the data and charts in a worksheet as an HTML document.

Designing the Excel-to-HTML Program

Before writing a more challenging program, I spend a few minutes writing a general statement that describes the program, including its basic function and the type of interface I want to use. Next, I write out a list of the most significant programming objects I will use to write the program. I also write a reasonably detailed algorithm listing the order of tasks I want to complete while writing the program.

Describing the Excel-to-HTML Program

The Excel-to-HTML converter program will have a simple interface created from a Userform to provide the user with the ability to select a single worksheet (or range) for conversion to a static HTML document. The program will then generate two text files and as many image files as there are charts within the worksheet being converted. One text file is the HTML document (.html extension), and the other text file is the style sheet for the page (.css extension). The tags used to construct the text files will follow XHTML standards (see Appendix B). The program will also make it possible to save all generated files on a local or networked computer. Finally, the entire project will be converted to an Excel add-in that can be initiated from a custom toolbar. Additional projects will be included with the add-in as they are discussed in later chapters.

The Excel-to-HTML converter is not necessarily a complete project. The goal is to create a program that does a fair job of reproducing the most common formatting elements (color, fonts, and borders) and any charts that might be included in a worksheet. The program does not reproduce all the formatting available to an Excel user; however, after reviewing its construction, you should be able to tailor the program to fit your needs by adding desired elements that were not included.

Choosing the Project Tools and Algorithm

With a well-defined statement describing the function of the program, the next step is deciding what programming tools to use and the algorithm to follow in the program's construction.

As with any project, there are numerous approaches to solving the problems it presents. After considering the preceding requirements, I decided to write the major elements of the project using the following VBA components:

♦ Userform/Active X controls
♦ File I/O objects
♦ Class modules
♦ Toolbar

The Userform and ActiveX controls will provide the interface in which the user selects a worksheet or worksheet range. The file I/O objects in VBA (see Chapter 8, "Understanding File I/O, Debugging, and Error Handling in VBA") will allow for text file creation and selection of the path in which to store them. Class modules are for creating custom classes that will manage the data being converted to a Web page. This project could certainly be written without class modules, but using them will greatly simplify the programming. Finally, a custom toolbar provides the interface that initiates the program.

Here are the steps you follow to write the program:

1. Design the Userform including ActiveX controls and describe their function.

2. Design the object model for managing the data content and formatting in an Excel worksheet. Include any necessary properties and methods. The object model should include many of the same classes as the Excel object model starting at the worksheet level.

3. Create each class included in the object model and test for proper behavior. Create instances of each class and initialize the objects properties; then read each property to test for accuracy. Remember that many of the formatting properties that describe a table element must be converted to the proper String values for HTML tag attributes (for example, color should be a hexadecimal String).

4. Write the program that creates the HTML document. All code should reside in the Userform's code module.

5. Initialize the Userform's ActiveX controls.

6. Write the code that allows the user to select a folder in which to save the files generated by the program.

7. Instantiate all required objects for holding worksheet data. Assign property values of custom objects to hold the data from a worksheet.

8. Create the style sheet file. Include styles for every cell used on the worksheet.

9. Create the HTML file.

Defining the Classes

The object model required for this project is very similar to the Excel object model starting at the worksheet level, albeit greatly simplified. The goal is to create a model that is sufficient for reproducing a worksheet as a Web page and flexible enough to make it easily expandable if desired. For example, if you want the ability to create multiple Web pages, you can add a Pages collection object that will hold multiple instances of the Page class. Figure 12.1 shows the object model for the project.

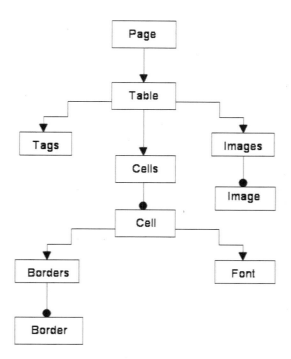

FIGURE 12.1 *The Excel-to-HTML object model.*

The Page Class

Although at the top of the object model, the `clsPage` class is short and simple and could just as easily have been left as a standalone class; that is, the current project does not require that this class be at the top of the object hierarchy. The project requires a title along with opening and closing HTML tags, and it makes the most sense to put these items in the `clsPage` class because they represent basic tags that enclose the content of a Web page. The `clsPage` class is at the top of the object hierarchy because that is the natural place for it in terms of its relationship with the other objects and because it makes the model more conducive to expansion (that is, adding a `Pages` collection object).

The `clsPage` class contains a read-write `BackColor` property to represent the background color of the Web page and two read-only properties that contain the opening and closing tags for an HTML document. The `Title` property is a simple `Public` declaration that will hold the title of the HTML document (name of the worksheet), and the `Table` property returns a new `clsTable` object, thus defining a relationship in the object model.

```vb
Option Explicit
Public Title As String
Public Table As New clsTable
Private backColorP As String

Public Property Get HtmlEnd() As String
    HtmlEnd = "</body>" & vbCrLf & "</html>"
End Property

Public Property Get HtmlBegin() As String
'Build opening string for HTML document
    Dim docType As String

    'Specify XHTML compliant document
    docType = "<!DOCTYPE html PUBLIC " & Chr(34) & "-//W3C//DTD " & _
            "XHTML 1.0 Transitional//EN" & Chr(34) & " " & Chr(34) & _
            "http://www.w3.org/TR/xhtml1/DTD/xhtml1-transitional.dtd" & _
            Chr(34) & ">"

    'Add opening and closing tags for head and title.
    'Include link to css file
    HtmlBegin = docType & vbCrLf & "<html>" & vbCrLf & "<head>" & vbCrLf
    HtmlBegin = HtmlBegin & "<title>" & Title & "</title>"
    HtmlBegin = HtmlBegin & vbCrLf & "<link rel=stylesheet type=" & _
                Chr(34) & "text/css" & Chr(34) & vbCrLf & "href=" & _
                Chr(34) & Title & ".css" & Chr(34) & vbCrLf & _
                "title=" & Chr(34) & "xls" & Title & Chr(34) & ">" & _
                vbCrLf & "</head>" & vbCrLf

    'Add opening body tag
    HtmlBegin = HtmlBegin & vbCrLf & "<body>"
End Property

Public Property Get BackColor() As String
    BackColor = backColorP
End Property
```

```
Public Property Let BackColor(ByVal pageColor As String)
'Convert input string to hexadecimal string
'representing an HTML color.
'Correct string if Hex function reverses RGB components.
    pageColor = Hex(pageColor)
    Select Case Len(pageColor)
        Case Is = 1
            backColorP = pageColor & "00000"
        Case Is = 2
            backColorP = pageColor & "0000"
        Case Is = 4
            backColorP = Right(pageColor, 2) & Left(pageColor, 2) & "00"
        Case Is = 6
            backColorP = Right(pageColor, 2) & Mid(pageColor, 3, 2) & _
                Left(pageColor, 2)
        Case Else
            backColorP = pageColor
    End Select
End Property
```

The Table Class

The clsTable class is the simplest class in the model. It defines an HTML table that is used to hold the content of the worksheet being converted. The Cells, Tags, and Images properties establish relationships to subordinate objects, and the TableRange property sets a Range object that represents a range of cells on a worksheet. The TableRange property will have to be set by the program that uses this object to include not only all worksheet cells that are in use but also those cells that are covered by an embedded chart.

```
Option Explicit
Private rangeP As Range
Public Cells As New clsCells
Public Tags As New clsTableTags
Public Images As New clsImages
Public ID As String

Public Property Get TableRange() As Range
    Set TableRange = rangeP
End Property
```

```
Public Property Set TableRange(ByVal tabRange As Range)
'Input range represents used range on a worksheet, including charts
    Set rangeP = tabRange
End Property
```

The TableTags Class

The clsTableTags class is included as a convenience to the programmer who uses this object. It contains read-only properties with String values that represent the HTML tags used to construct a table in a Web page (table, row, and cell). You can easily expand this class to include more properties that represent HTML tags for different parts of a document.

```
Option Explicit
Public Property Get TableStart() As String
'Opening table tag
    TableStart = "<table>"
End Property


Public Property Get TableEnd() As String
'Closing table tag
    TableEnd = "</table>"
End Property


Public Property Get RowStart() As String
'Opening row tag
    RowStart = "<tr>"
End Property


Public Property Get RowEnd() As String
'Closing row tag
    RowEnd = "</tr>"
End Property


Public Property Get CellStart(Optional cellName As String) As String
'Open column tag. Include class attribute for css
    If cellName <> "" Then
        CellStart = "<td " & "class=" & Chr(34) & cellName & _
            Chr(34) & ">"
```

```
    Else
        CellStart = "<td>"
    End If
End Property


Public Property Get CellEnd() As String
'Closing column tag
    CellEnd = "</td>"
End Property
```

The Image and Images Collection Classes

An instance of the `clsImage` class holds information pertaining to the image of an embedded Excel chart that must be added to the HTML document. It includes `Width` and `Height` properties to hold the size of the image, a `Path` property to hold the file path for the image, and a `Location` property to hold a `Range` object representing the worksheet cells over which the chart was placed. You can add each instance of the `clsImage` class to a `clsImages` collection object.

```
Option Explicit
Public Width As Integer
Public Height As Integer
Public ID As String
Public Path As String
Private locationP As Range


Public Property Get Location() As Range
    Set Location = locationP
End Property


Public Property Set Location(chLocation As Range)
'Worksheet range underneath an embedded chart
    Set locationP = chLocation
End Property
```

The `FindLocation` method determines the range of cells covered by an embedded chart on a worksheet. The `Chart` object of interest is passed to the procedure where its `Left`, `Top`, `Width`, and `Height` properties are compared with the cumulative width and height of the worksheet cells until the range of cells masked by the chart is determined.

```
Private Function FindLocation(myChart As ChartObject) As Range
'Finds the range of cells covered by an embedded chart on the wksheet
    Dim topRow As Integer, bottomRow As Integer
    Dim leftCol As Integer, rightCol As Integer
    Dim shWidth As Integer, shHeight As Integer
    Dim I As Integer

    Do          'Find columns at the left and right edges of chart
        I = I + 1
        If shWidth < myChart.Left Then leftCol = I
        shWidth = shWidth + Cells(1, I).Width
        rightCol = I
    Loop While shWidth < myChart.Left + myChart.Width
    I = 0
    Do          'Find the rows at the top and bottom edges of chart
        I = I + 1
        If shHeight < myChart.Top Then topRow = I
        shHeight = shHeight + Cells(I, 1).Height
        bottomRow = I
    Loop While shHeight < myChart.Top + myChart.Height

    Set FindLocation = Range(GetColumnRef(leftCol) & topRow & ":" & _
                    GetColumnRef(rightCol) & bottomRow)

End Function
```

The GetColumnRef() Function procedure is used in Chapter 6, "Creating VBA Loops and Arrays." The FindLocation method uses this Function procedure to convert a numerical column index to a String representing a worksheet column reference. You declare it with Private scope to encapsulate it with the clsImage object's FindLocation method.

```
Private Function GetColumnRef(columnIndex As Integer) As String
'Converts column index number to a textual reference
    Dim numAlpha As Integer
    Dim firstLetter As String
    Dim secondLetter As String
    Dim remainder As Integer

    'Calculate the number of characters needed
    numAlpha = columnIndex \ 26
```

```
    Select Case columnIndex / 26
        Case Is <= 1      'Column ref is between A and Z
            firstLetter = Chr(columnIndex + 64)
            GetColumnRef = firstLetter
        Case Else    'Column ref has two letters
            remainder = columnIndex - 26 * (columnIndex \ 26)
            If remainder = 0 Then
                firstLetter = Chr(64 + (columnIndex \ 26) - 1)
                secondLetter = "Z"
                GetColumnRef = firstLetter & secondLetter
            Else
                firstLetter = Chr(64 + (columnIndex \ 26))
                secondLetter = Chr(64 + remainder)
                GetColumnRef = firstLetter & secondLetter
            End If
    End Select
End Function
```

You can use an instance of the clsImages class to hold any instance of the clsImage class created in a program. Add each clsImage object using the Add method of the clsImages object. You need to add one clsImage object to the collection for each embedded chart on a worksheet. In Chapter 11, I describe the clsImages class as a basic collection class; however, clsImages includes two methods that aren't described in that chapter. The GetMaxRow and GetMaxColumn methods are included here to provide a convenient way for you, as a programmer, to return the maximum row and column indices from the Location property of the clsImage objects that are added to the collection.

```
Option Explicit
Private imagesP As Collection


Property Get Item(ByVal imageID As Variant) As clsImage
'Identify clsImage object by ID number
    Set Item = imagesP(imageID)
End Property


Public Property Get Count() As Integer
'Return number of images in collection
    Count = imagesP.Count
End Property
```

```
Public Sub Add(aImage As clsImage)
'Add new clsImage object to collection
'ID property serves as key field
    On Error GoTo AddError
    imagesP.Add aImage, aImage.ID
    Exit Sub
AddError:
    Err.Raise Number:=vbObjectError + 516, Source:="clsImages.Add", _
        Description:="Add Method of Image Collection Object Failed"
End Sub


Public Sub Remove(ByVal imgIndex As String)
'Remove image from collection by specifying index
'that correlates to ID property of clsImage object
    On Error GoTo RemoveError
    cellsP.Remove imgIndex
    Exit Sub
RemoveError:
    Err.Raise Number:=vbObjectError + 517, Source:="clsImages.Remove", _
        Description:="Unable to Remove clsImage object " & _
                            "from the collection"
End Sub

Public Function GetMaxColumn() As Integer
'Find the max column index in collection
    Dim aImage As New clsImage
    For Each aImage In imagesP
        If GetMaxColumn < aImage.Location.Column + _
                aImage.Location.Columns.Count Then
            GetMaxColumn = aImage.Location.Column + _
                aImage.Location.Columns.Count
        End If
    Next
End Function


Public Function GetMaxRow() As Integer
'Find the max row index in collection
    Dim aImage As New clsImage
```

```
      For Each aImage In imagesP
          If GetMaxRow < aImage.Location.Row + _
                  aImage.Location.Rows.Count Then
              GetMaxRow = aImage.Location.Row + aImage.Location.Rows.Count
          End If
      Next
  End Function


  Private Sub Class_Initialize()
      Set imagesP = New Collection
  End Sub


  Private Sub Class_Terminate()
      Dim I As clsImage
      For Each I In imagesP
          Set I = Nothing
      Next
      Set imagesP = Nothing
  End Sub
```

You can find the code for the remaining classes of the project's object model (refer to Figure 12.1) in Chapter 11. These classes include the clsCell and clsCells collection classes, as well as their subordinate clsFont, clsBorder, and clsBorders collection classes.

Designing the User Interface

You have a number of choices when designing an interface to use with an Excel-VBA application. You can use ActiveX controls on a worksheet or Userform, create a custom toolbar or menu, create an add-in, or use a combination of these items. The question to ask is this: What is the best method to give the user for loading and interacting with a program? Ideally, the interface is simple, intuitive, and not obtrusive. The interface should blend into the Excel application window and give the user the ability to easily initiate the program. The interface that best suits the Excel-to-HTML program is as an add-in that creates a toolbar when the program is loaded and destroys the toolbar when the program is unloaded. You can use the toolbar to initiate several programs (perhaps with a common element — for example, Web Utilities), and it should contain at least one button for each program. The Excel-to-HTML program is initiated from a single toolbar button that, when pressed, loads and shows a Userform. As you complete more projects, they are easily included with the same add-in (if applicable), and you can add more buttons to the toolbar to initiate the new programs.

The Excel Utilities Toolbar

The major difference between an Excel add-in file and a workbook file is that the workbook/worksheet GUI is unavailable to the user with the add-in. Yet, the add-in must still contain a workbook with the same number of worksheets as existed when the file was created. Figure 12.2 shows the Project Explorer window with an Excel workbook project file (Book1.xls) and two add-in files (FUNCRES.XLA and Excel_Utilities.xla).

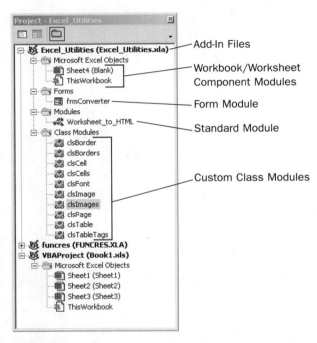

FIGURE 12.2 *The Project Explorer window showing the objects included with a custom add-in.*

Notice that the custom add-in Excel_Utilities.xla contains one Workbook object with the minimum requirement of one Worksheet object. So, the properties, methods and events of the Workbook and Worksheet objects are still available for use in a program.

 TIP

The Worksheet object in an add-in is an excellent location for holding data required by a VBA program. You achieve read-write access to the data in an add-in's worksheet using the normal object path (Workbook.Worksheet.Range). What makes an add-in's worksheet special is that it is protected from contamination by users, because they have no access (not even visual) to it through the Excel application window.

The event procedures of the Workbook object serve as ideal locations for the code used to create a custom toolbar. In Chapter 9, I write that toolbars are represented as CommandBar objects in VBA and are included in the CommandBars collection object.

The following code is from the code module of the Workbook object (named ThisWorkbook — refer to Figure 12.2) in the Excel_Utilities.xla add-in. A module-level variable of type CommandBar represents the custom toolbar. The Open() event of the Workbook object is triggered when the add-in is loaded and serves to call the procedures that create and remove the custom toolbar. The BeforeClose() event of the Workbook object ensures that the custom toolbar is deleted when the add-in is unloaded.

```
Option Explicit
Private tlbProjects As CommandBar
Private Sub Workbook_Open()
'Delete the toolbar just in case the toolbar already exists
    RemoveToolbar ("Excel Projects")
    AddToolbar
End Sub


Private Sub Workbook_BeforeClose(Cancel As Boolean)
    RemoveToolbar ("Excel Projects")   'Deletes the toolbar
End Sub
```

The AddToolbar() Sub procedure sets the reference to the module-level variable tlbProjects and creates the custom toolbar. A single button referenced by the variable tlbSaveAsWebPage is added to the toolbar, and its properties are set to display a caption and call a procedure (WorksheetToHTML).

```
Private Sub AddToolbar()
'Create a custom toolbar
    Dim tlbSaveAsWebPage As CommandBarButton
    '------------------------------
    'Set reference to new toolbar
    '------------------------------
    Set tlbProjects = Application.CommandBars.Add( _
        Name:="Excel Projects", _
        Temporary:=True)
    '-------------------------------------
    'Set reference to button(s) on toolbar
    '-------------------------------------
```

```
        Set tlbSaveAsWebPage = tlbProjects.Controls.Add( _
            Type:=msoControlButton, _
            Temporary:=True)
        tlbSaveAsWebPage.Style = msoButtonCaption
        tlbSaveAsWebPage.Caption = "Web Page"
        tlbSaveAsWebPage.OnAction = "WorksheetToHTML"
        tlbProjects.Visible = True
End Sub
```

The RemoveToolbar() Sub procedure loops through the CommandBars collection object searching for the custom toolbar and deleting it if found.

```
Private Sub RemoveToolbar(tlbarName As String)
'Delete the specified toolbar
    Dim cBar As CommandBar
    For Each cBar In Application.CommandBars
        If cBar.Name = tlbarName Then
            cBar.Delete
            Exit For
        End If
    Next
End Sub
```

Adding more buttons to the custom toolbar will simply require having more CommandBarButton objects in the AddToolbar() Sub procedure and setting their properties.

The HTML Converter Userform

Pressing the Web Page button on the custom toolbar calls the Sub procedure WorksheetToHTML(), which contains one line of code that loads and shows the frmConverter Userform. The Userform must be shown modally (this is the default behavior of a Userform; therefore, no argument is passed to the Show method), regardless of which version of Excel is being used as a requirement of the RefEdit control that is on the Userform.

```
Public Sub WorksheetToHTML()
    frmConverter.Show
End Sub
```

Figure 12.3 shows the frmConverter Userform, and Table 12.1 lists and describes the ActiveX controls it contains.

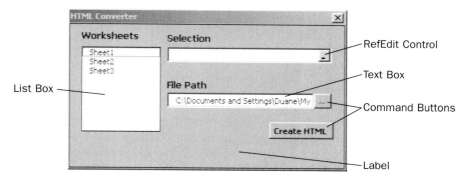

FIGURE 12.3 *The Userform interface for the Excel-to-HTML program.*

Table 12.1 Functional ActiveX Controls Contained on the Excel-to-HTML Project Userform

ActiveX control	Name	Description
List Box control	lstWkSheets	Provides a list of all worksheets in the active workbook.
RefEdit control	refSelection	Allows the user to select a range in the active worksheet.
TextBox control	txtPath	Displays a file path for storing HTML files.
Command Button control	cmdChangePath	Allows the user to select a new file path.
Command Button control	cmdCreate	Creates the HTML files.
Label control	lblOutput	Outputs messages to the user.

All remaining code for the project is contained in the form module of the `frmConverter` Userform. The module-level variable `aPage` represents an object variable of the `clsPage` custom class. It's accessed by several Sub procedures and will represent the HTML page and the data it contains. The `Initialize()` event of the `Userform` object fills the List Box control with the names of all worksheets in the active workbook. The default file path is set to the `Path` property of either the active workbook or the add-in.

```
Option Explicit
Private aPage As clsPage
Private Sub UserForm_Initialize()
'Initialize the list box and text box controls
    Dim ws As Worksheet
    'Add names of all worksheets to list box
```

```
    For Each ws In Worksheets
        lstWkSheets.AddItem ws.Name
    Next
    'Provide default file path
    If ActiveWorkbook.Path <> "" Then
        txtPath.Text = ActiveWorkbook.Path
    Else
        txtPath.Text = ThisWorkbook.Path
    End If
End Sub
```

The QueryClose() event, which is triggered by pressing the close icon (the x in upper-right corner), contains the code that releases the system memory holding the Userform object and ends the program.

```
Private Sub UserForm_QueryClose(Cancel As Integer, CloseMode As Integer)
'Clear the userform from memory and end the program
    Unload Me
    End
End Sub
```

The Click() event of the Command Button control cmdChangePath uses a FileDialog object (see Chapter 8) to give the user a way to change the path in which to save the HTML files. Alternatively, the user can type a new path in the text box.

```
Private Sub cmdChangePath_Click()
'User selects path to save HTML files
    Dim fd As FileDialog
    Dim I As Integer
    'Use the folder dialog
    Set fd = Application.FileDialog(msoFileDialogFolderPicker)
    With fd
        .AllowMultiSelect = False   'Allow only one selection
        .Title = "Select Folder"
        .InitialFileName = ""
        If .Show = -1 Then   'Add selected folder path to text box
            txtPath.Text = .SelectedItems(1)
        End If
    End With
    Set fd = Nothing
End Sub
```

The `Click()` event of the CommandButton control `cmdCreate` serves as the main procedure for the program. First, calls to the `ValidPath()` and `ValidSelection()` Sub procedures ensure that the file path in `txtPath` is valid and that the user has selected either a range or a worksheet. If the user input is valid, several more procedure calls create and initialize the properties of the custom objects used to hold the data from the worksheet. Finally, the CSS (Cascading Style Sheets) and HTML files are created before memory used to hold the module-level variable `aPage` is released.

```vba
Private Sub cmdCreate_Click()
    '...........................
    'Validate selection and path
    '...........................
    If Not ValidPath Then
        lblOutput.Caption = "Invalid Path!"
        Exit Sub
    ElseIf Not ValidSelection Then
        lblOutput.Caption = "Make a Selection!"
        Exit Sub
    End If
    '.................
    'Object Creation
    '.................
    CreatePage
    CreateTableImages
    SetTableRange
    CreateCells
    ModifyCells
    '...........
    'Write files
    '...........
    WriteStyles (ActiveSheet.Name & ".css")
    WritePage (ActiveSheet.Name & ".html")

    Set aPage = Nothing
End Sub


Private Function ValidPath() As Boolean
'Validate the file path
    Dim fPath As String
```

```
        fPath = txtPath.Text
        If Dir(fPath, vbDirectory) = "" Or fPath = "" Then
            ValidPath = False
        Else
            ValidPath = True
        End If
End Function


Private Function ValidSelection() As Boolean
'Validate that the user has made a selection
    If lstWkSheets.Value <> "" Then
        Worksheets(lstWkSheets.Value).Activate
        ValidSelection = True
    Else
        If refSelection.Value = "" Then
            lblOutput.Caption = "Make a Selection!"
            ValidSelection = False
        Else
            ValidSelection = True
        End If
    End If
End Function
```

Creating the Objects

After user input validation, you create instances of the custom classes and set their properties to hold the formatting and content of the worksheet. The Sub procedure `CreatePage()` instantiates the module-level variable **aPage** and sets its `Title` and `BackColor` properties. The title of the HTML page will be the title of the worksheet, and its color is set to the color of the used or selected range. The object variable **aPage** represents the top-level object in the hierarchy and will be used throughout the program to access subordinate objects and set their properties. Accessing subordinate objects through the **aPage** variable is not a requirement because separate objects can be instantiated for the `clsTable` and `clsCells` classes; however, following the hierarchy simplifies and better documents the code.

```
Private Sub CreatePage()
'Create an instance of the Page object and set its properties
    Set aPage = New clsPage
    If refSelection.Value <> "" Then
```

```
        aPage.Title = Left(refSelection.Value, InStr( _
            1, refSelection.Value, "!") - 1)
        aPage.BackColor = Range(refSelection.Value).Interior.Color
    Else
        aPage.Title = lstWkSheets.Value
        aPage.BackColor = Worksheets( _
            aPage.Title).UsedRange.Interior.Color
    End If
End Sub
```

The `CreateTableImages()` Sub procedure fills a `clsImages` collection object with `clsImage` objects representing the embedded charts on a worksheet. If the user chooses to convert an entire worksheet, then all charts are located and saved as JPEG images using the `Export` method of the `Chart` object. The file path has already been validated, so no error handling is required in this procedure. If the user selects a specific range on the worksheet, charts are ignored.

```
Private Sub CreateTableImages()
    Dim myChart As ChartObject, aChart As clsImage
    Dim imageID As Integer
    Dim fPath As String
    Dim chCorner As Range
    '....................................................
    'Find all embedded charts, create images of them,
    'set their properties, and add to Images collection
    '....................................................
    On Error GoTo ErrorHandler
    If refSelection.Value <> "" Then Exit Sub
    For Each myChart In Worksheets(lstWkSheets.Value).ChartObjects
        fPath = txtPath.Text & "\" & myChart.Name & ".jpg"
        myChart.Chart.Export Filename:=fPath, FilterName:="JPG"
        imageID = imageID + 1
        Set aChart = New clsImage
        aChart.ID = imageID
        aChart.Path = fPath
        'Find range covered by the chart
        Set chCorner = aChart.FindLocation(myChart)
        Set aChart.Location = chCorner .
        aPage.Table.Images.Add aChart
```

```
            Set aChart = Nothing
        Next
        Set chCorner = Nothing
        Set myChart = Nothing
        Exit Sub
ErrorHandler:
        MsgBox Err.Description & "   ", vbInformation, Err.Source
        End
End Sub
```

The size of the HTML table is directly correlated to the size of the used range on the worksheet. If charts are included, the used range includes the cells underneath any chart. The SetTableRange() Sub procedure sets the TableRange property of the clsTable object that holds the data for the HTML table that must be created for the Web page. If the user selects a worksheet range, the HTML table will match exactly the selected range. If the user selects a worksheet, the HTML table will match the size of the worksheet starting at cell A1 and extending to the last cell used (including charts).

```
Private Sub SetTableRange()
'Create Table object and set properties
    Dim curRange As Range
    Dim maxCol As Integer, maxRow As Long
    '...............................................................
    'Set the range of the table that holds the content of the web page
    'If range is not selected by user then get used range starting
    'with cell A1
    '...............................................................

    If refSelection.Value <> "" Then
        Set curRange = Range(refSelection.Value)
    Else
        maxCol = Worksheets(lstWkSheets.Value).UsedRange.Column + _
                 Worksheets(lstWkSheets.Value).UsedRange.Columns.Count
        maxRow = Worksheets(lstWkSheets.Value).UsedRange.Row + _
                 Worksheets(lstWkSheets.Value).UsedRange.Rows.Count
        If maxCol < aPage.Table.Images.GetMaxColumn Then
            maxCol = aPage.Table.Images.GetMaxColumn
        End If
        If maxRow < aPage.Table.Images.GetMaxRow Then
            maxRow = aPage.Table.Images.GetMaxRow
        End If
```

```
        Set curRange = Range("A1:" & GetColumnRef(maxCol) & maxRow)
    End If


    Set aPage.Table.TableRange = curRange
    Set curRange = Nothing
End Sub
```

You include the `GetColumnRef()` Sub procedure in the form module code because the `SetTableRange()` Sub procedure needs it.

```
Private Function GetColumnRef(columnIndex As Integer) As String
'Converts column index number to a textual reference
    Dim numAlpha As Integer
    Dim firstLetter As String
    Dim secondLetter As String
    Dim remainder As Integer


    'Calculate the number of characters needed
    numAlpha = columnIndex \ 26
    Select Case columnIndex / 26
        Case Is <= 1    'Column ref is between A and Z
            firstLetter = Chr(columnIndex + 64)
            GetColumnRef = firstLetter
        Case Else    'Column ref has two letters
            remainder = columnIndex - 26 * (columnIndex \ 26)
            If remainder = 0 Then
                firstLetter = Chr(64 + (columnIndex \ 26) - 1)
                secondLetter = "Z"
                GetColumnRef = firstLetter & secondLetter
            Else
                firstLetter = Chr(64 + (columnIndex \ 26))
                secondLetter = Chr(64 + remainder)
                GetColumnRef = firstLetter & secondLetter
            End If
    End Select
End Function
```

The last set of custom objects that must be instantiated are the `clsCell` and subordinate objects, whose object model is discussed in Chapter 11. The `CreateCells()` Sub procedure sets the properties of a `clsCell` object and adds it to a `clsCells` collection object.

A new `clsCell` object is created and added to the collection for every cell included in the used range on the worksheet being converted to an HTML document. If a `clsCell` object represents the location of the upper-left corner of a chart, its `HasChart` property is set to `True`.

```vba
Private Sub CreateCells()
'Create instances of cell objects and set properties
    Dim c As Range, img As clsImage
    Dim aCell As clsCell
    Dim I As Integer

    On Error GoTo ErrorHandler
'Loop through all cells in used range
    For Each c In aPage.Table.TableRange
        Set aCell = New clsCell
        aCell.CellValue = c.Value
        aCell.CellWidth = c.Width
        aCell.CellHeight = c.Height
        aCell.Alignment = c.HorizontalAlignment
        Set aCell.CellRange = Range(c.Address)

        'Test for image placement
        For I = 1 To aPage.Table.Images.Count
            If c.Address = Left(aPage.Table.Images.Item(I).Location _
                    .Address, InStr(aPage.Table.Images.Item(I) _
                    .Location.Address, ":") - 1) Then
                aCell.HasChart = True
                Exit For
            End If
        Next I

        'Read border properties of cells
        aCell.ReadBorders aCell, c
        If c.Borders.LineStyle = xlLineStyleNone Then
            aCell.HasBorder = False
        Else
            aCell.HasBorder = True
        End If
```

```
            'Read font, backcolor properties and add cell to collection
            aCell.ReadFont aCell, c
            aCell.BackColor = c.Interior.Color
            aPage.Table.Cells.Add aCell
            Set aCell = Nothing
        Next
        Set c = Nothing
        Set img = Nothing
        Exit Sub
ErrorHandler:
        MsgBox Err.Description & "   ", vbInformation, Err.Source
        End
End Sub
```

The `ModifyCells()` Sub procedure loops through each cell that was added to the `clsCells` collection in the `CreateCells()` Sub procedure and sets the `WriteCell` property accordingly. A separate procedure is used because the process of editing the `WriteCell` property requires nested loops, and the code is easier to follow if it is isolated from other procedures. The `WriteCell` property is tested when writing the HTML file; if the value is `False`, the cell is not included in the file. If the cell is beneath a chart, it will not be included in the HTML document, which prevents the creation of ghost cells created by the `colspan` and `rowspan` attributes of the `<td>` tag.

```
Private Sub ModifyCells()
'Set WriteCell property of all clsCell objects in collection
    Dim c As Range, img As clsImage, cl As clsCell
    Dim I As Integer, K As Integer

    For I = 1 To aPage.Table.Images.Count  'Loop thru all images
        Set img = aPage.Table.Images.Item(I)
        For Each c In img.Location     'Loop thru range covered by image
            'Loop thru collection of cells
            For K = 1 To aPage.Table.Cells.Count
                Set cl = aPage.Table.Cells.Item(K)
                If cl.CellRange.Address = c.Address Then
                    cl.WriteCell = False
                    Exit For
                End If
            Next K
```

```
          Next
      Next I
      Set cl = Nothing
  End Sub
```

Building the Files

After the objects are created and their properties are set to the values of the data in a worksheet, you must write the style sheet and HTML file to disk. Style sheets are text files that define a set of styles (fonts, colors, and so on) for a Web site. They offer the advantage of one document as the source of styles for multiple pages. They also allow you to remove numerous tags and tag attributes from the HTML document, making it more readable. Thus, Web sites are easier to maintain when style sheets are used. You can, of course, include styles with an HTML document; my preference is to separate style sheets to avoid unnecessary clutter.

The CSS file

The style sheet file written by the `WriteStyles()` Sub procedure writes the styles for every cell used in a worksheet. This includes those cells that have no content but are below an embedded chart. You must include all cells in order to set the height and width of the cell; otherwise, the browser's interpretation of the document might collapse the cell. For example, an empty column with a 48-point width in an Excel worksheet will be collapsed to a much smaller width in the browser. This will certainly degrade the capability of the program to reproduce the original worksheet.

Although the collapse of empty table columns and rows in a browser is dependent on other attributes set in the style sheet and HTML document, this problem has many other solutions. One solution is to include width and height attributes in the `<td>` tags of the HTML document. However, one goal of this project is to create a simple HTML document. Therefore, the width and height attributes for every cell used in a worksheet are included in a separate style sheet. A total of 13 attributes are written to the CSS file for each cell. The 13 attributes are read from the properties of each `clsCell` object that was added to the `clsCells` collection object in the `CreateCells()` Sub procedure.

Several instances of the `WriteLine` method of the `TextStream` object write the data to the file. The file is well formed and conforms to XHTML standards (see Figure 12.4). The file consists of blocks of text where a single block represents the styles for a single cell in an HTML table.

FIGURE 12.4 *Part of a sample CSS file created by the Excel-to-HTML converter program.*

The WriteStyles() Sub procedure follows:

```
Private Sub WriteStyles(fName As String)
'Writes the style sheet (text file) with .css extension
'for the web page.
    Dim fso As FileSystemObject, txtStr As TextStream
    Dim fPath As String
    Dim cl As clsCell
    Dim I As Integer

    On Error GoTo ErrorHandler
    fPath = txtPath.Text & "\" & fName
    Set fso = New FileSystemObject
    Set txtStr = fso.CreateTextFile(fPath, True)

    'Write body and initial table style
    txtStr.WriteLine "body {background-color: #" & aPage.BackColor & "}"
    txtStr.WriteLine "table {border-collapse: collapse}"
```

```
'Loop through all cells in HTML table and
'write a new line for each attribute of a cell
For I = 1 To aPage.Table.Cells.Count
    Set cl = aPage.Table.Cells.Item(I)
    txtStr.WriteLine "td." & cl.CellRange.Address(False, False) & _
                     " {background-color: #" & cl.BackColor & ";"
        txtStr.WriteLine "          color: #" & cl.Font.Color & ";"
        txtStr.WriteLine "          width: " & cl.CellWidth & "pt;"
        txtStr.WriteLine "          height: " & cl.CellHeight & "pt;"
        txtStr.WriteLine "          text-align: " & cl.Alignment & ";"
        txtStr.WriteLine "          border-top: " & cl.Borders(1) _
                            .BorderWeight & " " & cl.Borders(1) _
                            .BorderStyle & " #" & cl.Borders(1) _
                            .BorderColor & ";"
        txtStr.WriteLine "          border-right: " & cl.Borders(2) _
                            .BorderWeight & " " & cl.Borders(2) _
                            .BorderStyle & " #" & cl.Borders(2) _
                            .BorderColor & ";"
        txtStr.WriteLine "          border-bottom: " & cl.Borders(3) _
                            .BorderWeight & " " & cl.Borders(3) _
                            .BorderStyle & " #" & cl.Borders(3) _
                            .BorderColor & ";"
        txtStr.WriteLine "          border-left: " & cl.Borders(4) _
                            .BorderWeight & " " & cl.Borders(4) _
                            .BorderStyle & " #" & cl.Borders(4) _
                            .BorderColor & ";"
        txtStr.WriteLine "          font-family: " & cl.Font.Name & ";"
        txtStr.WriteLine "          font-weight: " & cl.Font.Bold & ";"
        txtStr.WriteLine "          font-size: " & cl.Font.Size & "pt;"
        txtStr.WriteLine "          font-style: " & cl.Font.Style & _
                            "}" & vbCrLf
Next I
txtStr.Close
Set cl = Nothing

Exit Sub
'
```

```
ErrorHandler:
    MsgBox Err.Description & " " & Err.Source
    End
End Sub
```

The HTML File

You create the HTML file using the `WritePage()` Sub procedure. The bulk of the procedure involves writing the lines that define the rows and columns of the table. If an image tag is to be included in a table cell, you set the `colspan` and `rowspan` attributes of the cell to the number of rows and columns that are masked by the embedded chart in the Excel worksheet (which are determined from the `Location` property of the `clsImage` object). When the `colspan` and `rowspan` attributes are used, it is important that the same numbers of column and row tags that follow the image tag are left out of the HTML table. This prevents the browser from creating ghost cells and subsequent distortion of the Web page relative to the original worksheet. You handle this task by reading the value of the `WriteCell` property of the `clsCell` object.

The resulting HTML document is well formed and easy to read because a single table dominates it. Figure 12.5 shows an example of a text file created by the `WritePage()` Sub procedure.

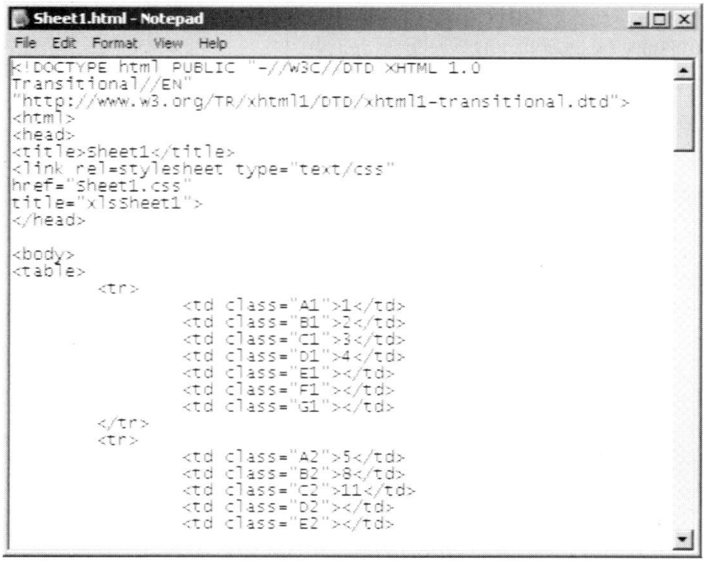


```
<!DOCTYPE html PUBLIC "-//W3C//DTD XHTML 1.0
Transitional//EN"
"http://www.w3.org/TR/xhtml1/DTD/xhtml1-transitional.dtd">
<html>
<head>
<title>Sheet1</title>
<link rel=stylesheet type="text/css"
href="Sheet1.css"
title="xlsSheet1">
</head>

<body>
<table>
        <tr>
                <td class="A1">1</td>
                <td class="B1">2</td>
                <td class="C1">3</td>
                <td class="D1">4</td>
                <td class="E1"></td>
                <td class="F1"></td>
                <td class="G1"></td>
        </tr>
        <tr>
                <td class="A2">5</td>
                <td class="B2">8</td>
                <td class="C2">11</td>
                <td class="D2"></td>
                <td class="E2"></td>
```

FIGURE 12.5 *A sample HTML file created by the Excel-to-HTML converter program.*

The `WritePage()` Sub procedure follows:

```
Private Sub WritePage(fName As String)
'Write page to text file as html
    Dim I As Integer, K As Integer, J As Integer
    Dim cl As clsCell
    Dim tg As New clsTableTags
    Dim aChart As clsImage
    Dim fso As FileSystemObject, txtStr As TextStream
    Dim fPath As String

    On Error GoTo ErrorHandler
    fPath = txtPath.Text & "\" & fName
    Set fso = New FileSystemObject
    Set txtStr = fso.CreateTextFile(fPath, True)

    'Write initial block of HTML tags
    txtStr.WriteLine aPage.HtmlBegin
    txtStr.WriteLine tg.TableStart          '<table>

    For K = 0 To aPage.Table.TableRange.Rows.Count - 1
        txtStr.WriteLine vbTab & tg.RowStart     'New row <tr>
        'Add columns <td></td>
        For I = 1 To aPage.Table.TableRange.Columns.Count
            Set cl = aPage.Table.Cells _
                .Item(I + aPage.Table.TableRange.Columns.Count * K)
            If cl.HasChart Then       'Add image if required
                For J = 1 To aPage.Table.Images.Count
                    Set aChart = aPage.Table.Images.Item(J)
                    'Add image tag if cell represents upper left
                    'corner of a chart
                    If Left(aChart.Location.Address, InStr( _
                        1, aChart.Location.Address, ":") - 1) = _
                        cl.CellRange.Address Then
                            txtStr.WriteLine vbTab & vbTab & _
                                "<td colspan=" & Chr(34) & _
```

```
                              aChart.Location.Columns.Count & _
                                Chr(34) & " rowspan=" & Chr(34) & _
                                aChart.Location.Rows.Count _
                              & Chr(34) & ">" & "<img src=" & Chr(34) & _
                              aChart.Path & Chr(34) & ">" & tg.CellEnd
                         Exit For
                    End If
                Next J
            Else        'Write the value if not hidden by an image
                If cl.WriteCell Then
                    txtStr.WriteLine vbTab & vbTab & tg.CellStart( _
                        cl.CellRange.Address(False, False)) & _
                        cl.CellValue & tg.CellEnd
                End If
            End If
            Set cl = Nothing
        Next I
        txtStr.WriteLine vbTab & tg.RowEnd
    Next K


    'Write closing tags for document
    txtStr.WriteLine tg.TableEnd
    txtStr.WriteLine aPage.HtmlEnd
    txtStr.Close
    lblOutput.Caption = fName & " successfully created!"
    Exit Sub
ErrorHandler:
    MsgBox Err.Description & "   " & Err.Source
    End
End Sub
```

This completes the coding phase of the project. All that remains is testing and debugging the program.

Testing and Debugging

Prior to writing the program that actually creates the style sheet and HTML documents, I tested the object model as described in Chapter 11. I instantiated individual classes, initialized their properties to random values, and read the property values using a series of `Debug.Print` statements.

I tested the program code from the form module by creating several sample worksheets in Excel with random data tables and charts at various locations. The data was formatted with different colors, fonts, and borders. Then I reproduced the worksheet as an HTML document and compared it to the original worksheet looking for a similar appearance. Because the objects had already been tested, they didn't present a problem when I tested the program code from the form module. I encountered the most serious debugging when setting the location of the images and reproducing the widths of the Excel tables. As a result, I added the `WriteCell` and `HasChart` properties to the `clsCell` class to encapsulate these problems within the object model. Figures 12.6 and 12.7 show a comparison of a sample Excel worksheet and the resulting Web page created by the Excel-to-HTML program.

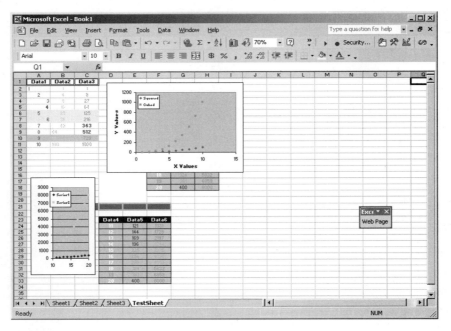

FIGURE 12.6 *A sample Excel worksheet to be converted to a Web page.*

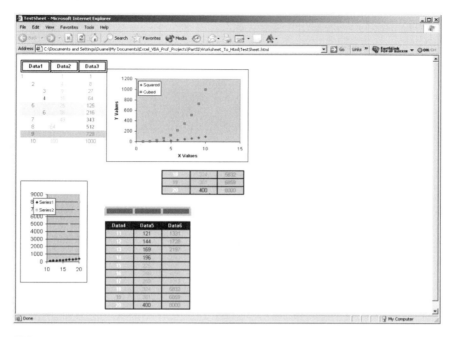

FIGURE 12.7 *The Web page resulting from the conversion of the worksheet shown in Figure 12.6.*

The reproduction is reasonable, but not perfect by any means. One problem is that the charts are assumed to completely mask cells around their borders. Thus, the program ignores the content (value and formatting) of partially masked cells around the border of a chart. This can also displace images and tables in the HTML document relative to the original worksheet. Other problems are related mostly to the limited formatting that the program can reproduce. These problems are correctable: Just add more code to address the issues that concern you the most.

Summary

This chapter constructed a program that reproduces existing Excel worksheets as static Web pages with reasonable accuracy. The text files produced by the program are well formed, and even beginning Web developers will find them easy to read. The program is meant to be stored as an Excel add-in file and executed from a custom toolbar. The program involved the use of objects discussed in Chapters 9–11, but made the most extensive use of class modules. The Chart object made only a minor appearance in the Excel-to-HTML program, but you will see it again in later projects.

PART III

Professional Project 2 — Data Analysis for Pear Tree Used Cars, Inc.

Parts I and II of this book use programming structures and common objects in VBA and the Excel object model to create custom applications for Excel. Most of the objects discussed thus far are fairly well documented in the VBA online help included with Office. However, many of the solutions required by Office applications involve objects that are not installed, or no help is included with Office. This is especially true of data control objects used in applications requiring access to a database. The most common object models used in VBA are ActiveX Data Objects (ADO) and Data Access Objects (DAO). Unfortunately, no help is provided for these through the Office interface, making it harder to learn how to use them without seeking external sources.

Many of your database solutions for Excel will involve Access, which is a component of the Microsoft Office suite. You are not limited by VBA to writing applications only for Access databases, but it is the only database application covered in this book.

Access is a relational database management system (RDBMS) developing desktop and client-server database applications under Windows. Although an RDBMS is wonderful for storing, retrieving, and otherwise managing large volumes of data, it is appropriate mostly for trivial data analyses. Conversely, Excel (or any other spreadsheet application) is excellent for simple-to-complex data analyses but is not particularly good at data management. So, Access and Excel complement each other nicely.

The chapters in Part III teach you how to build applications using Excel and VBA to read and update data from an Access database. Specifically, you learn about the following:

- ◆ Creating and normalizing an Access database
- ◆ The Microsoft Jet database engine
- ◆ Using the DAO and ADO object models to import and export data between Excel and Access
- ◆ Creating and manipulating Excel pivot tables and pivot charts

The last chapter in Part III uses these newly introduced objects to construct a business analysis program for a fabricated group of car dealerships.

Chapter 13

You will not find a more complementary application to a relational database management system (RDBMS) than a spreadsheet application such as Excel. The two applications work so well together because the RDBMS organizes and retrieves information quickly, whereas the spreadsheet provides the tools to effectively analyze the data.

Office comes with Excel and Access, a powerful RDBMS for creating database applications that run under Windows. (Access is differentiated from most database applications by its strong graphical interface, which enables users with little or no database experience to develop a relational database, albeit ineffectively.) Despite the fact that Office comes with Access and Excel, many people use only Excel, for storing data, never bothering to learn to use Access or basic database theory. Doing so is fine for a very small database; however, Excel does not have the tools needed for managing data as Access does and, therefore, should not be used for anything other than the most trivial database applications (flat-file phone directories, address books, checkbooks, and so on).

This chapter includes a brief description of how to create and define an Access database using its GUI. (Although, you can use VBA to create and define an Access database, it is much simpler to create the database from the Access GUI.) I then show you how to use VBA to update and query an Access database from Excel.

You can use two similar but distinct object models in VBA with an Access database: the Data Access Object (DAO) model, an outdated object model no longer updated by Microsoft, and the ActiveX Data object (ADO) model, the preferred and versatile object model that is extended to the latest version of Visual Basic (.Net) as ADO.Net. The ADO object model allows you to connect to any database provider included with the objects and is simpler than the DAO model. I include a discussion of the DAO object model in this chapter because it is easy to use and is still supported by and included with Office.

Using DAO or ADO requires knowledge of the Structured Query Language (SQL), a standard language used for querying, manipulating, and defining a relational database. Access supports a version of SQL that is not too different from the ANSI standard version. See Appendix C for the basic SQL commands for querying and manipulating an Access database.

Creating a Database with Microsoft Access

For simplicity, let me say that a *relational database* is a collection of related data tables where each table describes a single entity. The nature of these tables and their relationships in terms of the rules governing how they are created determines a database's qualification as relational. Ideally, your database is *normalized* (more about this later) and well defined with key fields, indices, and other constraints. However, neither Access nor any other RDBMS will check for proper normalization, and most constraints are not required. So, it is up to the user to define and build a normalized database with proper constraints.

Consider an example of a database for a business that tracks customer and product information. A table that holds customer information (call it Customers) in this database can be defined by the names, addresses, and phone numbers of the customers and will include columns for each of these fields. The data that defines the products sold by the business cannot be included in the Customers table because it does not describe a customer (even though customers do purchase products). Combining the customer and product data into a single table will result in inconsistencies and redundancies and will make updates difficult if not impossible (as I discuss in the next section). Therefore, the fields that define the products sold by the business will have to be included in another table (for example, Products). The relationship between the Customers and Products tables in the database is indirect and will probably follow through a table called Orders or something similar. The point of all this is that you should not start creating a database before designing it, even if the database is relatively small.

Before you create a database in Access, you should first design a set of normalized tables for holding the required data. Each table should define a component of the data and include natural relationships to one or more other tables in the database. Once this is accomplished, the database is said to be "normalized," and you can proceed to create it in Access.

 NOTE

Avoid creating a database that is not properly normalized as doing so will lead to constant restructuring of your tables and relationships making the database hard to maintain. The end result will be frustration, more work, and potential errors when accessing the data. In addition, a non-normalized relational database wastes storage space.

Normalization: Creating Effective Database Tables

Normalization is the process of identifying and correcting potential problems in the design of a relational database. Improper normalization causes redundancies that can lead to inconsistent data and update anomalies.

To illustrate the process of normalization, consider an example of a business's database holding information regarding its customers and the products they have purchased. Data includes the customer name (first and last), address, and phone number, along with each product they have purchased, the description of the product, number of products purchased, and the price paid for each product.

Table 13.1 shows the result when all of the aforementioned data is entered into a single table. The phone number serves as the primary key for the table.

 NOTE

A *primary key* is the column or combination of columns that uniquely identifies the rows in a table.

Table 13.1 An Unnormalized Customer/Products Database Table

First Name	Last Name	Address	City	State	Zip Code	Phone	Product Name	Product Description	Number Purchased	Product Price
John	Smyth	123 Spring Mill Blvd.	Indianapolis	IN	46200	555-0234	Widget	A basic widget	1	$99.99
Jack	Jons	456 Meridian Rd.	Indianapolis	IN	46210	555-0876	Gadget	A basic gadget	2	$79.99
Jane	Roe	789 Michigan Ct.	Indianapolis	IN	46222	555-0678	Widget, Gadget	A basic widget, A basic gadget	2,3	$99.99 $79.99
John	Smyth	345 W 86th	Indianapolis	IN	46250	555-0567	Gadget	A basic gadget	3	$79.99

Primary keys are essential for distinguishing one row from another in a table. A RDBMS uses a primary key to quickly identify unique records in a database. Ensuring the uniqueness of the records in a database reduces data redundancies and inconsistencies that can impede its utility. For example, without the phone number field shown in Table 13.1, it would be hard to distinguish customers who have the same first and last name, making it more difficult to write a practical query on this table. A primary key should be defined for every table in a relational database.

It may be tempting to include all of the data in a single table as shown in Table 13.1; however, with the addition of a few records of data, you will start to see some problems. First, any record for a customer who has purchased more than one product includes multiple entries in the fields related to the products. These multiple entries are known as *repeating groups* and must be avoided at all times. Problems with repeating groups include the following:

◆ **Data handling errors.** Any RDBMS considers each cell in a table as single-valued. Returning data from repeating groups in a query can cause run-time errors. For example, a query that returns the sum of the purchase price column will result in an error because of the non-numerical field that must be used to store multiple entries.

◆ **Redundancies.** The product name, description, and price are often repeated in the table, resulting in inefficient use of disk space.

◆ **Update anomalies.** Changing a product description means altering every record that includes the product, which could easily result in multiple descriptions of the same product if some records are missed. Also, you cannot add a new product that has not been ordered because there is no customer information. Similarly, you cannot delete a record without the risk of losing all information about a product (if, for example, only one customer has ordered a certain product).

Any record with repeating groups can be split into multiple records to eliminate the repeating groups from the table (see Table 13.2). The table is now said to be in *first normal form* if the primary key is redefined as the combination of the Phone and Product Name columns.

Table 13.2 Customer/Purchased Products Database Table in First Normal Form

First Name	Last Name	Address	City	State	Zip Code	Phone	Product Name	Product Description	Number Purchased	Product Price
John	Smyth	123 Spring Mill Blvd.	Indianapolis	IN	46200	555-0234	Widget	A basic widget	1	$99.99
Jack	Jons	456 Meridian Rd.	Indianapolis	IN	46210	555-0876	Gadget	A basic gadget	2	$79.99
Jane	Roe	789 Michigan Ct.	Indianapolis	IN	46222	555-0678	Widget	A basic widget	2	$99.99
Jane	Roe	789 Michigan Ct.	Indianapolis	IN	46222	555-0678	Gadget	A basic gadget	3	$79.99
John	Smyth	345 W 86th	Indianapolis	IN	46250	312-4567	Gadget	A basic gadget	3	$79.99

A table that is in first normal form will still have the redundancy and updating problems previously listed. The nature of the problem with Table 13.2 is the dependencies of non-key columns on only a portion of the primary key. For example, the product description is dependent only on the product name and not on the customer's phone number.

 NOTE

A column that is not part of the primary key is a *non-key* column.

To further normalize Table 13.2, the incomplete dependencies of non-key columns on only a portion of the primary key must be removed. The easiest way to do this is to add another column and assign it a unique value for each record, as shown in Table 13.3. The primary key is now the ID column. This effectively removes the incomplete dependencies of non-key columns on only a portion of the primary key and places the table in *second normal form.*

Table 13.3 Customer/Purchased Products Database Table in Second Normal Form

ID	First Name	Last Name	Address	City	State	Zip Code	Phone	Product Name	Product Description	Number Purchased	Product Price
1	John	Smyth	123 Spring Mill Blvd.	Indianapolis	IN	46200	555-0234	Widget	A basic widget	1	$99.99
2	Jack	Jons	456 Meridian Rd.	Indianapolis	IN	46210	555-0876	Gadget	A basic gadget	2	$79.99
3	Jane	Roe	789 Michigan Ct.	Indianapolis	IN	46222	555-0678	Widget	A basic widget	2	$99.99
4	Jane	Roe	789 Michigan Ct.	Indianapolis	IN	46222	555-0678	Gadget	A basic gadget	3	$79.99
5	John	Smyth	345 W 86th	Indianapolis	IN	46250	555-0567	Gadget	A basic gadget	3	$79.99

NOTE

Any table that is in first normal form and that contains a primary key defined with only one column is automatically in second normal form.

Unfortunately, problems still exist with Table 13.3. Namely, redundancies, update anomalies, and data inconsistencies are still present or likely to occur. The nature of the problem now lies with the dependencies of non-key columns on columns other than the primary key. For example, the product description and price are dependent on the product name as well as the primary key (ID). The next step in the normalization process is to remove the dependencies of non-key columns on columns other than the primary key. This can be accomplished only by splitting the table into multiple tables. The number of required tables depends on the number of dependent groups within the original table. The following is a list of the dependencies of non-key columns on the Phone and Product Name columns in Table 13.3:

◆ **Phone.** First Name, Last Name, Address, City, State, Zip Code

◆ **Product Name.** Product Description, Number Purchased, Product Price

With two dependent groups, the original table is now split into two (see Tables 13.4 and 13.5). The phone number once again serves as the primary key for the Customers table, and the product name is the primary key for the Products table. Both tables are now in *third normal form* because all non-key columns are dependent on only the primary key.

Table 13.4 The Customers Table in Third Normal Form

First Name	Last Name	Address	City	State	Zip Code	Phone
John	Smyth	123 Spring Mill Blvd.	Indianapolis	IN	46200	555-0234
Jack	Jons	456 Meridian Rd.	Indianapolis	IN	46210	555-0876
Jane	Roe	789 Michigan Ct.	Indianapolis	IN	46222	555-0678
John	Roe	345 W 86th	Indianapolis	IN	46250	555-0567

Table 13.5 The Products Table in Third Normal Form

Product Name	Product Description	Product Price
Widget	A basic widget	$99.99
Gadget	A basic gadget	$79.99

It is now possible to properly update the Customers and Products tables without the worry of creating redundancies or data inconsistencies. Ensuring that the tables in a database are all in third normal form is usually sufficient for removing update anomalies, inconsistent data, and redundancies. Yet there is still a problem with the Customer and Products tables shown in Tables 13.4 and 13.5. How do you define the relationship between these two tables? Clearly a relationship must exist because customers order products. If you want to track what customers purchase and how much they spend, a relationship between these tables will have to be defined. Unfortunately, adding product information to the Customers table or vice versa will violate the rules of normalization. In this case, the only way to define a relationship between the Customers and Products tables is to create a third table to serve as a link between them. The natural relationship between the Customers and Products tables defines the third table; a Products Purchased table is required to link the customers to the products they have purchased (see Table 13.6).

Table13.6 The Products Purchased Database Table in Third Normal Form

Phone	Product Name	Number Purchased
555-0234	Widget	1
555-0876	Gadget	2
555-0678	Widget	2
555-0678	Gadget	3
555-0567	Gadget	3

The Products Purchased table includes three fields: the customer's phone number, the product name, and the number of products ordered. The primary key is the combination of the Phone and Product Name fields. The table is in third normal form because the only non-key column (number purchased) is dependent on both components of the primary key.

Creating and Defining Tables Using the Access GUI

As I mentioned previously in this chapter, Access comes with a considerable GUI interface complete with wizards for creating all available object types (tables, queries, forms, reports, and Web pages). Access may actually be too easy to use because it is possible for someone with little or no background in relational database theory to become quite proficient with the GUI. Of course, this can lead to serious problems down the road, when it is learned that the company database must be completely restructured because of a poor design.

When creating a new Access database, you are prompted to save the database before adding components or entering data. After you enter a descriptive name, Access will create a file with the .mdb extension at the specified location. As you build your database by adding tables, queries, and so on, the .mdb file is updated to include all components, so there is never more than one file associated with a single database (with the exception of image files that may be used with forms, reports, and Web pages).

After a new database is created, the Database window appears. This window serves as the interface to the objects the database contains (see Figure 13.1).

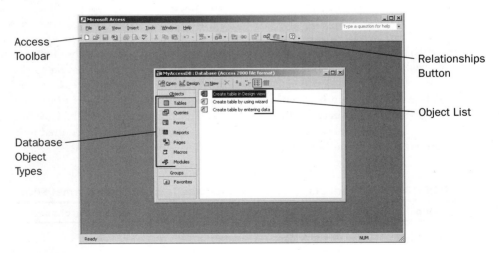

FIGURE 13.1 *The Access Database window for a new, blank database.*

Use the Database window to create new objects for a database including tables. Creating a database table requires that you define the fields (columns) and their data types (String,

`Integer`, `Boolean`, and so on). Key fields (primary, foreign), and any other desired constraints are optional but highly recommended. Access includes a wizard for creating tables, but it is useless unless your table will include only fields from its limited selection. To create a new table in Design view, start with a blank database and your definitions of a normalized set of tables. Then follow these steps:

1.   Select Tables from the list of available objects and double-click the Create table in Design view icon. A Design view table window appears containing a grid with three columns for the field names, data types, and description (see Figure 13.2). The field properties are listed at the bottom of the window.

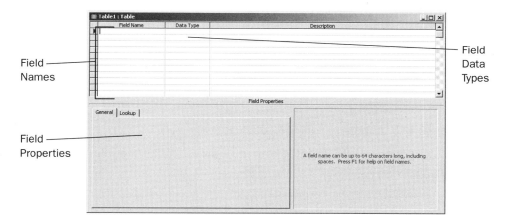

FIGURE 13.2   *Creating an Access database table from Design view.*

2.   Enter the names of the fields. Use descriptive names, don't over abbreviate, and avoid spaces.

3.   Select the appropriate data type from the drop-down list that appears in the Data Type column after entering the name of a field. The data types are essentially the same as those used in VBA. Choose the appropriate type for the data that will be stored within the given field.

4.   Edit the default value for the size of the field. For text and numerical data types, enter or select a value for the Field Size in the Field Properties list at the bottom of the window (see Figure 13.3).

5.   Add additional constraints. At a minimum, select (or at least note) values for the Indexed and Required properties for a field. You can also set additional formatting constraints for textual and numerical data using the, Format, and Input Mask properties (see Figure 13.3).

6.   Create the primary key. Select all fields (or field) you want to define as the primary key and the press primary key button (the little yellow key near the middle of the toolbar).

7.   Repeat for each table required for your database.

Primary Key Button

Field Size Property

Required Property

Indexed Property

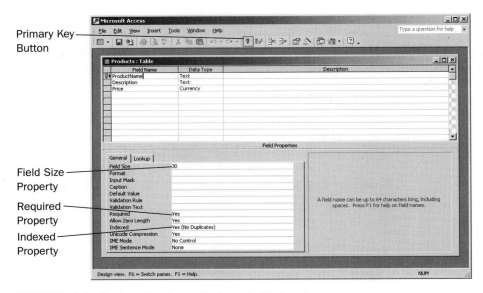

FIGURE 13.3 *An Access database table shown in Design view.*

Once you create all the tables, you need to define the relationships (foreign keys). To define the foreign keys follow these steps:

1. Select the Database window and click the Relationships button on the toolbar (refer to Figure 13.1). The Show Table dialog box appears (see Figure 13.4).

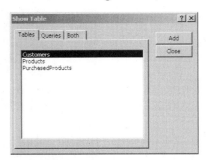

FIGURE 13.4 *The Show Table dialog box used to define relationships between tables.*

2. In the Show Table dialog box, add all tables to the Relationships window by selecting them and clicking Add.

3. Create a relationship. From the main menu, select Relationships, Edit Relationship or drag the field name from one table to the related field in another table in the Relationships window.

4. Select or ensure that the proper fields and tables are entered in the Edit Relationships dialog box (see Figure 13.5).

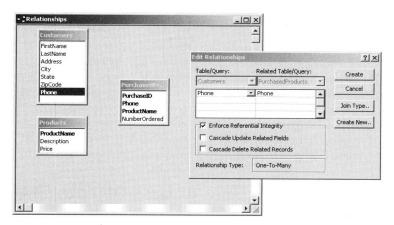

FIGURE 13.5 *The Edit Relationships dialog box used to create relationships between tables.*

5. Choose whether to Enforce Referential Integrity (usually a good idea) and click Create. Access draws a line between the key fields in the Relationships window (see Figure 13.6).

6. Repeat these steps for all other foreign keys.

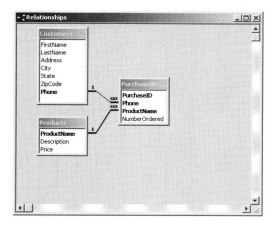

FIGURE 13.6 *The Relationships window after all relationships are defined.*

You can edit your relationships at any time by displaying the Relationships window and right-clicking the line that defines the relationship of interest.

Only after all tables, keys, constraints, and relationships are defined, do you begin to enter data into your database.

The Microsoft Jet Database Engine

Microsoft's Jet database engine is the desktop RDBMS behind the Access GUI. The Jet database engine is installed with any version of Office that includes Access. It is also installed with Visual Basic or Visual Studio. The Jet database engine has a built-in query processor and optimizer for supporting the creation, manipulation, and querying of a database. Furthermore, it supports access to other database engines through ODBC (open database connectivity), although performance will vary with each database. Since this book deals in Excel-VBA programming and Excel and Access are both components of Office, I will limit programming examples to accessing a Jet database (.mdb file extension).

Programming in Excel with Data Access Objects (DAO)

The Data Access Object (DAO) model serves as a programmer's interface to the Jet database engine. It contains several objects that are used to transfer data to and from a database. In addition, it exposes its objects in a COM library so they can be used in other applications (for example, Visual Basic, Excel). To use the DAO object model in Excel, you must set a reference to the COM library Microsoft DAO 3.6 Object Library (or earlier version) listed with the available references. To access these references from the Excel-VBA IDE, select Tools, References. The References - VBAProject dialog box opens (see Figure 13.7).

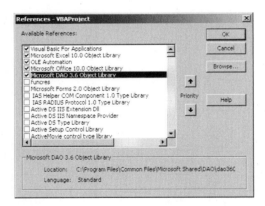

FIGURE 13.7 *Setting a reference to the DAO COM library from the Excel-VBA IDE.*

The DAO Object Model

A diagram of the DAO object model is shown in Figure 13.8. The model is fairly complex, but the `Recordset` object is the workhorse object in the model, so it will receive most of the attention here.

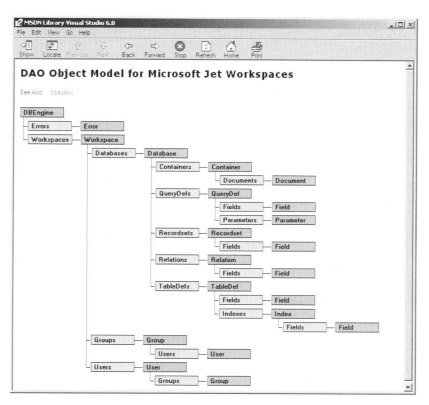

FIGURE 13.8 *The DAO object model.*

Workspaces and the DBEngine Object

The DBEngine object is the top-level object in the DAO object hierarchy. It is not part of a collection, and you cannot create additional DBEngine objects. As the top-level object, its existence is implied, and it will rarely have to be qualified in an object path. Typically, it is explicitly referenced when creating a new Access database using the CreateDatabase method.

```
Dim myDB As DAO.DBEngine
Set myDB = New DBEngine
myDB.CreateDatabase Name:="C:\MyNewDatabase.mdb", _
    locale:=dbLangGeneral
```

The preceding code creates a new Jet database named MyNewDatabase.mdb at the specified path. The new database is empty, but components (tables, queries, and so on) can be created using the objects and methods included in the DAO object model. However, if Access is already available, there is little point to creating the database programmatically, so I don't discuss such methods any further.

The Workspaces collection object contains all active Workspace objects under the DBEngine object. A Workspace object represents a user's session, controls the data source (Jet or ODBC), may contain multiple open databases, and manages the transactions that occur during the session. The Microsoft Jet workspace is the default Workspace object and is used to access a Jet database. So, if your intention is to access a Jet database within a single session, you don't have to specify the DBEngine object and Workspace object in your code.

 NOTE

Multiple Workspace objects are required when creating multiple sessions or when you need to access both Jet and ODBC database engines.

In the remaining code examples, I assume that a single session is accessing an existing Jet database.

Opening an Existing Jet Database with DAO

The Database object represents a single database, and you can use its properties and methods to retrieve and manipulate data in an open database. To open an existing Jet database (.mdb file), use the OpenDatabase method of the Workspace object.

```
Dim database As DAO.Database
Set database = workspace.OpenDatabase ( _
    dbname, options, read-only, connect)
```

First, the variable database is declared as a Database object. The DAO type library reference is included in the declaration only as a precaution. If a program references more than one database object model (for example, DAO and ADO), including the type library in the variable declaration removes any ambiguity. The Workspace object is optional, and if it's not specified, the default (Jet) is used.

The OpenDatabase method accepts up to four arguments. The dbname argument is required and specifies the name and path to the database file. The options argument is optional and accepts a Boolean value indicating whether the database is to be opened for exclusive (True) or shared use (False, default). The read-only argument is also optional and should be set to True to open the database with read-only access or False (default) to allow read-write access. The connect argument is for passing strings representing various connection parameters, such as a password or data source name and driver for an ODBC data source (not considered here). The following opens the sample Access database Northwind.mdb for shared read-write access:

```
Dim dbNorthwind As DAO.Database
Dim dbPath As String
```

```
DbPath = " C:\Program Files\Microsoft Office\Office\" & _
    "Samples\Northwind.mdb"
Set dbNorthwind = OpenDatabase(dbPath)
```

Once the database is open, you can manipulate it using the objects, properties, and methods subordinate to the `Database` object. Three of the more useful objects include the `TableDef`, `QueryDef`, and `Recordset` objects used to represent stored definitions of tables, queries, and the records in a base table or query, respectively. Ultimately, when you use DAO objects, data is manipulated almost exclusively with the `Recordset` object. This is also true when importing and updating data in a database from Excel.

Using the Recordset Object for Data I/O Between Excel and Access

The `Recordset` object represents all records in a base table or query. To create a `Recordset` object, use the `OpenRecordset` method of the `Database` object.

```
Set recordset = object.OpenRecordset (source, type, options, lockedits)
```

The `source` argument (required) is a `String` that specifies the source of the records in the Jet database (defined table, query, or SQL statement). The `type` argument specifies a `Recordset` type as described in Table 13.7.

Table 13.7 Recordset Types

Type Constant	Description
dbOpenTable	Opens a database table and populates the `Recordset` immediately. You must specify the name of the table in the source argument. The resulting table is updatable.
dbOpenDynaset	Query based `Recordset` that is populated as needed. Data is updatable.
dbOpenSnapshot	Query based `Recordset` that is populated as needed. Data is not updatable.
dbOpenForwardOnly	Same as snapshot `Recordset`, except you can only move forward through the records.

If the type does not provide enough control, the `options` argument (optional) may be used to specify one or more characteristics of the `Recordset`. Named constants included with the DAO object model for use with the `options` argument in the `OpenRecordset` method are listed in Table 13.8.

Table 13.8 Recordset Options

Option Constant	Description
dbAppendOnly	Data can be appended to the `Recordset`, but existing records cannot be edited or deleted.
dbSQLPassThrough	Passes an SQL statement to a data source for processing (snapshot-type `Recordset` only).
dbSeeChanges	In applications where multiple users have simultaneous read/write access to the same data, a run-time error is generated if one user is changing data that another user is editing (dynaset-type `Recordset` only).
dbDenyWrite	Prevents other users from modifying or adding records.
dbDenyRead	Prevents other users from reading data in a table (table-type `Recordset` only).
dbInconsistent	Allows inconsistent updates (dynaset-type and snapshot-type `Recordset` objects only).
dbConsistent	Allows only consistent updates (dynaset-type and snapshot-type `Recordset` objects only).

Finally, the `lockedits` argument (optional) determines the locking for the `Recordset`. Again one of several constants may be used to specify the locking (`dbReadOnly`, `dbPessimistic`, or `dbOptimistic`). The constants `dbPessimistic` and `dbOptimistic` set the locking time in a multiuser environment. With `dbPessimistic`, a record that is being edited is locked as soon as the `Edit` method is invoked. With `dbOptimistic`, a record is not locked until the `Update` method is invoked. Use either `dbPessimistic` or `dbOptimistic` if read-write access to the database is required.

You can create as many `Recordset` objects as required by your program, and they can access the same data without conflicts. The following code creates two `Recordset` objects representing the `Employees` and `Customers` tables in the Northwind.mdb database:

```
Dim rsEmployees As DAO.Recordset
Dim rsCustomers As DAO.Recordset
Set rsEmployees = dbNorthwind.OpenRecordset("Employees", dbOpenTable)
Set rsCustomers = dbNorthwind.OpenRecordset("Customers", dbOpenTable)
```

After a `Recordset` object is instantiated, its properties and methods are used to navigate through the records and access the data. The number of records in a `Recordset` is read with the `RecordCount` property. Table-type recordsets are immediately filled with all records from the specified table, but dynaset and snapshot-type recordsets are populated as needed and hold only one record when first created. Thus, the `RecordCount` property will return the value 1 when a dynaset or snapshot `Recordset` is first created. If you need an accurate record count when the `Recordset` is first created, move the data pointer to the last record with the `MoveLast` method before using the `RecordCount` property to read the number of records.

```
rsCustomers.MoveLast
numCustomers = rsCustomers.RecordCount
```

The methods `MoveFirst`, `MoveLast`, `MoveNext`, and `MovePrevious` are used to navigate through the records contained in a `Recordset` object and are especially convenient when used with loops. Use the `Boolean` properties `BOF` (beginning of file) or `EOF` (end of file) to establish a loop's conditional statement when navigating through a `Recordset`.

The find methods (`FindFirst`, `FindLast`, `FindNext`, and `FindPrevious`) locate the first, last, next, or previous record in a dynaset or snapshot-type `Recordset` that satisfies a specified criterion (input as a `String` that includes a field name). The first record found that matches the specified criterion is made the current record. If no record is found, the `NoMatch` property is set to `True`, and the record pointer is unknown.

```
With rsEmployees
    .FindFirst "City = 'Seattle'"
    If .NoMatch Then
        MsgBox ("No Records Found!")
        .MoveFirst
    Else
        MsgBox ("Found " & .Fields(2).Value & " " & .Fields(1).Value & _
            " in Seattle")
    End If
End With
```

Accessing Data with the Fields Collection and Field Objects

After a `Recordset` object has been created and populated with records, you can access the data in a record using the `Fields` collection object. Specific data elements of the record are accessed via the `Value` property of the `Field` object that was returned from the `Fields` collection object. Indices for the `Fields` collection object start at zero, so the `Fields` collection for a `Recordset` with five columns includes indices between 0 and 4. The following code outputs all employee names from the Northwind.mdb database to an Excel worksheet:

```
I = 2
With rsEmployees
    If Not .BOF Then .MoveFirst
    Do While Not .EOF
```

```
        Cells(I, 1).Value = .Fields(2)    'First name in third column
        Cells(I, 2).Value = .Fields(1)    'Last name in second column
        .MoveNext
        I = I + 1
    Loop
End With
```

Creating a Database Form from an Excel Worksheet

Data I/O between Excel and a Jet database is a very common programming task when using DAO objects in VBA. The worksheet shown in Figure 13.9 demonstrates data I/O between an Excel worksheet and Jet database. The worksheet is designed to display, edit, and create new records in the `Categories` table of the Northwind.mdb database.

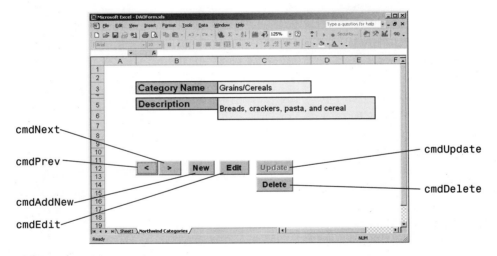

FIGURE 13.9 *An Excel worksheet serving as a database form.*

To make the form functional, all code is written in the worksheet's code module after setting a reference to the DAO object library. Module-level variables are declared for the `Database` and `Recordset` objects (`dbNorthwind` and `rsCategories`, respectively).

```
Option Explicit
Private dbNorthwind As DAO.Database
Private rsCategories As DAO.Recordset
```

The `Activate()` event of the `Worksheet` object initializes the `dbNorthwind` and `rsCategories` object variables. A table-type `Recordset` is then filled with the records from the `Categories` table using the `OpenRecordset` method of the `Database` object.

The name and description fields of the first record are then written to cells in the work-sheet (C3 and C5). The `Deactivate()` event of the `Worksheet` object closes the database and releases system memory.

```
Private Sub Worksheet_Activate()
'Initialize variables and display the first record
    Dim dbpath As String

    dbpath = "C:\Program Files\Microsoft Office\Office10\" & _
        "Samples\Northwind.mdb"
    Set dbNorthwind = OpenDatabase(dbpath)
    Set rsCategories = dbNorthwind.OpenRecordset( _
        "Categories", dbOpenTable)
    With rsCategories
        If Not .BOF Then .MoveFirst
        Cells(3, 3).Value = .Fields(1).Value    'Name
        Cells(5, 3).Value = .Fields(2).Value    'Description
    End With
End Sub
Private Sub Worksheet_Deactivate()
'Close database if worksheet is made inactive
    If IsNull(rsCategories) Then
        rsCategories.Close
        dbNorthwind.Close
        Set rsCategories = Nothing
        Set dbNorthwind = Nothing
    End If
End Sub
```

You use the `Click()` events of the Command buttons `cmdNext` and `cmdPrev` to display the next or previous record in the `Recordset`. Some care is needed here because the `MoveNext` and `MovePrevious` methods of the `Recordset` object will generate a run-time error if the record pointer is moved beyond the limits of the `Recordset`. Therefore, the `MoveLast` and `MoveFirst` methods are used to ensure that the record pointer never passes these limits.

```
Private Sub cmdNext_Click()
'Move to next record in recordset and display fields
    With rsCategories
        If Not .EOF Then
```

```
        .MoveNext
        If .EOF Then .MoveLast
        Cells(3, 3).Value = .Fields(1).Value    'Name
        Cells(5, 3).Value = .Fields(2).Value    'Description
      End If
    End With
End Sub
Private Sub cmdPrev_Click()
'Move to previous record in recordset and display fields
    With rsCategories
        If Not .BOF Then
            .MovePrevious
            If .BOF Then .MoveFirst
            Cells(3, 3).Value = .Fields(1).Value    'Name
            Cells(5, 3).Value = .Fields(2).Value    'Description
        End If
    End With
End Sub
```

The remaining procedures are all Click() events of the Command buttons used to add a new record, edit the current record, delete the current record, and update changes made to the Recordset. To save changes made to the Recordset with the AddNew or Edit methods, you must invoke the Update method before moving the record pointer.

```
Private Sub cmdAddNew_Click()
'Create a new blank record. Must be updated or new data is lost.
    Range("C3").Value = ""
    Range("C5").Value = ""
    cmdUpdate.Enabled = True
    With rsCategories
        .AddNew
    End With
End Sub
Private Sub cmdEdit_Click()
'Edit the current record. Must be updated or new data is lost
    rsCategories.Edit
    Range("C5").Select
    cmdUpdate.Enabled = True
End Sub
```

```
Private Sub cmdUpdate_Click()
'Update new records and edited records
    With rsCategories
        .Fields(1).Value = Cells(3, 3).Value
        .Fields(2).Value = Cells(5, 3).Value
        rsCategories.Update
    End With
    cmdUpdate.Enabled = False
End Sub
Private Sub cmdDelete_Click()
'Delete the current record
    rsCategories.Delete
End Sub
```

As you can see, little code is required to effectively manipulate a database with the DAO object model. However, because Microsoft is no longer updating the DAO object model, you should probably limit its use. It is hard to say how much longer Office will include the DAO object model.

Programming in Excel with ADO

ADO (ActiveX data objects) is the successor to DAO and has been evolving for a few years. These objects allow access to data through any OLE database provider. The object model is greatly simplified relative to DAO but still remains very robust, giving a consistent interface to a wide variety of data sources. The connection to these data sources is actually implemented with the OLE DB set of COM interfaces, but ADO greatly simplifies this interface with its objects, properties, and methods. It is the preferred object model to use in database applications. In essence, it's a lightweight but powerful model for database development.

 NOTE

Before programming with the objects included in the ADO object model, you must set a reference to its type library Microsoft ActiveX Data Objects 2.7 Library. If the library is not listed, you can download version 2.7 or later from Microsoft's Web site at http://msdn.microsoft.com/downloads/list/dataaccess.asp.

The ADO Object Model

The ADO object model is greatly simplified from DAO, as shown in Figure 13.10.

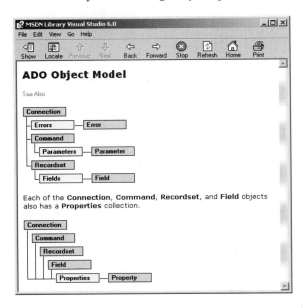

FIGURE 13.10 *The ADO object model.*

The `Connection` object is the top-level object in the model and represents an open connection to a data source. Use the properties and methods of the `Connection` object to configure the connection before opening it. Data source providers are installed with ADO, so all you have to do is include the provider in the `ConnectionString` or `Provider` properties of the `Connection` object. To open a Jet database, use `"Microsoft.Jet.OLEDB.4.0"` as the provider `String` (the version number may be different on your computer).

```
Dim conn As ADODB.Connection
Dim connStr As String
connStr = "Data Source=" & ActiveWorkbook.Path & "\myDB.mdb"
Set conn = New ADODB.Connection
With conn
    .Provider = "Microsoft.Jet.OLEDB.4.0"
    .Mode = adModeReadWrite       'allow read-write access
    .ConnectionTimeout = 10
    .ConnectionString = connStr
    .Open
End With
```

The ConnectionString property contains the information required to open a connection. ADO supports only four arguments for the ConnectionString property (Provider, File Name, Remote Provider, and Remote Server). If more information is required to open a data source (for example, driver, userID, password, and so on), ADO simply passes the String directly to the provider without any processing. The String arguments included with the ConnectionString property must be separated by semicolons.

After a database is opened, commands can be executed against it to return records in a Recordset object (from a base table or query) or otherwise manipulate the database. A Command object represents a specific command to be executed against an open data source. To execute a query against a database, set the CommandText property of the Command object to a String holding an SQL statement. Then use the Execute method to return the results of the query to a Recordset object.

```
sqlStr = "SELECT * FROM MyDBTable;"
Set rs = New ADODB.Recordset
Set comm = New ADODB.Command
With comm
     .ActiveConnection = conn
     .CommandTimeout = 10
     .CommandText = sqlStr
     Set rs = .Execute
End With
```

NOTE

To execute a query without using a Command object, pass a query String to the Execute method of a Connection object or to the Open method of a Recordset object.

The ADO Recordset object is very similar to that of DAO and is used to store all records from a base table or the results from an executed query String. The Recordset object must be used to add, retrieve, and manipulate data in a database.

Manipulating a Database from Excel with ADO

A simple and common example using ADO with Excel involves importing data from a database for subsequent viewing and analysis in a worksheet. Once data is in a Recordset variable, you can use Excel-VBA to write it to any desired cell or cells in a worksheet. Alternatively, you may need to delete, append data to, or edit existing data in a database.

The worksheet displayed in Figure 13.11 and the program initiated by its Button controls allow the user to write the SQL statement to be executed against the Northwind.mdb sample database. The program supports common SQL query types including the definition and manipulation components of the language (`Select`, `Insert`, `Create`, `Update`, `Delete`, and `Drop`).

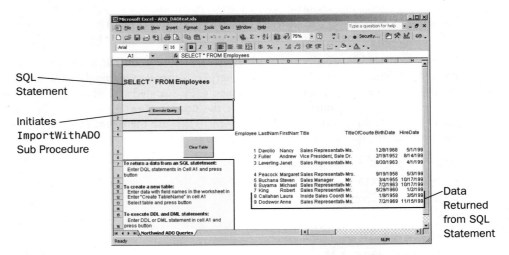

SQL Statement

Initiates ImportWithADO Sub Procedure

Data Returned from SQL Statement

FIGURE 13.11 *Executing an SQL statement against the Northwind.mdb sample database from Excel.*

The program is entered into a standard code module. You must enter the SQL statement in cell A1 before pressing the button that activates the `ImportWithADO()` procedure listed next. The `ImportWithADO()` procedure serves as the main Sub procedure for the program and calls other procedures that create the ADO `Connection`, `Command`, and `Recordset` objects in the same manner as previously described. The connection is always to the same database regardless of the type of SQL statement. Any errors that may occur (file path, SQL syntax, and so on) are output to cell A3 of the worksheet.

```
Option Explicit
Private conn As ADODB.Connection
Private comm As ADODB.Command
Private rsQuery As ADODB.Recordset
Private sqlType As String
Private tlbName As String


Public Sub ImportWithADO()
'Main sub procedure for executing queries against Northwind db
    Dim I As Integer
```

```
    On Error GoTo ADOError
    CreateConnection     'Set connection to database
    CreateCommand        'Execute command against database
    If sqlType = "DQL" Then
        WriteData     'Write records to worksheet
    End If


    'If recordset object has been set then close and delete it
    If Not rsQuery Then
        rsQuery.Close
        Set rsQuery = Nothing
    End If
    Set comm = Nothing
    conn.Close
    Set conn = Nothing
    Exit Sub
ADOError:
    Range("A3").Value = Err.Description
End Sub
Private Sub CreateConnection()
'Create a connection to Northwind
    Dim connStr As String
    Dim dbpath As String


    'Provide path to database. You may need to change this path.
    dbpath = "C:\Program Files\Microsoft Office\Office10\" & _
        "Samples\Northwind.mdb"
    connStr = "Data Source=" & dbpath
    Set conn = New ADODB.Connection
    With conn
        .Provider = "Microsoft.Jet.OLEDB.4.0"
        .Mode = adModeReadWrite
        .ConnectionTimeout = 10
        .ConnectionString = connStr
        .Open
    End With
End Sub
```

Depending on the nature of the SQL statement (DQL, DDL, or DML), the `Command` object has to be set somewhat differently. DQL commands require a `Recordset` variable to which records are returned, whereas DDL commands don't. If the user intends to create a new table with a DDL statement, an additional procedure (`BuildSQL`) is used to build the statement for them.

```
Private Sub CreateCommand()
'Create a Command to Northwind DB
    Dim sqlStr As String

    sqlStr = Range("A1").Value
    'Determine query type
    Select Case Trim(LCase(Left(sqlStr, 6)))
        Case "select"
            sqlType = "DQL"
        Case "create"
            sqlType = "DDL"
        Case Else
            sqlType = "ANY"
    End Select
    Set rsQuery = New ADODB.Recordset
    Set comm = New ADODB.Command
    'Execute query.  If DQL-type then set Recordset object
    With comm
        .ActiveConnection = conn
        .CommandTimeout = 10
        .CommandText = sqlStr
        If sqlType = "DQL" Then
            Set rsQuery = .Execute
        ElseIf sqlType = "DDL" Then
            .CommandText = BuildSQL     'Build DDL string
            .Execute
            AddRecords     'Adds data to new db table
        Else
            .CommandText = sqlStr
            .Execute
        End If
    End With
End Sub
```

The BuildSQL() Function procedure builds an SQL data definition statement based on the current selection in the worksheet. The first row in the selected data is assumed to contain the field names used, and data types are assigned as VARCHAR. This makes it easy to add numerical or textual data to the table without error; however, it would be better if the data types were recognized before building the statement. One additional column named ID is added to the user's selection to serve as the primary key.

 NOTE

The ADOX object model is available for defining components of a database if you don't want to use SQL. To use ADOX objects, set a reference to the COM library Microsoft ADO Ext. 2.7 for DDL and Security (or later version).

```
Private Function BuildSQL() As String
'Builds an SQL statement for creating a new table
'from a worksheet selection
'The first row is assumed to be the field names.
'An additional column is added to the table to serve as primary key
    Dim sqlStr As String
    Dim tabRange As Range, tabRow As Range, tabCell As Range

    tlbName = Right(Range("A1").Value, Len(Range("A1").Value) - 7)
    sqlStr = "CREATE TABLE " & tlbName & vbCrLf
    sqlStr = sqlStr & "(ID  INTEGER PRIMARY KEY, " & vbCrLf
    Set tabRange = ActiveWindow.Selection

    'Retrieve column header to use as field name
    'Add field name and data type to sql string
    For Each tabRow In tabRange.Rows
        For Each tabCell In Range(tabRow.Address)
            sqlStr = sqlStr & tabCell.Value & "  VARCHAR," & vbCrLf
        Next
        sqlStr = Left(sqlStr, Len(sqlStr) - 3) & ");"
        Exit For
    Next
    Range("A1").Value = sqlStr
    BuildSQL = sqlStr
End Function
```

For SQL statements that retrieve data from the database, the WriteData() Sub procedure writes the data into the worksheet with column B4 as the upper-left corner of the table. Field names are written first, followed by the data.

```
Private Sub WriteData()
'Writes data from recordset to worksheet
    Dim I As Integer, K As Integer
    Dim numCols As Integer

    I = 5
    With rsQuery
        If Not .BOF Then .MoveFirst
        numCols = .Fields.Count
        For K = 1 To numCols        'Write column headers
            Cells(4, K + 1).Value = .Fields(K - 1).Name
        Next K

        Do While Not .EOF    'Write data to worksheet
            For K = 1 To numCols
                Cells(I, K + 1).Value = .Fields(K - 1).Value
            Next K
            I = I + 1
            .MoveNext
        Loop
    End With
    Range("B:Z").Columns.AutoFit
End Sub
```

After a table is created, records are added with the AddRecords() Sub procedure. A Recordset object is opened using the newly created table as its source. The AddNew method of the Recordset object creates a single record whose field values are copied from the worksheet. After each record is added, the Update method must be called to save the changes, or they will be lost with the next call to the AddNew method.

```
Private Sub AddRecords()
'Adds data to newly create table
    Dim I As Integer, K As Integer
    Dim tabRange As Range
```

```
    Set tabRange = ActiveWindow.Selection
    'Create a recordset object and fill it with records.
    'Add each record to table with Update method
    Set rsQuery = New ADODB.Recordset
    With rsQuery
        .ActiveConnection = conn
        .Source = tlbName
        'Lock records only when Update method is invoked
        .LockType = adLockOptimistic
        .Open    'Establish connection to newly created table
        For I = 1 To tabRange.Rows.Count - 1
            'Add new record and fill fields with data
            .AddNew
            .Fields(0) = I
            For K = 1 To tabRange.Columns.Count
                .Fields(K).Value = tabRange.Cells(I + 1, K).Value
            Next K
            .Update    'Update new record
        Next I
    End With
End Sub
Public Sub ClearTable()
'Clear the table content of the worksheet
    Dim lastRow As Long
    Dim lastCol As Integer

    lastCol = ActiveSheet.UsedRange.Columns.Count + 2
    lastRow = ActiveSheet.UsedRange.Rows.Count + 5
    Range(Cells(4, 2), Cells(lastRow, lastCol)).Clear
End Sub
```

These procedures illustrate the most common methods needed to read and manipulate data in a database using the ADO object model. As was the case with the DAO object model, the ADO object model involves significant use of the `Recordset` object.

Summary

You have just concluded one of the most important chapters in this book. Database applications dominate the custom software field and are commonly used in custom solutions with Excel. In this chapter, you learned how to create a relational database using MS Access after first designing a set of normalized tables. You also learned how to retrieve and manipulate the data in a Jet database using the DAO and ADO object models through VBA.

Chapter 14

*Using and
Creating Excel
Pivot Tables
for Fast Data
Analyses*

Pivot tables are one of the most powerful data analysis tools available in Excel. With them, users can quickly perform summary analyses on large volumes of data. The source data for a pivot table can be an Excel worksheet, external file (for example, text file or Access database), or another pivot table. Once a pivot table is created, the user can easily manipulate it to cross-tabulate a variety of different fields with varying detail in order to summarize the data for a report. Users manipulate pivot tables by dragging fields to different sections (row, column, page, and data) of the table. If desired, users can even add their own calculated fields to further customize a report. In addition, users can create pivot chart reports from an existing pivot table and quickly change them by moving fields around on the pivot chart.

This chapter shows you how to create and use pivot tables and pivot chart reports from the Excel application window. I also show you how to create and manipulate a pivot table and pivot chart programmatically with VBA. Because pivot tables represent a dynamic and easy-to-use data analysis tool, other than what is needed to create them, very little programming is required. Manipulating a pivot table or pivot chart programmatically actually makes little sense because these tasks are just as easily accomplished through the Excel application window.

Creating a Pivot Table from the Application Window

Like any other data table, a pivot table is constructed from a set of rows and columns. Pivot tables are unique because of their capability to quickly transform by the addition of more data, by filtering of existing data, or by transposition of rows and columns, after which the data is quickly analyzed with a basic (or custom) summary function. You can easily swap rows and columns in a pivot table, group or expand them on a data field, and quickly chart the results. For example, you can group a column or row of data containing dates so that the data is summarized by period (day, month, quarter, year, and so on) and so that a column or row of categories can be expanded or compressed to include or exclude subcategories.

Because pivot tables are unfamiliar to many Excel users, I'm including a brief tutorial on how to create and manipulate them. Once you see how easy it is to begin using a pivot table, I am sure you will begin to apply them in your analyses when appropriate.

 NOTE

Data displayed in the pivot tables in this chapter is from the sample Northwind.mdb database included with Microsoft Access.

Components of a Pivot Table

To better understand my discussion on creating a pivot table with VBA and then to actually create one, you need to understand the terminology used with a pivot table. The terms associated with a pivot table are categorized by the field types, data, and the layout. The terms that describe the components of a pivot table are intuitive in that they represent the typical components of a table.

 NOTE

Though pivot tables can also be created from OLAP (Online Analytical Processing) data sources, I don't cover such sources in this book. To learn more about OLAP data sources for pivot tables, consult the Microsoft developer network at http://msdn.microsoft.com.

Field Types

The field types of a pivot table include the row, column, data, and page fields. Each of the four field types is shown in a basic pivot table in Figure 14.1. In this example, the pivot table includes a single row field containing a series of categories that represent food products. There is also just one column field representing the years in which data is available. You can use a page field to filter the data in a pivot table to include all items or just a single item. The page field in the pivot table in Figure 14.1 is constructed to use the date (grouped by quarters) so that the data in the table can be summarized according to specific quarters.

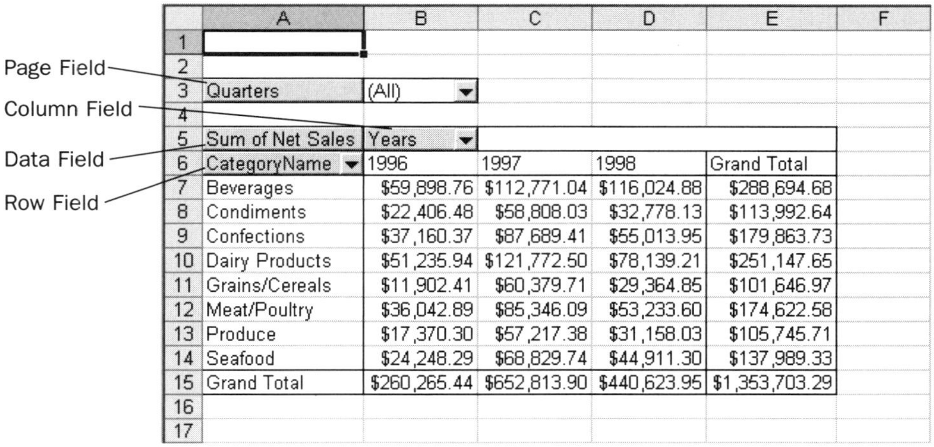

	A	B	C	D	E	F
1						
2						
3	Quarters	(All) ▼				
4						
5	Sum of Net Sales	Years ▼				
6	CategoryName ▼	1996	1997	1998	Grand Total	
7	Beverages	$59,898.76	$112,771.04	$116,024.88	$288,694.68	
8	Condiments	$22,406.48	$58,808.03	$32,778.13	$113,992.64	
9	Confections	$37,160.37	$87,689.41	$55,013.95	$179,863.73	
10	Dairy Products	$51,235.94	$121,772.50	$78,139.21	$251,147.65	
11	Grains/Cereals	$11,902.41	$60,379.71	$29,364.85	$101,646.97	
12	Meat/Poultry	$36,042.89	$85,346.09	$53,233.60	$174,622.58	
13	Produce	$17,370.30	$57,217.38	$31,158.03	$105,745.71	
14	Seafood	$24,248.29	$68,829.74	$44,911.30	$137,989.33	
15	Grand Total	$260,265.44	$652,813.90	$440,623.95	$1,353,703.29	
16						
17						

Page Field → (row 3)
Column Field → (row 4)
Data Field → (row 6)
Row Field → (row 7)

FIGURE 14.1 *A simple pivot table.*

You can add more than one row, column, or data field to a pivot table as long as the data does not exceed the row and column limits for a worksheet (65536 and 256, respectively). For example, the pivot table in Figure 14.2 includes a second row field for the product names. The product names represent subcategories of the food category field that was already added to the table as a row field. You can arrange column fields in a similar fashion.

Row Fields →

	A	B	C	D	E	F
3	Quarters	(All)				
4						
5	Sum of Net Sales		Years			
6	CategoryName ▼	ProductName ▼	1996	1997	1998	Grand Total
7	Beverages	Chai	$2,007.00	$5,063.40	$6,295.50	$13,365.90
8		Chang	$3,772.45	$7,647.50	$6,299.45	$17,719.40
9		Chartreuse verte	$4,447.80	$4,623.30	$4,260.60	$13,331.70
10		Côte de Blaye	$31,093.00	$55,479.93	$67,324.25	$153,897.18
11		Guaraná Fantástica	$695.93	$1,762.43	$2,317.50	$4,775.86
12		Ipoh Coffee	$6,164.00	$11,419.50	$7,525.60	$25,109.10
13		Lakkalikööri	$2,557.80	$7,667.10	$6,335.10	$16,560.00
14		Laughing Lumberjack Lager	$52.50	$910.00	$1,444.80	$2,407.30
15		Outback Lager	$2,261.25	$5,755.50	$3,395.25	$11,412.00
16		Rhönbräu Klosterbier	$923.03	$4,594.98	$2,953.53	$8,471.54
17		Sasquatch Ale	$1,253.00	$2,244.90	$3,241.00	$6,738.90
18		Steeleye Stout	$4,671.00	$5,602.50	$4,632.30	$14,905.80
19	Beverages Total		$59,898.76	$112,771.04	$116,024.88	$288,694.68
20	Condiments	Aniseed Syrup	$300.00	$1,860.00	$1,080.00	$3,240.00
21		Chef Anton's Cajun Seasoning	$2,314.40	$5,271.20	$1,501.50	$9,087.10
22		Chef Anton's Gumbo Mix	$2,425.36	$373.63	$3,042.38	$5,841.37
23		Genen Shouyu	$387.50	$1,474.83		$1,862.33
24		Grandma's Boysenberry Spread	$900.00	$2,500.00	$3,917.00	$7,317.00
25		Gula Malacca	$2,562.54	$7,296.68	$1,135.89	$10,995.11

FIGURE 14.2 *A pivot table with two row fields.*

The *data field* is the area of the pivot table that actually contains the numerical (or textual) information. In Figure 14.2, the data field includes the sum total of the net sales for the products. The pivot table will filter and summarize the data in the table based on the selections for the row, column, and page fields.

Pivot Table Data

Data included in a pivot table must come from another source, either from an Excel worksheet, external file (text, database, and so on), or another pivot table. The underlying data for a pivot table is referred to as the *source data*.

A *pivot table field* refers to a category of data that's derived from a column in the source data. The category name and product names in Figures 14.1 and 14.2 represent fields in the pivot tables. Fields can be added to any of the field types (row, column, page, or data) in a pivot table.

A member of a field in a pivot table is referred to as an *item*. For example, the category Beverages in Figure 14.1 and the product name Chai in Figure 14.2 are examples of items.

Finally, the term *summary function* refers to the type of Excel function used to summarize the data. For numerical data, the default function is Sum, and for textual data, it is Count. However, you can choose from several other functions (Average, Max, Min, Product, StDev, Var) or create one of your own. In the pivot table of Figures 14.1 and 14.2, Sum is used as the summary function.

If your pivot table is based on data from an external source, then you may want to refresh the pivot table to reflect any updates that have been made to the underlying data source.

Pivot Table Layout

The layout of a pivot table includes four drop areas for each field type (row, column, data, and page — see Figure 14.3). At a minimum, a pivot table should contain fields in the data drop area and in at least one row or column drop area. To add fields to a pivot table, you drag items from the pivot table field list to one of the four drop areas. The pivot table field list shows all available fields from the source data.

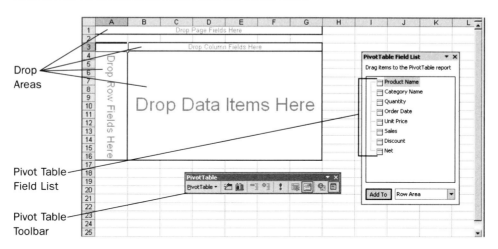

FIGURE 14.3 *Pivot table layout prior to the addition of data.*

A pivot field drop-down list displays the items in each field added to a pivot table (see Figure 14.4). Use the field drop-down list to select which items to display in the pivot table.

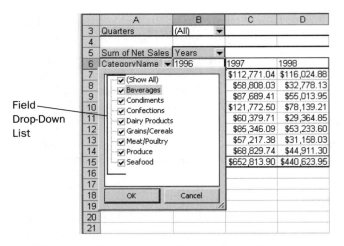

Field Drop-Down List

FIGURE 14.4 *Field drop-down list in a pivot table.*

To format a pivot table report, you can either format the cells as you normally would in Excel or choose one of the auto format options from the Pivot Table toolbar. Select Pivot Table, Format Report from the Pivot Table toolbar (see Figure 14.5) to display the AutoFormat dialog box for pivot tables, which is shown in Figure 14.6.

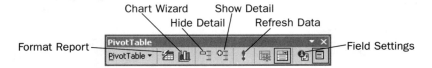

Chart Wizard   Show Detail
Hide Detail   Refresh Data
Format Report   Field Settings

FIGURE 14.5 *The pivot table toolbar.*

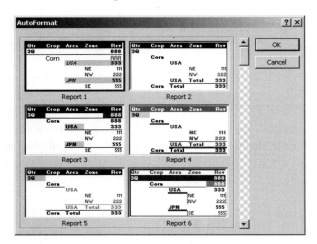

FIGURE 14.6 *Use the AutoFormat dialog box to quickly set formatting in a pivot table.*

Using the PivotTable and PivotChart Wizard to Create a Pivot Table

I don't always recommend using wizards because they often make too many assumptions for you; however, the PivotTable and PivotChart Wizard does represent the easiest method for creating a pivot table or pivot chart report in Excel. To initiate the PivotTable and PivotChart Wizard and begin creating a pivot table from data within a worksheet, follow these steps:

1. From the Excel menu bar, click Data.

2. From the drop-down menu that appears, select PivotTable and PivotChart Report. The PivotTable and PivotChart Wizard appears (see Figure 14.7).

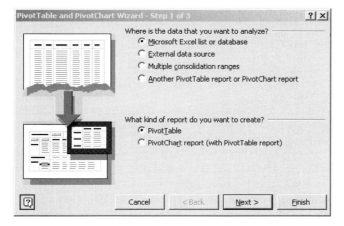

FIGURE 14.7 *Step 1 of the PivotTable and PivotChart Wizard.*

3. Check the appropriate option for "Where is the data that you want to analyze?"

   When the data is already in an Excel worksheet, simply select any cell within the block of data before initiating the wizard. The wizard will find the contiguous block of cells that represents the data.

4. Check the appropriate option for "What kind of report do you want to create?" and click Next to proceed to Step 2 of the wizard. When the data is already in Excel, the wizard will display a worksheet range as shown in Figure 14.8.

5. If the wizard does not display the desired range, select the range holding the data for the pivot table and click Next to proceed to the final step of the wizard.

FIGURE 14.8 *Step 2 of the PivotTable and PivotChart Wizard.*

The final step of the wizard is to specify a new worksheet or existing worksheet in which to place the new pivot table (see Figure 14.9).

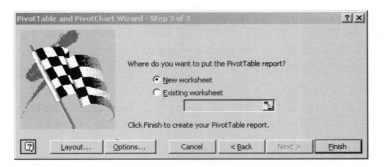

FIGURE 14.9 *Step 3 of the PivotTable and PivotChart Wizard.*

After the data is imported to a worksheet, the PivotTable and PivotChart Wizard creates a pivot table layout with four drop areas, as shown earlier in Figure 14.3.

NOTE

To create a pivot table in Excel from data in an external database, you must specify the type of database and its location in Step 2 of the wizard after selecting External data source in Step 1. The wizard then loads and initiates Microsoft Query for selecting the database and specific components within the database for importing into Excel. (Microsoft Query must be installed before you can create a pivot table from an external data source.) With Microsoft Query, you essentially build an SQL statement to be executed against the selected database. The queried data is then returned to an Excel worksheet.

Creating Pivot Table Reports

After the source data is imported into Excel and the pivot table layout is created, you are ready to create a pivot table report. With a layout similar to that shown earlier in Figure 14.3, all that is required to create the report is to drag the fields from the pivot table field list to the appropriate drop areas in the pivot table. In most reports, textual data serves as row and column headers, so you can drag these fields to the row, column, or page field drop areas in the pivot table. You typically drag numerical fields to the data field drop area in the pivot table.

Consider the sample data shown in Figure 14.10. I selected the data via a custom query from the Northwind.mdb database and copied it into an Excel worksheet. The data represents the products ordered for the years 1996–1998 from the mythical Northwind Traders Company and contains fields for the product and category names, the order date, unit price, quantity, and discounts given on an item. After copying the data to Excel, I calculated additional fields for gross sales and total discounts.

	A	B	C	D	E	F	G	H
1	ProductName	CategoryName	Quantity	UnitPrice	Discount	OrderDate	Gross Sales	Total Discounts
2	Chai	Beverages	45	$18.00	0.2	8/20/1996	$810.00	162
3	Chai	Beverages	18	$18.00	0	8/30/1996	$324.00	0
4	Chai	Beverages	20	$18.00	0	9/30/1996	$360.00	0
5	Chai	Beverages	15	$18.00	0.15	11/7/1996	$270.00	40.5
6	Chai	Beverages	12	$18.00	0	11/14/1996	$216.00	0
7	Chai	Beverages	15	$18.00	0.15	12/3/1996	$270.00	40.5
8	Chai	Beverages	10	$18.00	0	1/7/1997	$180.00	0
9	Chai	Beverages	24	$18.00	0	1/14/1997	$432.00	0

FIGURE 14.10 *Source data for a pivot table report.*

One of the more obvious reports desired from this data is a sales report broken down by category, product, and date. To create the sales pivot table report, follow these steps:

1. Drag the Order Date field from the Pivot Table Field List to the row field drop area. The pivot table now appears as shown in Figure 14.11.

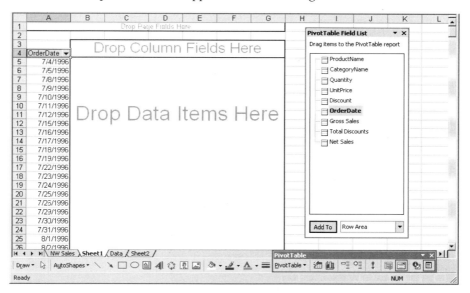

FIGURE 14.11 *A pivot table report with a single column of dates in a row field.*

2. Group the Order Date field by month, quarter, and year. To group date fields by several different periods (second, day, quarter, year, and so on), select the field and from the Pivot Table toolbar (see Figure 14.5) select Pivot Table, Group and Show Detail, Group. The Grouping dialog box appears with a list of available time periods to choose from.

3. Select the desired time periods in the Grouping dialog box (see Figure 14.12) and click OK.

FIGURE 14.12 *The Grouping dialog box used to group date fields in a pivot table.*

The result of grouping the Order Date field by years, quarters, and months is shown in Figure 14.13. You will notice that what was a single field in the pivot table (OrderDate) is now three fields (Years, Quarter, and OrderDate).

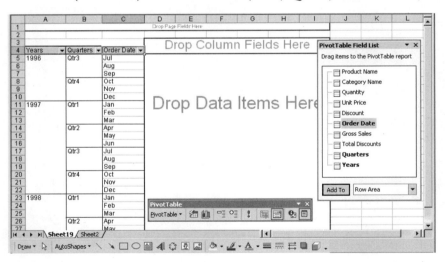

FIGURE 14.13 *Pivot Table layout with three Order Date fields added to the row field drop area.*

4. Drag all three Order Date fields to the page field drop area. With the date grouped by year, there are basically four choices in the drop-down list for the Order Date field (All, 1996, 1997, and 1998). You can use any page field to filter data in the pivot table according to the period selected (see Figure 14.14).

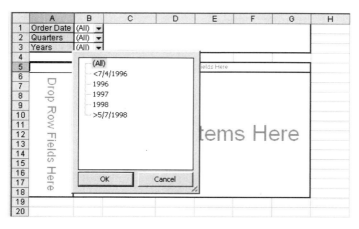

FIGURE 14.14 *Pivot table layout with the Order Date field added to the page field drop area.*

5. Drag the Category Name and Product Name fields to the row field drop area. Because Product Names is a subcategory of Category Names, you place it to the right, as shown in Figure 14.15.

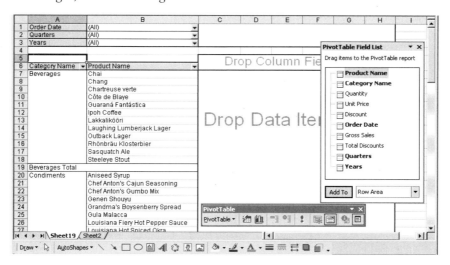

FIGURE 14.15 *Pivot table with dependent row fields.*

6. Drag the Gross Sales and Total Discounts fields to the data drop area on the pivot table. Numerical information added to the data drop area will automatically be summarized with the Sum function.

7. Create a custom field to calculate net sales by selecting Pivot Table, Formulas, Calculated Field from the Pivot Table toolbar. The Insert Calculated Field dialog box appears (see Figure 14.16).

8. Name the field and enter the formula using the fields listed. Click Add to include the custom field in the pivot table field list then click OK. You can also use constants or Excel functions as needed. The calculated field is added to the data drop area of the pivot table, resulting in the table shown in Figure 14.17.

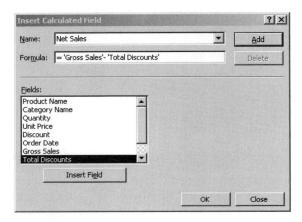

FIGURE 14.16 *Use the Insert Calculated Field dialog box to create custom functions for a pivot table.*

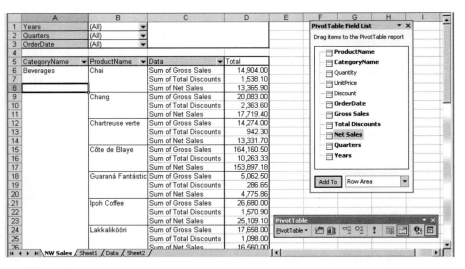

FIGURE 14.17 *A completed pivot table summarizing the sales for the Northwind Traders Company.*

After the pivot table is created, you can manipulate it to display the desired summary analysis.

Manipulating Reports

Pivot tables are dynamic in the sense that they enable you to easily add new fields, swap existing fields, and expand the summary analyses to include more data. The pivot table report just shown in Figure 14.17 contains row fields for the category names and product names, page fields for the date (month, quarter, and year), and data fields for the gross sales, total discounts, and the net sales. No column fields are added to the pivot table. There are numerous possible useful configurations of the pivot table shown in Figure 14.17. The following list instructs you on how to create a few of these configurations by manipulating the existing pivot table:

- Select 1996 in the Order Date field that is grouped by years to filter the summarized data to display only the sales for 1996.
- Select the entire column of category names and select Hide Detail from the Pivot Table toolbar. This hides the subcategory product names resulting in data summarized by category only.
- Drag the Order Date field grouped by years to the column field drop area of the pivot table.
- Drag the Order Date field that is grouped by quarters to the column drop area of the pivot table. The resulting pivot table now displays the sales for each year and quarter as shown in Figure 14.18.
- Swap fields in the column and row drop areas to completely pivot (transpose) the table (see Figure 14.19).

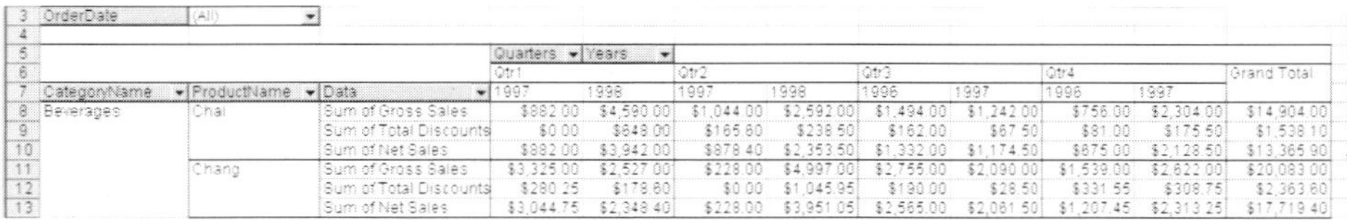

3	OrderDate	(All)									
4											
5				Quarters / Years							
6				Qtr1		Qtr2		Qtr3		Qtr4		Grand Total
7	CategoryName	ProductName	Data	1997	1998	1997	1998	1996	1997	1996	1997	
8	Beverages	Chai	Sum of Gross Sales	$882.00	$4,590.00	$1,044.00	$2,592.00	$1,494.00	$1,242.00	$756.00	$2,304.00	$14,904.00
9			Sum of Total Discounts	$0.00	$648.00	$165.60	$238.50	$162.00	$67.50	$81.00	$175.50	$1,538.10
10			Sum of Net Sales	$882.00	$3,942.00	$878.40	$2,353.50	$1,332.00	$1,174.50	$675.00	$2,128.50	$13,365.90
11		Chang	Sum of Gross Sales	$3,325.00	$2,527.00	$228.00	$4,997.00	$2,755.00	$2,090.00	$1,539.00	$2,622.00	$20,083.00
12			Sum of Total Discounts	$280.25	$178.60	$0.00	$1,045.95	$190.00	$28.50	$331.55	$308.75	$2,363.60
13			Sum of Net Sales	$3,044.75	$2,348.40	$228.00	$3,951.05	$2,565.00	$2,061.50	$1,207.45	$2,313.25	$17,719.40

FIGURE 14.18 *The Northwind Traders pivot table report after rearrangement of its fields.*

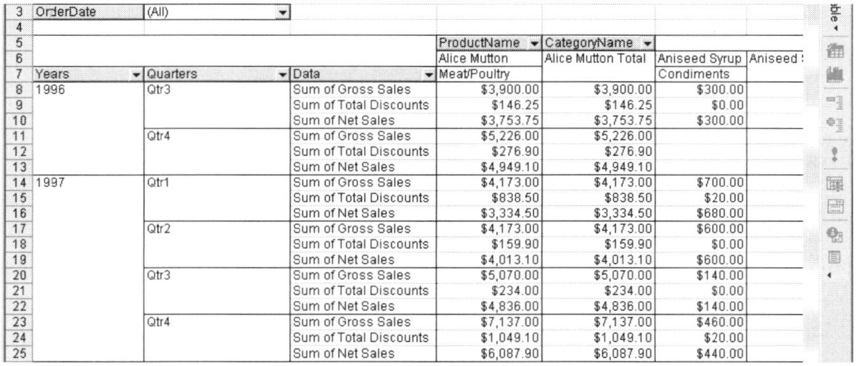

3	OrderDate	(All)					
4							
5				ProductName	CategoryName		
6				Alice Mutton	Alice Mutton Total	Aniseed Syrup	Aniseed S
7	Years	Quarters	Data	Meat/Poultry		Condiments	
8	1996	Qtr3	Sum of Gross Sales	$3,900.00	$3,900.00	$300.00	
9			Sum of Total Discounts	$146.25	$146.25	$0.00	
10			Sum of Net Sales	$3,753.75	$3,753.75	$300.00	
11		Qtr4	Sum of Gross Sales	$5,226.00	$5,226.00		
12			Sum of Total Discounts	$276.90	$276.90		
13			Sum of Net Sales	$4,949.10	$4,949.10		
14	1997	Qtr1	Sum of Gross Sales	$4,173.00	$4,173.00	$700.00	
15			Sum of Total Discounts	$838.50	$838.50	$20.00	
16			Sum of Net Sales	$3,334.50	$3,334.50	$680.00	
17		Qtr2	Sum of Gross Sales	$4,173.00	$4,173.00	$600.00	
18			Sum of Total Discounts	$159.90	$159.90	$0.00	
19			Sum of Net Sales	$4,013.10	$4,013.10	$600.00	
20		Qtr3	Sum of Gross Sales	$5,070.00	$5,070.00	$140.00	
21			Sum of Total Discounts	$234.00	$234.00	$0.00	
22			Sum of Net Sales	$4,836.00	$4,836.00	$140.00	
23		Qtr4	Sum of Gross Sales	$7,137.00	$7,137.00	$460.00	
24			Sum of Total Discounts	$1,049.10	$1,049.10	$20.00	
25			Sum of Net Sales	$6,087.90	$6,087.90	$440.00	

FIGURE 14.19 *The Northwind Traders pivot table report after transposition of its row and column fields.*

Creating Pivot Chart Reports

Pivot charts are column charts of the summary data displayed in the data drop area of a pivot table. To create a pivot chart, select the Chart Wizard from the Pivot Table toolbar. The pivot chart is immediately created as a new chart sheet in the existing workbook. The pivot chart created from the pivot table in Figure 14.2 is shown in Figure 14.20.

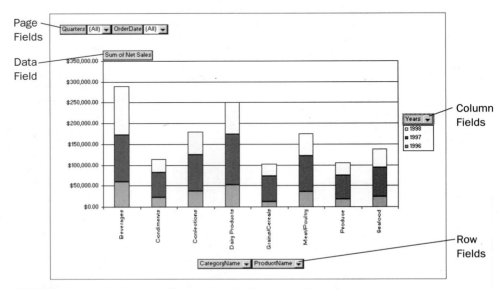

FIGURE 14.20 *A pivot chart illustrating sales by category for each year.*

As with regular Excel charts, pivot charts are automatically updated if the underlying data source is altered in some way. What differentiates a pivot chart from a regular Excel chart is the capability to swap component fields. The four field areas of the pivot table are included in the pivot chart and can be dragged to any other area (refer to Figure 14.20) on the pivot chart to alter its appearance. Note that altering the pivot chart has the equivalent effect on the underlying pivot table from which it was created.

Creating a Pivot Table with VBA

Excel's pivot tables are easy to create and manipulate from the application window. Because pivot tables are dynamic and easy to use, there isn't much need for VBA programs that automate tasks involving pivot tables. In most cases, you simply can't make it any easier for the user. This is not to say that users don't have problems with pivot tables, because they do. However, the nature of these troubles mostly arise because of a general lack of understanding about which fields must be included in the source data or how the fields should be added to the table. Consequently, a VBA program can't really help with problems like these. The Query Wizard can also cause significant problems for the user when importing data from an external data source (for example, Access database) due to a lack of understanding of relational database structure. Thus, the most useful VBA routines involving pivot tables are those that create the tables by importing the data and defining the layout. You've already seen how to create a pivot table from the Excel application window, so now I will show you how to create one using VBA.

The pivot table object model is fairly extensive, but it is also intuitive if you are familiar with pivot tables and their components. As with most object models in VBA, the best way to learn to program using the pivot table object model is by recording macros and studying the resulting code.

 NOTE

It has been my experience that the objects included in the pivot table object model are somewhat buggy. Problems include an inability to use For/Each loops with some of the collection objects, the failure of some methods to function properly when working with the data, and a few other quirks that can cause frustration when working with these objects. I will draw attention to some of these problems as they arise in the examples that follow.

The PivotCache and PivotTable Objects

A `PivotCache` object represents the memory cache for a pivot table. For every pivot table, there exists a `PivotCache` object. Use the `Add` method of the `PivotCaches` collection object to create a new `PivotCache` object. You must specify the `SourceType` argument using one of five possible values (the VBA constants `xlConsolidation`, `xlDatabase`, `xlExternal`, `xlPivotTable`, and `xlScenario`). If the `SourceType` is anything other than `xlExternal`, the data source is ultimately a worksheet, and the `SourceData` argument must also be specified. The following code creates a new `PivotCache` object from data in the active worksheet using the specified range (as a `String`):

```
Dim pivCache As PivotCache
Set pivCache = ActiveWorkbook.PivotCaches.Add( _
    SourceType:=xlDatabase, SourceData:="A1:I2156")
```

When importing data from an external database, use the `Connection` and `CommandText` properties of the `PivotCache` object to establish the connection to the database and set the SQL `String`.

```
Dim sqlStr As String, dbPath As String, connStr As String
sqlStr = "SELECT * FROM Sales;"
dbPath = "C:\MyDbase.mdb"
```

```
connStr = "ODBC;DSN=MS Access Database;DBQ=" & dbPath
Set pivCache = ActiveWorkbook.PivotCaches.Add(SourceType:=xlExternal)
With pivCache
    .Connection = connStr
    .CommandText = sqlStr
End With
```

Alternatively, you can create an ADO `Recordset` object (see Chapter 13, "Data I/O Between Excel and Access," for information on using the ADO object model to return a set of records from a query or base table in a database and set it to the `Recordset` property of the `PivotCache` object. In the next example, the variable `rsQuery` is of type `ADO.Recordset` and is assumed to already contain records resulting from a query.

```
pivCache.Recordset = rsQuery
```

After creating the `PivotCache` object, use its `CreatePivotTable` method to add a pivot table to a worksheet. The `CreatePivotTable` method accepts up to four arguments (`TableDestination`, `TableName`, `ReadData`, and `DefaultVersion`). The `TableDestination` argument is required and specifies the location of the upper-left cell of the pivot table. The remaining arguments are optional and are used to assign a name to the pivot table, create a PivotTable cache (if that's not already done), and specify the default version of the pivot table report, respectively. At the very least, a descriptive name should be assigned to the pivot table to prevent VBA from assigning a non-descriptive name (for example, PivotTable1).

```
Dim pivTab As PivotTable
Set pivTab = pivCache.CreatePivotTable(TableDestination:=Range("L4"), _
    TableName:="MyPivTable")
```

After the PivotCache and PivotTable objects are created, fields are ready to be added to the report.

Using the PivotField Object to Add Fields to a Pivot Table

The `PivotField` object represents one of four possible fields (row, column, page, or data) in a pivot table. Each `PivotField` object is a member of the `PivotFields` collection object. Since there is no `Add` method for the `PivotFields` collection object, you should use the `AddFields` and `AddDataFields` methods of the `PivotTable` object to add a new field to an existing pivot table. The `RowFields`, `ColumnFields`, and `PageFields` arguments of the `AddFields` method are used to add row, column, and page fields to the pivot table, respectively. The `AddToTable` argument specifies whether to replace existing fields in the pivot table (`False` replaces existing fields). Use a parameter array when adding more than one field to the same field type.

```
With pivTab.AddFields( _
        RowFields:=Array("MyRowField1", "MyRowField2"), _
        ColumnFields:=("MyColumnField"), _
        PageFields:=("MyPageField"), _
        AddToTable:=False)
End With
```

Use the `AddDataField` method of the `PivotTable` object to add data fields to the pivot table. The `AddDataField` method accepts three arguments (`Field`, `Caption`, and `Function`) used to specify the pivot field (required), the field caption, and the summary function to be applied to the data (the default is `Sum`). The following code adds a data field named `"MyData"` to an existing pivot table:

```
Dim pivField As PivotField
pivTab.AddDataField pivTab.PivotFields("MyData")
Set pivField = pivTab.DataFields(1)
With pivField
    .Caption = "My Caption"
    .Function = xlAverage
End With
```

The `PivotField` object contains numerous properties and methods from which you can read information and manipulate the object. In the preceding example, the `Caption` and `Function` properties of the `PivotField` object set the caption displayed in the pivot table and the summary function used in the field calculation. Other notable members of the `PivotField` object include the `DataRange`, `DataType`, `Formula`, `NumberFormat`, and `Orientation` properties.

Creating a Sales Report for Northwind Traders

The pivot table report, created earlier in this chapter, showing product sales for the mythical Northwind Traders Company is repeated here using a few short VBA procedures. The program copies the necessary data to an Excel worksheet before creating a pivot table and pivot chart.

You use an ADO `Recordset` object to retrieve the data from the Northwind.mdb database. There are disadvantages to importing the data before creating the pivot table. Most notable is the time it takes to copy the large volume of data typically used in pivot tables to the worksheet. However, in this example, it is highly desirable to group the dates by period (month, quarter, year, and so on), which you can accomplish only if the source data is in an Excel worksheet (more on that topic later in this section).

You add the code to a standard module, and you must set a reference to the ADO object library. By design, the program is initiated from any blank Excel worksheet. Data is copied to the active worksheet, and the pivot table is added to a new worksheet. The pivot chart is embedded on the same worksheet as the pivot table.

```
Option Explicit
Private conn As ADODB.Connection
Private comm As ADODB.Command
Private rsQuery As ADODB.Recordset
Private tlbName As String
Private fieldNum As Integer
Private pivTab As PivotTable
Private srcRange As String
```

The Sub procedure `SalesReport()` serves as the main procedure for the program and contains calls to the procedures that import the data from the Access database and create the pivot table and pivot chart. The `ScreenUpdating` property of the `Application` object is turned off to speed up execution of the code.

```
Public Sub SalesReport()
'Main sub procedure for creating sales report from Northwind db
    On Error GoTo ADOError
    Application.ScreenUpdating = False
    CreateConnection    'Create connection to Northwind database
    'Execute command query against database.
    'Set recordset object to hold result.
    CreateCommand
    CopyRecords       'Copy records to worksheet
    CreatePivTab      'Create pivot table
    FormatTable       'Format the pivot table
    PivotChart        'Create pivot chart
    Range("D1").Select
    Set pivTab = Nothing
    Set rsQuery = Nothing
    Set comm = Nothing
    conn.Close
    Set conn = Nothing
    Application.ScreenUpdating = True
    Exit Sub
ADOError:
```

```
        MsgBox (Err.Description)
        End
End Sub
```

The Sub procedures CreateConnection() and CreateCommand() are similar to those from Chapter 13 and are used to set the connection and retrieve the data from the Northwind.mdb database. The SQL statement is rather lengthy, but it represents a fairly straightforward join operation. The point of creating a pivot table for a user is to deliver a large volume of data that they can manage from Excel, so SQL statements may have to retrieve data from several fields and database tables.

```
Private Sub CreateConnection()
'Create a connection to Northwind
    Dim connStr As String
    Dim dbpath As String

    'You may need to alter this file path
    dbpath = "C:\Program Files\Microsoft Office\Office10\" & _
            "Samples\Northwind.mdb"
    connStr = "Data Source=" & dbpath
    Set conn = New ADODB.Connection
    With conn
        .Provider = "Microsoft.Jet.OLEDB.4.0"
        .Mode = adModeRead      'read-only permission
        .ConnectionTimeout = 10     'Wait 10 seconds to connect
        .ConnectionString = connStr
        .Open
    End With
End Sub


Private Sub CreateCommand()
    Dim sqlStr As String, sqlSel As String,
    Dim sqlFrom As String, sqlWhere As String

    'Build the SQL statement
    sqlSelect = "SELECT P.ProductName, C.CategoryName, " & _
            "OD.Quantity, P.UnitPrice, OD.Discount, " & _
            "FORMAT(O.OrderDate,'m/d/yyyy') AS OrderDate, " & _
            "OD.Quantity*P.UnitPrice AS [Gross Sales], " & _
            "OD.Quantity*OD.Discount*P.UnitPrice AS " & _
```

```
            "[Total Discounts], " & _
            "[Gross Sales]-[Total Discounts] As [Net Sales] "
    sqlFrom = "FROM [Order Details] AS OD, Orders AS O, " & _
            "Products AS P, Categories AS C "
    sqlWhere = "WHERE OD.OrderID=O.OrderID And " & _
            "C.CategoryID=P.CategoryID " & _
            "And P.ProductID=OD.ProductID;"
    sqlStr = sqlSelect & sqlFrom & sqlWhere
    Set rsQuery = New ADODB.Recordset
    Set comm = New ADODB.Command

    'Use current connection and execute SQL statement
    With comm
        .ActiveConnection = conn
        .CommandTimeout = 10
        .CommandText = sqlStr
        Set rsQuery = .Execute
    End With
End Sub
```

The `CopyRecords()` Sub procedure copies the data from a `Recordset` object into the active worksheet. The `Recordset` variable `rsQuery` is module-level and is filled with data after the `CreateCommand()` Sub procedure executes.

```
Private Sub CopyRecords()
'Copy records to a worksheet.
'This is required for grouping the date data
'in the pivot table
    Dim I As Integer, K As Integer
    I = 2
    With rsQuery
        If Not .BOF Then .MoveFirst
        '--------------
        'Copy headers
        '--------------
        For K = 0 To .Fields.Count - 1
            Cells(1, K + 1).Value = .Fields(K).Name
        Next K
        '----------
```

```
            'Copy Data
            '-----------
            Do While Not .EOF
                For K = 0 To .Fields.Count - 1
                    Cells(I, K + 1).Value = .Fields(K).Value
                Next K
                I = I + 1
                .MoveNext
            Loop
            .MoveFirst
        End With
        ActiveSheet.Name = "Data"      'Name worksheet
        'Set mod-level string variable to hold source range for pivot table
        srcRange=ActiveSheet.Name & "!A1:" & Chr( _
            64 + rsQuery.Fields.Count) & I - 1
End Sub
```

The Sub procedure `CreatePivTab()` adds a new worksheet to the active workbook and then adds a new pivot table to it. Some of the frustrations of programming with pivot tables show up with this procedure. First, the pivot table must be created from data within a worksheet because you cannot group fields from a `Recordset` object, even if the field is of type `Date`. Second you cannot group a field that has been added to the page field drop area of a pivot table (although this is also true when creating a pivot table from the Excel application). Third, you must set the `DefaultVersion` argument of the `CreatePivotTable` method to `xlPivotTableVersion10`, or you will be unable to group a field. Setting the `DefaultVersion` argument of the `CreatePivotTable` method to `xlPivotTableVersion10` creates a layout like the one shown previously in Figure 14.3. As a result of these requirements, the `CreatePivTab()` Sub procedure must add the `OrderDate` field to the row field drop area of the pivot table and then group the field as desired (month, quarters, and years) before moving the three date fields to the page field drop area. The `Orientation` property of the `PivotField` object is used to move the date fields to the page field drop area.

```
Private Sub CreatePivTab()
'Create the pivot table and add necessary fields
    '---------------------------
    'Add table to new worksheet
    '---------------------------
    Worksheets.Add
    ActiveSheet.Name = "NW Sales"
```

```
With ActiveWorkbook.PivotCaches.Add( _
        SourceType:=xlDatabase, SourceData:=srcRange)
    Set pivTab = .CreatePivotTable( _
                    TableDestination:=Range("A4"), _
                    TableName:="NWSales", _
                    DefaultVersion:=xlPivotTableVersion10)
End With


'-------------------------
'Add fields to pivot table
'-------------------------

With pivTab
    .AddFields RowFields:="OrderDate"
    .PivotFields("OrderDate").DataRange.Select
    Range("A5").Select
    'Group by months, quarters, and years
    Selection.Group Start:=True, End:=True, Periods:=Array(False, False, _
        False, False, True, True, True)
    .PivotFields("OrderDate").Orientation = xlPageField
    .PivotFields("OrderDate").Position = 1
    .PivotFields("Quarters").Orientation = xlPageField
    .PivotFields("Quarters").Position = 2
    .PivotFields("Years").Orientation = xlPageField
    .PivotFields("Years").Position = 3
    .AddFields RowFields:=Array("CategoryName", "ProductName"), _
        AddToTable:=True
    .AddDataField pivTab.PivotFields("Gross Sales")
    .AddDataField pivTab.PivotFields("Total Discounts")
    .AddDataField pivTab.PivotFields("Net Sales")
End With

Range("A:D").Columns.AutoFit
Range("A1").Select
HideDetails
End Sub
```

The HideDetails() Sub procedure simply hides the product names from being displayed in the pivot table. This is the equivalent of pressing the Hide Detail button on the Pivot Table toolbar. The product names are still part of the pivot table, and the user can easily show them by pressing the Show Detail button on the Pivot Table toolbar.

```
Private Sub HideDetails()
'Hide details of row field
    Dim pItems As PivotItems
    Dim I As Integer

    If fieldNum = 0 Then fieldNum = 3
    Set pItems = ActiveSheet.PivotTables("NWSales") _
        .PivotFields("CategoryName").PivotItems
    For I = 1 To pItems.Count
        pItems(I).ShowDetail = False
    Next I
End Sub
```

The `FormatTable()` Sub procedure uses the `NumberFormat` property of the `PivotField` object (returned by `DataFields` property of the `PivotTable` object) to format the fields in the data area of the pivot table as currency. I could not use a `For/Each` loop to iterate through the `PivotFields` collection object due to a lack of support with this particular collection object. Furthermore, the `NumberFormat` property was effective only when I used the `DataFields` property of the pivot table object, even though the `PivotFields` property should have worked just as well. In fact, when using the `PivotFields` property, the code that changes the number format does execute, but it has no effect on the display in Excel. Undoubtedly, other bugs such as these are in the objects of the pivot table object model, and you will have to use workarounds when you find them.

```
Private Sub FormatTable()
    Dim pf As PivotField
    Dim I As Integer
    For I = 1 To pivTab.DataFields.Count
        Set pf = pivTab.DataFields(I)
        If pf.Name = "Sum of Gross Sales" Or _
           pf.Name = "Sum of Total Discounts" Or _
           pf.Name = "Sum of Net Sales" Then
            pf.NumberFormat = "$#,##0.00"
        End If
    Next I
    Set pf = Nothing
End Sub
```

The `PivotChart()` Sub procedure adds an embedded pivot chart to the worksheet holding the pivot table. By default, pivot charts are added as a new chart sheet when created from the Excel application. If you prefer embedded charts, use this procedure; otherwise, you will have to copy and paste the pivot chart from the Excel application window. See

Chapter 10, "Creating and Manipulating Excel Charts," for a discussion on programming charts with Excel's Chart object model.

```
Private Sub PivotChart()
'Embed a pivot chart on the worksheet
    Dim pivChart As ChartObject
    Dim sh As Worksheet

    Set sh = ActiveSheet
    sh.ChartObjects.Add Left:=Range("A1:D1").Width, Top:=20, _
        Width:=400, Height:=300
    sh.ChartObjects(1).Activate
    With ActiveChart
        .ChartType = xlColumnClustered
        .SetSourceData Source:=Worksheets("NW Sales").Range("A1")
        .Location Where:=xlLocationAsObject, Name:="NW Sales"
    End With
End Sub
```

The pivot table and pivot chart created by this program is shown in Figure 14.21.

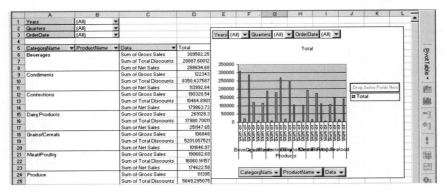

FIGURE 14.21 *A pivot table and embedded pivot chart created from a VBA program.*

Summary

In this chapter, you learned how to create and manipulate pivot tables and pivot charts from both the Excel application and VBA. You learned about the components of a pivot table and how they can be arranged and manipulated to display the desired summary analysis.

Chapter 15

Pear Tree Used Cars, Inc., consists of three fictitious dealerships that use an Access database to store employee, customer, inventory, and sales data. The owner and managers of the dealerships need a VBA program that can retrieve data from the Access database into Excel for performing analyses and generating reports. The program should provide the owner and managers with inventory search capabilities as well as reports that analyze the data according to units sold, sales by period (month, quarter, and year), and sales by employee (sales rep). The cars sold by each dealership should also be included in the reports.

This chapter takes you through the design and construction of the Access database and VBA program created for carrying out the required analyses. Although the project is not meant to represent a complete database and data analysis tool for a business, it does represent a subset of the typical data retrieval and analysis routines that can be used for such an application.

Project Description

The database for Pear Tree Used Cars, Inc., consists of a set of normalized tables holding customer, sales rep, inventory, and vehicle sales information for each of its three dealerships. The VBA program is created in Excel and must provide the user with a simple interface for retrieving inventory and sales information from the Access database. With regard to inventory, the program should allow the user to easily search for specific vehicles based on typical information (make, model, color, and so on). In addition, the program should allow the user to update the database with new inventory that has been entered into an Excel worksheet. The program should also retrieve sales data for each dealership that includes the make and model of the car, the date each car was sold, the sales rep responsible for the sale, and the net profit for the dealership. The user should be able to add sales data to a pivot table for fast-and-easy analyses and report generation.

Project Tools/Algorithm

The components used in the program (toolbars, Userforms, ActiveX controls, ADO objects, worksheets, and pivot tables) are all discussed in previous chapters. Most notably, the program involves the ADO and PivotTable objects discussed in Chapter 13, "Data I/O Between Excel and Access," and Chapter 14, "Using and Creating Excel Pivot Tables for Fast Data Analyses."

The project for Pear Tree Used Cars, Inc., will include the following set of Office components and VBA programming tools:

◆ **An Access database for data storage.** The database includes current and past inventory and customer and sales information for each dealership.

◆ **A VBA program stored as an Excel add-in.** When loaded, the add-in creates a toolbar that provides an interface for searching and updating inventory as well as for generating various sales reports.

◆ **An ADO object for interfacing with the Access database.** The ADO object is used to retrieve data from and add data to the database.

◆ **A formatted Excel worksheet for adding new inventory to the database.** The user creates the worksheet from the toolbar, which also provides a common-sense interface for adding new inventory and updating the database.

◆ **Pivot tables for generating sales reports.** The user can create pivot tables for displaying vehicle sales, company profits, and sales rep commissions using a VBA program initiated from another toolbar button.

◆ **A VBA Userform for searching the current inventory.** The Userform is loaded via a toolbar button and provides the user with the ability to quickly search the database for specific cars based on desired criteria. The program associated with the Userform will output results to a formatted worksheet for printing as a report.

The design of this project is based on the assumptions that a majority of the tables in the database are maintained by another program and that Excel is desired for its ability to quickly perform data analysis and generate reports based on these analyses.

 NOTE

I created the database for Pear Tree Used Cars, Inc., using Access. I carefully added reasonably credible data to the database (for example, the car makes, models, and engines are fairly accurate). However, because some of the data was generated randomly, some inconsistencies and inaccuracies may appear in the figures (data was randomly generated for car accessories, car prices and sales, and sales rep and customer information). If you are a car aficionado, you will probably notice some inconsistencies; however, these errors in no way detract from the validity of the discussion and program code in this chapter.

Creating the Database

The components of the database for Pear Tree Used Cars, Inc., considered here represent only a subset of the tables that would realistically be needed even for a small business. However, the database I created demonstrates several VBA programming principles. The database will track each dealership's inventory and its sales, customers, and sales representatives. The database must be normalized to prevent errors in data retrieval and updates.

The normalized database contains the six related tables shown in Figure 15.1. The database tables `Vehicles` and `Packages` hold the current and past inventory for the three dealerships. You could combine these two tables into one table without violating the rules of normalization because every field depends only on the `VehicleID`. However, I preferred not to create a table with that many fields, so I split the table into two tables with the `Packages` table containing those fields defined with a `Boolean` data type (Yes or No in Access). The `Customers`, `SalesReps`, and `Dealerships` tables are all intuitive with foreign keys used to relate specific customers to their purchases, sales reps to their customers and dealerships, and dealerships to their automobiles. The `CustomerPurchases` table stores the information used to track specific customers to their purchases and is required to ensure proper normalization.

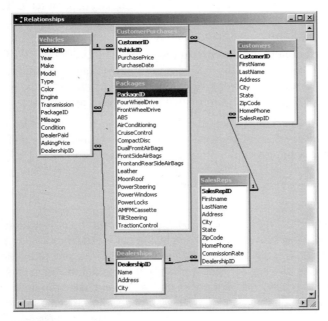

FIGURE 15.1 *The relational database used to track sales and inventory for Pear Tree Used Cars, Inc.*

Designing the User Interface

When designing a program, convenience and ease of use for the user is a high priority. For Excel users, an add-in represents an easy method for loading a program, and I use them often in Office applications. Furthermore, custom toolbars provide an easy-to-use and nonintrusive interface for initiating a program. Therefore, the Pear Tree sales and inventory analysis program is stored as an Excel add-in that uses a programmatically created toolbar to initiate each component of the program. The program has three main components: one for viewing and searching current inventory, one for adding new inventory to the database, and one for creating various sales reports. Other than the custom toolbar, the user interface includes a Userform designed for searching the database for current inventory, an Excel worksheet for adding new inventory to the database, and additional worksheets for holding pivot table reports that summarize various aspects of company sales.

Creating the Toolbar

I discuss custom toolbars in Chapter 9, "Custom Menus and Toolbars." The program for Pear Tree Used Cars, Inc., requires four buttons on the toolbar to initiate the various components of the program. Enter the code into the code module for the Workbook object for creating custom toolbars dynamically when an Excel workbook (.xls or .xla file) is loaded. The following code creates a custom toolbar with four buttons whose captions are View Inventory, Add Inventory, Update Inventory, and View Sales. When clicked, each button initiates a Public procedure in a standard code module.

```
Option Explicit
Private tlbPearTree As CommandBar


Private Sub Workbook_BeforeClose(Cancel As Boolean)
'Remove the toolbar when add-in is closed
    RemoveToolbar ("Pear Tree Used Cars")
End Sub


Private Sub Workbook_Open()
'Remove toolbar (if it exists due errors) before re-creating it
    RemoveToolbar ("Pear Tree Used Cars")
    AddToolbar
End Sub


Private Sub AddToolbar()
'Create one custom toolbar with four buttons
    Dim tlbViewInventory As CommandBarButton
    Dim tlbAddInventory As CommandBarButton
    Dim tlbUpdateInventory As CommandBarButton
    Dim tlbSales As CommandBarButton


    '- - - - - - - - - - - - - - - - - - - - - - - - - - - -
    'Set reference to new toolbar
    '- - - - - - - - - - - - - - - - - - - - - - - - - - - -
```

```vba
Set tlbPearTree = Application.CommandBars.Add( _
    Name:="Pear Tree Used Cars", _
    Temporary:=True)


'-------------------------------------
'Set reference to buttons on toolbar
'-------------------------------------
Set tlbViewInventory = tlbPearTree.Controls.Add( _
    Type:=msoControlButton, _
    Temporary:=True)
With tlbViewInventory
    .Style = msoButtonCaption
    .Caption = "View Inventory"
    .OnAction = "ShowInventory"        'Displays a userform
End With


Set tlbAddInventory = tlbPearTree.Controls.Add( _
    Type:=msoControlButton, _
    Temporary:=True)
With tlbAddInventory
    .Style = msoButtonCaption
    .Caption = "Add Inventory"
    .BeginGroup = True
    .OnAction = "AddNewInventory"    'Formats a worksheet
End With


Set tlbUpdateInventory = tlbPearTree.Controls.Add( _
    Type:=msoControlButton, _
    Temporary:=True)
With tlbUpdateInventory
    .Enabled = False
    .Style = msoButtonCaption
    .Caption = "Update Inventory"
    .BeginGroup = True
    'Updates database with new inventory
    .OnAction = "UpdateInventory"
End With
```

```
    Set tlbSales = tlbPearTree.Controls.Add( _
        Type:=msoControlButton, _
        Temporary:=True)
    With tlbSales
        .Style = msoButtonCaption
        .Caption = "View Sales"
        .BeginGroup = True
        .OnAction = "PearTreeSales"      'Creates pivot table reports
    End With

    tlbPearTree.Visible = True
End Sub


Private Sub RemoveToolbar(tlbarName As String)
'Deletes the custom toolbar
    Dim cBar As CommandBar

    For Each cBar In Application.CommandBars
        If cBar.Name = tlbarName Then
            cBar.Delete
            Exit For
        End If
    Next
End Sub
```

The resulting toolbar is shown in Figure 15.2. The button labeled Update Inventory is initially disabled because the user must input records into a worksheet before the database can be updated. The OnAction property of the CommandBarButton object is used to set the name of the VBA Public procedure that will be initiated when the toolbar button is clicked.

FIGURE 15.2 *The Pear Tree Used Cars custom toolbar.*

The Userform

Selecting the button labeled View Inventory on the custom toolbar loads and displays a Userform. The Userform (in Design view) is shown in Figure 15.3.

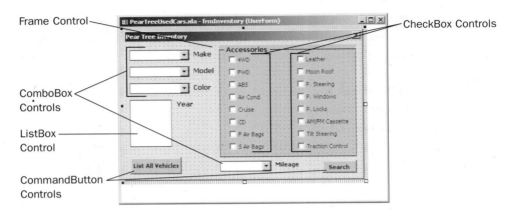

FIGURE 15.3 *The Pear Tree Used Cars view inventory Userform.*

The Userform shown in Figure 15.3 provides an interface that enables the user to search the database for existing inventory based on a car's make, model, color, and year in a successive fashion using a series of ComboBox controls. The user can also search for specific accessories (without specifying make, model, and so on) by selecting one or more check boxes grouped in a Frame control. Approximate mileage can also be used as search criteria through another ComboBox control.

Properties of the ActiveX controls altered from their default values at design time include `Name`, `Caption`, and various appearance properties (`Width`, `Height`, `Font`, `BackColor`, and so on). In addition, the `Style` properties of all ComboBox controls are set as a drop-down list (`fmStyleDropDownList`).

The code module for the Userform contains procedures for connecting to the Access database and retrieving records based on various queries. The queries are constructed from user input via the ActiveX controls on the Userform and return records that represent the dealership's current inventory. The code entered into the Userform code module is listed below. The code contains references to variables and procedures contained in other code modules that are listed later in this chapter. You must set a reference to the ADO object library (Microsoft ActiveX Data Objects 2.7 Library or later version) before executing this program.

```
Option Explicit
Private comm As ADODB.Command
```

The `Activate()` event of the `Userform` object initializes the ComboBox control used to hold the Make of the car (Ford, Chevrolet, Toyota, and so on). The query executed against the PearTreeUsedCars.mdb database returns a list of car manufacturers (based on existing inventory) that is stored in the `Public` variable `rsVehicles` (type `Recordset`). The `AddItem` method of the ComboBox control adds the list of vehicle manufacturers to `cmbMake`. The ComboBox control `cmbMileage` is also initialized with a series of mileage ranges before the worksheet used to hold the results of the search is found or created.

> **NOTE**
>
> Because Access does not support difference (minus) SQL operations, you must use a sub-query to return only those records representing existing inventory.

```
Private Sub UserForm_Activate()
'Initialize file path to the database, ActiveX controls, and the
'Excel worksheet for holding retrieved records.
    Dim sqlStr As String
    Dim ws As Worksheet, addSheet As Boolean


    '- - - - - - - - - - - - - - - - - - - - - - - - - - - - - - - - - - - - - - - - -
    'Create connection to database and execute SQL statement
    'for populating combo box holding the auto 'Make'
    '- - -'- - - - - - - - - - - - - - - - - - - - - - - - - - - - - - - - - - -
    On Error GoTo ADOError
    dbPath = ActiveWorkbook.Path & "\PearTreeUsedCars.mdb"
    cmbModel.Enabled = False
    sqlStr = "SELECT DISTINCT Make " & _
        "FROM Vehicles " & _
        "WHERE VehicleID NOT IN " & _
            (SELECT VehicleID FROM CustomerPurchases) " & _
        "ORDER BY Make;"
    CreateConnection            'Call to public sub in standard module
    CreateCommand (sqlStr)


    '- - - - - - - - - - - - - - - - - - - - - - - - - - -
    'Add unique "Make" to combo box
    '- - - - - - - - - - - - - - - - - - - - - - - - - - -
    cmbMake.Clear
    cmbMake.AddItem "*"
    With rsVehicles                 'Public variable
        If .EOF Then .MoveFirst
        Do While Not .EOF
            cmbMake.AddItem .Fields(0).Value
            .moveNext
        Loop
```

```
        .MoveFirst
        cmbMake.Text = "*"
    End With
    ClearMemory        'Call to sub that releases system memory


    '.............................................
    'Populate mileage combo with constants
    '.............................................
    cmbMileage.AddItem "<10000"
    cmbMileage.AddItem "<20000"
    cmbMileage.AddItem "<30000"
    cmbMileage.AddItem "<50000"
    cmbMileage.AddItem "<75000"
    cmbMileage.AddItem "<100000"
    cmbMileage.Text = "<100000"


    '...................................................
    'Create/find worksheet for holding retrieved records
    '...................................................
    addSheet = True
    For Each ws In Worksheets
        If ws.Name = "Current Inventory" Then
            ws.Activate
            addSheet = False
            Exit For
        End If
    Next
    If addSheet Then
        Worksheets.Add
        ActiveSheet.Name = "Current Inventory"
    End If
    Exit Sub


ADOError:
    MsgBox (Err.Description)
    End
End Sub
```

The connection to the database is established with a call to a `Public` Sub procedure in a standard code module (`CreateConnection`, which is listed later in this chapter in the section "Public Procedures"). After the connection to the database is created, the `CreateCommand()` Sub procedure is called in order to execute an SQL statement against the database. All SQL statements from the Userform code module will return records from the database to the `Public Recordset` variable `rsVehicles`. The elements of the SQL statement will depend on the user's selections on the Userform and, therefore, may differ with each call to the `CreateCommand()` Sub procedure.

```
Private Sub CreateCommand(sqlStr As String)
'Create/execute the SQL Command to Pear-tree database
'Must be preceded with call to connection sub procedure.
    Set rsVehicles = New ADODB.Recordset
    Set comm = New ADODB.Command
    With comm
        .ActiveConnection = conn
        .CommandTimeout = 10
        .CommandText = sqlStr
        Set rsVehicles = .Execute
    End With
End Sub
Private Sub ClearMemory()
'Release system memory for public/module variables
    Set rsVehicles = Nothing
    Set comm = Nothing
    conn.Close
    Set conn = Nothing
End Sub
```

The `Change()` events of the ComboBox controls are used to build the SQL statements executed against the database when the user selects a value from the list. This happens successively starting from the ComboBox control that lists the make of car (`cmbMake`, populated from code in the `Activate()` event of the `Userform` object). Initially, all combo boxes are empty except `cmbMake`. Selecting a make of car from the drop-down list triggers the `Change()` event of the control. A query returns all records for the selected make, which are then copied to the worksheet with a call to the `Public` procedure `CopyRecords()`. Another query returns the available models and populates the ComboBox control named `cmbModel`. When the user selects a car model, the `Change()` event of `cmbModel` is triggered and records based on the selected make and model are returned from the database and copied to the worksheet. Another query then populates the ComboBox control listing available colors. This process is repeated for the ListBox control that displays available years for a car based on the make, model, and color (1stYear). The logic in each of these Change() event procedures is essentially identical. The code differs only in the SQL strings and controls altered by each procedure's execution.

```
Private Sub cmbMake_Change()
'Copy records to worksheet based on selected 'Make' of car.
'Populate 'Model' combo box when the user selects a new 'Make' of car.
    Dim sqlStr As String
    On Error GoTo ADOError
    sqlStr = "SELECT Make, Model, Type, Year, Mileage, AskingPrice, " & _
                    "Engine, Transmission, Color " & _
            "FROM Vehicles " & _
            "WHERE Make='" & cmbMake.Text & "' AND " & _
                    "VehicleID NOT IN (" & _
                    "SELECT VehicleID FROM CustomerPurchases) " & _
            "ORDER BY Model;"
    cmbModel.Clear
    If cmbMake.Text <> "*" Then
        ClearAccessories               'Clear check boxes
        cmbModel.Enabled = True
        CreateConnection          'Execute query to return selected Make
        CreateCommand (sqlStr)
        CopyRecords              'Public sub that copies records to worksheet
        FormatTable
        Set rsVehicles = Nothing
        '-----------------------------------------------------------------
        'Create and execute another query that populates
        'the 'Model' combo box
        '-----------------------------------------------------------------
        sqlStr = "SELECT Distinct Model " & _
            "FROM Vehicles " & _
            "WHERE Make='" & cmbMake.Text & "' AND " & _
                "VehicleID NOT IN (" & _
                    "SELECT VehicleID FROM CustomerPurchases);"
        CreateCommand (sqlStr)
        With rsVehicles
            If Not .BOF Then .MoveFirst
```

```
                Do While Not .EOF
                    cmbModel.AddItem .Fields(0).Value
                    .moveNext
                Loop
            End With
            ClearMemory
        End If
        Exit Sub
ADOError:
    MsgBox (Err.Description)
    End
End Sub


Private Sub cmbModel_Change()
'Copy records to worksheet based on selected 'Make' and 'Model' of car.
'Populate 'Color' combo box when the user selects a new 'Model' of car.
    Dim sqlStr As String
    On Error GoTo ADOError
    sqlStr = "SELECT Make, Model, Type, Year, Mileage, " & _
                "AskingPrice, Engine, Transmission, Color " & _
            "FROM Vehicles " & _
            "WHERE Make='" & cmbMake.Text & "' AND " & _
                "Model='" & cmbModel.Text & _
            "' AND VehicleID NOT IN (" & _
                "SELECT VehicleID FROM CustomerPurchases);"
    cmbColor.Clear
    If cmbModel.Text <> "" Then
        ClearAccessories
        CreateConnection
        CreateCommand (sqlStr)
        CopyRecords
        FormatTable
        Set rsVehicles = Nothing
        sqlStr = "SELECT Distinct Color " & _
            "FROM Vehicles " & _
            "WHERE Make='" & cmbMake.Text & "' AND " & _
                "Model='" & cmbModel.Text & _
```

```
                    "' AND VehicleID NOT IN (" & _
                       "SELECT VehicleID FROM CustomerPurchases);"
            CreateCommand (sqlStr)
            With rsVehicles
                If Not .BOF Then .MoveFirst
                Do While Not .EOF
                    cmbColor.AddItem .Fields(0).Value
                    .moveNext
                Loop
            End With
            ClearMemory
        End If
        Exit Sub
ADOError:
    MsgBox (Err.Description)
    End
End Sub
Private Sub cmbColor_Change()
'Copy records to worksheet based on selected 'Make', 'Model',
'and 'Color' of car. Populate 'Year' list box when the user
'selects a new 'Color' of car.
    Dim sqlStr As String
    On Error GoTo ADOError
    sqlStr = "SELECT Make, Model, Type, Year, Mileage, AskingPrice, " & _
                "Engine, Transmission, Color " & _
            "FROM Vehicles " & _
            "WHERE Make='" & cmbMake.Text & "' AND " & _
                "Model='" & cmbModel.Text & _
            "' AND Color='" & cmbColor.Text & "' AND VehicleID " & _
                "NOT IN (SELECT VehicleID FROM CustomerPurchases);"
    lstYear.Clear
    If cmbColor.Text <> "" Then
        ClearAccessories
        CreateConnection
        CreateCommand (sqlStr)
        CopyRecords
```

```
        FormatTable
        Set rsVehicles = Nothing
        sqlStr = "SELECT Distinct Year " & _
            "FROM Vehicles " & _
            "WHERE Make='" & cmbMake.Text & "' AND " & _
                "Model='" & cmbModel.Text & "' AND " & _
                "Color='" & cmbColor.Text & "' AND VehicleID " & _
                "NOT IN (SELECT VehicleID FROM CustomerPurchases);"
        CreateCommand (sqlStr)
        With rsVehicles
            If Not .BOF Then .MoveFirst
            Do While Not .EOF
                lstYear.AddItem .Fields(0).Value
                .moveNext
            Loop
        End With
        ClearMemory
    End If
    Exit Sub
ADOError:
    MsgBox (Err.Description)
    End
End Sub


Private Sub lstYear_Click()
'Copy records to worksheet based on
'selected 'Make', 'Model', 'Color', and 'Year' of car.
    Dim sqlStr As String
    On Error GoTo ADOError
    sqlStr = "SELECT Make, Model, Type, Year, Mileage, AskingPrice, " & _
                "Engine, Transmission, Color " & _
            "FROM Vehicles " & _
            "WHERE Make='" & cmbMake.Text & "' AND " & _
                "Model='" & cmbModel.Text & "' AND " & _
                "Color='" & cmbColor.Text & "'  AND " & _
                "Year='" & lstYear.Text & "' AND " & _
```

```
                    "VehicleID NOT IN (" & _
                    "SELECT VehicleID FROM CustomerPurchases);"
        If lstYear.Text <> "" Then
            ClearAccessories
            CreateConnection
            CreateCommand (sqlStr)
            CopyRecords
            FormatTable
            Set rsVehicles = Nothing
            ClearMemory
        End If
        Exit Sub
ADOError:
        MsgBox (Err.Description)
        End
End Sub
```

The `Click()` event procedure of the CommandButton control `cmdListAll` executes a query against the database that returns a `Recordset` holding all cars currently in stock at the three dealerships.

```
Private Sub cmdListAll_Click()
'Copy all cars in stock to worksheet
    Dim sqlStr As String

    sqlStr = "SELECT Make, Model, Type, Year, Mileage, AskingPrice, " & _
                "Engine, Transmission " & _
            "FROM Vehicles " & _
            "WHERE VehicleID NOT IN (" & _
                "SELECT VehicleID FROM CustomerPurchases)" & _
            "ORDER BY Make, Model;"

    On Error GoTo ADOError
    Application.ScreenUpdating = False
    CreateConnection
    CreateCommand (sqlStr)
    CopyRecords
    FormatTable
```

```
    Range("A1").Select
    ClearMemory
    Exit Sub
ADOError:
    MsgBox (Err.Description)
    End
End Sub
```

The Click() event of the CommandButton control cmdSearch holds the code that will query the database for records based on the criteria specified in all CheckBox controls and the ComboBox control cmbMileage. Other search criteria (make, model, color, and year) are ignored. The query String is constructed from the selected check boxes and the mileage ComboBox control. Because the query can potentially be quite long, a separate procedure (BuildSQL) is used to construct the SQL String.

```
Private Sub cmdSearch_Click()
'Search for cars in stock based on selected check boxes
    Dim sqlStr As String

    cmbMake.Text = "*"
    'Use separate procedure to build lengthy query
    sqlStr = BuildSQL
    If BuildSQL = "" Then
        MsgBox "Select at least one accessory!", _
            vbOKOnly, "Select Accessory"
        Exit Sub
    End If
    On Error GoTo ADOError
    CreateConnection
    CreateCommand (sqlStr)
    CopyRecords
    FormatTable
    Range("A1").Select
    ClearMemory
    Exit Sub
ADOError:
    MsgBox (Err.Description)
    End
End Sub
```

The Function procedure BuildSQL() constructs an SQL String based on the user's selections in the cmbMileage ComboBox and all CheckBox controls. You use a parameter array (accessoryFields) to hold the field names in the database. The index values of the accessoryFields array correspond directly to the TabIndex property of the CheckBox controls. Therefore, the TabIndex property can be used to return the field names of the corresponding check boxes that have been selected by the user.

NOTE

The String variable returned from the BuildSQL() Function procedure when the user selects the check boxes labeled FWD, Air Cond., and ABS will have the following value:

```
SELECT Make, Model, Type, Year, Mileage, AskingPrice,
Engine, Transmission FROM Vehicles As V, Packages As P WHERE
V.PackageID=P.PackageID AND FrontWheelDrive=True AND
AirConditioning=True AND ABS=True   AND Mileage<100000AND
VehicleID NOT IN (SELECT VehicleID FROM CustomerPurchases);
```

```vb
Private Function BuildSQL() As String
'Builds the SQL statement when user chooses Search button.
'Statement is based on all userform input (Combo boxes and check boxes).
    Dim sqlStr As String, sqlWhere As String
    Dim ckAccessories As Control
    Dim accessoryFields
    Dim I As Integer

    accessoryFields = Array("FourWheelDrive", "FrontWheelDrive", "ABS", _
        "AirConditioning", "CruiseControl", "CompactDisc", _
        "DualFrontAirBags", "FrontSideAirBags", "Leather", _
        "MoonRoof", "PowerSteering", "PowerWindows", _
        "PowerLocks", "AMFMCassette", "TiltSteering", _
        "TractionControl")

    sqlStr = "SELECT Make, Model, Type, Year, Mileage, AskingPrice, " & _
                "Engine, Transmission " & _
            "FROM Vehicles As V, Packages As P "
```

```
        For Each ckAccessories In Frame1.Controls
            If ckAccessories.Value = True Then
                sqlWhere = sqlWhere & accessoryFields( _
                    ckAccessories.TabIndex) & "=True AND "
                I = I + 1
            End If
        Next
        If I = 0 Then
            BuildSQL = ""
            Exit Function
        End If
        sqlWhere = Left(sqlWhere, Len(sqlWhere) - 4)
        sqlStr = sqlStr & "WHERE V.PackageID=P.PackageID AND " & sqlWhere
        If cmbMake.Text <> "*" Then
            sqlStr = sqlStr & " AND Make='" & cmbMake.Text & "'"
        End If
        If cmbModel.Text <> "" Then
            sqlStr = sqlStr & " AND Model='" & cmbModel.Text & "'"
        End If
        If cmbColor.Text <> "" Then
            sqlStr = sqlStr & " AND Color='" & cmbColor.Text & "'"
        End If
        If lstYear.Text <> "" Then
            sqlStr = sqlStr & " AND Year='" & lstYear.Text & "'"
        End If
        sqlStr = sqlStr & " AND Mileage" & cmbMileage.Text & "AND " & _
            "VehicleID NOT IN (SELECT VehicleID FROM CustomerPurchases);"
        BuildSQL = sqlStr
End Function
```

The remaining procedures entered in the code module of the Userform object have the relatively simple tasks of formatting the worksheet that contains vehicle records (FormatTable), clearing all CheckBox controls (ClearAccessories), and releasing system memory when the Userform is closed (QueryClose() event of Userform object).

```
Private Sub FormatTable()
'Format the worksheet holding inventory records
    Dim numCols As Integer
```

```
    Dim headerRange As Range
    Dim tableRange As Range

    numCols = rsVehicles.Fields.Count
    Set headerRange = Range("A1:" & Chr(numCols + 64) & "1")
    Set tableRange = Range("A:" & Chr(numCols + 64))
    With headerRange
        .Interior.Color = RGB(150, 150, 150)
        .HorizontalAlignment = xlCenter
        .Font.Bold = True
        With .Borders(xlEdgeBottom)
            .LineStyle = xlDouble
            .Weight = xlThick
        End With
    End With
    With tableRange
        .Columns.AutoFit
        .HorizontalAlignment = xlCenter
    End With
End Sub
Private Sub ClearAccessories()
'Clear check box controls
    Dim ckAccessories As Control
    For Each ckAccessories In Frame1.Controls
        ckAccessories.Value = False
    Next
End Sub
Private Sub UserForm_QueryClose(Cancel As Integer, CloseMode As Integer)
    Unload Me
    End
End Sub
```

As an example, if the user searches the database for a black Toyota Land Cruiser, the resulting worksheet will appear as shown in Figure 15.4.

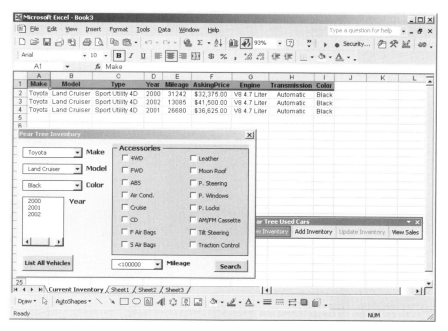

FIGURE 15.4 *Searching for a specific auto with a Userform interface.*

Adding Inventory to the Database

The remaining code for the Pear Tree database application is contained in standard code modules. Although only one module is required, the code is actually split into three modules to isolate procedures that have specific tasks and procedures that have general tasks used by other component modules.

An Excel worksheet serves as an excellent interface for adding new inventory to the database. There are numerous possibilities for formatting the worksheet that serves as a database form. The only requirement for this particular application is that the process must be initiated from the custom toolbar. I chose to use the simple form (Excel worksheet) shown in Figure 15.5.

FIGURE 15.5 *Excel worksheet serving as a database form for adding one or more records to the database.*

This worksheet is designed to input information to be added to the `Vehicles` and `Packages` tables in the database (refer to Figure 15.1) and is created by selecting Add Inventory on the custom toolbar (refer to Figure 15.2). The code used to create this worksheet is listed next. Two Sub procedures (`AddNewInventory` and `FormatWkSh`) create and format the worksheet within the active workbook. The code is fairly straightforward, with much of the `FormatWksh()` Sub procedure being recorded by Excel's macro recorder. The `FormatWksh()` Sub procedure uses a `Validation` object to provide some help for the user, because only the `Integer` values 0 and 1 (representing Yes and No fields in the Access database) should be entered into the cells of column B. To add data validation rules to a worksheet non-programmatically, select Data, Validation in the Excel application window. Records are added within worksheet columns so that an entire record can be viewed without having to scroll horizontally.

```
Option Explicit
Private comm As ADODB.Command


Public Sub AddNewInventory()
'Find/create the worksheet used to enter in new vehicles
'for adding to the database.
    Dim ws As Worksheet
    Dim addSheet As Boolean
```

```
        addSheet = True
        'Loop through worksheets to look for form.
        For Each ws In Worksheets
            If ws.Name = "Add Vehicles" Then
                ws.Activate
                addSheet = False
                Exit For
            End If
        Next
        If addSheet Then     'Add new worksheet to serve as form
            Worksheets.Add
            ActiveSheet.Name = "Add Vehicles"
        End If
        MsgBox "Enter records in consecutive columns before updating", _
            vbOKOnly, "Add Records"
        FormatWkSh
        Application.CommandBars("Pear Tree Used Cars").Controls( _
            "Update Inventory").Enabled = True
End Sub
Private Sub FormatWkSh()
'Format the worksheet used to add records to the database.
    Dim rowHeaders
    Dim c As Range
    Dim I As Integer

    rowHeaders = Array("VehicleID", "Year", "Make", "Model", "Type", _
        "Color", "Engine", "Transmission", "Mileage", "Condition", _
        "Dealer Paid", "Asking Price", "Dealership", "4 WD", "FWD", _
        "ABS", "AC", "CC", "CD", "DFAB", "SFAB", "FRSAB", "Leather", _
        "Moon Roof", "P.Steering", "P.Windows", "P.Locks", _
        "AM/FM/Cassette", "Tilt", "Traction Control")
    I = 1
    For Each c In Range("A1:A30")     'Add headers to column A
        c.Value = rowHeaders(I - 1)
        I = I + 1
    Next
```

```
With Range("A1:A30")    'Format headers
    .HorizontalAlignment = xlRight
    .Font.Bold = True
    .Borders(xlEdgeRight).LineStyle = xlContinuous
    .Borders(xlEdgeRight).Weight = xlThick
    .Borders(xlEdgeBottom).LineStyle = xlContinuous
    .Borders(xlEdgeBottom).Weight = xlThick
    .Columns.AutoFit
End With
With Range("A13")
    .Borders(xlEdgeBottom).LineStyle = xlContinuous
    .Borders(xlEdgeBottom).Weight = xlThick
End With
For Each c In Range("B14:B30")    'Add validation to Yes/No values
    With c.Validation
        .Delete
    .   .Add Type:=xlValidateWholeNumber, _
            AlertStyle:=xlValidAlertStop, _
            Operator:=xlBetween, Formula1:="0", Formula2:="1"
        .IgnoreBlank = True
        .InputTitle = "Input Value:"
        .ErrorTitle = "Input Error"
        .InputMessage = "0 or 1"
        .ErrorMessage = "Enter a zero (0) or one (1)!"
        .ShowInput = True
        .ShowError = True
    End With
    c.Value = 0
Next
End Sub
```

The user can enter 1 to 255 records in columns B through IV (column 256 of a worksheet) of the Add Vehicles worksheet before selecting Update Inventory on the custom toolbar. Doing so makes this worksheet a handy tool for batch updates to the database. The records are added to the database one at a time before being deleted from the worksheet. The process continues until an empty column is found.

TIP

There are a number of alternatives to creating a database form from an Excel work-sheet. One option is to format a worksheet with ActiveX controls that are able to connect to the database using VBA code contained in event procedures of the worksheet and controls. The Excel workbook containing the formatted worksheet can be saved as a template file (*.xlt) with its VBA code. Selecting a button on a custom toolbar will then trigger a procedure to load the template to serve as the database form for adding new vehicles to the database.

Presumably, the user selects Update Inventory on the custom toolbar after the data is entered or copied into the worksheet. The worksheet and VBA code triggered from this selection provide little validation of the user's entries simply because it's not necessary. Instead, validation is provided by the Jet database engine and violations returned to the user via a message box. Update errors include data type mismatches, key violations, and null values in required fields (among others). When an error occurs, the program ends with the record that generated the error listed in column B of the worksheet so the user can edit the record and start again.

The `UpdateInventory()` Sub procedure is triggered when the user selects the toolbar button with the same caption. This procedure inserts each record entered into the work-sheet into the PearTreeUsedCars.mdb database file provided no violations of the various constraints are raised. A `Do/Loop` iterates through each record (column) in the worksheet testing for uniqueness of the combination of fields that represents a record in the `Packages` table. If the combination is unique, a new `PackageID` number is generated for the key field. Otherwise, the existing `PackageID` number is used, and the only table updated with a new record is `Vehicles`. If the record is unique, a record is added to the `Packages` table first to avoid a foreign key violation with the `PackageID` field. When a record is successfully added to one or both tables, the next record is copied to column B from column C before column C is deleted. When column C is deleted, the remaining records are effectively shifted one column to the left in the worksheet, and the process repeats until an error is raised or no more records exist.

```
Public Sub UpdateInventory()
'Adds all records to the database. PackageID's are automatically
'found or created.
    Dim packageID As Integer, sqlStr As String
    Dim c As Range

    On Error GoTo ADOError
    Worksheets("Add Vehicles").Select
```

```
dbPath = ActiveWorkbook.Path & "\PearTreeUsedCars.mdb"
CreateConnection
Do
        '----------------------------------------
        'Find number of records in Packages table
        'and return/create a PackageID value.
        '----------------------------------------
        CreateCommand ("SELECT * FROM Packages", "DQL")
        packageID = FindMatch


        '--------------------------------------------------------------
        'Build the SQL statement for inserting data.
        'Exceute DML command against DB. If new record is required for
        'Packages table then build two SQL statements.
        '--------------------------------------------------------------
        If packageID > rsVehicles.RecordCount Then
            sqlStr = BuildInsert(True, packageID)
            CreateCommand (sqlStr, "DML")
        End If
        sqlStr = BuildInsert(False, packageID)
        CreateCommand (sqlStr, "DML")
        Range("C1:C30").Select
        Selection.Copy
        Range("B1:B30").Select
        ActiveSheet.Paste
        Range("C:C").Delete
        For Each c In Range("B14:B30")   'Assume Yes for non-zero values
            If c.Value <> 0 Then c.Value = 1
        Next
Loop While Range("B1").Value <> ""

Set rsVehicles = Nothing
Set comm = Nothing
conn.Close
Set conn = Nothing
Exit Sub
```

```
ADOError:

    MsgBox Err.Description, vbOKOnly, "ADO Error"

    End

End Sub
```

The `CreateCommand()` Sub procedure is similar to the command procedure listed previously in the code module of the `Userform` object. The procedure is called up to three times from `UpdateInventory()`: once to execute a query to return the entire contents of the `Packages` table, once to execute a query that inserts a new record into the `Vehicles` table, and, if required, once to execute a query that inserts a new record into the `Packages` table.

The first call to the `CreateCommand()` Sub procedure creates a `Recordset` (stored in the variable `rsVehicles`) that stores all the data in the `Packages` table. This `Recordset` must be tested for an available `PackageID` number (required as the foreign key in the `Vehicles` table) and the total number of records it contains. The combination of values in each record is also compared to the combination of values entered by the user in order to test for uniqueness. If the user's entries represent a unique combination, a new record will be added to the `Packages` table. If the combination of user's entries is not unique, the value of the `PackageID` field for the record in the `Packages` table that matches the user's entries is determined.

The curser type of the ADO `Recordset` object is changed to `adOpenStatic` to allow for more flexible movement through the `Recordset` (effectively enabling the `MoveLast` method and `RecordCount` property of the `Recordset` object). The default cursor type for an ADO `Recordset` object is `adForwardOnly`, which only allows you to move forward through the `Recordset` from the beginning, one record at a time, and effectively disables the `RecordCount` property (returns -1).

The type of SQL statement passed to the `CreateCommand()` Sub procedure is used to determine whether the `Execute` method of `Command` object will return a `Recordset`. The `Execute` method will return a `Recordset` if the SQL statement begins with the `Select` clause. No `Recordset` is returned by the `Execute` method if the SQL statement begins with the `Insert` clause.

```
Private Sub CreateCommand(sqlStr As String, qType As String)
'Create/execute the SQL Command to Pear-tree DB
    Set comm = New ADODB.Command
    With comm
        .ActiveConnection = conn
        .CommandTimeout = 10
        .CommandType = adCmdText
        .CommandText = sqlStr
        If qType = "DQL" Then
            Set rsVehicles = .Execute
```

```
                '- - - - - - - - - - - - - - - - - - - - - - - - - - - - - - - - - - - - - - -
                'Static cursor required for getting record count
                '- - - - - - - - - - - - - - - - - - - - - - - - - - - - - - - - - - - - - - -
                rsVehicles.Close
                rsVehicles.CursorType = adOpenStatic
                rsVehicles.Open
            Else
                .Execute
            End If
        End With
    End With
End Sub
```

The FindMatch()Function procedure is called from UpdateInventory() and loops through the contents of the Packages table (returned to rsVehicles) looking for a match to the combination of values in the worksheet range B14:B30. This range is used to hold the field values for the Packages table. If the combination is unique, the Function procedure returns the next number in the sequence for the PackageID field (primary key). Otherwise, it returns the PackageID number representing the record that matches the user's entries.

```
Private Function FindMatch() As Integer
'Find a match between user input and record in Packages table
'If no match, then return next number in sequence of primary key field
    Dim c As Range, I As Integer, moveNext As Boolean

    I = 1
    Do Until rsVehicles.EOF
        For Each c In Range("B14:B30")
            If rsVehicles.Fields(I).Value = CBool(c.Value) Then
                FindMatch = rsVehicles.Fields(0)
                moveNext = False
            Else
                FindMatch = rsVehicles.Fields(0) + 1
                moveNext = True
                Exit For
            End If
            I = I + 1
        Next
        I = 1
```

```
        If moveNext Then
            rsVehicles.moveNext
        Else
            Exit Do
        End If
    Loop
End Function
```

The BuildInsert() Function procedure constructs the SQL statements used to insert new records into the Vehicles and Packages tables. Depending on the value of the Boolean addPackage variable, the Function procedure creates one of two possible SQL statements. If addPackage is True, a SQL statement is constructed to add a new record to the Packages table; otherwise, the statement is constructed to add a new record to the Vehicles table.

```
Private Function BuildInsert(addPackage As Boolean, _
    packageID As Integer) As String
'Build the SQL string for inserting a record into a database table
    Dim c As Range


    If addPackage Then
        'Must build SQL string to add record to Packages table
        BuildInsert = "INSERT INTO Packages VALUES(" & packageID & ","
        For Each c In Range("B14:B30")
            If c.Value = 0 Then
                c.Value = False
            Else
                c.Value = True
            End If
            BuildInsert = BuildInsert & c.Value & ","
        Next
        BuildInsert = Left(BuildInsert, Len(BuildInsert) - 1) & ");"
    Else
        'Build SQL string to add record to Vehicles table
        BuildInsert = "INSERT INTO Vehicles VALUES("
        For Each c In Range("B1:B8")
            'Use Chr() function to add required quotation marks
            BuildInsert = BuildInsert & Chr(34) & c.Value & Chr(34) & ","
        Next
```

```
        BuildInsert = BuildInsert & packageID & ","
        BuildInsert = BuildInsert & Range("B9").Value & ","
        BuildInsert = BuildInsert & Chr(34) & Range("B10").Value & _
            Chr(34) & ","
        For Each c In Range("B11:B13")
            BuildInsert = BuildInsert & c.Value & ","
        Next
        BuildInsert = Left(BuildInsert, Len(BuildInsert) - 1) & ");"
    End If
End Function
```

After all records are inserted, the worksheet/database form will appear as it did when it was first created. The process of inserting records into a table is typically quite fast relative to a query that returns a `Recordset`. Therefore, even though the VBA code inserts records from the Excel worksheet/database form one at a time, the process executes quickly. SQL insert statements can be slowed by indexes and integrity constraints, but this is acceptable because of the benefits these factors create in a database.

You can create other forms from Excel worksheets to update the other tables in the database, but I'll leave these exercises for you to undertake.

Creating Pivot Table Reports

The last component of the Pear Tree inventory and sales analysis program creates a series of pivot table reports from a data set imported into an Excel worksheet from the Access database. I discuss pivot tables in Chapter 14. The primary function of a VBA project involving pivot tables is to provide the user with the ability to immediately manipulate and print various sales reports.

I created three pivot tables that analyze various aspects of the sales data for Pear Tree Used Cars, Inc. The pivot tables are all created from the same data set to alleviate time delays in retrieving new data from the database. The three pivot table reports summarize the following:

◆ **The most popular makes and models of cars sold.** The `Count` Function summarizes the data in the Make and Model fields from the `Vehicles` table for those cars that have been sold.

◆ **The net profits resulting from vehicle sales for each dealership.** The `Sum` Function summarizes the sales data for vehicles sold by each dealership. Net profits are calculated by subtracting the commissions and amount paid by the dealer from the price paid by the customer. Obviously, this is a simplified calculation of company profits because overhead costs and salary information are not included.

◆ **The commissions generated by sales reps at each dealership.** Commissions are calculated from the product of the commission rate and the difference of what the dealer paid and the final price of a vehicle.

The code for generating the pivot table reports is contained in a standard module and includes a `Public` procedure (`PearTreeSales`) that is initiated from the custom toolbar button labeled View Sales. The order of operations in the `PearTreeSales()` Sub procedure follows:

1. Create a connection to the database.

2. Execute a command against the database to return a set of records that includes numerous fields representing sales information.

3. Copy the records to an Excel worksheet. This is required in order to group date fields in the pivot tables.

4. Initialize `String` values representing row, column, data, and page fields in the pivot table and create the pivot table with an embedded pivot chart on the same worksheet. Repeat this step for each pivot table and chart required.

```
Option Explicit
Private comm As ADODB.Command
Private tlbName As String
Private fieldNum As Integer
Private pivTab As PivotTable
Private srcRange As String


Public Sub PearTreeSales()
'Main sub procedure for creating sales report from Pear-Tree database
    Dim rowFields() As String, colFields() As String
    Dim pageFields() As String, dataFields() As String

    On Error GoTo ADOError
    dbPath = ActiveWorkbook.Path & "\PearTreeUsedCars.mdb"
    CreateConnection
    CreateCommand
    CopyRecords


    '----------------------------------------------------------------
    'Create pivot table to show vehicle sales by Make, Model, and Date
    '----------------------------------------------------------------
    ReDim rowFields(1): ReDim colFields(0)
    ReDim pageFields(0): ReDim dataFields(1)
    rowFields(0) = "Make": rowFields(1) = "Model"
    colFields(0) = "DealershipName": pageFields(0) = "PurchaseDate"
    dataFields(0) = "Make": dataFields(1) = "Model"
```

```
CreatePivTab rowFields(), colFields(), pageFields(), dataFields(), _
     "Vehicle Sales Table", "VehicleSales"
GroupDateField "PurchaseDate", "VehicleSales"
PivotChart ("Vehicle Sales Table")
Range("D1").Select


'-------------------------------------------------
'Create pivot table to show profits grouped by date
'-------------------------------------------------
ReDim rowFields(0)
rowFields(0) = "DealershipName"
colFields(0) = "PurchaseDate"
pageFields(0) = ""
ReDim dataFields(0)
dataFields(0) = "NetProfit"
CreatePivTab rowFields(), colFields(), pageFields(), dataFields(), _
     "Profits Table", "Profits"
GroupDateField "PurchaseDate", "Profits"
FormatTable ("Sum of NetProfit")
PivotChart ("Profits Table")
Range("D1").Select


'-------------------------------------------------
'Create pivot table to show sales reps commissions
'-------------------------------------------------
ReDim rowFields(1)
rowFields(0) = "Firstname": rowFields(1) = "Lastname"
colFields(0) = "PurchaseDate"
pageFields(0) = ""
dataFields(0) = "Commissions"
CreatePivTab rowFields(), colFields(), pageFields(), dataFields(), _
     "Rep Sales Table", "RepSales"
GroupDateField "PurchaseDate", "RepSales"
FormatTable ("Sum of Commissions")
PivotChart ("Rep Sales Table")

Set pivTab = Nothing
Set rsVehicles = Nothing
```

```
        Set comm = Nothing
        conn.Close
        Set conn = Nothing
        Application.ScreenUpdating = True
        Exit Sub
ADOError:
        MsgBox (Err.Description)
        End
End Sub
```

The `CreateCommand()` Sub procedure is repeated here in order to execute the SQL statement that returns the desired sales information from the database. The SQL statement includes several calculated fields in addition to those fields taken directly from the database. The query must join five of the six tables in the database (to take advantage of the foreign key relationships), even though the data it returns originates from only four of the tables. More data is returned from the query than what is used in the three pivot tables so that the user can customize the pivot tables with different data if desired.

```
Private Sub CreateCommand()
'Create/execute the SQL Command to Pear-tree DB
    Dim sqlStr As String, sqlSelect As String, sqlFrom As String, sqlWhere As _
        String

    'Build the SQL string
    sqlSelect = "SELECT Make, Model, PurchaseDate, DealerPaid, " & _
        "PurchasePrice, PurchasePrice-DealerPaid As GrossProfit, " & _
        "DealershipName, S.Firstname, S.Lastname, CommissionRate, " & _
        "CommissionRate*GrossProfit As Commissions, " & _
        "GrossProfit-Commissions As NetProfit "
    sqlFrom = "FROM CustomerPurchases AS CP, Vehicles AS V, " & _
        "Dealerships AS D, SalesReps AS S, Customers C "
    sqlWhere = "WHERE CP.VehicleID=V.VehicleID And " & _
        "D.DealershipID=V.DealershipID And " & _
        "S.SalesRepID=C.SalesRepID AND C.CustomerID=CP.CustomerID;"

    sqlStr = sqlSelect & sqlFrom & sqlWhere
    Debug.Print sqlStr
    Set rsVehicles = New ADODB.Recordset
    Set comm = New ADODB.Command
    'Execute the SQL statement and return Recordset
```

```
        With comm
                .ActiveConnection = conn
                .CommandTimeout = 10
                .CommandText = sqlStr
                Set rsVehicles = .Execute
        End With
    End Sub
```

The CreatePivTab() Sub procedure was edited from the same procedure listed in Chapter 14 to allow for repetitive calls. The procedure accepts several arguments representing the fields to be added to a pivot table, the name that is to be assigned to the pivot table, and the name of the worksheet that will contain the pivot table. The data source for each pivot table that is created by this procedure must originate from the same location. This data source location is stored in a String variable named srcRange declared in a standard module named PublicSubs.

```
Private Sub CreatePivTab(rowFields() As String, colFields() As String, _
        pageFields() As String, dataFields() As String, wkShName As String, _
        pivTabName As String)
'Create the pivot table and add necessary fields
    Dim I As Integer
    '--------------------------
    'Add table to new worksheet
    '--------------------------
    Worksheets.Add
    ActiveSheet.Name = wkShName
    With ActiveWorkbook.PivotCaches.Add(SourceType:=xlDatabase, _
            SourceData:=PublicSubs.srcRange)
        Set pivTab = .CreatePivotTable( _
                        TableDestination:=Range("A4"), _
                        TableName:=pivTabName, _
                        DefaultVersion:=xlPivotTableVersion10)
    End With


    '--------------------------
    'Add fields to pivot table
    '--------------------------
    With pivTab
        For I = 0 To UBound(dataFields)
            .AddDataField pivTab.PivotFields(dataFields(I))
        Next I
```

```
        For I = 0 To UBound(rowFields)
            .AddFields rowFields:=rowFields(I), AddToTable:=True
        Next I
        For I = 0 To UBound(colFields)
            .AddFields ColumnFields:=colFields(I), AddToTable:=True
        Next I
        For I = 0 To UBound(pageFields)
            If pageFields(I) <> "" Then
                .AddFields pageFields:=pageFields(I), AddToTable:=True
            End If
        Next I
    End With
    ActiveSheet.UsedRange.Columns.AutoFit
    Range("A1").Select
End Sub
```

After the pivot table is created, a call to the GroupDateField() Sub procedure will group a specified date field (pfStr) in the specified pivot table (ptStr). You may recall that date fields must be in a column or row area of the pivot table when they are grouped. The GroupDateField() Sub procedure uses the Orientation property of the PivotField object to move the date fields between the row and page areas of the pivot table. Dates are grouped by month, quarter, and year.

The last two procedures in this module format currency data (FormatTable) and add a pivot chart to the worksheet containing the pivot table (PivotChart). You must deselect the chart before creating another pivot table.

```
Private Sub GroupDateField(pfStr As String, ptStr As String)
'Groups a date field by month, quarter, and year then moves them to page area
'of the pivot table.
    Dim pf As PivotField
    Dim pt As PivotTable

    Set pt = ActiveSheet.PivotTables(ptStr)
    For Each pf In pt.PivotFields
        If pf.Name = pfStr Then
            'Move date field to row area
            If pf.Orientation = xlPageField Then
                pf.Orientation = xlRowField
            End If
```

```
                    'Select and group date field by month, quarter, year
                    Cells(pf.DataRange.Row - 1, pf.DataRange.Column).Select
                    Selection.Group Start:=True, End:=True, Periods:=Array( _
                        False, False, False, False, True, True, True)
                    'Move date fields to page area
                    pf.Orientation = xlPageField
                    pf.Position = 1
                    pt.PivotFields("Quarters").Orientation = xlPageField
                    pt.PivotFields("Quarters").Position = 2
                    pt.PivotFields("Years").Orientation = xlPageField
                    pt.PivotFields("Years").Position = 3
            End If
        Next
        Set pt = Nothing
    End Sub


    Private Sub FormatTable(ParamArray fieldNames() As Variant)
    'Format input fields as currency
        Dim pf As PivotField
        Dim I As Integer, K As Integer
        For I = 1 To pivTab.dataFields.Count
            Set pf = pivTab.dataFields(I)
            For K = 0 To UBound(fieldNames)
                If pf.Name = fieldNames(K) Then
                    pf.NumberFormat = "$#,##0.00"
                End If
            Next K
        Next I


        Set pf = Nothing
    End Sub
    Private Sub PivotChart(wsStr As String)
    'Embeds a pivot chart on the worksheet containing the pivot table
        Dim pivChart As ChartObject
        Dim sh As Worksheet
```

```
Set sh = ActiveSheet
sh.ChartObjects.Add Left:=Range("A1:D1").Width, Top:=20, _
    Width:=400, Height:=300
sh.ChartObjects(1).Activate
With ActiveChart
    .ChartType = xlColumnClustered
    .SetSourceData Source:=Worksheets(wsStr).Range("A1")
    .Location WHERE:=xlLocationAsObject, Name:=wsStr
End With
End Sub
```

Creating these pivot tables is simply meant as a convenience for the user. Because all three pivot tables were created from the same data source, the user can manipulate any one table and reproduce the other two. The pivot table and pivot chart representing dealership profits as created by the preceding code is shown in Figure 15.6.

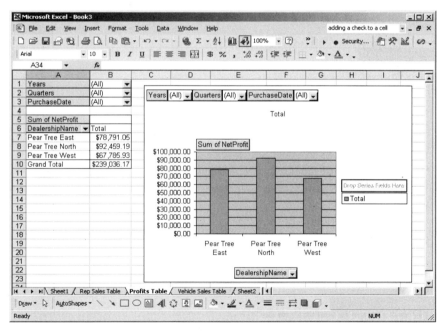

FIGURE 15.6 *Pivot table and pivot chart representing the net profits for Pear Tree Used Cars, Inc.*

Public Procedures

The last set of VBA procedures used by the Pear Tree inventory/sales program is included in a separate standard module for organizational purposes. You can better encapsulate your applications by isolating common procedures. These procedures are isolated in their own code module because they are called multiple times from procedures in the other code modules.

Three Sub procedures and one Function procedure are included in this module. The `ShowInventory()` Sub procedure is initiated from the custom toolbar (by selecting the button labeled View Inventory) and serves only to load and show the Userform named `frmInventory`. The `CreateConnection()` Sub procedure is called from procedures in each component module of the program and serves to create the connection to the Access database. The `Mode` property of the `ADO Connection` object is set to `adModeReadWrite` to allow for read-write access to the database (write access is required by the add inventory component of the program). If the Access database cannot be found, a call to the Function procedure `FindDBase()` will initiate a `FileDialog` object that allows the user to search for the file (if desired). If the user can find the Access file, the correct path is returned and the connection established. The last Sub procedure, `CopyRecords()`, copies the entire contents of the `Recordset` stored in the `Public` variable `rsVehicles` to a worksheet. The `CreateConnection()` Sub procedure is called numerous times from the inventory and sales components of the program.

```
Public conn As ADODB.Connection
Public rsVehicles As ADODB.Recordset
Public srcRange As String
Public dbPath As String
Public Sub ShowInventory()
    frmInventory.Show vbModal
End Sub
Public Sub CreateConnection()
'Create a connection to Northwind
    Dim connStr As String
    Dim ms As Integer

    On Error GoTo FileError
    If Dir(dbPath, vbNormal) = "" Then
        Err.Raise 513
    End If
    connStr = "Data Source=" & dbPath
    Set conn = New ADODB.Connection
    With conn
        .Provider = "Microsoft.Jet.OLEDB.4.0"
        .Mode = adModeReadWrite
        .ConnectionTimeout = 10
```

```
        .ConnectionString = connStr
        .Open
    End With
    Exit Sub
FileError:
    If Err.Number = 513 Then
        ms = MsgBox("Database not found. Do you want to search?", _
            vbYesNo, "Database File")
        If ms = 6 Then
            dbPath = FindDbase
            Resume Next
        Else
            End
        End If
    End If
End Sub
Public Sub CopyRecords()
'Copy records to a worksheet.
    Dim I As Integer, K As Integer

    Cells.Clear
    Application.ScreenUpdating = False
    I = 2
    On Error Resume Next
    With rsVehicles
        If Not .BOF Then .MoveFirst
        '-------------
        'Copy headers
        '-------------
        For K = 0 To .Fields.Count - 1
            Cells(1, K + 1).Value = .Fields(K).Name
        Next K
        '----------
        'Copy Data
        '----------
        Do While Not .EOF
```

```vba
                For K = 0 To .Fields.Count - 1
                    Cells(I, K + 1).Value = .Fields(K).Value
                Next K
                I = I + 1
                .moveNext
            Loop
            .MoveFirst
        End With
        Application.ScreenUpdating = True
        srcRange = "'" & ActiveSheet.Name & "'!A1:" & _
            Chr(64 + rsVehicles.Fields.Count) & I - 1
    '
    
End Sub
Private Function FindDbase()
'User selects path to find database file
    Dim fd As FileDialog
    Dim I As Integer
    
    Set fd = Application.FileDialog(msoFileDialogFilePicker)
    With fd
        .AllowMultiSelect = False
        .Title = "Find Access Database"
        .InitialFileName = ""
        If .Show = -1 Then
            FindDbase = .SelectedItems(1)
        Else
            End
        End If
    End With
    Set fd = Nothing
End Function
```

Summary

In this, chapter I walked you through the construction of an Excel-VBA application that manages and analyzes data for a mythical used car dealership (Pear Tree Used Cars, Inc.). The VBA program involved extensive use of the ADO object and its methods used to establish data I/O with an external database. The program also created several pivot tables based on sales data for each dealership.

The programming techniques used in the construction of the Pear Tree inventory and sales analysis program were covered in Chapters 13 and 14. In Chapter 13, you learned how to use DAO and ADO objects with VBA to establish data I/O operations between Excel and an Access database. You also learned in Chapter 13 that proper normalization of a relational database is critical for proper database management and avoiding updating anomalies. In Chapter 14, you learned how to create pivot tables from the Excel application and programmatically with VBA. The Pear Tree inventory and sales analysis program used all these elements to provide inventory and sales reports for the owner and managers of a series of used car dealerships.

PART IV

Professional Project 3 — Creating a Stock Ticker with VBA

Stock tickers are common applications that you can purchase or use for free at numerous Web sites. If you need real-time quotes, you will have to purchase a subscription; otherwise, if you don't mind a 20-minute delay, you can view the data from a Web site. The stock ticker program constructed in Chapter 18 will retrieve delayed stock quotes from a Web site.

The stock ticker is fun to create in VBA and will use familiar programming tools and introduce a couple of new tools. The ticker is constructed from a Userform using common ActiveX controls, custom VBA objects, and a third-party ActiveX control. Also, the Userform's appearance is dressed up using drawing functions from the Windows API. Data for the ticker is retrieved from Yahoo!'s financial Web site (although any number of other sites will work just as well) and stored in an Excel worksheet. Charts that allow the user to view daily, weekly, and monthly trends are created based on user input and copied to the Userform via a series of Windows API function calls. The stock ticker's programming tools that aren't yet introduced are discussed in the next three chapters. Specifically, the chapters in Part IV introduce the following topics:

◆ Importing data from the Web with the `QueryTable` object

◆ Creating hyperlinks and saving worksheets as Web pages with the `Hyperlink` and `PublishObject` objects

◆ Browsing the Web with the WebBrowser control and `InternetExplorer` object

◆ Using the Windows API to enhance a Userform's styles

◆ Using the Windows API to draw text and shapes on a Userform

◆ Adding a `Timer` object to your VBA programs for interval code execution

Chapter 16

**Web Queries and
Web-Related
Objects in VBA**

A large percentage of Part III is devoted to importing data from an Access database into Excel. This is because data I/O between Excel and Access is so common. Other sources (that is, sources not of Excel origin) from which you can import data include text files and the content of a Web page (or specific tables from a Web page). You can use the `TextStream` object (see Chapter 8, "Understanding File I/O, Debugging, and Error Handling in VBA"), the VBA `Open` statement, or the `Open` method of the `Workbook` object to import textual data into Excel. However, if you want to import data from a Web page (global Internet or local intranet) to a worksheet, you should use a Web query. Yes, the user can also retrieve data from a Web page using a simple copy and paste technique, but doing so can mean wasting time deleting unnecessary data and reformatting what remains. Furthermore, the user has to revisit the Web site in order to refresh the data.

In this chapter, you learn how to use the `QueryTable` object to import and refresh data from HTML tables into an Excel worksheet. Ultimately, the `QueryTable` object will be used to retrieve stock quotes from a Web site in the Stock Ticker program constructed in Chapter 18, "Constructing the Stock Ticker." In this chapter, you also learn how to use other Web-related objects from the Excel object model as well as objects from the Internet Explorer application that have been exposed through automation. The `WebBrowser` and `InternetExplorer` objects will be used to view Web pages from a Userform and to refresh data retrieved by a `QueryTable` object.

Importing Data from the World Wide Web into Excel

Although the data for a majority of your applications in Excel will be from relatively conventional sources (Excel files, Access or other database files, and text files), on occasion, you may need to draw data from a Web site. Whether it's a government or commercial Web site or company intranet site, Excel can import data from the entire Web page or from any and all of the tables it contains.

To import data from a Web page, from the Excel application window, select Data, Import External Data, New Web Query (see Figure 16.1).

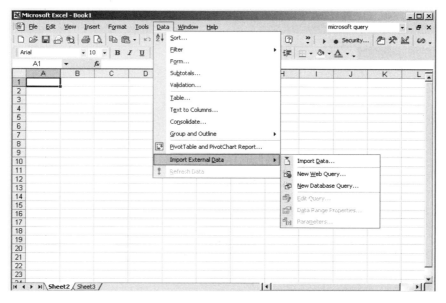

FIGURE 16.1 *Importing external data with Excel.*

The user can also utilize this feature to import data from other data sources, such as Access or Oracle, by selecting Import Data or New Database Query. Of course, anything that can be done from the Excel application window can also be done programmatically with VBA. If you record a macro while using the Import External Data feature, the recorded code will include a `QueryTable` object for importing and storing data in a worksheet. Because I discuss easier and more flexible methods for importing data from a database in previous chapters, here I consider only the `QueryTable` object when used to import data from a Web page.

Using the Excel Application

A Web query allows you to easily import data from a Web page provided your computer has access to the Internet or an intranet. After you select New Web Query from the Data menu (refer to Figure 16.1), the dialog box shown in Figure 16.2 appears. The New Web Query dialog box serves as a browser that you can use to navigate to the Web site of interest.

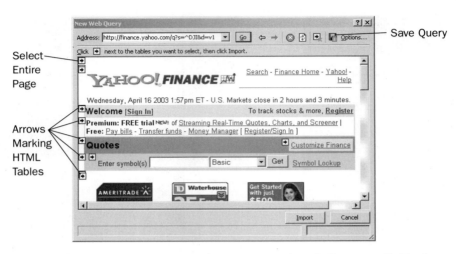

FIGURE 16.2 *The New Web Query dialog box selected from the Data menu in Excel.*

Enter the URL in the Address box to find the desired Web page. Although you can select all the contents of the Web page (text, tables, and images), because only the tables are of interest for the Stock Ticker application, that's all I cover here. To select a specific table, check one of the arrows marking a table on the displayed Web page. You can also choose how much formatting to apply to the table once it is imported into an Excel worksheet and save the query to run again at a later time. After you click Import, all the data from the selected tables in the specified Web page is loaded into Excel at the desired location.

Next, examine the VBA code that can be used to reproduce these actions and import data from a Web page into Excel.

Using VBA and the QueryTables Collection and QueryTable Objects

A `QueryTable` object represents a worksheet range built from data returned from an external data source (text, Web, or database files). As with other Excel objects, it follows that a `QueryTables` collection object represents a collection of `QueryTable` objects. To import data from a Web page, you must create a `QueryTable` object from a worksheet range. To create a new `QueryTable` object in the active worksheet, use the `Add` method of the `QueryTables` collection object.

```
ActiveSheet.QueryTables.Add (Connection, Destination, Sql)
```

The `Connection` argument (required) is much like the `ConnectionString` argument of the ADO `Connection` object (see Chapter 13, "Data I/O Between Excel and Access") and represents a `String` used to establish a connection to the file containing the data. The `Connection` argument must contain information about the type of file (text, Web, or database) and its path. A semicolon separates the different components of the `String` used to specify the information required for establishing a connection. The following example, when used with the `Add` method of the `QueryTables` collection object, establishes a connection to a Web page:

```
Connection:= "URL;http://www.anywebpage.edu"
```

The initial `String` `URL` establishes the type of connection. Other connection types include `TEXT` for a connection to a text file and `ODBC` for a connection to an ODBC data source. The second section of the `Connection` argument specifies the address or location of the Web page.

Regardless of the file type, the `Destination` argument (required) for the `Add` method of the `QueryTables` collection object denotes the upper-left cell of the worksheet to which the `QueryTable` object is inserted. In other words, it specifies the upper-left corner of the data table to be inserted into the worksheet.

```
Destination:=Range("A1")
```

The last named argument (`Sql`) of the `Add` method for the `QueryTables` collection object is used only with database files and represents a `String` that can be used to filter out some of the records returned by the `QueryTable` object. The `Sql` argument is not used with Web queries.

Manipulating the QueryTable Object

Once a link to a file is established, you can select and manipulate the `QueryTable` object using several of its properties and methods. Many of the properties of the `QueryTable` object are specific to the type of file accessed (text, Web page, or database). I will discuss only those properties specific to Web queries.

The following code creates a `QueryTable` object on the active worksheet and sets its data source to a single table from a Web page at the designated location:

```
Public Sub ImportWeb()
    Dim qt As QueryTable
    Set qt = ActiveSheet.QueryTables.Add( _
        Connection:="URL;http://finance.yahoo.com/q?s=^DJI&d=v1", _
        Destination:=Range("A1"))

    With qt
        .Name = "DJIQuery"
        .WebSelectionType = xlSpecifiedTables
        .WebTables = "16"     ' DJI table
        .WebFormatting = xlWebFormattingNone
        .EnableRefresh = True
```

```
        .RefreshPeriod = 5    'Unit in minutes
        .Refresh       'Execute query
    End With


    Set qt = Nothing
End Sub
```

The `WebSelectionType` property of the `QueryTable` object specifies how much information to import from the Web page (`xlAllTables`, `xlEntirePage`, or `xlSpecifiedTables`). Use the `WebTables` property to set a comma-delimited list of table names or table index numbers when importing specific tables for a Web query. This example imports a single table that contains data concerning the Dow Jones Industrial average from Yahoo!'s financial Web site.

 NOTE

> Because Web pages can change at any time, the sample code that returns the Dow Jones Industrial average from Yahoo!'s financial Web site may not be correct by the time you read this.

The `WebFormatting` property sets the amount of formatting preserved from the Web page when the data is imported into a query table (`xlWebFormattingAll`, `xlWebFormattingNone`, or `xlWebFormattingRTF`). The `EnableRefresh`, and `RefreshPeriod` properties are used to ensure that the query table is refreshed every five minutes. Finally, the `Refresh` method is called to invoke the query so data can be retrieved from the Web page and copied to the query table.

 NOTE

> Setting the `RefreshPeriod` property or invoking the `Refresh` method of the `QueryTable` object does not refresh the data retrieved from the specified Web page. Instead, the data is retrieved from the Web page cache stored in the temporary Internet files folder on your computer.

Web-Related Objects in Excel-VBA

The Excel object model includes a few objects that function to integrate Web content with Excel worksheets, and vice versa. You are probably aware that you can save an Excel workbook as a Web page for displaying in a browser (for example, Microsoft Internet Explorer or Netscape Navigator). You can also load Web pages directly into Excel for editing. On a related note, you can also add hyperlinks to a worksheet that can be used to reference Web pages, another worksheet range, or even another file. (See Appendix B for a brief HTML/XHTML tutorial.)

Saving Worksheets as Web Pages

The project in Part II of this book creates a program that saves Excel worksheets as static Web pages. The impetus for the Excel-to-HTML converter project is a desire to create well-formed HTML and CSS files, as opposed to the more chaotic files generated by Excel when you save a worksheet as a Web page. However, if you are not concerned about editing Web files created by Excel and need more formatting options than those the Excel-to-HTML converter program provides, you have two choices. You can modify the Excel-to-HTML converter program to include additional formatting options, or you can use existing Excel objects that can create Web files from existing worksheets. This section discusses the latter option.

You can save all or part of an Excel workbook as a Web page. Excel adds all necessary formatting tags to the HTML document so that it appears in a Web browser as it appears in Excel (or reasonably close).

To save the entire workbook as a Web page, use the `SaveAs` method of the `Workbook` object and specify the `Filename` and `FileFormat` arguments.

```
ActiveWorkbook.SaveAs _
      Filename:=ActiveWorkbook.Path & "\myXclfile.htm", _
      FileFormat:=xlHtml
```

The entire contents of the workbook will be saved within a single Web page. By setting the properties of the `WebOptions` object and/or the `DefaultWebOptions` object, you can customize the appearance of the Web page. However, the default values for the properties of these two objects are usually sufficient.

If you want to give the user the option of previewing a workbook before saving it as a Web page, you can use the `WebPagePreview` method of the `Workbook` object.

```
ActiveWorkbook.WebPagePreview
```

The active workbook will be displayed in the user's default browser.

The PublishObjects Collection and PublishObject Objects

The `SaveAs` method allows you to save the entire contents of a workbook as a static Web page. More valuable to the programmer are the abilities to save a single worksheet or even a selected range as a Web page and to enable some of the functionality of the worksheet. You can save different objects (`Worksheet`, `Range`, `Chart`, and so on) within a workbook using the `PublishObjects` collection and `PublishObject` objects.

The `PublishObject` object represents a component of a workbook or worksheet that has been saved to a Web page. The specific objects that can be saved to a Web page are listed in Table 16.1.

Table 16.1 Excel Source Components That Can Be Saved to a Web Page

Source Component	Description
`AutoFilter` object	An AutoFilter range
`Chart` object	A Chart
`PivotTable` object	A PivotTable
`PrintArea` object	A range of cells selected for printing
`QueryTable` object	A query table created from an external source
`Range` object	A range of cells
`Sheet` object	An entire worksheet

All `PublishObject` objects are members of the `PublishObjects` collection object. Use the `Add` method of the `PublishObjects` collection object to save an Excel component to a Web page.

```
ActiveWorkbook.PublishObjects.Add(SourceType, FileName, Sheet, _
    Source, HtmlType, DivID, Title)
```

Arguments for the `Add` method include `SourceType`, `Filename`, `Sheet`, `Source`, `HtmlType`, `DivID`, and `Title`. The arguments `SourceType` and `Filename` are required and refer to the source component (refer to Table 16.1) and filename or path, respectively. The `Sheet` argument refers to the name of the worksheet saved as a Web page or the name of the worksheet that contains the object that is to be saved as a Web page. The `Source` argument represents the name of the object (sheet, chart, range, and so on) that is to be saved as Web page and is correlated to the `SourceType` argument. For example, if `SourceType` is set as the constant `xlSourceChart`, `Source` should refer to the name of a chart (for example, `"Chart 1"`) on the specified worksheet. The argument `HTMLType` specifies whether the object is saved with interactivity or as a static Web page.

 NOTE

If you save an object such as a chart or range with interactivity, you will be able to edit the object directly in the Web browser. However, you will be able to view the Web page using only Microsoft Internet Explorer 4.01 or later with Microsoft Office Web components installed.

The argument `DivID` refers to a unique identifier used in the HTML DIV tag, and `Title` refers to the title of the Web page.

The following procedure saves the worksheet range `"$A$1:$B$11"` as a Web page without interactivity so that it can be viewed in any current browser:

```
Public Sub SaveRangeWeb()
'Creates a web page without interactivity from specified range
    ActiveWorkbook.PublishObjects.Add _
        SourceType:=xlSourceRange, _
        Filename:=ActiveWorkbook.Path & "\Sample1.htm", _
        Sheet:=ActiveSheet.Name, _
        Source:="$A$1:$B$11", _
        HtmlType:=xlHTMLStatic


    ActiveWorkbook.PublishObjects(1).Publish (True)
End Sub
```

If you run the `SaveRangeWeb()` Sub procedure after activating the worksheet shown in Figure 16.3, you will create the Web page displayed in Figure 16.4.

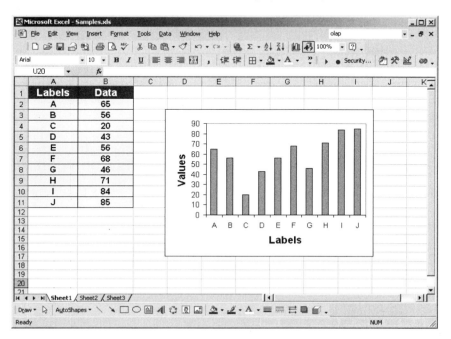

FIGURE 16.3 *A sample Excel worksheet before conversion to a Web page.*

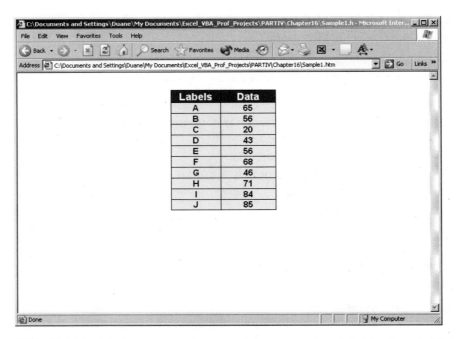

FIGURE 16.4 *A Web page created from a worksheet range using the* Publish *method (without interactivity) of the* PublishObject *object.*

To save a range, set the argument SourceType to the VBA constant xlSourceRange. The worksheet range is then specified as "$A$1:$B$11" on the active worksheet by the Source and Sheet arguments, respectively. The range is saved as a static Web page using the HtmlType argument set to the VBA constant xlHTMLStatic. To make a Range object interactive, set the HtmlType argument to the value of the constant xlHTMLCalc.

The Web page is not saved to a file until the Publish method of the PublishObject object is invoked. A Boolean argument is passed to the Publish method to specify whether an existing file is replaced (True) or appended (False).

In the next example, the Sub procedure SaveChartWeb() saves the Chart object named "Chart 1" located on the active worksheet to a Web page with interactivity. Differences from the SaveRangeWeb() Sub procedure include the constant assigned to the SourceType argument specifying a chart (xlSourceChart) instead of a range and the HtmlType argument specifying an interactive chart (xlHtmlChart) instead of a static Web page. When viewed with Internet Explorer, the resulting Web page allows you to edit the charted values directly in the browser.

```
Sub SaveChartWeb()
'Creates web page with interactivity from an embedded chart
'Assumes one PublishObject object already exists
```

```
ActiveWorkbook.PublishObjects.Add _
    SourceType:=xlSourceChart, _
    Filename:=ActiveWorkbook.Path & "\Sample2.htm", _
    Sheet:=ActiveSheet.Name, _
    Source:="Chart 1", _
    HtmlType:=xlHtmlChart


ActiveWorkbook.PublishObjects(2).Publish (True)
End Sub
```

If you run the `SaveChartWeb()` Sub procedure after activating the worksheet shown in Figure 16.3, you will create the Web page displayed in Figure 16.5.

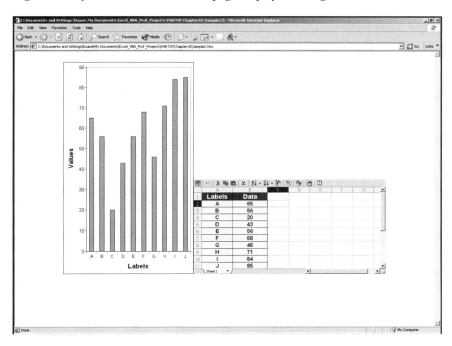

FIGURE 16.5 *A Web page created from an embedded chart using the* `Publish` *method (with interactivity) of the* `PublishObject` *object.*

The remaining constants that can be assigned to the `SourceType` argument include `xlSourceAutoFilter`, `xlSourcePivotTable`, `xlSourcePrintArea`, and `xlSourceSheet`, which are associated with the objects listed earlier in Table 16.1.

Hyperlinks

If you have ever browsed the Internet, you know that hyperlinks represent interactive text (or images) that reference other documents or components of the current document. When a hyperlink is selected, the browser window displays the referenced document. You can add hyperlinks to Excel worksheets via the Hyperlinks collection object and use them to reference another location in the active worksheet or workbook, another Excel file, a file on your hard drive or network, or an Internet address. Files referenced by a hyperlink are opened in the application that created them. Web addresses are opened in the user's default Web browser.

To add hyperlinks to a worksheet, use the Add method of the Hyperlinks collection object.

```
ActiveSheet.Hyperlinks.Add(Anchor, Address, SubAddress, _
    ScreenTip, TextToDisplay)
```

Arguments of the Add method include Anchor (required), Address (required), SubAddress, ScreenTip, and TextToDisplay. The Anchor argument specifies the object that holds the hyperlink; it can be a Range or Shape object. The location of the target file or document is set with the Address argument, and SubAddress specifies the location within the current workbook. The ScreenTip and TextToDisplay arguments denote the displayed text when the mouse is resting over the hyperlink and the text displayed for the hyperlink, respectively.

The Sub procedure AddHyperlinks() adds two hyperlinks to the active worksheet using the Add method of the Hyperlinks collection object (see Figure 16.6). The first hyperlink references cell A1 in the active worksheet of the active workbook. The Address argument is required, but is passed an empty String when a location within the active workbook is referenced. The SubAddress argument references the target location of the hyperlink. The second hyperlink references a Web page. For this hyperlink to function properly, you must be able to connect to the Internet. The Web page will be loaded in the user's default Web browser.

```
Public Sub AddHyperlinks()
'Adds two hyperlinks to active sheet
    ActiveSheet.Hyperlinks.Add _
        Anchor:=Range("A1"), _
        Address:="", _
        SubAddress:="'Sheet1'!A1", _
        ScreenTip:="Goes to Sheet1", _
        TextToDisplay:="Link to Sheet1"
    ActiveSheet.Hyperlinks.Add _
        Anchor:=Range("A3"), _
        Address:="http://www.microsoft.com/ms.htm", _
```

```
        ScreenTip:="Microsoft", _
        TextToDisplay:="Microsoft web site"
End Sub
```

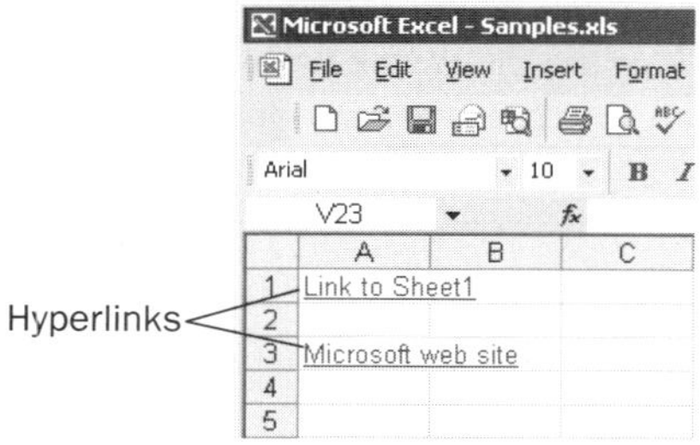

FIGURE 16.6 *Adding hyperlinks to the active worksheet.*

You can also activate the target document or file of a hyperlink using the `Follow` method of the `Hyperlink` object. This is the programming equivalent of the user selecting the hyperlink in the Excel application.

```
Worksheets("Sheet3").Hyperlinks(1).Follow
```

Finally, no event procedures are associated with the Web-related objects discussed previously; however, the `FollowHyperlink()` event procedure of the `Worksheet` object and the `SheetFollowHyperlink()` event procedure of the `Application` and `Workbook` objects are triggered when the user clicks a hyperlink in Excel. Use these event procedures when specific code needs to execute when the user clicks a hyperlink.

More ActiveX Controls Through Automation

The Control Toolbox accessible from either the Excel application window or the VBA IDE provides a minimal selection of ActiveX controls for use in Office applications (see Figure 16.7).

FIGURE 16.7 *The Control Toolbox from the VBA IDE containing the standard set of ActiveX controls available for use on a VBA Userform.*

The perceived lack of ActiveX controls is especially relevant if you have developed applications in Visual Basic and are use to the robust set of controls available in that environment. However, VBA programmers are not limited to the default selection of controls provided by Excel. In addition to the standard set of controls, you can find additional ActiveX controls on the Internet (often as freeware), build your own ActiveX controls using Visual Studio and Visual Basic 5.0 or 6.0, or use the ActiveX controls that have been exposed through automation by the installation of other programs on your computer.

NOTE

Licensing requirements may restrict the use of ActiveX controls that are not included with VBA.

To view the additional ActiveX controls that may be available on your computer, select Tools, Additional Controls in the VBA IDE (a Userform must be the active window). The Additional Controls dialog box appears with a list of available controls for use in your program (see Figure 16.8).

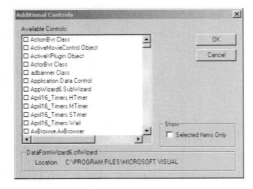

FIGURE 16.8 *The Additional Controls dialog box listing ActiveX controls exposed through automation.*

The controls listed in the Additional Controls dialog box represent those already registered with the computer's operating system. ActiveX controls can be compiled into .dll, .tlb, or .ocx files. To register library files such as these, select Tools, References from the VBA IDE. The References dialog box appears (see Figure 16.9). Choose Browse to select the library file and set the reference. You need to do this only once. ActiveX controls contained in these library files will then be available from the Additional Controls dialog box.

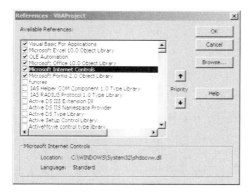

FIGURE 16.9 *Use the References dialog box to set references to object libraries for use in a VBA program.*

The functions of the additional controls available on a computer will vary. There are likely to be different versions of old standards including text boxes, buttons, labels, list boxes, combo boxes, and so on. In addition, there may be multimedia and animation controls, file I/O controls, data handling controls (ADO or DAO), and Web controls. Because this chapter focuses on data I/O between Excel and the Internet, the rest of the sections in this chapter introduce two objects that can be used in Excel to view and access Web pages on the Internet or a local networked computer. The WebBrowser control and the `Internet Explorer` object are registered with the operating system with the installation of Microsoft Internet Explorer, so they are available on any computer running Windows 98 or later.

The WebBrowser Control

The WebBrowser control is available on any computer running a recent version of Internet Explorer. The control is registered with the Windows operating system upon installation of Internet Explorer and can be added to the Control Toolbox by selecting Microsoft Web Browser from the Additional Controls dialog box (see Figure 16.10). Figure 16.11 shows the Control Toolbox with the WebBrowser control.

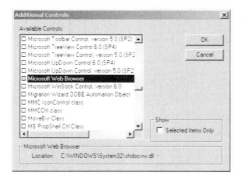

FIGURE 16.10 *Adding the WebBrowser control to the Control Toolbox.*

FIGURE 16.11   *The Control Toolbox including the Web Browser control.*

The WebBrowser control is drawn on a Userform (or worksheet) like any other ActiveX control. The size to which it is drawn on a Userform will represent the size of the browser window when the program is executed. The Userform shown in Figure 16.12 is designed to serve as a Web browser when the program contained in its code module is executed.

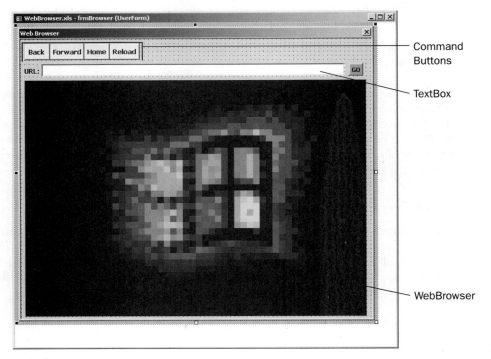

FIGURE 16.12   *A Userform designed to serve as a Web browser.*

The WebBrowser control has only a few functional properties used for setting its size and returning information about the displayed Web page or the current state of the browser. The control is intended for use with other ActiveX controls that can display the values of its properties and invoke its methods and events. The methods of the WebBrowser control are primarily used for navigation, and its events are triggered by changes that result from a navigation. Table 16.2 summarizes the unique and convenient members of the WebBrowser control.

Table 16.2 Members of the WebBrowser Control

Member	Type	Description
Busy	Property	Returns a `Boolean` value indicating whether the control is engaged in a navigation or a downloading operation.
LocationName	Property	Returns a `String` that contains the title of a Web page or path to the source file displayed in the control.
LocationURL	Property	Returns a `String` that contains the URL of the Web page currently displayed in the control.
ReadyState	Property	Retrieves the ready state of the control (`0`=uninitialized, `1`=loading, `2`=loaded, `3`=interactive, `4`=complete).
Silent	Property	Returns or sets a `Boolean` value indicating whether any dialog boxes can be shown.
GoBack	Method	Navigates backward one item in the history list.
GoForward	Method	Navigates forward one item in the history list.
GoHome	Method	Navigates to the home page specified in the Internet Explorer Options dialog box and Internet Control Panel.
Navigate	Method	Navigates to a Web page specified by a URL (`String`).
Refresh	Method	Reloads the page currently displayed in the control.
Stop	Method	Cancels all navigations and downloads.
CommandStateChange	Event	Triggered when the enabled state of a command changes.
DocumentComplete	Event	Triggered when the loading of the document being displayed in the control is complete.
DownloadBegin	Event	Triggered when a navigation begins.
DownloadComplete	Event	Triggered when a navigation finishes, is halted, or fails.
ProgressChange	Event	Triggered when the progress of a download operation is updated.

Constructing a Basic Web Browser from a Userform

Using the WebBrowser control is straightforward and makes the construction of a basic Web browser quite simple. The following code is from the code module of the Userform shown in Figure 16.12. In this program, the `Activate()` event of the Userform object invokes the `Navigate` method of the WebBrowser control to display the Web page at the location specified by the URL argument. When a document is finished loading, the `DocumentComplete()` event of the WebBrowser control is triggered, and the URL is displayed in a TextBox control (`txtURL`). Five of the remaining procedures are click events of CommandButton controls that invoke the `GoBack`, `GoForward`, `GoHome`, `Refresh`, and `Navigate` methods of the WebBrowser control when triggered. The `GoBack` and `GoForward` methods are not invoked unless the `Boolean` variables `navBack` and `navFor` are `True`. These variables are initialized to `False` in the `Activate()` event of the Userform object and altered when the `CommandStateChange()` event of the WebBrowser control is triggered. The `CommandStateChange()` event of the WebBrowser control is triggered when the enabled state of a command (forward or backward navigation) changes. Thus, the event is trigged whenever the WebBrowser control navigates to a new location and the forward or backward commands change their values. When the combination of `Command` and `Enable` arguments are set to 1 and `False`, respectively, the WebBrowser control has moved to the end of its history list, and the `GoForward` method should not be invoked. When the combination of `Command` and `Enable` arguments are set to 2 and `False`, respectively, the WebBrowser control has moved to the beginning of its history list, and the `GoBack` method should not be invoked.

```
Option Explicit
Private navBack As Boolean
Private navFor As Boolean

Private Sub UserForm_Activate()
'Initialize variables and navigate to
'specified URL
    navBack = False
    navFor = False
    WebBrowser1.Navigate URL:="http:\\www.premierpressbooks.com"
End Sub
Private Sub cmdBack_Click()
'Move back one document in history list
    If navBack Then WebBrowser1.GoBack
End Sub
Private Sub cmdForward_Click()
'Move forward one document in history list
    If navFor Then WebBrowser1.GoForward
End Sub
Private Sub cmdGo_Click()
```

```vba
'Navigate to URL in text box
    WebBrowser1.Navigate txtURL
End Sub
Private Sub cmdHome_Click()
'Navigate to URL specified as home page
    WebBrowser1.GoHome
End Sub
Private Sub cmdReload_Click()
'Reload the current web page
    WebBrowser1.Refresh
End Sub
Private Sub WebBrowser1_CommandStateChange( _
        ByVal Command As Long, ByVal Enable As Boolean)
'Triggered by a navigation
    If Command = 2 And Enable Then
        navBack = True    'Can navigate back in history list
    ElseIf Command = 2 And Not Enable Then
        navBack = False   'Cannot navigate back in history list
    End If
    If Command = 1 And Enable Then
        navFor = True    'Can navigate forward in history list
    ElseIf Command = 1 And Not Enable Then
        navFor = False    'Cannot navigate forward in history list
    End If
End Sub
Private Sub WebBrowser1_DocumentComplete( _
        ByVal pDisp As Object, URL As Variant)
'Triggered when document downloading is complete
    txtURL = WebBrowser1.LocationURL
End Sub
Private Sub UserForm_QueryClose(Cancel As Integer, CloseMode As Integer)
    Unload Me
    End
End Sub
```

When the Web browser Userform is shown from Excel, the specified Web site is displayed (see Figure 16.13) and the form may be used to navigate the World Wide Web or local file system.

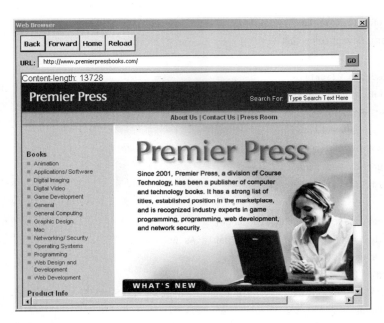

FIGURE 16.13 *The Userform Web browser running in Excel.*

The InternetExplorer Object

The WebBrowser control provides a visual interface to a Web document. If you need access to the Web but don't need the visual interface and don't want to include a Userform in your program, use the `InternetExplorer` object. To include the `InternetExplorer` object in a program, you must first set a reference to the Microsoft Internet Controls library (in the VBA IDE, select Tools, References). The Microsoft Internet Controls library is available on all machines with Windows and Internet Explorer installed.

The `InternetExplorer` object is essentially the same as the WebBrowser control without the visual interface. It contains the same properties, methods, and events as the WebBrowser control; however, you cannot draw an instance of the `InternetExplorer` object on a Userform. To create an instance of the `InternetExplorer` object that will include its event procedures, declare a variable using the `WithEvents` keyword in the general declarations section of a component (workbook, worksheet, or Userform) or class module.

```
Private WithEvents intExp As InternetExplorer
```

After the preceding statement is entered into the general declarations section, the event procedure definitions of the `InternetExplorer` object appear in the event drop-down list of the code module (see Figure 16.14).

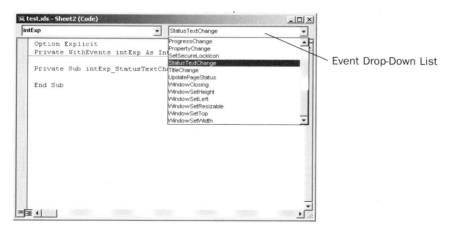

FIGURE 16.14 *The event procedure drop-down list for the* InternetExplorer *object.*

The variable that represents the InternetExplorer object must be instantiated in the appropriate procedure.

```
Set intExp = New InternetExplorer
```

Refreshing a Query Table

Unfortunately, the Refresh method of the QueryTable object cannot be configured to retrieve data from a newly refreshed Web page. Instead, it retrieves data from a cached document (if it exists). The cache of Web pages is controlled by your Web browser. You can configure Internet Explorer to automatically clear the cache only once per day (you can clear it manually at any time). This is a problem if you are retrieving data that is updated at relatively short intervals (for example, stock quotes). In such cases, the InternetExplorer object provides a nice complement to the QueryTable object because you can use it to refresh the Web page from which the QueryTable object retrieves data. When added to a worksheet module, the following program code will retrieve the data containing the Dow Jones Industrial average from Yahoo!'s financial Web site immediately after the Web page is refreshed.

The program is entered in the code module of a Worksheet object and begins with a call to the Sub procedure Main(). Instead of invoking the Refresh method of the InternetExplorer object to update the document cache, the Flags argument of the Navigate method is used to specify that the document not be read from the cache. If you omit the Flags argument, the document is loaded from the disk cache. Other values for the Flags argument include 1=Open the document in a new window, 2=Do not add the document to the history list, and 8=Do not write the results of this navigation to the disk cache.

```
Option Explicit
Private WithEvents intExp As InternetExplorer
```

```vba
Public Sub Main()
'Main sub that directs the program
    Set intExp = New InternetExplorer
    Application.StatusBar = "Getting data from web..."
    intExp.Navigate URL:="http://finance.yahoo.com/q?s=^DJI&d=v1", _
        Flags:=4    'Navigate to URL , do not read from cache
End Sub
```

The `DocumentComplete()` event procedure of the `InternetExplorer` object is triggered after the Web page download is finished. Therefore, you can use the `DocumentComplete()` event procedure to trigger the creation of the `QueryTable` object in the `CreateQTable()` Sub procedure that imports the data from the specified Web site into a worksheet. When you use the `DocumentComplete()` event procedure to trigger the creation of the query table, you ensure that current data is always imported to the worksheet.

```vba
Private Sub intExp_DocumentComplete(ByVal pDisp As Object, _
    URL As Variant)
'Create query table after web page is refreshed
'Delete IE object so this event procedure does not trigger
'after query table is created.
    Set intExp = Nothing
    CreateQTable
End Sub


Private Sub CreateQTable()
'Create a new query table on the active worksheet
    Dim qt As QueryTable
    Set qt = ActiveSheet.QueryTables.Add( _
            Connection:="URL;http://finance.yahoo.com/q?s=^DJI&d=v1", _
            Destination:=Range("A1"))
    With qt
        .Name = "DJIQuery"
        .WebSelectionType = xlSpecifiedTables
        'Index number of table on web page. This will probably change.
        .WebTables = "16"
        .WebFormatting = xlWebFormattingNone
        .Refresh BackgroundQuery:=False
    End With
```

```
        Range("A1").Select
        Application.StatusBar = "Done"
        Set qt = Nothing
    End Sub
```

The worksheet from which the preceding code was executed is shown in Figure 16.15. The query table was not formatted (`WebFormatting = xlWebFormattingNone`) and includes data from a single HTML table from the specified Web page.

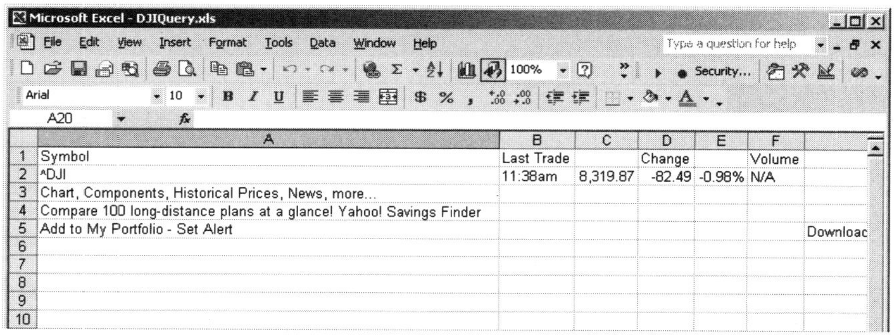

FIGURE 16.15 *Excel worksheet with a query table containing current data retrieved from a Web page.*

Summary

In this chapter, you learned how to create a Web query to retrieve data from a Web page into a worksheet using Excel and the `QueryTable` object. You also learned how to use other Web-related objects from the Excel object model including the `PublishObject` and `Hyperlink` objects. You use the `PublishObject` object to save workbooks (or components of workbooks) as Web pages, and you use the `Hyperlink` object to create hyperlinks in a worksheet. Hyperlinks can be used to send the focus to another component in a workbook or to open an existing file from the World Wide Web (or local computer). Finally, you learned how to use two similar objects for retrieving Web documents from the World Wide Web. The WebBrowser control and the `InternetExplorer` object are registered with the operating system by the installation of Internet Explorer and can be used to navigate through Web files. They differ by the lack of a visual interface with the `InternetExplorer` object.

Chapter 17

Accessing the
Windows API
with VBA

The Windows Application Programming Interface (API) is used to programmatically control the Windows operating system. The Windows API consists of numerous procedures that provide programmatic access to the features of the Windows operating system (for example, window functions, graphic functions, file functions, and so on). The API procedures are stored in the system directory of Windows as DLL (dynamic link library, .dll) files, and dozens of procedures can be stored within a single file. The API procedures are conceptually the same as the procedures used in any programming language, including VBA. However, because the API procedures are written in C/C++, accessing them via the VBA programming environment can be difficult and, in some cases, impossible.

Using the Windows API can be dangerous as it bypasses all the safety features built into VBA to prevent the misuse of system resources and the subsequent system crashes they might cause. However, the API can greatly extend the power of a program, making these risks acceptable.

 NOTE

If you are programming in a Windows 9x environment, you are more likely to experience system crashes when using the API. This is because Windows 9x operating systems do not adequately protect system memory from errant programs. If you are programming in Windows 2000 or XP with the API, you will spend less time waiting for the system to reboot as a result of an errant program.

This chapter shows you how to call API functions from a VBA program. The entire collection of API functions is too vast to show very many of them. However, this chapter demonstrates the use of some common API functions that you can use to extend the capabilities of your VBA programs. Examples include adding sound, manipulating windows and other graphics, and system memory.

Declaring API Functions in VBA

Using the Windows API is not like programming in VBA. When using the API, you are working directly with the operating system, so there are few protections (relative to VBA) to keep an errant program from causing some kind of a crash (application or system). This is particularly true with regard to system memory. In fact, one reason why the API is so useful to the VB/VBA programmer is that it provides a direct line to system memory that just isn't available in the highly protected VBA environment. As a result of the increased risk, you should close all nonessential applications and save your work often while writing and testing VBA applications that use the Windows API.

To call external functions that are embedded in DLL files, use a VBA `Declare` statement. You use these statements at module-level by entering them in the general declarations section of a code module. You may not use `Declare` statements at procedure-level. There are two possible types of statements, one for functions and one for Sub procedures.

```
Public/Private Declare Sub SubName Lib "LibName" Alias "AliasName" (argument list)
Public/Private Declare Function FunctionName Lib "Libname" alias "aliasname" _
(argument list) As Type
```

The scope can be specified with either `Public` or `Private` in a standard code module, but it must be `Private` in all other module types (class, Userform, workbook, or worksheet).

The *SubName* or *FunctionName* is replaced by the actual name of the procedure in the DLL file and represents the name that will be used when the procedure is called from VBA code. You can specify an alias for the name of the procedure, if desired, or in a few cases, when it is necessary. For example, if the DLL procedure name has the same name as a VBA keyword (for example, `SetFocus`) or uses characters that are illegal in VBA (leading underscore _), you must specify an alias. In addition, because DLL procedures are written in C++, they are case sensitive, so you must use the correct case for each character in the name. Unlike you do with VBA keywords, you cannot enter the wrong case for a DLL procedure name and have it automatically corrected for you.

The name of the DLL file containing the procedure being called must follow the `Lib` keyword and be encased within quotation marks. Only a handful of DLL files contain the thousands of procedures in the Windows API, and those I use in this chapter are summarized in Table 17.1. A majority of the Windows API procedures are included with the kernel32.dll, user32.dll, and gdi32.dll dynamic link library files.

Table 17.1 Dynamic Link Libraries

DLL	Description
kernel32.dll	Contains functions and procedures that manage memory, processes, and threads.
user32.dll	Contains functions and procedures that control the user interface (for example, windows).
gdi32.dll	Contains functions and procedures that draw and manipulate graphics, display text, and manipulate fonts.
winmm.dll	Contains multimedia-related functions and procedures.
comdlg32.dll	Contains functions and procedures that control the Windows common dialog boxes.

The *argument list* contains the parameters and their data types that must be passed to the DLL procedure. Typically, the individual arguments are preceded by `ByVal` or `ByRef` indicating, respectively, that either the value or the address of the argument is passed to the procedure. The data type of the argument that must be used follows the argument name. It is critical that arguments are passed appropriately to a DLL procedure to prevent general protection fault errors. The values of the arguments passed to a DLL procedure often require user-defined types and/or specific constants. All of this makes up-to-date documentation invaluable when programming with the Windows API.

 NOTE

You can download software that provides the proper syntax for more than 6,000 API procedures and 55,000 constants at http://www.allapi.net/agnet/apiguide.shtml. You will also find online documentation and sample programs at this site.

Finally, DLL functions return a value of a specific type and, as with a VBA function, you will often need to store the return value in a variable of the same type.

Now it is time to see the Windows API in action. Because of the risk involved with using DLL procedures in a VBA program, limit their use to tasks that cannot otherwise be accomplished with the objects available to you (VBA and Excel objects, or ActiveX controls, and so on). With this thought in mind, the examples I provide in this chapter are meant to complement, not replace, the objects in the VBA and Excel object models.

Adding Sound to a VBA Program

Excel 95 offered VBA programmers the ability to add sound to a program using the `SoundNote` property of the `Range` object. However, with the next version of Excel (Excel 97), support for playing sound files was removed from VBA, and the capability of playing sound is not in subsequent versions of Excel. This leaves two choices for playing sounds in Excel applications with VBA — ActiveX controls and the Windows API. Since no ActiveX controls for playing sound currently ship with VBA, the Windows API provides an excellent resource for adding sound to a VBA program.

 NOTE

If you have VB 6.0 installed on your system, you have access to Microsoft's multimedia control (check the additional controls list) that can be used to play sound files. However, the performance of this control is spotty at best, and I don't recommend using it rather than the Windows API.

You can use the sndPlaySound DLL function to play .wav (Wave Form Audio) files in a VBA program. You declare the function in the general declarations section of a code module.

```
Private Declare Function sndPlaySound Lib "winmm.dll" Alias _
    "sndPlaySoundA" (ByVal lpszSoundName As String, _
    ByVal uFlags As Long) As Long
```

Although you may not realize it, the previous statement is a relatively short call to a DLL function. The declaration creates a reference to the sndPlaySound() function found in the file winmm.dll. The declaration looks a lot like a function call in VBA, but it is only a declaration — the call to the function will come later. From the declaration, you can see that the function accepts two arguments. The argument lpszSoundName (type String) represents the name (including path) to the .wav file to be played, and the argument uFlags (type Long) denotes whether program execution should proceed immediately (1) or wait until after the file finishes playing (0). The sndPlaySound() function returns a value of type Long indicating whether the function succeeded in playing the .wav file. It is not necessary to provide a variable for holding the return value; so calls to the sndPlaySound() function from a VBA procedure can appear in one of two forms.

```
sndPlaySound "C:\myWave.wav file", 1
returnVal = sndPlaySound("C:\myWave.wav", 0)
```

When either of the previous statements executes, a sound file called myWave.wav located at the specified path is played on the system.

Playing sound files via the Windows API is about as easy as it gets. I consider it very simple because it doesn't involve any new concepts. It's just a straightforward function call without other requirements. Unfortunately, most tasks involving the Windows API are not as easy as playing sound files. The function calls may or may not be that involved, but often there are other considerations. For example, many API procedures reserve blocks of memory that are not automatically released after the program ends. Instead, it takes another function call to free the system memory that was used by the program. Knowing all the requirements of a particular API procedure is critical for the effective use of system resources when programming with the Windows API.

Manipulating Userforms with the Windows API

If you have experience programming in Visual Basic (VB), I am sure you find VBA Userforms every bit as annoying as I do. For some reason, Microsoft greatly stripped the VB form to create a VBA Userform, resulting in the inability to resize, minimize, maximize, restore, and include menus on a Userform. Furthermore, prior to Office 2000, you could not use VBA to create a modeless Userform. In addition to the stripped down form , VBA generally lacks ActiveX controls that can be used strictly for aesthetic purposes. The shape controls available in VB can be used to enhance the look of a form, but nothing similar is included in VBA. As a result, creating an aesthetically pleasing Userform with the tools that ship with Office is difficult. Fortunately, you can use the Windows API to extend the abilities and appearance of Userforms. In the next few sections, I introduce several useful DLL procedures that you can use to enhance the look and abilities of the Userform.

Object Handles

There are numerous types of objects in Windows including (among others) bitmaps, files, fonts, menus, and, of course, windows. When objects are created, Windows typically returns a *handle* to that object. A handle is a 32-bit integer that is used to represent an object in the Windows API. Don't confuse Windows objects with VBA objects such as Userforms and ActiveX controls, although VBA objects may or may not have handles associated with them. Userforms and ActiveX controls are manipulated by VBA and are not part of the Windows API.

Most DLL procedures that manipulate an object through the Windows API require a handle to that object. Because a handle is a 32-bit integer, you should use the VBA Long data type to store a handle to an object returned by a DLL function. The object handle can then be used to programmatically manipulate the object. So, in order to manipulate a VBA Userform using DLL procedures through the Windows API, you will first need to determine its handle.

Fortunately, Userforms are assigned handles when created, so retrieving that handle is just a matter of using the correct DLL function.

 NOTE

Unlike VB forms, VBA does not have a hWnd property of the Userform object that you can use to easily return the handle to a Userform.

The FindWindow() function finds the first top-level window in the window list that satisfies the specified arguments.

```
Public Declare Function FindWindow Lib "user32.dll" Alias "FindWindowA" _
    (ByVal lpClassName As String, ByVal lpWindowName As String) As Long
```

The VBA declaration for the FindWindow() function contains two String arguments, one for the class name (lpClassName), and the other for the window name (lpWindowName). The class name for a Userform is ThunderFrame with a reference to the version of Office from which it was created. For example, an Office 2000 or XP Userform has a class name

`ThunderDFrame`, and an Office 97 Userform has a class name `ThunderXFrame` (I don't know why!). The `lpWindowName` argument refers to a window's caption. Therefore, the following statement will retrieve the handle of a Userform created in Office 2000 or XP whose `Caption` property has been left as the default `"Userform1"`.

```
Dim hForm As Long
hForm = FindWindow("ThunderDFrame", "UserForm1")
```

One of the arguments can be passed a null `String` (`vbNullString`), and the `FindWindow` function will return a handle to the first window it finds that matches the one specified criterion. In fact, this is how I determined the class name of a Userform. Consider the following `FindHandle()` Sub procedure:

```
Private Sub FindHandle()
    Dim hForm As Long, rv As Long
    Dim s As String
    hForm = FindWindow(vbNullString, "UserForm1")
    Debug.Print hForm
    s = String(256, "x")    'Creates a string with 256 x's
    rv = GetClassName(hForm, s, 255)
    Debug.Print Left(s, rv)
End Sub
```

The function `GetClassName()` is another DLL procedure that retrieves the class name of a window specified by its handle. Its declaration should be written as follows:

```
Public Declare Function GetClassName Lib "user32.dll" Alias _
    "GetClassNameA" (ByVal hwnd As Long, _
    ByVal lpClassName As String, nMaxCount As Long) As Long
```

Note that the `GetClassName()` function returns a `Long` integer that represents the length in bytes of the class name (excluding the final null terminating character of a C++ string).

 NOTE

The C/C++ programming language does not support string variables. Instead, C/C++ uses something called a *character array* to store a string of characters. A C/C++ character array is analogous to a one-dimensional VBA array where each element in the array is allowed to hold only a single character. In order to specify the length of a string in C/C++, character arrays must end with a special character known as a *null terminator.*

The argument `lpClassName` should be passed a `String` variable of sufficient length for holding the class name. If the function is successful, the variable `s` will hold the class name plus extraneous characters left over from its initialization. The extra characters are easily removed with VBA's `Left()` function. When the `FindHandle()` Sub procedure is executed with the declarations for the `FindWindow()` and `GetClassName()` functions in the general declarations section of the code module, the output to the Immediate window will appear as shown in Figure 17.1 (although a different 32-bit integer will be output for each new instance of a `Userform` object).

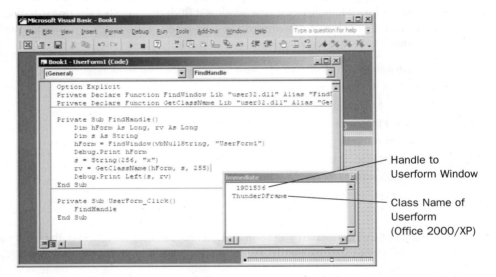

FIGURE 17.1 *Output to Immediate window after execution of* `FindHandle()` *Sub procedure.*

Once the handle to a window is known, specific details about the window can be read, or the window can be manipulated using one of several DLL procedures.

Changing a Userform's Style with the API

Window styles are those characteristics of a window that define its appearance. Styles include such things as the presence (or lack) of minimize and maximize buttons, a window menu, close button, title bar, and the ability to resize the window. Numerous styles can be included in a window, and all of them can be set by defined constants. There are too many styles to consider here, but I want to discuss some of the more interesting styles as they apply to Userforms.

Working with Styles

Many DLL procedures interpret their arguments as *bit fields* rather than actual numbers. Bit fields are a sequence of digits that represents which bits will be set by a bitwise operation between the bit field and another number. Bits are numbered from the least to the most significant, starting from the rightmost bit, which is bit zero. Because Windows is a 32-bit operating system, bit fields are represented by a maximum of 32 digits in binary, 10 digits in decimal (maximum value of 4294967295), and 8 digits in hexadecimal. In hexadecimal, each digit represents four bits with the first digit representing bits 0–3, the second digit representing bits 4–7, and so on. Thus, to set bit 5 in a bit field, you could use the binary value 100000, decimal value 32 (=2^5), or hexadecimal value 20 (second bit in second digit 2^1=2).

Constants used with Windows API procedures are often declared as `Long` integers using hexadecimal notation (specified by &H). For example, the constant *WS_EX_APPWINDOW* is used to set the bit that forces a window to appear in the task bar. The following declaration uses hexadecimal notation for the value of the *WS_EX_APPWINDOW* constant.

```
Private Const WS_EX_APPWINDOW As Long = &H40000&
```

It's fairly easy to recognize that the hexadecimal value 40000 sets bit 18 (3rd bit in 5th digit, 2^2=4) in a 32-bit integer. The decimal equivalent of the constant *WS_EX_APPWINDOW* is 262144. Certainly, it is considerably more difficult to recognize which bits are set by a decimal number.

The constants used to set window styles should be combined with `Boolean` operations using the operators `And`, `Or`, and `Not` before calling the DLL procedure that effects the changes.

NOTE

Not all window styles can be successfully changed at run time, but must be set when the window is first created. Significant experimentation may be required to learn which styles can be changed at run time.

The DLL functions `GetWindowLong()` and `SetWindowLong()` are used to retrieve and set the styles for a window, respectively.

```
Private Declare Function GetWindowLong Lib "user32.dll" Alias _
    "GetWindowLongA" (ByVal hWnd As Long, ByVal nIndex As Long) As Long
Private Declare Function SetWindowLong Lib "user32.dll" Alias _
    "SetWindowLongA" (ByVal hWnd As Long, ByVal nIndex As Long, _
    ByVal dwNewLong As Long) As Long
```

Both functions require a handle to the window of interest plus one or two constants that specify which set of styles to retrieve. The normal set of style bits is retrieved using the constant *GWL_STYLE* (−16) and the `GetWindowLong()` function. Use *GWL_EXSTYLE* (−20) to retrieve the extended set of style bits for a window.

```
curStyle = GetWindowLong(hForm, GWL_STYLE)
```

To set the normal or extended style bits for a window, use *GWL_STYLE* or *GWL_EXSTYLE* and SetWindowLong().

```
oldStyle = SetWindowLong(hForm, GWL_STYLE, newStyle)
```

The SetWindowLong() function returns the old set of style bits, which may be discarded since this number is normally retrieved with GetWindowLong(). One additional argument is required to set the style bits, and it should represent the desired combination of styles built from simple logic operations. For example, the following statement uses the Or operator to set the bits that tell Windows to show maximize and minimize boxes on the window:

```
curStyle = curStyle Or WS_MAXIMIZEBOX Or WS_MINIMIZEBOX
```

Other style constants for the normal and extended set of window styles are listed in Tables 17.2 and 17.3, respectively.

Table 17.2 Constants Used to Set Common Window Style Bits Using the API

Constant	Hexadecimal Value	Description
WS_BORDER	800000	Creates a window that has a border.
WS_CAPTION	C00000	Creates a window that has a title bar (implies the *WS_BORDER* style). Cannot be used with the WS_DLGFRAME style.
WS_CHILD	40000000	Creates a child window. Cannot be used with the *WS_POPUP* style.
WS_DISABLED	8000000	Creates a window that is initially disabled.
WS_DLGFRAME	400000	Creates a window with a double border but no title.
WS_HSCROLL	100000	Creates a window that has a horizontal scroll bar.
WS_MAXIMIZE	1000000	Creates a window of maximum size.
WS_MAXIMIZEBOX	10000	Creates a window that has a maximize button.
WS_MINIMIZE	20000000	Creates a window that is initially minimized. For use with the *WS_OVERLAPPED* style only.
WS_MINIMIZEBOX	20000	Creates a window that has a minimize button.

Constant	Hexadecimal Value	Description
WS_OVERLAPPED	0	Creates an overlapped window. An overlapped window usually has a caption and a border.
WS_OVERLAPPEDWINDOW	See description	Creates an overlapped window with the WS_OVERLAPPED, WS_CAPTION, WS_SYSMENU, WS_THICKFRAME, WS_MINIMIZEBOX, and WS_MAXIMIZEBOX styles.
WS_POPUP	80000000	Creates a pop-up window. Cannot be used with the WS_CHILD style.
WS_POPUPWINDOW	See description	Creates a pop-up window with the WS_BORDER, WS_POPUP, and WS_SYSMENU styles. The WS_CAPTION style must be combined with the WS_POPUPWINDOW style to make the Control menu visible.
WS_SYSMENU	80000	Creates a window that has a Control-menu box in its title bar. Used only for windows with title bars.
WS_THICKFRAME	40000	Creates a window with a thick frame that can be used to size the window.
WS_VISIBLE	10000000	Creates a window that is initially visible.
WS_VSCROLL	200000	Creates a window that has a vertical scroll bar.

Table 17.3 Constants Used to Set Extended Window Style Bits Using the API

Constant	Value	Description
WS_EX_APPWINDOW	40000	Creates a taskbar button for the window.
WS_EX_CLIENTEDGE	200	Specifies that a window has a 3D look — that is, a border with a sunken edge.

continues

Table 17.3 Constants Used to Set Extended Window Style Bits Using the API *(continued)*

Constant	Value	Description
WS_EX_DLGMODALFRAME	1	Designates a window with a double border that may (optionally) be created with a title bar when you specify the WS_CAPTION style flag in the GWL_Style argument.
WS_EX_OVERLAPPEDWINDOW	See description	Combines the WS_EX_CLIENTEDGE and WS_EX_WINDOWEDGE styles.
WS_EX_TOOLWINDOW	80	Creates a tool window, which is a window intended to be used as a floating toolbar. A tool window has a title bar that is shorter than a normal title bar, and the window title is drawn using a smaller font. A tool window does not appear in the task bar or in the window that appears when the user presses ALT+Tab.
WS_EX_TOPMOST	8	Specifies that a window created with this style should be placed above all nontopmost windows and should stay above them, even when the window is deactivated. An application can use the SetWindowPos member function to add or remove this attribute.
WS_EX_TRANSPARENT	20	Specifies that a window created with this style is to be transparent. That is, windows beneath the window are not obscured by the window. A window created with this style receives WM_PAINT messages only after all sibling windows beneath it have been updated.
WS_EX_WINDOWEDGE	100	Specifies that a window has a border with a raised edge.

Making a Sizable Userform with Minimize and Maximize Buttons

Some of my annoyances regarding Userforms are alleviated with the methods used in the following program. The program is a sample application with a single Userform. The run-time Userform is shown in Figure 17.2.

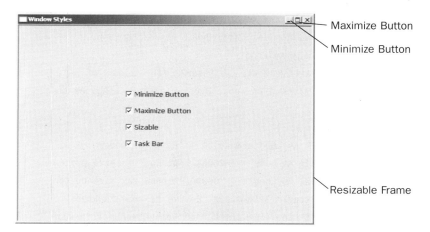

FIGURE 17.2 *A resizable Userform created with minimize and maximize buttons.*

The Userform contains four Check Box controls that are used to toggle four window styles on and off. The styles that can be toggled are the minimized and maximized buttons, making the Userform sizable and showing the Userform on the taskbar. All code is contained within the code module for the Userform.

 TIP

If you find yourself altering the style bits of Userforms on a regular or semi-regular basis, create a custom class that accomplishes the same task. You will save yourself considerable time and avoid the tedium of having to repeatedly write the same API declarations.

The general declarations section of the form module contains the API declarations, constants, and custom variable type definitions as well as a few module-level variable declarations.

```
Option Explicit
'********************
'API declarations
Private Declare Function FindWindow Lib "user32.dll" Alias _
    "FindWindowA" (ByVal lpClassName As String, _
    ByVal lpWindowName As String) As Long
Private Declare Function ShowWindow Lib "user32.dll" ( _
    ByVal hWnd As Long, ByVal nCmdShow As Long) As Long
Private Declare Function DrawMenuBar Lib "user32.dll" ( _
    ByVal hWnd As Long) As Long
```

```
Private Declare Function SetWindowLong Lib "user32.dll" Alias _
    "SetWindowLongA" (ByVal hWnd As Long, ByVal nIndex As Long, _
    ByVal dwNewLong As Long) As Long
Private Declare Function GetWindowLong Lib "user32.dll" Alias _
    "GetWindowLongA" (ByVal hWnd As Long, ByVal nIndex As Long) As Long
'***************
'Constants
Private Const WS_THICKFRAME As Long = &H40000    'Re-size window
Private Const WS_MINIMIZEBOX As Long = &H20000   'Window minimize button
Private Const WS_MAXIMIZEBOX As Long = &H10000   'Window maximize button
Private Const WS_POPUP As Long = &H80000000 'Remove to show taskbar
Private Const WS_VISIBLE As Long = &H10000000    'Remove to show taskbar
Private Const WS_EX_APPWINDOW As Long = &H40000 'Show window on taskbar
Private Const WS_EX_DLGMODALFRAME As Long = &H1& 'Show icon in title bar
Private Const WS_EX_CLIENTEDGE As Long = &H200&
Private Const GWL_STYLE As Long = -16    'Return/set window styles
Private Const GWL_EXSTYLE As Long = -20 'Return/set extended styles
Private Const SW_HIDE As Long = 0    'Hide window
Private Const SW_SHOW As Long = 5    'Show window
'************************
'Module-level variables
Private hForm As Long
Private prevStyle As Long
Private newStyle As Long
Private newXStyle As Long
Private curStyle As Long
Private curXStyle As Long
```

The `Activate()` event retrieves a handle to the Userform and calls the `SetStyles()` Sub procedure, which sets several normal styles and a couple of extended styles for the Userform. Some style settings are interdependent, and removing or adding a style can adversely affect the window unless another style is also removed or added. For example, *WS_POPUP*, *WS_VISIBLE*, and *WS_EX_APPWINDOW* are interdependent. The latter one adds the window to the taskbar, but pop-up windows are not allowed on the taskbar, so the *WS_POPUP* and *WS_VISIBLE* styles must be removed. Depending on the conflicting styles, disastrous results may occur; however, in this case, Windows just ignores the request to place the window on the taskbar if the *WS_POPUP* and *WS_VISIBLE* styles are not removed.

```
Private Sub UserForm_Activate()
'Get window handle/device context and set initial styles
```

```
    hForm = FindWindow(vbNullString, "Window Styles")
    SetStyles
End Sub
Private Sub SetStyles()
'Set initial styles to show min/max/taskbar buttons and sizable window
    prevStyle = GetWindowLong(hForm, GWL_STYLE)
    newStyle = prevStyle Or WS_MINIMIZEBOX
    newStyle = newStyle Or WS_MAXIMIZEBOX
    newStyle = newStyle Or WS_THICKFRAME 'Sizable window
    newStyle = newStyle And Not WS_POPUP   'Remove to show on taskbar
    newStyle = newStyle And Not WS_VISIBLE  'Remove to show on taskbar
    curStyle = SetWindowLong(hForm, GWL_STYLE, newStyle)
    'Retrieve and set extended styles
    curXStyle = GetWindowLong(hForm, GWL_EXSTYLE)
    newXStyle = curXStyle Or WS_EX_APPWINDOW      'taskbar button
    newXStyle = newXStyle Or WS_EX_CLIENTEDGE
    newXStyle = newXStyle And Not WS_EX_DLGMODALFRAME 'icon in title bar
    curXStyle = SetWindowLong(hForm, GWL_EXSTYLE, newXStyle)

    ShowWindow hForm, SW_SHOW    'Show changes
End Sub
Private Sub ckMaxButton_Click()
    ChangeStyle "Max"
End Sub
Private Sub ckMinButton_Click()
    ChangeStyle "Min"
End Sub
Private Sub ckSizeable_Click()
    ChangeStyle "Size"
End Sub
Private Sub ckTaskBar_Click()
    If Not ckTaskBar.Value Then
        ShowWindow hForm, SW_HIDE    'Hide taskbar button
    End If
    ChangeStyle "Task"
End Sub
```

NOTE

The task bar icon representing a Userform will not appear unless you deselect the auto-hide option in your task bar properties.

The `ChangeStyle()` Sub procedure serves to toggle styles on and off. A `Select/Case` structure sorts out specific calls from the `Click()` events of the Check Box controls and resets the styles appropriately. Changes do not take effect until the window is reshown and the title bar redrawn using the DLL functions `ShowWindow()` and `DrawMenuBar()`, respectively.

```
Private Sub ChangeStyle(winStyle As String)
'Change window style to reflect changes in check boxes
    prevStyle = GetWindowLong(hForm, GWL_STYLE)
    curXStyle = GetWindowLong(hForm, GWL_EXSTYLE)
    Select Case winStyle
        Case Is = "Min"
            If ckMinButton.Value Then
                newStyle = prevStyle Or WS_MINIMIZEBOX
            Else
                newStyle = prevStyle And Not WS_MINIMIZEBOX
            End If
        Case Is = "Max"
            If ckMaxButton.Value Then
                newStyle = prevStyle Or WS_MAXIMIZEBOX
            Else
                newStyle = prevStyle And Not WS_MAXIMIZEBOX
            End If
        Case Is = "Size"
            If ckSizeable.Value Then
                newStyle = prevStyle Or WS_THICKFRAME
            Else
                newStyle = prevStyle And Not WS_THICKFRAME
            End If
        Case Is = "Task"
            If ckTaskBar.Value Then
                newStyle = prevStyle And Not (WS_POPUP Or WS_VISIBLE)
                newXStyle = curXStyle Or WS_EX_APPWINDOW
```

```
        Else
            newStyle = prevStyle Or WS_POPUP
            newXStyle = curXStyle And Not WS_EX_APPWINDOW
        End If
    End Select
    curStyle = SetWindowLong(hForm, GWL_STYLE, newStyle)
    curXStyle = SetWindowLong(hForm, GWL_EXSTYLE, newXStyle)

    ShowWindow hForm, SW_SHOW
    DrawMenuBar hForm    'redraw menu/title bar to show changes made
End Sub
Private Sub UserForm_QueryClose(Cancel As Integer, CloseMode As Integer)
    Unload Me
    End
End Sub
```

You can use many more styles to alter the appearance and behavior of a Userform. One of the more curious styles is *WS_EX_TRANSPARENT*, which is used to create a transparent window (try it!). You should play with styles that are of interest, but keep in mind that some combinations of styles were not meant to be used together and can yield unpredictable results.

Drawing on a Userform

Although the shape controls and drawing methods available in VB are nothing special, they at least allow you to dress up your forms to make them more visually appealing. Because no shape controls or drawing methods are in VBA, you can use VB to create custom shape controls for use in your VBA projects, or you can use the Windows API to draw shapes on a Userform. Certainly, the API requires more effort than an ActiveX control, but it is just as effective and is always available.

Windows graphics-related procedures are stored in the Graphical Device Interface (GDI) library. This is the Gdi32.dll file stored in the system directory of Windows. The GDI contains procedures that allow you to draw (graphics and text) and manipulate images on any compatible device. A device may be physical such as a printer, or screen (or portion of a screen), or virtual (such as a window or a block of memory). Whatever the device you are drawing to, when using the API to draw or manipulate graphics, you must first create what is known as a *device context.*

Device Contexts

The concept of a device context is used in Windows to make drawing graphics and text device-independent. When using a device context, instead of having to consider the unique set of attributes for each different device, you have one independent set of attributes that is used to draw to any device. It then follows that a device context is a Windows object defined by a set of attributes that can be applied to any device. You can think of a device context as a scratch pad on which you can write text or draw graphics before pasting the drawing to a device (wall, refrigerator, and so on).

The general procedure for drawing to a device is as follows:

1. Obtain a device context.
2. Save the state of the device context.
3. Set the attributes and objects of the device context.
4. Apply desired drawing methods to the device context.
5. Destroy, restore, or release the device context as necessary.

API functions that are used to retrieve, release, and destroy a device context are summarized in Table 17.4.

Table 17.4 DLL Functions Related to a Device Context

Function	Description
GetDC	Retrieves a handle to a display device context for the client area of a specified window or for the entire screen. When finished with the device context, release it with `ReleaseDC`.
GetWindowDC	Retrieves the device context for the entire window, including title bar, menus, and scroll bars. When finished with the device context, release it with `ReleaseDC`.
CreateDC	Creates a device context for a device by using the specified name. When finished with the device context, delete it with `DeleteDC`.
CreateCompatibleDC	Creates a memory device context compatible with the specified device. When finished with the device context, delete it with `DeleteDC`.
WindowFromDC	Returns the handle of the window associated with the given display device context.
SaveDC	Saves the current state of the specified device context.
ReleaseDC	Releases a device context. Should be used with a common device context retrieved with `GetDC` or `GetWindowDC`.
RestoreDC	Restores a device context to the specified state.
DeleteDC	Deletes the specified device context. Should be used with a new device context created with `CreateDC` or `CreateCompatibleDC`.

Use `GetDC()` to return a device context for the client area of a specific window or use `GetWindowDC()` to retrieve the device context for the entire window. Device contexts returned by `GetDC()` or `GetWindowDC()` are obtained from a pool of device contexts available to any Windows program and should never be destroyed. Instead, release these device contexts with the `ReleaseDC()` function after the drawing operation is finished. Before altering the device context, save it with `SaveDC()` and restore it with `RestoreDC()` when drawing operations are finished. Declarations and sample calls to these DLL functions are listed here (note that this code is not meant to be executed in succession):

```
Private Declare Function GetDC Lib "user32.dll" ( _
    ByVal hwnd As Long) As Long
Private Declare Function GetWindowDC Lib "user32.dll" ( _
    ByVal hwnd As Long) As Long
Private Declare Function SaveDC Lib "gdi32.dll" ( _
    ByVal hdc As Long) As Long
Private Declare Function ReleaseDC Lib "user32.dll" ( _
    ByVal hwnd As Long, ByVal hdc As Long) As Long
dcForm = GetDC(hForm)   'Retrieves client-area DC from window handle
dcForm = GetWindowDC(hForm)   'Retrieves DC for entire window
oDC = SaveDC(dcForm)    'Saves current DC
ReleaseDC hForm, dcForm    'Releases the DC back to Windows pool
RestoreDC dcForm, oDC    'Restores the DC to saved state
```

 NOTE

The *client area* refers to the area of a window that can receive text or graphical output, excluding the title bar, borders, menus and toolbars, scroll bars, and rulers.

The `CreateDC()` and `CreateCompatibleDC()` functions return a new device context, and you can create as many as you like (limited only by memory). They can use a considerable amount of memory, so destroy them with the `DeleteDC()` function when the drawing operation is finished. Their declarations and sample calls are listed here:

```
Private Declare Function CreateCompatibleDC Lib "gdi32.dll" ( _
    ByVal hdc As Long) As Long
Private Declare Function DeleteDC Lib "gdi32.dll" ( _
    ByVal hdc As Long) As Long
dcbitForm = CreateCompatibleDC(dcForm)
DeleteDC (dcbitForm)
```

GDI Graphics Objects

Device contexts have some basic attributes, such as background color and background mode, but most of their attributes are also objects. The GDI graphics objects are summarized in Table 17.5.

Table 17.5 GDI Graphics Objects

Object	Description
Bitmap	A raster compatible data set that represents an image.
Brush	A graphic object that defines how to fill in drawing areas.
Pen	A graphic object that defines how to draw lines.
Font	A graphic object that defines the appearance of a set of characters.
Path	A sequence of drawing commands designed for a device context. A device context can contain only one path.
Region	A graphic object that defines an area within a device context.

After a device context is obtained, its attributes can be changed from their default settings by creating new drawing objects. For example, the function `CreatePen()` is used to specify the style, width, and color of the object used to draw lines. Table 17.6 summarizes some of the DLL procedures used to create GDI objects.

Table 17.6 DLL Procedures Used to Create Drawing Objects

Function	Description
`CreateEllipticRgn`	Creates an elliptical region using specified points.
`CreatePolygonRgn`	Creates a polygon region using specified points.
`CreateRectRgn`	Creates a rectangular region using specified points.
`CreatePen`	Creates a pen with the specified style, width, and color.
`ExtCreatePen`	Creates an extended pen.
`CreateSolidBrush`	Creates a brush with a solid color specified by an RGB integer.
`CreatePatternBrush`	Creates a brush using a bitmap to specify a pattern.
`CreateHatchBrush`	Creates a brush with one of several hatched patterns.
`GetStockObject`	Retrieves a stock object (standard Windows pen, brush, or font).

Function	Description
SetBkColor	Sets the background color for a specified device context.
SetArcDirection	Sets the direction (clockwise or counterclockwise) to use when drawing arcs.

Once the drawing object is created, it can be selected into any device context. The SelectObject() function is used to select a drawing object into a device context before applying any drawing functions. The declaration for SelectObject() specifies two arguments, one for the handle to the device context (hdc) and the other for the handle to the GDI object (hObject) created by one of the functions in Table 17.6. After finishing a drawing operation and when the drawing object is no longer needed, delete it with the DeleteObject() function.

```
Private Declare Function SelectObject Lib "gdi32.dll" ( _
     ByVal hdc As Long, ByVal hObject As Long) As Long
Private Declare Function CreateSolidBrush Lib "gdi32.dll" ( _
     ByVal crColor As Long) As Long
Private Declare Function CreatePen Lib "gdi32.dll" ( _
     ByVal nPenStyle As Long, ByVal nWidth As Long, _
     ByVal crColor As Long) As Long
Private Declare Function DeleteObject Lib "gdi32.dll" ( _
     ByVal hObject As Long) As Long
hBrush = CreateSolidBrush(RGB(255, 0, 0))
hPen = CreatePen(PS_SOLID, 2, RGB(0, 0, 255))
rv = SelectObject(dcForm, hBrush)
rv = SelectObject(dcForm, hPen)
DeleteObject hpen
DeleteObject hBrush
```

After obtaining the device context and defining the drawing objects, you are finally ready to draw. Multitudes of drawing functions are in the GDI; some of them are listed in Table 17.7.

Table 17.7 DLL Procedures Used to Draw

Function	Description
Arc	Draws an elliptical arc specified by a bounding rectangle and starting and ending points for the arc.
DrawEdge	Draws one or more edges of a rectangle using a specified style.

continues

Table 17.7 DLL Procedures Used to Draw *(continued)*

Function	Description
Ellipse	Draws an ellipse. The center of the ellipse is the center of the specified bounding rectangle.
FillPath	Closes any open figures in the current path and fills the path's interior by using the current brush and polygon-filling mode.
FillRect	Fills a rectangle by using the specified brush.
FloodFill	Fills an area of the device context with the current brush.
FrameRect	Draws a border around the specified rectangle by using the specified brush.
LineTo	Draws a line from the current position up to, but not including, the specified point.
MoveToEx	Moves the current position to the specified point and optionally returns the previous position.
InvertRect	Inverts a rectangle in a window by performing a logical NOT operation on the color values for each pixel in the rectangle's interior.
PaintRgn	Paints the specified region using the brush currently selected into the device.
Pie	Draws a pie-shaped wedge bounded by the intersection of an ellipse and two radials. The pie is outlined using the current pen and filled using the current brush.
PolyBezier	Draws one or more Bezier curves.
PolyDraw	Draws a set of line segments and Bezier curves.
Polygon	Draws a polygon consisting of two or more vertices connected by straight lines. The polygon is outlined using the current pen and filled using the current brush and polygon fill mode.
Rectangle	Draws a rectangle. The rectangle is outlined using the current pen and filled using the current brush.
RoundRect	Draws a rectangle with rounded corners. The rectangle is outlined using the current pen and filled using the current brush.

Putting all five steps together, the following procedure draws a rounded rectangle on a Userform. The procedure creates a pen and brush object to define the line and the fill for the rectangle. DLL function declarations are not listed here, but they must be included in the general declarations section of a code module in order for this procedure to execute.

```
Private Sub CommandButton1_Click()
    Dim rv As Long, hPen As Long, hBrush As Long
```

```
    Dim hForm As Long, dcForm As Long, oDC As Long
    Const HS_VERTICAL As Long = 1
    Const PS_SOLID As Long = 0

    'Get window handle and device context
    hForm = FindWindow(vbNullString, "Drawing Shapes with the API")
    dcForm = GetDC(hForm)
    oDC = SaveDC(dcForm)      'Save the DC for later restoration

    'Create drawing objects and draw a rounded rectangle
    hBrush = CreateHatchBrush(HS_VERTICAL, RGB(0, 255, 255))
    hPen = CreatePen(PS_SOLID, 4, RGB(0, 0, 0))
    rv = SelectObject(dcForm, hBrush)
    rv = SelectObject(dcForm, hPen)
    rv = RoundRect(dcForm, 20, 20, 300, 100, 200, 60)

    'Restore DC, release DC and delete drawing objects
    RestoreDC dcForm, oDC
    ReleaseDC hForm, dcForm
    DeleteObject hPen
    DeleteObject hBrush
End Sub
```

The rounded rectangle created by the procedure is shown in Figure 17.3.

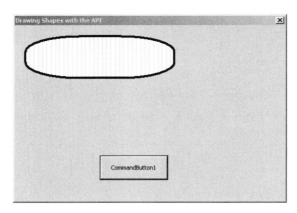

FIGURE 17.3 *Drawing a rounded rectangle on a Userform.*

Drawing Shapes on a Userform

The program in this section of the chapter exemplifies how to alter the appearance and draw shapes on a Userform using the Windows API. The program uses DLL functions through the Windows API to carry out the following tasks:

◆ Draw a wide edge around the Userform giving the Userform a sunken look.

◆ Draw a rectangle around a Command Button. The rectangle should follow the button regardless of where it is placed on the Userform.

◆ Provide a user interface to specify style, width, and color for a custom pen.

◆ Draw several shapes in the open area at the top of the Userform, including an arc, a series of lines, a filled rectangle, a polygon, and an ellipse.

◆ Clear the Userform of all drawings made with the API.

◆ Store an image of the Userform in memory for later restoration.

The code is contained within the code module of the Userform shown in Figure 17.4. The program provides an interface to the user for selecting a pen style, which they can use to add several different shapes to the upper section of the Userform. The user can also save an image of the Userform to memory for later restoration.

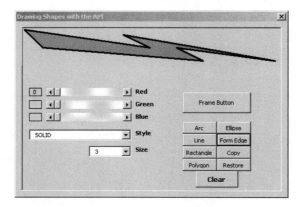

FIGURE 17.4 *Drawing shapes on a Userform with the API.*

The general declarations section of the code module includes the API declarations with required constants and type definitions.

```
Option Explicit
'-----------------------------------------------
'Demonstration of several API drawing functions
'Drawing to a userform
'*******************************************************
'API handle and device context function declarations
'These functions are used to retrieve a handle to the
```

```
'userform and get a device context for it. Other functions
'are for memory management.
Private Declare Function FindWindow Lib "user32.dll" Alias _
     "FindWindowA" (ByVal lpClassName As String, _
     ByVal lpWindowName As String) As Long
Private Declare Function GetDC Lib "user32.dll" ( _
     ByVal hwnd As Long) As Long
Private Declare Function SaveDC Lib "gdi32.dll" ( _
     ByVal hdc As Long) As Long
Private Declare Function SelectObject Lib "gdi32.dll" ( _
     ByVal hdc As Long, ByVal hObject As Long) As Long
Private Declare Function RestoreDC Lib "gdi32.dll" ( _
     ByVal hdc As Long, ByVal nSavedDC As Long) As Long
Private Declare Function ReleaseDC Lib "user32.dll" ( _
     ByVal hwnd As Long, ByVal hdc As Long) As Long
Private Declare Function DeleteDC Lib "gdi32.dll" ( _
     ByVal hdc As Long) As Long
'*****************************
'Misc window info. functions
'These functions are used return the dimensions of the
'userform and other misc information about it.
Private Declare Function GetWindowRect Lib "user32.dll" ( _
     ByVal hwnd As Long, lpRect As RECT) As Long
Private Declare Function GetClientRect Lib "user32.dll" ( _
     ByVal hwnd As Long, lpRect As RECT) As Long
'**********************************************************************
'API Drawing function declarations. Not all are used in this program
'These functions are used to draw shapes and lines to a device
'context. In this program the device context is associated with
'the userform.
Private Declare Function FrameRect Lib "user32.dll" ( _
     ByVal hdc As Long, lpRect As RECT, ByVal hBrush As Long) As Long
Private Declare Function CreateSolidBrush Lib "gdi32.dll" ( _
     ByVal crColor As Long) As Long
Private Declare Function DeleteObject Lib "gdi32.dll" ( _
     ByVal hObject As Long) As Long
```

```
Private Declare Function CreatePen Lib "gdi32.dll" ( _
    ByVal nPenStyle As Long, ByVal nWidth As Long, _
    ByVal crColor As Long) As Long
Private Declare Function DrawEdge Lib "user32.dll" ( _
    ByVal hdc As Long, qrc As RECT, ByVal edge As Long, _
    ByVal grfFlags As Long) As Long
Private Declare Function Arc Lib "gdi32.dll" (ByVal hdc As Long, _
    ByVal X1 As Long, ByVal Y1 As Long, ByVal X2 As Long, _
    ByVal Y2 As Long, ByVal X3 As Long, ByVal Y3 As Long, _
    ByVal X4 As Long, ByVal Y4 As Long) As Long
Private Declare Function MoveToEx Lib "gdi32.dll" (ByVal hdc As Long, _
    ByVal x As Long, ByVal y As Long, lpPoint As POINTAPI) As Long
Private Declare Function LineTo Lib "gdi32.dll" (ByVal hdc As Long, _
    ByVal x As Long, ByVal y As Long) As Long
Private Declare Function Polyline Lib "gdi32.dll" (ByVal hdc As Long, _
    lpPoint As POINTAPI, ByVal nCount As Long) As Long
Private Declare Function Rectangle Lib "gdi32.dll" (ByVal hdc As Long, _
    ByVal X1 As Long, ByVal Y1 As Long, ByVal X2 As Long, _
    ByVal Y2 As Long) As Long
Private Declare Function CreateHatchBrush Lib "gdi32.dll" ( _
    ByVal nIndex As Long, ByVal crColor As Long) As Long
Private Declare Function CreatePatternBrush Lib "gdi32.dll" ( _
    ByVal hBitmap As Long) As Long
Private Declare Function Polygon Lib "gdi32.dll" (ByVal hdc As Long, _
    lpPoint As POINTAPI, ByVal nCount As Long) As Long
Private Declare Function Ellipse Lib "gdi32.dll" (ByVal hdc As Long, _
    ByVal X1 As Long, ByVal Y1 As Long, ByVal X2 As Long, _
    ByVal Y2 As Long) As Long
Private Declare Function InflateRect Lib "user32.dll" (lpRect As RECT, _
    ByVal x As Long, ByVal y As Long) As Long
'**********************
'Bitmap functions
'These functions are used to create a bitmap image of
'the userform and copy it to memory or back to the userform.
Private Declare Function CreateCompatibleBitmap Lib "gdi32.dll" ( _
    ByVal hdc As Long, ByVal nWidth As Long, _
    ByVal nHeight As Long) As Long
```

```vba
Private Declare Function CreateCompatibleDC Lib "gdi32.dll" ( _
    ByVal hdc As Long) As Long
Private Declare Function BitBlt Lib "gdi32.dll" (ByVal hDestDC As Long, _
    ByVal x As Long, ByVal y As Long, ByVal nWidth As Long, _
    ByVal nHeight As Long, ByVal hSrcDC As Long, ByVal xSrc As Long, _
    ByVal ySrc As Long, ByVal dwRop As Long) As Long
'************
'Constants for CreatePen function
Private Const PS_SOLID As Long = 0   'Pen styles
Private Const PS_DASH As Long = 1
Private Const PS_DASHDOT As Long = 3
Private Const PS_DASHDOTDOT As Long = 4
Private Const PS_DOT As Long = 2


'Borders for DrawEdge function
Private Const BDR_SUNKENINNER As Long = &H8
Private Const BDR_RAISEDOUTER As Long = &H1
Private Const BDR_RAISEDINNER As Long = &H4
Private Const BDR_SUNKENOUTER As Long = &H2
Private Const BDR_INNER As Long = &HC
Private Const BDR_OUTER As Long = &H3
Private Const BDR_RAISED As Long = &H5
Private Const BDR_SUNKEN As Long = &HA


'Border flags for DrawEdge function
Private Const BF_MIDDLE As Long = &H800
Private Const BF_TOP As Long = &H2
Private Const BF_LEFT As Long = &H1
Private Const BF_RIGHT As Long = &H4
Private Const BF_BOTTOM As Long = &H8


'Brush constants for shape fills
Private Const HS_HORIZONTAL As Long = 0
Private Const HS_VERTICAL As Long = 1
Private Const HS_FDIAGONAL As Long = 2
Private Const HS_DIAGCROSS As Long = 5
Private Const HS_CROSS As Long = 4
Private Const HS_BDIAGONAL As Long = 3
```

```
'Simple copy for BitBlt
Private Const SRCCOPY As Long = &HCC0020
'*****************************************
'Common structures for API functions
'The RECT structure is used with API functions that
'will fill its components with the dimensions of a rectangle.
Private Type RECT
    Left As Long
    Top As Long
    Right As Long
    Bottom As Long
End Type

'This structure is used with API functions that fill its
'components with the values of an x-y coordinate pair (a point)
Private Type POINTAPI
    x As Long
    y As Long
End Type
'***********************
'Module-level variables for handles and device contexts
Private hForm As Long, dcForm As Long, oDC As Long
Private hPen As Long, hBrush As Long
Private ignoreChange As Boolean
Private hbitForm As Long
Private dcbitForm As Long
```

The program begins with the `Activate()` event of the `Userform` object where ActiveX controls are initialized, a handle and device context are retrieved for the Userform, and a custom pen is created.

```
Private Sub UserForm_Activate()
'Initialize combo boxes. Get userform handle and device context
    Dim myLabels
    Dim myValues
    Dim I As Integer

    'Don't want activate event to trigger change event
    'of the combo box controls.
    ignoreChange = True
```

```
    'Use parameter array to hold constants for CreatePen function
    'and add to a Combo Box
    myLabels = Array("SOLID", "DASH", "DASH-DOT", "DASH-DOT-DOT", "DOT")
    myValues = Array(PS_SOLID, PS_DASH, PS_DASHDOT, _
                                    PS_DASHDOTDOT, PS_DOT)
    For I = 0 To UBound(myValues)
        cmbPen.AddItem myLabels(I)
        cmbPen.List(I, 1) = myValues(I)
    Next I
    cmbPen.Text = "SOLID"


    'Used to set the line widths when drawing shapes
    For I = 0 To 9
        cmbSize.AddItem I + 1
    Next I
    cmbSize.Text = "1"


    GetDeviceContext    'Gets DC for userform
    SetPenAttr      'Creates a Pen object for drawing
    ignoreChange = False
End Sub


Private Sub GetDeviceContext()
'Get a handle and device context to/for the UserForm
    hForm = FindWindow(vbNullString, "Drawing Shapes with the API")
    dcForm = GetDC(hForm)
    oDC = SaveDC(dcForm)        'Save the DC for later restoration
End Sub
```

The SetPenAttr() procedure is called whenever the user changes the settings in the Combo Box or Scroll Bar controls. The procedure deletes the old pen object and creates a new pen based on the selections in these controls. The Combo Box controls set the style and width of the pen, and the Scroll Bar controls set the color. Note that the Min and Max properties of each scroll bar are set to 0 and 255, respectively.

```
Private Sub SetPenAttr()
'Create a new pen object for API functions
    Dim rv As Integer
```

```
    If hPen = 0 Then
        hPen = CreatePen(cmbPen.List(cmbPen.ListIndex, 1), cmbSize.Text _
            , RGB(scrRed.Value, scrGreen.Value, scrBlue.Value))
    Else
        DeleteObject hPen
        hPen = CreatePen(cmbPen.List(cmbPen.ListIndex, 1), cmbSize.Text _
            , RGB(scrRed.Value, scrGreen.Value, scrBlue.Value))
    End If
End Sub


Private Sub scrBlue_Change()
'Value property ranges from 0-255. This is used
'with RGB function to set color of drawing objects
    lblBlue.Caption = scrBlue.Value
    SetPenAttr
End Sub


Private Sub scrGreen_Change()
    lblGreen.Caption = scrGreen.Value
    SetPenAttr    'Create new pen object
End Sub


Private Sub scrRed_Change()
    lblRed.Caption = scrRed.Value
    SetPenAttr
End Sub


Private Sub cmbPen_Change()
'User has changed the pen style
    If Not ignoreChange Then SetPenAttr
End Sub


Private Sub cmbSize_Change()
'User has changed the pen size
    If Not ignoreChange Then SetPenAttr
End Sub
```

Anything drawn on the Userform with DLL functions through the Windows API is erased when the `Repaint` method of the `Userform` object is invoked. This is because the `Userform` object does not have an `AutoRedraw` property. Without this property, changes made to the client area of the Userform during run time are not saved to a persistent bitmap in memory. Instead, whenever the Userform is redrawn (either automatically by Windows or by invoking the `Repaint` method), Windows uses the persistent bitmap that represents the Userform's background image (as it appears when it is first loaded).

```
Private Sub cmdClear_Click()
    frmAPIdraw.Repaint   'Erases anything drawn with API
End Sub
```

The following `Click()` event procedures draw an ellipse, polygon, arc, line, and rectangle near the top of the Userform. If a new brush or pen is not defined in the procedure, the DLL functions will use the currently selected pen and/or brush to draw the shape. Note that one of the arguments (`lpPoint`) in the `Polygon()` and `Polyline()` functions requires the first `POINTAPI` structure in an array of `POINTAPI` structures. The `POINTAPI` structure is a user-defined type specifying an *x,y* coordinate, and its declaration is at module-level.

```
Private Sub cmdEllipse_Click()
'Draw an ellipse. Current pen and brush are used.
    Dim rv As Long

    frmAPIdraw.Repaint   'Erase other shapes
    'Always select drawing object into DC
    rv = SelectObject(dcForm, hPen)
    rv = Ellipse(dcForm, 25, 25, 450, 100)    'Draw an ellipse
End Sub


Private Sub cmdPolygon_Click()
'Draw a polygon. Current pen and brush are used.
    Dim rv As Long
    Dim pts(7) As POINTAPI

    frmAPIdraw.Repaint   'Erase other shapes

    '**********************************
    'Define array of points for polygon
    '**********************************
    pts(0).x = 15: pts(0).y = 15: pts(1).x = 50: pts(1).y = 50
    pts(2).x = 350: pts(2).y = 75: pts(3).x = 300: pts(3).y = 50
```

```
    pts(4).x = 485: pts(4).y = 75: pts(5).x = 200: pts(5).y = 25
    pts(6).x = 250: pts(6).y = 50


    rv = SelectObject(dcForm, hPen)
    rv = Polygon(dcForm, pts(0), UBound(pts))
End Sub


Private Sub cmdArc_Click()
'Draw an arc. Current pen is used.
    Dim rv As Long


    frmAPIdraw.Repaint
    rv = SelectObject(dcForm, hPen)
    rv = Arc(dcForm, 10, 10, 100, 100, 20, 20, 90, 20)
End Sub


Private Sub cmdLine_Click()
'Draw a few lines. Can also use Line function
    Dim rv As Long
    Dim pts(4) As POINTAPI, pt As POINTAPI


    'Move pen to new position on userform
    rv = MoveToEx(dcForm, 115, 25, pt)
    '*********************************************
    'Define an array of points to connect lines
    '*********************************************
    pts(0).x = 115: pts(0).y = 25: pts(1).x = 140: pts(1).y = 50
    pts(2).x = 150: pts(2).y = 45: pts(3).x = 140: pts(3).y = 30
    pts(4).x = 125: pts(4).y = 5


    frmAPIdraw.Repaint
    rv = SelectObject(dcForm, hPen)
    rv = Polyline(dcForm, pts(0), UBound(pts) + 1)
End Sub
```

```
Private Sub cmdRectangle_Click()
'Draw a rectangle and fill it with cross hatch pattern brush
    Dim rv As Long
    Dim hBrush As Long

    frmAPIdraw.Repaint
    hBrush = CreateHatchBrush(HS_CROSS, RGB( _
        scrRed.Value, scrGreen.Value, scrBlue.Value))
    rv = SelectObject(dcForm, hBrush)
    rv = Rectangle(dcForm, 20, 20, 400, 100)
    DeleteObject hBrush
End Sub
```

The Click() event of the CommandButton control named cmdFormEdge uses the DLL function GetClientRect() DLL to retrieve the coordinates of a rectangle representing the client region of the Userform (specified by its handle hForm). What is interesting about the GetClientRect() function is that the desired information is loaded in the variable frmrect (user-defined type RECT), which is passed to the function by reference. The RECT structure contains four fields representing the pixel position of the Left, Top, Right, and Bottom sides of the rectangle (the Left, and Top fields are always set to 0). The function's return value is assigned to the variable rv and specifies the function's success (nonzero) or failure (0) and is ignored in this program. The DLL function InflateRect() is then used to decrease the size of the RECT structure by 10 pixels on all sides. The DLL function DrawEdge() draws a sunken edge around all four sides of the rectangle for a three-dimensional effect (see Figure 17.4, shown earlier in this chapter).

```
Private Sub cmdFormEdge_Click()
'Draw an edge around form. Create a sunken look.
    Dim rv As Long
    Dim frmrect As RECT

    rv = GetClientRect(hForm, frmrect)
    rv = InflateRect(frmrect, -10, -10) 'Decrease rectangle
    rv = DrawEdge(dcForm, frmrect, BDR_SUNKEN, BF_BOTTOM _
        Or BF_RIGHT Or BF_TOP Or BF_LEFT)
End Sub
```

You use the DLL function FrameRect() to draw a rectangle around the button that triggers the Click() event procedure. The FrameRect() function draws a border one pixel wide around a specified rectangle. The point of interest here is that the procedure needs the location of the button to draw the border, but the button's coordinates cannot be directly determined using API calls. Instead, the dimensions of the client area of the Userform (in pixels) are returned from the RECT structure used with the GetWindowRect() function. The fields from the RECT structure are used with the Width and Height properties of the Userform object (in points) to determine the conversion factor between points and pixels. Finding the location of the Command Button control in pixels is then a simple operation involving its size properties and the point-to-pixel conversion factor.

```
Private Sub cmdFrameRect_Click()
'Draw a rectangle around the command button
    Dim hBrush As Long, rv As Long
    Dim cbRect As RECT, frmrect As RECT
    Dim ptPerPixelX As Single, ptPerPixelY As Single
    Dim scrWidth As Integer, scrHeight As Integer
    '
    'Create a solid brush
    hBrush = CreateSolidBrush(RGB(255, 0, 0))
    rv = SelectObject(dcForm, hBrush)

    'Get UserForm client coordinates and convert points to pixels
    rv = GetWindowRect(hForm, frmrect)
    ptPerPixelX = frmAPIdraw.Width / (frmrect.Right - frmrect.Left)
    ptPerPixelY = frmAPIdraw.Height / (frmrect.Bottom - frmrect.Top)

    'Set up array of points for a rectangle to be drawn around
    'the Command Button control
    cbRect.Left = cmdFrameRect.Left / ptPerPixelX - 1
    cbRect.Top = cmdFrameRect.Top / ptPerPixelY - 1
    cbRect.Right = (cmdFrameRect.Left + cmdFrameRect.Width) _
        / ptPerPixelX + 1
    cbRect.Bottom = (cmdFrameRect.Top + cmdFrameRect.Height) _
        / ptPerPixelY + 1
    rv = FrameRect(dcForm, cbRect, hBrush)

    DeleteObject hBrush
End Sub
```

Finally, because all drawings are lost when the Userform is repainted, a bitmap object representing an image of the Userform can be stored in system memory using the DLL functions CreateCompatibleBitmap(), CreateCompatibleDC(), and BitBlt(). First, you use the function CreateCompatibleBitmap() to create a device-dependent bitmap compatible with the device context for the Userform. The size of the bitmap is set to the size of the client area of the Userform because Windows repaints the non-client area. Next, you use the function CreateCompatibleDC()to create a memory device context that is compatible with the Userform's device context. This is necessary because any drawing operation requires a device context. The DLL function SelectObject() is then used to select the bitmap into the newly created memory device context just as it might be used to select a pen into the device context of a Userform before a drawing operation. The last step is to copy the bitmap of the Userform into the memory device context with the DLL function BitBlt().

The BitBlt() function can be used to manipulate the image in dozens of ways as it is copied to its new destination. The bitmap is altered using different combinations of constants for the dwRop argument. However, in this example, the bitmap is copied from the source to the destination unaltered (specified by SRCCOPY). The remaining arguments for the BitBlt() function specify the destination device context (hDestDc), the *x,y* coordinate of the upper-left corner of the destination rectangle in the destination device context (x, y), the width and height of the copied image (nWidth, nHeight), the source device context (hSrcDC), and the *x,y* coordinate of the upper-left corner of the source rectangle in the source device context.

```
Private Sub cmdCopyBM_Click()
'Copy the window image to memory
    Dim frmrect As RECT
    Dim rv As Long
    Dim nWidth As Long, nHeight As Long

    'Get dimensions of userform in pixels
    rv = GetWindowRect(hForm, frmrect)
    nWidth = frmrect.Right - frmrect.Left
    nHeight = frmrect.Bottom - frmrect.Top

    'Create bitmap and DC compatible with userform
    hbitForm = CreateCompatibleBitmap(dcForm, nWidth, nHeight)
    dcbitForm = CreateCompatibleDC(dcForm)
    rv = SelectObject(dcbitForm, hbitForm)

    'Straight copy of userform bitmap to memory
    rv = BitBlt(dcbitForm, 0, 0, nWidth, nHeight, dcForm, 0, 0, SRCCOPY)
End Sub
```

If the Userform is repainted, the bitmap stored in memory can be copied to the Userform using the BitBlt() function and switching the source and destination parameters.

```vba
Private Sub cmdRestoreBM_Click()
'Restore window with bitmap from memory
    Dim rv As Long
    Dim frmrect As RECT
    Dim nWidth As Long, nHeight As Long

    'Get dimensions of userform in pixels
    rv = GetWindowRect(hForm, frmrect)
    nWidth = frmrect.Right - frmrect.Left
    nHeight = frmrect.Bottom - frmrect.Top
    'Straight copy from memory to userform
    rv = BitBlt(dcForm, 0, 0, nWidth, nHeight, dcbitForm, 0, 0, SRCCOPY)
End Sub

Private Sub ClearDeviceContext()
'Release the handle, and restore the DC of userform to original
    RestoreDC dcForm, oDC
    ReleaseDC hForm, dcForm
    DeleteObject (hbitForm)
    DeleteDC (dcbitForm)
End Sub

Private Sub UserForm_QueryClose(Cancel As Integer, _
        CloseMode As Integer)
'Clear system memory
    DeleteObject hPen
    DeleteObject hbitForm
    ClearDeviceContext
    Unload Me
    End
End Sub
```

You now have a good start toward using DLL functions and the Windows API for drawing not only on Userforms but also to any other device for which you can obtain a device context. You might want to experiment with the functions I've shown you plus additional functions that interest you, but remember to save your work often because, as I've mentioned, programming with the API can cause disaster.

Adding Menus to Userforms

Now that you know how to alter the behavior and appearance of a Userform using the Windows API, I will address my final grievance about Userforms. Specifically, I am annoyed by the inability to add menus to a Userform using VBA. I suppose a menu editor is missing because Userforms were originally meant to serve as simple custom dialog boxes in Office applications, so the idea of adding a menu editor was rejected. However, as Windows and Office have evolved, applications written for Office have evolved as well and can really be quite complex. It's time for Microsoft to include a menu editor with the VBA IDE.

So, the obvious issue is how to add menus to Userforms with DLL functions and the Windows API. The solution is complex. In fact, it's a little too complex for the scope of this book. I address the basic issues here, but leave the essential problem as an exercise for further study. I suggest consulting books and the Internet for information on creating menus and subclassing with the Windows API.

Creating Userform Menus with the API

Creating menus on a Userform with DLL functions using the Windows API is relatively straightforward. The required functions are `CreateMenu()`, `CreatePopupMenu()`, `AppendMenu()`, `SetMenu()`, and `DestroyMenu()`. You must also use the `FindWindow()` function to return a handle to the Userform to which you are trying to add menus. To create menus on a Userform requires (at a minimum) the following API declarations in the general declarations section of a code module for a Userform:

```
Private Declare Function FindWindow Lib "user32.dll" _
    Alias "FindWindowA" (ByVal lpClassName As String, _
    ByVal lpWindowName As String) As Long
Private Declare Function CreateMenu Lib "user32" () As Long
Private Declare Function CreatePopupMenu Lib "user32" () As Long
Private Declare Function AppendMenu Lib "user32" Alias "AppendMenuA" _
    (ByVal hMenu As Long, ByVal wFlags As Long, _
    ByVal wIDNewItem As Long, ByVal lpNewItem As Any) As Long
Private Declare Function SetMenu Lib "user32.dll" (ByVal hWnd As Long, _
    ByVal hMenu As Long) As Long
Private Declare Function DestroyMenu Lib "user32" ( _
    ByVal hMenu As Long) As Long
Private Const MF_STRING = &H0&
Private Const MF_POPUP As Long = &H10&
Private hMenu As Long, hForm As Long, rv As Long
Private hPopUpMenu As Long
```

The idea is to first create a top-level menu for the Userform and then add as many pop-up menus to the top-level menu as desired. The `CreateMenu()` function creates a new top-level menu and returns a handle to the new menu. The `Initialize()` or `Activate()` events of the `Userform` object are ideal locations for the following code:

```
hForm = FindWindow("ThunderDFrame", "UserForm1")
hMenu = CreateMenu()
```

The new menu is empty and items are added as pop-up menus. The `CreatePopupMenu()` function creates an empty pop-up menu and returns a handle to the new menu. Items are added to the pop-up with the `AppendMenu()` function. The `AppendMenu()` function requires the handle of a pop-up menu, a flag representing the object that is to be added to the menu (for example, string, menu separator bar, check mark, or even another pop-up menu to serve as a submenu), a new command ID, and the item to add to the menu. The following statements add two strings to a newly created pop-up menu:

```
hPopUpMenu = CreatePopupMenu()
rv = AppendMenu(hPopUpMenu, MF_STRING, 40000, "Menu Item 1")
rv = AppendMenu(hPopUpMenu, MF_STRING, 40001, "Menu Item 2")
```

The constant *MF_STRING* (=&H0) specifies that the argument `lpNewitem` contains a `String` to be added to the pop-up menu. Command IDs specified by the `wIDNewItem` argument must not conflict with existing command IDs and are included in Windows event messages when a user selects the item at run time.

Next, the newly created pop-up menu is appended to the top-level menu using the `AppendMenu()` function. This time. the constant *MF_POPUP* (=&H10) specifies that the item being appended to the menu is a pop-up menu. The `wIDNewItem` argument must be a handle to a pop-up menu when *MF_POPUP* is used. The top-level menu is set to the Userform using the function `SetMenu()` and passing it the Userform and menu handles. The result of these statements is shown in Figure 17.5.

```
rv = AppendMenu(hMenu, MF_POPUP, hPopUpMenu, "Top-Level")
rv = SetMenu(hForm, hMenu)
```

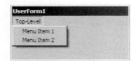

FIGURE 17.5 *A Userform containing menus created with the Windows API.*

When the Userform is closed, the menus should be destroyed with the `DestroyMenu()` function. You should add the following two statements to the `QueryClose()` event procedure of the `Userform` object:

```
DestroyMenu hPopUpMenu
DestroyMenu hMenu
```

As you can see, creating the menus is not too difficult. Of course, menus are normally used to trigger an event procedure that acts on the user's selection. However, no event procedures are automatically created for menus generated by DLL functions. Catching a menu event from a Userform menu created via the API requires a technique known as *subclassing*.

Subclassing a Userform

Windows are constantly receiving messages from the operating system. However, many of these messages don't trigger an action, so you don't notice changes to the window. The messages passed by the operating system can be intercepted by a custom window procedure that replaces the operating system's window procedure for a Userform.

 NOTE

Every window is associated with a special function called the *Windows function*. The function is named `WindowProc()`, and it receives messages from numerous sources including the Windows operating system.

Subclassing refers to a programming process that intercepts Windows messages before the target window processes them. The custom window procedure acts on the message or messages of interest before sending the remaining messages on to the original window procedure. It is critical that the original window procedure be called after the new window procedure acts on the messages of interest so that it can process all remaining messages. You have no way of knowing what messages are required by the original window procedure, and not passing the remaining messages will probably cause a general protection fault.

Subclassing a window is not difficult in theory, but it can be difficult in practice. The basic procedure for subclassing a window follows:

1. Use the `SetWindowLong()` function and pass it the following arguments: the handle to a window you want to subclass; the constant *GWL_WNDPROC* (=-4), which represents the memory address of the window function for the specified window; and the memory address of the custom window procedure that will be used to intercept window messages (use VBA `AddressOf` operator).

   ```
   hPrevWndProc = SetWindowLong(hForm, GWL_WNDPROC, AddressOf WindowProc)
   ```

2. Create a custom window procedure (`WindowProc`) for collecting all operating system messages passed by the subclassed window. The custom window procedure should act on the messages of interest before calling the original window procedure with the DLL function `CallWindowProc()`. The `CallWindowProc()` function should be passed the handle returned by the earlier call to the `SetWindowLong()` function along with the messages passed to the custom window procedure. The

definition of the custom window procedure and the declaration for the DLL function `CallWindowProc()` follow:

```
Public Function WindowProc(ByVal hWnd As Long, ByVal iMsg As Long, _
        ByVal wParam As Long, ByVal lParam As Long) As Long
    'Process message of interest here
    'Call original window procedure
End Function
Private Declare Function CallWindowProc Lib "user32.dll" Alias _
    "CallWindowProcA" (ByVal lpPrevWndFunc As Long, _
    ByVal hwnd As Long, ByVal msg As Long, ByVal wParam As Long, _
    ByVal lParam As Long) As Long
```

3. When it is no longer required, remove the subclassing with another call to the `SetWindowLong()` function that passes the handle to the original window procedure.

```
SetWindowLong(hForm, GWL_WNDPROC, hPrevWndProc)
```

Although the process of subclassing a window requires little code, it is not a trivial process. The operating system is very sensitive to bypassing the original `WindowProc()` Function procedure for a window, so I've had mixed success subclassing VBA Userforms, although my VBA programs that take advantage of subclassing techniques seem to be more stable in the Windows XP environment. Nevertheless, I don't recommend subclassing to the fainthearted. Save your work often and be prepared to reboot your computer or to frequently restart Excel.

Miscellaneous DLL Procedures

Finally, I have found a few miscellaneous, useful DLL functions. These functions are listed in Table 17.8, and their declarations follow the table.

Table 17.8 Miscellaneous DLL Functions

Function Name	Description
SleepEx	Delays program execution by a specified number of milliseconds.
GetSystemMetrics	Retrieves various system metrics and system configuration settings.
ScreenToClient	Converts the screen coordinates of a specified point on the screen to client coordinates.
GlobalMemoryStatusEx	Obtains information about the computer system's current usage of physical and virtual memory.

Function Name	Description
SetWindowPos	Sets the size, position, and Z order of a child, pop-up, or top-level window.
GetTopWindow	Retrieves a handle to a child window at the top of the Z order.
SetWindowPlacement	Sets the show state and the restored, minimized, and maximized positions of the specified window.
MoveWindow	Changes the position and dimensions of the specified window.

```
Private Declare Function SleepEx Lib "kernel32.dll" ( _
    ByVal dwMilliseconds As Long, ByVal bAlertable As Long) As Long
Private Declare Function GetSystemMetrics Lib "user32.dll" ( _
    ByVal nIndex As Long) As Long
Private Declare Function ScreenToClient Lib "user32.dll" ( _
    ByVal hwnd As Long, lpPoint As POINTAPI) As Long
Private Declare Function GlobalMemoryStatusEx Lib "kernel32.dll" ( _
    ByRef lpBuffer As MEMORYSTATUSEX) As Long
Private Declare Function SetWindowPos Lib "user32.dll" ( _
    ByVal hwnd As Long, ByVal hWndInsertAfter As Long, _
    ByVal x As Long, ByVal y As Long, ByVal cx As Long, _
    ByVal cy As Long, ByVal wFlags As Long) As Long
Private Declare Function SetWindowPlacement Lib "user32.dll" ( _
    ByVal hwnd As Long, lpwndpl As WINDOWPLACEMENT) As Long
Private Declare Function GetTopWindow Lib "user32.dll" ( _
    ByVal hwnd As Long) As Long
Private Declare Function MoveWindow Lib "user32.dll" ( _
    ByVal hwnd As Long, ByVal x As Long, ByVal y As Long, _
    ByVal nWidth As Long, ByVal nHeight As Long, _
    ByVal bRepaint As Long) As Long
```

Of particular interest is the GetSystemMetrics() function. Approximately 100 different constants can be used with the GetSystemMetrics() function to retrieve information about the Windows environment. When either of the constants *SM_CXSCREEN* (=0) or *SM_CYSCREEN* (=1) is passed to the GetSystemMetrics() function, it returns the screen width or height, respectively. This feature is not available in VBA as it is with the Screen object in VB, so I find it quite useful. Most of the system metrics are concerned with the size of the various components of a window or screen.

Summary

In this chapter, you learned how to incorporate the Windows API into a VBA program to greatly extend its power. Specifically, you learned how to add sound to a VBA program as well as manipulate the properties of a Userform. You also learned how to alter the appearance of a Userform by using drawing functions from the Windows API. Finally, I showed you how to add menus to a Userform and described the concept behind catching menu events.

Lastly, I want to reiterate that the Windows API should be used as a tool to extend the capability of your VBA program only when other methods are unavailable. For example, there is no discussion of the file I/O functions available through the Windows API in this chapter because VBA now includes adequate objects for handling file I/O operations.

Chapter 18

The previous two chapters introduce VBA objects and Windows API functions that you can use to view and retrieve data from the World Wide Web (WWW) and to enhance the look and capabilities of a VBA program. In this chapter, I use the tools discussed in the those two chapters to construct a stock ticker that retrieves stock quotes from the World Wide Web and displays them in a custom text box.

The stock ticker program uses an API-enhanced Userform as an interface for displaying stock quotes and related charts to the user. In addition to Web queries and API calls, the stock ticker program uses a third-party `Timer` object for animating the ticker and refreshing the Web query.

This chapter steps through the development of the stock ticker program while introducing more Windows API functions that draw text and retrieve bitmaps from the Windows clipboard.

Program Description

The interface for the stock ticker program is primarily within a single Userform that uses a custom text box built using Windows API functions to dynamically display relatively up-to-date (20 minute delay) stock quotes. In addition to the custom text box, the Userform contains Command Button controls and a Combo Box control that manages the list of company symbols currently being displayed. The user has the option of adding and removing company symbols from the ticker.

Stock quotes retrieved from the Web are stored in worksheets and can be viewed at any time as an Excel chart. Data from each Web query is temporarily stored in one worksheet, and the final daily value is stored permanently in another worksheet. Final daily values can be charted in order to display the history of stock prices for a company or market. The time period for a chart may range from either the current day or back to the start of the data set for a company. The charts essentially show the same data with more or less detail (daily, weekly, or monthly). The interface provides fast access to Excel charts by using Windows API calls to retrieve a bitmap of the desired chart from the clipboard and copy it to the Userform. The user can customize the ticker to include stock quotes for any company in the United States, Canada, or world markets listed at Yahoo!'s financial Web site (http://finance.yahoo.com). The ticker dynamically displays the data with either a horizontal or vertical scroll, and quotes are automatically refreshed every 20 minutes with a new Web query.

The stock ticker program is ideally suited for an Excel add-in because the interface can be entirely contained in a Userform, thus protecting the data in the worksheets. An example of the Userform used in the stock ticker program while the program is running is shown in Figure 18.1.

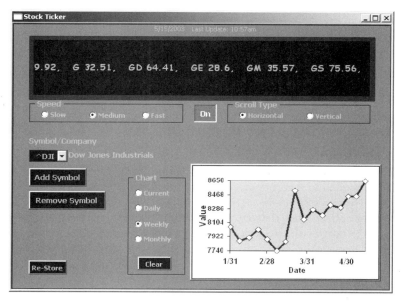

FIGURE 18.1 *An instance of the Userform from the stock ticker program as the program is running.*

Project Tools

Three main programming tools are used in the stock ticker program, although only one is visible to the user. First, a Userform serves as the interface for displaying the quotes and charts as previously described. Second, Windows API functions add styles to the User-form, draw shapes for the custom text box and charts, draw text representing the quotes, and copy bitmaps of Excel charts to the Userform. The third major tool is a third-party `Timer` object that controls the times at which the ticker is refreshed and the scrolling speed of the text in the custom text box.

I use these tools and other familiar components in VBA class modules and the Userforms that make up the stock ticker program.

Project Algorithm

While writing the stock ticker program, I followed an algorithm that listed the program's required components and a description of their function. For class modules, I describe the overall function of the class as well as the function of each of its members (properties and methods). The class modules included with the stock ticker program will customize the Userform, create the text box that dynamically displays the stock quotes, and manage the data.

Userforms serve as the interface for the program and are the only path for input by the user. When designing programs with Userforms, I sketch their appearance, including all ActiveX controls and then describe the function of each control. The main Userform in the stock ticker program should display the stock quotes and related charts and open a second Userform that allows the user to add and remove companies from the list as desired.

Finally, after the program is written and tested, it is embedded in the Excel utilities add-in created in Chapter 12, "Constructing the Excel-to-HTML Converter."

Custom Classes

When considering the design of the stock ticker program, I held to a requirement that two components be designed so that they can be easily incorporated into other VBA programs without editing. These two components are class modules, one that customizes a Userform (clsCustomForm) and another that creates a custom text box (clsDynamicTextBox). Other custom classes within the stock ticker program include a simple font class (clsFont) that is required to manage the appearance of the text displayed in the custom text box. Also, a symbol class (clsSymbol) and symbol collection class (clsSymbols) is written to manage the data retrieved from the Web queries. These two classes are specific to the stock ticker program and are not really suitable for use in other programs.

Although the stock ticker program does not require all members of the clsCustomForm class, every member is listed in Table 18.1. The properties defined by this class are used to set Userform styles that cannot be set from the VBA IDE. These properties must be set with Windows API functions declared in the class module. The stock ticker program may include repetitive declarations for some Windows API functions because these declarations must have Private scope in class modules. Methods of the clsCustomForm class will set the styles defined by its properties and copy bitmaps from system memory to a defined rectangle on the Userform.

Table 18.1 Members of the Custom Userform Class

Member	Type	Description
MinMaxButtons	Property	Boolean used to specify whether the Userform will contain minimize and maximize buttons.
Resizable	Property	Boolean used to specify whether the Userform will be resizable.
Taskbar	Property	Boolean used to specify whether the Userform will appear on the taskbar.

Member	Type	Description
FormIcon	Property	`Boolean` used to specify whether the Userform will contain an icon in its title bar.
Edge	Property	`Boolean` used to specify whether the Userform will have a specialized border.
UForm	Property	An object reference to the specific Userform to be customized.
SetStyles	Method	Sets the custom styles of the Userform.
CreateChartImage	Method	Copies an Excel chart to the customized Userform.
CopyFormImage	Method	Copies a bitmap of the customized Userform to memory.
RestoreFormImage	Method	Copies the memory bitmap (created by `CopyFormImage` method) back to the customized Userform.

The next custom class to describe is the one that constructs the text box used to display the stock quotes. I decided to create a custom text box rather than use existing ActiveX controls because drawing with Windows API functions is a much faster process than manipulating the strings representing the `Text` or `Caption` properties of Label and Text Box controls. You can also use the `Move` method of an ActiveX control to animate the text it contains, but this process is also relatively slow and can result in a "choppy" animation. As a result of the speed of the process, using Windows API functions creates a much smoother animation, making the text easier to read.

The class module that defines the `clsDynamicTextBox` class should contain properties that define its size, position, and formats (colors, font, and so on), much like a VBA Text Box control. In addition, the `clsDynamicTextBox` class will need style properties that define the dynamics of the text it displays (scroll type and speed). The custom text box should be drawn automatically when a variable of its type is instantiated in a program, so the only methods it needs are those for redrawing and clearing the area it defines. Properties and methods of the `clsDynamicTextBox` class are listed in Table 18.2.

 NOTE

The custom text box is not an ActiveX control and is in no way similar to the Label or Text Box controls included with VBA. It is simply a custom class that defines an area on a Userform on which shapes and text are drawn.

Table 18.2 Members of the Custom Text Box Class

Member Name	Type	Description
BackColor	Property	Long integer used to specify the RGB color of the background.
Border	Property	Boolean used to specify whether the text box has a border.
BorderColor	Property	Long integer used to specify the RGB color of the border.
BorderWidth	Property	Integer used to specify the width of the border in pixels.
Text	Property	String used to specify the text for display.
Style	Property	Integer used to specify whether the text box will have a raised of sunken appearance.
LeftSide	Property	Integer used to specify the location (in pixels relative to Userform coordinates) of the left side of the text box.
RightSide	Property	Integer used to specify the location (in pixels relative to Userform coordinates) of the right side of the text box.
Top	Property	Integer used to specify the location (in pixels relative to Userform coordinates) of the top of the text box.
Bottom	Property	Integer used to specify the location (in pixels relative to Userform coordinates) of the bottom of the text box.
Font	Property	Returns a Font object used to set the name, size, color, and style (italic or bold) of the text.
ScrollType	Property	Integer used to specify the direction of the scroll (horizontal or vertical).
Scroll	Property	Boolean used to toggle the animation on and off.
Speed	Property	Integer used to specify the speed of the text (three settings — slow, medium, and fast).
UForm	Property	An object that references the specific Userform to be customized.
Refresh	Method	Redraws the text box.
Clear	Method	Clears the text box.

In addition to its Public properties and methods, the clsDynamicTextBox class must contain Private procedures that draw the text box area and animate the text. A Timer object (see "The CCRP Timer Object" later in this chapter) embedded with the class controls the animation.

The two classes that are constructed specifically for the stock ticker program are the `clsSymbol` and `clsSymbols` collection classes. These classes will manage the data retrieved from the Web queries. The `clsSymbol` class is basic, containing properties that store the stock quotes for a single company along with the time and date of the quote and the company symbol used to retrieve the quote from the Yahoo! Web site. The `clsSymbols` collection class is more complex and includes the usual members for a collection class (`Add`, `Remove`, `Item`, and `Count`) along with a few methods used to update the text displayed in the custom text box. Members of the `clsSymbol` and `clsSymbols` collection classes are listed in Tables 18.3 and 18.4, respectively.

Table 18.3 Members of the Custom Symbol Class

Member	Type	Description
Symbol	Property	`String` representing a company's symbol as it appears on an exchange.
Value	Property	`String` representing the value of a company's stock.
DateTime	Property	`String` representing the date and time a quote was obtained from the Web.
ID	Property	`String` representing a unique identifier for a symbol. Required to add a `clsSymbol` object to the `clsSymbols` collection class.

Table 18.4 Members of the Custom Symbols Collection Class

Member	Type	Description
Count	Property	`Integer` representing the number of symbols stored in the collection.
Item	Method	Returns a `clsSymbol` object using its `ID` property as input.
Add	Method	Adds a new `clsSymbol` object to the collection.
Remove	Method	Removes a `clsSymbol` object from the collection.
FindBySymbol	Method	Returns a `clsSymbol` object using its symbol identifier as input.
GetSymbolString	Method	Returns a `String` that results from the concatenation of the `Symbol` property of all `clsSymbol` objects in the collection. Used for displaying in the custom text box.

continues

Table 18.4 Members of the Custom Symbols Collection Class (continued)

Member	Type	Description
GetSymbolWebQueryString	Method	Returns a `String` that results from the concatenation of the `Symbol` property of all `clsSymbol` objects in the collection. Contains the characters needed for submitting to Yahoo!'s financial Web site in order to return the stock quotes for each symbol included in the `String`.
Refresh	Method	Refreshes the Web query that returns new quotes for each `clsSymbol` object in the collection.

Finally, you use the `clsFont` class to set the properties of the `Font` object used with the `clsDynamicTextBox` class. The `clsFont` class contains simple `Public` properties used to set `Name`, `Size`, `Color`, `Bold`, and `Italic` properties of a `clsFont` object.

The User Interface

A single Userform provides the main interface to the stock ticker program and contains an instance of the `clsDynamicTextBox` class to serve as the ticker. ActiveX controls are used to display a list of companies currently contained in the ticker and to provide the ability to add or remove companies from this list. The interface also provides options for the scroll type and speed of the text animated in the custom text box and the specific chart to be copied to the Userform. The Design view image of the Userform interface is shown in Figure 18.2.

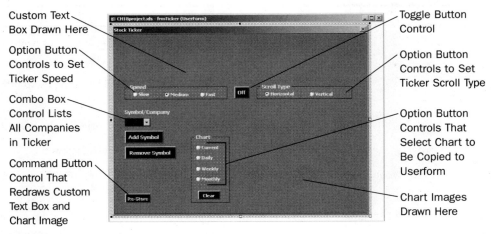

FIGURE 18.2 *Design view user interface used by the stock ticker program.*

Of course, one disadvantage of using the `clsDynamicTextBox` class to draw on a Userform is that you can't see the result until you run the program. Nevertheless, the custom text box will be drawn across the top of the Userform shown in Figure 18.2, and the area at the lower-right is reserved for chart images.

There's a problem with the Userform that you can't fix using techniques in this book: You can't automatically redraw custom areas of the Userform whenever necessary. Because Userform objects do not have an `AutoRedraw` property, the `Repaint` method does not redraw anything that was previously drawn with Windows API functions. I use a crude fix here consisting of a Command Button control (named `cmdRestore`) that invokes the appropriate methods of the `clsCustomForm` and `clsDynamicTextBox` classes to redraw any shapes or images that were on the Userform.

TIP

To effectively repaint a Userform that was drawn on using Windows API functions, the window must be sub-classed. With a sub-classed Userform, you can intercept operating system messages that are sent to repaint the window and invoke your own repainting method.

You can add a company symbol to the ticker with a click of a Command Button control named `cmdAddSymbol` (`Caption` property "Add Symbol"). Doing so will load and show a second Userform whose functions are to add a new symbol to the list of companies stored in an Excel worksheet, update the Combo Box control `cmbSymbols`, and update the `clsSymbols` collection object. The Design view Userform (`frmAddSymbol`) is shown in Figure 18.3, and the layout of the Excel worksheet that holds the company names and symbols is shown in Figure 18.4.

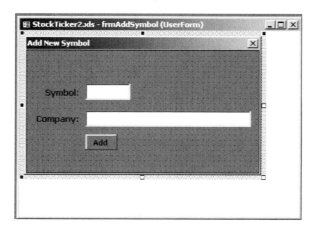

FIGURE 18.3 *Design view of Userform used to add new companies to the stock ticker.*

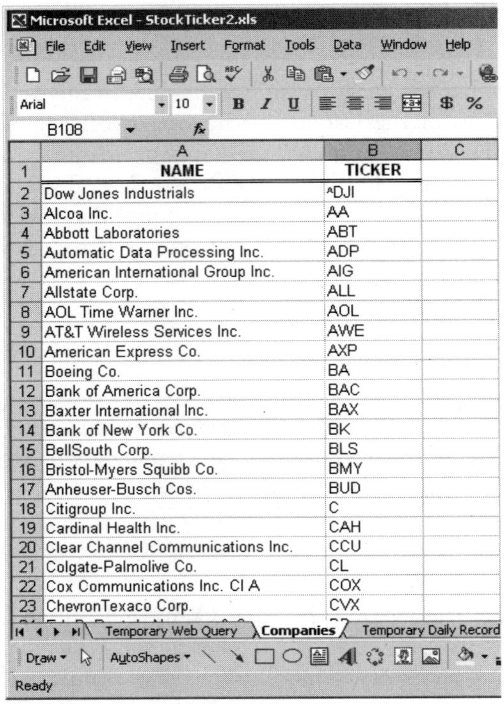

	A	B	C
1	NAME	TICKER	
2	Dow Jones Industrials	^DJI	
3	Alcoa Inc.	AA	
4	Abbott Laboratories	ABT	
5	Automatic Data Processing Inc.	ADP	
6	American International Group Inc.	AIG	
7	Allstate Corp.	ALL	
8	AOL Time Warner Inc.	AOL	
9	AT&T Wireless Services Inc.	AWE	
10	American Express Co.	AXP	
11	Boeing Co.	BA	
12	Bank of America Corp.	BAC	
13	Baxter International Inc.	BAX	
14	Bank of New York Co.	BK	
15	BellSouth Corp.	BLS	
16	Bristol-Myers Squibb Co.	BMY	
17	Anheuser-Busch Cos.	BUD	
18	Citigroup Inc.	C	
19	Cardinal Health Inc.	CAH	
20	Clear Channel Communications Inc.	CCU	
21	Colgate-Palmolive Co.	CL	
22	Cox Communications Inc. Cl A	COX	
23	ChevronTexaco Corp.	CVX	

FIGURE 18.4 *Excel worksheet used to hold company names and symbols.*

After you activate the Userform, follow these steps for the stock ticker program:

1. Customize the Userform by setting the properties of the `clsCustomForm` class.
2. Draw the custom text box on the Userform by instantiating a variable of the `clsDynamicTextBox` class.
3. Initialize ActiveX controls including the Combo Box control used to display companies whose stock quotes will be added to the ticker. Company symbols and names are stored in a worksheet (refer to Figure 18.4). When companies are added or deleted from the list, this worksheet is updated.
4. Initialize the worksheets storing the data. Two worksheets are used to store the data — one worksheet temporarily stores the daily quotes and another permanently stores the final daily value. When the program starts, it should copy the final value from the temporary worksheet to the permanent sheet, if necessary. Figures 18.5 and 18.6 show the layout of each worksheet.
5. The ticker begins with a click of a Toggle Button control. This initiates the Web query and starts the ticker. The Web query is refreshed every 20 minutes using the `InternetExplorer` and `QueryTable` objects. Data from the query is temporarily stored in another worksheet (see Figure 18.7) overwriting the

data from the previous query before it is copied to the worksheet shown in Figure 18.5.

6. By selecting the appropriate Option Buttons, you can enable the ticker to scroll text horizontally or vertically at three different speeds. These buttons simply change the properties of the object variable referencing the `clsDynamicTextBox` class.

7. A line chart showing the results from the current day, or the stored history of daily values for any company, is copied to the Userform when the user selects one of the chart options.

8. The custom text box and selected charts are redrawn with the click of a Command Button control.

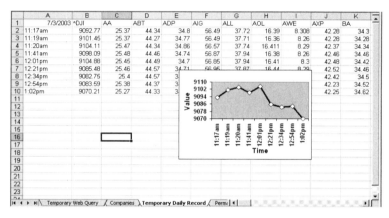

FIGURE 18.5 *Temporary Daily Record worksheet that stores the current (single day) quotes for companies listed in the stock ticker.*

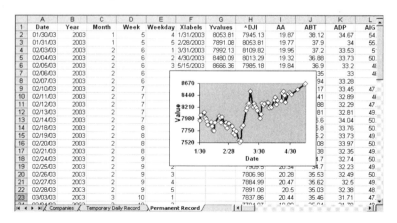

FIGURE 18.6 *Permanent Record worksheet that stores final daily values for companies listed in the stock ticker.*

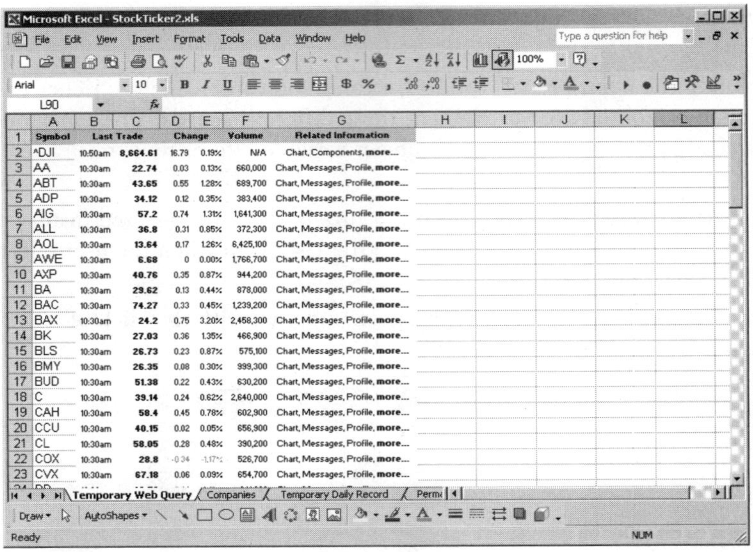

FIGURE 18.7 *Temporary Web Query worksheet that stores most recent stock quotes retrieved from a Web query.*

Interval Code Execution in VBA

Many programming languages provide the ability to create multiple processes (threads) within a program, or, at the very least, they provide tools for executing code at specific intervals. In VB (version 6 and earlier), interval code execution is provided by the Timer control. The VB Timer control contains an event procedure whose code is executed at time increments specified by the `Interval` property of the control. This makes the Timer control a powerful tool for the VB programmer; however, it does have some drawbacks. Namely, the VB Timer control must be drawn on a Form in order to use it, even if the Form is not needed in the program. Furthermore, the minimum time resolution is significantly higher than the allowed setting of one millisecond. In reality, the minimum interval is more than 50 milliseconds. However, I would happily take VB's Timer control over what is included with VBA's objects and ActiveX controls, which is next to nothing.

NOTE

Since VBA does not include a Timer control and the VB Timer control is inaccessible from VBA (even if VB 6.0 is installed on your computer), I will use a third-party Timer control in the stock ticker program. The CCRP Timer control is freely available for download from the Internet, and I discuss how to use it after a brief introduction to VBA's `OnTime` method.

The OnTime Method

The OnTime method is a member of Excel's Application object and can be used to initiate code execution at a specified time or at regular intervals. The syntax for the OnTime method follows:

```
Application.OnTime(EarliestTime, Procedure, LatestTime, Schedule)
```

Where the *EarliestTime* argument specifies the time you want the procedure specified in the *Procedure* argument to execute. The *LatestTime* and *Schedule* arguments are optional and specify the latest time at which the procedure can be run and a Boolean value indicating whether to schedule a new OnTime procedure or clear an existing one. The following statement schedules execution of the MyProc() procedure five seconds from the current system time:

```
Application.OnTime EarliestTime:=Now + TimeValue("00:00:05"), _
    Procedure:="MyProc"
```

The OnTime method can also be used to schedule a procedure's execution at regular intervals similar to the Timer() event of VB's Timer control. With each call to the MyProc() Sub procedure, the OnTime method schedules the next call to occur one second later. After the procedure executes 10 times, the next call to the procedure set with the OnTime method is cancelled. When the MyProc() Sub procedure executes, the numbers 0–9 are output to the Immediate window.

```
Sub MyProc()
    Static I As Integer
    Application.OnTime EarliestTime:=Now + TimeValue("00:00:01"), _
        Procedure:="MyProc", Schedule:=True
    Debug.Print I
    I = I + 1
    If I >= 10 Then
        Application.OnTime EarliestTime:=Now + TimeValue("00:00:01"), _
            Procedure:="MyProc", Schedule:=False
    End If
End Sub
```

Although the OnTime method can be used to initiate code execution at regular intervals in a VBA program, it has some serious limitations. First, its minimum time resolution is one second, so it is not particularly useful for animations. Second, its performance is spotty at best. The method often raises a failed to execute error. The work-around for this error is to construct a simple error handler that resumes program execution at the line that calls the OnTime method. This process is repeated until the OnTime method executes without error. However, this is a brute-force approach to solving the problem, and it doesn't always work. As a result of the problems inherent to the OnTime method, I don't recommend using it for anything other than scheduling one execution of an external procedure. Instead, I recommend finding or creating an ActiveX control or other object that can be used to initiate interval code execution in your program. Thankfully, such objects or controls already exist and are freely available for download from the Internet.

The CCRP Timer Object

The Common Controls Replacement Project (CCRP) is a group of VB programmers who got together and decided to create a series of ActiveX controls for the VB programming community. Some of the CCRP controls were meant to serve as replacements for the controls included with VB 6 with improved performance. One of these controls is the `Timer` object.

 NOTE

The CCRP `Timer` object and other timer-related objects can be downloaded at http://www.mvps.org/ccrp/download/ccrpdownloads.htm. You will notice that work was suspended on these objects and controls once Microsoft released VB.NET. As with any Web site mentioned in this book, there are no guarantees the content of the site will still exist at the time you read this.

Installation of the CCRP `Timer` objects is easy. Just unzip the file and move the files ccrpTmr6.dll, ccrpTmr6.dep, and ccrpTmr6.tlb to your Windows\System directory. You should also move the help file, ccrpTmr6.chm, to your Windows\Help directory.

Before you can use the CCRP `Timer` object in a VBA program, you must set a reference to its object library by selecting Tools, References from the VBA IDE and then choosing CCRP High Performance Timer Objects from the Available References dialog box as shown in Figure 18.8.

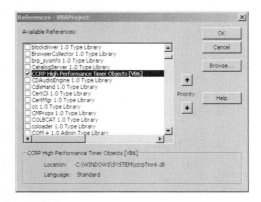

FIGURE 18.8 *Adding the CCRP* Timer *object to a VBA application.*

To create an instance of a CCRP `Timer` object, declare a module-level variable in the general declarations section of a Userform, class, or other component module (basically, anything but a standard module).

```
Private WithEvents Timer1 As ccrpTimer
```

Be sure to include the `WithEvents` keyword in the declaration to enable the `Timer()` event (defined in following code) for this object. To execute code at regular intervals, you must first set the `Enabled` (`Boolean`) property to `True` and then set the `Interval` (`Long`) property to a specified number of milliseconds.

```
Timer1.Enabled = True
Timer1.Interval = 100
Private Sub Timer1_Timer(ByVal Milliseconds As Long)
    'Code to be executed at a specified interval is entered here.
End Sub
```

The two great features of this object are that it doesn't have to be drawn on a Userform and its minimum resolution is truly one millisecond (assuming that your hardware is capable of processing at this time interval). `Timer` objects are very useful tools in any programming language, and the CCRP `Timer` object will play an important role in the stock ticker program.

Drawing Text Using the Windows API

Before continuing with the construction of the stock ticker program, allow me to introduce you to some more Windows API functions — namely, those API functions that you can use to draw text to a device context.

Drawing text using Windows API functions is very similar to drawing shapes or other graphics. In general, you follow these steps to draw text with Windows API functions:

1. Obtain a device context on which to draw the text.
2. Create a font to use for drawing.
3. Select the font into the device context.
4. Set text attributes such as colors and position.
5. Draw the text.
6. Restore objects as necessary.
7. Release memory as necessary.

As might be expected, drawing text can be complicated. Various font attributes, such as character cell dimensions and family (Decorative, Roman, Script, and so on), can influence the text output function you use. Of course, your program's requirements will also influence the text output function you will want to use.

API Text Output Functions

You can use several Windows API functions to output text to a device context (or support that output). These functions vary according to capability and complexity, and some of the more common ones are listed in Table 18.5.

Table 18.5 Windows API Functions for Outputting Text

Function	Description
CreateFont	Creates a Font object with specified attributes and returns a handle (Long) to the newly created object.
DrawText	Draws text into a specified rectangle on a device context and returns the height of the drawn text.
DrawTextEx	Similar to DrawText with additional formatting arguments.
ExtTextOut	Extended drawing function. Gives more control over the font spacing. Returns nonzero on success and zero on failure.
TextOut	Most basic text drawing function.
GetCharWidth32	Retrieves the width of one or more characters in a font.
GetTextExtentExPoint32	Determines the extents (the size that a block of text will take up on the output device) of a String.
GetTextAlign	Returns the current text alignment for a device context.
GetTextColor	Returns the current text color a device context.
GetTextMetrics	Returns information about the current Font object selected for a device context.
SetTextAlign	Sets the text alignment for a device context.
SetTextColor	Sets the text color for a device context.
SetBkColor	Sets the background color for a device context.

You can check in an up-to-date API viewer (for example, APIViewer 2003 available at www.allapi.net) for the declarations and supporting constants and structures for the functions listed in Table 18.5 that are not listed with the examples in this chapter. For now, take a closer look at the CreateFont() and DrawText() functions.

The CreateFont() function creates a logical font with the specified attributes. The declarative statement for the CreateFont() function includes a long list of arguments used to define the attributes of the font.

```
Private Declare Function CreateFont Lib "gdi32.dll" Alias _
    "CreateFontA" (ByVal H As Long, ByVal W As Long, ByVal E As Long, _
    ByVal O As Long, ByVal W As Long, ByVal I As Long, _
    ByVal u As Long, ByVal S As Long, ByVal C As Long, _
    ByVal OP As Long, ByVal CP As Long, ByVal Q As Long, _
    ByVal PAF As Long, ByVal F As String) As Long
```

The argument names are shortened here because of the length of the declaration. The arguments of the CreateFont() function are defined in Table 18.6. Several defined constants can be used with these arguments, and they can be found in any up-to-date API viewer.

Table 18.6 Arguments of the CreateFont API Function

Argument	Description
H	Specifies the height of the font in pixels.
W	Specifies the width of the font in pixels.
E	Specifies the font escapement or angle between the character and the x-axis of the device.
O	Specifies the font orientation or angle between each character and the x-axis of the device.
W	Specifies the font weight. Ranges from 0–1000. A value of 400 is normal, and 700 is bold.
I	Specifies that the font is italic. Use 1 to specify italic font, 0 for a normal font.
U	Specifies that the font is underlined (1 for underlined, 0 for no underline).
S	Specifies that the font has a strikethrough effect (1 for stikethrough, 0 for no strikethrough).
C	Specifies the character set. The defined constants end with CHARSET.
OP	Specifies the output precision. The output precision defines how closely the output must match the requested font's height, width, character orientation, escapement, pitch, and font type. Several defined constants begin with OUT.
CP	Specifies the clipping precision. The clipping precision defines how to clip characters that are partially outside the clipping region. Several defined constants begin with CLIP.

continues

Table 18.6 Arguments of the CreateFont API Function *(continued)*

Argument	Description
Q	Specifies the output quality. The output quality defines how carefully GDI must attempt to match the logical-font attributes to those of an actual physical font. The defined constants end with QUALITY.
PAF	Specifies the pitch and family of the font. The defined constants begin with FF.
F	Pointer to a null-terminated String that specifies the typeface name of the font. The length of this String must not exceed 32 characters, including the null terminator. In VBA, simply use a String containing the name of the font.

The following call to the CreateFont() function creates a Font object using the Times New Roman font face whose characters are 8 x 16 (width x height) pixels with a normal weight and no angles relative to the baseline of the characters (normal). The default attributes are used for all other arguments. The CreateFont() function returns a Long value representing a handle to the Font object that is created (hFont).

```
Private Const DEFAULT_CHARSET As Long = 1
Private Const OUT_DEFAULT_PRECIS As Long = 0
Private Const DEFAULT_PITCH As Long = 0
Private Const DEFAULT_QUALITY As Long = 0
Private Const CLIP_DEFAULT_PRECIS As Long = 0
hFont = CreateFont(16, 8, 0, 0, 400, 0, 0, 0, DEFAULT_CHARSET, _
    OUT_DEFAULT_PRECIS, CLIP_DEFAULT_PRECIS, DEFAULT_QUALITY, _
    DEFAULT_PITCH, "Times New Roman")
oObject = SelectObject(dcForm, hFont)
```

To draw text to a device context, you must select the Font object into the device context before using one of the text output functions such as DrawText().

```
Private Declare Function DrawText Lib "user32.dll" Alias "DrawTextA" ( _
    ByVal hdc As Long, ByVal lpStr As String, ByVal nCount As Long, _
    lpRect As RECT, ByVal wFormat As Long) As Long
```

The DrawText() function requires a handle to the device context in which to draw text (hdc), the String of characters that is to be drawn (lpStr), the number of characters within lpStr to draw (nCount, use −1 to draw all of them), a defining rectangle in which the text is to be drawn (lpRect), and, finally, the format to be used in drawing the text (wFormat, a combination of several defined constants beginning with DT). The DrawText() function returns the height of the text that was drawn. The following example assumes that a device context named dcForm has already been retrieved or created. The variable `frmRect` is of user-defined type `RECT` (defined in next example) and is filled with the boundaries of the drawing rectangle relative to the coordinates of the device context.

```
rv = DrawText(dcForm, "Drawing with the API", -1, frmRect, DT_CENTER _
    Or DT_VCENTER Or DT_SINGLELINE)
```

Some of the defined formatting constants used to format the justification of the text are listed next. The names of these constants describe their function.

```
Private Const DT_BOTTOM As Long = &H8
Private Const DT_CENTER As Long = &H1   'Center horizontally
Private Const DT_LEFT As Long = &H0
Private Const DT_NOCLIP As Long = &H100
Private Const DT_RIGHT As Long = &H2
Private Const DT_TOP As Long = &H0
Private Const DT_VCENTER As Long = &H4   'Center vertically
Private Const DT_WORDBREAK As Long = &H10
```

Next, take a look at an example of the `CreateFont()` and `DrawText()` functions in a VBA program that demonstrates how to draw text on a Userform.

Drawing Text on a Userform

When added to the code module of a VBA Userform, the following program will draw the `String` `"Drawing with the API"` at the center of the Userform. Several ActiveX controls, including Scroll Bars, a List Box, and two Check Boxes, are used to alter the appearance of the text. A running illustration of the program is shown in Figure 18.9.

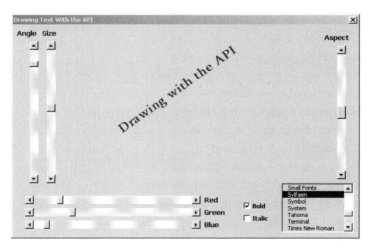

FIGURE 18.9 *Drawing text on a Userform using the Windows API.*

The names of the ActiveX controls are descriptive of their functions. The Min and Max properties of the Scroll Bars set the limits of their Value property (0–255 for the Scroll Bars that set the color of the font, 0–3600 for the angle, 6–64 for the size, and 10–50 for the Aspect ratio). You set the angle (specified in tenths of a degree) of the text with the *Escapement* and *Orientation* arguments of the CreateFont() function. You calculate the aspect ratio by dividing the Value property of its associated Scroll Bar by 10 so that font aspect ratios between 1 and 5 (graduated by tenths) are used to draw the text.

The general declarations section of the Userform's code module contains the API declarations, constants, and type definitions that are used in the program.

```
Option Explicit
'........................

'API Declarations
Private Declare Function FindWindow Lib "user32.dll" Alias _
     "FindWindowA" (ByVal lpClassName As String, ByVal _
     lpWindowName As String) As Long
Private Declare Function GetDC Lib "user32.dll" ( _
     ByVal hwnd As Long) As Long
Private Declare Function SaveDC Lib "gdi32.dll" ( _
     ByVal hdc As Long) As Long
Private Declare Function ReleaseDC Lib "user32.dll" ( _
     ByVal hwnd As Long, ByVal hdc As Long) As Long
Private Declare Function RestoreDC Lib "gdi32.dll" ( _
     ByVal hdc As Long, ByVal nSavedDC As Long) As Long
Private Declare Function CreateFont Lib "gdi32.dll" Alias _
     "CreateFontA" (ByVal h As Long, ByVal W As Long, ByVal E As Long, _
     ByVal O As Long, ByVal W As Long, ByVal I As Long, _
     ByVal u As Long, ByVal s As Long, ByVal c As Long, _
     ByVal OP As Long, ByVal CP As Long, ByVal q As Long, _
     ByVal PAF As Long, ByVal f As String) As Long
Private Declare Function DrawText Lib "user32.dll" Alias "DrawTextA" _
     (ByVal hdc As Long, ByVal lpStr As String, ByVal nCount As Long, _
     lpRect As RECT, ByVal wFormat As Long) As Long
Private Declare Function SetBkColor Lib "gdi32.dll" ( _
     ByVal hdc As Long, ByVal crColor As Long) As Long
Private Declare Function SetTextColor Lib "gdi32.dll" ( _
     ByVal hdc As Long, ByVal crColor As Long) As Long
Private Declare Function DeleteObject Lib "gdi32.dll" ( _
     ByVal hObject As Long) As Long
```

```
Private Declare Function SelectObject Lib "gdi32.dll" ( _
    ByVal hdc As Long, ByVal hObject As Long) As Long
Private Declare Function GetClientRect Lib "user32" ( _
    ByVal hwnd As Long, lpRect As RECT) As Long
'...................
'Constants and Types
Private Const DT_CENTER As Long = &H1
Private Const DT_SINGLELINE As Long = &H20
Private Const DT_VCENTER As Long = &H4
Private Const DEFAULT_CHARSET As Long = 1
Private Const OUT_DEFAULT_PRECIS As Long = 0
Private Const DEFAULT_PITCH As Long = 0
Private Const DEFAULT_QUALITY As Long = 0
Private Const CLIP_DEFAULT_PRECIS As Long = 0
Private Const RGB_RED = 200
Private Const RGB_GREEN = 200
Private Const RGB_BLUE = 200


Private Type RECT
    Left As Long
    Top As Long
    Right As Long
    Bottom As Long
End Type
```

The `Initialize()` event of the `Userform` object initializes the background color of the ActiveX controls it contains and the list box that holds the list of available fonts. You should use the same background color with the device context so that the drawing rectangle will not be visible to the user. You can retrieve a list of available fonts from the Combo Box control contained on Excel's formatting toolbar (see Figure 18.10). Specifically, the control that contains the font names is called a CommandBar Combo Box, and it is the first control on the toolbar. After you set an object reference to this control, its `List` property is used with the `AddItem` method of the List Box control (`lstFonts`) to display the available fonts.

CommandBar Combo Box Control

FIGURE 18.10 *Excel's formatting toolbar.*

```
Private Sub UserForm_Initialize()
    Dim c As Control
    Dim I As Integer
    Dim fCntrl As CommandBarComboBox
    '----------------------------------------------------
    'Set reference to font combo box on formatting toolbar
    '----------------------------------------------------
    Application.CommandBars("Formatting").Visible = True
    Set fCntrl = Application.CommandBars("Formatting").Controls(1)
    '--------------------
    'Add fonts to list box
    '--------------------
    lstFonts.Clear
    With fCntrl
        For I = 1 To .ListCount
            lstFonts.AddItem .List(I)
        Next I
    End With
    '--------------------
    'Set background color
    '--------------------
    frmAPIText.BackColor = RGB(RGB_RED, RGB_GREEN, RGB_BLUE)
    For Each c In frmAPIText.Controls
        c.BackColor = RGB(RGB_RED, RGB_GREEN, RGB_BLUE)
    Next
End Sub
```

The `DrawString()` Sub procedure is guided by the procedure listed earlier in this chapter for drawing text. First, a handle to the Userform is obtained with `FindWindow()` and immediately used to retrieve a device context using `GetDC()`. Next, the `Font` object is created with the `CreateFont()` function and selected into the device context with `SelectObject()`. Many of the arguments for the `CreateFont()` function are obtained from the values of the ActiveX controls contained on the Userform. For example, the font name is obtained from the `Text` property of the List Box control named `lstFonts`. The coordinates of the client region of the Userform are loaded into the `frmRect` (user-defined type `RECT`) variable after setting the text and background colors of the device context. The `frmRect` variable is then passed to the `DrawText()` function to output the `String` to the center of the Userform. Note that when centering text vertically with *DT_VCENTER*, you must also use the constant *DT_SINGLELINE*. Lastly, the font and device context objects are released from system memory.

```
Private Sub DrawString()
    Dim rv As Long
    Dim hForm As Long, dcForm As Long, oDC As Long
    Dim hFont As Long, oColor As Long, oObject As Long
    Dim frmRect As RECT
    Dim fAspect As Single, fBold As Long, fItalic As Long

    fAspect = scrAspect.Value / 10
    If ckBold Then fBold = 700 Else fBold = 400
    If ckItalic Then fItalic = 1 Else fItalic = 0


    '-----------------------------------------------
    'Get userform handle, DC, and create font object
    '-----------------------------------------------
    hForm = FindWindow(vbNullString, "Drawing Text With the API")
    dcForm = GetDC(hForm)
    oDC = SaveDC(dcForm)
    hFont = CreateFont(scrSize.Value, scrSize.Value / fAspect, _
        scrEsc.Value, scrEsc.Value, fBold, fItalic, 0, 0, _
        DEFAULT_CHARSET, OUT_DEFAULT_PRECIS, CLIP_DEFAULT_PRECIS, _
        DEFAULT_QUALITY, DEFAULT_PITCH, lstFonts.Text)
    oObject = SelectObject(dcForm, hFont)


    '------------------------
    'Set colors and draw text
    '------------------------
    oColor = SetTextColor(dcForm, RGB(scrRed.Value, scrGreen.Value, _
        scrBlue.Value))
    SetBkColor dcForm, RGB(RGB_RED, RGB_GREEN, RGB_BLUE)
    GetClientRect hForm, frmRect
    DrawText dcForm, "Drawing with the API", -1, frmRect, DT_CENTER Or _
        DT_VCENTER Or DT_SINGLELINE


    '---------
    'Clean up
    '---------
    SelectObject dcForm, oObject
    SetTextColor dcForm, oColor
```

```
        RestoreDC dcForm, oDC
        ReleaseDC hForm, dcForm
        DeleteObject hFont
    End Sub
```

The `Click()` events of the List Box and Check Box controls along with the `Change()` events of the Scroll Bar controls all contain the same two lines of code. The Userform is repainted before the `DrawString()` Sub procedure is called to redraw the `String` using the updated parameters with the `DrawText()` API function. Nine event procedures contain these two lines of code, but only one is listed here.

```
    Private Sub lstFonts_Click()
        frmAPIText.Repaint
        DrawString
    End Sub
```

The advantage to using the Windows API for drawing text on a Userform is that you can quickly draw text at any angle on the Userform. This is not possible using Label or Text Box controls that can only draw text at the normal angle.

Programming the Stock Ticker

Now that you are familiar with the program design and the tools used to write it, you are ready to begin building the stock ticker. You start with the custom classes before proceeding to the Userform code module. After testing the stock ticker, the individual modules are added to the Excel utilities add-in created in Chapter 12.

Custom Classes

The stock ticker program uses five custom classes, one for customizing the Userform, two more for creating and supporting the text box that will serve as the ticker, and two more for managing the data that is displayed in the ticker.

Custom Userform Class (clsCustomForm)

You use the class module named `clsCustomForm` to customize a Userform, and it contains members that set the window's styles and copy bitmaps from the clipboard to a defined area on the Userform. The class module contains a number of Windows API declarative statements and associated constants. I discussed most of these functions have in Chapter 17, "Accessing the Windows API with VBA"; however, the clipboard functions are new and are used to retrieve a handle to a bitmap that has been copied to the clipboard. I discuss them later in this section. The properties or this class are simple `Boolean` variables used to set a Userfom's styles with the exception of `UForm`, which is an object variable that represents the Userform to be customized.

```
Option Explicit
'----------------------------
'API Function Declarations
Private Declare Function FindWindow Lib "user32.dll" Alias _
    "FindWindowA" (ByVal lpClassName As String, ByVal _
    lpWindowName As String) As Long
Private Declare Function ShowWindow Lib "user32" ( _
    ByVal hwnd As Long, ByVal nCmdShow As Long) As Long
Private Declare Function DrawMenuBar Lib "user32" ( _
    ByVal hwnd As Long) As Long
Private Declare Function SetWindowLong Lib "user32.dll" Alias _
    "SetWindowLongA" (ByVal hwnd As Long, ByVal nIndex As Long, _
    ByVal dwNewLong As Long) As Long
Private Declare Function GetWindowLong Lib "user32.dll" Alias _
    "GetWindowLongA" (ByVal hwnd As Long, ByVal nIndex As Long) As Long
Private Declare Function BitBlt Lib "gdi32.dll" ( _
    ByVal hDestDC As Long, ByVal x As Long, ByVal y As Long, _
    ByVal nWidth As Long, ByVal nHeight As Long, _
    ByVal hSrcDC As Long, ByVal xSrc As Long, ByVal ySrc As Long, _
    ByVal dwRop As Long) As Long
Private Declare Function CreateCompatibleDC Lib "gdi32.dll" ( _
    ByVal hdc As Long) As Long
Private Declare Function CreateCompatibleBitmap Lib "gdi32.dll" ( _
    ByVal hdc As Long, ByVal nWidth As Long, _
    ByVal nHeight As Long) As Long
Private Declare Function GetDC Lib "user32.dll" ( _
    ByVal hwnd As Long) As Long
Private Declare Function SaveDC Lib "gdi32.dll" ( _
    ByVal hdc As Long) As Long
Private Declare Function ReleaseDC Lib "user32.dll" ( _
    ByVal hwnd As Long, ByVal hdc As Long) As Long
Private Declare Function RestoreDC Lib "gdi32.dll" ( _
    ByVal hdc As Long, ByVal nSavedDC As Long) As Long
Private Declare Function DeleteObject Lib "gdi32.dll" ( _
    ByVal hObject As Long) As Long
Private Declare Function DeleteDC Lib "gdi32.dll" ( _
    ByVal hdc As Long) As Long
```

```
Private Declare Function GetWindowRect Lib "user32.dll" ( _
    ByVal hwnd As Long, lpRect As RECT) As Long
Private Declare Function SelectObject Lib "gdi32.dll" ( _
    ByVal hdc As Long, ByVal hObject As Long) As Long
Private Declare Function GetClientRect Lib "user32" ( _
    ByVal hwnd As Long, lpRect As RECT) As Long
Private Declare Function DrawEdge Lib "user32.dll" (ByVal hdc As Long, _
    qrc As RECT, ByVal Edge As Long, ByVal grfFlags As Long) As Long
Private Declare Function InflateRect Lib "user32.dll" ( _
    lpRect As RECT, ByVal x As Long, ByVal y As Long) As Long
Private Declare Function IsClipboardFormatAvailable Lib "user32.dll" _
    (ByVal wFormat As Long) As Long
Private Declare Function OpenClipboard Lib "user32.dll" ( _
    ByVal hwnd As Long) As Long
Private Declare Function GetClipboardData Lib "user32.dll" ( _
    ByVal wFormat As Long) As Long
Private Declare Function CloseClipboard Lib "user32.dll" () As Long
Private Declare Function CopyImage Lib "user32.dll" ( _
    ByVal handle As Long, ByVal un1 As Long, ByVal n1 As Long, _
    ByVal n2 As Long, ByVal un2 As Long) As Long


'----------
'Constants
Private Const CF_BITMAP = 2      'Clipboard format
'Image type for CopyImage function
Private Const IMAGE_BITMAP As Long = 0
Private Const LR_COPYDELETEORG As Long = &H8
Private Const WS_THICKFRAME As Long = &H40000    'Re-size window
Private Const WS_MINIMIZEBOX As Long = &H20000   'Window minimize button
Private Const WS_MAXIMIZEBOX As Long = &H10000   'Window maximize button
'Window standard. Remove to show taskbar
Private Const WS_POPUP As Long = &H80000000
'Window standard. Remove to show task bar
Private Const WS_VISIBLE As Long = &H10000000
Private Const WS_EX_APPWINDOW As Long = &H40000 'Show window on task bar
'Show icon in window title bar
Private Const WS_EX_DLGMODALFRAME As Long = &H1&
```

```vb
'Edge the client region of window
Private Const WS_EX_CLIENTEDGE As Long = &H200&
Private Const GWL_STYLE As Long = -16    'Return/set window styles
Private Const GWL_EXSTYLE As Long = -20 'Return/set extended styles
Private Const SW_HIDE As Long = 0    'Hide window
Private Const SW_SHOW As Long = 5    'Show window
Private Const SRCCOPY As Long = &HCC0020      'Straight copy with BitBlt
'Borders for DrawEdge function
Private Const BDR_SUNKENINNER As Long = &H8
Private Const BDR_RAISEDOUTER As Long = &H1
Private Const BDR_RAISEDINNER As Long = &H4
Private Const BDR_SUNKENOUTER As Long = &H2
Private Const BDR_INNER As Long = &HC
Private Const BDR_OUTER As Long = &H3
Private Const BDR_RAISED As Long = &H5
Private Const BDR_SUNKEN As Long = &HA


'Border flags for DrawEdge function
Private Const BF_MIDDLE As Long = &H800
Private Const BF_TOP As Long = &H2
Private Const BF_LEFT As Long = &H1
Private Const BF_RIGHT As Long = &H4
Private Const BF_BOTTOM As Long = &H8


Private Type RECT
    Left As Long
    Top As Long
    Right As Long
    Bottom As Long
End Type


'-----------------------------------
'Public properties
Public MinMaxButtons As Boolean
Public Resizable As Boolean
Public Taskbar As Boolean
Public FormIcon As Boolean
```

```
Public Edge As Boolean
Public UForm As Object


'.................................
'Module-level handles and DC's
Private hForm As Long
Private dcForm As Long
Private oDC As Long
Private hbitForm As Long
Private dcbitForm As Long
```

The `Initialize()` event procedure of a class module is a great place to set default values for class variables. `Boolean` variables are initialized as `False` by VBA, so for the `clsCustomForm` class, you need to set only those properties whose default values you want to be `True`.

The `SetStyles()` method sets the Userform's styles as specified by the property values using the `GetWindowLong()` and `SetWindowLong()` functions as discussed in Chapter 17. The `SetStyles` method must be invoked from the program that incorporates this class for changes to take effect.

```
Private Sub Class_Initialize()
'Initialize default values for properties
    MinMaxButtons = True
    Taskbar = True
    Edge = True
End Sub
Public Sub SetStyles()
'Set form styles from specified properties
    Dim curStyle As Long, curXStyle As Long

    hForm = FindWindow(vbNullString, UForm.Caption)
    dcForm = GetDC(hForm)
    oDC = SaveDC(dcForm)
    If hForm = 0 Then
        Err.Raise 513, "clsCustomForm", "Unable to return pointer " & _
            "to Userform window!"
        Exit Sub
    End If
    If hForm <> 0 And UForm.Caption <> vbNullString Then
        curStyle = GetWindowLong(hForm, GWL_STYLE)
```

```
        If MinMaxButtons Then
            curStyle = curStyle Or WS_MINIMIZEBOX Or WS_MAXIMIZEBOX
        End If
        If Resizable Then curStyle = curStyle Or WS_THICKFRAME

        curXStyle = GetWindowLong(hForm, GWL_EXSTYLE)
        If Taskbar Then
            curXStyle = curXStyle Or WS_EX_APPWINDOW
            curStyle = curStyle And Not WS_POPUP And Not WS_VISIBLE
        End If
        If FormIcon Then
            curXStyle = curXStyle And Not WS_EX_DLGMODALFRAME
        End If
        If Edge Then curXStyle = curXStyle Or WS_EX_CLIENTEDGE

        curStyle = SetWindowLong(hForm, GWL_STYLE, curStyle)
        curXStyle = SetWindowLong(hForm, GWL_EXSTYLE, curXStyle)
        DrawMenuBar hForm
        ShowWindow hForm, SW_SHOW
    End If
End Sub
```

You use the CopyClipImage() method to copy a bitmap from the clipboard to a specified location on the Userform. You input the size and location of the image with the arguments imgLeft, imgTop, imgWidth, and imgHeight specified in points relative to the coordinate system of the Userform. The location and dimension of the image are converted to pixels and a raised rectangle is drawn with the DrawEdge() function.

Obtaining a handle to a bitmap that has been copied to the clipboard is fairly straightforward with Windows API functions. With any clipboard operation, you must first open the clipboard with the OpenClipboard() function and close it with the CloseClipboard() function after it is no longer needed. You use the IsClipboardFormatAvailable() function to test for the presence of text or images in a variety of formats. In this case, the function is used to test for the presence of a bitmap. If a bitmap exists on the clipboard, the function returns True, and the clipboard is opened. You obtain a handle to the bitmap with the GetClipboardData() function before the clipboard is closed. Of course, the bitmap must be present on the clipboard before it can be located with these functions. Copying an image of an Excel chart to the clipboard is left as a function of the interface's program code (discussed in the section "The Main Userform (frmTicker)"). Remember, I want to make this class easily portable to other programs, so the CopyClipImage() method can be used to copy any bitmap from the clipboard to any location on a Userform.

TIP

To test for or retrieve text on or from the clipboard, specify the constant *CF_TEXT* (`Const CF_TEXT As Long = 1`) in the appropriate clipboard functions.

Once a handle to the bitmap is obtained, you copy and resize it using the Windows API `CopyImage()` function. The `CopyImage()` function sets the size of the new bitmap to a size slightly less than that of the raised rectangle. The original bitmap is either stretched or compressed in order to obtained the specified size (nWidth, nHeight), and the original image is deleted (*LR_COPYDELETEORG*). The quality of an image suffers when its size is changed with the `CopyImage()` function, so it is best if the original charts are close to the desired size of the bitmap.

Before you can copy a bitmap to a Userform, you must create a memory device context compatible with the device context of the Userform using the `CreateCompatibleDC()` function. You can than select the bitmap into the compatible memory device context using the `SelectObject()` function. Once the bitmap is drawn to the memory device context (`dcBitmap`), you can copy it to another device context using the `BitBlt()` function. In this case, the memory device context with the bitmap drawn on it (`dcBitmap`) serves as the source of the `BitBlt()` operation that copies the bitmap to the destination device context (`dcForm`), which is on the Userform.

```
Public Sub CopyClipImage(imgLeft As Integer, imgTop As Integer, _
     imgWidth As Integer, imgHeight As Integer)
'Copies clipboard image to specified location on Userform. Bitmap of
'Excel chart must be copied to the clipboard prior to calling this method.
    Dim imgBaseRect As RECT, frmRect As RECT
    Dim rv As Long
    Dim ptToPixelX As Single, ptToPixelY As Single
    Dim hBitmap As Long, dcBitmap As Long, oldDC As Long
    Dim nWidth As Long, nHeight As Long
    Dim bmapExists As Boolean


    '-------------------------------
    'Draw a raised rectangle on form
    '-------------------------------
    rv = GetClientRect(hForm, frmRect)   'Get dimensions of client region
    ptToPixelX = UForm.Width / frmRect.Right
    ptToPixelY = UForm.Height / frmRect.Bottom
    imgBaseRect.Left = imgLeft / ptToPixelX
```

```
        imgBaseRect.Top = imgTop / ptToPixelY
        imgBaseRect.Right = (imgLeft + imgWidth) / ptToPixelX
        imgBaseRect.Bottom = (imgTop + imgHeight) / ptToPixelY
        rv = InflateRect(imgBaseRect, -2, -2)
        rv = DrawEdge(dcForm, imgBaseRect, BDR_RAISED, BF_BOTTOM Or _
            BF_RIGHT Or BF_TOP Or BF_LEFT)


        '----------------------------------------
        'Open clipboard and get handle to bitmap
        'Copy bitmap to transform its size
        '----------------------------------------
        bmapExists = IsClipboardFormatAvailable(CF_BITMAP)
        If bmapExists Then
            If OpenClipboard(0&) Then
                hBitmap = GetClipboardData(CF_BITMAP)
                CloseClipboard
            Else
                Err.Raise 516, "clsCustomForm", "Unable to retrieve " & _
                    image from clipboard."
            End If
        End If
        nWidth = imgBaseRect.Right - imgBaseRect.Left - 6
        nHeight = imgBaseRect.Bottom - imgBaseRect.Top - 6
        hBitmap = CopyImage(hBitmap, IMAGE_BITMAP, nWidth, nHeight, _
            LR_COPYDELETEORG)


        '----------------------------------------
        'Create bitmap DC and select bitmap into it
        '----------------------------------------
        dcBitmap = CreateCompatibleDC(dcForm)
        oldDC = SelectObject(dcBitmap, hBitmap)
        rv = BitBlt(dcForm, imgBaseRect.Left + 3, imgBaseRect.Top + 3, _
            nWidth, nHeight, dcBitmap, 0, 0, SRCCOPY)


        SelectObject dcBitmap, oldDC
        DeleteDC dcBitmap
End Sub
```

You use the next two methods, CopyFormImage() and RestoreFormImage(), to copy a bitmap of the Userform to memory and copy the bitmap stored in memory to the User-form, respectively. These are the same procedures listed in Chapter 17, and they serve to repaint a Userform that has been drawn on with API functions. The final procedure contained in the clsCustomForm class is the Terminate() event of the class, and you use this procedure to clean up memory used by this class to store the various GDI objects.

```
Public Sub CopyFormImage()
'Copy the window image to memory
    Dim frmRect As RECT
    Dim rv As Long
    Dim nWidth As Long, nHeight As Long

    'dcForm = GetDC(hForm)
    oDC = SaveDC(dcForm)      'Save the DC for later restoration

    rv = GetWindowRect(hForm, frmRect)
    nWidth = frmRect.Right - frmRect.Left
    nHeight = frmRect.Bottom - frmRect.Top
    hbitForm = CreateCompatibleBitmap(dcForm, nWidth, nHeight)
    dcbitForm = CreateCompatibleDC(dcForm)
    rv = SelectObject(dcbitForm, hbitForm)
    rv = BitBlt(dcbitForm, 0, 0, nWidth, nHeight, dcForm, 0, 0, SRCCOPY)
End Sub

Public Sub RestoreFormImage()
'Restore window with bitmap from memory
    Dim rv As Long
    Dim frmRect As RECT
    Dim nWidth As Long, nHeight As Long

    rv = GetWindowRect(hForm, frmRect)
    nWidth = frmRect.Right - frmRect.Left
    nHeight = frmRect.Bottom - frmRect.Top
    rv = BitBlt(dcForm, 0, 0, nWidth, nHeight, dcbitForm, 0, 0, SRCCOPY)
End Sub
```

```
Private Sub Class_Terminate()
'Memory clean-up
    SelectObject dcForm, oDC
    RestoreDC dcForm, oDC
    ReleaseDC hForm, dcForm
    DeleteObject (hbitForm)
    DeleteDC (dcbitForm)
End Sub
```

To include this class in another program, you must first export it (select File, Export File in the VBA IDE) as a .cls file. You can then import the .cls file to any VBA project. Once imported into a VBA project, you can instantiate an object of the clsCustomForm class in your program. Remember to set the UForm property and invoke the SetStyles() method before showing the Userform that incorporates this class.

Custom Text Box/Font (clsDynamicTextBox)

Deciding on how to create an animated ticker turned out to be a rather difficult process. Text Box and Label controls were unsatisfactory because they gave the ticker a choppy appearance when animated. I also considered the ScrollDC() and ScrollWindow() API functions that can be used to scroll all or part of a device context or client area of a window. However, these functions would have to be combined with text drawing functions anyway, so why complicate the process with extra API function calls? Ultimately, I decided a single Windows API text drawing function, ExtTextOut() is the best choice because it extends the control over the text that is drawn (relative to the DrawText() function).

The general declarations section of the clsDynamicTextBox class contains the API functions, constants, type definitions, and module-level variables required by the properties and methods of the class. Many of the API functions and constants are repeated from the clsCustomForm class. This is necessary to make the class reusable in other VBA projects.

```
Option Explicit
'.......................

'API Declarations
Private Declare Function FindWindow Lib "user32.dll" Alias _
    "FindWindowA" (ByVal lpClassName As String, _
    ByVal lpWindowName As String) As Long
Private Declare Function GetDC Lib "user32.dll" ( _
    ByVal hwnd As Long) As Long
Private Declare Function SaveDC Lib "gdi32.dll" ( _
    ByVal hdc As Long) As Long
```

```
Private Declare Function ReleaseDC Lib "user32.dll" ( _
    ByVal hwnd As Long, ByVal hdc As Long) As Long
Private Declare Function RestoreDC Lib "gdi32.dll" ( _
    ByVal hdc As Long, ByVal nSavedDC As Long) As Long
Private Declare Function CreatePen Lib "gdi32.dll" ( _
    ByVal nPenStyle As Long, ByVal nWidth As Long, _
    ByVal crColor As Long) As Long
Private Declare Function CreateFont Lib "gdi32.dll" Alias _
    "CreateFontA" (ByVal h As Long, ByVal W As Long, ByVal E As Long, _
    ByVal O As Long, ByVal W As Long, ByVal I As Long, _
    ByVal u As Long, ByVal s As Long, ByVal c As Long, _
    ByVal OP As Long, ByVal CP As Long, ByVal q As Long, _
    ByVal PAF As Long, ByVal F As String) As Long
Private Declare Function GetTextExtentPoint32 Lib "gdi32.dll" Alias _
    "GetTextExtentPoint32A" (ByVal hdc As Long, ByVal lpsz As String, _
    ByVal cbString As Long, lpSize As Size) As Long
Private Declare Function CreateSolidBrush Lib "gdi32.dll" ( _
    ByVal crColor As Long) As Long
Private Declare Function Rectangle Lib "gdi32.dll" (ByVal hdc As Long, _
    ByVal X1 As Long, ByVal Y1 As Long, ByVal X2 As Long, _
    ByVal Y2 As Long) As Long
Private Declare Function CreateRectRgn Lib "gdi32.dll" ( _
    ByVal X1 As Long, ByVal Y1 As Long, ByVal X2 As Long, _
    ByVal Y2 As Long) As Long
Private Declare Function FillRgn Lib "gdi32.dll" (ByVal hdc As Long, _
    ByVal hRgn As Long, ByVal hBrush As Long) As Long
Private Declare Function InflateRect Lib "user32" (lpRect As RECT, _
    ByVal x As Long, ByVal y As Long) As Long
Private Declare Function DrawText Lib "user32.dll" Alias "DrawTextA" _
    (ByVal hdc As Long, ByVal lpStr As String, ByVal nCount As Long, _
    lpRect As RECT, ByVal wFormat As Long) As Long
Private Declare Function SetBkColor Lib "gdi32.dll" ( _
    ByVal hdc As Long, ByVal crColor As Long) As Long
Private Declare Function SetTextColor Lib "gdi32.dll" ( _
    ByVal hdc As Long, ByVal crColor As Long) As Long
Private Declare Function SetTextAlign Lib "gdi32.dll" ( _
    ByVal hdc As Long, ByVal wFlags As Long) As Long
```

```vbnet
Private Declare Function ExtTextOut Lib "gdi32.dll" Alias _
    "ExtTextOutA" (ByVal hdc As Long, ByVal x As Long, _
    ByVal y As Long, ByVal wOptions As Long, lpRect As RECT, _
    ByVal lpString As String, ByVal nCount As Long, _
    lpDx As Long) As Long
Private Declare Function DeleteObject Lib "gdi32.dll" ( _
    ByVal hObject As Long) As Long
Private Declare Function SelectObject Lib "gdi32.dll" ( _
    ByVal hdc As Long, ByVal hObject As Long) As Long
Private Declare Function LineTo Lib "gdi32.dll" (ByVal hdc As Long, _
    ByVal x As Long, ByVal y As Long) As Long
Private Declare Function MoveToEx Lib "gdi32.dll" (ByVal hdc As Long, _
    ByVal x As Long, ByVal y As Long, lpPoint As POINTAPI) As Long
Private Declare Function GetClientRect Lib "user32" ( _
    ByVal hwnd As Long, lpRect As RECT) As Long


'-----------------
'API Constants
Private Const DT_CENTER As Long = &H1
Private Const DT_SINGLELINE As Long = &H20
Private Const DT_VCENTER As Long = &H4
Private Const DT_RIGHT As Long = &H2
Private Const DT_CALCRECT As Long = &H400
Private Const SW_ERASE As Long = &H4
Private Const SW_INVALIDATE As Long = &H2
Private Const SW_NORMAL As Long = 1
Private Const LF_FACESIZE As Long = 32
Private Const DEFAULT_CHARSET As Long = 1
Private Const ANSI_CHARSET As Long = 0
Private Const OUT_DEFAULT_PRECIS As Long = 0
Private Const DEFAULT_PITCH As Long = 0
Private Const DEFAULT_QUALITY As Long = 0
Private Const PS_SOLID As Long = 0
Private Const ETO_CLIPPED As Long = 4
Private Const ETO_GLYPH_INDEX As Long = &H10
Private Const ETO_OPAQUE As Long = 2
Private Const TA_UPDATECP As Long = 1
```

```vba
Private Const TA_BOTTOM As Long = 8
Private Const TA_CENTER As Long = 6
Private Const TA_TOP As Long = 0

Private Type RECT
    Left As Long
    Top As Long
    Right As Long
    Bottom As Long
End Type

Private Type POINTAPI
    x As Long
    y As Long
End Type

Private Type Size
    cx As Long
    cy As Long
End Type


'------------------------
'Public properties
Public BackColor As Long
Public Border As Boolean
Public BorderColor As Long
Public BorderWidth As Integer    'In pixels
Public Style As Integer          'Raised or sunken
Public LeftSide As Integer    'In pixels relative to userform coordinates
Public RightSide As Integer
Public Top As Integer
Public Bottom As Integer
Public Font As New clsFont
Public UForm As Object


'----------------
'Private vars
Private scrollP As Boolean   'Instance variables for properties
```

```
Private textP As String
Private speedP As Integer
Private scrollTypeP As Integer


'Handles and DC's
Private hPen As Long, hBrushBackColor As Long, hFont As Long
Private hOldPen As Long, hOldBrush As Long, hOldFont As Long
Private oldTxtColor As Long, oldTxtAlign As Long
Private hForm As Long, dcForm As Long, oDC As Long


Private frmRect As RECT, txtRect As RECT, clpRect As RECT
Private ptToPixelX As Single      'Point/pixel conversions
Private ptToPixelY As Single
Private xInc As Integer             'Scroll increments
Private yInc As Integer
Private lpSize As Size       'Extent sizes
Private ptText As String     'partial string for vertical scroll
Private strWidth As Long     'String extent
Private sp() As Long         'Character extents
Private WithEvents Timer1 As ccrpTimer
Private WithEvents Timer2 As ccrpTimer
Private Const ASPECT = 2.5
```

Properties of the clsDynamicTextBox class that cannot be defined by simple Public variables include ScrollType, Speed, Text, and Scroll. When the ScrollType property is changed, you must clear the text from the text box before the new String is drawn, because changing the scroll direction alters the drawing rectangle and some text may be left on the Userform from the previous scroll direction. I have included a CCRP Timer object in the clsDynamicTextBox class to handle text animation. You must update the Interval and Enabled properties of the Timer object when the Speed and Scroll properties are changed. Finally, the character extents (size of a character block in pixels) for each character in the Text property are loaded into an array for later use in the ExtTextOut() function.

```
Public Property Let ScrollType(sType As Integer)
    scrollTypeP = sType
    Clear    'Clear the text from text box
End Property
Public Property Get ScrollType() As Integer
    ScrollType = scrollTypeP
End Property
```

```vba
Public Property Let Speed(scrollSpeed As Integer)
    On Error Resume Next
    speedP = scrollSpeed
    SetSpeed          'Alter timer interval property
End Property
Public Property Get Speed() As Integer
    Speed = speedP
End Property


Public Property Let Text(cText As String)
    textP = cText
End Property
Public Property Get Text() As String
'Sets string value of text property. Also initializes the array holding
'the extents for each character in the string.
    Dim I As Integer

    Text = textP
    ReDim sp(Len(Text))
    strWidth = 0
    For I = 0 To Len(Text)
        GetTextExtentPoint32 dcForm, Mid(Text, I + 1, 1), 1, lpSize
        sp(I) = lpSize.cx   'Used by ExtTextOut function to draw text
        strWidth = strWidth + sp(I)
    Next I
End Property


Public Property Let Scroll(Toggle As Boolean)
'Toggle ticker on and off
    scrollP = Toggle
    If Toggle Then
        Timer2.Enabled = True
        SetSpeed
    Else
        Timer2.Enabled = False
    End If
End Property
```

```
Public Property Get Scroll() As Boolean
    Scroll = scrollP
End Property
```

You can use the `Clear()` method and `SetSpeed()` Sub procedure to clear the text from the text box and change the `Interval` property of the `Timer` object. These methods are called from some of the property and method procedures of the `clsDynamicTextBox` class.

```
Public Sub Clear()
'Clears the text from the text box by filling it with background color
    Dim hRgn As Long
    xInc = 0
    yInc = 0
    hRgn = CreateRectRgn(clpRect.Left, clpRect.Top, clpRect.Right, _
        clpRect.Bottom)
    FillRgn dcForm, hRgn, hBrushBackColor
End Sub
Private Sub SetSpeed()
    Select Case Speed
        Case Is = 0 'Slow
            Timer2.Interval = 50
        Case Is = 1 'Medium
            Timer2.Interval = 15
        Case Is = 2 'Fast
            Timer2.Interval = 1
        Case Else
            Timer2.Interval = 15
    End Select
End Sub
```

You use the `Initialize()` event of a custom class to initialize class variables. In the `clsDynamicTextBox` class, the `Initialize()` event also instantiates two `Timer` objects. The function of the first `Timer` object (`Timer1`) is to draw the text box after the Userform is made visible. You cannot enter the code that draws the text box in the `Initialize()` event because this event triggers before the Userform is visible. The operating system will not draw the text box when the Userform is first painted because any drawing done with API functions is not part of the window's persistent bitmap stored in memory. Therefore, the `Timer()` event procedure of the `Timer1` object is set to fire 200 milliseconds after the `Initialize()` event executes. The `Timer1` object is then disabled and not used again.

```
Private Sub Class_Initialize()
'Initialize properties and draw text box
    BackColor = RGB(255, 255, 255)
    scrollP = False
    BorderColor = RGB(0, 0, 0)
    Border = True
    BorderWidth = 2
    ScrollType = 0 'Ticker
    Style = 0 'sunken
    Speed = 1
    LeftSide = 0
    RightSide = 0
    Top = 0
    Bottom = 0

    Set Timer2 = New ccrpTimer
    Set Timer1 = New ccrpTimer
    Timer1.Enabled = True
    Timer1.Interval = 200
End Sub


Private Sub Timer1_Timer(ByVal Milliseconds As Long)
'Called only once after the class is instantiated.
    CreateTextBox
    Timer1.Enabled = False
End Sub
```

The `CreateTextBox()` Sub procedure is called once from the `Timer()` event procedure of the `Timer1` object. This procedure calls four other Sub procedures that define the area on the Userform for the text box along with the drawing objects used to draw both the text box and the text it will contain.

```
Private Sub CreateTextBox()
'Draws the text box on Userform
'Called once after custom class is instantiated
    CreateDrawingArea
    CreateDrawingTools
    CreateRect
    CreateBorder
End Sub
```

```
Private Sub CreateDrawingArea()
'Finds the client area of Userform and gets a DC for it.
'Also defines point per pixel values
    Dim rv As Long
    hForm = FindWindow(vbNullString, UForm.Caption)
    dcForm = GetDC(hForm)
    If hForm = 0 Or dcForm = 0 Then
        Err.Raise 517, "clsDynamicTextBox", "Cannot obtain handle " & _
            "to Userform!"
        Exit Sub
    End If
    oDC = SaveDC(dcForm)
    rv = GetClientRect(hForm, frmRect)
    ptToPixelX = UForm.Width / frmRect.Right
    ptToPixelY = UForm.Height / frmRect.Bottom
End Sub


Private Sub CreateDrawingTools()
'Creates the font, brush, and pen objects used to draw text box and text
    Dim fWeight As Long, fItalic As Long
    Dim rv As Long

    hPen = CreatePen(PS_SOLID, BorderWidth, BorderColor)
    hBrushBackColor = CreateSolidBrush(BackColor)
    rv = SetBkColor(dcForm, BackColor)
    fWeight = 400
    If Font.Bold Then fWeight = 700
    If Font.Italic Then fItalic = 1
    hFont = CreateFont(Font.Size, Font.Size / ASPECT, 0, 0, fWeight, _
        fItalic, 0, 0, DEFAULT_CHARSET, OUT_DEFAULT_PRECIS, _
        OUT_DEFAULT_PRECIS, DEFAULT_QUALITY, DEFAULT_PITCH, Font.Name)
    oldTxtColor = SetTextColor(dcForm, Font.Color)
    oldTxtAlign = SetTextAlign(dcForm, TA_TOP)
    hOldFont = SelectObject(dcForm, hFont)
    hOldPen = SelectObject(dcForm, hPen)
    hOldBrush = SelectObject(dcForm, hBrushBackColor)
End Sub
```

```
Private Sub CreateRect()
'Draws the background rectangle for the text box
    Dim rv As Integer
    rv = Rectangle(dcForm, LeftSide / ptToPixelX, Top / ptToPixelY, _
        RightSide / ptToPixelX, Bottom / ptToPixelY)
End Sub

Private Sub CreateBorder()
'Draws a border around the text box
    Dim rv As Long
    Dim I As Integer
    Dim pt1 As POINTAPI
    Dim offSet As Single

    offSet = BorderWidth / 2
    rv = MoveToEx(dcForm, LeftSide / ptToPixelX - offSet, _
        Bottom / ptToPixelY + offSet, pt1)
    rv = LineTo(dcForm, LeftSide / ptToPixelX - offSet, _
        Top / ptToPixelY - offSet)
    rv = LineTo(dcForm, RightSide / ptToPixelX + offSet, _
        Top / ptToPixelY - offSet)
    rv = LineTo(dcForm, RightSide / ptToPixelX + offSet, _
        Bottom / ptToPixelY + offSet)
    rv = LineTo(dcForm, LeftSide / ptToPixelX - offSet, _
        Bottom / ptToPixelY + offSet)
End Sub
Public Sub Refresh()
'Redraws the text box background and border
    CreateRect
    CreateBorder
End Sub
```

The most difficult tasks of the `clsDynamicTextBox` class are handled by the next three procedures: `ScrollText()`, `GetPartialString()`, and the `Timer()` event of the `Timer2` object. You use the `ScrollText()` Sub procedure to draw the text to the area on the Userform defined as the custom text box. You use the `GetPartialString()` Function procedure to build a `String` just long enough to fit in the area defined by the custom text box. You use the `GetPartialString()` function when the `ScrollType` property is set to vertical (1). The `Timer()` event procedure of the `Timer2` object effectively animates the output text by defining the coordinates of the rectangle to which text is drawn.

The `ScrollText()` Sub procedure uses the `ExtTextOut()` function to draw the text because it provides more control over the output relative to the `DrawText()` function. The downside is that the `ExtTextOut()` function is more difficult to use, with the main difficulty lying in the definition of the spacing between characters in the output `String` (defined by `lpDx` argument). You must define the character spacing accurately; if not, the `ExtTextOut()` function will draw the characters too close or too far apart.

CAUTION

If the `lpDx` is not used, `ExtTextOut()` will draw all characters in the `String` on top of each other.

To accurately return the correct spacing, use the `GetTextExtentPoint32()` function in the `Text` property procedure (listed earlier in this chapter) to return the extent for each character in the `String` to a variable array (`sp`). You can pass a pointer to the array variable holding the text extents to the `ExtTextOut()` function by specifying the first element in the array, `sp(0)`.

NOTE

A *text extent* refers to the space a block of text will occupy in an output device. Text extents can be obtained for a single character or a `String` of characters. The value of a text extent will vary with different characters, even when all other parameters are the same (that is, font type, font size, and so on).

Other arguments within the `ExtTextOut()` function include a handle to the device context in which to draw the text (`hdc`), the *x-y* point that specifies the start position for the drawing (`x`, `y` are calculated from a `RECT` structure), any desired flags (`wOptions`), a `RECT` structure that defines the rectangle in which to draw the structure (`lpRect`), the `String` to draw (`lpString`), and the number of characters within the `String` to draw (`nCount`). (See the declaration for the `ExtTextOut()` function and compare it to the function calls in the `ScrollText()` Sub procedure.)

To properly animate the text within the area defined by the custom text box, you need to alter the *x-y* point that specifies the starting position for the drawing and use the *ETO_CLIPPED* flag to ensure that the text is drawn within the specified rectangle. Text drawn outside the clipping rectangle (`clpRect`) will not be seen (see Figure 18.11).

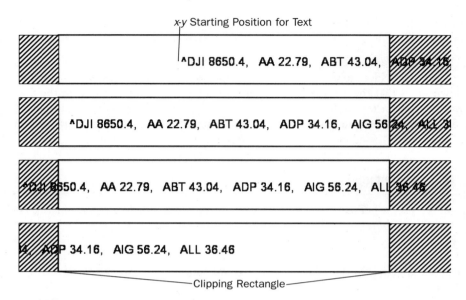

FIGURE 18.11 *Animating text with the* ExtTextOut *API function.*

The `clpRect` variable is defined in the `Timer()` event procedure of the `Timer2` object and essentially represents a rectangle the same size as the background area of the text box. If `ExtTextOut()` tries to draw text outside this rectangle, the drawing is clipped. The text appears to be animated because the `Timer()` event of the `Timer2` object redefines the `txtRect` variable each time it is triggered. When the text is scrolled horizontally, the value of x is decreased with each trigger of the `Timer()` event procedure, whereas y remains constant. Thus, the text appears to move from right to left. The opposite is true when the text is scrolled vertically; that is, the value of y is decreased so that the text moves from bottom to top.

```
Private Sub ScrollText()
'Draws the text at specified position.
'Different positions for horizontal or vertical scroll
'Positions updated in Timer event
    Dim rv As Long
    Dim x As Long, y As Long

    If ScrollType = 0 Then
        x = txtRect.Right
        y = (txtRect.Bottom + txtRect.Top) / 2 - Font.Size / 2
        rv = ExtTextOut(dcForm, x, y, ETO_CLIPPED, clpRect, Text, Len(Text), _
            sp(0))
```

```
    Else
        If yInc = 0 Then ptText = GetPartialString
        GetTextExtentPoint32 dcForm, ptText, Len(ptText), lpSize
        x = 0.5 * (clpRect.Right - clpRect.Left) - lpSize.cx / 2
        y = clpRect.Bottom - Font.Size
        rv = ExtTextOut(dcForm, x, y, ETO_CLIPPED, clpRect, _
                ptText, Len(ptText), sp(0))
    End If
End Sub
```

The `GetPartialString()` function is called from the `ScrollText()` Sub procedure when the `ScrollType` property is set to vertical. You use this function to split the `String` contained in the `Text` property into component strings that will fit just within the custom text box. As a result, the variable array holding the text extents must be redimensioned and filled with new values for use with the `ExtTextOut()` function. You construct each component `String` from a small number of elements that includes a company's symbol and stock quote. The static variable `I` is incremented with each call to this function. This ensures that all companies included in the `Text` property are output to the text box before the variable `I` is reset.

```
Private Function GetPartialString() As String
'Creates the segmented strings when the ticker scrolls vertically
    Dim textArray
    Dim strWidthV As Integer
    Dim tempStr As String
    Static I As Integer
    Dim K As Integer
    Dim elementLength As Integer, maxLength As Integer


    '---------------------------------------------------------------
    'Create array with individual elements representing symbol and price
    'Then get size of first element
    '---------------------------------------------------------------
    textArray = Split(Text, ",")
    GetTextExtentPoint32 dcForm, textArray(0), Len(textArray(0)), lpSize
    elementLength = lpSize.cx + 25


    '----------------------------------------------------
    'Build the partial string of symbols such that it
```

```
'fits in text area
'-----------------------------------------------
maxLength = (clpRect.Right - clpRect.Left)
Do While strWidthV < (maxLength - elementLength) And _
        I <= UBound(textArray)
    GetTextExtentPoint32 dcForm, textArray(I), Len(textArray(I)), lpSize
    'Add buffer between array elements
    strWidthV = strWidthV + lpSize.cx + 30
    tempStr = tempStr & "   " & textArray(I)
    I = I + 1
Loop
If I >= UBound(textArray) Then I = 0


'---------------------------------------------------------------
'Set array of character extents for ExtTextOut function
'---------------------------------------------------------------
tempStr = Trim(tempStr)
ReDim sp(Len(tempStr))
For K = 0 To Len(tempStr)
    GetTextExtentPoint32 dcForm, Mid(tempStr, K + 1, 1), 1, lpSize
    sp(K) = lpSize.cx + 2
Next K


    GetPartialString = tempStr
End Function
```

The Timer() event procedure of the Timer2 object is triggered at intervals set by the Speed property of the class. The Timer()event procedure will decrement either the Right or Bottom components of the variable txtRect, depending on the value of the ScrollType property (horizontal or vertical). This effectively moves the defining rectangle used by the ExtTextOut() drawing function, thus animating the text. The amount of the decrement is one or two pixels depending on the speed setting of the ticker. When the entire String has been scrolled through the ticker, you must reset the decrementing variables (xInc and yInc).

```
Private Sub Timer2_Timer(ByVal Milliseconds As Long)
'Triggered according to setting of Speed property.
'Alters the position text is drawn in text box
    txtRect.Left = LeftSide / ptToPixelX + 4
    txtRect.Top = Top / ptToPixelY + 4
```

```
    txtRect.Right = RightSide / ptToPixelX - (4 + xInc)
    txtRect.Bottom = Bottom / ptToPixelY - (4 + yInc)

    If xInc = 0 Then clpRect = txtRect

    If ScrollType = 0 Then   'Horizontal scroll
        ScrollText
        If Speed < 2 Then
            xInc = xInc + 1
        Else
            xInc = xInc + 2
        End If
        If xInc > strWidth + (RightSide - LeftSide) / ptToPixelX Then
            xInc = 0          'Reset ticker to start over
            strWidth = 0
            Clear
        End If
    Else                      'Vertical scroll
        ScrollText
        If Speed < 2 Then
            yInc = yInc + 1
        Else
            yInc = yInc + 2
        End If
        If clpRect.Bottom <= (clpRect.Top - Font.Size) Then
            yInc = 0          'Reset ticker to start over
        End If
    End If
End Sub
```

As always, you use the Terminate() event of the class to restore objects to their original configuration and release the memory used by the class.

```
Private Sub Class_Terminate()
'Memory clean-up
    SelectObject dcForm, hOldPen
    SelectObject dcForm, hOldBrush
    SelectObject dcForm, hOldFont
    SetTextColor dcForm, oldTxtColor
```

```
        SetTextAlign dcForm, oldTxtAlign
        DeleteObject hPen
        DeleteObject hBrushBackColor
        DeleteObject hFont
        RestoreDC dcForm, oDC
        ReleaseDC hForm, dcForm
        Set Timer1 = Nothing
        Set Timer2 = Nothing
    End Sub
```

The `clsDynamicTextBox` class uses the `clsFont` class to set the font's characteristics for the text drawn to the custom text box. The `clsFont` class is a simple class with properties used only to store the values set in the program. The `Initialize()` event of the class sets default values for the properties.

```
Option Explicit

Public Name As String
Public Size As Integer
Public Color As Long
Public Bold As Boolean
Public Italic As Boolean

Private Sub Class_Initialize()
    Name = "Tahoma"
    Size = 16
    Color = RGB(0, 0, 0)
    Bold = True
    Italic = False
End Sub
```

The combination of the `clsDynamicTextBox` and `clsFont` classes can be imported into any VBA project that requires a scrolling text box.

The Symbol and Symbols Collection Objects (clsSymbol and clsSymbols)

You construct the `clsSymbol` and `clsSymbols` collection classes to specifically manage the data for the stock ticker program. The `clsSymbol` class consists of four basic read-write properties (`Symbol`, `Value`, `DateTime`, and `ID`). The `Symbol` property holds a

`String` representing a company's identification in the stock market. The `Value` and `DateTime` properties hold the quote and time of the last trade, respectively. You must ensure that each instance of a `clsSymbol` class has a unique `ID` property so that it can be easily retrieved from the `clsSymbols` collection class.

```
Option Explicit
Public Symbol As String
Public Value As String
Public DateTime As String
Public ID As String


Private Sub Class_Initialize()
    ID = Trim(Str(CLng(Rnd * (2 ^ 31))))
End Sub
```

The `clsSymbols` collection class contains the usual members of a collection class, including `Add`, `Remove`, and `Item` methods as well as a `Count` property. In addition, there are methods used to return a specific `clsSymbol` object from an identifying `String` (`FindBySymbol`), to concatenate all symbols and their values into a single `String` (`GetSymbolString`) and to build the `String` that must be sent to Yahoo! in order to return the stock quotes (`GetSymbolWebQueryString`).

```
Option Explicit
Private Const navNoReadFromCache = 4
Private symbolsP As Collection
Private WithEvents intExp As SHDocVw.InternetExplorer
Private refreshComplete As Boolean


Public Property Get Count() As Integer
    Count = symbolsP.Count
End Property
Public Function Item(ByVal sID As String) As clsSymbol
    Set Item = symbolsP(sID)
End Function


Public Sub Add(aSymbol As clsSymbol)
    On Error GoTo AddError
    symbolsP.Add aSymbol, aSymbol.ID
    Exit Sub
```

```vba
AddError:
    Err.Raise Number:=vbObjectError + 514, Source:="clsSymbols.Add", _
        Description:="Unable to Add clsSymbol object to the collection"
End Sub
Public Sub Remove(ByVal ID As String)
    On Error GoTo RemoveError
    symbolsP.Remove ID
    Exit Sub
RemoveError:
    Err.Raise Number:=vbObjectError + 515, _
        Source:="clsSymbols.Remove", _
        Description:="Unable to Remove clsSymbol object " & _
            "from the collection"
End Sub
Public Function FindBySymbol(Symbol As String) As Long
'Find a symbol object using input string
    Dim s As clsSymbol
    For Each s In symbolsP
        If s.Symbol = Symbol Then
            FindBySymbol = s.ID
            Exit Function
        End If
    Next
    FindBySymbol = 0
End Function


Public Function GetSymbolString() As String
'Build single string from all symbols in collection
    Dim s As clsSymbol

    For Each s In symbolsP
        GetSymbolString = GetSymbolString & s.Symbol & " " & _
            s.Value & ",    "
    Next
    GetSymbolString = Trim(GetSymbolString)
End Function
Public Function GetSymbolWebQueryString() As String
```

```
'Build the string required for query by Yahoo's financial Web site
    Dim s As clsSymbol

    For Each s In symbolsP
        GetSymbolWebQueryString = GetSymbolWebQueryString & _
            s.Symbol & "%2C"
    Next
    GetSymbolWebQueryString = Left(Trim(GetSymbolWebQueryString), _
        Len(GetSymbolWebQueryString) - 3)
End Function
```

You should invoke the `Refresh()` method of the `clsSymbols` class to refresh the Web query that retrieves the stock quotes. This method is necessary because of a bug in Excel's `QueryTable` object that prevents it from refreshing a Web query based on current data from a Web site. If a Web page is available from the cache, the `QueryTable` object will refresh from the old document. Therefore, you can use the `InternetExplorer` object to refresh the Web page containing the stock quotes as described in Chapter 16, "Web Queries and Web-Related Objects in VBA."

 TIP

You can also use the `InternetExplorer` object via its associated API functions. You can use a series of API functions beginning with "`Internet`" to navigate the Internet and download Web pages.

The `Refresh()` method of the `clsSymbols` class invokes the `Navigate` method of the `InternetExplorer` object specifying not to use the file cache (`Flags:=navNoReadFromCache`). You can use an empty loop at the end of the procedure (as I have done here) to tie up the program while the Web document is downloading to prevent further code execution. Alternatively, you can allow program execution to proceed, but the ticker will always display the prior set of downloaded quotes. When the download is complete, the `DocumentComplete()` event procedure of the `InternetExplorer` object is triggered. The `QueryTable` object is then allowed to retrieve the document from the cache, and the refreshed data is copied to a worksheet. The `Update()` procedure then updates the `clsSymbols` collection object and the daily worksheet.

```
Public Sub Refresh()
'Refresh the Web query using Internet explorer
    Dim connStr As String
    Dim ws As Worksheet
```

```vba
        refreshComplete = False
        Set intExp = New SHDocVw.InternetExplorer
        connStr = "http://finance.yahoo.com/q?s=" & _
            GetSymbolWebQueryString & "&d=v1"
        intExp.Navigate connStr, Flags:=navNoReadFromCache

        For Each ws In Worksheets
            If ws.Name = "Temporary Web Query" Then
                ws.Activate
                Exit For
            End If
        Next

        Do      'Delay program execution until Web page is done downloading
            DoEvents
        Loop Until refreshComplete
        Update
End Sub

Private Sub intExp_DocumentComplete(ByVal pDisp As Object, _
        URL As Variant)
'After Web page is refreshed create the query table
'and import refreshed data
        Dim qtStock As QueryTable
        Dim connStr As String
        Dim h As Hyperlink

        Set intExp = Nothing
        '-------------------------------------------------------
        'Send the connection string to Yahoo to get the quotes.
        '-------------------------------------------------------
        connStr = "URL;http://finance.yahoo.com/q?s=" & _
            GetSymbolWebQueryString & "&d=v1"
        Set qtStock = ActiveSheet.QueryTables.Add(Connection:=connStr, _
            Destination:=Worksheets("Temporary Web Query").Range("A1"))
        With qtStock
            .FieldNames = False
            .RowNumbers = False
```

```
            .RefreshStyle = xlOverwriteCells
            .RefreshPeriod = 0
            .WebSelectionType = xlSpecifiedTables
            .WebTables = "16"
            .Refresh BackgroundQuery:=False
        End With


        '................................................
        'Remove the objects added by the Web query
        '................................................
        ActiveSheet.Names(1).Delete
        qtStock.Delete
        For Each h In ActiveSheet.Hyperlinks
            h.Delete
        Next
        refreshComplete = True
        Set qtStock = Nothing
End Sub


Private Sub Update()
'Update the data in collection and daily worksheet
        Dim s As clsSymbol
        Dim nextRow As Integer
        Dim K As Integer
        Dim ws As Worksheet
        Dim numSymbols As Integer


        numSymbols = symbolsP.Count
        'Set Value property of Symbol objects in collection
        On Error Resume Next
        For Each s In symbolsP
            Range("A1:A" & numSymbols + 1).Find(What:=s.Symbol, _
                LookAt:=xlWhole).Activate
            s.Value = Cells(ActiveCell.Row, ActiveCell.Column + 2)
            s.DateTime = Cells(ActiveCell.Row, ActiveCell.Column + 1)
        Next
        '
        'Update Temporary daily worksheet
```

```vba
    Set ws = Worksheets("Temporary Daily Record")
    nextRow = ws.UsedRange.Rows.Count + 1
    K = 2    'column index
    ws.Cells(nextRow, 1).Value = symbolsP(1).DateTime
    For Each s In symbolsP
        If ws.Cells(1, K).Value = "" Then    'Add symbols
            ws.Cells(1, K).Value = s.Symbol
            ws.Cells(nextRow, K).Value = s.Value
        Else
            If ws.Cells(1, K).Value = s.Symbol Then
                ws.Cells(nextRow, K).Value = s.Value
            End If
        End If
        K = K + 1
    Next

    Set ws = Nothing
End Sub
Private Sub Class_Initialize()
    Set symbolsP = New Collection
End Sub
Private Sub Class_Terminate()
    Dim c As clsSymbol
    For Each c In symbolsP
        Set c = Nothing
    Next
    Set symbolsP = Nothing
    Set intExp = Nothing
End Sub
```

That concludes the construction of the class modules used by the stock ticker program. The last components to write are for the Userforms that serve as the interface to the program.

The Main Userform (frmTicker)

The Userform interface that displays the stock quotes and related charts contains the code that incorporates the class modules just discussed for customizing the Userform, drawing the custom text box, and displaying and managing the data.

The general declarations section of the frmTicker code module contains the declarations for the module-level variables required by the program, including another reference to a

Timer object (TimerWebQ). This Timer object sets the interval for refreshing the Web query that returns the stock quotes.

```
Option Explicit
'----------------------
'Custom class variables
Private cTxtBox As clsDynamicTextBox
Public aSymbol As clsSymbol
Public aSymbols As clsSymbols
Dim cForm As clsCustomForm
'----------------------
Private numSymbols As Integer    'Number of companies in ticker
Private Const CFORECOLOR = 16762880      'Forecolor for controls
Private WithEvents TimerWebQ As ccrpTimer    '3rd-party timer-control
```

The Initialize() event of the Userform object contains the code that initializes its ActiveX controls and custom class variables. You should not use the Activate() event of the Userform object in this case because this code should be triggered only when the Userform is first loaded, not every time it is activated. Normally, this isn't an issue because Userforms cannot be minimized without API functions; therefore, their Activate() event will not trigger a second time.

The program initialization consists of setting a common value for the ForeColor property of the ActiveX controls, adding the company ticker symbols to the Combo Box control (cmbSymbols), setting the Userform's styles, drawing the custom text box, and setting other necessary object references and property values. The Sub procedures SetControlColors(), SetFormStyles(), AddTextbox(), CheckDate() and UpdatePermanentRecord() are all initialization procedures executed when the Userform is first loaded. The SetFormStyles() and AddTextbox() Sub procedures instantiate the clsCustomForm and clsDynamicTextBox classes and set several property values for the newly created objects. The CheckDate() and UpdatePermanentRecord() Sub procedures test to see if the temporary daily worksheet (refer to Figure 18-5 shown earlier in this chapter) contains data from a previous day. If the worksheet does contain old data, its last row is copied to the permanent record worksheet (refer to Figure 18.6).

```
Private Sub UserForm_Initialize()
'Initialize controls...forecolor properties and combo box
    Dim I As Integer, numCols As Integer
    Dim wsCompany As Worksheet, wsTDR As Worksheet

    On Error GoTo ActivateError
    Set wsCompany = Worksheets("Companies")
    Set wsTDR = Worksheets("Temporary Daily Record")
```

```vba
        Set aSymbols = New clsSymbols
        SetControlColors
        '------------------------------------------------------
        'Add symbols to the combo box control and initialize
        'custom object variables that hold data.
        '------------------------------------------------------
        numSymbols = wsCompany.UsedRange.Rows.Count - 1
        numCols = wsTDR.UsedRange.Columns.Count
        cmbSymbols.Clear
        For I = 0 To numSymbols - 1
            Set aSymbol = New clsSymbol
            cmbSymbols.AddItem wsCompany.Cells(I + 2, "B").Value
            aSymbol.Symbol = wsCompany.Cells(I + 2, "B").Value
            aSymbol.Value = "0.00"
            aSymbols.Add aSymbol
            Set aSymbol = Nothing
        Next I
        SetFormStyles
        AddTextbox   'Initializes the ticker
        lblTimeStamp.Caption = Date
        Set TimerWebQ = New ccrpTimer
        CheckDate

        Set wsCompany = Nothing
        Set wsTDR = Nothing

        Exit Sub
    ActivateError:
        MsgBox Err.Description, vbOKOnly, "Error: " & Err.Source
        End
    End Sub
    Private Sub SetControlColors()
    'Loop through all controls and set their Forecolor property
        Dim ctr As Control

        For Each ctr In frmTicker.Controls
            ctr.ForeColor = CFORECOLOR   'RGB(0, 200, 255)
        Next
```

```
End Sub
Private Sub SetFormStyles()
'Initialize style variables for custom form class
    Set cForm = New clsCustomForm
    Set cForm.UForm = Me
    cForm.Taskbar = True
    cForm.Resizable = False
    cForm.MinMaxButtons = True
    cForm.FormIcon = True
    cForm.Edge = True
    cForm.SetStyles
End Sub
Private Sub AddTextbox()
'Create the custom text box
    Set cTxtBox = New clsDynamicTextBox

    With cTxtBox      'Initialize properties of custom text box
        .BackColor = RGB(0, 0, 0)
        .Border = True
        .BorderColor = RGB(0, 0, 175)
        .BorderWidth = 5
        .Bottom = 100        'Dimensions in points
        .LeftSide = 24
        .RightSide = 456
        .Top = 20
        'Builds string of symbols and values
        .Text = aSymbols.GetSymbolString
        .ScrollType = 0
        .Speed = 1
        .Font.Bold = True
        .Font.Color = RGB(0, 200, 255)
        .Font.Name = "Comic Sans MS"
        .Font.Size = 20
    End With

    'Tell textbox the userform object to which it belongs
    Set cTxtBox.UForm = Me
End Sub
```

```vba
Private Sub CheckDate()
'Test the date in the Temporary Daily Record worksheet
'to see if its a new day
    Dim ws As Worksheet
    Dim testDate As Date

    Set ws = Worksheets("Temporary Daily Record")
    testDate = ws.Cells(1, 1)
    If testDate = Date Then
        Exit Sub
    Else
        UpdatePermanentRecord
        ws.Cells.Clear
        ws.Cells(1, 1).Value = Date
    End If

    Set ws = Nothing
End Sub
Private Sub UpdatePermanentRecord()
'Copies data from temporary record to permanent record
    Dim wsT As Worksheet, wsP As Worksheet
    Dim nextRowT As Long, nextRowP As Long
    Dim nextColT As Long, nextColP As Long
    Dim K As Integer
    Dim curSymbol As String
    Dim targetCell As Range
    Dim newCol As Boolean

    On Error GoTo RangeNotSetError
    Set wsT = Worksheets("Temporary Daily Record")
    Set wsP = Worksheets("Permanent Record")
    nextRowT = wsT.UsedRange.Rows.Count + 1
    nextRowP = wsP.UsedRange.Rows.Count + 1
    nextColT = wsT.UsedRange.Columns.Count + 1
    nextColP = wsP.UsedRange.Columns.Count + 1

    '-------------------------------------------------
    'Create formulas for holding components of the date
```

```
'--------------------------------------------------
wsP.Cells(nextRowP, 1).Value = wsT.Cells(1, 1)
wsP.Cells(nextRowP, 2).Formula = "=YEAR(A" & nextRowP & ")"
wsP.Cells(nextRowP, 3).Formula = "=MONTH(A" & nextRowP & ")"
wsP.Cells(nextRowP, 4).Formula = "=WEEKNUM(A" & nextRowP & ",1)"
wsP.Cells(nextRowP, 5).Formula = "=WEEKDAY(A" & nextRowP & ",2)"


'--------------------------------------------------------------------
'Copy data for each symbol. Add new column to
'permanent record if needed
'--------------------------------------------------------------------
For K = 2 To nextColT
    curSymbol = wsT.Cells(1, K)
    Set targetCell = wsP.Range("1:1").Find(What:=curSymbol, _
        LookAt:=xlWhole)
    If newCol Then
        wsP.Cells(1, nextColP).Value = curSymbol
        wsP.Cells(nextRowP, nextColP + 1).Value = wsT.Cells( _
            nextRowT, K)
        nextColP = nextColP + 1
    Else
        wsP.Cells(nextRowP, targetCell.Column).Value = wsT.Cells( _
            nextRowT - 1, K)
    End If
Next K


Set wsT = Nothing
Set wsP = Nothing
Exit Sub
RangeNotSetError:
    If Err.Number = 91 Then
        newCol = True
        Resume Next
    End If
End Sub
```

A user can add or remove company symbols from the ticker using the cmbSymbols, cmdAddSymbol, and cmdRemoveSymbols Combo Box and Command Button controls. Selecting a company symbol from cmbSymbols triggers its Change() event, which is coded to find the company listing in the Companies worksheet (refer to Figure 18-4 shown earlier in this chapter) and return the name of the company to a Label control (lblCompanyName). The Change() event procedure also copies a chart to the Userform if a user selects one of the chart Option Button controls.

To completely remove a company from the program, you must first select it in the cmbSymbols Combo Box control before pressing the cmdRemoveSymbol Command Button control. This triggers its Click() event procedure whose code removes the company from the Companies worksheet, cmbSymbols Combo Box control, and clsSymbols collection class.

A new company is added to all three components (Combo Box, worksheet, and clsSymbols collection object) via another Userform (frmAddSymbol) whose code is listed later in this section.

The frmTicker Userform as it appears while running but before the ticker has been started is shown in Figure 18.12.

FIGURE 18.12 *Selecting a company symbol in the Stock Ticker program.*

```
Private Sub cmbSymbols_Change()
'Display company name when symbol is selected from
'combo box and update chart
    Dim Symbol As String
    Dim c As Range
```

```
    '--------------------
    'Display company name
    '--------------------
    Symbol = cmbSymbols.Value
    Set c = Sheets("Companies").Range("B:B").Find(What:=Symbol, _
        LookAt:=xlWhole)
    lblCompanyName.Caption = Sheets("Companies").Range( _
        "A" & c.Row).Value
    '----------------------------------
    'Update chart if option is selected
    '----------------------------------
    If optDaily.Value Then
        CopyChartToClip "Daily"
        cForm.CopyClipImage 225, 190, 245, 165
    ElseIf optWeekly.Value Then
        CopyChartToClip "Weekly"
        cForm.CopyClipImage 225, 190, 245, 165
    ElseIf optMonthly.Value Then
        CopyChartToClip "Monthly"
        cForm.CopyClipImage 225, 190, 245, 165
    ElseIf optCurrent.Value Then
        CopyChartToClip "Current"
        cForm.CopyClipImage 225, 190, 245, 165
    End If

    Set c = Nothing
End Sub


Private Sub cmdAddSymbol_Click()
'Show userform used to add new companies to the ticker
    frmAddSymbol.Show vbModal
End Sub


Private Sub cmdRemoveSymbol_Click()
'Remove selected symbol from combo box and cell in Companies worksheet
    Dim ws As Worksheet
    Dim rmSymbol As String, rmCell As Range
```

```
Dim sID As Long
Dim lastRow As Long


'--------------------------------
'Remove symbol from the combo box
'--------------------------------
If cmbSymbols.Text = "" Then Exit Sub
Set ws = Worksheets("Companies")
lastRow = ws.UsedRange.Rows.Count
rmSymbol = cmbSymbols.Text
cmbSymbols.RemoveItem cmbSymbols.ListIndex
cmbSymbols.ListIndex = 1


'----------------------------------------------------------
'Delete cells from the worksheet and remove from collection
'----------------------------------------------------------
Set rmCell = ws.Range("B1:B" & lastRow).Find( _
    What:=rmSymbol, LookAt:=xlWhole)
ws.Cells(rmCell.Row, rmCell.Column - 1).Delete Shift:=xlUp
rmCell.Delete Shift:=xlUp
sID = aSymbols.FindBySymbol(rmSymbol)
aSymbols.Remove sID


Set ws = Nothing
Set rmCell = Nothing
End Sub
```

A user starts the ticker by clicking a Toggle Button control (`tglScrollOn`). This triggers the `Click()` event of the Toggle Button control that starts the ticker running. First, the `Refresh()` methods of the `cTxtBox` object (`clsDynamicTextBox` class) and `aSymbols` object (`clsSymbols` class) are invoked in order to redraw the text box area and initiate a new Web query. Next, you must set the `Scroll` property of the `cTxtBox` object to `True` to enable the ticker and set the `Interval` property of the `TimerWebQ` object to the desired time interval between stock quote updates (in this case, 20 minutes). This sets the `Timer()` event procedure of the `TimerWebQ` object to trigger every 20 minutes where another Web query is initiated by refreshing the `aSymbols` object.

```
Private Sub tglScrollOn_Click()
'Toggle ticker on and off. Refresh the symbols and toggle the timer.
    Dim lastRow As Integer
```

```
    cForm.CopyFormImage
    cmdRestore.Enabled = True
    If Application.WorksheetFunction.Weekday(Date, 2) = 6 Or _
        Application.WorksheetFunction.Weekday(Date, 2) = 7 Then
        tglScrollOn.Value = False
        tglScrollOn.Caption = "Off"
        Exit Sub
    End If
    'Refresh symbol string and start display
    If tglScrollOn.Caption = "Off" Then
        cTxtBox.Refresh
        aSymbols.Refresh
        cTxtBox.Text = aSymbols.GetSymbolString
        cTxtBox.Scroll = True
        tglScrollOn.Caption = "On"
        tglScrollOn.ForeColor = RGB(255, 255, 255)
        TimerWebQ.Interval = 1200000
        TimerWebQ.Enabled = True
        lastRow = Worksheets( _
            "Temporary Daily Record").UsedRange.Rows.Count
        lblTimeStamp.Caption = Date & "    " & "Last Update: " & _
            Worksheets("Temporary Daily Record").Range( _
                "A" & lastRow).Value
    Else
        tglScrollOn.Caption = "Off"
        tglScrollOn.ForeColor = RGB(0, 200, 255)
        cTxtBox.Scroll = False
        TimerWebQ.Enabled = False
    End If
End Sub
Private Sub TimerWebQ_Timer(ByVal Milliseconds As Long)
'This Timer is set to a 20 minute interval.
    aSymbols.Refresh
    cTxtBox.Text = aSymbols.GetSymbolString
End Sub
```

A user can choose between three sets of Option Button controls to set the ticker speed and scroll type (horizontal or vertical) and select a chart to be copied to the Userform. You set the ticker speed and scroll type by setting the corresponding property values of the cTxtBox object variable. The clsDynamicTextBox class then handles any changes in its ScrollType and Speed properties.

```
Private Sub optFast_Click()
    cTxtBox.Speed = 2
End Sub
Private Sub optMedium_Click()
    cTxtBox.Speed = 1
End Sub
Private Sub optSlow_Click()
    cTxtBox.Speed = 0
End Sub
Private Sub optHorizontal_Click()
    cTxtBox.Clear
    cTxtBox.ScrollType = 0
End Sub
Private Sub optVertical_Click()
    cTxtBox.Clear
    cTxtBox.ScrollType = 1
End Sub
```

Before a chart can be copied to the Userform, you must first copy it to the clipboard. To copy a chart to the clipboard, you must first activate the chart and then use the CopyPicture method of the Chart object to copy a bitmap image of the chart to the clipboard. This task is accomplished with a call to the CopyChartToClip() Sub procedure.

The Temporary Daily Record and Permanent Record worksheets already contain an embedded chart. You must update these charts with the desired data before copying them to the clipboard. This is the function of the UpdateChart() Sub procedure. This procedure is fairly long but involves only Excel-VBA objects and methods. An object reference to the correct worksheet containing the desired chart is set before the column ranges representing the data to be charted are located. To select the data for a chart, you can specify a range or formula string (begin with "=") with the XValues and Values properties of the Series object, but if you use a formula String, the String must not exceed 256 characters in length. If the weekly or monthly chart is selected, the UpdateChart() Sub procedure copies the data to new columns so a contiguous range of cells are used to set the values for the chart. Excel does not require a data range specified for a chart to be contiguous, but if it's not, a formula String will have to be used to set the XValues and Values properties. If a formula String is used to set the chart values, the limit of 256 characters will be exceeded in only a few weeks.

The UpdateChart() Sub procedure also sets the minimum and maximum y-axis scale values for the chart rather than leaving Excel's automatic selections. You can use Excel worksheet functions to round the values for the y-axis scale since VBA does not contain Min, Max, RoundUp, and RoundDown functions.

```
Private Sub optCurrent_Click()
    If cmbSymbols.Text = "" Then Exit Sub
    CopyChartToClip ("Current")
    cForm.CopyClipImage 225, 190, 245, 165
End Sub


Private Sub optDaily_Click()
    If cmbSymbols.Text = "" Then Exit Sub
    CopyChartToClip ("Daily")
    cForm.CopyClipImage 225, 190, 245, 165
End Sub


Private Sub optWeekly_Click()
    If cmbSymbols.Text = "" Then Exit Sub
    CopyChartToClip ("Weekly")
    cForm.CopyClipImage 225, 190, 245, 165
End Sub


Private Sub optMonthly_Click()
    If cmbSymbols.Text = "" Then Exit Sub
    CopyChartToClip ("Monthly")
    cForm.CopyClipImage 225, 190, 245, 165
End Sub


Private Sub cmdClear_Click()
    Dim c As Control
    For Each c In fmCharts.Controls
        If Left(c.Name, 3) = "opt" Then c.Value = False
    Next
    frmTicker.Repaint
    cTxtBox.Refresh
End Sub


Private Sub CopyChartToClip(chType As String)
'Find Chart and copy it to the clipboard
```

```vba
        Dim myChart As ChartObject
        Dim curWs As Worksheet, chWs As Worksheet

        Set curWs = ActiveSheet
        If chType = "Current" Then
            Set chWs = Worksheets("Temporary Daily Record")
        Else
            Set chWs = Worksheets("Permanent Record")
        End If
        For Each myChart In chWs.ChartObjects
            myChart.Activate
            UpdateChart myChart, chType
            ActiveChart.CopyPicture xlScreen, xlBitmap, xlScreen
        Next
        curWs.Select

        Set curWs = Nothing
        Set chWs = Nothing
End Sub

Private Sub UpdateChart(curChart As ChartObject, chType As String)
'Update the chart that is to be copied to the clipboard
        Dim lastRow As Long
        Dim symRange As Range, c As Range
        Dim valRangeStr As String
        Dim ws As Worksheet
        Dim curPeriod As Integer, curCell As Range
        Dim chSym As String
        Dim dataCol As Integer
        Dim I As Integer
        Dim ymin As Long, yMax As Long

        On Error GoTo ErrorHandler
        '....................................................................
        'Set data source worksheet and find the desired column of data
        '....................................................................
        chSym = cmbSymbols.Text
```

```
If chType <> "Current" Then
    Set ws = Worksheets("Permanent Record")
Else
    Set ws = Worksheets("Temporary Daily Record")
End If
lastRow = ws.UsedRange.Rows.Count
'Finds desired column in row 1
Set symRange = ws.Range("1:1").Find(What:=chSym, LookAt:=xlWhole)
valRangeStr = GetColumnRef(symRange.Column) & _
        Trim(Str(2)) & ":" & GetColumnRef(symRange.Column) & lastRow


    '----------------------------------------------------------
    'Search through columns to find the end of a week or month
    '----------------------------------------------------------
Select Case chType
    Case Is = "Weekly"
        curPeriod = ws.Cells(2, 4).Value
        dataCol = 4
    Case Is = "Monthly"
        curPeriod = ws.Cells(2, 3).Value
        dataCol = 3
End Select
I = 2
If (chType <> "Current") And (chType <> "Daily") Then
    ws.Range("F2:G" & lastRow).Clear
    For Each c In Range(valRangeStr)
        If ws.Cells(c.Row, dataCol).Value = curPeriod Then
            Set curCell = c
        Else
            ws.Cells(I, "F").Value = ws.Cells(c.Row - 1, 1).Value
            ws.Cells(I, "G").Value = curCell.Value
            curPeriod = ws.Cells(c.Row, dataCol).Value
            I = I + 1
        End If
    Next
    'Add last value in column
    ws.Cells(I, "F").Value = ws.Cells(lastRow, 1).Value
```

```vba
            ws.Cells(I, "G").Value = ws.Cells(lastRow, curCell.Column).Value
        End If


        '--------------------------
        'Update chart with new data
        '--------------------------
        With curChart
            If (chType <> "Current") And (chType <> "Daily") Then
                .Chart.SeriesCollection(1).XValues = ws.Range( _
                    "F2:F" & lastRow)
                .Chart.SeriesCollection(1).Values = ws.Range( _
                    "G2:G" & lastRow)
                ymin = Application.WorksheetFunction.Min( _
                    ws.Range("G2:G" & lastRow))
                ymin = Application.WorksheetFunction.RoundDown(ymin, -1)
                yMax = Application.WorksheetFunction.Max( _
                    ws.Range("G2:G" & lastRow))
                yMax = Application.WorksheetFunction.RoundUp(yMax, -1)
            Else
                .Chart.SeriesCollection(1).XValues = ws.Range( _
                    "A2:A" & lastRow)
                .Chart.SeriesCollection(1).Values = ws.Range(valRangeStr)
                ymin = Application.WorksheetFunction.Min(ws.Range( _
                    valRangeStr))
                ymin = Application.WorksheetFunction.RoundDown(ymin, -1)
                yMax = Application.WorksheetFunction.Max(ws.Range( _
                    valRangeStr))
                yMax = Application.WorksheetFunction.RoundUp(yMax, -1)
            End If
        End With
        With curChart.Chart.Axes(xlValue)
            .MinimumScale = ymin
            .MaximumScale = yMax
            .MajorUnit = Round(yMax - ymin) / 5
            .MinorUnit = .MajorUnit / 4
        End With
```

```
        Set symRange = Nothing
        Set ws = Nothing
        Set curCell = Nothing
        Exit Sub


ErrorHandler:
        If Err.Number = 91 Then
            MsgBox "No current data"
            Exit Sub
        End If
End Sub
```

The remaining procedures in the frmTicker code module contain straightforward or familiar code. The RedrawUForm() Sub procedure repaints the Userform including the custom text box and chart image if one was selected. This procedure is called from the Click() event procedure of the Command Button control cmdRestore and the Resize() event of frmTicker. The GetColumnRef() Sub procedure is an old standard and is used by the UpdateChart() Sub procedure to construct a range String representing data to be charted. Finally, the QueryClose() event of frmTicker disables the timer and clears system memory.

```
Private Sub cmdRestore_Click()
'Redraws the custom text box and chart
        RedrawUForm
End Sub
Private Sub RedrawUForm()
        Dim c As Control
        Dim chType As String

        For Each c In fmCharts.Controls
            If c.Value = True Then
                chType = c.Caption
                Exit For
            End If
        Next
        frmTicker.Repaint
        cTxtBox.Refresh
        If chType <> "" And cmbSymbols.Text <> "" Then
            cForm.CopyClipImage 225, 190, 245, 165
        End If
End Sub
```

```vba
Private Function GetColumnRef(columnIndex As Integer) As String
'Converts column index number to a textual reference
    Dim numAlpha As Integer
    Dim firstLetter As String
    Dim secondLetter As String
    Dim remainder As Integer
    '
    'Calculate the number of characters in the column string
    numAlpha = columnIndex \ 26
    Select Case columnIndex / 26
        Case Is <= 1     'One character column
            firstLetter = Chr(columnIndex + 64)
            GetColumnRef = firstLetter
        Case Else      'Two character column
            remainder = columnIndex - 26 * (columnIndex \ 26)
            If remainder = 0 Then
                firstLetter = Chr(64 + (columnIndex \ 26) - 1)
                secondLetter = "Z"
                GetColumnRef = firstLetter & secondLetter
            Else
                firstLetter = Chr(64 + (columnIndex \ 26))
                secondLetter = Chr(64 + remainder)
                GetColumnRef = firstLetter & secondLetter
            End If
    End Select
End Function


Private Sub UserForm_Resize()
    On Error Resume Next     'Ignore error if object ref. not set
    RedrawUForm
End Sub


Private Sub UserForm_QueryClose(Cancel As Integer, CloseMode As Integer)
    TimerWebQ.Enabled = False
    Set TimerWebQ = Nothing
    Set aSymbols = Nothing
    Set cTxtBox.UForm = Nothing
    Set cTxtBox = Nothing
```

```
    Set cForm.UForm = Nothing
    Set cForm = Nothing
    Unload Me
End Sub
```

An example of the `frmTicker` Userform running with an active ticker is shown in Figure 18.13.

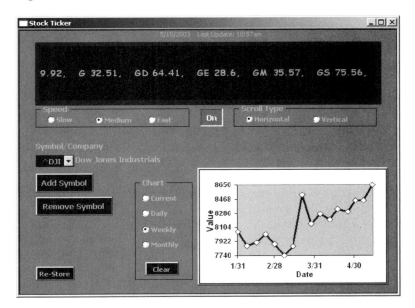

FIGURE 18.13 *The stock ticker userform in action.*

The last component of the stock ticker program is the `frmAddSymbol` Userfom that functions to add a company to the ticker (see Figure 18.3). Its code module contains a single procedure for the `Click()` event of the Command Button control named `cmdAddSymbol`. This procedure adds the user input to the Companies worksheet, Combo Box control, and `aSymbols` collection object. The new company symbol will be included in the `String` sent to Yahoo!'s financial page, and if it is a valid symbol, a stock quote will be retrieved by the Web query.

```
Option Explicit


Private Sub cmdAddSymbol_Click()
'Add new company to worksheet, combo box, and symbols collection
    Dim aSymbol As New clsSymbol
    Dim ws As Worksheet
    Dim nextRow As Long
```

```
    If txtCompany = "" Or txtSymbol = "" Then Exit Sub

    Set ws = Worksheets("Companies")
    nextRow = ws.UsedRange.Rows.Count + 1
    ws.Cells(nextRow, 1).Value = txtCompany.Text
    ws.Cells(nextRow, 2).Value = txtSymbol.Text

    frmTicker.cmbSymbols.AddItem txtSymbol.Text
    aSymbol.Symbol = txtSymbol.Text
    aSymbol.Value = "0.00"
    frmTicker.aSymbols.Add aSymbol

    Set aSymbol = Nothing
    Set ws = Nothing
    Unload Me
End Sub
```

This concludes the code listings for the stock ticker program. The next phase of the design is testing the program for fatal errors, nonfatal errors, and overall behavior. When debugging this program, I focused on each component starting with the custom classes before moving on to the main Userform. This works well because the program is created by encapsulating the problems into smaller more manageable components. Why not follow the same procedure when debugging?

Of course, a program is never really finished. While writing the stock ticker, I thought of several other functions that would be nice to include. For example, a symbol lookup feature would be helpful, as well as the ability to specify a beginning and ending time period for a chart, to name just a couple. I am sure you can think of others.

Creating the Add-In

The final phase of the project is to include the stock ticker in the Excel utilities add-in that was created in Chapter 12 for the Excel-to-HTML converter. The process is relatively simple, but can be tedious and somewhat frustrating.

First, you should ensure that the merger of objects proceeds from the add-in to the .xls file containing the stock ticker project. The transfer should proceed from the add-in to the .xls file because you cannot copy worksheets to an add-in, and the StockTicker2.xls file has several worksheets that contain data, whereas the add-in does not have any. With both files open (Excel_Utilities.xla and StockTicker2.xls), I opened the Project Explorer window in the VBA IDE. All components contained in the open projects are listed in the Project Explorer window as shown in Figure 18.14.

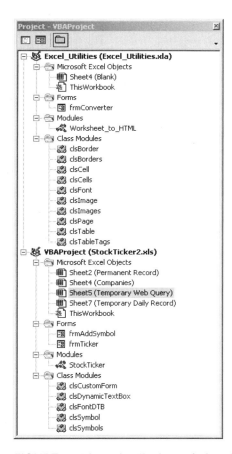

FIGURE 18.14 *Project Explorer window showing components of the Excel_Utilities.xla and StockTicker2.xls files.*

From the Project Explorer window, you can copy Userforms, Modules, and Class Modules from one open project to another simply by dragging their icons. Unfortunately, the same cannot be done with the Excel objects listed in the Project Explorer window. Therefore, you should copy the components from the Excel_Utilities.xla project to the StockTicker2.xls project. Note that you must rename the clsFont class before copying to avoid a naming conflict. It follows that all instances of the clsFont class in the stock ticker program must also be renamed (one declaration in clsDynamicTextBox class). You also must copy the code from the ThisWorkbook code module in the add-in to the ThisWorkbook code module in the .xls file and add an additional CommandBarButton object to the AddToolbar() Sub procedure. The AddToolbar() Sub procedure was originally listed in Chapter 12 and is repeated here with extra code that adds another button to the toolbar. The ShowTicker() Sub procedure referenced with the OnAction property of the CommandBarButton object contains one line of code that loads the frmTicker Userform.

```
Private Sub AddToolbar()
    Dim tlbSaveAsWebPage As CommandBarButton
    Dim tlbStockTicker As CommandBarButton


    '..............................
    'Set reference to new toolbar
    '..............................
    Set tlbProjects = Application.CommandBars.Add( _
        Name:="Excel Projects", _
        Temporary:=True)


    '.......................................
    'Set reference to buttons on toolbar
    '.......................................
    Set tlbSaveAsWebPage = tlbProjects.Controls.Add( _
        Type:=msoControlButton, _
        Temporary:=True)
    tlbSaveAsWebPage.Style = msoButtonCaption
    tlbSaveAsWebPage.Caption = "Web Page"
    tlbSaveAsWebPage.OnAction = "WorksheetToHTML"

    Set tlbStockTicker = tlbProjects.Controls.Add( _
        Type:=msoControlButton, _
        Temporary:=True)
    tlbStockTicker.Style = msoButtonCaption
    tlbStockTicker.Caption = "Stock Ticker"
    tlbStockTicker.OnAction = "ShowTicker"
    tlbStockTicker.BeginGroup = True


    tlbProjects.Visible = True
End Sub
```

The toolbar created by the AddToolbar() Sub procedure is shown in Figure 18.15.

FIGURE 18.15 *Custom toolbar created by the* AddToolbar() *Sub procedure.*

After all objects and the code from the `ThisWorkbook` code module are copied to the StockTicker2.xls project, you can resave the project as an add-in (.xla extension). However, the stock ticker program will not run properly without a couple more changes. First, you must alter all references to `Worksheet` objects to contain a reference to the Excel_Utilities.xla workbook. This is because an add-in can never serve as the active `Workbook` object. So, the reference `Worksheets("Temporary Daily Record")` becomes `Workbooks("Excel_Utilities.xla").Worksheets("Temporary Daily Record")`. Second, you should add a reference to the class name of a VBA Userform "ThunderDFrame" ("ThunderXFrame" in Office 97) to all calls to the `FindWindow()` API function. Without this reference, the `FindWindow()` function may return a handle to a window of the `OfficeTooltip` class — an odd occurrence considering the only difference is that the program is initiated from a custom toolbar rather than the run macro toolbar button. Alternatively, you can hide toolbar ScreenTips by selecting Tools, Customize, Options and deselecting the Show ScreenTips on toolbars checkbox. After making these changes, both Excel-to-HTML converter and Stock Ticker programs are available through a common interface.

Summary

The stock ticker project included extensive use of Windows API functions and COM objects to construct a program that retrieved stock quotes from the Internet and displayed them in a Userform. Using Windows API functions, you learned how to customize a Userform's styles, draw shapes and text on a Userfom, and copy bitmaps from system memory to a Userform. You also learned how to include Microsoft Internet controls and the CCRP Timer objects in a VBA program by using automation to reference their object libraries.

PART V

Professional Project 4 — Data Analysis Automation and Curve-Fitting with Excel-VBA

This book provides examples of using VBA to extend Excel's capabilities through tasks that are difficult (if not impossible) from the Excel window. However, you can also use VBA to perform routine tasks that are just as easily accomplished from Excel. When routine data analysis tasks become repetitive, it is time to use VBA programs to handle the analyses. The savings in time to complete an analysis using VBA versus Excel can be dramatic. Multiply the difference by the number of times an analysis is repeated, and you might save hundreds of hours over a few months.

In these last three chapters, I show you how to use simple VBA programming techniques to optimize repetitive tasks in Excel. You also learn how to model data by using Excel's built-in mathematical expressions or by building custom expressions. Although Microsoft puts a business slant in the online help associated with the use of Excel's data modeling methods, data modeling is not limited to business applications. Scientists and engineers can also use these methods for simple or complex data analyses.

Excel has never been the choice of scientists and engineers for data analysis because better software packages have been available, but with the high cost of software and Microsoft's domination of the market, many companies don't provide employees with any choice but Excel. Fortunately, Excel provides the tools scientists and engineers need to perform complex data modeling. Because these methods are not particularly well known, I want to introduce you to Excel's data-modeling methods. In these last chapters, you learn about the following topics:

◆ Writing fast and efficient code for automating repetitive tasks

◆ Data modeling with Excel's `Trendline` object

◆ Custom data modeling with the Solver add-in

◆ Using class modules and the Windows API to create interactive charts

The last chapter walks you through a sample data automation application that involves fitting data to a custom expression based on the equation for a Guassian distribution. The method discussed for fitting the data can be applied to other problems simply by defining a new data model.

Chapter 19

*Reducing the
Workload by
Automating Data
Analyses*

People who use Excel on a regular basis will eventually find themselves repeatedly using an analysis on identically structured data sets. The data may be repetitive measurements on the same source or identical measurements from difference sources. In either case, the analysis is identical, and repeating it using only the Excel application is not without risk.

The risks involved in data analyses are mostly associated with the human element of reading and writing data to and from Excel. For example, consider a situation in which an Excel template requires raw data to be entered in specific cells in order for the formulas contained in the template to calculate the correct values. If an operator then mistakenly enters data into the wrong cells or enters the wrong data, the analysis will be incorrect. If the error in the analysis is not immediately noticed, it might propagate and lead to serious errors somewhere down the road.

Using VBA to automate an analysis can reduce the probability of an error by eliminating much of the human element. Instead of hand-entering the data, a VBA program can be used to import the data into the proper cell locations, carry out the analysis, and output the results. Of course, significant testing of the program is required for validation of the analysis. But once the automation program is validated, it can be used without worrying about random mistakes tainting the analysis. This will never be true if too much of the analysis is left in human hands. In addition, automation can save many hours of labor thereby reducing costs.

Common Automation Tasks

Several tasks are common to automating an analysis in Excel. I will proceed through some of these tasks with an emphasis on writing a minimal amount of code that will execute as efficiently as possible.

Importing Data (File I/O and SQL)

Importing data is typically the slowest phase in an analysis. Reading or writing data to a permanent storage location can be time-consuming. To make your VBA code as efficient as possible, you should minimize the number of read-write operations in your program. This is true whether the file I/O operations involve opening and importing data from text files or database files.

Text Files

When using text files to support an automation procedure, you can take a few steps to reduce the time involved in a file I/O operation. If possible, do not save temporary or supporting data in Excel format. As you are about to see, file I/O operations for Excel files (.xls extension) can take considerably longer than for text files.

Consider the next four Sub procedures that save data from a single Excel worksheet (see Figure 19.1). Three of the procedures use different methods to save the data in an identical tab-delimited text format. The other procedure saves the workbook in an Excel format (.xls).

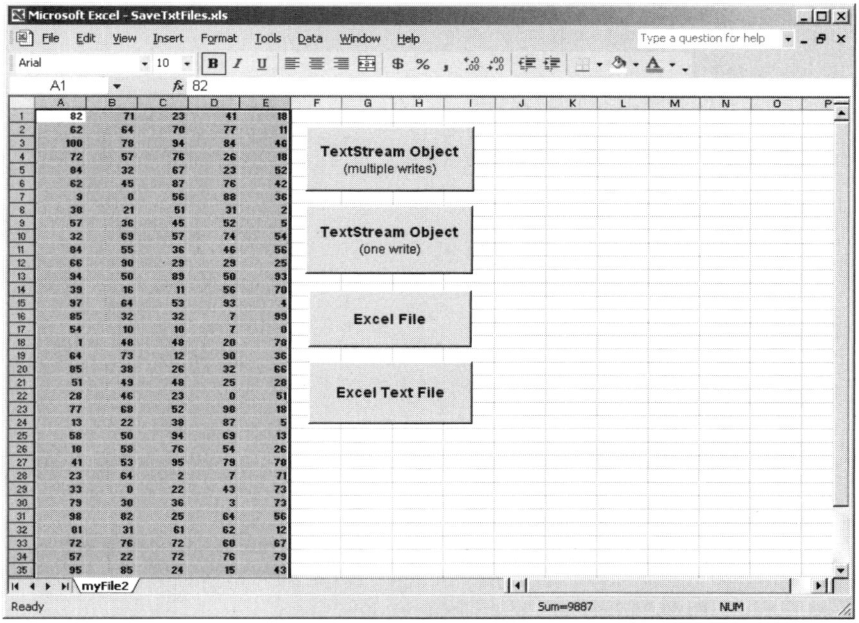

FIGURE 19.1 *Random integers used to time various methods for saving data using Excel-VBA.*

The `CreateTxtFile()` Sub procedure saves data from the highlighted range on the active worksheet to a text file called `myFile.txt`. The data is written to disk as a tab-delimited text file one value at a time with line breaks every five values. The process takes about 40 milliseconds on my computer (1.4 GHz processor, Windows/Office XP) to write 200 integers to a hard drive (7500 RPM) as measured by VBA's `Timer` function and the variables `sTime` and `fTime`.

```
Public Sub CreateTxtFile()
'Save as tab-delimited text file one cell at a time
    Dim fso As FileSystemObject
    Dim aFile As TextStream
    Dim c As Range
    Dim curRow As Integer
    Dim sTime As Single, fTime As Single
```

```
'---------------------------------------------------
'Set object references and loop through selected range
'to write each value to the file.
'---------------------------------------------------
Set fso = New FileSystemObject
Set aFile = fso.CreateTextFile("C:\myFile.txt", True)
curRow = ActiveWindow.Selection.Row
sTime = Timer
For Each c In ActiveWindow.Selection
    If c.Row <> curRow Then      'Test for the next row
        aFile.WriteLine
        curRow = c.Row
    End If
    aFile.Write (c.Value & vbTab)    'Write tab-delimited text
Next
aFile.Close            'Close file and clear memory
fTime = Timer
MsgBox fTime - sTime
Set fso = Nothing
Set aFile = Nothing
End Sub
```

You can optimize the `CreateTxtFile()` Sub procedure by using just one write operation to save the file. The `CreateTxtFile2()` Sub procedure first writes all the data (using the same format) to the `String` variable `outputStr` before writing it to disk. The same 200 integers previously saved by the `CreateTxtFile()` Sub procedure are now written to my hard drive in approximately 8 milliseconds.

```
Public Sub CreateTxtFile2()
'Save as tab-delimited text file with one output statement
    Dim fso As FileSystemObject
    Dim aFile As TextStream
    Dim c As Range
    Dim curRow As Integer
    Dim outputStr As String
    Dim sTime As Single, fTime As Single


    '---------------------------------------------------
    'Set object references and loop through selected range
    'to write each value to the file.
    '---------------------------------------------------
```

```
    Set fso = New FileSystemObject
    Set aFile = fso.CreateTextFile("C:\myFile3.txt", True)
    curRow = ActiveWindow.Selection.Row
    sTime = Timer
    For Each c In ActiveWindow.Selection
        If c.Row <> curRow Then        'Test for the next row
            outputStr = outputStr & vbCrLf
            curRow = c.Row
        End If
        outputStr = outputStr & c.Value & vbTab
    Next
    aFile.Write outputStr
    aFile.Close            'Close file and clear memory
    fTime = Timer
    MsgBox fTime - sTime
    Set fso = Nothing
    Set aFile = Nothing
End Sub
```

In this example, the method used to write the text file to disk is not important since the difference between 8 and 40 milliseconds is imperceptible to the user. However, the time required to save a file will increase with its size and the medium used (that is, it takes longer to write to a zip or floppy drive), so consideration of the number of write operations to a single file may become important.

The next two Sub procedures save the same data as an Excel file and tab-delimited text file using the SaveAs method of the Workbook object. Saving the workbook, which was comprised of just one worksheet holding the same 200 integers and no applied formatting, took more than 600 milliseconds on my computer, whereas saving the data from the worksheet as a tab-delimited text file (FileFormat:=xlText) took approximately 80 milliseconds. So, even though you can use the SaveAs method of the Workbook object to save tab-delimited text files, doing so is not nearly as efficient as using one write operation with the FileSystemObject and TextStream objects.

```
Public Sub SaveAsExcel()
'Save workbook as Excel file
    Dim sTime As Single, fTime As Single
    sTime = Timer
    Workbooks(1).SaveAs "C:\myFile.xls"
    fTime = Timer
    MsgBox fTime - sTime
End Sub
```

```
Public Sub SaveAsExcelTxt()
'Save sheet as tab-delimited text file
    Dim sTime As Single, fTime As Single
    sTime = Timer
    Workbooks(1).SaveAs Filename:="C:\myFile2.txt", FileFormat:=xlText
    fTime = Timer
    MsgBox fTime - sTime
End Sub
```

 NOTE

The execution time of these procedures may vary significantly from one computer to the next, but the order of execution from slowest to fastest will not change. In addition, the relative difference in speeds will not vary significantly. That is, saving a tab-delimited text file with the `CreateTxtFile2()` Sub procedure will always be about 75 times faster (600/8) than saving the data as an Excel workbook file.

Database Files

Accessing database files efficiently follows a similar line of reasoning to that of text files. When using SQL to access a database, keep the number of queries used in a program and the amount of data retrieved by a query to a minimum. In essence, keep the number of file I/O operations to the smallest number possible, and don't read in any more data than what is required.

After the database file has been opened, an SQL statement sent to the DBMS will initiate some action. The action taken by the DBMS will be the slow step in the process, regardless of the statement's type (DQL, DML, or DDL). Therefore, a program with fewer SQL statements will execute faster (all else being equal). Similarly, the more work that has to be done as the result of an SQL statement, the longer VBA will take to execute the statement. For example, the following SQL statement returns nine columns of data from five different tables in the PearTreeUsedCars.mdb Access database.

```
SELECT V.Make, V.Model, C.FirstName, C.LastName, S.FirstName, S.LastName,
D.DealershipName, CP.PurchaseDate, CP.PurchasePrice
FROM Vehicles V, Customers C, CustomerPurchases CP, SalesReps S, Dealerships D
WHERE V.VehicleID=CP.VehicleID AND CP.CustomerID=C.CustomerID
    AND S.SalesRepID=C.SalesRepID AND D.DealershipID=S.DealershipID
    AND CP.PurchaseDate BETWEEN #2/1/03# AND #2/28/03#
ORDER BY CP.PurchaseDate;
```

It is the number of tables involved in the join operation that will slow the creation of the resultant recordset, because the DBMS must first build the Cartesian product (see Appendix C, "Basic SQL Tutorial," for more on Cartesian products) and then filter records from this product. As long as all the data returned by the query is required, it is okay (even better) to send lengthy SQL statements. However, if only the purchase date and price are required, the following SQL statement will execute much faster and should be used instead of the previous statement.

```
SELECT PurchaseDate, PurchasePrice
FROM   CustomerPurchases
WHERE PurchaseDate BETWEEN #2/1/03# AND #2/28/03#
ORDER BY PurchaseDate;
```

Whatever the data source might be for an automation program, chances are that if it is input to Excel through a file I/O operation, you can take some measures to make the process operate more efficiently.

TIP

Use the program shown in Figure 13-11 (Chapter 13, "Data I/O Between Excel and Access") modified to query the PearTreeUsedCars.mdb database to test the queries listed in this chapter.

Formatting a Worksheet

After you enter the data into a worksheet, you will need to apply at least a minimal amount of formatting to make the worksheet more "readable." If the worksheet represents a report, more formatting may be required. Using VBA to format items such as the color, font, and size of a cell or range of cells is straightforward programming. Doing so can also be quite tedious, as you find yourself moving from one range of cells to another in a program to apply yet another set of formats. To reduce or even eliminate the tedium, you can create custom formatting classes or use Excel templates.

Custom Format objects

Instead of writing a lot of formatting code in your automation projects, you can create a custom class with methods that apply predefined formats on a given range. After the members of the custom class are written, formatting a range of cells is as simple as invoking a method. By defining a series of methods in the custom class, you can define formatting styles for headers, data blocks, charts, and so on.

The following custom class (clsCustomFormats) contains just two methods. The HeaderFormat method is meant to be used to format column headers and the DataFormat1 method to format a block of data. Both methods accept a single argument specifying the range of cells in which to apply the formatting.

```
Option Explicit
Public Sub HeaderFormat(cfRange As Range)
'Header format. Centered, bold, italics, black text
'with red-orange background
    cfRange.Font.Bold = True
    cfRange.Font.Color = RGB(0, 0, 0)
    cfRange.Font.Italic = True
    cfRange.Font.Name = "Times New Roman"
    cfRange.Font.Size = 20
    cfRange.Interior.Color = RGB(255, 150, 150)
    cfRange.HorizontalAlignment = xlCenter
    With cfRange.Borders(xlEdgeBottom)
        .LineStyle = xlDouble
        .Weight = xlThick
        .Color = RGB(255, 0, 150)
    End With
    cfRange.Columns.AutoFit
End Sub


Public Sub DataFormat1(cfRange As Range)
'Data block format. Centered black text with gray background
    cfRange.Font.Color = RGB(0, 0, 0)
    cfRange.Font.Name = "Times New Roman"
    cfRange.Font.Size = 14
    cfRange.Interior.Color = RGB(200, 200, 200)
    cfRange.HorizontalAlignment = xlCenter
    With cfRange.Borders(xlEdgeLeft)
        .LineStyle = xlContinuous
        .Weight = xlMedium
        .ColorIndex = xlAutomatic
    End With
    With cfRange.Borders(xlEdgeTop)
        .LineStyle = xlContinuous
```

```
        .Weight = xlMedium
        .ColorIndex = xlAutomatic
    End With
    With cfRange.Borders(xlEdgeBottom)
        .LineStyle = xlContinuous
        .Weight = xlMedium
        .ColorIndex = xlAutomatic
    End With
    With cfRange.Borders(xlEdgeRight)
        .LineStyle = xlContinuous
        .Weight = xlMedium
        .ColorIndex = xlAutomatic
    End With
    With cfRange.Borders(xlInsideVertical)
        .LineStyle = xlContinuous
        .Weight = xlMedium
        .ColorIndex = xlAutomatic
    End With
    With cfRange.Borders(xlInsideHorizontal)
        .LineStyle = xlContinuous
        .Weight = xlMedium
        .ColorIndex = xlAutomatic
    End With
    With cfRange.Borders(xlEdgeBottom)
        .LineStyle = xlDouble
        .Color = RGB(0, 0, 0)
    End With
End Sub
```

 NOTE

I named the method `DataFormat1` under the assumption that more data formatting methods will be added to the class in the future.

The `TestCustomFormatClass()` Sub procedure invokes both methods of the `clsCustomFormats` class to apply formatting to the ranges A1:D1 and A2:D10 in the active worksheet. The result is shown in Figure 19.2.

```
Public Sub TestCustomFormatClass()
    Dim cf1 As clsCustomFormats
    Set cf1 = New clsCustomFormats
    cf1.HeaderFormat Range("A1:D1")
    cf1.DataFormat1 Range("A2:D10")
    Set cf1 = Nothing
End Sub
```

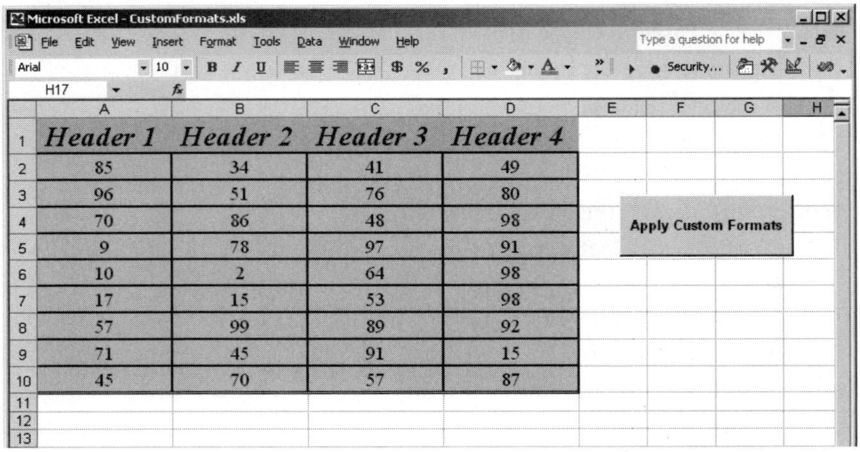

FIGURE 19.2 *Using a custom class to format a worksheet.*

After writing a custom class containing numerous methods that format headers, blocks of data, and charts, you will be able to quickly apply worksheet formatting to future automation projects.

Using a Template

If the project involves adding data to a static worksheet or worksheets, the formatting becomes trivial and hardly involves VBA. Instead of using a VBA program to create the formatting, charts, and formulas in a worksheet, simply use the Excel application window as you normally would. After the worksheets appear and function as desired, delete the data from the worksheets, but leave all formatting, charts, and formulas. Next, save the workbook as an Excel template (.xlt extension).

The program that automates the analysis can open the template file with the Open method of the Workbooks collection object. One line of code replaces all code that would have been required to format the worksheet.

```
Workbooks.Open "C:\MyTemplate.xlt"
```

Opening a template will create a new Workbook object named MyTemplate1 (assuming the template name is MyTemplate.xlt) that is an exact copy of the template file. Subsequent calls to open the template will increment the number at the end of the name of the Workbook object created (for example, MyTemplate2, MyTemplate3, and so on). After the new Workbook object is created, it becomes the active workbook. The data automation process should then proceed to add the required data to the appropriate cells in the template before it is saved (presumably as an Excel workbook — .xls).

Finding the Next Available Cell

Finding the next available or *empty* cell in a worksheet is a relatively common task in automation programs, especially in situations where you have to add a new row of data to an existing table. You can use a couple of methods to find the next available cell. One approach is to use a For loop that searches for empty strings in the Value property of a Range object returned from the current iteration of the loop.

```
Dim I As Long
For I = 1 To Range("A:A").Count
    If Cells(I, "A").Value = "" Then
        Cells(I, "A").Select
        Exit For
    End If
Next I
```

However, this approach can be slow, especially if it takes a large number of iterations through the loop to find an empty cell. A better approach is to use the Find method of the Range object.

The VBA Find method is the equivalent of selecting Edit, Find from the Excel application window (see Figure 19.3). This method is very efficient for finding a specific cell in a worksheet based on several criteria that may be specified as arguments passed to the method. The only required argument (What) tells the Find method what to look for and can be specified using any valid Excel data type. To find an empty cell, you specify an empty String ("") for the What argument. Optional arguments of the Find method are listed in Table 19.1 and directly correlate to the inputs on the Find and Replace dialog box shown in Figure 19.3.

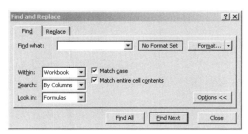

FIGURE 19.3 *Using the Find and Replace dialog box in Excel.*

Table 19.1 Arguments of VBA's Find Method

Argument	Description
What	Specifies what to search for. Can be any Excel data type.
After	Specifies the cell after which you want the search to begin.
LookIn	Specifies the type of information in which to search (formulas, values, or constants). Use constants `xlFormulas`, `xlValues`, or `xlConstants`.
LookAt	Specifies whether to look at all (`xlWhole`) or part (`xlPart`) of the contents of the cells.
SearchOrder	Specifies whether to search by rows (`xlByRows`) or columns (`xlByColumns`).
SearchDirection	Specifies the search direction (`xlNext` or `xlPrevious`).
MatchCase	True to make the search case sensitive. The default value is `False`.
SearchFormat	Specifies the formatting to search for.

The `Find` method returns a `Range` object that represents the first cell where the information specified by the `What` argument is found.

The `FindNextEmptyCell()` Sub procedure uses the `Find` method of the `Range` object to search for an empty worksheet cell. The arguments of the procedure are used to denote whether to search by columns or rows (`SearchByCol`) and where to begin the search (`StartCell`). You immediately select the cell returned by the `Find` method by invoking its `Activate` method.

```
Public Sub FindCell()
    Dim curCell As Range
    Set curCell = Range("A1")
    FindNextEmptyCell True, curCell
End Sub
Private Sub FindNextEmptyCell(searchByCol As Boolean, _
            startCell As Range)
    If searchByCol Then
        Cells.Find(What:="", After:=startCell, _
            SearchOrder:=xlByColumns, _
            SearchDirection:=xlNext).Activate
    Else
        Cells.Find(What:="", After:=startCell, _
            SearchDirection:=xlNext).Activate
```

```
    End If
End Sub
```

The `Find` method of the `Range` object will locate the empty cell quickly, regardless of the size of the worksheet; whereas, the time required by a `For` loop to find an empty cell will be a function of the number of cells searched — a potentially lengthy process.

Copying Formulas

Adding formulas to worksheets in an automation project is almost inevitable. Whenever possible, you should take advantage of the spatial relationships between cell references to create a formula with relative or absolute references (see Appendix A, "Basic Excel Tutorial"). Consider an example that converts several angles from degrees to radians. If the angles specified in degrees are contained in column A of a worksheet and the angles in radians are to be calculated in column B, the formula entered in cell B2 should be "=RADIANS(A2)" (see Figure 19.4). The formula uses a relative reference to cell A2, which contains an angle in degrees. Rather than type more formulas in the remaining cells of column B, you can copy and paste (or autofill) the existing formula down the column, and the relative reference to the row index will increment accordingly (see Figure 19.4). This is a great timesaver when using Excel. It is also a great timesaver when writing formulas with VBA.

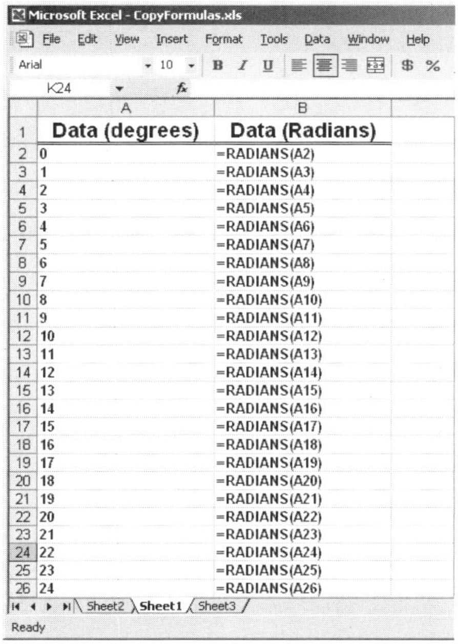

	A	B
1	Data (degrees)	Data (Radians)
2	0	=RADIANS(A2)
3	1	=RADIANS(A3)
4	2	=RADIANS(A4)
5	3	=RADIANS(A5)
6	4	=RADIANS(A6)
7	5	=RADIANS(A7)
8	6	=RADIANS(A8)
9	7	=RADIANS(A9)
10	8	=RADIANS(A10)
11	9	=RADIANS(A11)
12	10	=RADIANS(A12)
13	11	=RADIANS(A13)
14	12	=RADIANS(A14)
15	13	=RADIANS(A15)
16	14	=RADIANS(A16)
17	15	=RADIANS(A17)
18	16	=RADIANS(A18)
19	17	=RADIANS(A19)
20	18	=RADIANS(A20)
21	19	=RADIANS(A21)
22	20	=RADIANS(A22)
23	21	=RADIANS(A23)
24	22	=RADIANS(A24)
25	23	=RADIANS(A25)
26	24	=RADIANS(A26)

FIGURE 19.4 *Copying as formula with a relative reference in Excel.*

Consider the following `For/Next` loop that writes a formula to 360 cells in column B of the worksheet shown in Figures 19.4.

```
For I = 2 To 361
        Cells(I, 2).Formula = "=RADIANS(A" & I & ")"
Next I
```

The time the loop takes to execute is relatively long (200 milliseconds on my computer), and this time will increase if more formulas must be written (approximately linearly with the number of formulas). It doesn't take much more than one thousand formulas to delay a program by one second (longer for an older processor). Because creating a few thousand formulas is not uncommon in an automation project, you should avoid using loops when creating formulas (if possible).

Rather than use a loop, use the `Copy` or `AutoFill` methods of the `Range` object to create formulas in a worksheet.

```
Range("B2").Formula = "=RADIANS(A2)"
Range("B2").Copy Destination:=Range("B2:B361")
```

The `Copy` method of the `Range` object copies the contents of the existing cell and pastes it to all cells specified in the `Destination` argument. Alternatively, you can use the `AutoFill` method to gain the same result.

```
Range("B2").Formula = "=RADIANS(A2)"
Range("B2").AutoFill Destination:=Range("B2:B361")
```

The `Copy` and `AutoFill` methods execute much faster than a `For/Next` loop (10 milliseconds to run the previous code on my computer or 20 times faster than the `For/Next` loop), and the magnitude of the difference increases with the number of formulas created.

Of course, if the spatial relationships do not exist, the formulas will have to be written to their cells with individual lines of code.

Screen Updating

If you have watched the Excel application window while running a macro (recorded or otherwise), you have noticed that Excel refreshes the screen with each line of code that alters its appearance. Whether it's adding values to a cell or formatting various components of a chart, the screen is updated with each change made by the program. Updating the screen with each alteration can greatly slow the execution speed of a program. Fortunately, it's incredibly easy to turn off the screen updates by using the `ScreenUpdating` property of the `Application` object. Simply place the following line of code just before the execution of a code block that will alter the appearance of the Excel application window.

```
Application.ScreenUpdating = False
```

After setting the `ScreenUpdating` property to `False`, any changes to the Excel application window are delayed until the property is set to `True` or program execution ends.

Printing Reports

Finally, the last stage of a data automation project usually involves preparing the worksheet or worksheets for printing. I presume that you have already formatted the worksheets using printer friendly styles (colors, widths, heights, and so on), so all that remains is to define the page or pages that represent a report so that inconvenient page breaks (for example, down the middle of a chart) are avoided.

Page Breaks in Excel

You can add horizontal and vertical page breaks to a worksheet using the `Add` method of the `HPageBreaks` and `VPageBreaks` collection objects. The `Before` argument specifies the location at which the horizontal or vertical page break is placed.

```
ActiveSheet.VPageBreaks.Add Before:=Range("K1")
```

```
ActiveSheet.HPageBreaks.Add Before:=Range("A25")
```

To view page breaks from the Excel application window, select View, Page Break Preview. Existing page breaks appear as horizontal and vertical lines on the worksheet (see Figure 19.5).

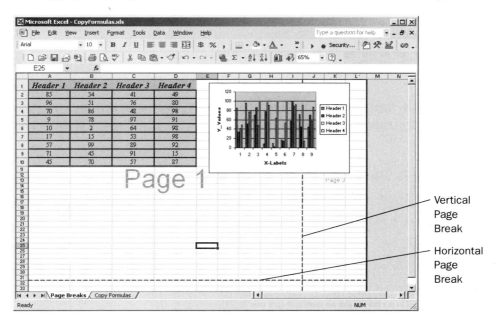

FIGURE 19.5 *Viewing page breaks in Excel.*

Page breaks that appear as dashed lines are automatically set by Excel and cannot be deleted, but you can move them using the Drag method of the HPageBreak or VPageBreak objects. The PageBreaks() Sub procedure formats the page setup and page breaks for the document shown in Figure 19.5. The worksheet is set to landscape before any automatic page breaks are moved to the next region. All page breaks in the worksheet will be automatic because the ResetAllPageBreaks method of the Worksheet object is invoked at the start of the procedure.

```
Public Sub PageBreaks()
    Dim curSh As Worksheet
    Dim hBreak As HPageBreak, vBreak As VPageBreak

    ActiveSheet.ResetAllPageBreaks    'Reset to default
    ActiveWindow.View = xlPageBreakPreview
    ActiveSheet.PageSetup.Orientation = xlLandscape

    Set curSh = ActiveSheet
    For Each hBreak In curSh.HPageBreaks    'Move horizontal break
        hBreak.DragOff Direction:=xlDown, RegionIndex:=1
    Next

    For Each vBreak In curSh.VPageBreaks    'Move vertical break
        vBreak.DragOff Direction:=xlToRight, RegionIndex:=1
    Next

    curSh.VPageBreaks.Add Before:=Range("M1")    'Add vertical break
    curSh.HPageBreaks.Add Before:=Range("A14")    'Add horizontal break

    Set curSh = Nothing
End Sub
```

The worksheet from Figure 19.5 that results after the execution of the PageBreaks() Sub procedure is shown in Figure 19.6.

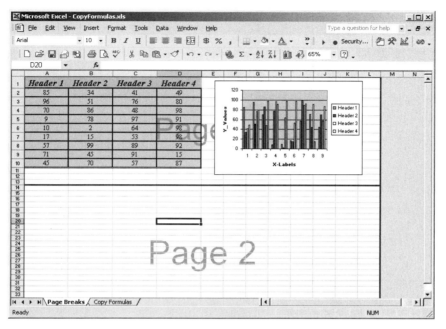

FIGURE 19.6 *Customizing page breaks with VBA.*

TIP

Use the `PrintArea` property of the `PageSetup` object to set vertical and horizontal page breaks at the worksheet row and column specified in a `String` using the A1 style reference notation.

`ActiveSheet.PageSetup.PrintArea = "A1:L12"`

Automatic page breaks located within the defined area will not be moved or deleted.

Summary

In this chapter, you learned some straightforward but essential techniques for writing VBA code efficiently. The techniques discussed were applied to the problem of creating data automation programs for Excel. The data automation process was split into three categories: data I/O, worksheet formatting, and printing reports.

Chapter 20

**Advanced Data
Analysis Using
Curve-Fitting and
Interactive Charts
with Excel-VBA**

This chapter continues the process of automating data analyses using VBA and Excel. Specifically, this chapter shows you how to model data in Excel using both the application window and VBA. In addition, you learn how to make a chart interactive so that it provides the user with specific information based on a chart selection.

Data Modeling

Excel has a good set of tools for modeling data based on a mathematical expression. The basic concept of data modeling involves the calculation of a dependent variable (Y) based on a mathematical equation that is a function of an independent variable (X). The idea is to reproduce the observed values (Y measured) at the given X-Y data points. Most of the functions of interest can be expressed as a linear combination of simpler functions with coefficients that represent unknown constants, as shown here:

$Y = f(X)$

$f(X) = c_1{}^*f_1(X) + c_2{}^* f_2(X) = \ldots + c_n {}^*f_n(X)$

The calculated values are "fit" to a data set using the method of least squares and should be a fair reproduction of the original data. The method of least squares calculates an error (SSE) in the fit from the summation of the squared differences between the calculated and observed values. The SSE represents the sum of squared error for each observable (i) up to the total number of points (N).

$SSE = \Sigma (f(X_i) - Y_i)^2$

By minimizing the SSE with respect to each coefficient, the best mathematical expression reproducing a set of observables is then returned. Minimizing the SSE involves calculating the partial derivatives of the SSE with respect to each coefficient in the model expression and setting the result equal to zero.

For example, if the model expression $f(X)$ is that of a straight line ($f(X) = c_1{}^*X + c_2$), there are two coefficients, and the derivatives will generate two independent equations with two unknowns that are easily solved. The derivates are given by the following two equations:

$\partial SSE/\partial c_1 = 0 = c_1{}^*\Sigma X_i^2 + c_2{}^*\Sigma X_i - \Sigma X_i Y_i$

$\partial SSE/\partial c_2 = 0 = c_1{}^*\Sigma X_i + N^*c_2 - \Sigma Y_i$

Simultaneously solving these two equations produces the solutions for the slope and intercept for the equation of a straight line that best reproduces the data.

$$c_1 = slope = (N^* \Sigma X_i Y_i - \Sigma X_i \Sigma Y_i)/(N^* \Sigma X_i^2 - (\Sigma X_i)^2)$$

$$c_2 = intercept = (\Sigma X_i^2 Y_i - \Sigma X_i \Sigma X_i Y_i)/(N^* \Sigma X_i^2 - (\Sigma X_i)^2)$$

For a linear least squares fit, you need to calculate only four different summations to determine the slope (c_1) and y-intercept (c_2) for the model.

After a model equation is calculated by the method of least squares, the values of the coefficients extracted from the calculation can be used in further analyses. In addition, the model can be used to predict new values for the dependent variable for any given value of the independent variable. Common mathematical expressions used to model multivariate data (dependent data sets) provided by Excel are listed in Table 20.1. Excel uses the method of least squares when fitting these expressions to a data set.

Table 20.1 Excel's Mathematical Expressions for Data Modeling

Name	Expression	Description
Linear	$Y = c1^*X + c2$	Y is linearly dependent on X (straight line). The coefficient $c1$ is the slope, and $c2$ is the Y-intercept.
Logarithmic	$Y = c1^*Ln(X) + c2$	Y is dependent on the natural logarithm of X. The coefficient $c1$ represents an amplitude, and $c2$ is the Y-asymptote.
Polynomial	$Y = c1 + c2^*X + c3^*X^2 +$	Y is dependent on the polynomial expression of X. The polynomial order is the largest power of X used in the expression.
Power	$Y = c1^*X^{c2}$	Y is dependent on the value of X raised to an unknown power.
Exponential	$Y = c1^*e^{c2^*X}$	Y is dependent on the base e exponential raised to the power of the parameter $c2$ times X.

 NOTE

Excel also provides an option for a moving average that can be charted with a data set. A moving average calculates the average value for a specified number of data points as the series progresses. The calculation of a moving average is not data modeling because the expression is not "fit" to the data.

Excel Functions and Add-Ins

Numerous Excel worksheet functions use the method of least squares to model data and then return some component of the result. Like other Excel worksheet functions, the data modeling functions can be added to worksheet cells with VBA as a formula sting. For example, functions that use a linear model include SLOPE(), INTERCEPT(), LINEST(), TREND(), and FORECAST(). To add a formula that includes one of these functions, use the Formula or FormulaArray properties of the Range object.

```
Range("A20").Formula = "=SLOPE(B2:B5,A2:A5)"
Range("B20").Formula = "=INTERCEPT(B2:B5,A2:A5)"
Range("A20:B20").FormulaArray = "=LINEST(B2:B5,A2:A5)"
```

Note that the LINEST() worksheet function returns two values to the worksheet; thus, the FormulaArray property is used with a Range object that includes two cells.

Other data modeling-related functions include LOGEST(), GROWTH(), and STEYX(). You can use any of these functions in an automation program simply by copying a formula String to the appropriate worksheet cell. Consult Excel's online help for an understanding of the arguments required by these functions.

To use these functions in a VBA program without creating a formula in a worksheet cell, use the WorksheetFunction property of the Application object as previously discussed on several occasions in this book.

```
Dim myVar()
myVar2 = Application.WorksheetFunction.Slope(Range("B2:B5"), _
        Range("A2:A5"))
myVar() = Application.WorksheetFunction.LinEst(Range("B2:B5"), _
        Range("A2:A5"))
For I = 1 To 2
    Debug.Print myVar(I)
Next I
```

Again, functions that return more than one value receive special treatment. The LinEst() function of the WorksheetFunction object must be used with a dynamic variable array (Variant). Furthermore, the LinEst() function returns its two values to the array indices 1 and 2 rather than 0 and 1, even if the Option Base is zero.

Add-Ins

The Analysis ToolPak add-in comes with Excel and includes numerous tools for conducting data analyses and returning the results to a worksheet. Some of the tools included with the Analysis ToolPak can be used to model data. You load the Analysis ToolPak add-in by selecting Tools, Add-Ins from the Excel application window. After it is loaded, you can access its functions by selecting Tools, Data Analysis. The resulting dialog box is shown in Figure 20.1.

FIGURE 20.1   *The Data Analysis dialog box listing tools available with the Analysis ToolPak add-in.*

Excel add-ins are briefly discussed in Chapter 9, "Custom Menus and Toolbars," where you learn how to load the Analysis ToolPak add-in and execute its random number generator using VBA code. As stated in Chapter 9, the only way to learn how to use the components of the Analysis ToolPak is to record a macro and examine the resulting code.

The following line of code was recorded by selecting Regression from the Data Analysis dialog box:

```
Application.Run "Regress", ActiveSheet.Range("$B$2:$B$5"), _
    ActiveSheet.Range("$A$2:$A$5"), False, False, , ActiveSheet.Range( _
    "$I$2"), True, False, True, True, , False
```

The `Boolean` values represent the values of the check boxes and option buttons in the Regression dialog box shown in Figure 20.2. At a minimum, you must input an X and Y range and select an output option.

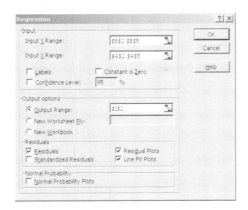

FIGURE 20.2   *The Regression dialog box used to carry out a linear regression analysis on selected data in Excel.*

The results from the regression analysis created by the previous line of code are shown in Figure 20.3. The chart labels created by the regression tool leave something to be desired, but that can be remedied with a little more code. Just consult references to the Chart object throughout this book and the online help.

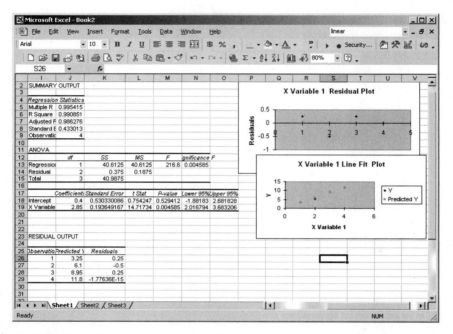

FIGURE 20.3 *Results of a regression analysis carried out by the Regression tool from the Analysis ToolPak.*

The *X-Y* Scatter Chart

Scatter charts plot *X-Y* data points on a grid represented by perpendicular axes with an origin at *x=y=0*. The quality of a model is best illustrated using an *X-Y* scatter chart. For example, the chart shown in Figure 20.4 contains two series that represent arbitrary data (column B) and the values reproduced from a linear fit to this data (column C). The linear model was computed with the SLOPE() and INTERCEPT() worksheet functions in cells E2 and F2, which were used to calculate the values in column C.

NOTE

Excel's bubble chart is another example of an *X-Y* scatter chart that includes a third dimension represented by the relative size of the data markers.

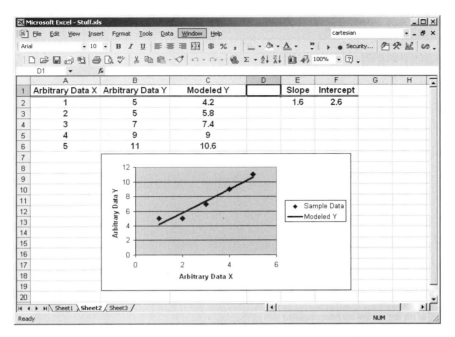

FIGURE 20.4 *An X-Y scatter chart containing an arbitrary data series and another series representing a linear model for the data.*

You can create scatter charts from VBA using a procedure like the `CreateScatterChart()` Sub procedure listed next. The procedure creates an embedded scatter chart on the active worksheet. The procedure's arguments represent the worksheet ranges that contain the data, the chart position, and titles for the legend and axes.

```
Private Sub CreateScatterChart(xRange As Range, yRange As Range, _
    cLeft As Integer, cTop As Integer, cWidth As Integer, _
    cHeight As Integer, xTitle As String, yTitle As String)
'Embeds a scatter chart on the active worksheet
    Dim curSh As Worksheet

    Set curSh = ActiveSheet
    curSh.ChartObjects.Add(Left:=cLeft, Top:=cTop, Width:=cWidth, _
        Height:=cHeight).Activate

    'Format the chart and add data
    With ActiveChart
        .ChartType = xlXYScatter
        .SeriesCollection.NewSeries
```

```
            .HasLegend = True
            .Legend.Position = xlLegendPositionRight
            .Axes(xlCategory, xlPrimary).HasTitle = True
            .Axes(xlCategory, xlPrimary).AxisTitle.Characters.Text = xTitle
            .Axes(xlValue, xlPrimary).HasTitle = True
            .Axes(xlValue, xlPrimary).AxisTitle.Characters.Text = yTitle
            .SeriesCollection(1).MarkerSize = 8
            .SeriesCollection(1).Name = "Sample Data"
            .SeriesCollection(1).XValues = xRange     'X-data range
            .SeriesCollection(1).Values = yRange      'Y-data range
        End With
        Set curSh = Nothing
    End Function
```

The AddChart() Sub procedure calls the CreateScatterChart() procedure and adds a second series that should represent the best fit to the data. The second series is added to the chart via the Copy method of the Range object and Paste method of the SeriesCollection collection object. The second series is formatted as a solid line (refer to Figure 20.4).

```
Public Sub AddChart()
'Creates an embedded scatter chart and adds a
'second series formatted as a line
    Dim s As Integer


    '-------------------------------------
    'Call the function to create the chart
    '-------------------------------------
    CreateScatterChart Range("A2:A6"), Range("B2:B6"), 100, 100, 350, _
        200, Range("A1").Value, Range("B1").Value
    Range("C1:C6").Copy


    '---------------------------------
    'Add the second series to the chart
    '---------------------------------
    ActiveChart.SeriesCollection.Paste Rowcol:=xlColumns, _
        SeriesLabels:=True, CategoryLabels:=False, _
        Replace:=False, NewSeries:=True


    '---------------------------------------------------
```

```
    'Re-format the second series to look like a trend line
    '------------------------------------------------------
    Application.CutCopyMode = False
    ActiveChart.SeriesCollection(2).Select
    With Selection.Border
        .ColorIndex = 25
        .Weight = xlThick
        .LineStyle = xlContinuous
    End With
    Selection.MarkerStyle = xlNone
End Sub
```

Alternatively, data can be modeled directly from the Chart object using the Trendline and Trendlines collection objects.

Trendlines

Trendlines are added to a chart from the Excel application window by first activating the chart and then selecting Chart, Add Trendline. The resulting dialog box is shown in Figure 20.5.

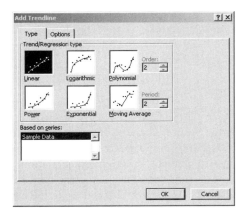

FIGURE 20.5 *The Add Trendline dialog box for selecting built-in models to be applied to charted data.*

Select a model from the available choices (refer to Table 20.1) and click OK. To add the best-fit equation to the chart, select Options, Display equation on chart from the Add Trendline dialog box.

To add a trendline to an existing chart with VBA, use the Add method of the Trendlines collection object. The Type and DisplayEquation properties of the Trendline object are used in the AddChart2() Sub procedure to select the built-in model (xlLinear) and display the resulting equation. Other constants for the Type property of the Trendline object include xlExponential, xlLogarithmic, xlPolynomial, xlPower, and xlMovingAvg. Other arguments for the Add method of the Trendlines collection object include Order (specifies the order of the polynomial), Period (specifies the period for a moving average), Forward (the number of periods the trendline extends forward), Backward (the number of periods the trendline extends backward), Intercept, DisplayRSquared (True to display the R-squared value of the trendline on the chart), and Name (the name of the trendline as text).

```
Public Sub AddChart2()
    CreateScatterChart Range("A2:A6"), Range("B2:B6"), 100, 100, 350, _
        200, Range("A1").Value, Range("B1").Value
    ActiveChart.SeriesCollection(1).Trendlines.Add Type:=xlLinear, _
        DisplayEquation:=True
End Sub
```

The chart resulting from the execution of the AddChart2() Sub procedure is shown in Figure 20.6.

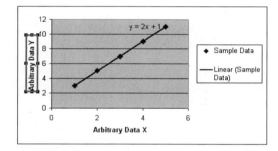

FIGURE 20.6 *A scatter chart with a linear regression trendline.*

Displaying the equation on the chart is only for the user's benefit. In order to use the coefficients from the model in further calculations, you should repeat the analysis using the appropriate formulas as discussed earlier in this chapter. The trendline equation can be returned from the DataLabel property of the Trendline object using the following line of code. This copies the trendline equation to the clipboard. You can paste the equation to a worksheet cell using the Paste method of the Worksheet object.

```
ActiveChart.SeriesCollection(1).Trendlines(1).DataLabel.Select
Range("G19").Select
ActiveSheet.Paste
```

However, you will have to use several String manipulation functions to extract the coefficients from the String representing the model expression.

Custom Models

Excel's built-in expressions for data modeling are useful only when the data is best represented by one of these expressions. In many analyses, the built-in expressions will be of no use because the data is not described by these equations. In such cases, you must construct a custom model with which to fit the data.

Building the Model

To fit a custom model to a data set, first define the model and add its coefficients to the worksheet. Next, enter a first guess for the coefficients and use them to calculate an estimate of the Y values that represent the fit to the data. Finally, create an X-Y scatter chart that includes series for the measured and calculated values.

Consider the data entered into the worksheet shown in Figure 20.7. The custom model $Y = C1 + C2/X$ is used to reproduce the data entered in column B. (The data in this example is real. I removed descriptive labels because they are irrelevant to this discussion.)

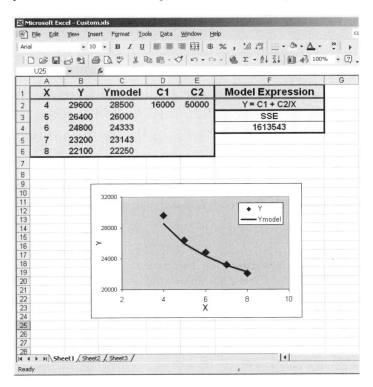

FIGURE 20.7 *Building a custom model to fit to a data set.*

Initial guesses for the coefficients C1 and C2 were used to calculate the values in column C (Ycalc) using the equation shown in cell F2. The SUMXMY2() worksheet function returns the sum of squared error (SSE) to cell F4. Everything included in the worksheet can be created from VBA using methods discussed in this chapter and previous chapters.

The Y values calculated from the model are not yet optimized but the worksheet is ready for the Solver add-in to accomplish this task.

The Solver Add-In

The Solver add-in extends the capabilities of Excel to include custom modeling of data in an analysis. Solver is used to optimize (in our case, minimize) the value in a worksheet cell (target cell) by adjusting the values in other cells. The cells whose values are adjusted represent the desired coefficients from the model and should be directly or indirectly related to the value being minimized. You can apply constraints to restrict the values Solver can use in the model, and the constraints can refer to other cells that affect the target cell formula. You can use a number of optional parameters to set details such as the maximum time and iterations allowed to find a solution, the desired precision of the solution, the tolerance, and so on.

 NOTE

The Microsoft Excel Solver tool uses a nonlinear optimization method developed by Leon Lasdon, University of Texas at Austin, and Allan Waren, Cleveland State University.

Linear and integer problems use the simplex method with bounds on the variables, and the branch-and-bound method, implemented by John Watson and Dan Fylstra, Frontline Systems, Inc.

Solver is not installed with the normal installation of Excel. If Solver is not listed in the Add-Ins dialog box (to access it, select Tools, Add-Ins), you will have to install it from the product CD.

After Solver is loaded, you can show the Solver Parameters dialog box (see Figure 20.8) by selecting Tools, Solver from the Excel application window.

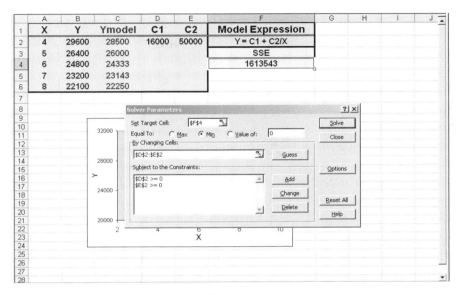

	A	B	C	D	E	F	G	H	I	J
1	**X**	**Y**	**Ymodel**	**C1**	**C2**	**Model Expression**				
2	4	29600	28500	16000	50000	Y = C1 + C2/X				
3	5	26400	26000			SSE				
4	6	24800	24333			1613543				
5	7	23200	23143							
6	8	22100	22250							

FIGURE 20.8 *The Solver Parameters dialog box used to set the parameters for fitting data to a custom model.*

You set the Solver parameters to minimize the SSE by adjusting the values of the coefficients in the custom model expression. Constraints are not required, but you should include them (if possible) in order to decrease the time Solver will require to find a solution. To access the Solver Options dialog box (see Figure 20.9), you click the Options button. You should also set optional parameters so that the solution is the desired precision, without taking an excessive amount of time to calculate.

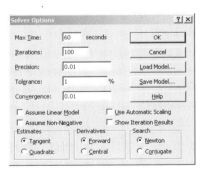

FIGURE 20.9 *The Solver Options dialog box with additional parameters to be used in a custom fit to a data set.*

Once Solver is initiated, it will calculate a solution using the input parameters. The coefficients to the model are updated on the worksheet after the Solver Results dialog box is addressed. The update to the coefficients is reflected in all dependent cells. The solution returned by Solver with the worksheet in Figure 20.7 is shown in Figure 20.10.

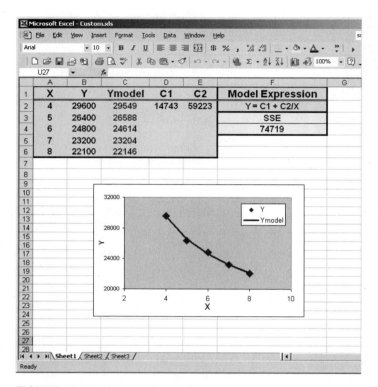

FIGURE 20.10 *A custom fit to a data set as determined by the Solver add-in.*

Although unusual for an add-in, to invoke Solver from a VBA program, you must first set a reference to the Solver object library by selecting Tools, References, SOLVER in the VBA IDE. After the reference is set, calls to the Solver function library can be used to set up the parameters and initiate a custom fit to a data set.

The InvokeSolver() Sub procedure calls several Solver functions that are used to fit the data in the worksheet of Figure 20.7. Using the SolverReset function, you clear the parameters before using the SolverOk function to define a basic Solver model. The SolverAdd function adds the same constraints shown in Figure 20.8, and the SolverOptions function sets the parameters shown in the Solver Options dialog box shown earlier in Figure 20.9. You start the optimization with the SolverSolve function specifying True for the UserFinish argument, which tells Solver to return the solution without showing the Solver Results dialog box.

```
Public Sub InvokeSolver()
    SolverReset
    SolverOk SetCell:="$F$4", MaxMinVal:=2, ValueOf:="0", _
        ByChange:="$D$2:$E$2"
    SolverAdd CellRef:="$D$2", Relation:=3, FormulaText:="0"
```

```
    SolverAdd CellRef:="$E$2", Relation:=3, FormulaText:="0"
    SolverOptions MaxTime:=60, Iterations:=100, Precision:=0.1, _
        IntTolerance:=1, Convergence:=0.1
    SolverSolve UserFinish:=True
End Sub
```

Although the optimization of a data set to a custom model can be carried out in the Excel application window, it is a good idea to add it to a VBA program, because the methods are fairly advanced and the user may not understand how to set the parameters.

Interactive Charts

In Chapter 10, "Creating and Manipulating Excel Charts," you learn that event procedures for chart sheets are automatically enabled and available through their code window. However, when the chart is embedded on a worksheet, a separate class module is required to initialize the event procedures of the `Chart` object. The obvious significance of this is that making a chart interact with the user requires the use of event procedures.

Displaying Data Labels

One application of an interactive chart is to allow the user to add a data marker to a chart by selecting a specific point. You add data markers to individual points from the Excel application window using the Format Data Point dialog box. To access this dialog box, select a data series and double-click a specific point. Next, you select the Data Labels tab and the desired check boxes (see Figure 20.11). The process is somewhat cumbersome and can be simplified with a simple event procedure of the `Chart` object.

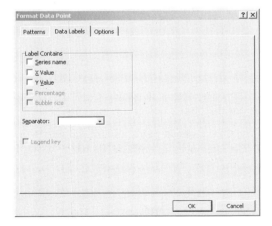

FIGURE 20.11 *Adding data labels to a data marker using the Format Data Point dialog box.*

The Select() event procedure of the Chart object is probably the most useful of the Chart object's events because it identifies the specific components of the chart selected by the user. You may remember that the Select() event procedure accepts three arguments. The argument ElementID is a Long integer that refers to the object or element selected by the user (ChartArea, PlotArea, Series, and so on), and Arg1 and Arg2 are Long integers that refer to specific components of the selected object.

The Select() event procedure is the ideal location for code that adds data labels to a data point. You can add data labels to individual points using the ApplyDataLabels method of the Point object. When the user selects a data series, the ElementID argument is 3, and the Arg1 argument holds the number of the selected series according to the order in which it was added to the chart. The Arg2 argument holds the value −1 until an individual point is selected by the user, at which time, the argument holds the number of the data point as it exists in the specific series.

```
Public WithEvents myChartClass As Chart
Private Sub myChartClass_Select(ByVal ElementID As Long, ByVal _
        Arg1 As Long, ByVal Arg2 As Long)
'Add/remove data label to selected point
    If ElementID = 3 And Arg2 > 0 Then
        With ActiveChart.SeriesCollection(Arg1).Points(Arg2)
            If .HasDataLabel Then
                .HasDataLabel = False
            Else
                .ApplyDataLabels ShowCategoryName:=True, ShowValue:=True
            End If
        End With
    End If
End Sub
```

The preceding Select() event procedure is that of an embedded chart, so it is contained in a custom class module. In this case, the class module is named clsChartEvents, and a declaration is included in the module for the Chart object it represents.

You initialize the event procedures of the Chart object in a standard module by instantiating the clsChartEvents class so that it references an embedded chart.

```
Private myClassModule As New clsChartEvents
Public Sub InitializeChart()
    Set myClassModule.myChartClass = ActiveSheet.ChartObjects(1).Chart
End Sub
```

The result of selecting a specific data point from a chart with the previously listed Select() event procedure is shown in Figure 20.12.

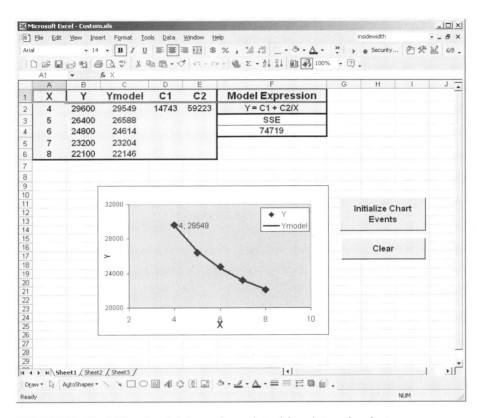

FIGURE 20.12 *Adding data labels to a data point with an interactive chart.*

Returning an Arbitrary Point from the Plot Area of a Chart

Not every application involving interactive charts requires the user to select data points. There are occasions when you require knowledge of the *X-Y* point selected by the user in the plot area of a chart, but not necessarily from a data point. For example, you may require specific input from the user before continuing a calculation concerning the data that is charted. This typically means you must know the *X-Y* values of a selection in the same units of the data points.

The MouseDown() event procedure of the Chart object provides the *X-Y* coordinates of the user's selection relative to the coordinate system of the chart (that is, the upper-left corner of the chart is point 0,0). However, the values of the x and y arguments are in pixels, whereas the size properties of the ChartArea and PlotArea objects contained in a Chart object are all in points. The challenge is to first convert the values of the x and y arguments of the MouseDown() event procedure to points before making the final conversion to the units of the data. Once again, I will use the Windows API to convert between pixels and points. This requires getting a handle to the Chart object.

The following code is added to a custom class module named `clsChartEvents`. The `Chart` object referenced by this procedure is named `myChartClass`. The bulk of the program is contained in the `MouseDown()` event procedure of the `Chart` object that converts the *X-Y* point selected by the user to values in the same units as the data. A second procedure, `GetChartSize()`, gets the dimensions of the `Chart` object using Windows API functions and fills the module-level variable `chRect` (type `RECT`) with the size and position of the chart.

```
Option Explicit
'-----------------------------
'API Function Declarations
Private Declare Function FindWindow Lib "user32.dll" Alias _
    "FindWindowA" (ByVal lpClassName As String, _
    ByVal lpWindowName As String) As Long
Private Declare Function FindWindowEx Lib "user32.dll" Alias _
    "FindWindowExA" (ByVal hWnd1 As Long, ByVal hWnd2 As Long, _
    ByVal lpsz1 As String, ByVal lpsz2 As String) As Long
Private Declare Function GetClientRect Lib "user32.dll" ( _
    ByVal hwnd As Long, lpRect As RECT) As Long


Private Type RECT
    Left As Long
    Top As Long
    Right As Long
    Bottom As Long
End Type


Public WithEvents myChartClass As Chart
Private chRect As RECT
```

The `MouseDown()` event procedure starts with the user's selection in points and converts the *X-Y* values to the units of the data. Note the use of the `InsideHeight`, `InsideTop`, `InsideWidth`, and `InsideLeft` properties of the `PlotArea` object, which return the dimensions of the chart's plot area excluding the axis labels. The `Height`, `Top`, `Width`, and `Left` properties of the `PlotArea` object include the axis labels, so you must not use these properties when converting the units of a selected point. Also note that the chart area does not quite encompass the entire contents of the embedded chart. There is a three-point padding around the chart area as determined by the `Left` and `Top` properties of the `ChartArea` object (code not listed here). This padding appears to be constant regardless of the size of the chart, but test it on your computer to be sure.

If the user selects a point within the chart's plot area, a marker is added to the chart, and the converted *X-Y* values are output to a set of merged cells, as shown in Figure 20.13.

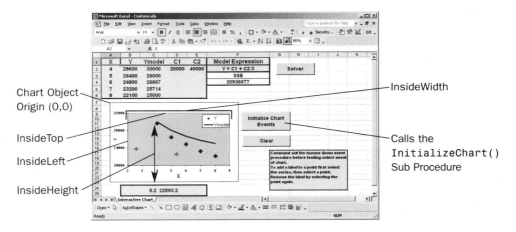

FIGURE 20.13 *Returning a user's selection from the plot area of a chart in the units of the data.*

```
Private Sub myChartClass_MouseDown(ByVal Button As Long, _
        ByVal Shift As Long, ByVal x As Long, ByVal y As Long)
    Dim newX As Single, newY As Single
    Dim pixelPerPtX As Single, pixelPerPtY As Single
    Dim xMin As Long, xMax As Long, yMin As Long, yMax As Long
    Dim pa As PlotArea, ca As ChartArea
    Dim paXleft As Single, paXright As Single
    Dim paYtop As Single, paYbottom As Single

    Set pa = myChartClass.PlotArea
    Set ca = myChartClass.ChartArea

    GetChartSize    'Fills chRect variable with dimension of chart
    Range("A1").Select
    pixelPerPtX = (chRect.Right) / (ca.Width + 6)   'Conversion factors
    pixelPerPtY = (chRect.Bottom) / (ca.Height + 6)

    newX = x / pixelPerPtX  'Convert x,y arguments to points
    newY = y / pixelPerPtY
```

```
'........................
'Get axes scale values
'........................
With myChartClass.Axes(xlValue)
    yMin = .MinimumScale
    yMax = .MaximumScale
End With
With myChartClass.Axes(xlCategory)
    xMin = .MinimumScale
    xMax = .MaximumScale
End With


'..............................
'Convert points to units of data
'..............................
paXleft = pa.InsideLeft + 3
paXright = pa.InsideLeft + pa.InsideWidth - 6
paYtop = pa.InsideTop + 3
paYbottom = pa.InsideTop + pa.InsideHeight - 6
If newX >= paXleft And newX <= paXright Then
    If newY >= paYtop And newY <= paYbottom Then
        myChartClass.Shapes.AddShape msoShape4pointStar, _
            newX, newY, 10, 10
        newX = (newX - paXleft) / (paXright - paXleft)
        newX = newX * (xMax - xMin) + xMin
        'y-values must be flipped because direction of increasing y
        'is opposite between coord. system of chart and that of data
        newY = 1 - (newY - paYtop) / (paYbottom - paYtop)
        newY = newY * (yMax - yMin) + yMin
        Range("B24").Value = Format(newX, "#0.0") & "  " & Format(newY, _
            "#0.0")
    End If
End If
Range("A1").Select
Set pa = Nothing
Set ca = Nothing
End Sub
```

NOTE

You can add the four-point star to the chart via the AddShape method of the Shapes collection object. The Shapes collection object represents the shapes contained on the Drawing toolbar that comes with most Office applications. Adding shapes from the Drawing toolbar with VBA is relatively straightforward programming and is not discussed in this book.

The GetChartSize() Sub procedure is called from the MouseDown() event procedure and serves to fill the module-level variable chRect with the dimensions of the embedded chart in pixels. Before you can return a handle to a chart with an API function, you must first show the chart as a window. To show a chart window, you use the ShowWindow method of the Chart object. Invoking the ShowWindow method is the equivalent of selecting Chart Window from the short-cut menu of a chart in the Excel application window. After selecting Chart Window from a chart's shortcut menu, the chart will appear as shown in Figure 20.14. Because a chart window is not a top-level window, you must use the FindWindowEx() function to return its handle. The path to the chart window follows from the parent Excel window (class name XLMAIN) to that of the child workbook window (class name XLDESK) to the child chart window (class name EXCELE).

```
Private Sub GetChartSize()
'Determines the size of a chart in pixels
    Dim hParent As Long, hChild As Long, hChart As Long
    Dim chWindowName As String

    chWindowName = "[" & ActiveWorkbook.Name & "]" & myChartClass.Name
    myChartClass.ShowWindow = True
    'Excel application is a top-level window
    hParent = FindWindow("XLMAIN", vbNullString)
    'Workbook window is a child of the main Excel window
    hChild = FindWindowEx(hParent, 0, "XLDESK", vbNullString)
    'Chart window is a child of the workbook window
    hChart = FindWindowEx(hChild, 0, "EXCELE", chWindowName)
    GetClientRect hChart, chRect
    myChartClass.ShowWindow = False
End Sub
```

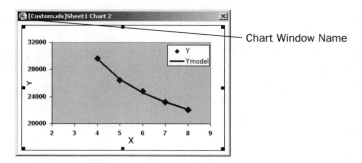

Chart Window Name

FIGURE 20.14 *An Excel chart window.*

Although converting arbitrary points selected by the user within the plot area of a chart is by no means a simple operation, it is at least fairly short. The Sub procedures listed here can be incorporated into any interactive charting application that requires knowledge of a user's selection converted to units of the data.

Summary

In this chapter, you learned how to use Excel's built-in expressions for data modeling to fit specific equations to a data set. The process of modeling data can involve creating formulas with the appropriate worksheet functions or adding a trendline to a chart.

Next, you learned how to use the Solver add-in to fit custom expressions to a data set and illustrate the quality of the fit using an *X-Y* scatter chart.

Finally, you learned how to create interactive charts in Excel. Specifically, you learned how to return data markers from a user's selection in the plot area of a chart.

Chapter 21

Two of the previous projects constructed in this book (HTML converter and the stock ticker) are general applications created to demonstrate various VBA programming techniques. In addition, these programs are intended for general use by anyone interested in their function. The third project (Pear Tree Used Cars database application) was designed as a specific business application for a fictitious company to demonstrate the use of `ADO` and `PivotTable` objects in a VBA-Excel program. The final project constructed in this book is also specific to a particular company, although, in this case, the company and project are real.

This chapter steps you through the process of automating a data analysis procedure using VBA and Excel. Although the program created in this chapter was originally designed for a specific company and is not suitable for general use, the overall automation process illustrates some of the common components that are used in data analysis programs. You may find many of the procedures and methods found in this chapter useful in your own projects.

Project Description

Biogel Technology, Inc. is a small biotechnology company that manufactures biodegradable and biocompatible microparticles (particles between 0.01 and 1 millimeter in diameter) for the controlled release of pharmaceutical agents. In a recent study, the company needed to analyze sample formulations of microparticles for their size distribution as the particles degraded in solution over a period of time. As part of the analysis, it is desirable to view the size distributions of specific microparticle formulations simultaneously and generate summary reports. Unfortunately, the software that comes with the instrumentation used to acquire the data cannot adequately analyze the data it measures. The instrument's software can load only one data file for analysis, and the process of extracting various details from the particle size distribution is lengthy and difficult. As a result of these deficiencies, the data must be transferred to Excel for analysis, where the process of formatting the worksheets, creating charts, and constructing reports is time-consuming. The need for an automation procedure is apparent when you consider that each of the dozens of samples generates approximately two dozen data files.

The automation process involves importing a series of data files (stored as tab-delimited text files) into Excel worksheets for analysis. Specifically, the automation program must carry out the following tasks:

◆ Provide a user interface for selecting the data files.
◆ Add each data set to a preformatted worksheet stored as an Excel template. There must be one worksheet per file.

- Calculate descriptive statistics for each data set using the preformatted template or VBA code.

- Chart the microparticle size distribution using an *X-Y* scatter chart. This is not the ideal chart for a distribution, but it is required for charting the modeled data that reproduces the measured values.

- Model the measured size distributions using the equation for a normal (Gaussian) distribution. The program should estimate initial values for each parameter used in the expression that reproduces the size distribution before invoking Solver in order to optimize these parameters.

- Provide the user with the ability to customize the fit by selecting a subset of the data and/or a non-zero baseline.

- Calculate the area under the curve representing the modeled data.

- Generate a summary report for a sample that contains the following:

  - The average particle size as calculated by the fit (center of normal distribution)

  - The standard deviations obtained from the fit

  - The areas calculated from fitting each particle size distribution

Project Tools/Algorithm

The tools required in the data automation procedure are introduced in previous chapters and include a Userform, a custom toolbar, and a workbook template file with one preformatted worksheet. The template includes basic formatting (colors, fonts, borders, and so on) as well as several formulas and an *X-Y* scatter chart. The program requires VBA and Excel objects for creating a toolbar and Userform, manipulating the components of the worksheet (especially the chart), and fitting the data to a custom model (Solver). The code is contained in workbook, form, standard, and class modules. Because the program manipulates objects in a separate workbook, it is saved as an add-in.

The first step in the automation is creating the custom toolbar with buttons used to initiate the various components of the program. The custom toolbar (see Figure 21.1) contains five buttons that initiate the tasks listed in Table 21.1.

Table 21.1 Tasks Initiated by the Toolbar Created for the Data Automation Project

Toolbar Button	Task
Data Files	Shows Userform used to select specific data files.
Guass Fit	Automatically fits each distribution in the worksheets to a Gaussian function.

continues

Table 21.1 Tasks Initiated by the Toolbar Created for the Data Automation Project *(continued)*

Toolbar Button	Task
Custom Baseline	Enables chart events to allow the user to customize a fit with a linear baseline.
Zoom	Enables chart events to allow the user to zoom in on a portion of the distribution to customize a fit using only the selected points.
Summary	Creates a summary report that includes the vital fit parameters from each worksheet and a chart of the Gaussian centers as a function of degradation time.

FIGURE 21.1 *Custom toolbar used to initiate components of the data analysis automation program.*

The user must select the data to be analyzed. A basic Userform with a Combo Box, List Box, and Command Button controls serve as the interface for file I/O operations. The Userform (Design view) is shown in Figure 21.2.

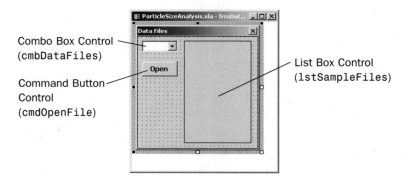

Combo Box Control (cmbDataFiles)

Command Button Control (cmdOpenFile)

List Box Control (lstSampleFiles)

FIGURE 21.2 *Userform interface used for selecting data to be added to worksheet template for analysis.*

The form module associated with the Userform interface (frmDataFiles) uses event procedures of the ActiveX controls along with custom procedures in accordance with the following algorithm:

1. Read the names of distinct samples from a text file and add them to the Combo Box control (cmbDataFiles).

2. When the user selects one sample name from the Combo Box control, add its associated data files to the List Box control (`lstSampleFiles`). Use the `Click()` event procedure of the Combo Box control to handle this process.

3. When the user clicks the Command Button control (`cmdOpenFile`) or double-clicks the List Box control, load the names of the selected files into an array variable using the `Click()` or `DblClick()` events of these controls, respectively.

4. Load the template file and make a sufficient number of copies within the same workbook to accommodate the number of selected data files.

5. Add the data to the workbook, one data file per worksheet.

After the data is added to the workbook, the user has the option of fitting each distribution to a Gaussian expression. The components of the program that fit the data are added to a standard module and must include procedures for obtaining initial estimates of the fit parameters, invoking the Solver add-in for fitting the data, adding the modeled data to the chart, and calculating the area under the curve.

After the data is fit to a Gaussian expression, the user may customize each fit to include a linear baseline and/or a smaller sample from the data. This requires a class module that enables the event procedures of the embedded `Chart` object. You use the `MouseDown()` event procedure of the `Chart` object along with a few Windows API functions to return user selections on the chart (in the units of the data). The two points selected by the user determine either the initial guess for the linear baseline or the bounding rectangle that is used to reset the scale values of the chart.

Finally, you use a separate standard module in conjunction with custom class modules to dynamically create a summary report worksheet. The worksheet contains the fit parameters from each data worksheet along with a chart of the Gaussian centers. The chart must contain error bars representing the standard deviations obtained from the model.

Worksheet Formatting

Writing code that formats the worksheet used to hold the data can be a time-consuming and tedious process. However, in this project, you can use a template because the structure of the data files does not change. This project requires only one template for the data and one dynamically created worksheet for the summary report. You can preformat a template from the Excel application window to include all the borders, colors, fonts, formulas, and charts required by the analysis, resulting in an easy-to-read report ready for printing. Because you save time by not having to write as much code, using a template is always the preferred method for creating a data report.

The Worksheet Template

The template required by the analysis of microparticle size distributions is shown in Figure 21.3 (Page Break Preview). When formatting a template, you should include the sample data in order to test for correctness of the formulas and also for the desired appearance of the cells and charts. After completing the formatting, you should remove the data and store the template with an .xlt extension.

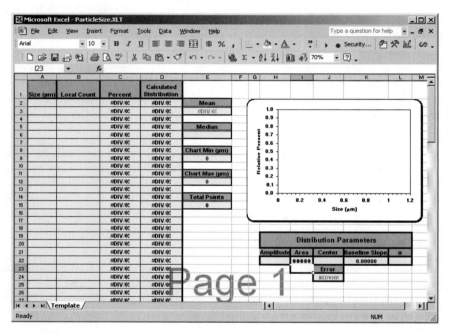

FIGURE 21.3 *Worksheet template (shown in Page Break Preview) used in data analysis automation of microparticle size distributions.*

There are two distinct regions on the template. The largest region is represented by columns A through E, which are used to contain the measured and calculated data values along with some summary statistics. The second region contains the chart and a few cells below it that hold the values of the parameters used in the custom model.

The data from a file contains two columns and 101 rows of numbers. The first column represents the size ranges in which the microparticles were grouped (as measured by the instrumentation). The second column represents the relative number of particles measured within a given size range (although the units reflect particle volumes in cubic meters). The data measured by the instrumentation is stored as text files and must be added to columns A and B in the template.

Columns C and D contain formulas that calculate the relative percentage of particles within a given size range and the Gaussian expression used to reproduce the values in Column C, respectively. The two formulas contained in cells C2 and D2 are listed here (note the use of relative references, because these formulas are copied down the length of each column):

C2 = B2/SUM(B$2:B$102)*100

D2 = ($H$22/SQRT(2*PI()*$L$22))*EXP(-((A2-$J$22)^2)/(2*$L$22^2))

Additional formulas are included in the template for the mean, chart min/max, total points, and sum of squared error (SSE). You cannot calculate the median until the data has been entered into the chart, because the median is only an estimate based on the particle counts in each range. The `Integrate()` Function procedure is a custom function that I wrote for the data analysis automation program. The `Integrate()` Function procedure calculates the area under a curve identified by two arrays (X-Y data points) and discussed in section "Gaussian Fit" later in this chapter.

E3 = SUMPRODUCT(A2:A102,C2:C102)/100

E9 =MIN(A2:A102)

E12 =MAX(A2:A102)

E15 =COUNT(A2:A102)

I22 =ParticleSizeAnalysis.xla!Integrate(A2:A102,D2:D102 ,K22,0)

J24 =SUMXMY2(C2:C102,D2:D102)

NOTE

Any given measurement of a microparticle size distribution involved several hundred thousand to more than one million counts. Because the counts are so high, the instrument software does not permanently record each particle size as it is measured. If each individual size measurement were recorded, the resulting data files would be too large, even for a new computer. Instead, as particle sizes are measured, they are immediately grouped into size ranges, and the total counts per size range are stored. This reduces the resulting file size by several orders of magnitude.

Finally, the template contains an embedded chart (type X-Y scatter) preformatted to plot the size distribution (columns A and C). The calculated values from column D are added to the chart only after the user chooses to model the data.

The Custom Toolbar

By now, you probably realize that I'm fond of custom toolbars and that I recycle the same general procedure when creating them. As always, the code that creates the custom toolbar is added to the code module of the `Workbook` object. Although somewhat redundant, the code module of the Workbook object for the data analysis automation is listed in the following:

```
'.....................
'Workbook code module
'.....................
Private Sub Workbook_BeforeClose(Cancel As Boolean)
    RemoveToolbar ("Data Automation")
End Sub
Private Sub Workbook_Open()
    RemoveToolbar ("Data Automation")
    AddToolbar
End Sub
Private Sub AddToolbar()
'Creates a custom toolbar with 5 buttons.
'Initiates automation procedures for microparticle data analysis
    Dim tlbGetSample As CommandBarButton
    Dim tlbGauss As CommandBarButton
    Dim tlbInitChart As CommandBarButton
    Dim tlbZoom As CommandBarButton
    Dim tlbSummaryReport As CommandBarButton

    '----------------------------
    'Set reference to new toolbar
    '----------------------------
    Set tlbAutomation = Application.CommandBars.Add( _
        Name:="Data Automation", _
        Temporary:=True)

    '-------------------------------------
    'Set references to buttons on toolbar
    '-------------------------------------
    Set tlbGetSample = tlbAutomation.Controls.Add( _
        Type:=msoControlButton, _
        Temporary:=True)
    tlbGetSample.Style = msoButtonCaption
    tlbGetSample.Caption = "Data Files"
    tlbGetSample.OnAction = "DisplayDataFiles"
```

```
Set tlbGauss = tlbAutomation.Controls.Add( _
    Type:=msoControlButton, _
    Temporary:=True)
tlbGauss.Style = msoButtonCaption
tlbGauss.Caption = "Gauss Fit"
tlbGauss.OnAction = "FitOneGaussian"
tlbGauss.Enabled = False
tlbGauss.BeginGroup = True


Set tlbInitChart = tlbAutomation.Controls.Add( _
    Type:=msoControlButton, _
    Temporary:=True)
tlbInitChart.Style = msoButtonCaption
tlbInitChart.Caption = "Custom Baseline"
tlbInitChart.OnAction = "InitializeChart"
tlbZoom.Enabled = False
tlbInitChart.BeginGroup = True


Set tlbZoom = tlbAutomation.Controls.Add( _
    Type:=msoControlButton, _
    Temporary:=True)
tlbZoom.Style = msoButtonCaption
tlbZoom.Caption = "Zoom"
tlbZoom.OnAction = "InitializeChartII"
tlbZoom.Enabled = False
tlbZoom.BeginGroup = True


Set tlbSummaryReport = tlbAutomation.Controls.Add( _
    Type:=msoControlButton, _
    Temporary:=True)
tlbSummaryReport.Style = msoButtonCaption
tlbSummaryReport.Caption = "Summary"
tlbSummaryReport.OnAction = "SummaryReport"
tlbSummaryReport.Enabled = False
tlbSummaryReport.BeginGroup = True


tlbAutomation.Visible = True
```

```
        Set tlbGetSample = Nothing
        Set tlbGauss = Nothing
        Set tlbInitChart = Nothing
        Set tlbZoom = Nothing
        Set tlbSummaryReport = Nothing
        Set tlbAutomation = Nothing
    End Sub
Private Sub RemoveToolbar(tlbarName As String)
    Dim cBar As CommandBar

    For Each cBar In Application.CommandBars
        If cBar.Name = tlbarName Then
            cBar.Delete
            Exit For
        End If
    Next
End Sub
```

The custom toolbar created from the previous code listing contains five buttons (refer to Figure 21.1) that initiate the procedures declared in the `OnAction` property of the `CommandBarButton` objects. Note that four of the five buttons are initially disabled via their `Enabled` property (Gauss Fit, Custom Baseline, Zoom, and Summary). The idea is to lead the user along in the automation process by allowing only certain selections on the toolbar.

Importing the Data

Each microparticle sample is associated with multiple data files representing measured size distributions at different time periods. The sample names are stored in a small text file named Samples.txt in the same directory as the data files. This makes it easy to retrieve unique sample numbers for display in the Combo Box control on the Userform. The name of a data file includes the sample name and the number of days the sample has been in solution when its size distribution is measured (for example, S78 V D14.txt). The structure of the Sample.txt file and a typical data file are shown in Figures 21.4 and 21.5, respectively. The data files are tab-delimited resulting in two columns of numbers in each file. The first column represents the measured particle size range and the second column the measured volume of particles in the associated size range.

Samples.txt - ...
File Edit Format View
Help
S77
S78
S120
S121
S122
S125
S126
S127
S128

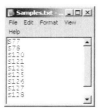

FIGURE 21.4 *The structure of the Samples.txt file used to hold the names of the samples included in the study.*

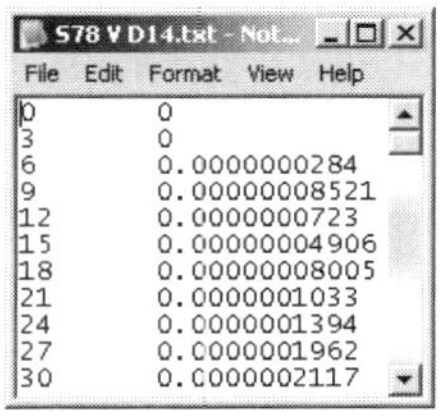
S78 V D14.txt - Not...
File Edit Format View Help
0 0
3 0
6 0.0000000284
9 0.00000008521
12 0.0000000723
15 0.00000004906
18 0.00000008005
21 0.0000001033
24 0.0000001394
27 0.0000001962
30 0.0000002117

FIGURE 21.5 *The structure of a data file used to hold the size distribution of a microparticle sample at a specified time.*

The Userform is displayed when the user selects the custom toolbar button labeled Data Files. This initiates the `DisplayDataFiles()` Sub procedure contained in a standard module. The `DisplayDataFiles()` procedure loads and shows the Userform and disables the last three buttons on the custom toolbar (if they are not already disabled).

```
'Procedure from standard module named "Gaussian"
Public Sub DisplayDataFiles()
    Dim I As Integer

    For I = 3 To 5
        Application.CommandBars("Data Automation") _
            .Controls(I).Enabled = False
    Next I
    frmDataFiles.Show vbModal
End Sub
```

To load the data from a data file into the worksheet template, the user must first select a sample name from the Combo Box control on the Userform. Once a sample name is selected, the List Box control is filled with a list of files associated with the selected sample name. The run-time appearance of the Userform is shown in Figure 21.6.

FIGURE 21.6 *Userform that serves as the interface for selecting data files for the automation.*

The code module of the Userform object `frmDataFiles` contains the following declarations and procedures. The `FileSystemObject` and `TextStream` objects handle the data input from the text files, so a reference must be set to the Microsoft Scripting Runtime library (select Tools, References in the VBA IDE). The module-level array variable `sampleFiles` holds the names of the data files associated with the sample selected by the user, and `basePath` holds the `String` representing the path to the Excel template and data.

```
'..............................
'Form  module "frmDataFiles"
'..............................
Option Explicit
Private sampleFiles() As String
Private basePath As String
```

The `Initialize()` event of the Userform object initializes the variable `basePath` and fills the Combo Box control (`cmbDataFiles`) with the names of the samples. An error handler is included in case the `Samples.txt` file cannot be found. The `FindFile()` Function procedure is called by the error handler to show a file dialog box that allows the user to search for the file if desired.

```
Private Sub UserForm_Initialize()
'Load list box with distinct sample names.
'Names are read from a simple text file.
    Dim filePath As String
    Dim fso As FileSystemObject, ts As TextStream
    Dim ms As Integer, msg As String

    On Error GoTo FileError
    Set fso = New FileSystemObject
    basePath = Workbooks("ParticleSizeAnalysis.xla").Path & "\Data\"
    filePath = basePath & "Samples.txt"
    'Open the text file at the specified path
```

```
    Set ts = fso.OpenTextFile(filePath)
    Do While Not ts.AtEndOfStream
        'Read one line and add to Combo Box
        cmbDataFiles.AddItem ts.ReadLine
    Loop
    ts.Close

    Set ts = Nothing
    Set fso = Nothing

    Exit Sub
FileError:
    If Err.Number = 53 Then
        msg = filePath & vbCrLf & _
            " cannot be found. Do you want to search?"
        ms = MsgBox(msg, vbYesNo, "File Error")
        If ms = 6 Then   'User selected Yes
            filePath = FindFile   'Show file dialog
            If fso.GetFileName(filePath) = "Samples.txt" Then
                Resume    'Return with new path
            Else   'User could not find file
                MsgBox "Looking for a file named Samples.txt"
                End
            End If
        Else   'User selected No
            End
        End If
    Else
        MsgBox Err.Description
    End If
End Sub
```

When the user triggers the `Click()` event of the Combo Box control (`cmbDataFiles`), the List Box control (`lstSampleFiles`) is filled with the data files associated with the selected sample number using a call to the `GetSampleList()` Sub procedure.

```
Private Sub cmbDataFiles_Click()
'User has selected a sample. Add associated data files to list box.
    lstSampleFiles.Clear
```

```
        lstSampleFiles.SpecialEffect = fmSpecialEffectSunken
        GetSampleList
End Sub


Private Sub GetSampleList()
'Load list box with data file names associated with selected sample.
        Dim fso As FileSystemObject, f As File

        On Error GoTo SampleFileError
        Set fso = New FileSystemObject
        'List files from selected data folder
        For Each f In fso.GetFolder(basePath).Files
            If Left(f.Name, Len(cmbDataFiles.Text)) = cmbDataFiles.Text Then
                lstSampleFiles.AddItem f.Name   'Add filename to list box
            End If
        Next
        If lstSampleFiles.ListCount = 0 Then
            lstSampleFiles.AddItem "No files found"
        End If

        Set fso = Nothing
        Exit Sub
SampleFileError:
        MsgBox "An error was encountered while trying to " & _
            retrieve the sample list.", vbOKOnly, Err.Description
        End
End Sub


Private Sub cmdOpenFile_Click()
'Load data into worksheet template. One worksheet per data file.
        If lstSampleFiles.ListCount < 1 Then
            MsgBox "Select one or more files from the list.", _
                vbOKOnly, "Select File"
        End If
        LoadData    'Loads data from file into template
        Unload Me
End Sub
```

```
Private Sub lstSampleFiles_DblClick( _
        ByVal Cancel As MSForms.ReturnBoolean)
    LoadData    'Loads data from file into template
    Unload Me
End Sub
```

The data is loaded into a workbook using the `LoadData()` Sub procedure whenever the `Click()` event or `DblClick()` event of the Command Button or List Box controls are triggered. These event procedures also unload the `Userform`. When the `Userform` is unloaded from memory, the second button on the custom toolbar is enabled from the `QueryClose()` event procedure.

The `LoadData()` Sub procedure selects each worksheet in the workbook while selecting different cells and charts — a time-consuming process if you have to watch it take place in the application window. When your VBA program contains numerous lines that alter the appearance of a worksheet, you should first set the `ScreenUpdating` property of the `Application` object to `False`, as is done in the `LoadData()` Sub procedure. Next, the template file is loaded, and a sufficient number of copies made (within the same workbook) to accommodate the number of data files selected by the user. A `For/Each` loop handles the process of activating each worksheet and adding the contents of a data file to columns A and B. Note the use of two `Split()` functions in the procedure. The first `Split()` function divides the contents of the data file into individual rows for storage in the array variable `sData`. The second `Split` function divides each element of `sData` into two values that are stored in the array variable `sLine`.

```
Private Sub LoadData()
'Load data into worksheets. Load template once, then create a
'copy for each data file.
    Dim I As Integer
    Dim ws As Worksheet, c As Range
    Dim fso As FileSystemObject, ts As TextStream, s As String
    Dim sData() As String, sLine() As String

    On Error GoTo TemplateFileError
    Application.ScreenUpdating = False
    '------------------------------------------------
    'Build file list. Open template and add data
    '------------------------------------------------
    GetSelectedFiles
    Workbooks.Open basePath & "ParticleSize.XLT"
    'Create copies of template for each data file
```

```
For I = 0 To UBound(sampleFiles) - 1
    Worksheets("Template").Copy After:=Worksheets(Worksheets.Count)
Next I

On Error GoTo SampleFileError
'Add data to worksheets
I = 0
Set fso = New FileSystemObject
For Each ws In ActiveWorkbook.Worksheets
    ws.Activate
    ws.Name = Left(sampleFiles(I), Len(sampleFiles(I)) - 4)
    Set ts = fso.OpenTextFile(basePath & sampleFiles(I))
    s = ts.ReadAll
    'Split data by rows. Two values in each row
    sData = Split(s, vbCrLf)
    ts.Close
    For Each c In ws.Range("A2:A102")
        sLine = Split(sData(c.Row - 2), vbTab)
        c.Value = sLine(0)
        ws.Cells(c.Row, "B").Value = sLine(1)
    Next
    ws.Cells(6, "E").Value = CalculateMedian(ws)
    UpdateChart ws
    s = ""
    Set ts = Nothing
    I = I + 1
Next
Application.ScreenUpdating = True

Set fso = Nothing
Set ws = Nothing
Exit Sub
TemplateFileError:
    MsgBox "There was an error opening the template file. " & _
        "Check the file before trying again."
    End
```

```
SampleFileError:
    MsgBox "There was an error opening the sample data file " & _
        sampleFiles(I) & ". Check the file and try again."
    End
End Sub
```

The GetSelectedFiles() Sub procedure is called from LoadData() to fill the module-level array variable sampleFiles with the names of the data files selected by the user. The UpdateChart() and CalculateMedian() procedures are also called from LoadData() with the specific purposes of calculating the median particle size and determining the maximum *X*-axis scale on the chart.

```
Private Sub GetSelectedFiles()
'Retrieve selected data file names into an array.
'There are multiple data files for each sample.
    Dim I As Integer, J As Integer

    If lstSampleFiles.ListCount = 0 Then Exit Sub
    For I = 0 To lstSampleFiles.ListCount - 1
        If lstSampleFiles.Selected(I) = True Then
            ReDim Preserve sampleFiles(J)
            sampleFiles(J) = lstSampleFiles.List(I)
            J = J + 1
        End If
    Next I
End Sub
Private Sub UpdateChart(ws As Worksheet)
'Update chart x-axis maximum scale using maximum value from data.
    Dim chAxis As Axis

    Set chAxis = ws.ChartObjects("Chart 1").Chart.Axes(xlCategory)
    chAxis.MaximumScale = Application.WorksheetFunction.Max( _
        ws.Range("A2:A102"))
    Set chAxis = Nothing
End Sub
Private Function CalculateMedian(ws As Worksheet) As Single
'Calculate the median particle size
    Dim colSum As Single
    Dim I As Integer
```

```
    I = 2
    Do
        colSum = colSum + ws.Cells(I, "C").Value
        I = I + 1
    Loop Until colSum >= 50
    I = I - 1
    CalculateMedian = 1 - (colSum - 50) / ws.Cells(I, "C").Value
    CalculateMedian = CalculateMedian * (ws.Cells(I, "A").Value - _
        ws.Cells(I - 1, "A").Value) + ws.Cells(I - 1, "A").Value
End Function
Private Function FindFile() As String
'User selects path to save HTML files
    Dim fd As FileDialog
    Dim I As Integer

    Set fd = Application.FileDialog(msoFileDialogFilePicker)
    With fd
        .AllowMultiSelect = False
        .Title = "Find Samples.txt"
        .InitialFileName = ""
        If .Show = -1 Then
            FindFile = .SelectedItems(1)
        End If
    End With
    Set fd = Nothing
End Function
Private Sub UserForm_QueryClose(Cancel As Integer, CloseMode As Integer)
    Application.CommandBars("Data Automation").Controls( _
        "Gauss Fit").Enabled = True
End Sub
```

After the data has been loaded into the appropriate worksheets, the ScreenUpdating property of the Application object is set to True, and the user sees a worksheet similar to what is shown in Figure 21.7. The data in the worksheets is now ready for modeling with a custom expression.

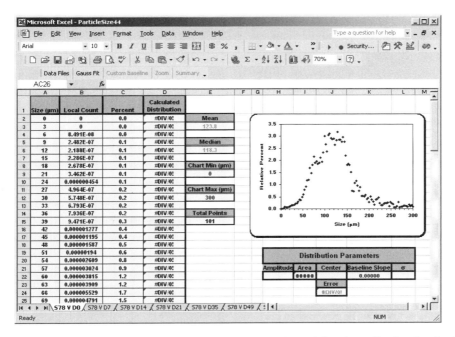

FIGURE 21.7 *The appearance of a microparticle sample worksheet immediately after the data has been entered.*

Modeling the Data

The data analysis automation program provides the user with the ability to model the data with a custom expression based on the equation for a Gaussian (normal) distribution. The modeling is not carried out automatically after the data is loaded in order to give the user the option of deleting worksheets where there may be problems with the data.

The data in each worksheet is fit with the custom expression when the user selects the button labeled Gauss Fit on the custom toolbar. This initiates a Sub procedure called `FitOneGaussian()` contained in a standard code module.

The custom expression that reproduces the data has already been entered into column D of the template, so the process of fitting the data consists of the following:

1. Estimate initial values for the fit parameters (amplitude, Gaussian center, and standard deviation). These parameters are used in the formula entered into column D of the worksheet that reproduces the measured particle size distribution.

2. Invoke Solver in order to optimize the parameters from Step 1.

3. Add the optimized data series in column D of the worksheet to the chart.

Gaussian Fit

The process of modeling data in order to obtain a mathematical expression that can be used to accurately reproduce the measured values is often referred to as *fitting* the data. In the automation of the analyses used with the measured particle size distributions, you want to fit the data to a Gaussian expression. The interest in modeling the data is driven by a need for returning a calculated center and standard deviation for a particle size distribution because the measured values are often skewed by various noise factors (mostly particle aggregates). The measured size distribution is expected to appear as a normal curve — therefore the use of a Gaussian expression for modeling the data.

Here is the mathematical expression you should use to fit data that approximates a Gaussian:

$$f(X) = A/(2\pi\sigma)^{1/2} * exp-[(X- X_0)^2/(2\sigma^2)]$$

The three parameters that must be adjusted to fit the data include the amplitude *(A)*, the standard deviation *(σ)*, and the Gaussian center *(X_0)*. Depending on the data set, a nonzero sloping baseline may be required to accurately reproduce the data. In these situations, an extra term is added to the expression (*m*X*, where *m* is the slope of a line that reproduces the measured baseline) to provide a linear baseline. In this case, four parameters are optimized when fitting the data.

The VBA code that accomplishes the task of fitting the preceding expression to the data sets contained in the worksheets is listed next. There are just four short procedures for fitting the data, starting with `FitOneGaussian()`. This procedure loops through the worksheets in the active workbook and calls the `InitialGuess()`, `StartSolver()`, and `AddFitToChart()` Sub procedures after each worksheet is selected.

```
'Standard module named "Gaussian"
Public Sub FitOneGaussian()
'Initiated by toolbar button labeled "Gauss Fit".
'Fits a Gaussian distribution to each data set in the workbook.
    Dim ws As Worksheet
    Dim I As Integer


    '-----------------------------------------------------------
    'Calculate initial guess to fit parameters and start the fit
    '-----------------------------------------------------------
    Application.ScreenUpdating = False
    For Each ws In Worksheets
        ws.Select
        If ws.Range("H22").Value = "" Then InitialGuess ws, 2, 102
        StartSolver False
        AddFitToChart
```

```
    Next

    Application.ScreenUpdating = True


    '-------------------------------------------

    'Enable/disable appropriate toolbar buttons

    '-------------------------------------------

    Application.CommandBars("Data Automation").Controls( _

        "Gauss Fit").Enabled = False

    For I = 3 To 5

        Application.CommandBars("Data Automation").Controls(I) _

            .Enabled = True

    Next I

End Sub
```

The `InitialGuess()` Sub procedure obtains initial estimates of the fit parameters and enters them into the appropriate worksheet cells. You do not have to calculate initial estimates that are very close to the final optimized values, but the closer they are, the less time it takes Solver to find a solution.

The amplitude is assigned the maximum *Y*-value in the data series. This value is subsequently used to determine the estimates for the Gaussian center and the standard deviation. The estimate for the Gaussian center is set to the size value (*X*-value) at the maximum *Y* (amplitude). To estimate the standard deviation, you first find the *X*-value when *Y* is half the value of the amplitude and subtract it from the Gaussian center before multiplying by two. This is essentially an estimate of the full width at half the maximum of the distribution.

The estimation of these parameters relies on a couple of assumptions. First, I am assuming that the initial estimate of the amplitude is close to the center of the distribution. Second, I assume the distribution is a single modal. If these assumptions are not valid, the initial estimates of the fit parameters may be too far off for Solver to optimize. In these cases, the user must supply the estimates by entering them directly into the worksheet cells after inspecting the initial fit.

```
Private Sub InitialGuess(ws As Worksheet, row1 As Integer, row2 As Integer)

'Sets the initial guess parameters for the fit

'Determine initial guess parameters for Amplitude,

'Gaussian center and StDev.

    Dim c As Range

    Dim halfX As Single, halfY As Single

    Dim gAmp As Single, gCenter As Single, sDev As Single

    Dim I As Integer
```

```
'Amplitude is maximum y-value
gAmp = Application.WorksheetFunction.Max(ws.Range( _
    "C" & row1 & ":C" & row2))
Set c = ws.Range("C" & row1 & ":C" & row2).Find( _
    What:=Format(gAmp, "#0.0"), LookIn:=xlValues)
gCenter = ws.Cells(c.Row, "A").Value

'Determine StDev estimate
I = 2
Do
    halfY = ws.Cells(I, "C").Value
    halfX = ws.Cells(I, "A").Value
    I = I + 1
Loop Until (halfY > gAmp / 2)
sDev = (gCenter - halfX) * 2
gAmp = gAmp * Sqr(6.28 * sDev)

'Add fit parameters to worksheet
ws.Range("H22").Value = gAmp
ws.Range("J22").Value = gCenter
ws.Range("L22").Value = sDev

Set c = Nothing
End Sub
```

The `StartSolver()` Sub procedure invokes the Solver add-in that optimizes the parameters used in the calculation of the Gaussian curve.

 NOTE

You must set a reference to the SOLVER object library (select Tools, References in the VBA IDE) before you can program with the Solver object model.

If a baseline term is required (as specified by the variable `useBaseline`), Solver must optimize a fourth parameter whose value is entered in cell K22 of the worksheet. As discussed in Chapter 20, "Advanced Data Analysis Using Curve-Fitting and Interactive Charts with Excel-VBA," Solver is asked to optimize the parameters by minimizing the SSE. The SSE is calculated with a formula in cell J24 of the worksheet using the worksheet function SUMXMY2.

```
Public Sub StartSolver(useBaseLine As Boolean)
'Begin crunching numbers for fit.
'Minimize SSE between Ymeas and Ycalc
'This part uses Excel's solver
'Must set a reference to solver library in VBA IDE or this sub will fail.


    SolverReset
    If useBaseLine Then
        SolverOk SetCell:="$J$24", MaxMinVal:=2, ValueOf:="0", _
            ByChange:="$H$22,$J$22,$L$22,$K$22"
    Else
        SolverOk SetCell:="$J$24", MaxMinVal:=2, ValueOf:="0", _
            ByChange:="$H$22,$J$22,$L$22"
    End If
    SolverAdd CellRef:="$H$22", Relation:=3, FormulaText:="0"
    SolverAdd CellRef:="$J$22", Relation:=3, FormulaText:="0"
    SolverAdd CellRef:="$L$22", Relation:=3, FormulaText:="0.1"
    SolverOptions MaxTime:=30, Precision:=0.0001, Iterations:=100, _
        IntTolerance:=0.01, Convergence:=0.0001
    SolverSolve (True)
End Sub
```

The AddFitToChart() Sub procedure adds the contents of column D (the calculated Gaussian distribution) to the *X-Y* scatter chart as a new series. The series represented by column D is formatted as a continuous line with no data markers.

```
Private Sub AddFitToChart()
'Adds column D to the chart and formats the curve as a solid line
    Range("D2:D102").Copy
    ActiveSheet.ChartObjects("Chart 1").Activate
    ActiveChart.SeriesCollection.Paste Rowcol:=xlColumns, _
        NewSeries:=True
    Application.CutCopyMode = False
    ActiveChart.SeriesCollection(2).Select
    With Selection
        .MarkerStyle = xlNone
        .Border.Color = RGB(0, 0, 255)
        .Border.Weight = xlMedium
        .Border.LineStyle = xlContinuous
```

```
        End With
        Range("A1").Select
End Sub
```

The area under the curve representing the calculated expression is estimated using the `Integrate()` Function procedure. This function is utilized in the formula for cell I22 in the template and uses a trapezoidal approximation to calculate the area under the curve. The trapezoidal approximation adds the areas of a series of trapezoids that can be drawn under a curve as shown in Figure 21.8. The shaded area in the figure represents the error in the calculation. When the shaded area lies above the trapezoid, the contribution to the sum total area under the curve is underestimated. When the shaded area lies within the trapezoid, the contribution to the sum total area under the curve is overestimated. The errors contributed from each trapezoid tend to cancel each other out when they are all added together. Therefore, the approximation is quite reliable.

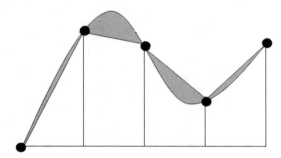

FIGURE 21.8 *The trapezoid approximation for estimating the area under a curve.*

```
Public Function Integrate(xRange As Range, yRange As Range, _
        Optional YBaseline As Single, Optional mSlope As Single, _
        Optional Yintercept As Single) As Single
'Integrates the area under a curve using trapezoidal approximation.
        Dim I As Integer
        Dim iTerm As Single
        Dim yBaseline As Single

        For I = 1 To xRange.Count - 1
            iTerm = xRange.Cells(I + 1, 1).Value - xRange.Cells(I, 1).Value
            yBaseline = mSlope * xRange.Cells(I, 1).Value + Yintercept
            iTerm = iTerm * ((yRange.Cells(I + 1, 1).Value - yBaseline) - _
                0.5 * (yRange.Cells(I + 1, 1).Value - _
                    yRange.Cells(I, 1).Value))
```

```
        Integrate = Integrate + iTerm
    Next I
End Function
```

After the data in each worksheet has been fit to a Gaussian expression, a worksheet similar to the one shown in Figure 21.9 appears.

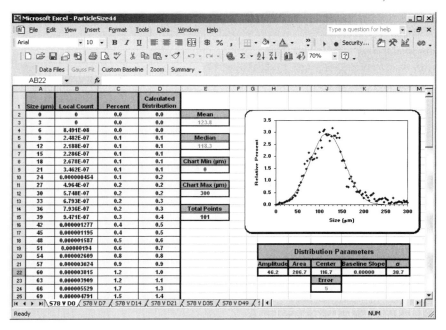

FIGURE 21.9 *The appearance of a microparticle sample worksheet after the data has been fit to a Gaussian expression.*

Adding a Linear Baseline

In certain instances, a measured particle size distribution has an increasing baseline (see Figure 21.10 later in this section). Because the custom expression used to fit the data assumes a zero baseline, the accuracy of the fit suffers as the baseline slope increases. To correct for an increasing linear baseline, the user can further customize the fit by adding another term to the expression.

The process of adding a linear baseline to the custom expression that fits the data is initiated when the user selects the button on the custom toolbar labeled Custom Baseline. This triggers the InitializeChart() Sub procedure contained in a standard code module where the event procedures of the embedded Chart object are initialized.

The MouseDown() event procedure of the Chart object previously listed in Chapter 20 is recycled here (with some modifications) to collect two X-Y points selected by the user.

After the second point is selected, a call to the `NewBaseline()` Sub procedure from the `MouseDown()` event procedure updates the formula in column D of the worksheet to include an additional term for the non-zero baseline. The linear term is added to the existing equation using an absolute reference to cell K22 and a relative reference to cells in column A (*X*-values). Cell K22 must be included in the list of parameters passed to the Solver add-in when refitting the data. The two points selected by the user serve only to provide an initial estimate for the baseline slope. The Solver add-in optimizes the slope when it fits the data.

```vba
'Standard module named "Gaussian"
Private myClassModule As New clsChartEvents
Public Sub InitializeChart()
    Set myClassModule.myChartClass = ActiveSheet.ChartObjects(1).Chart
    Range("A1").Select
End Sub
Public Sub NewBaseline()
    Dim curFormula As String
    Dim GaussRange As Range, c As Range


    '--------------------------------------------------
    'Add/update baseline term to Gaussian formula.
    'Use loop instead of copy/paste due to formatting
    '--------------------------------------------------
    Application.Calculation = xlCalculationManual    'Saves time
    Set GaussRange = Range("D2:D102")
    If Right(Range("D2").Formula, 9) Like "*K$22*" Then
        For Each c In GaussRange
            curFormula = Left(c.Formula, InStrRev(c.Formula, "+") - 1)
            c.Formula = curFormula & "+K$22*A" & c.Row
        Next
    Else
        For Each c In GaussRange
            curFormula = c.Formula
            c.Formula = curFormula & "+K$22*A" & c.Row
        Next
    End If
    Application.Calculation = xlCalculationAutomatic
    Range("I22").Formula = "=ParticleSizeAnalysis.xla!Integrate( _
        A2:A102,D2:D102,K22,0)"
```

```
        Set GaussRange = Nothing
End Sub
```

The code contained in the class module that includes the MouseDown() event procedure for the embedded chart is listed next. The MouseDown() event procedure has been modified from the listing in Chapter 20 to account for selecting a new baseline or zooming in on a section of the chart (otherwise, the code in this module is unchanged). In either case, after the user has selected two points, Solver is invoked in order to refit the data.

```
'----------------------------------------
'Custom class  module 'clsChartEvents'
'----------------------------------------
Option Explicit
'API Function Declarations
Private Declare Function FindWindow Lib "user32.dll" Alias _
    "FindWindowA" (ByVal lpClassName As String, _
    ByVal lpWindowName As String) As Long
Private Declare Function FindWindowEx Lib "user32.dll" Alias _
    "FindWindowExA" (ByVal hWnd1 As Long, ByVal hWnd2 As Long, _
    ByVal lpsz1 As String, ByVal lpsz2 As String) As Long
Private Declare Function GetClientRect Lib "user32.dll" ( _
    ByVal hwnd As Long, lpRect As RECT) As Long


Private Type RECT
    Left As Long
    Top As Long
    Right As Long
    Bottom As Long
End Type


Public WithEvents myChartClass As Chart
Private chRect As RECT


Private Sub myChartClass_MouseDown(ByVal Button As Long, _
    ByVal Shift As Long, ByVal x As Long, ByVal y As Long)
'Convert x,y arguments to the units of the data
    Dim newX As Single, newY As Single
    Dim pixelPerPtX As Single, pixelPerPtY As Single
    Dim xMin As Long, xMax As Long, yMin As Long, yMax As Long
    Dim pa As PlotArea, ca As ChartArea
```

```
Dim paXleft As Single, paXright As Single
Dim paYtop As Single, paYbottom As Single
Static nCount As Integer
Static xpt1 As Single
Static ypt1 As Single

Set pa = myChartClass.PlotArea
Set ca = myChartClass.ChartArea

GetChartSize     'Fills chRect variable with dimension of chart

Range("A1").Select
pixelPerPtX = (chRect.Right) / (ca.Width + 6)    'Conversion factors
pixelPerPtY = (chRect.Bottom) / (ca.Height + 6)

newX = x / pixelPerPtX   'Convert x,y arguments to points
newY = y / pixelPerPtY

'----------------
'Get axes scales
'----------------
With myChartClass.Axes(xlValue)
    yMin = .MinimumScale
    yMax = .MaximumScale
End With
With myChartClass.Axes(xlCategory)
    xMin = .MinimumScale
    xMax = .MaximumScale
End With

'-------------------------------
'Convert points to units of data
'-------------------------------
paXleft = pa.InsideLeft + 3
paXright = pa.InsideLeft + pa.InsideWidth - 6
paYtop = pa.InsideTop + 3
paYbottom = pa.InsideTop + pa.InsideHeight - 6
If newX >= paXleft And newX <= paXright Then
```

```
        If newY >= paYtop And newY <= paYbottom Then
            With myChartClass.Shapes.AddShape( _
                    msoShape4pointStar, newX, newY, 5, 5).Line
                .ForeColor.RGB = RGB(0, 0, 255)
            End With
            newX = (newX - paXleft) / (paXright - paXleft)
            newX = newX * (xMax - xMin) + xMin
            newY = 1 - (newY - paYtop) / (paYbottom - paYtop)
            newY = newY * (yMax - yMin) + yMin
            If nCount = 0 Then xpt1 = newX
            If nCount = 0 Then ypt1 = newY
        Else
            Exit Sub
        End If
    Else
        Exit Sub
    End If


    nCount = nCount + 1      'Allow only two selections on chart
    '----------------------------------------------------------
    'Re-scale chart to user's selection and re-fit the data or
    'Calculate baseline estimate and re-fit the data
    '----------------------------------------------------------
    If nCount = 2 Then
        Application.ScreenUpdating = False
        If zoomSelected Then
            Gaussian.ZoomChart xpt1, ypt1, newX, newY
            Gaussian.StartSolver False
        Else
            Range("K22").Value = (newY - ypt1) / (newX - xpt1)
            Gaussian.NewBaseline
            Gaussian.StartSolver True
        End If
        Gaussian.ClearShapesFromChart
        Set pa = Nothing
        Set ca = Nothing
        Gaussian.ClearMemory
        Application.ScreenUpdating = True
```

```
        End If
        Set pa = Nothing
        Set ca = Nothing
    End Sub
    Private Sub GetChartSize()
    'Determines the size of a chart in pixels
        Dim hParent As Long, hChild As Long, hChart As Long
        Dim chWindowName As String

        chWindowName = "[" & ActiveWorkbook.Name & "]" & myChartClass.Name
        myChartClass.ShowWindow = True
        hParent = FindWindow("XLMAIN", vbNullString)
        hChild = FindWindowEx(hParent, 0, "XLDESK", vbNullString)
        hChart = FindWindowEx(hChild, 0, "EXCELE", chWindowName)
        GetClientRect hChart, chRect
        myChartClass.ShowWindow = False
    End Sub
```

After a custom baseline has been added to a fit, a worksheet appears similar to the one shown in Figure 20-10.

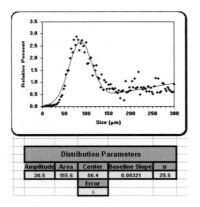

FIGURE 21.10 *Adding a custom baseline to the Gaussian expression used to fit the data.*

Chart Zoom

The chart zoom feature allows the user to select a rectangle on the chart that is expanded to fill the entire plot area, thus obtaining a zoom effect. Only the data points included in the zoomed area are refit to the Gaussian expression. This allows for zeroing in on smaller sections of the particle size distribution that are of interest or filtering out those areas that are undesirable.

To zoom in on an area of the chart, the user must first select the button on the custom toolbar labeled Zoom, which executes the `InitializeChartII()` Sub procedure and initializes the event procedures of the `Chart` object. The zoom area is defined by selecting two points on the chart representing opposite corners of a rectangle. The `MouseDown()` event procedure listed earlier calls the `ZoomChart()` Sub procedure that alters the chart to include only those points in the selected area.

```
'Standard module named "Gaussian"
Public zoomSelected As Boolean
Public Sub InitializeChartII()
    Set myClassModule.myChartClass = ActiveSheet.ChartObjects(1).Chart
    Range("A1").Select
    zoomSelected = True
End Sub
Public Sub ZoomChart(x1 As Single, y1 As Single, x2 As Single, y2)
'Change x and y scales to selected values
'Update worksheet cells
    Dim curChart As Chart
    Dim I As Integer
    Dim x1Row As Integer, x2Row As Integer
    Dim newDataRange As String

    Set curChart = ActiveSheet.ChartObjects("Chart 1").Chart

    With curChart.Axes(xlCategory)
        .MinimumScale = Round( _
            Application.WorksheetFunction.Min(x1, x2), 0)
        .MaximumScale = Round( -
            Application.WorksheetFunction.Max(x1, x2), 0)
        Range("E9").Value = .MinimumScale
        Range("E12").Value = .MaximumScale
    End With
    With curChart.Axes(xlValue)
        .MinimumScale = Round( _
            Application.WorksheetFunction.Min(y1, y2), 1)
        .MaximumScale = Round( _
            Application.WorksheetFunction.Max(y1, y2), 1)
    End With
```

```
Range("A1").Select
For I = 2 To 102
    If x1 >= Cells(I, "A").Value Then
        x1Row = I + 1
    End If
    If x2 >= Cells(I, "A").Value Then
        x2Row = I
    End If
Next I
newDataRange = "C" & x1Row & ":C" & x2Row & _
    ",D" & x1Row & ":D" & x2Row
Range("J24").Value = "=SUMXMY2(" & newDataRange & ")"
Range("E15").Value = x2Row - x1Row - 1

InitialGuess ActiveSheet, x1Row, x2Row
Set curChart = Nothing


End Sub
```

The appearance of a chart before and after an area has been zoomed is shown in Figures 21.11 and 21.12. In Figure 21.11, a rectangle was added for illustration purposes only; the program does not add this shape.

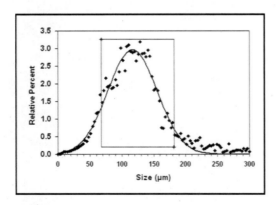

FIGURE 21.11 *An embedded chart showing an area selected for zooming.*

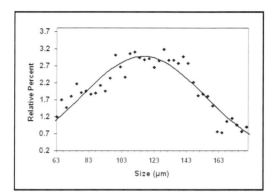

FIGURE 21.12 *The chart from Figure 21.11 after the area in the rectangle was used to rescale the axis.*

The remaining procedures included in the standard code module named Gaussian are used to clear the markers from the chart and the reference to the `clsChartEvents` class module.

```
Public Sub ClearShapesFromChart()

    Dim chShape As Shape


    For Each chShape In ActiveSheet.ChartObjects("Chart 1").Chart.Shapes
        chShape.Delete
    Next
End Sub
Public Sub ClearMemory()
    Set myClassModule.myChartClass = Nothing
    Range("A1").Select
    End
End Sub
```

Summary Report

After the analysis of the individual files is complete, each worksheet can be printed as a report sheet. Alternatively (or additionally), the data can be summarized in a new report. This report must be created dynamically because you cannot possibly know how many files are selected by the user and included in a workbook.

The creation of the summary report is straightforward. The `SummaryReport()` Sub procedure adds a new worksheet to the workbook and copies the fit parameters from each worksheet to columns B, C, and D. Two class modules (`clsCustomFormats` and `clsEmbeddedChart`) are used to format the worksheet and add the embedded line chart.

```
'.................................
'Standard module named "Report"
'.................................
Option Explicit
Public Sub SummaryReport()
'Create summary report
    Dim ws As Worksheet, curSheet As Worksheet
    Dim myFormat As clsCustomFormats
    Dim chLine As clsEmbeddedChart
    Dim I As Integer

    'Add column headers
    Set curSheet = Worksheets.Add(After:=Worksheets(Worksheets.Count))
    ActiveSheet.Name = "Summary Data"
    Range("A1").Value = "Filename"
    Range("B1").Value = "Gaussian Center"
    Range("C1").Value = "Stan. Dev."
    Range("D1").Value = "Area"

    'Loop through worksheets and add data to report sheet
    I = 2
    For Each ws In Worksheets
        If ws.Name = "Summary Data" Then Exit For
        curSheet.Range("A" & I).Value = ws.Name
        curSheet.Range("B" & I).Value = ws.Range("J22").Value
        curSheet.Range("C" & I).Value = ws.Range("L22").Value
        curSheet.Range("D" & I).Value = ws.Range("I22").Value
        I = I + 1
    Next

    'Format worksheet cells
    Set myFormat = New clsCustomFormats
    myFormat.HeaderBackColor = RGB(12, 228, 255)
    myFormat.HeaderForeColor = RGB(0, 0, 0)
    myFormat.DataBackColor = RGB(0, 255, 255)
```

```
    myFormat.DataForeColor = RGB(0, 0, 0)
    myFormat.DataFormat1 Range("A2:D" & I - 1)
    myFormat.HeaderFormat Range("A1:D1")

    'Create embedded chart
    Set chLine = New clsEmbeddedChart
    Set chLine.XRange = Range("A2:A" & I - 1)
    Set chLine.YRange = Range("B2:B" & I - 1)
    Set chLine.ErrorRange = Range("C2:C" & I - 1)
    Set chLine.CurrentSheet = curSheet
    chLine.ChartLeft = 0.5 * Range("A1").Width
    chLine.ChartTop = Range("A1:A" & I).Height
    chLine.ChartWidth = Range("B1:D1").Width
    chLine.ChartHeight = Range("A1:A12").Height
    chLine.XTitle = "Day"
    chLine.YTitle = "Dist. Center"
    chLine.CreateLineChart

    Range("A1").Select
    Set myFormat = Nothing
    Set chLine = Nothing
    Set curSheet = Nothing
End Sub
```

You can use the custom class modules listed next to add worksheet formatting and a line chart to the summary worksheet. These modules are abbreviated to show only the properties and methods used in the data analysis automation project. Normally, these code modules contain several methods that can be invoked to add different formatting and chart types to a worksheet. Using custom classes saves time you would otherwise have to spend writing lengthy procedures to format a worksheet.

```
'......................................
'Class module named "clsCustomFormats"
'......................................
Option Explicit
Public HeaderForeColor As Long
Public HeaderBackColor As Long
Public DataForeColor As Long
Public DataBackColor As Long
```

```vba
Public Sub HeaderFormat(cfRange As Range)
'Header format. Centered, bold, italics, black text
'with red-orange background
    cfRange.Font.Bold = True
    cfRange.Font.Color = HeaderForeColor
    cfRange.Font.Italic = True
    cfRange.Font.Name = "Times New Roman"
    cfRange.Font.Size = 20
    cfRange.Interior.Color = HeaderBackColor
    cfRange.HorizontalAlignment = xlCenter
    With cfRange.Borders(xlEdgeBottom)
        .LineStyle = xlDouble
        .Weight = xlThick
        .Color = RGB(0, 0, 0)
    End With
    cfRange.Columns.AutoFit
End Sub


Public Sub DataFormat1(cfRange As Range)
'Data block format. Centered black text with gray background
    cfRange.Font.Color = DataForeColor
    cfRange.Font.Name = "Times New Roman"
    cfRange.Font.Size = 14
    cfRange.Interior.Color = DataBackColor
    cfRange.HorizontalAlignment = xlCenter
    With cfRange.Borders(xlEdgeLeft)
        .LineStyle = xlContinuous
        .Weight = xlMedium
        .Color = RGB(0, 0, 0)
    End With
    With cfRange.Borders(xlEdgeTop)
        .LineStyle = xlContinuous
        .Weight = xlMedium
        .Color = RGB(0, 0, 0)
    End With
```

```vbnet
    With cfRange.Borders(xlEdgeBottom)
        .LineStyle = xlContinuous
        .Weight = xlMedium
        .Color = RGB(0, 0, 0)
    End With
    With cfRange.Borders(xlEdgeRight)
        .LineStyle = xlContinuous
        .Weight = xlMedium
        .Color = RGB(0, 0, 0)
    End With
    With cfRange.Borders(xlInsideVertical)
        .LineStyle = xlContinuous
        .Weight = xlMedium
        .Color = RGB(0, 0, 0)
    End With
    With cfRange.Borders(xlInsideHorizontal)
        .LineStyle = xlContinuous
        .Weight = xlMedium
        .Color = RGB(0, 0, 0)
    End With
    With cfRange.Borders(xlEdgeBottom)
        .LineStyle = xlDouble
        .Color = RGB(0, 0, 0)
    End With
End Sub


'.....................................
'Class module named "clsEmbeddedChart"
'.....................................

Option Explicit
Public XRange As Range
Public YRange As Range
Public ErrorRange As Range
Public ChartLeft As Integer
Public ChartTop As Integer
Public ChartWidth As Integer
```

```
Public ChartHeight As Integer
Public XTitle As String
Public YTitle As String
Public CurrentSheet As Worksheet


Public Sub CreateLineChart()
'Embeds a line chart on the active worksheet
    CurrentSheet.ChartObjects.Add(Left:=ChartLeft, Top:=ChartTop, _
        Width:=ChartWidth, Height:=ChartHeight).Activate


    With ActiveChart
        .HasLegend = False
        .ChartType = xlLineMarkers
        .SeriesCollection.NewSeries
        .Axes(xlCategory, xlPrimary).HasTitle = True
        .Axes(xlCategory, xlPrimary).AxisTitle.Characters.Text = XTitle
        .Axes(xlValue, xlPrimary).HasTitle = True
        .Axes(xlValue, xlPrimary).AxisTitle.Characters.Text = YTitle
        .Axes(xlValue).HasMajorGridlines = False
        .PlotArea.Interior.ColorIndex = xlNone
        .SeriesCollection(1).MarkerSize = 8
        .SeriesCollection(1).Name = "Sample Data"
        .SeriesCollection(1).XValues = XRange
        .SeriesCollection(1).Values = YRange
        .SeriesCollection(1).ErrorBar Direction:=xlY, Include:=xlBoth, _
            Type:=xlCustom, Amount:=ErrorRange, MinusValues:=ErrorRange
    End With


End Sub
Private Sub Class_Terminate()
    Set XRange = Nothing
    Set YRange = Nothing
    Set ErrorRange = Nothing
    Set CurrentSheet = Nothing
End Sub
```

An example of a report sheet created from these procedures is shown in Figure 21.13.

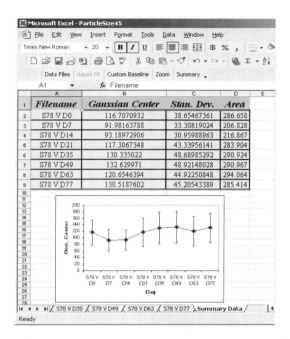

FIGURE 21.13 *Summary report created dynamically for the automation of the particle size analysis.*

The creation of the summary report is the final step in the automation of the particle size analysis. After the analysis of a specific sample is complete, the user can proceed to load more data if desired. However, the automation project is not really complete. Some items were left out for reasons of brevity, and because they mostly involve redundant code. First, the project requires some routine error handling procedures that would prevent the user from selecting the wrong toolbar button. Also, there is a need for more functionality that allows the user to insert data sheets into an existing workbook.

As a final note, I want to emphasize that, even if your comfort level with a particular subject is not really high, you should be able to complete the task at hand. Automation projects often involve analysis procedures that you will not fully understand. However, as long as you are comfortable with VBA and Excel, you should be able to get all the help you need from the person or persons requiring the automation. Whatever the requirements, be sure you understand them before doing any programming; otherwise, you will certainly waste time.

Summary

In this chapter, I used a real-world example of a data analysis automation project I created a couple of years ago to demonstrate some common techniques you may want to use when creating your own projects. Specifically, the project automated an analysis of microparticle size distributions as the particles degraded in solution over a fairly lengthy period of time (several months). The analysis consisted of loading data from a series of text files into an Excel workbook generated from a preformatted template. Basic statistical parameters were calculated from the data and a chart of the size distribution included in each worksheet. Additional features were added to the project that allowed the user to model the data based on a custom mathematical expression. Finally, the automation project allowed for the creation of a report that summarized the analyses for a specific microparticle sample.

PART VI

Appendixes

Appendix A

I assume that this book will attract three types of readers: experienced Excel users with some programming experience, experienced programmers with little Excel experience, and those with little programming or Excel experience. This appendix is intended for the latter two types of readers or anyone needing an Excel refresher. Obviously, I cannot cover the scope of the Excel application in one appendix; instead, I focus on the most common objects used in Excel, in particular, those objects most often cited in this book. If you need additional help, check out a book dedicated to the Excel application such as *Microsoft Excel Fast and Easy* by Faith Wempen.

The Excel Application Window

Excel opens with a single window that serves as a container window for a number of other objects. These objects include the menu bar, toolbars, and most importantly a workbook window (see Figure A.1).

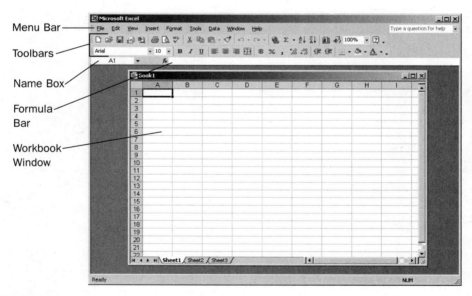

FIGURE A.1 *The Excel application window.*

All user interaction with Excel occurs through the application window. Data content and the analysis of that data are contained entirely within workbook windows. The menu bar and toolbars provide access to the functions used to enter, edit, format, and analyze the data in a workbook window.

The Menu Bar

The menu bar in the Excel application window has many of the items you expect in a high-end application, including File, Edit, and Help items in addition to the other items shown in Figure A.1. It is not possible to discuss the function of each and every item in the menu bar. Suffice it to say that the main menu items are descriptive of the sub-items they contain. For example, the File menu item contains sub-items that allow you to open and save Excel-compatible files.

Several items included in the menu bar are discussed in the book, and a few more are mentioned in this appendix. The one feature you will want to examine immediately after installing Excel is the Options item located in the Tools menu. Selecting this item displays the Options dialog box (see Figure A.2), which is used to set default values for your Excel application.

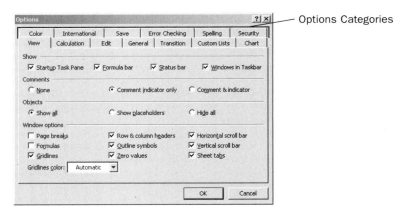

FIGURE A.2 *The Options dialog box.*

The Options dialog box contains several tabs representing the categories for setting the default values of components in the Excel application. Categories you will want to explore include General, View, Calculation, Save, and Edit. Setting default values saves you the time of having to reset these settings every time you open Excel or a new workbook. For example, from the General tab, you can set the default number of worksheets that will be included with a new workbook (see Figure A.3).

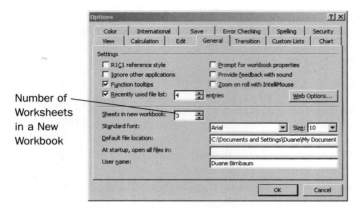

Number of Worksheets in a New Workbook

FIGURE A.3 *The General tab in the Options dialog box.*

Toolbars

Excel has a number of toolbars that you can use to provide fast access to the different functions and components of the application. The Standard, Formatting, Visual Basic, Forms, and Control Toolbox toolbars are referenced extensively in the book. To access a toolbar, select View, Toolbars from the menu bar and select the desired item from the list (see Figure A.4). Custom toolbars will also appear in the list.

FIGURE A.4 *Available Excel toolbars.*

The Standard Toolbar

The standard toolbar is included with many of the Office applications and is shown in Figure A.5. The standard toolbar provides immediate access to file I/O operations; cut, copy, and paste methods; printing; and several Excel specific functionalities (AutoSum, Chart Wizard, sorting, among others). You can also access every item on the standard toolbar from the menu bar; however, you may need to work through one or two menu sub-items in order to find the item of interest, whereas you can get to that same item with one click of a toolbar button.

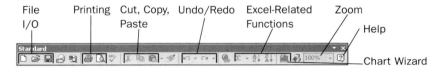

FIGURE A.5 *The Standard toolbar.*

The Formatting Toolbar

The Formatting toolbar is also common to many Office applications and is used in Excel to quickly define formatting (font, colors, borders, and so on) in a worksheet. The Formatting toolbar is shown in Figure A.6.

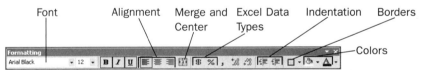

FIGURE A.6 *The Formatting toolbar.*

To format a cell or group of cells, simply highlight them and make a selection from the Formatting toolbar. In Figure A.6, the contents of cells A1 through B9 were formatted using a 12-pt Arial Black font face in bold, italics, and underlined. The text is left-justified, and a heavy weight border surrounds the worksheet selection.

The Workbook

A workbook window is a separate window contained within the application window and includes its own title bar, minimize, maximize, and close buttons. You can open as many workbook windows as memory will allow by selecting File, New from the menu bar or Standard toolbar. The application window in Figure A.7 contains three workbook windows.

File Menu Item

Standard
Toolbar

Workbook
Windows

Worksheet
Tabs

FIGURE A.7 *The Excel application window containing three workbook windows.*

The default file extension for a workbook is "xls." All content (worksheets and numbers, text, charts, and images within) in a single workbook is saved to one file when you select File, Save, or Save As from the menu bar and save the file with the xls extension. Even if you have data in multiple worksheets within the same workbook, it is all saved to one xls file. You can save the content of a workbook using different file types that include Web pages, previous versions of Excel, and csv files (among others) by selecting file type from the Save As file dialog box (see Figure A.8).

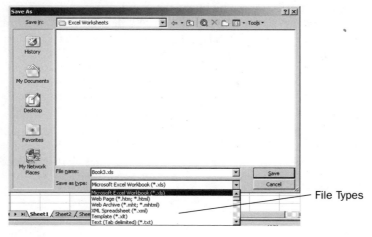

File Types

FIGURE A.8 *The Save As file dialog box.*

Any workbook can contain multiple worksheets. Different worksheets are selected by clicking a tab at the lower-left corner of the workbook window (see Figure A.7). The number of worksheets allowed is only limited by system memory. To add more worksheets to a workbook select Insert, Worksheet from the menu bar. To delete one or more worksheets, select the worksheet or worksheets (hold shift or control key while selecting the worksheet) and choose Edit, Delete Sheet from the menu bar.

The Worksheet

An Excel worksheet represents the spreadsheet part of the application. Worksheets may contain data, charts, images, or any other available objects desired by the user. You select a worksheet by selecting the tab at the lower-left corner of the workbook (refer to Figure A.7). To rename a worksheet double-click the tab and enter a new name.

A worksheet consists of a grid of columns and rows. A single worksheet cannot contain more than 256 columns and 65,536 rows. So, a maximum of 16,777,216 cells are allowed in any single worksheet. A single cell is the smallest component of a worksheet and may contain text, numbers, or formulas. Worksheet cells are also referred to as a *range of cells*. A cell range may consist of one cell or a series of contiguous cells in a worksheet. Understanding how to reference a range is one of the most critical concepts pertaining to spreadsheet applications.

Referencing Cells/Denoting a Cell Range

A cell reference is built from two indexes. The column index is a reference to the letter or letters at the top of the column in a worksheet. A row index is a reference to the number at the far left of a worksheet. You reference a single worksheet cell by combining the column and row indexes. For example, the cell reference A1 refers to the worksheet cell located in column A and row 1 (see Figure A.9). To reference a contiguous range of cells, you must denote references to the two cells at the upper-left and lower-right corners of the range and separate them by a colon. For example, the reference C3:G6 references the block of cells in columns C through G and rows 3 through 6 for a total of 20 cells (see Figure A.9). To reference more than one cell in a non-contiguous block, separate the references by commas instead of a colon. The cell reference A1, A3 refers only to the two cells listed. Several examples of cell references are listed in Table A.1 and illustrated in Figure A.9

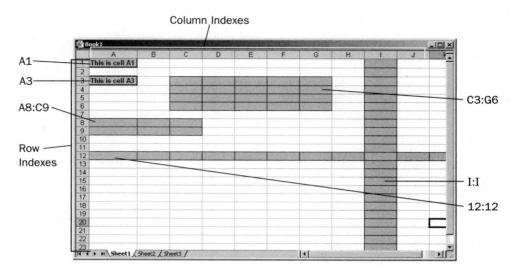

FIGURE A.9 *Understanding cell references in an Excel worksheet.*

Table A.1 Denoting Worksheet Cell References

Reference	Number of Cells Referenced	Description
A1	1	References a single worksheet cell.
C3:G6	20	References a contiguous range of worksheet cells.
A1, A3	2	References two worksheet cells.
I:I	Up to 65,536	References an entire column of worksheet cells.
12:12	Up to 256	References an entire row of worksheet cells.
C3:G6, A8:C9	26	References two contiguous blocks of worksheet cells.

References may also be written using a dollar sign ("$") before the column and row indexes (for example, $C$5). Dollar signs are used to denote absolute references to a row or column index as opposed to a relative reference that does not use the dollar sign. Absolute and relative references may also be mixed when referencing a worksheet cell. The reference C$5 is relative with respect to the column index and absolute with respect to the row index. The use of absolute and relative references is important when writing formulas in worksheet cells and will be discussed in "Absolute and Relative References" later in this appendix.

Cell Formatting

A cell's appearance may be altered in one of two ways. First, appearance properties such as the font, colors, alignment, and borders can be formatted using the Formatting toolbar in the same way you might format text in a Word document (refer to Figure A.6). Second, the cell content can also be formatted by data type.

Data types are manually set by selecting Format, Cells, and the Number tab from the menu bar (see Figure A.10). Available data types include General (default), several numerical types (Number, Currency, Accounting, Percentage, Fraction, Scientific), Date, Time, Text, Special, and Custom.

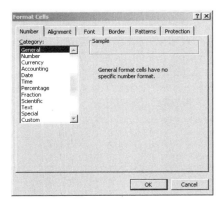

FIGURE A.10   *The Number tab of the Format Cells dialog box.*

When worksheet cells are formatted with the General data type, Excel tries to guess the data type and usually (but not always) guesses correctly. However, there are times when you will want to apply a specific format to the content of a cell. For example, if you want numbers in a range of cells to display a precision of two decimal places, select the range of cells and set the data type according to that shown in Figure A.11.

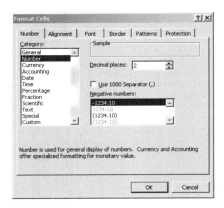

FIGURE A.11   *Formatting worksheet cells to display a precision of two decimal places.*

NOTE

The Format Cells dialog box can also be used to format appearance properties of a cell or range of cells to more detail than what is available from the Formatting toolbar through the other tabs located in the dialog box.

Formulas

Any data analysis in a spreadsheet application relies on formulas to do much of the work, and Excel is no exception. Even a relatively simple analysis will require formulas to be entered into several dozen cells. You enter formulas directly into worksheet cells the same way you enter a number or string. Alternatively, you can enter a formula in the formula bar of the application window (refer to Figure A.1). What differentiates a formula from text is that a formula must begin with an equal sign "=". When Excel evaluates the contents of a cell and finds an equal sign as the first character, it triggers an event that calculates the entered expression. Worksheet formulas may contain any valid combination of numbers, text, cell references, and functions.

NOTE

You may also begin a worksheet formula with the plus sign "+" rather than an equal sign. As a personal preference, I use only the equal sign because it makes more sense when reading formulas in a spreadsheet. For example, if there is a formula in cell A1 of a worksheet, I read the worksheet as saying "The content of cell A1 equals this expression."

A few examples of worksheet formulas are listed next. These examples use text and cell references in expressions that return the result of each expression to the cell that contains them.

= 5/2 + 3*(9–7)

= 5* A2

= $F$2*A2 + $G$2

= A2^2

= 20%

= "Text " & "Concatenation"

= A2 < B2

NOTE

You can permanently set formulas to be displayed in a worksheet by selecting Tools, Options, View tab from the menu bar and then checking the Formulas checkbox.

The mathematical operators available for use in formulas are listed in Table A.2. Use these operators to perform basic mathematical operations such as addition, subtraction, multiplication, and division.

Table A.2 Mathematical Operators Available in Worksheet Formulas

Operator	Description
+	Plus sign performs addition.
−	Minus sign performs subtraction.
*	Asterisk performs multiplication.
/	Forward slash performs division.
%	Percent sign converts a percentage to its fraction.
^	Caret sign raises a value to its exponent.

Comparison operators may also be used in worksheet formulas with expressions that return a logical value (TRUE or FALSE). Comparison operators are listed in Table A.3.

Table A.3 Comparison Operators Available in Worksheet Formulas

Operator	Description
=	Equal sign. Returns TRUE if two sides of the expression are equal.
>	Greater than sign. Returns TRUE if left side is greater than right side.
<	Less than sign. Returns TRUE if right side is greater than left side.
>=	Greater than or equal to sign. Returns TRUE if left side is greater than or equal to right side.
<=	Less than or equal to sign. Returns TRUE if right side is greater than or equal to left side.
<>	Not equal to sign. Returns TRUE if two sides are not equal.

Other available operators include the text concatenation operator (&) and three reference operators (colon, comma, and space). Descriptions and examples of these operators are listed in Table A.4.

Table A.4 Text Concatenation and Reference Operators Available in Worksheet Formulas

Operator	Description	Example
&	Concatenation operator. Combines text into one continuous string.	= "D" & "B"
: (colon)	Range operator. Creates one reference to all cells in the contiguous reference.	=A1:A10
, (comma)	Union operator. Creates one reference from multiple references.	= SUM(A1, B1:B10)
(space)	Intersection Operator. Creates one reference common to two references.	A1:C5 B2:D8 produces reference to the range B2:C5

When you use several operators in a single formula, the formula is evaluated in a specific order. The order follows the rules of operator precedence. The order of operator precedence is listed in the following with operators of highest precedence listed first. If a formula contains operators with the same precedence (for example, multiplication and division), the operators are evaluated from left to right.

: (colon)

 (space)

, (comma)

− (negative)

%

^

* and /

+ and −

&

= < > <= >= <>

Absolute and Relative References

Even with the help given by formulas, writing them can still be a time-consuming and tedious process. However, since many formulas required in a worksheet will be essentially identical (differing only in a cell reference), you can take advantage of relative and absolute references to eliminate most of the work. To illustrate the effect of absolute and relative references in a worksheet formula, consider the arbitrary formula "=B3+$B$2+A$5+$C3" entered into cell C10 of a worksheet. When this formula is copied from cell C10 and pasted to other cells in the worksheet, Excel adjusts the relative column and row indexes in the formula according to the spatial relationships between the original and destination cells. Thus, if the formula is copied to cell D9, the net change in the column index between original and destination cells is +1, and the net change in the row index is −1. The resulting formula in cell D9 is then "=C2+$B$2+B$5+$C2". All relative references to column indexes were increased by one, and all relative references to row indexes were decreased by one. All absolute references were left unchanged. Be careful not to allow a net change that creates an impossible cell reference (column index less than A or a row index less than 1). For example, the reference C5 cannot be decreased by more than two columns and 4 rows; otherwise, a reference error occurs (see Figure A.12).

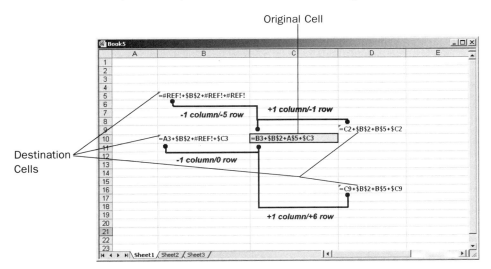

FIGURE A.12 *Copying a formula within a worksheet.*

To illustrate the benefits of using relative references in formulas, consider the worksheet shown in Figure A.13. The worksheet was created to convert a column of distances from units of miles to kilometers.

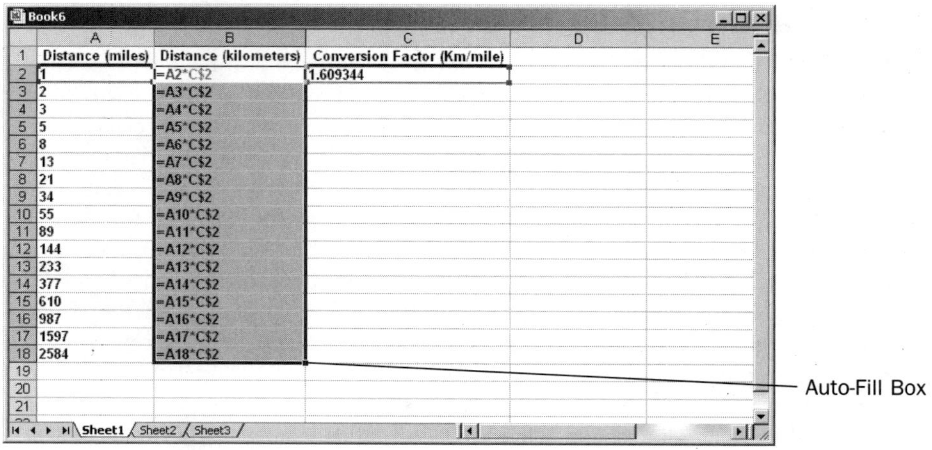

	A	B	C	D	E
	Distance (miles)	Distance (kilometers)	Conversion Factor (Km/mile)		
1					
2	1	=A2*C$2	1.609344		
3	2	=A3*C$2			
4	3	=A4*C$2			
5	5	=A5*C$2			
6	8	=A6*C$2			
7	13	=A7*C$2			
8	21	=A8*C$2			
9	34	=A9*C$2			
10	55	=A10*C$2			
11	89	=A11*C$2			
12	144	=A12*C$2			
13	233	=A13*C$2			
14	377	=A14*C$2			
15	610	=A15*C$2			
16	987	=A16*C$2			
17	1597	=A17*C$2			
18	2584	=A18*C$2			
19					
20					——— Auto-Fill Box
21					

Sheet1 / Sheet2 / Sheet3 /

FIGURE A.13 *Copying a formula within a column.*

The distances in miles are entered into column A, the conversion factor is in cell C2, and the distances in kilometers are calculated in column B. The fastest method for completing the worksheet is to enter the formula "= A2*C$2" into cell B2 and then copy and paste (or auto-fill) the formula down the column. This is much faster than typing each formula from scratch, even if there are only a few cells.

> **NOTE**
>
> Formulas copied and pasted within the same row can use an absolute or relative reference with the row index, and it will not change. Likewise, when pasting formulas within the same column, the references to the column indexes will not change with either an absolute or relative reference. For example, the following formula works identically to the one listed in Figure A.13: =A2*$C$2

Referencing Worksheets and Workbooks

You can include references in formulas to cells in other worksheets as well as other workbooks. References to the worksheet and/or workbook are added to the left of the cell reference with each increase in the level of the hierarchy. The following formulas reference cells from other worksheets in the same and different workbooks:

=Sheet2!$A$2 (reference to another worksheet within the same workbook)

=[Book6]Sheet1!$A$2 (reference to another open workbook)

='C:\Windows\[Book6.xls]Sheet1'!$A$25 (reference to a workbook file)

In the last example, the reference is to a workbook file saved at the specified path. Formulas that contain links to other workbooks are acceptable, but be aware that, as the files are moved or deleted, these links are broken, and Excel will prompt you with an error message when you open the workbook file that contains the formulas with the external links. Large workbooks with numerous broken links are difficult to maintain.

Functions

Excel includes several dozen functions you can use in formulas to calculate quantities that might otherwise take considerable effort to calculate (if it can be done at all). In general, you pass one or more arguments (as cell references) to a function, and after performing some operation on these arguments, the function returns a single value to the calling formula. All functions require parentheses to immediately follow the function name. Any arguments passed to the function must be inside the parentheses.

 NOTE

Not all functions will accept arguments. The PI() function does not accept any arguments and returns the value of pi (3.14159 . . .). Likewise, not all functions return a single value. The LINEST() function returns the slope and intercept calculated from the linear regression analysis of a set of *x-y* coordinate pairs.

Functions can be included in formulas along with text and numbers as long as the syntax rules of the function and Excel formulas are satisfied. Examples of formulas that contain functions are listed here:

= SUM(1,3,45)

= SUM(A2:A11)/10

= AVERAGE($A$2:$A$11)

=PMT(G2/12,H$2,F$2,0,0)

= IF(A$1="Age", A1, B1)

Each of these functions was passed one or more values, and each function will return a single value to the cell in which the formula was entered.

Categories

A complete list of functions available for use in formulas can be viewed from the Insert Function dialog box (see Figure A.14). To show the Insert Function dialog box select Insert, Function from the menu bar or click the script *fx* next to the formula bar.

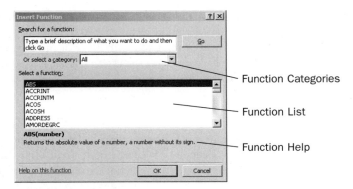

FIGURE A.14 *The Insert Function dialog box used to add a specific function to a formula.*

The Insert Function dialog box allows you to sort the list of available functions by category (for example, Financial, Math & Trig, Statistical, and so on) and provides a short help message when a function is selected. Once a function is found, it provides some help with its syntax via the Function Arguments dialog box (see Figure A.15). Required arguments are listed in bold; the other arguments are optional.

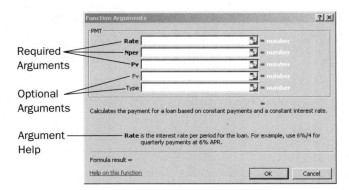

FIGURE A.15 *The Function Arguments dialog box for the PMT() function.*

Select the text box associated with each argument to display a brief help message at the bottom of the dialog box. The Insert Function dialog box for the PMT() function (see Figure A.15) shows that the function requires three arguments and that two other arguments are optional. A help message for the Rate argument is displayed at the bottom of the dialog box.

Nesting

Nesting refers to embedding a function within the argument list of another function. For example, the following formula nests the SUM() function within the SQRT() function:

=SQRT(SUM(A2:A21))

You can nest functions in your formulas as much as seven levels deep, although I would hate having to interpret a formula with functions nested to such a degree.

Named Ranges

To aid in the interpretation of a formula, you can assign a name to a range of worksheet cells and then use that name in a formula. For example, if sales figures for the month of June are entered in cells C2 through C11 of a worksheet, the sum of these values can be calculated with the following formula:

=SUM($C$2:$C$11)

However, the formula can be rendered more readable if the range C2:C11 is first assigned a name.

=SUM(June_Sales)

To assign a named range, first highlight the range and then enter the name in the Name Box (refer to Figure A. 1). You should use descriptive names for a range and avoid the use of unusual characters and spaces. The name must begin with an alphabetical character. Named ranges are always absolute references to the specified cells. To edit the named ranges in a workbook (or add new names), select Insert, Name, Define from the menu bar and display the Define Name dialog box (see Figure A.16).

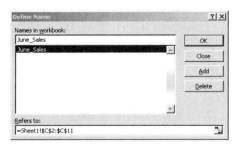

FIGURE A.16   *The Define Name dialog box used to add new or to edit existing named ranges in a workbook.*

Common Errors

There are several errors that commonly occur when writing formulas. When Excel encounters an error in a formula, it returns a message to the worksheet cell that holds the formula. The most common errors that occur are summarized in Table A.5.

Table A.5 Common Errors Associated with Worksheet Formulas

Error Message	Description
#DIV/0!	Divide by zero error.
Circular reference prompt	Circular reference error caused by including a reference to the cell containing the formula within the formula itself (for example, entering the formula =SUM(A1:A5) in cell A5 will generate a circular reference error.
#####	Insufficient column width to display value. Not really an error. Just increase the width of the column so the value can be displayed.
#VALUE	Value error. A formula contains a reference to a textual value when Excel expected a numerical value.
#NAME	Name error. A formula contains a wrong or misspelled named range or function name.

Charts

Charts are used for data interpretation to illustrate the behavior or trend of a data set or to compare values within and between data sets. It is much easier to view a chart in order to interpret a behavior or trend than it is to interpret a long series of numbers.

Although not its strongest feature, Excel provides you with the ability to create a number of different chart types that can be used in data interpretation. The first decision that you must make is deciding on the chart type that best illustrates the behavior or properties of a given data set.

Creating Charts

Excel provides a wizard that can be used to create embedded charts or chart sheets. To activate the wizard select Insert, Chart from the menu bar or press the Chart Wizard icon from the Standard toolbar (refer to Figure A.5). The Chart Wizard consists of four dialog boxes, the first of which is shown in Figure A.17.

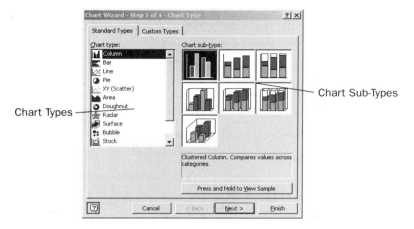

FIGURE A.17 *The first step in creating a chart using the Chart Wizard.*

Chart Types

Although it may seem as though Excel has dozens of different chart types, there are actually only about seven different types (depending on your point of view). These types include the column, line, area, pie, scatter, surface, and radar charts. It seems as though there are more chart types because Excel includes a couple of different versions of the pie (doughnut) and scatter (bubble) charts and numerous versions of the column chart (bar, stock, cylinder, cone, and pyramid). In addition, each main chart type has several associated subtypes that essentially are different only aesthetically.

When choosing a chart type, you must decide which one of the seven main types is best suited to illustrate the data. Once that decision is made, you can base the decision of which subtype to use on what is most visually pleasing. Summary descriptions of the seven main chart types are listed in Table A.6. Use these descriptions as a guide to selecting the best chart for your data set.

Table A.6 Main Chart Types Available in Excel

Chart Type	Description	Use
Column/Bar	Charts a series of values across a set of categories using vertical columns or horizontal bars.	Illustrates a single data set or compare values of multiple data sets across same set of categories.
Line	Charts a series of values across a set of categories as points connected by a line.	Illustrates one or more trends over time (that is, categories should be a unit of time such as hours, days, months, years, and so on).

continues

Table A.6 Main Chart Types Available in Excel (continued)

Chart Type	Description	Use
Pie/Doughnut	Charts a series of values as a percentage of the whole.	Illustrates the contribution of each value in the data set to a total. Number of values in the data set should be minimal (approximately less than ten).
Scatter/Bubble	Charts *X,Y* coordinate pairs.	Illustrates the dependence of one set of values (*Y*) on another (*X*).
Area	Combines the properties of a line and pie chart to chart a series of values across a set of categories as a continuous area.	Illustrates a trend across a set of categories or time.
Surface	Charts two series of values across a set of categories in two dimensions.	Illustrates a trend in values across two dimensions in a continuous curve.
Radar	Charts changes in values relative to a center point.	Illustrates the differences of each value from the average value in a distribution.

After selecting a chart type, proceed through the remaining three steps of the Chart Wizard to finish your chart. Step two involves selecting the data to be charted. From the Data Range tab shown in Figure A.18, enter the worksheet range containing the data to be charted. Alternatively, you can highlight the range before initiating the Chart Wizard (recommended).

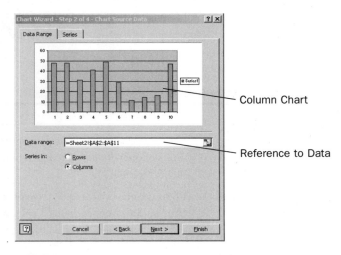

Column Chart

Reference to Data

FIGURE A.18 *Step two of the Chart Wizard: selecting the data.*

If each unique series to be charted has been entered into worksheet columns (typical), be sure that the option button labeled Columns is selected in step two of the wizard; otherwise, each row in the data column will be charted as a separate series. Next, select the Series tab in step two of the wizard (see Figure A.19) to add more descriptive labels to the data.

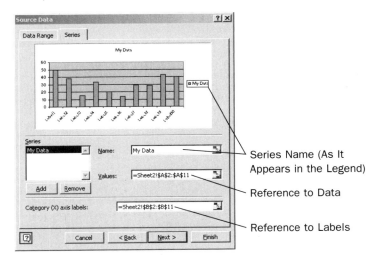

FIGURE A.A.19 *Step two of the Chart Wizard: customizing the data series.*

You can use the Series tab to add or remove data, edit the name of a series, and reference series labels for the chart. Note that depending on the chart type, this dialog box may appear somewhat different. For example, the Series tab of the Chart Wizard for a scatter chart contains a text box for X values and Y values, but not for X-axis labels.

Step three of the Chart Wizard contains tabs that allow you to customize the appearance of the chart by adding titles, gridlines, a legend, data labels, and so on (see Figure A.20). Select each tab and choose or enter the desired options and values. Any changes you make will be immediately applied to the displayed chart.

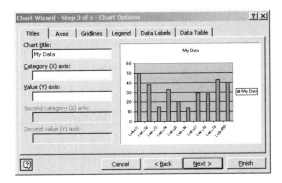

FIGURE A.20 *Step three of the Chart Wizard: customizing the chart appearance.*

The final step of the Chart Wizard allows you to create an embedded chart or new chart sheet (see Figure A.21). Make the desired selection and click Finish.

FIGURE A.21 *Step four of the Chart Wizard: creating an embedded chart or chart sheet.*

It is inevitable that once you create a chart, you will need to edit those features that are unavailable from the Chart Wizard.

Editing Charts

Editing a chart is a fairly straightforward process, but you have to be willing to experiment with the numerous dialog boxes available for changing the appearance and content of a chart. After obtaining some experience editing the different chart types, you will become familiar with the different components of the chart, and it will all be second nature.

The first step in editing an existing chart is double-clicking the area of the chart you want to edit. Figure A.22 illustrates the common components of a chart that will each invoke a different dialog box when double-clicked.

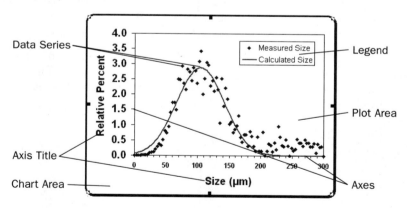

FIGURE A.22 *Common components of an Excel chart.*

The dialog boxes that are displayed by double-clicking a chart component are used to edit the appearance or content of the selected component. For example, the Format Axis dialog box (see Figure A.23) is displayed when you double-click either the X or Y axis of the chart.

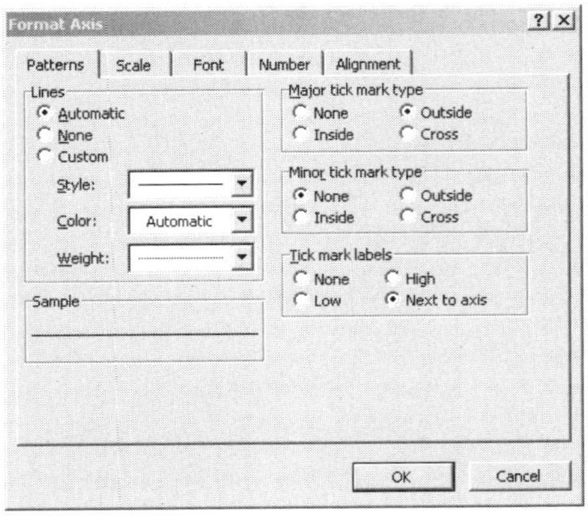

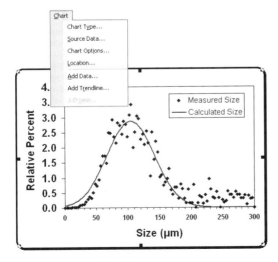

FIGURE A.23 *The Format Axis dialog box.*

The Format Axis dialog box contains several tabs that allow you to format the axis lines, tick marks, font, numbers, and alignment, as well as set the scale values (min and max). The best way to learn how to use the Format Axis dialog box and all the other available dialog boxes is to show each dialog box, make a selection, and see how it alters the appearance of the chart.

In addition to the chart dialog boxes just mentioned, you can also edit a chart by showing the dialog boxes from steps two and three of the wizard. To show these dialog boxes, select Chart, Source Data (or Chart Options) from the menu bar while the chart is selected. The chart menu also contains other options related to the selected chart, as shown in Figure A.24.

FIGURE A.24 *The Chart menu item.*

Appendix B

**Basic
HTML/XHTML
Tutorial**

Learning Hypertext Markup Language (HTML) and Extensible Hypertext Markup Language (XHTML) is much easier than learning a programming language. I say this because HTML/XHTML is not really programming. Instead, it is document editing, which, conceptually, is a pretty simple idea. If you are old enough to remember a time when word processors didn't exist and documents were created on machines called typewriters, you will remember how documents use to be edited for changes and corrections. You would write instructions on the paper for the author to use as a guide on how the document should appear. For example, a note with a caret symbol would tell the author to insert the hand-written text at the specified location. Other conventions used symbols that would tell the author to reverse the order of two words, start a new paragraph, or check the spelling of a word. This is similar to HTML/XHTML in that you mark up a document using standard symbols called *tags*. The tags are then interpreted by the browser as instructions that tell it how to display the document.

Similar to a programming language, HTML is constantly evolving with more improvements added to each version. In fact, HTML is slowly being phased out in favor of the Extensible Markup Language (XML) with XHTML as an intermediary. But if you are just getting started making Web documents, don't worry about what language you should learn because browsers will continue to support HTML for quite some time, and HTML/XHTML is a good place to start.

This appendix teaches you how to create basic HTML and XHTML documents for viewing in a Web browser. Only the basic features of HTML and XHTML and style sheets are covered in this appendix. For a more complete review of HTML, XHTML, or XML, you may want to purchase one or more books, such as *XHTML Fast & Easy Web Development*, by Brian Proffitt and Ann Zupan, and *Learn XML In a Weekend*, by Erik Westermann.

HTML/XHTML Introduction

HTML is a set of rules that relies on special directions known as tags (special characters and words enclosed in the symbols < >) to define a document's layout. HTML defines the rules for the placement of these directions in a document in order to display text, images, and other media. A Web browser such as Microsoft Internet Explorer or Netscape Navigator understands these directions and displays the intended content of the document without the tags.

XHTML is very similar to HTML and serves as the bridge for the eventual migration to XML. Because the World Wide Web is ultimately a tool for the dissemination of vast amounts of data, it was decided that a language better suited than HTML was required to manage that data. Thus, XML was developed. The idea is to use XML for managing data and HTML for displaying it. Unfortunately, HTML is not XML-compliant, so an intermediary language was required, and XHTML was born. I will adhere to XHTML conventions with the examples included in this appendix and point out the differences in HTML. This appendix does not cover XML.

Requirements

All that is required to create a Web page is a simple text editor that can save files in ASCII text format (for example, Notepad). You can use higher end applications to create Web documents; however, if you are just learning HTML, it's best to start with something simple. You will learn a language faster when you do the work rather than have an application generate your code for you.

You will also need a browser such as Microsoft Internet Explorer or Netscape Navigator in which to view your documents.

 NOTE

Depending on the browser and version, you will have mixed results displaying your HTML documents, especially when using style sheets. Support for style sheets was not added to Internet Explorer or Navigator until after version 4.0 and has been improving since (although Netscape remained far behind). I recommend using Internet Explorer 5.5 or later when creating Web documents that include style sheets.

The text files you create with a text editor will look nothing like the document that appears when you load the file into a browser (of course, the whole objective is to be able to create simple small files that can be downloaded from the Internet quickly but still look cool). In order to view a document created with your text editor, you must save the file with the htm or html extension so that a browser can recognize it. It is still an ASCII text file, but the extension has been changed from txt. With a text editor and browser open simultaneously, you can quickly view the results of your labor by saving the text file and clicking the Refresh button in the browser.

A Basic HTML Document

All Web pages require a minimum number of tags before anything will be displayed in a browser. I will start with a document that shows you the minimum number of tags that should be included (but are not required) in a document, and then I will show you how HTML lets you get away with using much less.

When the following text is stored with the html extension and loaded into a browser, one line of text is displayed in the browser window along with a title in the title bar of the window (see Figure B.1):

```
<html>
     <head>
          <title>A basic Web Page</title>
     </head>
     <body>
          This is the body of the web page.
     </body>
</html>
```

 TIP

Indentation is not a requirement of HTML/XHTML. However, as with your VBA program code, it is a good idea to indent your HTML code to improve the readability of the document.

Title ———

File Path ———

Body ———

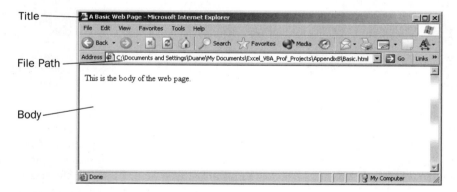

FIGURE B.1 *A minimal Web page.*

The previous listing includes the four sets of tags that should be included with all HTML documents. The `<html>` and `</html>` tags always start and end an HTML document. The first tag (`<html>`) is referred to as an *opening tag,* and the second one (`</html>`) is referred to as a *closing tag* because it contains a forward slash.

Although HTML does not strictly require most closing tags, you should always include them because XHTML requires them. They also make the document more readable for an experienced HTML author. Imagine what your VBA code would look like without `End Sub` statements!

In addition to the `<html>` and `</html>` tags, the document contains `<head>` and `</head>` tags plus `<body>` and `</body>` tags. These two sets of tags represent the main sections of an HTML document. Most of the content enclosed inside the `<head>` and `</head>` tags is not visible in the browser. Instead, this section of the document includes various document properties such as the title, name, links, version, and any embedded programs (JavaScript, VBScript). Much of the information intended for the `<head>` and `</head>` tags is omitted by HTML authors, but, at the very least, you should include a title within the `<title>` and `</title>` tags. The visible content of the document should be included within the `<body>` and `</body>` tags. This includes text, images, tables, forms, and other components that make up an HTML document as viewed from a browser window.

Now, just to illustrate how loose the syntax rules are in HTML, the following document will appear in a Web browser exactly as shown in Figure B.1:

```
<title>A basic Web Page</title>
This is the body of the web page.
```

Although it may appear to be the better document because there are only two lines of text, in reality your documents will include a lot more information than this example, and all the tags should be included to help organize and understand the content of the document.

 NOTE

You probably noticed that I used all lowercase characters in the tags. This is not a requirement of HTML. In fact, the HTML convention is to write them in all uppercase, even though HTML is not case sensitive. However, XHTML is case sensitive, and its convention is to use all lowercase characters in tags, so you might as well get used to writing the tags this way.

Tag Attributes

If HTML authors were allowed to use only basic tags as I've written them thus far, all documents would have white backgrounds and black text, which is pretty boring. The attributes assigned to a tag are what make a document stand out. Almost every HTML tag includes a set of attributes that are used to set the properties of that section of the document defined by the tag. Attributes are analogous to the properties that describe a VBA programming object. They set values for the properties of a document component such as color, border, font, and so on. Attributes of a tag must be included within the tag's brackets (`< >`).

Attributes of the `<body>` tag

The `<body>` tag has more than two dozen attributes that are used to control the appearance of your document and initiate embedded scripts. I will discuss the appearance attributes only in this appendix. Attributes that set the color and background of your HTML document are described in Table B.1.

Table B.1   Color and Background Attributes of the \<body\> Tag

Attribute	Description
alink	Sets the color of the hyperlink text for active links in the document specified as an HTML standard color or 6-digit hexadecimal RGB value.
background	Sets the background image of the document specified as a URL to the image file.
bgcolor	Sets the background color of the document specified as an HTML standard color or 6-digit hexadecimal RGB value.
class	Sets the name of the style class used to define body attributes in a style sheet.
link	Sets the color of hyperlink text for unused links in the document specified as an HTML standard color or 6-digit hexadecimal RGB value.
text	Sets the color of the text in the document specified as an HTML standard color or 6-digit hexadecimal RGB value.
vlink	Sets the color of hyperlink text for visited links in the document specified as an HTML standard color or 6-digit hexadecimal RGB value.

Color attributes in HTML can be expressed using standard color names or RGB values represented as hexadecimal numbers. Sixteen standard colors represent the most common colors (for example, black, blue, green, yellow, red, and so on). You may be used to expressing RGB values as three integers between 0 and 255. With HTML, you must first convert these integers to their two-digit hexadecimal equivalent, concatenate the three values, and precede the resulting six digit hexadecimal number with the pound sign (#). For example, the following statement sets the background color of a document to yellow and the text color to blue (red=00, green=00, and blue= FF).

```
<body bgcolor="yellow" text="#0000FF">
```

Values of attributes should be assigned within quotes. This is not a requirement of HTML, but it is required with XHTML.

More Tags

Beside the skeleton tags discussed in the last section, many more tags are available for use in your HTML documents. I will show you how to use some of the more common tags along with their attributes for creating relatively simple Web documents. The following tags are meant to be used within the \<body\> and \</body\> tags of an HTML document.

Line Breaks

HTML does not automatically add a line break to a document when it encounters the carriage return and line feed characters in a text file. Instead, it will continue to display text on a single line until it runs out of room in the browser window and wraps the text to the next line. To insert a line break in HTML, use the `<br/>` tag. This tag does not have a closing tag in HTML — thus the use of the forward slash at the end to make it XHTML-compliant.

Images

Images are embedded in documents using the `<img>` tag. Again, there is no closing tag in HTML, so you should use a forward slash at the end of the tag to make it XHTML-compliant. The location of the image in the document will appear near the location specified in the document text. The document layout will, of course, depend on the size of the image, so you will need to view your document in a browser to ensure that it appears as desired.

Table B.2 Selected Attributes of the `<img>` Tag

Attribute	Description
align	Sets the image alignment with the surrounding text. Standard values are left, right, top, middle, and bottom.
alt	Use with text-only browsers to specify text alternative.
border	Sets the width (in pixels) of the image border.
class	Sets the name of the style class used to define image attributes in a style sheet.
height	Sets the height of the image in pixels.
src	Sets the path to the image file.
width	Sets the width of the image in pixels.

The following example loads an image called test.gif that is 200 x 100 pixels in size and adds a 2-pixel border around its edge. The URL of the image file is specified as a relative path, so it must be included in the same directory as the source document.

```
<img src="test.gif" width="200" height="100" border="2"/>
```

Adding the previous statement to the basic document listed earlier in this chapter creates the document shown in Figure B.2.

```
<html>
    <head>
```

```
        <title>A basic Web Page</title>
    </head>
    <body>
        This is the body of the web page.
        <br/><br/>
        <img src="test.gif" width="200" height="100" border="2"/>
    </body>
</html>
```

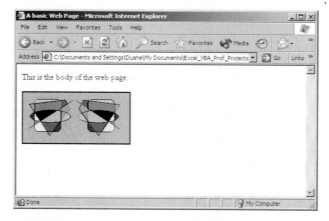

FIGURE B.2 *Basic HTML document including an image.*

Links

Most Web pages contain hyperlinks that, when selected, initiate the loading of another document in the browser window. The new document is referred to as the *hyperlink's target*. Hyperlinks are added to an HTML document using the <a> and </a> tags.

There are several attributes of the hyperlink tag; the most critical (and often the only one used) is the href attribute, which is used to specify the URL of the target. The text embedded between the opening and closing hyperlink tags will appear underlined and in the color specified by the alink attribute of the body tag. If no alink attribute is used, the browser will use its default value. Adding a hyperlink to the previous basic HTML document creates the document shown in Figure B.3.

```
<html>
    <head>
        <title>A basic Web Page</title>
    </head>
    <body>
```

```
        This is the body of the web page.
        <br/><br/>
        <img src="test.gif" width="200" height="100" border="2"/>
        <br/><br/>
        <a href="MyDoc.html">Click Me</a>
    </body>
</html>
```

When the text Click Me is selected in the browser, the MyDoc.html document is loaded into the browser window.

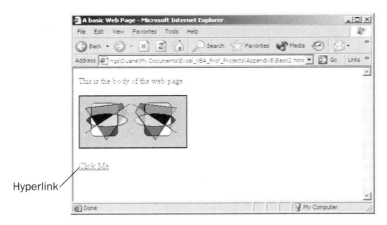

Hyperlink

FIGURE B.3 *Basic HTML document including an image and hyperlink.*

You can also use images as hyperlinks by embedding the `<img>` tag within the `<a>` and `</a>` tags as follows:

```
<a href="MyDoc.html"><img src="test.gif"/></a>
```

Tables

Tables are among the most common elements of an HTML document, even if you don't notice them in the browser. Tables are very popular because they provide a lot of control over document layout. Viewers may not notice them because their borders do not have to be visible if the author doesn't want them to be. In fact, a zero width or invisible border is the default setting of an HTML table.

Tables are created with the `<table>` and `</table>` tags and are meant to be used with the `<tr>` and `</tr>` tags and the `<td>` and `</td>` tags for defining rows and columns within the table, respectively. The following table structure creates an HTML table with two rows and three columns. The row and column numbers are entered into each table cell.

```
<table>
     <tr>
          <td>Row 1, Column 1</td>
          <td>Row 1, Column 2</td>
          <td>Row 1, Column 3</td>
     </tr>
     <tr>
          <td> Row 2, Column 1</td>
          <td> Row 2, Column 2</td>
          <td> Row 2, Column 3</td>
     </tr>
</table>
```

Adding this table structure to an HTML skeleton creates the document shown in Figure B.4.

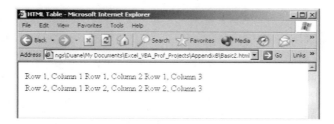

FIGURE B.4 *Basic HTML document including a table.*

 TIP

Use the <th> and </th> tags within the first row of a table to define column headers. The content of the <th> and </th> tags will automatically be centered and appear in boldface type.

Selected attributes of the <table> tag are listed in Table B.3. Use the border attribute to specify a border width (in pixels) that will surround the table and its cells. Use the cellspacing and cellpadding attributes to control the amount of space between cells and between cell edges and their contents, respectively. Finally, use the width attribute to set the maximum allowable width of the table. This is a very useful attribute as it can be used to ensure that viewers of your document will not have to use the horizontal scroll. For example, by setting the width attribute of a table to 600 pixels and enclosing the entire content of the document within this table, you ensure that the document is not too wide to fit on even the lowest resolution monitor. The following HTML statement creates a red table that is 100 pixels wide with a five pixel border:

```
<table border="5" bgcolor="red" width=100>
```

Table B.3 Selected Attributes of the <table> Tag

Attribute	Description
bgcolor	Sets the background color of the table. Use an RGB hexadecimal triplet or HTML standard color.
border	Sets the width of the table border in pixels. Omit to use the default value of 0 (no border).
cellpadding	Sets the amount of space between adjacent cells in a table and along its outer edge.
cellspacing	Sets the amount of space between the edge of a cell and its content.
class	Sets the name of the style class used to define table attributes in a style sheet.
width	Sets the width of the table in pixels.

The <tr> tag also has attributes that can be used to control the color and alignment of a table (see Table B.4). The <td> tag includes additional attributes that help control a table's layout (see Table B.5). The colspan and rowspan attributes are used to merge cells into a single table cell. When using colspan and rowspan, the value of the attribute includes the current and subsequent rows or columns. For example, the following HTML table contains six rows and four columns, but cell 1 is the merged area of three rows and two columns. Subsequent HTML statements involving rows must reflect this merged area. The resulting document is shown in Figure B.5.

```
<table border="5"  width=400>
    <tr>
        <th>Table Heading 1</th>
        <th>Table Heading 2</th>
        <th>Table Heading 3</th>
        <th>Table Heading 4</th>
    </tr>
    <tr>
        <td rowspan="3" colspan="2">Cell 1</td>
        <td>Cell 2</td>
        <td>Cell 3</td>
```

```
          </tr>
          <tr>
                  <td>Cell 4</td>
                  <td>Cell 5</td>
          </tr>
          <tr>
                  <td>Cell 6</td>
                  <td>Cell 7</td>
          </tr>
          <tr>
                  <td>Cell 8</td>
                  <td>Cell 9</td>
                  <td>Cell 10</td>
                  <td>Cell 11</td>
          </tr>
          <tr>
                  <td>Cell 12</td>
                  <td>Cell 13</td>
                  <td>Cell 14</td>
                  <td>Cell 15</td>
          </tr>
  </table>
```

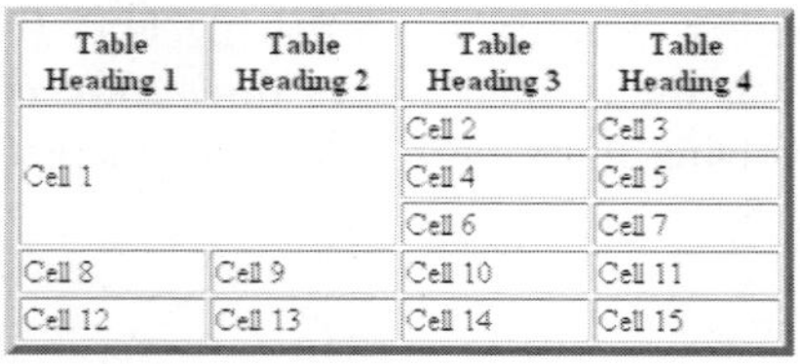

Table Heading 1	Table Heading 2	Table Heading 3	Table Heading 4
Cell 1		Cell 2	Cell 3
		Cell 4	Cell 5
		Cell 6	Cell 7
Cell 8	Cell 9	Cell 10	Cell 11
Cell 12	Cell 13	Cell 14	Cell 15

FIGURE B.5 *A basic HTML document containing a table with merged cells.*

Table B.4 Selected Attributes of the <tr> Tag

Attribute	Description
bgcolor	Sets the background color of the row. Use an RGB hexadecimal triplet or HTML standard color.
class	Sets the name of the style class used to define row attributes in a style sheet.
valign	Sets the vertical alignment of the row. Use values top, bottom, or baseline.

Table B.5 Selected Attributes of the <td> Tag

Attribute	Description
bgcolor	Sets the background color of a cell. Use an RGB hexadecimal triplet or HTML standard color.
class	Sets the name of the style class used to define cell attributes in a style sheet.
colspan	Sets the number of columns in a merged area.
height	Sets the minimum height of a cell.
nowrap	Prevents word-wrapping in a cell.
rowspan	Sets the number of rows in a merged area.
valign	Sets the vertical alignment of a cell. Use values of top, bottom, middle, or baseline.
width	Sets the width of a cell.

You can also nest tables to add even more control over the document layout. The following HTML table contains four rows and three columns with another table of four rows and two columns nested in row 3, column 2 of the original table. The resulting document is shown in Figure B.6.

```
<table border="5"  width=400>
    <tr>
        <th>Table Heading 1</th>
        <th>Table Heading 2</th>
        <th>Table Heading 3</th>
    </tr>
    <tr>
        <td>Cell 1</td>
        <td>Cell 2</td>
        <td>Cell 3</td>
    </tr>
    <tr>
        <td>Cell 4</td>
        <td>
            <table border="3">
                <tr>
                    <td>Nested Table</td>
                    <td>Nested Table</td>
```

```
                    </tr>
                    <tr>
                         <td>Nested Table</td>
                         <td>Nested Table</td>
                    </tr>
                    <tr>
                         <td>Nested Table</td>
                         <td>Nested Table</td>
                    </tr>
                    <tr>
                         <td>Nested Table</td>
                         <td>Nested Table</td>
                    </tr>
               </table>
          </td>
          <td>Cell 6</td>
     </tr>
     <tr>
          <td>Cell 7</td>
          <td>Cell 8</td>
          <td>Cell 9</td>
     </tr>
</table>
```

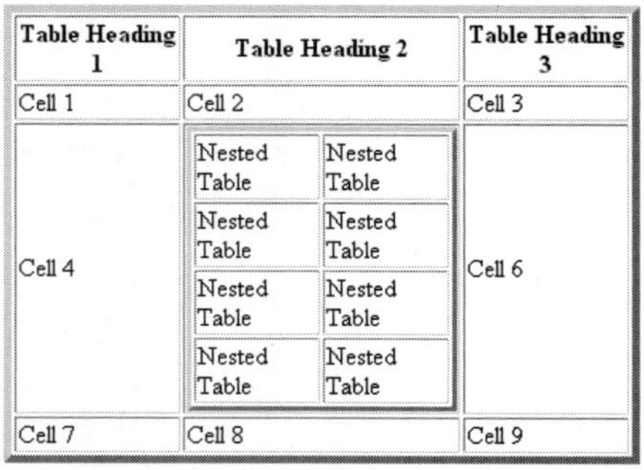

Table Heading 1	Table Heading 2		Table Heading 3
Cell 1	Cell 2		Cell 3
Cell 4	Nested Table	Nested Table	Cell 6
	Nested Table	Nested Table	
	Nested Table	Nested Table	
	Nested Table	Nested Table	
Cell 7	Cell 8		Cell 9

FIGURE B.6 *A basic HTML document containing a table with a single nested table.*

More HTML Tags

There are many more tags that can be used to control the content and layout of an HTML document. However, it is not my intention to give you a full introduction to HTML but just enough to provide a general understanding and help you get through Part III of this book. Table B.6 contains a description of more HTML tags that you will need to understand if interested in authoring HTML documents.

Table B.6 Additional HTML Tags

Tag	Description
`<p></p>`	Paragraph tag.
`<ul></ul>`	Unordered list. Use for bulleted list.
`<ol></ol>`	Ordered list. Use for a numbered list.
`<li></li>`	Defines an element in a list.
`<h1></h1>`	Headings. Use numbers 1–6. Number 1 will create the largest heading.
`<hr/>`	Horizontal rule.
`<i></i>`	Italics.
`<b></b>`	Bold.
`<u></u>`	Underline.
`<map></map>`	Image map.
`<area></area>`	Use to define hyperlink area in an image map.
`<base/>`	Defines the base URL for other anchors in the document.
`<link/>`	Defines a relationship between two documents.
`<meta/>`	Supplies information about the document.
`<script></script>`	Contents include embedded programming scripts (JavaScript, VBScript, and so on).
`<form></form>`	Creates an HTML form.
`<frame></frame>`	Defines a single frame within a `<frameset>`.
`<frameset></frameset>`	Defines a collection of frames.
`<!-- -->`	Comment. Enclosed text is not visible in the browser.

Style Sheets

Style sheets are used to control the appearance of a Web document. Style sheets are great tools for defining the aesthetic aspects of a Web site because they make it easy to bring consistency in its appearance. Support for style sheets has been added to Web browsers to separate the content and style sections of a document. Content should always be an author's first consideration when creating a Web document, but style does play an important role. Style sheets mostly replace the need for attributes of HTML tags and even some of the tags themselves. By eliminating the clutter created by the use of numerous tag attributes, an HTML document will appear cleaner and easier to read. With the use of style sheets, you can focus your attention entirely on the content of the document when editing the html file. Similarly, you can focus your attention entirely on presentation when editing the CSS file.

Styles can be embedded within an HTML document or maintained in a separate file. Since style sheets were created in order to separate style and content, I'm not sure why anyone would want to embed styles within a document. So, I will show only examples that use separate files for the HTML document and the style sheet document.

You store style sheets as ASCII text files just like you do HTML files, only you use a CSS extension when saving a style sheet. To link a style sheet to an HTML document, use the `<link>` tag in the header section of the document.

```
<html>
    <head>
        <title>Sheet1</title>
        <link rel=stylesheet type="text/css"  href="Sheet1.css"/>
    </head>
    <body>
        <!—Body content here-->
    </body>
</html>
```

The `href` attribute of the `<link>` tag specifies the URL of the style sheet that will be used to define the appearance of all or part of the document. The `rel` attribute specifies the relationship between the source and target documents. The `type` attribute defines the type of linked style sheet (CSS for cascading style sheet).

Style Classes

To distinguish between different sections of a document, you can create classes within a document using the `class` attribute of an HTML tag. For example, to distinguish between two different paragraphs in the same document, assign different class names.

```
<p class="abstract"> Abstract text is entered here.</p>
<p class="body">Body of text is entered here.>/p>
```

To set different styles for each of these paragraphs, use a style sheet stored as a separate file and reference the paragraph tag and class name using dot notation.

```
p.abstract {font-family: Times New Roman;
      color: rgb(255,0,0);
      font-weight: bold;
      font-size: 10pt;
      margin-left: 3.5 cm;
      margin-right: 3.5 cm;}


p.body {font-family: Times New Roman;
      color: rgb(0,0,0);
      font-weight: normal;
      font-size: 14pt;
      margin-left: 1 cm;
      margin-rightL 1 cm}
```

Sections of an HTML document are defined by their tag or combination of tag and class name. The style sheet defines the appearance of these sections by referencing either the tag or the combination of tag.class (read as, tag name dot class name). This is followed by brackets ({ }) that enclose the sections' attributes. A semicolon separates each attribute.

You do not have to use the class attribute of a tag if you want the style to apply to the entire content of the document associated with a particular tag. For example, to set properties of a document's body, simply specify CSS properties of the <body> tag. The following sets the background color of the body to light gray:

```
body {background-color: rgb(200,200,200)}
```

A sample document that incorporates these styles is listed next, and its result is shown in Figure B.7. The HTML document uses styles stored in the file myDoc.css to set its appearance properties. The file myDoc.css contains the styles previously listed for the <body> and <p> tags.

```
<html>
    <head>
        <link rel=stylesheet type="text/css"  href="myDoc.css"  title="style1"/>
        <title>Style Sheets</title>
    </head>
    <body>
```

```
        <p class="abstract"> This is the abstract section of my document. The
text is in a Times New Roman font with a red color and bold weight. The size of
the font is 10 pt and the margins are set to 3.5 cm on the left and right. </p>
        <p class="body"> This is the main body of my document. The text is in a
Times New Roman font with a black color and normal weight. The size of the font is
14 pt and the margins are set to 1 cm on the left and right.</p>
    </body>
</html>
```

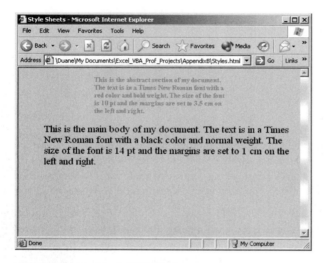

FIGURE B.7 *A basic HTML document that uses a style sheet.*

Although this is only a terse introduction to HTML and style sheets, it should provide you with a feel for how static Web documents are created. This appendix provides you with enough information to understand the content of the HTML and CSS files created by the Excel-to-HTML converter program. It is not my intention to provide a reference source for creating HTML documents. If your intention is to author Web documents, I suggest you pick up one or more books from your favorite bookseller.

Appendix C

Basic SQL Tutorial

SQL (Structured Query Language) was originally developed by IBM about 30 years ago as the data manipulation language for a new relational DBMS (Database Management System). SQL has since become the standard language for the manipulation of a relational database and is supported by all major providers of DBMS software (albeit slightly different versions).

With SQL, you execute commands against a relational database to obtain a desired result. The three basic types of commands are summarized as follows:

- ◆ **DQL (Data Query Language).** Retrieves data from the database.
- ◆ **DML (Data Manipulation Language).** Updates the data in a database. Adds, deletes, or edits records.
- ◆ **DDL (Data Definition Language).** Defines the structure of the database (tables, fields, relationships, constraints, and so on).

This appendix focuses on the DQL component of SQL by showing you how to write queries that retrieve data from a relational database. Examples of single table queries and multitable joins against the Northwind.mdb database are used to illustrate the functionality of the DQL component of SQL. You also learn how to write basic SQL statements that add, delete, and edit the data within a database as well as define its structure.

Creating and Executing a Query in Access

Microsoft Access is the relational database application included with Office. Access uses a graphical interface and includes numerous wizards in an attempt to help the user construct and maintain a database. As a result of the GUI (graphical user interface) and numerous wizards, Access allows introductory users to build simple databases without learning advanced textual commands. A downside to this approach is that users with little knowledge of database theory can become quite proficient with the Access GUI. Such users build databases from tables that are not normalized, making them difficult to maintain. The end result is more work and potentially serious errors involving the storage and retrieval of data from the database.

Regardless of the DBMS used, anyone who designs or maintains a relational database should be proficient with table normalization and SQL. I discuss table normalization in

Chapter 13, "Data I/O between Excel and Access." My discussion of SQL is reserved for this appendix. I have used references to Access throughout this book because it is part of the Office suite of programs and is an excellent DBMS application, even with its propensity to attract users with little or no background in database theory.

Although Access is a GUI-based DBMS, it does provide support for writing SQL statements. To write and execute a SQL statement in Access, you should follow these steps:

1. Open the desired Access database.

2. From the Database Objects window, select Queries from the list of objects and create a new Design view query (see Figure C.1).

3. Close the Show Table dialog box without adding any tables and then select SQL view for the Design view query window (see Figure C.2).

4. Enter the SQL statement and click the Run icon on the Query Design toolbar (see Figure C.3).

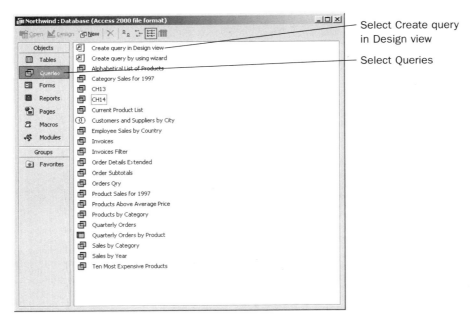

FIGURE C.1 *Access Database Objects window showing stored queries in the Northwind.mdb sample database.*

SQL View   Close Show Table Dialog Box

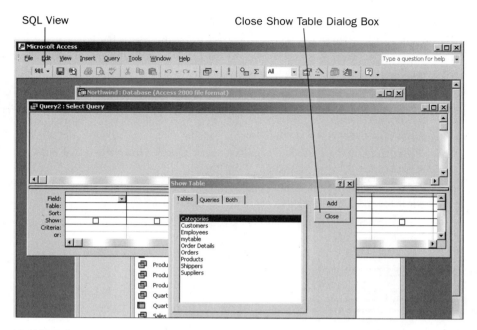

FIGURE C.2 *Creating a new Design view query with Access.*

Run Query Icon

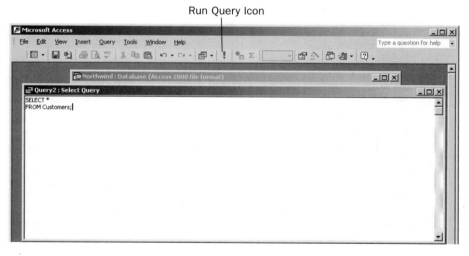

FIGURE C.3 *Executing a SQL statement in Access.*

DQL (Data Query Language)

The DQL component of SQL retrieves data from one or more tables in a relational database. DQL commands allow you to select specific fields (columns) from one or more tables and then filter these records based on specific criteria. To begin, I will show you how to select one or more fields from a database table. I will illustrate the results of sample queries executed against the Northwind.mdb sample database included with Microsoft Office. The basic structure and relationships of the Northwind.mdb database are shown in Figure C.4

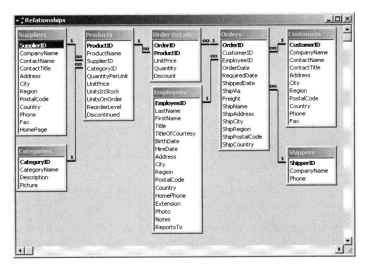

FIGURE C.4 *The Northwind.mdb sample relational database.*

 NOTE

The SQL statements in this appendix are all supported by Access. In many cases, the statements conform to ANSI standard SQL and should therefore execute without error in most DBMS applications. However, you should be aware that the syntax used in this appendix may not execute in another DBMS (for example, Oracle). Every DBMS application supports its own version of SQL, but none of the basic commands differ too much from the ANSI standard version.

Selecting Fields and Tables with SELECT and FROM

The minimum requirement of any DQL statement is that it contain the keywords SELECT and FROM. You use the SELECT keyword to select specific fields (columns) from a table, and the FROM keyword to select the table that contains these fields. The following query returns the `CompanyName`, `City`, and `Phone` fields from all records (rows) in the `Customers` table of the Northwind.mdb database. The first few records of the resulting table are shown in Figure C.5

```
SELECT CompanyName, City, Phone
FROM Customers;
```

Selected Fields

Company Name	City	Phone
Alfreds Futterkiste	Berlin	030-0074321
Ana Trujillo Emparedados y helados	México D.F.	(5) 555-4729
Antonio Moreno Taquería	México D.F.	(5) 555-3932
Around the Horn	London	(171) 555-7788
Berglunds snabbköp	Luleå	0921-12 34 65
Blauer See Delikatessen	Mannheim	0621-08460
Blondel père et fils	Strasbourg	88.60.15.31
Bólido Comidas preparadas	Madrid	(91) 555 22 82
Bon app'	Marseille	91.24.45.40
Bottom-Dollar Markets	Tsawassen	(604) 555-4729
B's Beverages	London	(171) 555-1212
Cactus Comidas para llevar	Buenos Aires	(1) 135-5555
Centro comercial Moctezuma	México D.F.	(5) 555-3392
Chop-suey Chinese	Bern	0452-076545
Comércio Mineiro	São Paulo	(11) 555-7647
Consolidated Holdings	London	(171) 555-2282
Drachenblut Delikatessen	Aachen	0241-039123
Du monde entier	Nantes	40.67.88.88
Eastern Connection	London	(171) 555-0297

Record: |◄|◄| 1 |►|►||►*| of 91

Number of Returned Records

FIGURE C.5 *Table that results from selecting indicated fields from the* `Customers` *table in the Northwind.mdb database.*

When selecting more than one field, be sure to separate the field names with commas, or you will get an error. Also, you will notice that the keywords in the DQL statement are written with uppercase letters. This is not a requirement of SQL but a convention that helps isolate the keywords in the statement and make it more readable. Another convention is to enter the `FROM` clause on a new line rather than continue it on the same line as the `SELECT` clause.

 TIP

To return records from every field in a table use the asterisk (*) with the `SELECT` clause in the DQL statement.

```
SELECT *
FROM Customers;
```

Returning Calculated Fields

Field selections in a query are not limited to just the columns in a table. You can also return fields that are calculated from any mathematically valid expression. Typically, the expression will include one or more fields from a database table, but this is not a requirement. The following statement calculates the stock value of all products in the Northwind.mdb database. The resulting query table is shown in Figure C.6.

```
SELECT ProductName, UnitPrice*UnitsInStock AS [Value In Stock]
FROM Products;
```

It is also a good idea to assign an alias to the calculated field so the query table will have a sensible column header for the calculated field. You assign an alias using the keyword AS. If the alias string contains spaces, it must be enclosed in brackets or quotes.

 NOTE

Any SQL statement that references a field, table, or alias with a name that contains a space from an Access database must enclose that name within brackets ([ ]). Most other DBMS applications, such as Oracle, do not support spaces in table or field names, so brackets are not required.

Product Name	Value In Stock
Chai	$702.00
Chang	$323.00
Aniseed Syrup	$130.00
Chef Anton's Cajun Seasoning	$1,166.00
Chef Anton's Gumbo Mix	$0.00
Grandma's Boysenberry Spread	$3,000.00
Uncle Bob's Organic Dried Pears	$450.00
Northwoods Cranberry Sauce	$240.00
Mishi Kobe Niku	$2,813.00
Ikura	$961.00
Queso Cabrales	$462.00
Queso Marchego La Pastora	$3,268.00
Konbu	$144.00
Tofu	$813.75
Genen Shouyu	$604.50
Pavlova	$506.05

Record: 1 of 77

— Calculated Field with Alias

FIGURE C.6 *Query table resulting from a DQL statement that returns a calculated field.*

Returning Distinct Values

Many queries will return multiple instances of the same value. If that is not the desired result, you can add the DISTINCT keyword just before the field name in the SELECT clause to return just one instance of each unique value in the column.

```
SELECT DISTINCT ProductID
FROM [Order Details];
```

The Order Details table contains numerous instances of the same ProductID. Without the DISTINCT keyword in the previous statement, the query returns the value of the

ProductID for every record in the Order Details table with many instances of the same ProductID. Using DISTINCT in the DQL statement forces the query to return only one instance of a unique ProductID that results in a much smaller table.

Establishing Criteria with WHERE

The SELECT and FROM keywords in a DQL statement filter out columns from a database table, but all records are returned by the query. Queries of this type are of limited use since you will rarely need to return every record from a table. To filter records, you must use a WHERE clause in the DQL statement. You use SQL's WHERE clause to define the criteria by which records are removed from the table created by the SELECT and FROM clauses.

The following statement includes a WHERE clause to filter the records from a previously listed query such that the resulting table includes only those customers living in the USA. The resulting table is shown in Figure C.7.

```
SELECT CompanyName, City, Phone
FROM Customers
WHERE Country="USA";
```

A WHERE clause relies on one or more conditional statements (very much like the conditional statements in a VBA decision structure) to filter the records returned by the SELECT and FROM clauses. You can use comparison operators (=, <, >, <=, >=, <>), logical operators (AND, OR, NOT), and other SQL keywords when constructing a conditional statements for a WHERE clause.

 NOTE

When writing conditional statements in the Access version of SQL, you must enclose strings within single or double quotes and dates within pound signs (#).

Query2 : Select Query			_□×
Company Name	City	Phone	
Great Lakes Food Market	Eugene	(503) 555-7555	
Hungry Coyote Import Store	Elgin	(503) 555-6874	
Lazy K Kountry Store	Walla Walla	(509) 555-7969	
Let's Stop N Shop	San Francisco	(415) 555-5938	
Lonesome Pine Restaurant	Portland	(503) 555-9573	
Old World Delicatessen	Anchorage	(907) 555-7584	
Rattlesnake Canyon Grocery	Albuquerque	(505) 555-5939	
Save-a-lot Markets	Boise	(208) 555-8097	
Split Rail Beer & Ale	Lander	(307) 555-4680	
The Big Cheese	Portland	(503) 555-3612	
The Cracker Box	Butte	(406) 555-5834	
Trail's Head Gourmet Provisioners	Kirkland	(206) 555-8257	
White Clover Markets	Seattle	(206) 555-4112	

Record: ◄◄ ◄ 1 ► ►► ►* of 13 — Number of Records

FIGURE C.7 *Effect of a WHERE clause on the table returned by selecting the indicated fields from the Customers table in the Northwind.mdb database.*

Multiple Conditionals and IN

As with VBA decision structures, multiple conditionals in a WHERE clause must include logical operators (AND, OR, NOT, and so on). To return customers from North America, you can add two more conditional statements to the WHERE clause in the previous DQL statement.

```
SELECT CompanyName, City, Phone
FROM Customers
WHERE Country="USA" OR Country="Mexico" OR Country="Canada";
```

Alternatively, you can use the IN keyword to compare the value of a field to those from a list. Values in the list must be in parentheses separated by commas, and strings must be enclosed within quotes.

```
SELECT CompanyName, City, Phone
FROM Customers
WHERE Country IN ("USA","Mexico","Canada");
```

BETWEEN

Conditional expressions that compare a single value to a range of values can use SQL's BETWEEN keyword. Typically, you use this type of comparison with numerical values and dates. The following statement returns the CustomerID and OrderDate from the Orders table for those orders placed in August 1996.

```
SELECT CustomerID, OrderDate
FROM Orders
WHERE OrderDate BETWEEN #8/1/1996# AND #8/31/1996#;
```

Alternatively, the WHERE clause could have been written using two comparison expressions with the <= and >= operators.

```
WHERE OrderDate >= #8/1/1996# AND OrderDate<=#8/31/1996#;
```

SQL Functions

Every DBMS provides a handful of functions you can use in your DQL statements to quickly evaluate an expression and return a single result. The functions common to most DBMS applications are listed in Table C.1. These functions are referred to as *aggregate* or *group* functions because they return a result based on multiple rows.

Table C.1 SQL Aggregate (Group) Functions

Function	Description
SUM()	Returns the sum of the numerical values in a field.
COUNT()	Returns the number of values in a field.
AVG()	Returns the average or mean of the numerical values in a field.
MAX()	Returns the maximum numerical value in a field.
MIN()	Returns the minimum numerical value in a field.
STDEV()	Returns the standard deviation of the numerical values in a field.
VAR()	Returns the variance of the numerical values in field.

The following statement uses the SUM() function to calculate the total value of Northwind's inventory.

```
SELECT SUM(UnitPrice*UnitsInStock) AS [Value In Stock]
FROM Products;
```

Since SUM() is an aggregate function, it will return only one value, so any attempt to return additional fields will generate an error. In order to use aggregate functions with queries that return multiple fields, you must group the data by type.

 NOTE

Access includes many more functions for use in DQL statements that operate on numerical, string, and date fields. Many of these functions are equivalent to the VBA functions of the same name. For example, you can use the string functions LEN(), LEFT(), RIGHT(), and INSTR() in your DQL statements that execute against an Access database. Other DBMS applications will support their own set of functions.

Grouping Data by Type Using the GROUP BY Clause

To group data of similar type, you must use the GROUP BY clause in a DQL statement. A statement containing a GROUP BY clause returns one record for each unique value in the column that is grouped.

The following statement returns the value of each order (excluding discounts) from the Order Details table in the Northwind.mdb database. The statement groups the data by a single field (OrderID), and the aggregate function calculates a value based on the grouping rather than the entire column.

```
SELECT OrderID, SUM(UnitPrice*Quantity) AS [Order Value]
FROM [Order Details]
GROUP BY OrderID;
```

For example, three of the records in the `Order Details` table are identified by the `OrderID` number 10248. These three specific records are listed in Table C.2. Using a `GROUP BY` clause, the statement returns one record that groups all the items with an `OrderID` of 10248 and returns the sum of the product of the `UnitPrice` and `Quantity` fields for the grouped records (see Figure C.8).

Table C.2 Selected Records from the Order Details Table in the Northwind.mdb Database

Order ID	Product	Unit Price	Quantity
10248	Queso Cabrales	$14.00	12
10248	Singaporean Hokkien Fried Mee	$9.80	10
10248	Mozzarella di Giovanni	$34.80	5

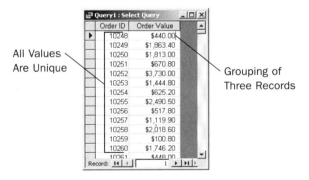

All Values Are Unique

Grouping of Three Records

FIGURE C.8 *Query table resulting from grouping records in the* `Order Details` *table by the* `OrderID` *field.*

You may also group data by more than one field by listing each field in the `GROUP BY` clause. The following statement groups data from the `Orders` table by `CustomerID`. The `COUNT()` function returns the number of occurrences for each unique value of the `CustomerID` field. The first few records of the resulting query table are shown in Figure C.9.

```
SELECT CustomerID, COUNT(*) AS [Orders Placed]
FROM Orders
GROUP BY CustomerID;
```

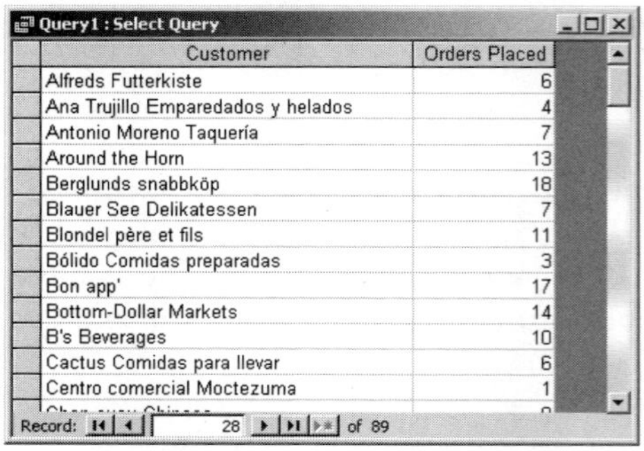

Customer	Orders Placed
Alfreds Futterkiste	6
Ana Trujillo Emparedados y helados	4
Antonio Moreno Taquería	7
Around the Horn	13
Berglunds snabbköp	18
Blauer See Delikatessen	7
Blondel père et fils	11
Bólido Comidas preparadas	3
Bon app'	17
Bottom-Dollar Markets	14
B's Beverages	10
Cactus Comidas para llevar	6
Centro comercial Moctezuma	1

FIGURE C.9 *Query table generated by a DQL statement that groups records in the* `Orders` *table by the* `CustomerID` *field.*

To group the data by a second field, you must add the field to the `SELECT` and `GROUP BY` clauses. The sequence of the fields in the `GROUP BY` clause does not affect the result. The following statement groups data from the `Orders` table by the `CustomerID` and `EmployeeID` fields. The first few records of the resulting query table are shown in Figure C.10.

```
SELECT CustomerID, EmployeeID, COUNT(*) AS [Orders Placed]
FROM Orders
GROUP BY CustomerID, EmployeeID;
```

You must include both the `CustomerID` and `EmployeeID` fields in the `GROUP BY` clause if they are listed in the `SELECT` clause, or the statement will generate an error when executed.

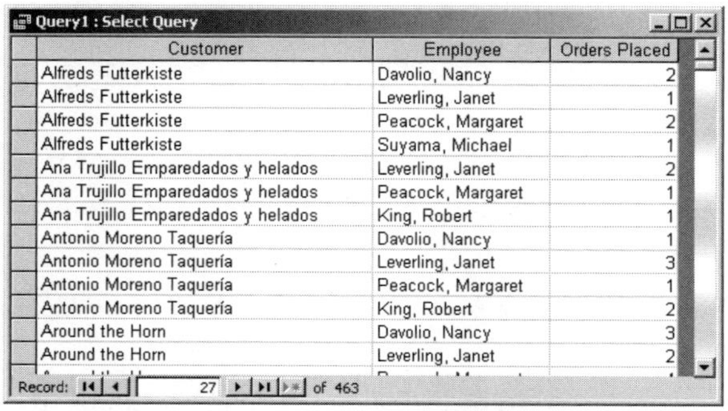

Customer	Employee	Orders Placed
Alfreds Futterkiste	Davolio, Nancy	2
Alfreds Futterkiste	Leverling, Janet	1
Alfreds Futterkiste	Peacock, Margaret	2
Alfreds Futterkiste	Suyama, Michael	1
Ana Trujillo Emparedados y helados	Leverling, Janet	2
Ana Trujillo Emparedados y helados	Peacock, Margaret	1
Ana Trujillo Emparedados y helados	King, Robert	1
Antonio Moreno Taquería	Davolio, Nancy	1
Antonio Moreno Taquería	Leverling, Janet	3
Antonio Moreno Taquería	Peacock, Margaret	1
Antonio Moreno Taquería	King, Robert	2
Around the Horn	Davolio, Nancy	3
Around the Horn	Leverling, Janet	2

FIGURE C.10 *Query table generated by a DQL statement that groups records by the* `CustomerID` *and* `EmployeeID` *fields.*

Sorting Data with ORDER BY

You can sort data returned from a query on one or more columns using the `ORDER BY` clause at the very end of a DQL statement. For example, the following statement returns the names and prices of all products sorted by price in descending order. The resulting table is shown in Figure C.11.

```
SELECT ProductName, UnitPrice
FROM Products
ORDER BY UnitPrice DESC;
```

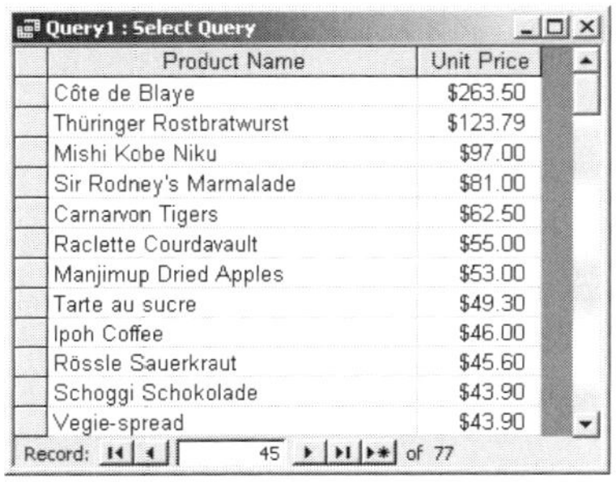

Product Name	Unit Price
Côte de Blaye	$263.50
Thüringer Rostbratwurst	$123.79
Mishi Kobe Niku	$97.00
Sir Rodney's Marmalade	$81.00
Carnarvon Tigers	$62.50
Raclette Courdavault	$55.00
Manjimup Dried Apples	$53.00
Tarte au sucre	$49.30
Ipoh Coffee	$46.00
Rössle Sauerkraut	$45.60
Schoggi Schokolade	$43.90
Vegie-spread	$43.90

FIGURE C.11 *Query table generated by a DQL statement with an* `ORDER BY` *clause for sorting records on the* `UnitPrice` *field.*

The default sort order in an `ORDER BY` clause is ascending unless `DESC` is specified. You can sort on more than one field by adding the field name to the list. For example, `ORDER BY LastName, FirstName` sorts a query table alphabetically in ascending order by last name, then first name.

Sub-queries

A sub-query is used to retrieve one or more values that are used in the evaluation of a conditional expression in a `WHERE` clause. The DQL statement included with the `WHERE` clause is referred to as the *inner query*. The following statement returns the quantity of products ordered for those products currently not in stock.

```
SELECT ProductID, COUNT(OrderID) AS [Orders Placed],
                SUM(Quantity) AS [Quantity Ordered]
FROM [Order Details]
WHERE ProductID IN (SELECT ProductID
                                        FROM Products
                                        WHERE UnitsInStock=0)
GROUP BY ProductID;
```

The inner query returns the `ProductID` from the `Products` table for any product not in stock. Since more than one item may be returned by the inner query, the `IN` keyword is used to compare it to the value of the `ProductID` field in the `Order Details` table. You can only use the equal (=) comparison operator with a sub-query when the result of the inner query is single-valued. The rest of the query uses two aggregate functions to group the products by their `ProductID`. The resulting table is shown in Figure C.12.

Query2 : Select Query		_ □ ×
Product	Orders Placed	Quantity Ordered
Chef Anton's Gumbo Mix	10	298
Alice Mutton	37	978
Thüringer Rostbratwurst	32	746
Gorgonzola Telino	51	1397
▶ Perth Pasties	30	722

Record: |◄| ◄ | 5 | ► |►I|►*| of 5

FIGURE C.12 *Query table generated by a DQL statement written with a sub-query.*

A sub-query can include data from more than one table in the database, and does so in the previous example. However, data can be returned from only a single table unless the outer query involves a join operation.

Joins

Querying a single table in a database has its usefulness, but most queries require data from more than one table. In the previous section, you saw how a sub-query could be used to retrieve data from a single table based on values in a different table. Joins take sub-queries a step further by allowing you to return data from more than one table.

NOTE

Often (but not always), you can write a DQL statement in either the form of a sub-query or in the form of a join, and the query will return the same result from the database.

To include additional tables in a query, you must list each table in the `FROM` clause. You can list as many tables as allowed by system memory.

```
SELECT P.SupplierID, ProductName, S.SupplierID, CompanyName
FROM Products AS P, Suppliers AS S
```

Note that an alias is assigned to each table to identify common fields. You reference fields using the dot operator with the alias and field name (for example, `P.SupplierID`).

Cartesian Products

When a DQL statement that joins multiple tables is executed, a table referred to as a *Cartesian product* is created in system memory. A Cartesian product is the combination of every record in a table with each record in every other table. So, for a two-table join, where one table contains 50 records and the other table 40 records, the resulting Cartesian product contains 2,000 records! If a multitable DQL statement is executed without a WHERE clause (or INNER JOIN clause), the Cartesian product of the tables listed in the FROM clause is returned by the query. The previous query listing the Products and Suppliers tables in the FROM clause returns every field from both tables in a Cartesian product that contains 2,233 records (77 records in Products table and 29 records in Suppliers table). The first few records are shown in Figure C.13.

FIGURE C.13   *Cartesian product of the* Products *and* Suppliers *table in the Northwind.mdb database.*

Natural or Inner Joins

Natural joins (also referred to as *inner joins* and *equi-joins*) query multiple tables in a relational database and rely on the defined relationships (foreign keys) between tables to properly filter the result set.

When writing a natural join, you not only consider the fields you want returned by the query but also the relationships between the tables that contain the desired fields. Use the SELECT clause to list the fields you want returned in the query. These fields may originate from any table listed in the FROM clause. In addition, there must be a set of relationships that allow you to trace a path between every table listed in the FROM clause. For example, you can write a three-table join between the Suppliers, Categories, and Products tables in the Northwind.mdb database because there are defined relationships that establish a connection between each of these tables (refer to Figure C.4). However, you cannot (or should not) write a three-table join between the Suppliers, Categories, and Order Details tables because there is no relationship between the Order Details table and either of the other two tables (you can actually write the query, but the results will be a partial Cartesian product and not particularly useful).

To prevent a Cartesian product from being returned by the execution of a query, you must use a WHERE or INNER JOIN clause.

> **NOTE**
>
> Because WHERE clauses are easier to write for joins involving more than two tables, I will use only the WHERE clause when joining tables.

You use the WHERE clause to list the conditional statements that filter the records contained in the Cartesian product of the tables listed in the FROM clause. At a minimum, any join operation should contain as many conditional statements as the number of tables listed in the FROM clause, less one. So, if three tables are used in a query, the WHERE clause should contain at least two conditional statements that compare the values of the foreign key fields between two tables. You can add more conditional statements as required by the query. The previous query is then written as follows (see the result in Figure C.14):

```
SELECT P.SupplierID, ProductName, S.SupplierID, CompanyName
FROM Products AS P, Suppliers As S
WHERE P.SupplierID=S.SupplierID;
```

P.SupplierID	Product Name	Supplier ID	Company Name
1	Chai	1	Exotic Liquids
1	Chang	1	Exotic Liquids
1	Aniseed Syrup	1	Exotic Liquids
2	Chef Anton's Cajun	2	New Orleans Cajun Delights
2	Chef Anton's Gumb	2	New Orleans Cajun Delights
2	Louisiana Fiery Hot	2	New Orleans Cajun Delights
2	Louisiana Hot Spice	2	New Orleans Cajun Delights
3	Grandma's Boysenl	3	Grandma Kelly's Homestead
3	Uncle Bob's Organi	3	Grandma Kelly's Homestead
3	Northwoods Cranbe	3	Grandma Kelly's Homestead
4	Mishi Kobe Niku	4	Tokyo Traders
4	Ikura	4	Tokyo Traders
4	Longlife Tofu	4	Tokyo Traders
5	Queso Cabrales	5	Cooperativa de Quesos 'Las Cabras'
5	Queso Manchego L	5	Cooperativa de Quesos 'Las Cabras'
6	Konbu	6	Mayumi's

Record: 1 of 77

Values of Common Fields Are Equivalent

FIGURE C.14 *Query table generated from a join of the* Products *and* Suppliers *tables in the Northwind.mdb database.*

The join removes those records from the table shown in Figure C.13 where the SupplierID fields from the two tables are not equal. The query is written using one natural relationship in the WHERE clause because it is a two-table join. Additional criteria can be added to further filter the result.

In many cases, you will have to include a table in the join to serve as a bridge between two other tables. The following statement returns the names of the employees who served Northwind's customers and the total value of their orders grouped by employee. The DQL statement is a three-table join, even though data is retrieved from only two tables (Employees and Order Details). The Orders table is required to bridge the relationship between the

`Employees` and `Order Details` tables (refer to Figure C.4). The resulting query table is shown in Figure C.15.

```
SELECT FirstName, LastName,SUM(UnitPrice*Quantity) AS [Total Sales]
FROM Employees AS E, Orders AS O, [Order Details] AS OD
WHERE E.EmployeeID=O.EmployeeID AND OD.OrderID=O.OrderID
GROUP BY FirstName, LastName;
```

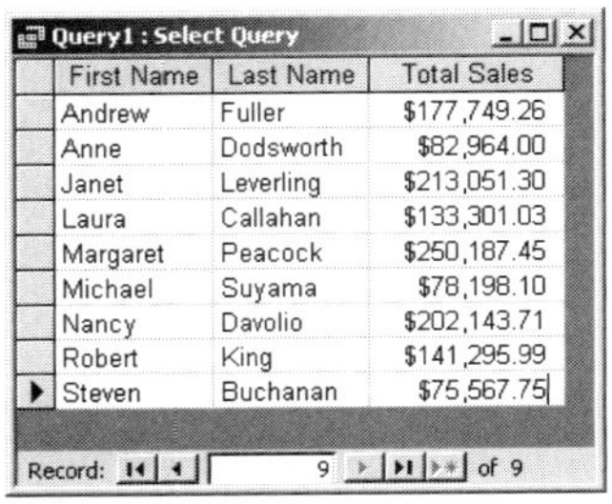

First Name	Last Name	Total Sales
Andrew	Fuller	$177,749.26
Anne	Dodsworth	$82,964.00
Janet	Leverling	$213,051.30
Laura	Callahan	$133,301.03
Margaret	Peacock	$250,187.45
Michael	Suyama	$78,198.10
Nancy	Davolio	$202,143.71
Robert	King	$141,295.99
Steven	Buchanan	$75,567.75

FIGURE C.15 *Query table generated from a three-table join of the* `Employees`, `Orders`, *and* `Order Details` *tables in the Northwind.mdb database.*

Outer Joins

In a natural join, only those records in the Cartesian product with equivalent values of the common fields that define the relationship are returned by the query. In some cases, desired information may be lost if a natural join is used. For example, a natural join between the `Products` and `Order Details` tables will exclude any products that have never been ordered. To include such products, you must use an outer join. The following statement uses a `LEFT OUTER JOIN` that will return all records from the left table (`Products` in this example) even if there are no equivalent values for the `ProductID` field in the records of the right table (`Order Details`).

```
SELECT P.ProductID, ProductName, OrderID, O.ProductID
FROM Products AS P LEFT OUTER JOIN [Order Details] AS O ON
     O.ProductID=P.ProductID;
```

You can also use `RIGHT OUTER JOIN` to return all records from the right table even if there are no equivalent values for the joined field in the records of the left table. If you switch the order of the tables and switch from `LEFT` to `RIGHT` (or vice versa), you will get the same result from the outer join.

DML (Data Manipulation Language)

The DML component of SQL contains just a few basic commands that alter the content of the database. The three commands I discuss in this appendix are INSERT, UPDATE, and DELETE.

Inserting Data into a Table with INSERT

There are two common methods for inserting data into a database table with the DML component of SQL. The first method adds a single record to a database table by listing the values for the record with the INSERT INTO and VALUES keywords. The following statement inserts a single record into the Shippers table of the Northwind.mdb database:

```
INSERT INTO Shippers
VALUES (4,"USPS","(503) 555-2001");
```

The number of values in the list must match the number of fields in the table. You also need to match data types and ensure that any integrity constraints (primary or foreign key) are not violated or an error will result.

The second common method for inserting data into a table adds the records returned from a query to a specified table. The following statement inserts the result of a query into a table called EmployeeSales (created just to hold this set of records).

```
INSERT INTO EmployeeSales
SELECT FirstName, LastName,SUM(UnitPrice*Quantity) AS Sales
FROM Employees AS E, Orders AS O, [Order Details] AS OD
WHERE E.EmployeeID=O.EmployeeID AND OD.OrderID=O.OrderID
GROUP BY FirstName, LastName;
```

The EmployeeSales table must contain the three fields listed in the query (FirstName, LastName, and Sales), or an error will result. The EmployeeSales table can contain other fields, but they must allow null values or, in the case of an Access database, be an auto-number field.

Editing Data with UPDATE

You use UPDATE statements to edit the values of an existing record in a table. You must specify the name of the table and use the SET keyword to identify the specific fields to edit. To identify the record or records that will be edited, you must use a WHERE clause. The following DML statement changes the address and phone number of the employee named Steven Buchanan listed in the Employees table.

```
UPDATE Employees
SET Address='123 Anywhere St', HomePhone='(206) 555-1234'
WHERE LastName='Buchanan' AND FirstName='Steven';
```

Removing Data with DELETE

You can also delete records from a table with a simple DML statement that identifies a specific record or records. You must specify the table and use a WHERE clause to identify one or more records in that table.

```
DELETE FROM Shippers
WHERE ShipperID=4;
```

DDL (Data Definition Language)

The data definition language component of SQL is used to define the structure of a relational database. With DDL statements, you can create and delete tables or alter the definition of a table by adding or removing fields, indexes, and constraints. I will show you how to use three basic DDL statements that are used to create, alter, and delete a database table.

Create

Creating a new table involves the DDL keywords CREATE TABLE along with specifications for the components of the new table. At a minimum, you must identify the table name, its fields, and their data types. You can also identify different constraints, key fields (primary, foreign), and indexes.

The following DDL statement creates a new table called EmployeeSales with four fields (ID, FirstName, LastName, and Sales). The ID field is identified as the primary key and, along with the LastName field, is constrained as a required field (every record must contain a value for these fields). Note the placement of parentheses and commas, because they are critical for proper execution of the statement. Each field is defined with a data type followed by any desired constraints. You must separate field definitions with commas.

```
CREATE TABLE EmployeeSales(
ID          INTEGER PRIMARY KEY NOT NULL,
FirstName   VARCHAR(15),
LastName    VARCHAR(20) NOT NULL,
Sales       CURRENCY);
```

Different DBMS applications will require slightly different syntax for a CREATE TABLE statement. The INTEGER and CURRENCY data types are Access-specific. The VARCHAR data type is for variable length strings up to the specified number of characters. Fixed length strings are identified with the CHAR data type, but Access treats all string fields as VARCHAR. Access does not allow much more than what is shown with the exception of foreign key definitions (not used in this example).

Changing a Table with ALTER

To change the definition of a table by adding a new field, you use the ALTER TABLE keywords and specify the name and data type of the new field. The following adds a new field called Commission to the EmployeeSales table. The data type of the new field is set to CURRENCY.

```
ALTER TABLE EmployeeSales
ADD Commission    CURRENCY;
```

You can change the data type of a column with another ALTER TABLE statement.

```
ALTER TABLE EmployeeSales
ALTER COLUMN Commission  NUMBER;
```

You may or may not be able to delete fields from a table depending on whether the records contain data for the field or the field is restricted by various constraints. To delete a column, replace ADD with DROP in the previous statement.

```
ALTER TABLE EmployeeSales
DROP Commission;
```

Deleting Tables with DROP

Finally, you can delete components of a table or delete the entire table using the DROP keyword. You must specify the component to be deleted (TABLE or INDEX) and the name of the component. The following deletes the table named EmployeeSales:

```
DROP TABLE EmployeeSales;
```

Index